"An eloquent synthesis of evidence. Readers of this masterful book will recognize the extent to which so much of the literature on the First World War, with its focus on secret treaties, bumbling diplomacy, inept military leaders, and particular battles simply obscures the fundamental character of the war and its differential impacts on various groups of people."
— *Alvin Finkel, Professor Emeritus at Athabasca University and author of Our Lives: Canada After 1945 and Social Policy and Practice in Canada: A History*

"With this engagingly written account, Jacques Pauwels delivers a popular counter-history of the conflict whose dissenting verve seems long overdue."
— *Geoffrey Eley, Karl Pohrt Distinguished University Professor of Contemporary History at the University of Michigan, Ann Arbor*

"A panoramic and persuasive history of the First World War . . . Pauwels convincingly disposes of two familiar views of the war: the reactionary myth that the war was glorious, and the liberal belief that it was meaningless. In fact, this book shows, the war makes more sense if you grasp the ideological motivation of the elites, which was to crush the working class and strengthen the hierarchies of old Europe."
— *David Tough, Trent University*

THE GREAT CLASS WAR
1914–1918

JACQUES R. PAUWELS

JAMES LORIMER & COMPANY LTD., PUBLISHERS
TORONTO

Notice to educators:
This book is available for purchase in print and ebook form. Copies can be purchased from our website at www.lorimer.ca. Copies of individual chapters or portions of the full text in print or digital form are also available for sale at reasonable prices. Contact us for details at rights@lorimer.ca.

The publisher and the author of this work expect that portions of this work will be useful for education, and expect reasonable compensation for this use. This can be readily achieved by arranging to purchase these portions from the publisher. Contrary to the view of university administrators and their legal advisors, it is unlikely that use of a chapter or 10% of this work for educational purposes with no payment to the publisher or author would be found to be fair dealing under the Canadian Copyright Act.

James Lorimer & Company Ltd., Publishers acknowledges the support of the Ontario Arts Council. We acknowledge the support of the Canada Council for the Arts which last year invested $24.3 million in writing and publishing throughout Canada. We acknowledge the Government of Ontario through the Ontario Media Development Corporation's Ontario Book Initiative.

Canadä

Canada Council   Conseil des Arts
for the Arts   du Canada

Front cover image: *The Stretcher-bearer Party*, Cyril Henry Barraud, 1918
Back cover image and on pp. 166-167: *German Prisoners*, Frederick Varley, 1919
pp. 22-24: *Frankfurt am Main Barrikade*, Jean Nicolas Ventadour, 1848
pp. 522-523: *For What?* Frederick Varley, 1918

Library and Archives Canada Cataloguing in Publication

Pauwels, Jacques R.
[Groote Klassenoorlog 1914-1918. English]
       The great class war 1914-1918 / Jacques R. Pauwels.

Translation of: De Groote Klassenoorlog 1914-1918.
Includes bibliographical references and index.
Issued in print and electronic formats.
ISBN 978-1-4594-1105-0 (paperback).--ISBN 978-1-4594-1106-7 (hardback).--ISBN 978-1-4594-1107-4 (epub)

       1. World War, 1914-1918--Causes. 2. World War, 1914-1918--Social aspects. I. Title. II. Title: Groote Klassenoorlog 1914-1918. English.

D511.P3913 2016   940.3'11   C2016-900036-2
                                             C2016-900037-0

James Lorimer & Company Ltd., Publishers
117 Peter Street, Suite 304
Toronto, ON, Canada
M5V 2G9
www.lorimer.ca

Printed and bound in Canada.

To the next generation: Charlotte, Olivia, Chapelle, Reed, and Lyra

CONTENTS

Foreword: The Great War in Dali-Vision 9

PART ONE: THE LONG NINETEENTH CENTURY, "MOTHER" OF THE GREAT WAR

Chapter 1. The Revolutions of 1789, 1830, and 1848:
First Steps toward Democracy 25

Chapter 2. The Nobility and the Bourgeoisie:
A Counterrevolutionary Symbiosis 38

Chapter 3. Socialism and Democratization 56

Chapter 4. Nationalism and "Social Imperialism" 67

Chapter 5. Nietzsche and Social Darwinism: Ode to War 83

Chapter 6. Imperialist Friends and Foes on the Road to a Great War 102

Chapter 7. Bourgeoisie, Aristocracy, Church, and Socialists
Confront War and Revolution 121

Chapter 8. Fear and Tensions in the *Belle Époque* 134

Chapter 9. Reactionary and Bellicose Policies 145

PART TWO: THE GREAT CLASS WAR, 1914–1918

Chapter 10. August 1914: Enthusiasm and Resignation (1) 169

Chapter 11. August 1914: Enthusiasm and Resignation (2) 185

Chapter 12. The End of Politics 203

Chapter 13. Gentlemen and Plebeians on the War Path 225

Chapter 14. Fall 1914: Disillusion 234

Chapter 15. Friends and Enemies 257

Chapter 16. Militaria 1914: Aborted Plans   283

Chapter 17. Human Moles in the "Lovely Land of War"   295

Chapter 18. Militaria 1915: The Great Offensives   325

Chapter 19. From the Dolomites to the Dardanelles   336

Chapter 20. Tired of War   352

Chapter 21. Militaria 1916: Materiel and Human Material   373

Chapter 22. Disgruntled Soldiers and Civilians   387

Chapter 23. Militaria 1917: Catastrophes at Caporetto and Elsewhere 409

Chapter 24. 1917: The Year of Troubles   419

Chapter 25. The Yanks Are Coming!   443

Chapter 26. Revolution in Russia, on the Way to Revolutions in Asia 460

Chapter 27. Militaria 1918: German Spring Offensive,
             Allied Final Offensive   476

Chapter 28. Revolution, Counterrevolution, and Reforms   491

Chapter 29. Versailles: Peace or Armistice?   516

PART THREE: THE LONG SHADOW OF THE GREAT WAR

Chapter 30. Via Fascism to a Second World War, 1918–1945   525

Chapter 31. Class Wars from 1945 to the Present   550

Acknowledgements   573

Endnotes   574

Bibliography   606

Index   619

About the author   632

FOREWORD

THE GREAT WAR IN DALI-VISION

Our house stood beside the railway, in a village halfway "between the towers of Bruges and Ghent," as Jacques Brel used to sing in a popular chanson about the Flemish countryside, *Marieke*.[1] During the First World War, my grandmother used to watch German trains roll by, full of soldiers and loaded with all sorts of war equipment, on their way to the front in the extreme west of Flanders, the famous Flanders' Fields. An English war poet killed in 1916, Raymond Asquith, son of Britain's wartime Prime Minister Herbert Henry Asquith, actually devoted a few verses to this railway line in a poem entitled "Liquid Fire and Poison Gas":

> *Only insignificant*
> *Traffic passed from Bruges to Ghent*
> *But the line from Ghent to Bruges*
> *Is quite another pair of shoes.*
>
> . . . .
> *They are moving troops from Ghent*
> *To the Ypres Salient.*[2]

Occasionally one of these trains would stop in "our" little station, and my grandmother would talk the engineer into treating her to a few kilos of coal, enough fuel to feed the hungry old-fashioned stove in her kitchen for a day or so. The German soldiers who passed through our village ate pumpernickel, a very dark type of bread, sliced and topped with a thick layer of real butter (which shocked the thrifty folks of our village), and they accompanied that with a generous helping of liverwurst or cheese. That must have been in the early stage of the war, since from 1916 on, German soldiers and civilians experienced serious food shortages. The situation would be even worse for the people in occupied Belgium.

In 1914, when the Germans invaded Belgium, my father, still a young child, had fled to France with his parents and siblings, like thousands of other Belgians. They were to spend the four long years of the war in Thieulloy-l'Abbaye, a village near Amiens, capital of the province of Picardy. My father went to school there, which is why even late in life he still spoke French fluently. His mother — my other grandmother — I have never known, since she died there and lies buried in the churchyard of that Picardian parish. My godfather, the brother of my mother, was a carpenter just like his father, and during the 1920s they helped to rebuild the "devastated regions" around the town of Ieper (Ypres), the urban hub of Flanders' Fields.

On November 11, after the high mass, a ceremony would take place at the war memorial. Proud chests loaded with decorations helped me recognize the "war veterans," the "heroes" of whom it was respectfully whispered that they "had been in the trenches," but I had no idea what this was supposed to mean. I was told that the Allies had won the war because those smart little Belgians had flooded the plain of the Yser River, thus halting the hitherto irresistible advance of the German juggernaut. In high school we had a teacher — a priest, no less — who demonstrated enthusiastically how a soldier would pierce an enemy's belly with his bayonet during the Great War. He also proclaimed loudly that in this conflict the French had been the bravest and therefore the best soldiers. And I gobbled it all up.

As an adolescent, to improve my high-school French, I was made to spend a holiday with a family in the village of Brimeux, in the north of France, close to the town of Montreuil-sur-Mer where, in 1914–1918, the British commander-in-chief, Douglas Haig, had his headquarters. There I met a man in his sixties who had fought in the First World War and who told me about his experiences. He had served in the army of Charles Mangin, a general known as "the butcher." It was only years later that I realized that he had not meant "butcher" of Germans, or *"Boches,"* as the French called them, but of his own soldiers.

And then I saw the brilliant film Stanley Kubrick directed in 1957, *Paths of Glory*. It was inspired by a book of the same name, written in 1935 by Humphrey Cobb, an American born in Italy who, during the Great War, had joined the Canadian army as a volunteer.[3] The film was never formally prohibited in France, but it was not screened there in theatres until 1975. The reason for this was undoubtedly because it offered a very unconventional view of the French army of 1914–1918 and, indeed, a very different view of the First World War in general. It amounted to a ruthless settlement of accounts with the illusions, the myths, and the nonsense we had been served — and are still being served — with respect to the complex drama of that war.

Paths of Glory dealt with the Great War, but not in the conventional way, that is, as a conflict between the French and the Germans and their respective allies. The camera hovers on the French side and it even fearlessly accompanies the *poilus*, as the French soldiers were known, into the sinister no man's land, once on a night patrol, and once during a large-scale daytime attack.[4] But not a single German soldier makes an appearance in the film, not a single specimen of France's great official enemy. It is only at the very end that someone from "the other side of the Rhine," as they say in France, shows up on the screen. But instead of a stereotypically boorish *Boche*, it turns out to be a pretty young woman, who is supposed to entertain a crowd of French soldiers during a pause in the fighting. She tries hard, in spite of her timidity and clumsiness, to perform a traditional German love song, with as theme a hussar who had to leave his love to go to war: *"Es war einmal ein treuer Hussar"* ("There Once was a Faithful Hussar"). The Frenchmen do not understand one iota of the song's lyrics, but the melody, sad and catchy at the same time, reminds them of their own loved ones, left behind at home in order to fight a bloody war — God knows why! — against people just like them, of whom they know only too well that they too would have preferred to stay in the heimat with their mother, wife, or fiancée. The film, which was introduced noisily by the music of the militaristic and bloodthirsty French national anthem, the *"Marseillaise,"* ends emphatically with the *poilus* humming a German love song.[5]

"Wheels within wheels" is an expression that alludes to hidden or little-known aspects that make it difficult to understand complex phenomena, including complex historical phenomena. What was to be called the "Great War," and was later known as the first of two "World Wars," constitutes a complex historical phenomenon featuring "wheels within wheels." The exterior wheel is that of the military events. That wheel has been examined in great detail by countless historians and has benefited from an inordinate amount of attention from the media, for example in the form of TV documentaries. The public is therefore most familiar with that aspect of the war. But within the military wheel of the Great War there were other wheels, less visible perhaps, but which also played important roles in the historical reality of 1914–1918. Within the mechanism of the Great War, a cultural wheel also happened to be turning, and it is also possible to study and interpret the Great War from a cultural perspective. This is what a Canadian historian, Modris Eksteins, achieved in a book published in 1989, *Rites of Spring: The Great War and the Birth of the Modern Age*; and just recently, in 2013, a similar study was published in Germany, namely, Ernst Piper's *Nacht über Europa* (Night over Europe). But the general public is far less familiar with this type of approach and interpretation.

Even less known are the social-economic wheels that turned within the mechanism of the Great War, and yet they were of paramount importance. They were not ordinary wheels, but "cogwheels" or "ratchets" that transmitted movement to other wheels, wheels of the war that were perhaps more visible but ultimately less important, including the wheel of military events. Nevertheless, it is almost exclusively specialists in the history of the two World Wars and of the nineteenth and twentieth centuries in general who focus on the social and economic sides of the Great War, and their studies rarely receive much attention outside of the ivory towers. What is possibly the best published example of this kind of approach is already more than fifty years old, but is still waiting to be discovered by the general public in many countries: *Germany's Aims in the First World War*, by the German historian Fritz Fischer.[6]

In order to understand the mechanism of the Great War in all its complexity, one must concentrate on the social-economic wheels turning in its interior, and this is the purpose of this book. *Paths of Glory* provided inspiration primarily with respect to the social aspects. The conflict that is the subject of the film is indeed a "wheel within a wheel," a conflict within a conflict, a war within the war. It is a conflict between two types of Frenchmen: on the one hand, the generals and other superior officers, upper-class gentlemen, snooty and arrogant; on the other hand, the ordinary soldiers, the plebeian *poilus*. But Stanley Kubrick could also have set his story in the German, British, or Russian camps, because there, too, a blatant polarity prevailed between superior officers and simple soldiers. The film rightly conveys the fact that the First World War was not just a conflict pitting Frenchmen against Germans, but also of Frenchmen against Frenchmen and Germans against Germans. In this war, a certain class of Frenchmen, Germans, and British confronted another class of Frenchmen, Germans, and British.

The theme of *Paths of Glory* is a conflict between *"ceux d'en haut"* and *"ceux d'en bas,"* as they say in French — "those above" and "those below." "Those above" were the members of the upper class, an elite of people who command great wealth and power and enjoy all sorts of privileges. In *Paths of Glory*, they are incarnated by generals who reside literally "up there," in lofty chateaux, where they stroll on Persian carpets. "Those below" are the poor and powerless, the plebs, including peasants, workers, and craftsmen. In the film, they are incarnated by the rugged *poilus*, living literally "down there," namely in the trenches, with their feet stuck in the mud. In the social no man's land between the two frontlines, were to be found the lower levels of the middle class, the petty bourgeoisie, including white-collar workers, shopkeepers, teachers, small businessmen, etc. They tended to identify with the elite, but occasionally also displayed solidarity with the plebeians. In the film, the main actor, Kirk Douglas, embodies this class. He is Colonel Dax, an officer of intermediate rank who has to decide whether he will identify with his superiors or with his subordinates. With the consequences of this decision he will have to live or, more likely, die — at least, if he takes the side of the simple soldiers and thus shares their unenviable fate in the trenches. This choice is far from easy, because the *poilus* are not idealized, but rather presented as uncouth characters. Moreover, Dax happens to be a lawyer and

13

therefore more naturally a member of the higher class, to which the high-ranking army officers belong. He can hope to land a relatively easy and safe appointment at a safe distance from the front, perhaps even in one of those comfortable chateaux where the generals are at home and where they plan the next offensive that will bring them glory and advancement, but will mean certain death to countless ordinary soldiers.

The Great War was obviously a "vertical" war in the sense that a vertical obstacle, the "wall" of the frontline, separated countries, including their upper as well as their lower classes. But *Paths of Glory* rightly suggests that it was simultaneously a "horizontal" war, in that a horizontal rampart segregated "those above" from "those below," the superior from the inferior classes, within each belligerent country. The Great War was therefore also the Great Class War. Only by understanding this can one begin to understand that war, and begin to understand why it came to this catastrophic massacre of millions of people a century ago. It was a holocaust that would leave its imprint on the history of the rest of the twentieth century and even on our own era. It is not without reason that the Great War has been described as the "original catastrophe" (*Ur-katastrophe* in German) of the twentieth century.

We perceive the Great War primarily — or even exclusively — as a "vertical" war, as a traditional armed conflict between countries and as a primarily military enterprise, because that is how it was presented at the time by political and military leaders, and the great majority of historians have interpreted the Great War in the same way ever since. In order to understand that 1914-1918 was also a class war, one has to examine it from a different angle. In this respect, the phenomenon of the Great War resembles a painting by Salvador Dali, *Lincoln in Dali-vision*, displayed in the "theatre-museum" of that artist in the small Catalan town of Figueres.[7] The centre of the painting features a naked Gala, Dali's wife, and it is only natural that our attention is immediately drawn to her. But when the spectator moves a few steps and reexamines the painting, she or he recognizes clearly on the canvas — superimposed on, or interwoven with, the image of Gala — a portrait of Abraham Lincoln. In the same way, one can recognize the class war in the Great War. It suffices to examine this war "in Dali-vision," which implies moving to a different vantage

14

point, blinking, and looking again, to see something entirely different.

In order to discern the class war in the great but somewhat blurry "painting" of the Great War, we have to distance ourselves chronologically from "1914–1918" and take a few steps back in time. We have to follow the advice of the great French historian Fernand Braudel and examine that conflict within the *"longue durée,"* that is, within the long-term historical context. The great conflict of 1914–1918 was the product of the nineteenth century. Many historians consider that century to have been a "long" century. It ended, symbolically and belatedly, in 1914, but it had also started prematurely, in 1789, in fact, with the outbreak of the French Revolution. That "long" nineteenth century was the child of the French Revolution and the parent of the Great War. Of the French Revolution, it cannot be denied that, other than a political upheaval, it also constituted a social tempest. It was obviously a conflict between classes: on the one hand, the landowning nobility (or aristocracy), intimately connected with the Catholic Church, and on the other hand, the commercial and industrial bourgeoisie, or middle class, which enjoyed the support of the "little" or "common" people — in other words the populace, the popular masses — composed of peasants, workers, craftsmen, above all the famous Parisian "sans-culottes."[8]

The French Revolution led to a series of international wars that dragged on until 1815. The main cause of these wars was the fact that the aristocratic upper class of France's neighbours could not tolerate that in a major country the traditional, established order, the *"ancien régime"* was overthrown to the benefit of another class, the bourgeoisie. Conversely, the revolutionary French bourgeoisie felt that it had to export its revolution to other countries, to the disadvantage, obviously, of the local nobility (and clergy). Quite obviously, then, these wars were not merely "vertical" but also "horizontal" conflicts, that is, wars between countries and simultaneously wars between classes. Furthermore, the international wars also gave the French bourgeoisie the opportunity to direct the dangerous revolutionary energy of the French (and above all the Parisian) plebs against a foreign enemy. That way, it became possible for the bourgeoisie to "externalize" the revolution, thus "cooling down its temperature," instead of running the risk of seeing it being "internalized," in other words, "radicalized."[9]

The subsequent history of the "long" nineteenth century was characterized by new explosions of the class struggle, and certainly not only in France. In 1830, for example, a revolution broke out in Paris, but also in Brussels. In retrospect, the 1830 uprising in Brussels (and elsewhere in what was to become Belgium) looks like a national revolution of the independent-minded Belgians against their Dutch rulers; however, it began as a revolt of the lower classes in the southern regions of the contemporary Kingdom of the Netherlands, a combination of what are now the three Benelux countries. It was essentially a social revolution that was "hijacked" or "kidnapped" by the bourgeoisie and transformed into a "national" revolution that was far less threatening, and even advantageous, to bourgeois interests.[10] And in 1848 the fire of revolution swept through virtually all of Europe. It is remarkable that virtually all these revolutions were accompanied by foreign wars. The Franco-Prussian conflict of 1870 1871, for example, produced the Paris Commune, and the Russian-Japanese war of 1905 proved to be the catalyst of a revolution in Russia in that same year. Is it realistic to think that the war that broke out in 1914, after a "long" century of relentless dialectic of revolution and war, might not have had something to do with class struggle? In the titanic clash of 1914–1918 too, we encounter the same intertwining of war and class struggle, this "horizontal" dimension of a conflict between countries, a conflict which, at first sight, looms as merely "vertical."

It is evident that 1914–1918 was not only a class war. Class conflicts appear rarely, if ever, in a pure form, i.e., as purely social revolts and revolutions, but are virtually always associated with other types of conflict, such as traditional wars between countries and religious and linguistic feuds.[11] The peasant rebellions of sixteenth-century Germany come to mind, an eruption of class war that cannot be dissociated from the religious revolution that the Protestant Reformation, launched by Luther, happened to be. That the Great War was not only a class war, but that it was certainly also a class war, is also made obvious by the fact that it produced a wave of social revolutions. It led to authentic revolutions in Germany and Hungary that were repressed; to embryonic revolutions, characterized by huge strikes and massive demonstrations, in countries such as Great Britain; and — last but certainly not least — to a great revolution that actually succeeded, namely the Russian Revolution of 1917.

It is only when one does not take into account the historical connection between the Great War and the French Revolution and the nineteenth-century dialectic of war and revolution, and when one leaves out of the chronicles of 1914–1918 not only the Russian Revolution but also the other, embryonic and repressed revolutions — as most historians unfortunately tend to do — that it becomes possible to perceive the First World War as something that it was definitely not: an event of a nearly exclusively politico-military nature, a tragic "accident" of history, a typical but ultimately incomprehensible and inexplicable case of collective "human folly." Put differently: a historical phenomenon in which social problems and class struggle did not play a role, or at least no role worth mentioning.[12]

In this book, however, the Great War will most certainly be portrayed as a class war, and even as the "Great Class War." First, we will distance ourselves chronologically from the world conflict of 1914–1918 in order to examine it in "Dali-vision." In order to achieve this, we will take a step back in time, namely to the historical pinnacle of 1789; hence we will descend the great current of history, via the revolutionary rapids of 1830, 1848, 1871, and 1905, to the fateful falls of 1914. En route, we will briefly describe the paramount developments of the social-economic history of the "long" nineteenth century. We will come to the realization that the Great War was wanted and unleashed by a European elite that was essentially a "symbiosis" of the nobility, that is, the large landowners, and the haute bourgeoisie or "upper middle class," the latter consisting above all of industrialists and bankers. The nobility — not only in France, but everywhere in the Europe of the *ancien régime* — was counterrevolutionary from the very moment when, in 1789, the "great" revolution broke out in France. The bourgeoisie had been revolutionary in 1789, but it became counterrevolutionary after its traumatic experiences during the revolutions of 1848 and 1871. These new revolutions made the bourgeoisie understand that the rights and privileges it had acquired via the French Revolution were threatened by the aspirations of the lower classes in general and the working class in particular; from the perspective of the bourgeoisie these were henceforth the "dangerous classes" (*classes dangereuses*), the "vile multitude." The working class loomed more and

17

more menacing because it had discovered a potent emancipatory strategy in Marxist socialism. Moreover, it had developed forms of organization, especially workers' parties and trade unions, and had thus managed to obtain more and more political and social reforms, such as a widening of the electoral franchise. The fear of revolution and even of a seemingly irresistible democratization — the "rise of the masses" — convinced the elite that Nietzsche and the apostles of Social Darwinism were right; these intellectuals propounded that only war could eliminate the grave risks associated with democratization and above all the mortal danger of revolution.

In addition, a victorious war would bring territorial acquisitions, within and/or without Europe. Of these acquisitions, the nobility as well as the industrial and financial bourgeoisie could expect enormous advantages. They could serve as markets for finished industrial products and investment capital, and as sources of important raw materials and cheap labour. Furthermore, they might function as faraway planets where one could dump the demographic surplus of restless, troublesome, often rebellious, and generally dangerous proletarians. This raises the issue of imperialism and of the economic causes of the Great War, which will also be dealt with.

After a first part in which we will analyse the "long" nineteenth century, we will focus in a second part on the Great War itself. Why and how did this miserable war break out in the glorious summer of 1914? Were the populations of the belligerent countries really enthusiastic at first, or are we dealing with a kind of optical illusion? How did the war metamorphose from a "war of movement" into the "stationary warfare" associated with the trenches? Why did the soldiers resign themselves to lead such a horrible existence in the trenches for so many years? What was the situation in the rear, on the "home front"? What were the real reasons why the Americans entered the war rather late, namely in 1917? What caused a revolution to break out in Russia in that same year, in the middle of the war? Why and how did the Allies finally manage to win the war?

In any event, the Great War would turn out very differently from what the elite had hoped for and expected in 1914. It is one of the great ironies of history that the war gave birth, at least in Russia, to precisely the kind of revolution that it was supposed to have prevented. The war was also supposed to have halted, and even to have "rolled back" the democratization process; but when it ended, the elite was forced to introduce even more political and social reforms in order to forestall revolutions *à la russe* in countries such as Great Britain and Belgium. On the other hand, the Great War did shower considerable economic advantages on the elite of the great — and even small — powers that emerged victoriously from the bloody ordeal. On the economic level, this war can and must be interpreted as a merciless imperialist struggle over sources of raw materials and markets — as Lenin correctly pointed out, in the middle of the war, in his famous book entitled *Imperialism, the Highest Stage of Capitalism*.[13]

As a settling of accounts among imperialist rivals, however, the conflict of 1914–1918 also produced losers. In Germany, for example, the elite was traumatized by the losses it suffered as a result of defeat; but it would seek ways to compensate for the losses and try again to realize the ambitions it had cherished in 1914. It is with those objectives in mind that, in 1933, it would hoist Hitler into the saddle of power and, as expected, his policies would lead to a new war. It was confidently expected that this war would achieve for German imperialism what the Reich's elite had hoped in vain with respect to the first world conflict — and also that it would lead to the annihilation of the Soviet Union, the country that had been the fruit of the revolution of 1917 and that incarnated the revolution.

The Great War and the Russian Revolution — understandable only in light of the French Revolution and its offspring, the nineteenth century — constitute together the hinge of contemporary history, the bridge between, on the one hand, the "long" century that preceded 1914 and, on the other hand, the hundred years that have elapsed since that fateful year. As in the case of the French Revolution, one can say of the 1914–1918 nexus of war and revolution that it was a phenomenon that shook the world. And the dramatic historical developments that followed, including those we are witnessing today, can only be fully understood in light of it.

In order to understand the Great War, we have to revert to 1789 and examine that war in "Dali-vision." Similarly, in order to understand the history of the twentieth and the beginning of the twenty-first century, we must go back to 1914-1918 and examine our own era in "Dali-vision." While the nineteenth century, which started symbolically in 1789, was to engender the Great War, the Great War in turn produced the twentieth century, including the Second World War, the Cold War, and even the current so-called "War on Terror." These conflicts, too, can be interpreted as class wars, and this will be done in the third part of this book.

In order to examine the Great War in "Dali-vision," one has to distance oneself from it not only chronologically, but also geographically. Thus it becomes clear that the colonies and the "semi-colonies" of Europe's imperialist powers in Africa and elsewhere were also very much involved in the drama of 1914-1918; in other words, that 1914-1918 was also a conflict for or against the emancipation of exploited and oppressed countries and peoples. In this context the great Italian philosopher and historian Domenico Losurdo emphasizes the fact that, according to Marx, class conflict is not only a matter of social conflict within a country, in other words, a case of the struggle for or against the emancipation of the exploited and oppressed lower classes. Another form of class struggle is the struggle for the emancipation of countries and peoples that are oppressed and exploited by other countries and peoples — not only the colonies of European powers, but also certain countries within Europe itself, such as Ireland. In such cases, we are dealing with a struggle between "classes" of countries, a struggle in which a "proletarian" country (or people) seeks to emancipate itself via a national movement (and a national revolution), just as the proletarians of a country seek to do via a social movement (and a social revolution).[14] This dimension of the class war which the Great War happened to be will also receive attention here.

The fact that the United States and Japan also became involved in Europe's Great War, that heavy fighting took place in Africa and in Asia, and that 1914-1918 revealed itself to be very important to the history of China and India, had of course a lot to do with the fact that this war was an imperialist war. It was a conflict fought by powers that felt they had the right to control countries anywhere in the world, and especially countries inhabited by nonwhite and therefore supposedly inferior women and men, and to run them as colonies or, at the very least, to penetrate them economically *ad libitum*. To powers such as Great Britain, the United States, and

Japan, the following question played an important role in 1914–1918: how can one obtain control, preferably exclusive control, over the raw materials and markets, not only of the hostile Ottoman Empire enemy (with its oil-rich Mesopotamia), but also of neutral countries such as China and Persia? The Great War was definitely an imperialist project and, in order to fully understand it, we have to understand the history of imperialism. This book therefore also purports to explain how nineteenth-century imperialism produced the Great War and how this war left its mark on the further development of imperialism in the course of the twentieth and early twenty-first centuries.

PART ONE

THE LONG NINETEENTH CENTURY, "MOTHER" OF THE GREAT WAR

CHAPTER 1

THE REVOLUTIONS OF 1789, 1830, AND 1848: FIRST STEPS TOWARD DEMOCRACY

The French Revolution of 1789, in which the bourgeoisie, the peasants and the workers challenge the king, the nobility, and the church, sets in motion the march toward democracy, the emancipation of the "little" people. In spite of the triumph of the counterrevolution in 1815 and a new, romantic and conservative spirit of the times, the democratization continues to make progress in 1830 and 1848 via reforms and new revolutions, at least in Western Europe . . .

In order to understand the First World War, it is necessary to understand the French Revolution, which started in 1789 and lasted about ten years.[1] It was a conflict between social entities, in other words, between "classes" of Frenchmen. On the one hand, there was the nobility — of which the king, Louis XVI, was the *primus inter pares* — and the clergy. In pre-1789 France, during what has been called the *ancien régime*, these two classes benefited from a plethora of privileges and, not surprisingly, they did not want any societal changes. This *ancien régime* front was opposed by a heterogeneous coalition of peasants and other inhabitants of the countryside, and of the cities' bourgeoisie as well as artisans, workers and other "little people" (*menu peuple*) or, to use ancient Roman terminology, "plebeians." In Paris, the artisans and the (not yet very numerous) factory workers formed the revolutionary shock troops, the famous *"sans-culottes."* It was they who would pull the chestnuts out of the fire on behalf of the revolutionary cause, for example by taking up arms and storming the Bastille on July 14, 1789.

The revolutionaries wanted change, but had very different opinions about how much change was desirable, and how far-reaching the changes should be; in others words, about how radical the revolution ought to be. The traditionally conservative peasants were already satisfied with the abolition of the ancient "feudal" privileges of the noble landowners, privileges which had weighed heavily on their shoulders. Once this was settled, in 1789, the peasants did not want any further changes and ceased to play a revolutionary role. Put differently, the peasantry ceased to be a revolutionary class. And later, when the Revolution clashed with the Catholic Church (to which the peasantry remained attached) and also came to recruit its sons for the defence of the nation, it was only logical that the peasants allowed themselves to be mobilized on behalf of the counterrevolutionary, monarchist, and clerical cause. This development was tragically reflected in uprisings in the Vendée region and in the famous "peasant war" in Belgium, which had been annexed by revolutionary France.

The haute bourgeoisie — France's upper middle class, which then still consisted primarily of merchants and bankers, as well as lawyers, medical doctors, and other members of the liberal professions — wanted major political changes. It wanted to be able to use the state in order to promote, via the introduction of "liberal" or *"laissez-faire"* laws and regulations, not only its traditional *commercial* and *financial* interests, but also its more and more important *industrial* interests, and not just the interests of the landowning nobility and clergy, as had been the case under the *ancien régime.* (A good example of such liberal legislation was the law Le Chapelier of 1791, which prohibited workers' associations and strikes in the name of liberty.) In the fall of 1791, when that objective had been largely achieved, the bourgeoisie in its turn decided that the revolution had gone far enough. Finally, the urban "little people," the *sans-culottes* and other representatives of what Karl Marx would later call the "proletariat," expected that the revolution would bring improvements to their often miserable existence in the form of higher wages, lower prices, and equality not only before the law (which was also wanted by the bourgeoisie), but also *social* equality, which was abhorred by the bourgeoisie. (Most if not all members of the bourgeoisie desired equality with the class above itself, the nobility, but not equality with the class below itself, the working class.) With the collaboration of a minority within the bourgeoisie, or at least the petty bourgeoisie, the lower middle class, represented by personalities such as Maximilien Robespierre, the Revolution moved into a radical phase in the years 1792–1794. This era was characterized by the replacement of the monarchy by a new, republican form of government and by the execution, by means of the guillotine, of the king and of countless other enemies of the Revolution, in other words, by the "Terror."

France's respectable burghers were terrified and conservative French historians such as François Furet condemn this episode as a deplorable kind of "derailment" of the Revolution. That a great deal of bloodshed was involved is undeniable. However, as the great American historian Arno Mayer has shown, the bloodshed can certainly not only be blamed on allegedly bloodthirsty revolutionaries such as Robespierre; the counterrevolutionaries who abhorred the Revolution because it deprived them of the privileges they had enjoyed had even more blood on their hands.[2] What terrified the bourgeoisie much more than the Terror were the overly egalitarian and democratic measures introduced by Robespierre and consorts; for example, elections on the base of universal suffrage instead of the censal suffrage favoured by the bourgeoisie, as well as the extremely antiliberal forms of state intervention in the economy, such as price controls and public aid to the needy; and of course the abolition of slavery, on February 2, 1794, which was condemned as a violation of the principle of private property, because slaves were then still seen as a form of property. (A considerable part of the bourgeoisie — not only in France, but also in the Netherlands and Great Britain, and above all in seaports such as Nantes, Amsterdam, and Liverpool — had accumulated colossal riches in the course of the eighteenth century thanks to slavery and the slave trade.) Revolutionary France was the very first country in Europe to abolish slavery, an admirable achievement to which historians hardly ever pay any attention.

The haute bourgeoisie rushed to put an end to the "terror regime" of

Robespierre and thus to the radical phase of the Revolution by means of two coups d'état: first the one of July (known as "Thermidor") 1794, which introduced the authoritarian but unstable "Directoire" regime, then that of November ("Brumaire") 1799, which brought Napoleon Bonaparte to power, first as "consul" and then as emperor. The dictatorship of Napoleon consolidated the revolutionary gains of the bourgeoisie in the face of two menaces: first, the national and international counterrevolution and, second, the radical revolution of Robespierre. There was no more talk of universal suffrage, and slavery was reintroduced by Napoleon.

As for the wars waged by the Directoire and above all by Napoleon, they served not exclusively, but certainly in part to "externalize" the revolution, that is, to export its moderate, liberal version to the advantage of the French bourgeoisie and the European bourgeoisie in general; this contrasted dramatically with the attempt to "interiorize," that is, to radicalize and intensify the Revolution in France itself for the benefit of the plebeians, as Robespierre and consorts had done by means of the Terror. The wars associated with this "externalization" of the Revolution — in which many businessmen made huge profits thanks to state orders for weapons, uniforms, etc. — also served to neutralize the restless *sans-culottes* and other representatives of the "populace," removing them physically from the country and above all from Paris, and metamorphosed their revolutionary enthusiasm, all too dangerous from the bourgeois point of view, into French nationalism (known as "chauvinism"), fanatical but socially inoffensive.[3] The French Revolution revealed itself not only to be a powerful stimulus of nationalism in France, but also in other countries, especially those that were occupied by France, such as Germany and Italy, where the reaction against French chauvinism and Bonapartist imperialism involved the blossoming of a homegrown patriotic fever.

The Revolution thus led to a series of wars. But it should not be forgotten that it was another series of wars, namely, the Seven-Years War (1756–1763), a world war *avant la lettre*, and the American War of Independence (1775–1783), that had put the kingdom of the Louises deeply into debt and had thus led to a fiscal crisis that was in many ways responsible for the outbreak of the "Great Revolution" in Paris in 1789. In view of this, it will hardly come as a surprise that in the century following 1789, wars would again engender revolutions and vice versa. The Franco-Prussian war of 1870–1871 comes to mind, which produced the Paris Commune, and so does the Russian-Japanese war of 1905, catalyst of a revolution in Russia. And was the First World War not to be the "mother" of the Russian Revolution of 1917?

In spite of the Terror and the wars associated with it, the French Revolution amounted to a genuine "great leap forward" in the history of mankind. The "Great Revolution" established important principles such as liberty and equality, even if it was a mere equality before the law. The revolutionaries also formulated a very solemn "declaration of the rights of men and of the citizen" and introduced "enlightened" and "modern" reforms such as the separation of church and state. The French Revolution was in many ways a first attempt to "emancipate" or to "liberate" the members of the lower classes, not only politically, but also socially and economically. One can say that the French Revolution inaugurated the era of *democracy*, a *political* but also a *social-economic* system in which power is exercised by and for the entire people, including the lower-class majority — or, to use ancient Greek terminology, the *demos*, the *polloi* or "numerous ones," as opposed to the *oligoi* or "few" of the upper class; the Romans similarly spoke of the plebeians and the patricians.[4] (The undeniable fact that countless members of the lower class believe that they belong to the middle class is an issue that cannot be discussed here.)

The *ancien régime* had been the golden age of the aristocratic and ecclesiastical elite, Europe's original, quintessential "upper class." With the Revolution, the French were suddenly transformed from impotent subjects (*sujets*) of a crowned head to full-fledged citizens (*citoyens*) of a state that was to function in their interests, as opposed to being a kind of personal possession of kings such as Louis XIV. (The latter had even famously proclaimed that he *was* the state — "*L'État, c'est moi!*") Henceforth, even "commoners" had a say, not only the members of the middle class but even the "little people" of the lower class, the plebeians, such as the peasants, artisans, and workers. The French Revolution pointed the way toward democracy, starting the process of democratization that is still ongoing today and that, after more than two centuries of highs and lows, continues to be incomplete and unfinished.

In 1815, the battlefield of Waterloo witnessed the triumph of the counterrevolution, that is, of the lords of Europe's *ancien régime*, the crowned heads, the landowning nobility, and also of the churches that were connected like Siamese twins to the great monarchies, namely the Catholic Church in the Habsburg Empire, Lutheranism in Prussia, Anglicanism in Great Britain, and the Orthodox Church in the Russian Empire. The achievements of the Revolution were undone, at least as much as possible, not only in France, where another Louis ascended the throne thanks to the British, Russians, and other victors, but in all countries — for example in Belgium — where the Directoire and Napoleon had exported the Revolution's moderate, bourgeois manifestation. The crowned heads came together in the famous Vienna Congress in order to set the clock back as much as possible to the "good old" times before the French Revolution. A kind of neofeudal order was thus established throughout Europe, whose basic structure was to survive until 1914. In Russia, serfdom — a typically feudal, medieval institution — was to be maintained until 1861!

With the triumph of the counterrevolution in 1815, the intellectual and cultural tide also turned in Europe. In many ways, the French Revolution had found inspiration in the ideas of the Enlightenment, a cultural move-ment associated with critical, logical, and even scientific thinking, not only with respect to nature, but also to human society, including problems of a political and social nature. Somewhat optimistically, the Enlightenment considered human beings as intrinsically good, endowed with reason and therefore capable of rational thinking, of identifying and understanding issues and of finding solutions — including solutions to political and social-economic problems. From Voltaire, Rousseau, and other "enlight-ened" philosophers, the revolutionaries had learned that it was possible to create a better society. The models they had in mind stemmed from clas-sical Antiquity, for example, Athenian democracy and the Roman repub-lic. The radical phase of the Revolution thus revived a "classical" form of government, the republic. Like the philosophers of the Enlightenment, the revolutionaries firmly believed in the existence of rights and values that applied to all men, in other words, *universal* values, such as liberty and equality. In this sense, the French Revolution was much more than a revo-lution *made in France*: it was an international revolution, a revolution with a universal mission and with worldwide repercussions. (It is true, of course, that all sorts of rationales were invented to restrict the newly proclaimed rights to human being of the male and white variety.)

The Enlightenment also inspired a new *economic*, rational and supposedly scientific theory that differed greatly from the hitherto prevailing protectionist, "mercantilist" ideas and practices. This kind of thinking has gone down in history under the label of "liberalism." It preached the advantages of the "free" circulation of goods and of labour, of competition between producers and merchants, and of the greatest possible restriction of the role of the state in economic life, essentially reducing it to that of "night watch." In economic life one had to allow the actors as much freedom of action as possible, an attitude summed up in the slogan *"laissez faire,"* for it was believed that the "invisible hand" of the "free market" ensured that each individual's quest for personal advantage would produce the greatest possible advantage for the entire community. Liberalism functioned as an ideology; that is, it reflected and favoured the interests of the mainly bourgeois owners of capital, of the commercial and industrial means of production, of "mobile" assets as opposed to the "immobile" assets that constituted the wealth of the nobility and the Church. Liberalism thus actually served as a blueprint for a capitalist economy and society.

It is generally known that the Bible of this new kind of social-economic thinking was the book *Inquiry into the Nature and Causes of the Wealth of Nations*, written by a Scot, Adam Smith (1723–1790). This book, published in 1776, on the eve of the French Revolution, served as perfect intellectual grist for the mill of the bourgeoisie of Great Britain, a country where the industrial revolution was already in full swing. Like other Enlightenment ways of thinking, however, the new liberal ideas were "universal" and appealed also to the rising middle class of other countries, including France, where the bourgeoisie had started to put into practice all sorts of enlightened ideas during the Revolution.

But after the battle of Waterloo, the ideas of the Enlightenment quickly went out of fashion. Henceforth the tone was set by Romanticism, an intellectual and cultural current that emphasized the helplessness, the limitations, and the base instincts of human beings, as well as their powerlessness in their confrontation with God or nature. Romanticism presented the world and our existence as unfathomable mysteries instead of objects of scientific research; and glorified sentiment and intuition rather than rational thinking, faith and religion at the expense of knowledge and science. The Romanticists also denied the existence of universal values and rights: not only each individual, but each people was unique and had its own soul — a *Volksgeist*, as the German philosopher Johann Gottfried von Herder called it — reflected by its own language, traditions and values, its own past (or history) and its own destiny, determined by the divine providence or by some mysterious but omnipotent destiny.

Romanticism was to function as a mighty stimulus for nationalism, likewise a product of the French Revolution, as we have seen. Nationalism, which would very much leave its mark on the nineteenth and twentieth centuries, was an ambiguous phenomenon. It could be and often was progressive in nature, particularly in France, and associated with typically bourgeois Enlightenment ideas, especially with liberalism, but sometimes also with radical revolutionary notions, such as the "Jacobin" ideas of Robespierre, and later also with socialism. But outside of France, nationalism often revealed itself to be counterrevolutionary, closely tied to religion in general and Christianity in particular, to the monarchy, the nobility, and the *ancien régime* in general, and to conservative and Romanticist thinking. Even today, nationalism can be conservative and even reactionary, but also progressive and "emancipatory."[5]

It is not a coincidence that Romanticism found inspiration in the Middle Ages, the golden age of the nobility, the traditional upper class which, after 1815, having overcome the challenge of the French Revolution, found itself firmly back in the saddle of power, or so it believed, and the Church which, after the outburst of anticlericalism engendered by the French Revolution, dreamed of a glorious comeback. Romanticism reflected a nostalgia for the "good old days" before the French Revolution, when everyone — the lord as well as his subjects — knew and accepted their supposedly natural or God-given role in society. The heroes of Romantic literature were crusaders and proud knights like Ivanhoe, pretty but chaste virgins, pious monks, and simple but hard-working and, of course, humble and docile peasants. For the benefit of the readers, the authors extolled the virtues of chivalry, of feudal loyalty to the sovereign and to the nation's glorious dynasty and, last but not least, of Christian devotion. Countless British citizens who in 1914 would respond enthusiastically to the intrinsically feudal "summons" to go to war "for king and country" had read *Ivanhoe*, an archetypical Romantic opus, written in 1820 by a Scotsman, Sir Walter Scott. Architecture likewise reflected the spirit of the time: neomedieval churches and castles — such as the very *kitsch* "fairytale castles" of King Ludwig II of Bavaria — rose up everywhere like mushrooms. Even the temples of modern science, the universities, of which many were founded at the time, were constructed in neo-Gothic or some other form of medieval revivalism.

Romanticism had a Siamese twin on the political and social level, namely the ideology known today as "conservatism." Its protagonists — above all Edmund Burke, author of *Reflections on the Revolution in France*, a book published in 1790 and immediately translated into French — were the contemporaries of the great male and female figures of Romanticism such as François René de Chateaubriand, who allegedly invented the term "conservatism" in 1819. They were all, without exception, mortal enemies of the French Revolution and simultaneously partisans of the counterrevolution or, as one can also say, of the "reaction." They preached that all that exists is natural or wanted by God and that, as a consequence, all that is must also be — and may not be modified in any way by man. Similarly, a hierarchical human society was said to be natural or wanted by God; any attempt to improve this society is therefore condemned to fail — to fail catastrophically, because such hubris is immediately punished by nature or by God. The tragedy of the French Revolution, with all its bloodshed, had presumably demonstrated this truth. Change, it was proclaimed, could only result from a slow and gradual "organic growth," never from human meddling and certainly not from revolution. The book that disseminated this ideology most effectively, though not necessarily deliberately, was *Frankenstein; Or, the Modern Prometheus*, written by Mary Shelley and published in 1818. In this "gothic" novel, the experiments of a scientist, Dr. Frankenstein, produce to his consternation a horrible monster. The moral of the story was this: first, man does not have the right to tinker with God's creation and, consequently, not even with human society; second, it is not surprising that the great political experiment of the French Revolution had fathered the Terror!

33

Romanticism was not fond of change, and certainly not of rapid change, but in the golden age of Romanticism a lot of things were changing very rapidly. The nineteenth century not only witnessed the famous industrial revolution, but also an agricultural revolution, which, on account of factors such as mechanization, became more productive and thus less labour intensive. Simultaneously, Europe experienced a demographic revolution, a spectacular population growth whose causes cannot be elucidated here. In any event, all this produced a demographic surplus in the countryside. These rural poor sought salvation in emigration, either to the far side of the Atlantic Ocean, where land was to be had at low prices or even totally free of charge — for example in the form of the land of the Indians who were being massacred in what has been called the "American Holocaust" by some historians — or to the new industrial centres that were emerging in Europe itself, such as the English Midlands or the German Ruhr area. Even so, the European working class would long remain composed mostly of poor peasants. In 1900, 36 per cent of the Germans and 43 per cent of the French still made a living in agriculture. In Belgium, on the eve of the First World War, the peasants still formed a quarter of the active population. And during that war, the majority of the soldiers would consist of peasants. In 1914–18, no less than 3.7 million of them served in the French army alone![6]

In Europe, a large part of the rural population thus migrated to the industrial cities in order to find work in the factories. And so the working population of the cities grew dramatically in the course of the nineteenth century, but it was composed increasingly of low-paid wage-earning factory workers rather than the "independent" artisans, shopkeepers, etc., just like the Parisian "*sans-culottes*" of the time of the French Revolution of 1789. These factory workers were concentrated in the sinister kind of slums described so vividly in the novels of Charles Dickens; however, the classic scientific study of the fate of English workers of the nineteenth century is of course *The Situation of the Working Class in England in 1844*, a work written by Friedrich Engels in 1844–1845. In contrast to the craftsmen, these poor labourers had no possessions other than their children, which is actually the meaning of a famous term that originated in that era, "proletarians," in which one can recognize the Latin word *proles*, "progeniture," "offspring," or "family."

34

Everybody was aware of the extreme poverty of the industrial proletariat. But what could be done about it? Since time immemorial, the nobility had been used to seeing most of the people wallow in misery, and it found nothing particularly wrong or unusual about that. The Church endorsed this attitude by traditionally preaching that the poor would always be among us (and that they would surely inherit the kingdom of God), but that Christian charity could bring some relief. As for the bourgeoisie, it derived an explanation from its sacrosanct ideology, liberalism, and insisted that nothing could be done, since the "invisible hand" of the market was doing its work. Learned colleagues of Adam Smith, such as Thomas Malthus, explained that poverty was the inevitable result of natural demographic growth. Poverty existed because there were simply too many people in comparison to the available land, because not enough food could ever be produced to feed the all-too-rapidly increasing number of human beings. The poor, in particular, reproduced too quickly — in other words, the poor were to blame for their own poverty — and the solution to the problem of poverty was therefore to be found in the reduction of the number of paupers. The state could lend a helping hand in this respect by causing the poor to disappear; for example, by encouraging emigration and also by deporting people for the slightest misdeed to distant penal colonies such as Australia. But the ranks of the poor were thinned out primarily by diseases such as tuberculosis and by starvation, as was the case in Ireland during the "great famine" of 1845–1850. Malthus identified diseases and undernourishment as "positive checks" introduced by Mother Nature herself for the purpose of reducing the number of paupers and thus solving the problem of poverty. War was another one of these positive checks according to Malthus, which functioned to thin out the *army* of the poor. We will later see that during the years preceding 1914, many respectable burghers firmly believed that war might provide an excellent Malthusian solution to the problem of the surfeit of poor and therefore miserable, unruly, and dangerous folks.

To ameliorate their truly miserable condition, which actually inspired Victor Hugo's monumental novel *Les Misérables*, the poor could thus only count on themselves. And indeed, it was obvious that they were far from satisfied with their lot. The proletariat took its cue from the French Revolution and revealed itself on many occasions and in many countries, regions, and cities to be unhappy, rebellious, and on occasion even revolutionary — for example, in 1830 in Paris and in Brussels, and in 1848 in Paris again and in many other European cities.

After 1815, in spite of the Romantic and conservative spirit of the time, the bourgeoisie — the haute bourgeoisie as well as the petty bourgeoisie — continued to be well-disposed toward revolution, and not only in France. It looked out for an opportunity to try again to overthrow the old feudal order that had been restored after Waterloo. With the rapid development of typically bourgeois activities, namely commerce and above all industry (i.e., the rapid development of capitalism), the haute bourgeoisie, now consisting increasingly of industrialists, grew richer and richer. Conversely, the nobility, whose wealth was based on land ownership, and thus above all on agriculture, became *relatively* less wealthy. Incidentally, the members of the landowning nobility, associated with agriculture and often residing in ancestral country estates of the type featured in the popular TV series *Downton Abbey*, were referred to as the "agrarians," as opposed to the bourgeois "industrialists" (and bankers) who were typically at home in cities, where they lived in comparatively modern but equally imposing great houses.[7]

The bourgeoisie was rather timid and meek in the period immediately after Waterloo, in an era known in German as *Biedermeier*; however, as this class was quickly accumulating great riches, it also became increasingly self-assured and therefore politically and socially more ambitious. In France, the revolutionary fire soon flared up again in the camp of the bourgeoisie, and via the revolutions of 1830 and 1848, during which the proletariat again made the bulk of the necessary sacrifices, bourgeois regimes were installed in Paris. Elsewhere too, the "rising" bourgeoisie displayed its ambition and revolutionary energy. Such was the case in the Kingdom of the Netherlands, for example, where in 1830 a proletarian uprising in the rapidly industrializing southern part of the country was "hijacked" by the local bourgeoisie and subtly transformed into a "national revolution." The result was a new country, called Belgium, which was actually the Latin name used by the sixteenth-century humanists to refer to the Netherlands. The new nation was predestined to be ruled by its haute bourgeoisie, albeit in collaboration with the nobility and the Catholic Church. This compromise was reflected in the form of government, a monarchy, which pleased the nobility, headed by a king who was a (converted) Catholic, which pleased the Church. But this was a *constitutional* monarchy, endowed with a very liberal constitution, which suited the industrialists, bankers, and other upper-middle-class types. It was no coincidence that Marx was to describe Belgium as a "paradise for capitalists."[8]

In Great Britain also, where the industrial revolution had made the most progress by far, and where the upper-middle class had therefore become extremely rich, this class was able to play an increasingly important role in political and social life. After a series of reforms introduced in the 1830s and 1840s, the British bourgeoisie, represented in the political arena by the Liberal Party, managed to increase its political influence and social prestige without having to have recourse to a revolution. But the nobility would continue to remain the most powerful class, thanks primarily to institutions such as the monarchy itself and the unelected House of Lords. Throughout the 19th century, all the key positions in diplomacy, the army, and the judiciary remained securely in the hands of the nobility.[9]

The bourgeoisie did not fare nearly as well in Central and Eastern Europe, for example in Prussia and in the other states of Germany, which was not yet unified, or in the Habsburg Empire. The revolutions that broke out in Berlin, Vienna, etc., in the great revolutionary year — "the crazy year" (*das tolle Jahr*) — which 1848 happened to be, coupled with attempts to install "liberal" bourgeois systems (with the indispensable help of the proletariat), failed lamentably. The crowned heads and noble lords of the *ancien régime* briefly panicked but soon bounced back and managed to preserve their monopoly of political power. In Russia, the bourgeoisie simply never had a chance to even dream of grabbing a share of power.

CHAPTER 2

THE NOBILITY AND THE BOURGEOISIE: A COUNTERREVOLUTIONARY SYMBIOSIS

After its traumatic experiences of 1848 and 1871 — respectively "the crazy year" and the annus horribilis of the Paris Commune — the bourgeoisie ceases to be revolutionary and joins the nobility and the Church in the counterrevolutionary camp . . .

After 1815 the European bourgeoisie, though temporarily chastened, had remained a progressive and revolutionary class, keen to achieve its liberal objectives via reforms or, if necessary, via revolution. But it is doubtful that the bourgeoisie would have been able to come to power, or at least grab a major share of power, in France and in Belgium in 1830 and in France again in 1848, without the active support of that other revolutionary class, the working people of Paris and other great cities, who had already done most of the heavy lifting in 1789. Under the *ancien régime*, life for the "lower orders" had never been anything but "nasty, brutish, and short," to quote the seventeenth-century English philosopher Thomas Hobbes;[1] and in the summer of 1789, when bread had become rare and extremely expensive, the Parisian populace had had enough of this misery and took up arms. This type of scenario was to repeat itself in 1830 and 1848. Then too, hunger and misery in general motivated the "little people" of Paris (and of Brussels in 1830) to commit great revolutionary deeds. Reflecting on this, Marx drew the conclusion that increasing misery or "pauperization" would necessarily drive the proletariat into the arms of revolution.

Of the revolution of 1830, the bourgeoisie could still easily control the development and outcome. Thus was born the very haut-bourgeois reign of Louis-Philippe, the "bourgeois king." The "little" people, on the other hand, who had made the success of the revolution possible, were left empty-handed. In 1848, however, a very different revolutionary scenario unfolded in Paris. It came to a veritable *social* revolution through which the lower classes threatened to come to power at the expense not only of the nobility, but also of the bourgeoisie itself. In order to prevent the worst, the bourgeoisie reluctantly had to satisfy certain radical demands by the people. Universal suffrage was reintroduced, and this time slavery was definitively abolished. But when, exactly as at the time of Robespierre, the revolution threatened to radicalize even more, the bourgeoisie decided that it had had enough. Troops were mobilized to teach the "insurgents" good manners, a new *brumaire* was orchestrated, and another Bonaparte appeared on the scene like a *deus ex machina* in order to hold his protective hand over the heads of the French bourgeoisie.

This "Second Empire" of Napoleon III, nephew of the first Napoleon, revealed itself to be the golden age of the haute bourgeoisie in France. This idyll turned out to be short-lived, however, expiring ingloriously in a humiliating defeat during the Franco-Prussian War of 1870–1871. Once again, war led to a revolution, and this revolution arrived in the spring of 1871 in the guise of the Paris Commune, which was to be smothered in blood by the army. When the smoke of war and revolution finally dissipated, France was saddled with a new bourgeois regime, the Third Republic, a system that was to survive until 1940. In this state, not only the upper but also the lower-middle class, the petty bourgeoisie, had a say in the realm of politics, although comparatively little in the case of the latter. But in the state administration, in diplomacy, and above all in the army, the old landowning and essentially Catholic nobility remained in control. In 1914, a disproportionally high percentage of the generals and other high officers would still be of noble origin.[2]

For the bourgeoisie as well as for the nobility, not only in France but in all of Europe and even in the distant United States, the Paris Commune proved to be an extremely traumatic event. This uprising in the French capital, which was condemned by the very influential elitist bourgeois philosopher Friedrich Nietzsche as the handiwork of "barbarian slaves,"[3] looked like it had been a genuine proletarian revolution. It was generally believed that it would have sounded the death knell of the established political and social-economic order if the authorities had not intervened so resolutely.[4] In any event, as a result of its experiences with the revolutions of 1848 and of the Paris Commune, the international bourgeoisie was henceforth saddled with a great angst and horror with respect to revolutions, and it joined the nobility and the Church in the counterrevolutionary camp.

Until 1848, the bourgeoisie and the proletariat had been progressive and even revolutionary allies in the class struggle against the counterrevolutionary nobility and Church. After 1871, the bourgeoisie and the nobility constituted a conservative and counterrevolutionary common front against the proletariat and the popular masses in general. "The industrial revolution," writes a German historian, H.W. Koch,

> *Had not only created a new middle class, but also a growing urban proletariat, which in time began to formulate its own political and social demands. Vis-à-vis this new working class, liberals now began to defend the political and social status quo and consequently were bound to appear as conservatives and reactionaries.*[5]

Indeed, the bourgeoisie was now conservative and reactionary. After the revolutionary year of 1848, and certainly after the Paris Commune of 1871, a kind of partnership or "active symbiosis," as the Austrian-American economist and political scientist Joseph Schumpeter would call it,[6] of the two "propertied classes" was forged. In many ways, the traditional upper class, the nobility, and the upper level of the middle class, the haute bourgeoisie, were merging into one single upper class, one single "power elite" or "establishment." This was so even though, on the political level, the nobility preferred conservative (and/or Christian) parties while the haute bourgeoisie favoured liberal parties. (The Italian historian and philosopher Domenico Losurdo speaks in this context of "a fusion of the ancient and of the new dominant class," *fusione tra vecchia e nuova class dominante.*)[7] What united the two was their common fear (and, indeed, loathing) of the potentially revolutionary "underclass" of the proletariat. The latter would henceforth increasingly be referred to as the "dangerous classes" (*classes dangereuses*) or the "vile multitude." It is important to note, finally, that the propertied classes' great fear of revolution went hand-in-hand with a determination to fight tooth and nail against any reforms that might undermine its own privileges, which happened to be the case with most reforms, but especially with radical reforms. On the other hand, reforms of the moderate variety were considered acceptable if they could be useful for the purpose of forestalling radical reforms and, above all, revolutions. We will soon see that *war* was viewed as an effective stratagem in the fight against reforms and revolution, and that the First World War must be understood in this light.

The *modus vivendi* that emerged between the nobility and the bourgeoisie went hand-in-hand with a social and economic "interpenetration" of these two classes. Aristocrats married members of the haute bourgeoisie, and vice versa. On occasion, meritorious members of the bourgeoisie were "elevated" into the nobility; thus they contributed to a kind of "bourgeoisification" (*embourgeoisement*) of the old aristocracy. Aristocrats also invested more and more in industrial projects, particularly when their vast land holdings turned out to contain minerals important to industry. Conversely, well-to-do burghers often invested part of their fortunes in vast rural domains, prestigious country homes, and other forms of landed or "immobile" property. (Such property, hitherto the monopoly of the nobility, continued to be considered as the primordial and genuinely legitimate form of wealth, and was therefore known as "real estate.") In any case, as seen from the viewpoint of the proletariat, the haute bourgeoisie and the nobility henceforth constituted one single superior class of rich and powerful, of "plutocrats."[8]

On account of its great wealth, the haute bourgeoisie unquestionably now formed part, together with the nobility, of the *ruling class*, but it was not necessarily part of the *governing class*, that is, the class that enjoyed political power. Put differently, while everywhere the bourgeoisie held considerable (and rapidly growing) *economic* and *financial* power, it did not always possess a lot of *political* power, and in many states it was virtually impotent, politically speaking. The bourgeoisie did rule *and* govern in France, in Belgium, and in Great Britain, but in partnership with the nobility. Even in France, the latter class was far from eliminated in spite of a string of revolutions. It was only on the far side of the Atlantic Ocean, in the United States, that the industrial upper-middle class managed to achieve a monopoly of political power, namely after having eliminated — during the civil war of 1861–1865 — the "agrarian" competition, that is, the quasi-aristocracy of the large landowners in the southern states, the slave-owning "cotton barons." Everywhere else — for example, in the gigantic German, Russian, and Habsburg Empires — the nobility was and remained the sole governing class.

One can say that in Europe the nobility generally continued to set the tone on the political and social level, as Arno Mayer has emphasized in a remarkable study, *The Persistence of the Old Regime: Europe to the Great War*, originally published in 1981. This noble governing class, writes Mayer, was solidly retrenched behind the walls of "absolutist authoritarian systems of different degrees of enlightenment and headed by hereditary monarchs" and it was supported unconditionally by the Church, itself a large landowner, whose bishops and other prelates or "princes" were generally scions of noble families. Mayer cites Friedrich Engels, who noted that while "society became more and more bourgeois . . . the political order remained feudal."[9]

It was above all in Germany and in the Habsburg Empire — known as Austria-Hungary, the Danube Monarchy, or the Dual Monarchy after a major constitutional reform in 1867, the so-called *Ausgleich*, or "compromise" — that the political system had remained essentially feudal. In 1848, in Berlin and in Vienna, the bourgeoisie still dreamed of a liberal republic and had manned the barricades. But after that "crazy year" it abandoned its revolutionary aspirations and opted for a counterrevolutionary course. The nobility could thus continue to enjoy a monopoly of political and military power and social prestige while also continuing to set the tone on the cultural level, as reflected in operettas with aristocrats as stars and heroes. With respect to Germany's bourgeois industrialists, Arno Mayer observes that "once they perceived [the rise of socialism] as a clear and present danger, they practically abandoned what remained of their bid for a share of political power commensurate with their newly acquired material positions."[10] The Central-European bourgeoisie henceforth concentrated on its economic vocation, the accumulation of riches, the famous "accumulation process," which was in fact also the main concern of their counterparts in all other countries. The German and Austro-Hungarian upper-middle class was obviously motivated by the fear of a proletarian revolution and by the realization that an autocratic monarchist state run by aristocrats with impeccable counterrevolutionary credentials offered the best insurance against this danger. "We need a strong monarchy," wrote the famous historian Heinrich von Treitschke in 1869, "in order to maintain peace in our society."[11]

The political system that best exemplified this new *modus vivendi* of nobility and haute bourgeoisie was undoubtedly that of the new German Empire, born in 1871 and ruled for many years with an iron hand by Otto von Bismarck. In this state, the agrarian nobility, represented primarily by the landowning Prussian junkers such as Bismarck himself, monopolized political, bureaucratic, judicial, and military power and continued to set the tone on the social, cultural, and intellectual levels. As the French political scientist Nicos Poulantzas has emphasized, what prevailed in Germany was

> the feudal ideology of the nobility, characterised by militarism, respect for the authority of the state and the superior classes, social discipline, the Christian faith, etc.; conversely, in this Germany 'liberalism', the bourgeois ideology par excellence in the European context, never had the slightest chance of taking root.[12]

However, simultaneously, the state made it possible for the upper-middle class and above all for industrialists like Krupp to enrich themselves spectacularly thanks to state orders — for cannons, for example! — and to bask in considerable social prestige, sometimes via the acquisition of a noble title. Bismarck himself described this *modus vivendi* of agrarian aristocrats and haut-bourgeois industrialists as "a marriage of iron and rye." In spite of their liberal preferences, Germany's industrialists (and financiers) thus reconciled themselves with the feudal political system of the Bismarckian state. And they became quite fond of the authoritarian way in which that state maintained domestic order and of the aggressive foreign policy and the wars that permitted the "iron chancellor" to create a great and mighty German Empire, both of which offered them considerable advantages. (After the Great War, when Germany became a liberal and relatively democratic republic, a majority of the country's big industrialists and bankers would experience a great nostalgia for the era of the pre-1914 authoritarian Empire.)

Whether the nobility dominated on the political level or, as in France, became a junior partner of the haute bourgeoisie, everywhere in Europe these two classes henceforth collaborated closely in the service of the counterrevolutionary cause, and the feudal-bourgeois states did everything in their power to defend and promote the interests of these two classes. Between the nobility and the bourgeoisie there remained important differences of opinion, for example with respect to the importation of agricultural products; the agrarian conservatives wanted to maintain high import duties in order to protect the prices of their own agricultural products, while the liberal industrialists preferred to eliminate such tariffs in order to lower the prices of foodstuffs and thus be able to pay low wages to their workers.[13] What was more important, however, was that under the auspices of the "marriage of convenience" of nobility and upper-middle class, the European states undertook certain projects that revealed themselves to be particularly profitable to both classes.

The nineteenth century was the age of the industrial revolution and was characterized by rapid economic growth in all countries that experienced that kind of revolution. This was the case above all in Western Europe, especially in Great Britain, France, and Belgium, as well as in the most important country of Central Europe, namely Germany. Symptomatic of this development was the appearance, during the 1870s, of a new type of economic crisis, a crisis that reflected the growth of industrial productivity.

Typical for the pre-industrial, essentially agriculture-based economy, had been crises of underproduction. These were situations in which the supply did not meet demand, which produced all sorts of shortages that in turn triggered famines and diseases. Such crises of the old type persisted in the 1840s in Ireland (the infamous potato famine!), in the 1860s in Spain, and in the 1890s in Russia. On the other hand, the new type of economic crisis, typical for an economy based primarily on industry, an increasingly productive economy, was — and continues to be — a crisis of *overproduction*, in which supply exceeds demand, thus resulting in slowdowns and even closings of businesses, layoffs, wage reductions, unemployment, etc.; this leads to a reduction of purchasing power and a further constriction of demand.

The latter type of crisis first manifested itself during the 1870s, and this "depression" had profound consequences. First, countless small industrial producers became its victims and disappeared from the economic scene, at least in the most developed countries, that is, in Western and Central Europe and in the US. The industrial landscape was henceforth dominated by a relatively restricted group of gigantic enterprises, mostly incorporated, joint-stock companies or "corporations," as well as associations of firms known as cartels, and of course big banks. These "big boys" did compete with each other, but increasingly they also concluded agreements and collaborated in order to share raw materials and markets, set prices, and find other ways to limit as much as possible the disadvantages of competition in a theoretically "free" market — and in order to defend and aggressively promote their common interests against foreign competitors and, of course, against their own workers and other employees. In this system, the big banks played an important role. They provided the credit required by large-scale industrial production and, at the same time, they looked all over the world for opportunities to invest the surplus capital produced by megaprofits. (In this context it ought to be emphasized that colonies — and "semi-colonies" — were not only important as sources of raw materials and cheap labour as well as markets for finished industrial products, but also as regions offering lucrative opportunities for investment capital.) Big banks thus became partners and even owners, or at least major shareholders, of corporations. Concentration, gigantism, oligopolies, and even monopolies characterized this new stage in the development of capitalism. The term "imperialism" had already been used in connection with the establishment of worldwide empires such as that of Great Britain, but it was Lenin who would use it to refer to this phase, to this manifestation of capitalism.

The industrial and financial bourgeoisie had hitherto been very much attached to the liberal, laissez-faire thinking of Adam Smith, who had assigned to the state only a minimal role in economic life, namely that of "night watch." The role of the state was becoming increasingly important, however, for example as buyer of industrial products such as guns and other arms from Krupp. One also counted on the state's intervention to protect the country's corporations against foreign competition by means of tariffs on the importation of finished products, even though this violated the classical liberal dogma of free markets and free competition. "National economic systems" or "national economies" thus emerged everywhere, which proceeded to compete fiercely against each other.[14] The best-known example of this type of "rat race" is the rivalry between the industrial super-power that Great Britain then happened to be, and the rising star in the industrial firmament, Germany. This rivalry was particularly keen and was predestined to lead to war between those two countries in 1914; an English historian, Neil Faulkner, recently proclaimed it to have been "the main axis of the European crisis of 1914." But he simultaneously emphasized that "the growth of giant monopolies and the fusion of industrial, bank, and state capital had created a dangerous world of competing nationalisms," which were "the most deep-rooted cause of the First World War."[15]

State intervention — to be labelled "dirigism" or "statism" by economists — was also indispensable for the acquisition of sources of raw materials, new markets, and cheap labour. In the nineteenth century the industrialists were already what they still are today, namely "raw material hunters"[16] as well as "market conquerors," and they counted on the state to hunt for raw materials and to conquer markets all over the world on their behalf. Moreover, the industrialists as well as the large landowners were always looking out for the cheapest possible labour. Slavery had long been useful from this point of view, but in the course of the nineteenth century it had to be abolished for reasons that cannot be examined here.[17] It is in this context that the resourceful British developed the infamous "coolie" system, that is, the systematic deportation of Indians and Chinese to any parts of the Empire where hard, dirty, and/or dangerous work had to be performed, for example backbreaking work on the sugar plantations of the Caribbean or the construction of railroads in the Canadian Rocky Mountians. Other European colonial powers similarly helped themselves to this kind of pseudo-slavery, such as the French in Indochina, the Dutch in Indonesia, and the Belgians in the Congo.

Cheap labour and raw materials were highly prized assets that were generally not available in sufficient quantities or at sufficiently low prices in the industrialized countries, and the domestic scene did not offer enough opportunities for the profitable investment of accumulated capital. The industrialists and bankers therefore appreciated that the state also sought to resolve this problem by means of the acquisition of direct or indirect control over regions where there still existed a considerable potential for such investments. Wherever that was feasible, one went to work next door, in neighbouring lands. That course of action was long the specialty of the United States, who grabbed the vast territories of the Native Americans, stretching from the "frontier" all the way to the coast of the Pacific Ocean, and also managed to grab a large part of the territory of neighbouring Mexico. But in Europe, one could only dream of such grandiose achievements. And indeed, numerous were the Germans who, at the time, were inspired by the American conquest of the "Wild West" and fantasized about similarly large-scale conquests in Europe's vast eastern stretches; in other words, who dreamed of a new edition of the legendary medieval Germanic *Drang nach Osten*. Consequently, in 1914 territorial annexations in Eastern Europe would not be missing from Germany's extensive list of war objectives. Even after its defeat in 1918, this dream of territorial conquest in the east would live on in Adolf Hitler's ambition of conquering "living space" (*Lebensraum*) for the German people in the eastern reaches of Europe. Hitler was born in 1889 under the Dual Monarchy, but close to the German border; he was a child of his era and of the society that had produced him.

It was generally more realistic, however, to dream of great territorial acquisitions in faraway lands, above all in Africa. That part of the world was abundantly blessed with important raw materials such as copper and rubber, impressive quantities of commodities such as coffee, bananas, and exotic edibles for which Europe was then developing a great appetite and even a dependency; and the millions of natives seemed to hanker for an opportunity to receive the benefits of British or French culture and of the Christian religion, a favour for which they would gladly reciprocate by slaving away for the white man in some mine or plantation. Furthermore, virtually nowhere in Africa were there any large and powerful states that might have been capable of mounting an effective resistance to colonial penetration by Europeans. (The exception to the latter rule was provided by Ethiopia, an empire that defeated an invading Italian army at Adowa in 1896.)

And so, during the second half of the nineteenth century — and above all during its last two decades, this on account of the rise of the imperialist avatar of capitalism — the European powers and the US, a transatlantic "neo-Europe," gained control over huge territories just about everywhere in the world. The famous "scramble for Africa" and the conquest of the American West were the most spectacular examples of that. But the imperialist rivalries among the great powers inevitably led to war, including the Great War, which Faulkner calls "an imperialist war."[18] On the other hand, imperialist aspirations also inspired the formations of short- and even long-term alliances between players in the great imperialist game. We will soon return to the theme of imperialist rivalries, alliances, and war.

France of the Third Republic, essentially bourgeois, profoundly feudal Bismarckian Germany, and half-bourgeois, half-feudal Great Britain eagerly took part in the rush to colonize most of Africa and much of the rest of the world. But they did not all enjoy the same measure of success. During the second half of the nineteenth century, Great Britain acquired approximately 12 million square kilometres of territory, France 9 million, but Germany "only" 2.5 million. In any event, together with their colonies, all European powers together occupied no less than 67 per cent of the land surface of the planet in 1878, and by 1914 that figure had risen to 84 per cent.[19] In each European state, the bourgeoisie enthusiastically embraced the aforementioned benefits of imperialism to their industry and to their "national economy" in general, in the form of important raw materials, exclusive markets, and a huge pool of cheap labour.

In order to conquer faraway lands, an army was required, and so were a navy and a merchant marine in order to transport personnel and merchandise back and forth; equally useful were modern weapons, needed to teach good manners to recalcitrant natives. This turned out to be a boon for the bourgeoisie as well as for the nobility. The ever-increasing production of modern weapons brought unprecedented profits to the kind of industrialists of whom Krupp was one of the outstanding examples. Already at that time there emerged what would later be called a "military-industrial complex," a nexus of private enterprises and state bureaucracies, industrialists and bankers, political and military leaders of noble as well as upper-middle-class origin with a common interest in the production and sale of weapons and in the expansion of armies. For bourgeois industrialists such as Krupp, that translated into orders and profits, and for the nobility — traditionally the military class in all European countries — it meant careers, promotions, and glory.

The scramble for colonies, mostly but not exclusively in Africa, did of course exacerbate competition and tensions between countries, above all between the great powers. In 1898, Britain and France came perilously close to war in Fashoda, in distant Sudan. The scramble for colonial possessions also engendered enormous tensions between Great Britain and Russia with respect to Central Asian territories near the borders with British India, such as Afghanistan. It is most remarkable that in 1914 the British would actually go to war on the side of France and Russia against Germany, a country that had not been a major competitor in the race for colonies. We will later see why this was so.

In any event, it is obvious that imperialist appetites would play a major role in the outbreak of the First World War. It is in fact on account of its imperialist origins that this war ended up being a *world* war. And while Europe's great powers would confront each other most spectacularly in Europe, they would descend like vultures on each other's colonial possessions in Africa, in the Middle East, and even in China. Finally, in Versailles, the victors would divide and claim not only to the relatively modest booty represented by Germany's former colonies, but especially the petroleum-rich regions of the Middle East that had belonged to the Ottoman Empire.

In the context of the scramble for Africa and the concomitant arms race, we can understand why propaganda in favour of the military was made systematically and aggressively virtually everywhere in Europe. Society was being militarized. Kings, emperors, and other political leaders were proud to appear in public like gamecocks, dressed in dazzling uniforms, shiny helmets on their heads, their chests loaded with decorations.[20] Uniformed men in general radiated prestige and enjoyed considerable success with women. Military parades frequently invaded squares and avenues, especially in the numerous garrison towns, and army bands enthralled the burghers and were trailed by enthusiastic children. In Germany, after their military service, members of the upper-middle class were proud to remain reserve officers for many years, which allowed them to don their uniforms at the drop of a hat. But most important of all, the army was lionized as a "training school" for the nation. In other words, compulsory military service was used to inculcate respect and obedience in the recruits, vis-à-vis both the military and other "superiors," and thus to integrate them better into the established order. As Eric Hobsbawm has written:

> *For governments and ruling classes, armies were not only forces against internal and external enemies, but also a means of securing the loyalty, even the active enthusiasm, of citizens with troubling sympathies for mass movements which undermined the social and political order. Together with the primary school, military service was perhaps the most powerful mechanism at the disposal of the state for inculcating proper civic behaviour and, not least, for turning the inhabitant of a village into the (patriotic) citizen of a nation.[21]*

The language used here by Hobsbawm reflects the modern social scientist's urge to appear objective. But a critical contemporary observer, the German socialist Karl Liebknecht, a notorious critic of militarism, was far less charitable in his own description of this kind of role of military service, at least in his German heimat. In 1907 he wrote the following in a pamphlet on the theme of militarism as an instrument of class hegemony:

> *In this manner [i.e. via conscription] they try to tame people like they tame animals. The recruits are anesthetized, confused, oppressed, incarcerated, dragged along, beaten up*

THE NOBILITY AND THE BOURGEOISIE: A COUNTERREVOLUTIONARY SYMBIOSIS

> . . . In this manner a bastion is built up against anything
> that is subversive . . . The goal of instilling the required
> subservience and resignation is achieved by means of
> unconditional compliance with the rules, iron discipline . . . in
> one word, whatever holds the soldier, uniformed or not, in an
> iron grip whenever he thinks or acts.[22]

Germany was naturally the militarist country *par excellence*. An extremely conservative officer corps enjoyed total control over its army and took advantage of the opportunity offered by military service to purge young workers of any subversive thoughts and to metamorphose the recruits into compliant subjects. The result was that the army was a most useful instrument for teaching good manners to strikers, demonstrators, and other plebeians who were perceived as a threat to the established order.[23]

Even voluntary military service, which existed in Great Britain, contributed to socialize the potentially recalcitrant lower classes. Service in the army may not have been well paid and was in many ways not very pleasant, but to many it loomed as a more attractive option than unemployment or equally poorly paid and often unhealthy and dangerous work in a Newcastle mine or a Manchester cotton mill. Moreover, room and board were included, and one had an opportunity to visit distant parts of the world. Rather attractive, at least from the perspective of youngsters of modest origin, was the prospect of a career as a sergeant. Countless members of the lower classes, not only proletarians but also lower-middle-class folks, were thus integrated into the existing political and social-economic order. It is not a coincidence that it was mainly Scotsmen and Irishmen who served in the armies that conquered a gargantuan empire for Great Britain, even though their own countries had been the first victims of the same imperialism in its embryonic phase, namely the expansion of English feudalism during the Middle Ages. (American blacks and Hispanics similarly provide the manpower for the Marines and other troops that are presently at work all over the world to "defend" the interests of the United States.)

It was certainly not only in Germany that the army was acclaimed as the *nec plus ultra* of human organization, as a model that other organizations ought to emulate. Youth organizations such as the Boy Scouts, founded

51

by Robert Baden-Powell in 1908, and even charitable organizations such as the Salvation Army, already established in 1865, were designed according to the military model; and in the factories workers were increasingly treated as "soldiers of industry," that is, subjected to the control of an entire hierarchy of low- and high-ranking superiors — corresponding to army corporals, sergeants, and officers — and to a quasi-military discipline, as Marx already noted in *The Communist Manifesto* of 1848.[24] This military style of worker discipline was only a short step away from the organization of forced labour, a form of labour that offered the advantage of being not only extremely disciplined, but also very cheap. Forced labour was used on a large scale in the colonies from the Congo to Vietnam, and during the Great War it would make its appearance in Europe itself; for example, in German-occupied Belgium.[25]

We have already seen that, on account of the considerable advantages of state intervention and the emergence in each country of a national economy, the European bourgeoisie ceased to favour classical liberal economic ideas such as free trade, especially in the wake of the economic crisis of the 1870s. Buried at the same time were numerous universal ideas of the Enlightenment, such as the belief in the international solidarity or "fraternity" of men and of peoples that had been written, together with liberty and equality, on the banner of the bourgeois French Revolution of 1789. From the idea of equality, the bourgeoisie had already disengaged at the time of the Great Revolution, namely by restricting the equality discourse to judicial equality and refusing even to consider the merits of, let alone pursue, any form of social or economic equality.

Imperialism and militarism, accompanying the emergence of "national economies," also caused the bourgeoisie to be increasingly enamoured of nationalism, which, catalyzed by the French Revolution and the cultural reaction against that same revolution, Romanticism, had already blossomed in the early nineteenth century. The passage of the bourgeoisie from universalism to nationalism, like its passage from classical liberalism to statism, was determined by the fact that high volumes of business and plentiful profits henceforth depended greatly on the ups and downs of national economic systems and consequently also on the strength — including the military prowess — of each nation.

Converts are often particularly ardent defenders of their faith. It is therefore hardly surprising that the bourgeois variety of nationalism of the second half of the nineteenth (and the beginning of the twentieth) century revealed itself in each country to be an extreme, blind, and aggressive form of nationalism. It became known as "jingoism," and its motto was "my country, right or wrong!" The term stems from a song that was written on the occasion of a threat of war between Great Britain and Russia in 1878. Its refrain goes as follows:

> *We don't want to fight*
> *But, by Jingo, if we do*
> *We've got the ships,*
> *We've got the men,*
> *We've got the money, too.*[26]

While jingoism obviously refers first and foremost to an extreme form of British nationalism, Germany, Russia, the United States, and quite a few other countries also developed forms of jingoism. In the case of France, that kind of nationalism usually goes by its aforementioned older name, *chauvinisme*. In any event, this extreme, unthinking bourgeois nationalism, this jingoism would survive well into the twentieth century and would reach a pinnacle of sorts in 1914.

Nationalism was an ambiguous phenomenon. In the early nineteenth century, having been stimulated by the French Revolution, it could function in favour of the bourgeoisie, which was still revolutionary (or at least progressive) at that time, and of the plebeians. But nationalism was also promoted by the cultural reaction against the Revolution, Romanticism, and by conservative thinking, and as such it was useful to the nobility and the church. Particularly in the first half of the nineteenth century, nationalism was often associated with progressive, liberal movements, for example during the revolutions that broke out in 1848 in Budapest and elsewhere in the Habsburg Empire, collectively known as the "Springtime of the Peoples." During the second half of the nineteenth century, however, nationalism was increasingly associated just about everywhere — even in France! — with Romantic-conservative, counterrevolutionary ideas and values that served the interests of the nobility and the church, such as the Christian religion in general and the concept of a "*Volk*" or "nation."[27] By embracing nationalism (and, by association, militarism) on account of the economic advantages connected with it, the bourgeoisie thus adopted the conservative, counterrevolutionary thinking of the *ancien régime*. "In exchange for help in acquiring state assistance," writes Arno Mayer,

> *[bourgeois] business leaders jettisoned their liberal beliefs, embraced the conservative world-view of the traditional elites, and supported the politics of illiberalism. This realignment reduced elite conflicts and ideological debates [that is, between the nobility and the bourgeoisie] in favor of a consensus heavily weighed toward the old moral, cultural, and political order.*[28]

Indeed, on the cultural level too, the bourgeoisie proceeded to adopt the "ancient," "traditional," or "classical" values; in other words, the values of the nobility and the *ancien régime* in general. Vis-à-vis modernist and avant-garde movements, the upper-middle class revealed itself to be unreceptive, except for the Jewish burghers in cities such as Berlin and Vienna, because the blue-blooded nobility wanted nothing to do with Jews under any circumstances. The bourgeoisie raved about "classical" art and music as well as neo-Gothic and other "historicist" (or "revivalist") forms of architecture, all of which happened to reflect the values of the feudal, preindustrial world and glorified it in many ways. With just as much enthusiasm as the aristocrats, members of the haute bourgeoisie flocked to imposing theatres to revel in Wagner's Romantic operas with their medieval themes and heroes such as the warrior Siegfried and troubadours like Tannhäuser. (The fact that the plot sometimes also revolved around *gold* — the potent symbol of money, of wealth, of capital — made Wagnerian operas extra sexy in the eyes of the businessmen and bankers that many burghers happened to be!) Yet another symptom of this "aristocratization" of the bourgeoisie — the complement of the already mentioned "bourgeoisification" of the nobility — was the tendency of the German bourgeoisie to send its sons to study at universities rich in tradition, such as the one in Heidelberg — scene of the adventures of the Student Prince — where they could join student associations (*Landsmannschaften*) profoundly penetrated by a "quasi-feudal ethos."[29] It is hardly surprising that in 1914 countless German university students of bourgeois origin would go to war voluntarily and enthusiastically in order to sacrifice their lives in a kind of Wagnerian "twilight of the gods" (*Götterdämmerung*).

Finally, it ought to be noted that while Europe's elite preached nationalism, it was itself rather internationally inclined. The nobility and the upper-middle class of Germany, Russia, France, etc., had much more in common among themselves than with the lower classes of their own countries, and the daughters and sons of the aristocracy often married foreign princes and princesses. The royal families were frequently of foreign origin and closely related to their counterparts in other countries. The British and Belgian dynasties, for example, were of German origin, which would prove somewhat awkward in 1914. Emperor Wilhelm II was a grandson of Queen Victoria. "The extended royal and aristocratic families," writes Arno Mayer, "shared a pan-European predilection for the French language, the English hunt, and the Prussian monocle, which they displayed at the Continent's fashionable resorts."[30] The upper-middle class shared this internationalist outlook, at least to some extent. The Rothschild family, for example, had branches in Germany, France, and England. Thus it is not without reason that, in *Paths of Glory*, Stanley Kubrick shows us supposedly patriotic French generals and their ladies waltzing happily to music composed by a national of an enemy country, the Austrian Johann Strauss.[31]

CHAPTER 3
SOCIALISM AND DEMOCRATIZATION

The elite tries to exorcize the proletarian threat not only by using the "stick" of bloody repression but also the "carrot" of social legislation and political reforms. And it invents all sorts of tricks to combat socialism and slow down the democratization process . . .

We return to the crucial fact that the alliance of the upper-middle class and the nobility was rooted in a common fear of "those below" (*ceux d'en bas*), the proletariat. This potentially revolutionary proletariat had to be tamed, and such a task required a strong, authoritarian state and, above all, a strong army that one could count on to maintain or restore order in case of a possible resurgence of the social troubles of 1848 and 1871. As we have seen, militarism was useful for this purpose, and that is why the supposedly peaceable burghers embraced it. During the second half of the nineteenth century, the repressive role of the state continued to expand for the simple reason that the proletarian danger kept increasing relentlessly. The proletariat was no longer the impetuous populace that had stormed the Bastille in 1789 and had manned the barricades in 1830 and 1848. At that time, they had not yet formed a class consciousness, they had not yet been armed with a program or ideology, had few or no capable leaders, and could therefore easily be manipulated and ultimately — when the revolutionary dirty work was done — sent packing by more astute fellow revolutionaries of the bourgeois variety. But now, things were different.

SOCIALISM AND DEMOCRATIZATION

Already in 1848, it became obvious that the proletariat, still consisting mainly of craftsmen, but also increasingly of factory workers, had discovered capable leaders and had developed not only a strong class consciousness, but also a coherent ideology, called socialism. The *Manifesto of the Communist Party*, the first Marxist socialist program, was drawn up by Karl Marx and Friedrich Engels in 1847 and published in February 1848, barely a few days before a revolution broke out in Paris. Like liberalism, socialism was a child of the Enlightenment; however, in addition to the "liberty" that was also written on the banner of liberalism, socialism preached equality and, more precisely, *social* equality instead of the mere equality *before the law* that had been introduced by the French Revolution. According to Marx and Engels, this equality could only become reality via a revolution, a revolution that would bring down the existing capitalist social and economic order together with its political superstructures; thus creating a better, more equitable, and truly egalitarian society. If the Paris Commune terrified the European bourgeoisie as much as it did, it was precisely because it seemed to be a socialist revolution, an attempt to overthrow the entire established social, economic, and political order.

Even after the bloody repression of this insurrection, the bourgeoisie and the nobility were not rid of their fear of the proletarians and the abominable revolutionary socialism embraced by the latter. In fact, there emerged within Europe a major labour movement, well organized and militant, with trade unions, cooperatives, and political parties that mostly subscribed to the ideology and program of revolutionary, *Marxist* socialism. (It should not be forgotten that other varieties of socialism also existed.) The British historian Eric Hobsbawm has described the contemporary atmosphere as follows:

> The mass of workers was large, was indisputably growing, and threw a dark shadow over the established ordering of society and politics. What indeed would happen if, as a class, they organized politically? This is precisely what happened, on a European scale, suddenly and with extraordinary speed . . . Mass parties based on the working class, for the most part inspired by an ideology of revolutionary socialism and led

57

by men — and even sometimes by women — who believed
in such an ideology, appeared on the scene and grew with
startling rapidity. [1]

Indeed, during the years 1870–1880 the socialist parties rose like mushrooms and were generally partisans of Marxist revolutionary socialism. But they also formulated concrete and practical demands, such as the extension of the right to vote, higher wages, fewer work days, and shorter working hours, as well as restrictions on child labour. (In this field, the socialist parties discovered useful allies in socialist and other trade unions that knew how to use the feared weapon of the strike.) Put differently, the socialists aimed not only at a revolutionary overthrow of the established order: they also demanded political reforms and social-economic change within that order. They stood for *revolution*, for radical change, but also for *evolution*, for progressive, gradual change. In any event, with this ambivalent and somewhat contradictory program they enjoyed considerable success among the plebeians, not only among the factory workers, the "blue-collar workers," but also, albeit to a lesser extent, among the lower-middle class, the petty bourgeoisie, composed of craftsmen, shopkeepers, and "white-collar workers." This lower-middle class was caught between the capitalist Charybdis of the aristocratic-bourgeois elite and the socialist Scylla of the rising labour movement. It was traumatized by being squeezed from above as well as from below, by being looked down upon by social superiors and being subjected to competition from big industry, from "big business," as well as by the fear of being swallowed up by the socially inferior working class, by being "proletarianized"; and so it developed anticapitalist as well as antisocialist tendencies. (It is on account of this that the petty bourgeoisie was receptive to anti-Semitism, a Janus-faced phenomenon with an anticapitalist and an antisocialist side, thus seeming to reconcile both tendencies.)

In any event, from the viewpoint of the aristocratic and bourgeois elite, it seemed as if the restless popular masses in their entirety were poised to overthrow the established order. How could one exorcize this danger? In order to keep the "dangerous classes" under control and abort embryonic revolutions, one needed those same armies that also happened to be useful for the achievement of imperialist objectives. This was one of the most important reasons why in many countries the bourgeoisie had graciously ceded the domain of politics to representatives of the *ancien régime*, that is, to people with centuries of military experience, particularly experience in the ruthless struggle against anything that was revolutionary. Of the king and the nobility, one could also hope that their authority and prestige might contribute to keep ordinary people respectful and submissive. In 1878, the following could be read in the liberal German newspaper *National-Zeitung*:

> The king [of Prussia] is the master par excellence of the existing order . . . In the face of the [socialist] tsunami the monarchy is our strongest bastion, the dam that protects our peace and our rights, our property, and our erudition against the deluge of barbarity.[2]

One could similarly count on the church, yet another pillar of the *ancien régime*, to keep the people under control. After the experiences of 1848 and 1871, for example, the French bourgeoisie, though essentially free-thinking, was happy to abandon primary school education to the clerical authorities. Napoleon had already been keenly aware of the utility of religion in this respect. He made frequent remarks to the effect that religion "is excellent for keeping common people quiet" and "keeps the poor from murdering the rich."[3]

In order to protect the rights, the property, and the entire "civilization" of the bourgeoisie, the nobility, and the church, in other words, the interests of the propertied classes, against proletarian "barbarity" and to teach good manners to the restless plebeian masses, all means were good, including bloody repression. In this field too, the autocratic crowned heads and the aristocratic military leaders were the great specialists. They had provided a prototypical example of their skills in this respect in 1819, on St. Peter's Field in Manchester, when the cavalry attacked a crowd of 60,000 demonstrators and caused such a bloodbath that the massacre went down in history under the name of "Battle of Peterloo"; this name being a sarcastic allusion to the fact that one of the men responsible for this repression of what appeared to be an imminent revolution was the Duke of Wellington, who had already personally vanquished the international revolution incarnated by Napoleon's France, at the 1815 Battle of Waterloo. When it came to repression, however, bourgeois regimes were also quite capable of hitting hard; the best example of that was provided by the extremely bloody repression of the Paris Commune by the army of the French Third Republic. Thousands of Communards were massacred and thousands of others, including numerous women, were deported to penal colonies such as Devil's Island off the coast of French Guyana, to which revolutionaries had already been forcibly transported in 1848.

The bourgeoisie was not only ready and keen to quash revolutions (and any other form of lower-class agitation), it also collaborated closely with its partner, the nobility, to alienate the people from socialism. Bismarck, who according to certain historians was possessed by "fear of revolution" (*Revolutionsfurcht*)[4] became famous for his twin approach to the problem, known as the policy of "carrot and stick" (in German: *Zuckerbrot und Peitsche*, "egg bread and the whip"). Other than the "whip," for example in the form of his draconian "antisocialist laws" of 1878, including a prohibition of socialist associations and publications, the iron chancellor later also relied on the "egg bread" of concessions, notably via the establishment of a system of national sickness, and old age insurance. With this large-scale program of social legislation, predecessor of the later "welfare state" and of the post-1945 West-German "social state" (*Sozialstaat*), he hoped to captivate Germany's working class and take the wind out of the revolutionary sails of the socialists.

Bismarck also made seemingly generous concessions in the political field, most spectacularly by introducing universal suffrage for the Reichstag, the parliament of the unified, federal German Reich that had been created in 1871. But this sensational accomplishment was far less revolutionary than it appeared at first sight. First, the Reichstag was relatively powerless; it commanded less authority than the parliament of the greatest and most important member state (or *Land*) of the Empire, Prussia, where, thanks to a restricted voting system, the aristocratic Junkers enjoyed a virtual monopoly of power. (The Reichstag's major trump card was the fact that the Reich's budget had to be approved by a majority within this assembly, and in 1914 the Reichstag would thus have to authorize the war credits, a problem that will be discussed later.) Second, the federal cabinet was not accountable to the Reichstag, the country's legislative power, but to the executive power, that is, the person of the emperor. Consequently, in spite of its impressive electoral successes and the resulting spectacular increase of the number of its representatives in the Reichstag, the German socialist party, known as the Social Democratic Party (*Sozialdemokratische Partei Deutschland*, SPD) would long remain a lightweight in terms of political power, which is of course exactly what Bismarck had intended. In any event, during the second half of the nineteenth century, in countries such as Great Britain, Belgium, and Italy, the elite likewise made concessions in the form of a widening of the right to vote.

The emancipation of the "little people" on the political level was an important aspect of the democratization process that had started in 1789 and had made remarkable progress during the second half of the nine-teenth century. This progress was obviously achieved at the expense of the aristocratic and bourgeois elite, which had to relinquish a (usually small) part of its wealth, its privileges, and its prestige at each step in the process. It is therefore only logical that monarchs, aristocrats, members of the haute bourgeoisie, high-ranking government officials, church prelates, etc., abhorred democracy and fought tooth and nail to stop it during a rise that was slow and far from irresistible, even though at times it may have appeared to be so.

We should not overestimate the importance of this nineteenth-century democratization. Before the First World War, only very few countries had adopted universal suffrage. In 1914, a majority of countries, including Great Britain and Belgium, still did not allow the vote for all men, let alone for women. (Incidentally, New Zealand was the very first country in the world to introduce universal suffrage for women as well as men, in 1893.) The elite invented all sorts of stratagems to restrict the impact, overly democratic to elitist taste, of the universal right to vote. We have already seen how this was achieved in Germany. In Belgium, where the introduc-tion of universal suffrage could not be avoided, it made its appearance in the guise of a *plural* suffrage, in which people "involved in the mainten-ance of the social order on account of the possession of a family, a house, capital, a secure employment, or a diploma" were awarded more than one vote. (Plural suffrage was heartily recommended by the well-known British apostle of liberalism, John Stuart Mill, as a means to prevent too much power from being transferred from the hands of the rich to those of the poor.)[5] Another stratagem consisted in the manipulation of the geographic limits of electoral districts, so that those with few rich residents could send as many representatives to the legislative assemblies as those with a large population of poor people, which became known as gerrymandering. In certain countries, the potency of universal suffrage was sapped by means of an *indirect* voting system, in which one votes for "electors," virtually always members of the elite, who are then free to give their vote to the candidate they like the best; in the United States, the president is still elected by means of this undemocratic system. In Great Britain and many countries with a British political tradition, such as Canada, a "plurality voting system" (or "single-winner" system) was introduced to achieve the elite's antidemocratic objectives. This is a system whereby in each district one single seat in the assembly is available and goes to the candidate who harvests a plurality, and not necessarily a majority, of votes. In contrast to the more democratic system of "proportional representation," the plurality system favoured the existing, and usually conservative, big parties, and handicapped the small parties, including the socialist parties that had only just began to appear on the electoral scene in most countries.

While it is true that more and more people obtained the right to vote, it is also true that very few people actually happened to be *electable*. In practice, only rich burghers with plenty of leisure time qualified, because electoral campaigns and holding a public office involved high expenses. It is precisely for this reason that holding public office would long remain unremunerated, or poorly remunerated, and deliberately so. Finally, the elite learned very quickly that elections based on universal suffrage are most easily won by well-known personalities, and so they made it a habit to arrange for, and support, the candidacy of some "celebrity": a general, perhaps, or some scion of a prestigious family, someone who was said to have that *je ne sais quoi* called "charisma" and/or who could be said to be "above politics." What mattered was that such a person could be relied on to defend and promote the interests of the elite. This approach revealed itself to be particularly effective when universal suffrage was used to elect a president who would enjoy vast powers. The prototypical example was

Napoleon III, a nephew of "Napoleon the Great," who was elected in 1848 as president of a republic — the fruit of that year's revolution — in which universal suffrage had just been introduced. (A few years later, he would throw off his democratic mask and proclaim himself emperor.) This system thus became known as "bonapartism," and it is not a coincidence that it has enjoyed its greatest triumphs in France and the United States, countries endowed with "presidential regimes," namely in the form of the election of generals like de Gaulle and Eisenhower, or Hollywood stars like Ronald Reagan and (as governor of California) Arnold Schwarzenegger.

While the legislative assemblies composed of *elected* representatives of the people were the state's intrinsically democratic institutions, in many countries these assemblies enjoyed only very limited powers. Almost everywhere, the *executive* branch of government continued to command great power and numerous important prerogatives, and was most often embodied by crowned heads who had inherited their position from their father (or occasionally their mother). It was not unusual at all for a king or emperor to be commander-in-chief of the country's armed forces. Such was the case in Belgium, whose army would be commanded throughout the Great War by King Albert I. But the best example of a powerful monarch was obviously the emperor of Germany, who functioned as *Oberster Kriegsherr*, that is, supreme commander of the military forces, which he referred to as "his" army. (The popularly elected Reichstag, on the other hand, had no authority whatsoever over the army.) Even the president of one of the most democratic countries at the time, France of the bourgeois Third Republic, was endowed with enormous powers. He was a kind of pseudo-monarch who enjoyed all sorts of privileges and was elected for a term of no less than seven years. The American president likewise commanded extensive powers.

Furthermore, within the parliaments there often existed not only a lower chamber, consisting of elected representatives of the people, literally the "House of Commons," but also an upper chamber or senate, such as Britain's House of Lords, whose members were not elected, but appointed on the basis of their (upper-class) origin or their "merits," that is, the services they had rendered to the established order. These institutions were expected to function as a "saucer" into which one could "cool down" overly hot legislative concoctions served up by the potentially radical lower chamber. This is how George Washington delicately put it when the establishment of "a more thoughtful and deliberative" upper chamber, a senate, was being discussed shortly after the birth of the United States.[6]

Moreover, a large share of the powers of the modern state was concentrated in institutions whose officials were not elected but appointed: the judiciary, whose supreme court typically enjoyed the privilege of being able to reject as "unconstitutional" any laws made by the the parliaments; the high levels of the state bureaucracy and the army; and the diplomatic service. In these institutions too, officials were appointed virtually exclusively on the basis of a noble or very upper-middle class origin or an expensive higher education, preferably from elitist academic bastions such as Oxford and Cambridge; in other words, these loci of state power were de facto set aside for representatives of the upper classes and were off-limits to the plebeians. In Great Britain, Russia, Germany, and Austria-Hungary, the generals were essentially recruited from noble families, and to become an ambassador of countries such as Belgium, it would long remain *de rigueur* to be of aristocratic origin.

If in those days the state administration quickly gained importance in all countries, this was certainly not a coincidence. This "bureaucratization" did not happen *in spite of* the ongoing democratization, as the contemporary German sociologist Max Weber believed, but rather *because of* this democratization. For the elite, the bureaucratization was a means to counter democratization, to remove as much power as possible from the elected officials of the lower houses of the parliaments, over which the elite feared it might eventually lose control, and, at the same time, to stash away as much power as possible in institutions that could in fact be monopolized by the nobility and/or the haute bourgeoisie via the system of appointments. (In similar fashion, during the last few decades an enormous quantity of power has been transferred from elected — and therefore relatively democratic — institutions of individual countries toward supranational institutions whose decision-makers are mostly appointed.) Bureaucratization was certainly not a coincidental and unimportant byproduct of the democratization process. It was an instrument deliberately used by the elite for the purpose of neutralizing, or at least minimising, the impact of democratization.

A crucial institution in which all positions of importance continued to be filled by means of appointment and not election was the army. Just about everywhere, authority within the army remained a monopoly of the nobility and, to a lesser extent, of the haute bourgeoisie. The lower orders in general, and especially undesirable elements such as socialists and Jews, were absolutely not welcome there. This was dramatically illustrated with respect to the French army, a bastion of monarchists and clerical conservatives, by the Dreyfus Affair. In Germany, the army was and remained a kind of exclusively *aristocratic-feudal* state within the *aristocratic-bourgeois* state that the Reich happened to be. The high command was accountable only to the emperor, the army's commander-in-chief, and that would still be the case in 1914. (The infamous but capable General Ludendorff, a commoner, provided an exception to the general rule that the army's high command was monopolized by the nobility; Emperor Wilhelm despised him as an upstart and arranged for him to remain subordinated, at least in theory, to von Hindenburg, who was far less competent but was a 24-carat aristocrat.[7]) Militaristic Germany was clearly an extreme case, but even in less militaristic countries, the army likewise remained immune to all forms of democratization. Even the army of the relatively democratic French Republic cultivated a "certain type of military tradition, [namely] the principles of absolute authority, total and blind obedience, and the right to administer punishment." The military authorities tended to collaborate only reluctantly with governments that consisted of, or had to defer to, parliamentarians elected by the people, and they sometimes hatched all sorts of plans without informing the politicos. One of the reasons Great Britain would go to war in 1914 was that the high command of its army — in collaboration with the "war party" within the government, but unbeknownst to the House of Commons — had contracted obligations vis-à-vis the French army's high command, obligations that made it de facto impossible to remain neutral in case of war.[8]

In any event, the march toward democracy only moved at a glacial speed in late nineteenth-century Victorian Britain. Even in 1914, universal suffrage did not exist yet and the lower orders still had little or no say in political life. Similarly, the social services did not yet meet the criteria that one is entitled to expect of a modern democracy. Compulsory schooling at the primary level was only introduced in 1890, and in 1914 it was still not entirely free of charge. Great Britain would certainly not go to war for democracy and against autocracy, because in Germany universal suffrage had already existed, albeit in a far from perfect form, since 1871, and in the Austrian part of the Danube Monarchy, since 1907. (In Hungary, on the other hand, the right to vote remained reserved to only 6 per cent of the population.) And the popular masses were far better represented in the German Reichstag than in the British House of Commons.[9] It would only be at the end of the Great War that democracy would make its appearance in Britain, and we will soon learn why.

CHAPTER 4
NATIONALISM AND "SOCIAL IMPERIALISM"

As antidote against socialist internationalism, the elite stimulates nationalism. "Social imperialism" à la Cecil Rhodes simultaneously serves as a safety valve that reduces social pressure domestically by providing for the employment of proletarians in distant colonies as soldiers, missionaries, etc. Moreover, as imperialism is profitable, a cornucopia of raw materials and cheap labour, it becomes feasible to treat workers in Europe itself a little better . . .

A major cause of concern to the bourgeoisie and the nobility was the fact that the socialist movement organized itself on the international level. The "proletarians of all countries" were indeed uniting, as Marx had encouraged them to do. In March 1864, Marx himself had actually been one of the founders and leaders of the very first experiment in this sense, the International Workers' Association, better known as the First Socialist International, but this organization had foundered in 1876 as a result of internal conflicts. In 1889 — not coincidentally on July 14, the centenary of the storming of the Bastille — the Second International was founded in Paris, and this time it appeared in the form of an association of the big socialist parties that had meanwhile been established in most countries. The common anthem of the socialists of France, Germany, etc., written by the Communard Eugène Pottier and put to music by Pierre Degeyter, was called the *"Internationale"*; it became immensely popular as the battle hymn of the working-class movement.

The thought of a revolution in any single country was already disquieting, but now the elite was also tormented by the spectre of an international revolution, a revolutionary tsunami that might suddenly surge across the borders of all countries. Unity produces strength, and the international union of socialists enhanced the power of the socialist movement. In order to neutralize this power, the elite decided to rely on the old *divide et impera* approach. That is why it opted for nationalism, a movement that had emerged and expanded in the context of the French Revolution, Romanticism, and the rise of "national economies." With the instrument of nationalism, preferably in its extreme form, it became possible to undermine the international solidarity of the socialists and to divide the international proletariat. "Nationalism," wrote the Soviet historian P.J. Rachschmir in the early 1980s, "was considered an antidote to proletarian internationalism."[1] Focusing people's attention on an *external* enemy made it possible to divert their attention from the *internal* enemy, the class enemy, at whom socialism pointed its finger. If necessary, a class war at home could be avoided by means of a war against an enemy abroad. Such thoughts and expectations were very much on the minds of Europe's elite, and would lead it to think positively about war and to enthusiastically welcome it in 1914.

Nationalism insisted on the primordial character of the individual's identification, not with a *class* that transcended borders, such as the proletariat, but with a *people*, defined by its own ethnicity or "race," its own country, its language, its culture, and preferably also its religion or church, for example Catholicism in Poland, Ireland, and Flanders, and the Orthodox variety of Christianity among the Slavic and Greek minorities within the Ottoman Empire. (In Germany, the term for "nationalist" was *völkisch*, "of the people.") One's own *people* was of course superior to all others, and to belong to such a people was considered to be life's *nec plus ultra*. Conversely, those who were not satisfied with the traditional social order that existed among such a people could not possibly be genuine members of it! Seen from this nationalist viewpoint, the socialists, with their internationalism, were not patriots but rather traitors to their people, and socialism loomed as a sinister invention of the enemies of the people, the enemies of the country. In sharp contrast to socialism, nationalism preached that the people were homogeneous, not only in the ethnic, linguistic, and religious aspect, but also from the social point of view. Within the fundamentally idyllic "community of the people" (*Volksgemeinschaft* in German), antagonistic classes did not exist; there were no class enemies. It was therefore absurd to talk of class conflict. Instead of the socialist notion of *comrades* within the same class, nationalism glorified the idea of being a member of one's people (*Volksgenosse*) or, as one also used to say, a member of the same race, a "co-racialist."[2] When the war broke out in the summer of 1914, it seemed for one blissful moment that this nationalist ideal had become reality. In all countries, the socialists renounced the class struggle and proceeded instead to go to war for their fatherland and their people. There were apparently no longer any classes; there were only Germans, Frenchmen, Belgians, etc. But this euphoria would not last very long.

According to the nationalist credo, antagonistic classes within the people did not exist, and there were therefore no class enemies. But the people *did* have enemies: the enemy was the stranger — not the stranger who remained in his own (preferably distant) country, but the stranger who had infiltrated our people, who lived in our country as a parasite, as a germ that threatened to contaminate a healthy organism. This stranger, this "other," could be recognized by his appearance, his language, his religion, and even his smell! As the personification of this idea, nationalism targeted first and foremost the Jews, people who did not have a country of their own and who therefore lived everywhere as foreigners. The Jew was a stranger who could easily be recognized as the "other," the "germ," the "parasite" *par excellence*. But the Jew was certainly not the only "other" in this sense. In many countries, the Roma played this role, and in Germany, Poles and Slavs in general were considered as undesirable and parasitic foreign elements within the presumably homogeneous German people, as dangerous pathogens within the healthy body of the Germanic "race." In the United States, nationalism, known as "nativism," took aim at immigrants in general and of course at African Americans.

Nationalism thus often degenerated into virulent racism and anti-Semitism in particular. Like nationalism, anti-Semitism also featured an antisocialist dimension. Marx had had a Jewish background, and Jews were overrepresented in socialist parties in many countries, mainly because as members of an oppressed minority they had much to gain from revolutionary change. Socialism was thus perceived by many to be a Jewish ideology, an ideology concocted by an alien and hostile people, an ideology that was not only not *of* our people, but directed *against* our people, an ideology that was un-German, un-American, etc.

This fanatical variety of nationalism, tainted with xenophobia, racism, and anti-Semitism, was widespread at the time. The reason for this was that propaganda was systematically made for it in primary and secondary schools, in universities, in the media, and during the long compulsory military service that was being introduced at that time in most countries. For the purpose of spreading nationalist propaganda, the national symbols that were being introduced and increasingly widely used also proved to be particularly effective: flags, coats of arms, national hymns, and personifications such as the French Marianne, the British John Bull, and the American Uncle Sam.

In all countries, people were increasingly conditioned to believe that they were members of a people, nation, or "race" that was exceptional, chosen or at least blessed by God, and people everywhere were convinced that their own people or "race" had reached the highest possible degree of civilization. Conversely, the enemy of the people — whatever his identity, and that identity could and did change — was backward if not barbarian, biologically different and therefore inferior or barely human, and sometimes not even human at all.[3] This kind of enemy was capable of committing all sorts of atrocities, and was committed to eradicating "our" people. Hence we had the right to defend ourselves and, if necessary, to eradicate the hostile enemy, because in the final analysis that was the only real, the only "final" solution to the problem.

The fact that countless people subscribed to this way of thinking would have tragic implications with respect to the war that would break out in 1914. That conflict was to be presented by the authorities, the propagandists, the media, etc., as a war between peoples, between superior and inferior "races." The great English poet Rudyard Kipling, for example, would cry from the rooftops that the Germans — hitherto viewed by the

British as respectable "fellow Aryans" — were "a lesser breed," not really human beings, but "beasts,"[4] and the poet Gilbert Frankau reviled them as "beasts in gray" in a poem of the same title.[5] The journalist Horatio Bottomley claimed that the Germans were an inferior and incorrigible race and disparaged them as "Germhuns," thus suggesting that they were a kind of pathogen that needed to be destroyed — a course of action he actually recommended.[6] As for the French, they would revile the Germans as *Boches*, supposedly wretched creatures with all sorts of deficiencies, including chronic constipation and a correspondingly nasty body odour.[7] Conversely, the Germans spoke disdainfully of the French as a "bastard-ized" people and considered Russians and Slavs in general as inferior, sworn enemies of their supposedly highly civilized selves. The Austrians, finally, were contemptuous above all of the Serbs.

Racist nationalism (or nationalist racism) blossomed in the context of the battle fought by the elite against internationalist socialism (or social-ist internationalism), in other words, in the context of the class conflict between the elite and the lower classes. Nationalism and racism, wrote a British-German historian, Hansjoachim Wolfgang Koch, were supposed to serve as "antidotes to potential social revolution," were supposed to "push the class struggle into the background."[8] The contempt for other peoples was therefore interwoven with contempt for supposedly inferior classes. This is illustrated by the disdainful commentary offered by Viscount Northcliffe, owner and editor of *The Times*, a mouthpiece of the British elite, after a visit to a camp with German prisoners of war in 1917:

> It was regrettable that gentlemen had to fight such an enemy; these were not only barbarians, but also lower-class barbarians.[9]

It is hardly surprising that Northcliffe made a great impression on, and served as model for, the German who would later serve as Hitler's minister of propaganda, namely Josef Goebbels.[10]

Nationalism contaminated all layers of the population, but above all the petty bourgeoisie, for whom the notion of belonging to a suppos-edly classless people's community provided a certain compensation for its social inferiority vis-à-vis the upper-middle class and the nobility, as well as its fear of proletarization. Even some members of the working class proved receptive to the slogans of nationalism and racism, particularly when foreigners arrived to compete for jobs and thus helped keep wages at low levels. It is for this reason that American trade unions would long remain anti-Hamitic, i.e., hostile to blacks, as well as sinophobic.[11] In general, however, the proletarians — or at least the socialists among them — resisted the siren song of nationalism. They remained internationalists and condemned nationalism as a petit-bourgeois phenomenon and as a "right-wing" ideology. Significant in this respect is the fact that the Paris Communards proclaimed themselves to be internationalists, determined to create a "universal republic" (*République universelle*).[12]

From the viewpoint of the elite, nationalism was an extremely useful weapon in its struggle against socialism. Consequently, conservative thinking became closely associated with nationalism and vice versa. "[The concept of the nation] came to embody the established order and the political forces sworn to uphold it," writes Arno Mayer, and he adds that "the most zealous nationalists [were] the most radical conservatives."[13] But nationalism was a double-edged sword; it also featured a "dysfunctional" dimension.

The chauvinistic glorification of one's own people, nation, language, culture, and religion implied the denigration of other peoples; first and foremost, the rivals in the "imperialist" contest for advantage. And indeed, the already antagonistic relations among the great powers, for example between a hyperpatriotic Germany and an increasingly chauvinist and — with respect to Alsace-Lorraine — "revanchist" France, deteriorated inexorably. This increased the danger of war: a major war, a war that might reveal itself to be extremely traumatic, even fatal, to the elites of the losing countries — and maybe even those elite of the victorious powers. Regardless, nobody gave any thought to the possibility of such a catastrophe. The kind of Wagnerian demise that did in fact cause the elite great headaches was the social revolution, the possibility of a triumph of internationalist socialism, and it was precisely the spectre of this revolution that could be exorcized by waving the wand of nationalism, or so it was believed. In any event, it is a fact that the kind of nationalism that helped cause the Great War was stimulated by the European elites in order to combat the danger of revolutionary socialism. In this sense, the Great War may be said to have been a counterrevolutionary and antisocialist project.

Nationalism happened to be extremely dangerous in other ways for the aristocratic and bourgeois elite that promoted it. While it shored up the established order in ethnically and linguistically homogeneous countries, the nationalism of ethnic *minorities* such as the Poles, the Czechs, the Irish, and the Flemish constituted a threat to this same order in multi-ethnic and multi-linguistic states such as Austria-Hungary, Russia, the Ottoman Empire, and Belgium. And the rising nationalism in colonies such as India — and in "semi-colonies" such as China — represented a formidable challenge to the imperialist powers. In many countries, nationalist movements sprang up like mushrooms, and while some of them were happy with reforms to the existing state, others pursued nothing less than full independence, to be achieved if necessary via revolution. To the menace of *social* revolutions was thus added the menace of *national* revolutions, and national revolutions did indeed break out, namely in 1830 in the Polish regions of the Russian Empire and in 1848 in Hungary, which at that time still belonged to the Habsburg Empire. These revolutions were crushed mercilessly, but that did not completely eliminate the threat. Obviously, this threat loomed larger wherever *national* movements were simultaneously *social* movements, and when the champions of such movements made plans for revolutions or radical reforms with a social as well as a national character.

The great hero of the Italian *Risorgimento*, Giuseppe Garibaldi, the freedom fighter in the red shirt, incarnated this danger and was therefore thoroughly despised by monarchs such as Queen Victoria. But even more repugnant to the arch-conservative British sovereign were of course the Irish nationalists within her own British Empire, especially when those nationalists, for example James Connolly, were simultaneously separatists, republicans, and socialists who had joined the Second International and persuaded it to recognize Ireland as a separate nation.[14] As for the czar of Russia, he had to worry about the fact that the nationalist leaders of his Polish and Finnish minorities likewise joined the Second International and thus openly subscribed to a *revolutionary* form of socialism. In Belgium, Daensism was a movement that combined Flemish nationalism with socialism, or at least populism, and therefore offended the Flemish, Belgian, and European elites personified respectively by the Bishop of Ghent, King Leopold II, and the Pope.[15] Later, after the Great War, the simultaneous struggle for a national and social revolution would become associated with yet another outstanding revolutionary like Garibaldi, namely Ho Chi Minh, the "father" of independent Vietnam.

In the countries that were colonized and/or exploited or oppressed in other ways, such as Poland and Ireland, nationalism and socialism were not irreconcilable enemies, but were often allies. The struggle for national emancipation — a variety of class struggle, as we have seen — often went hand-in-hand with the struggle for social emancipation. Ireland functioned as a "colony" where English aristocrats — the Anglo-Irish gentry — had appropriated the land and whence wool and meat were exported to England while the Irish themselves, robbed of their land, died of starvation or had to emigrate; the struggle for social emancipation was therefore simultaneously a struggle for national emancipation, a struggle in which socialist champions of the social revolution collaborated with the liberal and even conservative (or clerical) proponents of a national revolution. "The national issue and the class one were interlinked," is how an Irish historian, Nuala C. Johnson, has recently put it.[16]

So there existed national movements that were primarily or even exclusively right-wing, conservative, clerical, and bourgeois, as well as national movements that incorporated both right-wing, conservative as well as left-wing, socialist (or at least socially-oriented) parties that competed with each other. The nationalist movement of Europe's Jews was one of those that featured two tendencies. Many Jews in Russia and Eastern Europe in general joined the "Bund" (officially known as the "General Union of Jewish Workers of Lithuania, Poland, and Russia"), a Marxist party that was a member of the Second International. Other Jews found a home in Zionism, a Jewish nationalist movement that had been founded in 1897 by Theodor Herzl, with as objective the establishment of a purely Jewish state in Palestine. Everywhere, the right-wing nationalists were great enemies of nationalists of the left, who were socialists, sometimes petty-bourgeois, but mostly proletarian. The elite obviously found it advantageous to stimulate and manipulate nationalism of the right-wing variety.[17]

The aristocratic-bourgeois power elite thus waved the banner of the right-wing, conservative, antisocialist, and counterrevolutionary nationalism of the existing state, and fought tooth and nail against all forms of nationalism expressed by the state's ethnic, linguistic, and religious minorities — and especially against the left-wing, radical, and above all revolutionary varieties of that nationalism. As in the case of the struggle against rising *social* movements in general and against socialism in particular, both the "stick" of repression and the "carrot" of concessions were used in the struggle against the rising national movements, and especially against potential national *revolutions*; here too, the concessions that were made consisted mostly of modest reforms, often of a mostly symbolic nature. A good example was provided by the British policy with respect to Ireland: ruthless repression on the one hand, but on the other hand also reforms conjuring up a form of Irish independence, or rather, less visible dependence vis-à-vis London, the system euphemistically referred to as "Home Rule." As in the case of the aforementioned political and social reforms, this carrot-like approach was quite successful. The concept of Home Rule seduced countless Irish nationalists and took a lot of wind out of the sails of the republican, socialist, and other radical Irish nationalists. But reforms did not really resolve the situation of the minorities, which actually continued to deteriorate. This was the case not only in Ireland, but also in the Balkans, that is, on the opposite side of Europe. The Habsburgs were driven to despair by the aspirations and agitation of the "South-Slav" minorities within the Dual Monarchy, over which the Austrians and the Hungarians were already at loggerheads, and by the dissatisfaction of their Czech, Slovak, Polish, and other fellow citizens.

The very thorny problem of undesirable nationalist movements also created new opportunities, however, especially when such movements reared their heads in rival states. One could in fact weaken rivals by encouraging and supporting the nationalist aspirations of their minorities, and even of their colonial subjects. The temptation was great and irresistible. The Russian Empire, for example, which lusted after Constantinople and control over the straits between the Black Sea and the Mediterranean, supported the nationalism of the Ottoman Empire's Slav subjects, who were mostly Orthodox Christians. A prime example is the Bulgarians, who were thus able to gain their independence in 1908. The Russians actually encouraged all Balkan and Caucasian Christians to rise up against their Ottoman overlords. The latter reacted by abandoning their customary religious tolerance in favour of a systematic pro-Islamic policy — in 1876 Islam was proclaimed the Empire's official religion — and a ruthless anti-Christian repression. (Confronted with the Russian menace, the Ottomans would also ally themselves with Germany, as we will examine later.) This policy led to massacres of Christian Greeks and Armenians during the 1890s, on the island of Crete and elsewhere, and was to culminate in the Armenian genocide of 1915, during the Great War. The nationalist and antisocialist policy of the aristocratic and bourgeois elite of Europe thus contributed not only to provoking the Great War, as we have already seen, but also to making possible some of its most awful horrors.

It was not only the great imperialist powers that inflamed the nationalism of their rivals' minorities. Even minor states believed they could profit from this kind of intrigue. Serbia comes to mind: a small country that systematically encouraged "South-Slav" nationalism in the Bosnian, Croatian, and Slovenian regions of its big neighbour, Austria-Hungary. Nationalists of this type would assassinate the Habsburg crown prince and his wife in Sarajevo in the summer of 1914, an event that may be said to have sparked — but not *caused* — the Great War. And during that Great War, the antagonists would immediately go to work to support with word and deed the nationalist (and preferably revolutionary) movements within the enemy's European and colonial possessions. The British, for example, would provide military assistance to independence-minded movements among the Arab denizens of the Ottoman Empire, an ally of Germany, and the French made all sorts of promises to the Polish minority in Germany and the Czech minority in the Dual Monarchy. Conversely, the Germans would encourage independence movements of the Poles within the Russian Empire, of the Irish and the Indians within the British Empire, and promoted Flemish separatism in occupied Belgium. Lenin was to remark cynically that "the chauvinists only make propaganda in favour of civil war in the enemy camp, but they never defend the right of their own colonies and oppressed peoples to secede."[18] During the First World War, the Germans would go so far as to support movements aiming at a *social* revolution in

76

the camp of the enemy, notably by facilitating Lenin's voyage to Russia during the summer of 1917. The elites were keen to support radical and even revolutionary national and even social movements within enemy countries, but it was a strategy fraught with great "blowback" risks, as Germany, for example, would find out when at the end of the war the revolutionary winds would blow from the Russian to the Prussian capital.

Domestically, the elite fought the danger of social as well as national revolution on all fronts and with all means at its disposal. Imperialism admittedly served first and foremost for the purpose of acquiring raw materials, markets, and cheap labour, all for the benefit of the national economy. But it also proved useful as a means to exorcise the spectre of gradual as well as revolutionary change in the socialist sense and thus to preserve the established order to which the nobility and upper-middle class were attached. By mobilizing them for colonial projects in Africa, Southeast Asia, and other distant parts of the world, it was possible to wean a goodly part of the proletarians and petit bourgeois from socialism. In the colonies these folks could be put to work as soldiers, employees, and foremen on plantations and in mines (where the natives served as slaves), low-ranking bureaucrats in the colonial administration, and even missionaries. "The empire was also a market for men," remarks the French historian Michel Winock, and he emphasizes the fact that colonies functioned to a large extent as "a way out of misery" for the inhabitants of the least privileged regions of the mother country, such as Corsica in the case of France.[19]

Even the people who, in their own country, belonged to the lowest classes, were thus offered the luxury of indulging in feelings of superiority far from home, with respect to "blacks" and other supposedly backward folks. The British historian Eric Hobsbawm draws attention to this psychological role of imperialism, which permitted ordinary people to feel superior and thus to identify with the state and be integrated into its established order. According to Hobsbawm, this

> *idea of superiority to, and domination over, a world of dark*
> *skins in remote places was genuinely popular . . . Th[is] sense*
> *of superiority thus united the western whites, rich, middle-*
> *class and poor . . . because all of them enjoyed the privileges*

of the ruler . . . in the colonies . . . the white worker was a commander of blacks.[20]

It was not a coincidence that Irishmen in particular were dispatched as soldiers to India — described on one occasion by Marx as the "Ireland of the East" — in order to lord it over the natives: in Albion itself, they were traditionally the ultimate example of the poor, powerless, and oppressed proletarians.[21]

The profits realized by the systematic and ruthless exploitation of the colonies not only made it possible to remunerate the colonial personnel relatively well, but also to offer slightly higher wages to the workers in the metropolis and to finance modest social services for their benefit. "Each nation's share in the economic control of the earth," explained the great German sociologist Max Weber in 1894, decides "its workers' earning potential." In Britain similar ideas were promoted by Austin Chamberlain, who proclaimed that "social reform was not possible without imperialism."[22] This development would give rise to the emergence of a so-called "labour aristocracy" in the imperialist countries of Western Europe, something about which we will hear more later on. Imperialism thus made it possible to improve the remuneration and treatment of the proletarians in the metropolises — and thus to take a lot of wind out of the sails of the socialists — at the expense of the oppressed and exploited denizens of the colonies. In other words, the most flagrant misery was exported from Europe (and the US) to the colonies, to what would later be called the "Third World." Imperialism thus served to "develop under-development" in Africa, Asia, and Latin America, a process already inaugurated in the so-called era of the "Great Explorations."[23]

This modest but certainly perceptible amelioration of the fate of working people in Europe's imperialist countries seemed to falsify Marxian theory. According to the latter's "theory of increasing pauperization," capitalism was to make the proletariat increasingly poorer and miserable and would thus cause it to overthrow the existing capitalist system sooner or later by means of a revolution; however, thanks to the "blessings" of imperialism, it looked as though Marx was wrong. Even many socialist leaders began to believe that the fate of the proletariat could and would improve within the capitalist system, and that a revolution was therefore no longer necessary.

Having listened to "wild speeches, which were just a cry for 'Bread! Bread!,'" at a meeting of unemployed people in London's miserable East End working-class district, Cecil Rhodes, the great champion of British imperialism, described as follows the counterrevolutionary function of imperialism, or "social imperialism," as he called it:

> On my way home I pondered over the scene and I became
> more than ever convinced of the importance of imperialism
> . . . My cherished idea is a solution for the social problem,
> i.e., in order to save the 40,000,000 inhabitants of the
> United Kingdom from a bloody civil war [i.e., revolution], we
> colonial statesmen must acquire new lands to settle the surplus
> population, to provide new markets for the goods produced in
> the factories and mines. The Empire, as I have always said,
> is a bread and butter question. If you want to avoid civil war,
> you must become imperialists.

This citation reflects not only Rhodes' conviction that colonial expansion was crucial as a weapon against socialist revolution, but also his Malthusian conviction that Britain's social problem itself was the result of overpopulation. This is why Rhodes — like many of his contemporaries who shared his Malthusian ideas — felt that it was absolutely necessary to rid the country of the restless and potentially revolutionary demographic surplus that the poor happened to be. As far as the propertied classes were concerned, imperialist projects were a perfect instrument in that sense, because they caused countless representatives of the "dangerous classes" to disappear from the social-economic and political scene of the metropolis. One can also express this viewpoint in social-psychological terms: Europe's proletarians could give free rein to their aggressive instincts not in the metropolis at the expense of the elite, but in distant colonies at the expense of the natives — and to the advantage of the metropolitan elite.

In France and Germany too, imperialism was viewed as an instrument for solving domestic social problems. In France, Maurice Wahl, a high-ranking colonial official, wrote the following in a book entitled *France in the Colonies*:

> *Owing to the growing complexities of life and the difficulties*
> *which weigh not only on the masses of the workers, but also*
> *on the middle classes, impatience, irritation and hatred are*
> *accumulating in all the countries of the old civilisation and*
> *are becoming a menace to public order; the energy which is*
> *being hurled out of the definite class channel must be given*
> *employment abroad in order to avert an explosion at home.*

As for Germany, as early as 1878 one could read in a newspaper there that the government ought to organize large-scale emigration to the colonies "as a safety valve against social problems." Colonial expansion was considered by the elite as an antidote to the German variety of socialism, social democracy. In another paper, which cited Australia as an example, the author stated that "the German state should find ways to remove 'seditious elements' from the country" and that "colonization within Europe, for example in Poland, could also be useful in this sense." An aristocratic partisan of colonialism expressed the opinion that "German social democracy could not be fought more effectively than by means of colonialism."[24]

Territorial expansion within and without Europe was seen to be indispensable for the purpose of solving domestic problems. In the case of Germany, however, expansion within Europe itself — and above all in Eastern Europe — seemed all the more necessary in that, in contrast to Great Britain, the Reich's relatively few colonies had insufficient potential for absorbing the demographic surplus. In this context it is understandable that the conquest of territory in Eastern Europe ranked high on Germany's long list of war aims in 1914. And Hitler, with his infamous lust for "living space" (*Lebensraum*) in Europe's east, would hardly be an anomaly, but rather a typical product of his time.

All over Europe, intellectuals and other leading personalities considered colonial expansion to be a means to resolve social problems and combat socialism. As a French example we can cite Ernest Renan, who declared that colonialism, which he believed France had "unfortunately" not yet sufficiently embraced on account of its many revolutions, "was the only way to counter socialism." "A nation that does not colonize," he explained, "is condemned to end up with socialism, to experience a war between rich and poor." Similarly, Theodor Herzl, the "father" of Zionism, felt that the colonization of Palestine could put a stop to the problem of the rise of revolutionary movements among the poor Jews of Europe.[25]

The imperialist powers' territorial ambitions inside and outside of Europe, which would make the Great War possible and even inevitable, had arisen as a means for the elites of these countries to combat the danger of socialism and to avoid social revolution. In this sense too, it can be said that the Great War was at least partly the result of an antidemocratic, antisocialist and counterrevolutionary policy; in other words, that it was an antidemocratic and counterrevolutionary project.

The conquest of colonies virtually always went hand-in-hand with wars against natives who dared to oppose the white man in spite of the latter's good intentions with respect to them. Did the white man not bring those people the blessings of "western" civilization in addition to that civilization's Siamese twin, the true Christian religion in its Catholic or Protestant manifestation? Did those who turned down such favours not deserve to be chastised? These wars generally amounted to unilateral massacres and usually finished with presumably glorious victories, which provided promotions for many army commanders, of whom many were to play important roles in the Great War, for example Joffre, von Falkenhayn, French, and Haig,[26] and also the American commander-in-chief, John J. Pershing, who had earned his stripes in "wars" of this kind against Indians, Filipinos, and Mexicans. The dead on the European (or American) side were not very numerous and belonged mostly to the unimportant lower orders.[27] These dead were unmourned because they could easily be replaced, and because in their own way they had made a contribution to the presumably necessary "culling" of the demographic surplus. As for the tens and even hundreds of thousands of massacred natives, did anybody care?[28] (One may ask the same question with respect to the natives killed in more recent colonial and neocolonial wars in Vietnam, Iraq, and Afghanistan.)

In 1914, when war erupted in Europe itself, many believed that the familiar scenario of the colonial wars would repeat itself: a war of a limited nature and of short duration, irresistible charges of our cavalry, ridiculously cheap and easy victories, quantitatively as well as qualitatively insignificant losses on our side, but masses of killed and wounded on the enemy side and, as the cherry on the cake, enormous economic advantages and eternal glory for the fatherland and its heroes. Thanks to the eager collaboration of the media, the colonial wars, for example the campaigns against the Zulus and the Boers or the American wars against the Indians, the Filipinos, the Mexicans, etc., revealed themselves to be particularly "popular" and thus made a significant contribution to the integration of the lower classes into the established order.[29]

CHAPTER 5
NIETZSCHE AND SOCIAL DARWINISM: ODE TO WAR

The process of democratization seems to be irresistible and, with the rise of the "masses," the elite, besieged and increasingly pessimistic, seeks remedies in Social-Darwinist fantasies and antidemocratic and racist Nietzschean schemes. War appears to offer the elite a way out of its labyrinth of problems. It is hoped that war will dispel the threat of revolutionary socialism, thin out the ranks of the dangerous popular masses, and integrate the lower orders into the existing political and social-economic order . . .

Around the turn of the century, it had become apparent that the aristocratic-bourgeois elite had achieved considerable success with its antidemocratic strategy. The symptoms of this success were visible everywhere: plenty of "little" people, particularly peasants and members of the lower-middle class, had embraced nationalism, anti-Semitism, militarism, and imperialism, and voted not for the socialists, but for conservative parties, such as Germany's Catholic Zentrum. In any event, in most countries the franchise was still a privilege of the "better" classes, and an enormous amount of state power remained concentrated in unelected institutions such as the parliaments' upper chambers, the bureaucracy, and the army; institutions in which the elite had solidly retrenched itself. The church still enjoyed a lot of influence, mostly among the peasants in the countryside, and worked hard to regain lost loyalty in the camp of the working class, which, under socialist influence, had abandoned Christianity *en masse* during the nineteenth century. The Catholic counter-offensive in this respect culminated in the 1891 proclamation of the encyclical *Rerum Novarum*, in which Pope Leo XIII condemned socialism as a "plague" and ordered the creation of Christian political parties and trade unions. During the "severe pontificate" of Leo XIII, the elite could also increasingly count on the Church to "glorify the throne, the sword, the flag, and the established social order" and, conversely, to condemn socialism and (non-Christian) trade union activism.[1] Nevertheless, the spectre of revolution — not only social, but also national revolution — continued to haunt Europe. Agitation and tension also affected distant parts of the world such as South America and China. The elite feared not only the possibility of a sudden and violent *revolution*, but also the pros-pect of a gradual and pacific *evolution* toward democracy, loathed as the rule of the presumably ignorant and vicious populace.

It was all too obvious: the relative success of the elite's antidemocratic strategy could slow down the rise of democracy, but in the long run this rise was irresistible. Governments were forced to multiply their concessions and introduce more and more reforms; for example, it proved necessary almost everywhere to widen the right to vote. The socialists continued to make headway among the lower classes, their parties kept growing in size and strength, they became more and more ambitious, and therefore loomed more and more menacing. It looked as if sooner or later the pro-letariat would achieve a great electoral victory, thus permitting the socialist revolutionaries to come to power in a nonrevolutionary manner. In that case, would the days of the established political and social order not be numbered as certainly as they would be in the case of a violent revolution? Was it possible to prevent this somehow?

Democracy was indeed something for which both the haute bourgeoisie and the nobility, from the most powerful monarch to the lowliest village squire, had nothing but contempt. The reason for this should be obvious: democracy, power exercised by and for the people, spelled the end of a system in which power was exercised by, and indeed for, a small part of the people, namely the tiny demographic minority that the combination of nobility and upper-middle class happened to be. Genuine democracy, that is, not only the political but also the social-economic emancipation of the lower orders, was not in the interest of the elite. Emperor Wilhelm II publicly denounced democracy, equating it with anarchy.[2] But at the time democracy was also a dirty word in Great Britain, because it stood for the power of the popular masses and not the supposedly normal, natural, or "God-given" power of the "better" classes, that is the propertied classes — or, as they used to say in French, the power of the *gens de rien*, the "people of nothing," instead of the *gens de bien*, the "people of substance."[3]

Ever since the epoch of the French Revolution, the noble (and conservative) elite had never dissimulated its antipathy toward the idea of liberty and progress for the benefit of the masses. The haute bourgeoisie was liberal by conviction and therefore partial to the concepts of liberty and progress, in theory for everybody, but in reality for itself; it detested the idea of democracy, which it perceived not as an ideal but a nightmare, rule by the stupid and cruel "masses."[4] A leading figure of French liberalism in the nineteenth century, Alexis de Tocqueville (1805–1859), explained in this context that he loved *liberty*, but not *democracy*.

The rise of the masses and the potentially catastrophic consequences of such a development constituted a theme that received a lot of attention around the turn of the century, as reflected in the success of a book published by Gustave Le Bon in 1895, *Psychologie des foules* (literally, "Psychology of Crowds," but published in English as *The Crowd: A Study of the Popular Mind*); of this book it was recently said that it "reflected the unrest of people at the time and their perplexity with respect to certain aspects of modernity." A similar bestseller reflecting the contemporary "cultural pessimism" was *Rembrandt als Erzieher* ("Rembrandt as Educator") by the German Julius Langbehn, published in 1890.[5]

If the masses came to power via elections, that too would constitute a catastrophe from the perspective of the elite. It was firmly believed that in this case the scenario of the Paris Commune would repeat itself, but on a much larger scale, with enormous effusions of blood and, as outcome, nothing less than the end of civilization, or at least of aristocratic-bourgeois civilization, and the birth of a monster: a socialist or, as they already said at the time, a "communist" society.[6]

The fear of the disagreeable consequences of the process of democratization and of the apparently irresistible rise of the masses that was linked to it loomed even worse when one considered the problem within a worldwide instead of merely national or even European context. Did democratization not similarly threaten to produce an equally irresistible rise of the masses of coloured folks in the colonies, to bloody "Communes" over there, and ultimately to the hegemony of the white man giving way, not only in the colonies but all over the world, to the rule of the inferior brown, black, and yellow masses? "The nightmares of empire merged with the fears of democracy," is how Eric Hobsbawm described this kind of angst.[7] Within the framework of the "world system" of imperialism, the coloured and therefore presumably inferior women and men of the colonies (and of semi-colonies such as China) loomed like dangerous proletarians constituting a menace to the "lords" in the metropolises; conversely, in elitist eyes the proletarians of the metropolises looked a lot like racially inferior foreigners. A reactionary French army officer thus wrote in 1914 — in a book published by the official publisher of the army! — that there existed "two Frances," "two races" of French:

> The ancient French race and a new social group, formed by
> a heterogeneous, motley crew, including outcasts of the old
> race as well as recent newcomers, not yet assimilated and . . .
> inassimilable, the extraordinary coalition of Protestants, Jews,
> Freemasons, socialists, and aliens [métèques].[8]

During the 1880s and 1890s, a gloomy pessimism thus pervaded the nobility and particularly the haute bourgeoisie, a widely shared feeling of living in an era of decadence and decline, an impression that together with the century civilization itself was approaching its end and that the superior "aryan" folk were menaced by hordes of inferior coloured people. This fin-de-siècle pessimism and nihilism contrasted dramatically with the optimism and the faith in progress that a dynamic and confident bourgeoisie, fired up by the Enlightenment, had displayed not so long before, notably during its "heroic," progressive, and even revolutionary epoch; this optimism had caved in like a failed soufflé in the revolutionary annus horribilis, 1848.

What had gone wrong, and what could be done? These were the urgent existential questions that the burghers asked themselves, and many found a soothing answer in a new, seemingly scientific ideology that was taking intellectual Europe by storm at the time, namely Social Darwinism. This worldview found inspiration in Darwin's theory of evolution and sought to apply to humans, peoples, "races," and countries concepts such as "natural selection," the "struggle for survival," and "survival of the fittest." Competition was considered as the basic principle of all forms of life, and success in the competition of life was seen as the *sine qua non* of survival and progress. The strongest triumphed in the struggle for survival, they were therefore considered to be the best, and thus they became even stronger; the weak, on the other hand, were the losers, they were left behind in the race for survival and were therefore doomed to extinction.

One can easily understand that this vulgar way of thinking managed to become "the dominant world-view of Europe's ruling and governing."[9] Concepts such as "natural selection" and "survival of the fittest" fit marvellously into the liberal theory that preached that competition separates the wheat from the chaff, so that the victors in the social and economic competition, that is, the prosperous businessmen and the elite in general, are manifestly the best and the fittest and thus merit being the "victors." And was it not evident that, in a race with countless competitors, there could only be a few winners? Consequently, the wealth and the power of a small number (the elite), as well as the poverty and powerlessness of the great number (the masses) were deserved and justified. The former did not have to be ashamed, and the latter did not have the right to complain, but had to shut up. The inequality of individuals and groups of people, such as classes, was the natural state of things (or, for the believers, the God-given and therefore immutable order of things). Any attempt to change that order, as the socialists and the nationalist champions of ethnic minorities proposed to do, was not only doomed to fail, but was in fact a senseless and even criminal undertaking.[10]

Social Darwinism was equally useful for the purpose of affirming and justifying the power of the white man in the colonies. All-too-easy conquests in Africa, the American "Wild West," and elsewhere convinced the Europeans and Americans that their own white "race," then still generally

known as "Aryan," though numerically insignificant in number, was qualitatively far superior to the huge masses of brown, black, and yellow folks.
But a hierarchy likewise prevailed within the "Aryan" family, even if it was
not entirely clear who occupied its summit. The "Anglo-Saxons" was the
answer given to that question in London, but in Berlin they were convinced
that on top were the Teutons, a "race" to which belonged not only the
Germans, but also other "Germanic" tribes such as the "Anglo-Saxons," the
Scandinavians, the Dutch, and the Flemish denizens of Belgium. In Paris
and Rome, it was firmly believed that superiority had been bestowed on
the French, Italians, and other "Latin" nations by virtue of their imperial
Roman pedigree. In the United States, finally, the palm was handed not
just to the presumably superior "Anglo-Saxons," but to "Nordic" people
in general, preferably those embracing a Protestant version of Christianity.
The anthropological *nec plus ultra* there would long remain the "WASP,"
that is, the American who was not only white, but also Anglo-Saxon and
Protestant.[11] Italians and other folks with a slightly darker skin, people
of the so-called "Mediterranean" type, generally shorter of stature, dark-
haired, and Catholic, and of course the "Celtic" Irish, also Catholics, were
perceived to inhabit a no man's land that separated the "Nordic" wheat
from the chaff of blacks and Indians or "redskins." For the latter, a special
term — with a Nietzschean ring to it — would be coined, namely "under-
men," by the American "scientific racist" Lothrop Stoddard. He first used
this term in a book published in 1920 entitled *The Rising Tide of Color
Against White World-Supremacy*. This opus was immediately translated into
German and impressed and inspired Hitler, who co-opted "under-man" in
its infamous German version, *Untermensch*.[12]

From a Social-Darwinist perspective, all the members of the superior
"Aryan" family had ample reason to be satisfied and happy. In their community, social or economic problems could not exist, and if somehow they
did appear, it was the fault of members of inferior "races" who, like a kind of
dangerous germ, had penetrated the healthy body of the "Aryan" community to contaminate it and make it sick. Revolutionary socialism was such a
disease, a potentially deadly disease, and the germs that had engendered it
were the Jews who had infiltrated the "Aryan" community. It was taken as
given that the Jews, like all other "inferiors," were envious of the superior

"Aryans" and dreamed of bringing them down from their lofty pedestal, using socialism as an instrument to achieve that evil objective. Thus we can understand why anti-Semitism was widespread at the time in conservative, antidemocratic, antisocialist, and counterrevolutionary circles.

Explaining social problems by pointing the finger at foreigners, not necessarily but preferably the Jews — in other words, making the Jew a scapegoat — already had a long tradition. Luther had blamed the Jews for the peasant revolts, and according to theorists of counterrevolutionary conservatism such as de Maistre, de Bonald, and Burke, it was the Jews — and the Freemasons — who had unleashed the French Revolution. Later, the Jews would similarly be accused of planning the Russian Revolution by people like Oswald Spengler, a German historian and philosopher who today no longer enjoys a good reputation, but also by personalities that many continue to admire, for example the American automobile manufacturer Henry Ford and the most famous of all British statesmen, Winston Churchill.[13]

Many champions of Social Darwinism were convinced that, within the "Aryan" family itself, certain groups were particularly vulnerable to contamination by foreign germs. Countless British conservatives firmly believed that the French suffered from a "revolutionary malady," of which the events of 1789, 1830, 1848, and 1871 had been the symptoms. And the reason for that was said to be that France had been "contaminated" by permitting the immigration of inferior people of the Mediterranean or even African type, which had allegedly led to a degeneration of its own "race"; "niggers begin in Calais!," was a line often dropped by British snobs with respect to France. In Germany and in the Dual Monarchy too, many felt that the French were a "bastardized" or "degenerated" lot; a young man named Adolf Hitler was one who thought so. A Frenchman who was himself convinced of this and who would actually inspire Hitler with his writings was Joseph de Gobineau, a royalist aristocrat who, during the 1850s, published a book entitled *Essay on the Inequality of the Human Races*. Gobineau proclamed the superiority of the "Aryan" race, warned of the dangers of sexual and other forms of "racial mixing," and blamed "racial pollution" for the revolutions and other social problems in France.[14]

The Social Darwinists believed that outside of Europe too, inferior peoples, green with jealousy, would try in one way or another to put an end to the legitimate worldwide hegemony of the "Aryans." For example, in Africa and the United States, or at least in the Southern states, blacks — who were only recently slaves — were presumed to always be looking for opportunities to rape white women, in the hope that they would thus pollute and ultimately destroy the "Aryan race." (In contemporary Europe, still extremely repressed on the sexual level, it was the Jews who were suspected of lusting after "Aryan" females.) Yet another menace lurked in the shape of the immense human masses of Chinese, simultaneously loathed and feared by whites as the "yellow peril." (The less numerous Japanese did not yet inspire such fear.) And the Chinese nationalists' Boxer Rebellion of 1899–1901 in Beijing was ruthlessly crushed by the combined armed forces of no less than eight imperialist powers, fraternally united for the occasion. In 1914, when these same powers rather unfraternally went to war against one another, the Germans, who had looked forward to a military contest among fellow "Aryans," were shocked that the French mobilized Senegalese and Moroccan troops against them and that the British called up Indians to fight on their side. *Noblesse oblige* and, confronted with the menace of inferior peoples, the "Aryans," no matter how divided they may have been among themselves, should maintain a common front, so the Germans believed. On the other hand, in the African theatre of operations, for example in East Africa, the Germans themselves did not hesitate to use black soldiers against the British and Belgian forces, which also consisted mostly of black recruits.

What had gone wrong, and what could be done about it? To find answers to these questions, the European and American elite sat down at the feet of the great German philosopher of the end of the century, Friedrich Nietzsche. Nietzsche has been described by Arno Mayer as

> *the chief minstrel of this battle [of the elite against all forms*
> *of equality] . . . [a man whose] thought was coherently and*
> *consistently antiliberal, antidemocratic, and antisocialist . . .*
> *He reviled his own age for permitting the masses to shackle*
> *the will to power of the 'highest specimens' . . . [so that] herd*
> *animals made themselves masters.*[15]

With the Enlightenment and liberalism, Europeans had gone astray, explained Nietzsche. Liberty, equality, and progress for all had been an impossible and dangerous ideal in a healthy society. An elite of superior beings must dominate and the masses must be dominated. To allow the inferior masses to come to power was not merely a mistake, but a crime. And, according to Nietzsche, the criminals who incited the people and fomented revolutions were the Jews, whom he called the "spiteful people *par excellence*."[16]

The elite can and must exercise power, said Nietzsche, and could find inspiration for that in the brilliant example of Ancient Greece, where a superior social layer of capable, wise, and courageous people ruled with an iron fist over a crowd of helots, aliens, and slaves, the inferior *hoi polloi,* "the multitude." In order to govern this way, one had to be tough, because showing compassion — something typical for Christianity — was a sign of weakness and therefore inferiority. The ruler is intelligent, courageous, and merciless. He is an *Übermensch,* a "super-man." In order to save civilization from decline, the citizens had to become such *Übermenschen,* ardently want to exercise power, and be prepared to launch a counteroffensive in order to stop the suicidal march toward democracy, ruthlessly repressing "slave revolts" such as the Paris Commune. (For Nietzsche, rebellious slaves were villains; the socialists whom he despised, on the other hand, admired rebellious slaves as heroes, and during the revolution in Germany at the end of the Great War radical socialists such as Rosa Luxemburg would call themselves Spartacists in honour of Spartacus.) Quite a few other intellectuals besides Nietzsche — for example the famous Italian sociologist, economist, political scientist, and philosopher Vilfredo Pareto — proclaimed the ineluctability and the virtues of elite rule. On the intellectual level, then, the European nobility and upper-middle class put up an increasingly stubborn resistance to the democratization process and proved more determined than ever before to keep power in their own hands.

In the Social-Darwinist and/or Nietzschean world-view, war played a crucial role. War was no longer abhorred but considered, as the Canadian historian Modris Eksteins has written, to be "the supreme test of spirit, and, as such, a test of vitality, culture, and life"; war was elevated to the rank of "life-giving principle."[17] Life itself was viewed as a form of war: one had to fight in order to survive and win, and victory was reserved for the best, for the *fittest*. This presumably applied not only to individuals but also to peoples, "races," and other human collectives. In Germany above all, war was glorified in this Social-Darwinist manner. After all, that country's unity had been achieved in the years 1864–1871 through "blood and steel," as Bismarck, the architect of that unification, had put it. The famous historian and politician Heinrich von Treitschke thus praised war as "the best remedy for sickly civilisations."[18] On the far side of the Rhine, a huge success was accorded to *Deutschland und der Nächste Krieg* ("Germany and the Next War"), a book published in 1911, only a few years before the outbreak of the Great War. In it the aristocratic German general Friedrich von Bernhardi glorified war as "something divine," a "biological imperative," and the supreme example of the "struggle for existence," a merciless test which, in the swarming of nations, separated the wheat from the chaff.

But Great Britain also boasted a tradition of glorification of war. In *The Crown of Wild Olive*, published in 1866, the great Victorian author John Ruskin, who remained very popular and influential until 1914, lauded war as follows:

> *War is the foundation of all the arts . . . it is the foundation*
> *of all the high virtues and faculties of men . . . All great*
> *nations learned their truth of word, and strength of thought,*
> *in war; that they were nourished in war, and wasted by peace;*
> *taught by war, and deceived by peace; trained by war, and*
> *betrayed by peace; in a word, that they were born in war, and*
> *expired in peace.*[19]

In the British monthly *The Nineteenth Century and After*, there appeared in 1911 an article entitled "God's Test by War," written by a certain H.F. Wyatt. "The biological law of competition," one could read there, "still rules the biological destiny of nations as of individual men." And to the question whether a country like Britain could still play a role in the competition, the answer was: "How shall we know? By the test. What test? That which God has given for the trial of peoples — the test of war."[20]

An almost identical tribute to war was featured in the catalogue of the

Universal Exposition of Paris in 1900, more specifically in a comment about the military section:

> War [is] 'natural to humanity . . . a school of the high-
> est qualities of man . . . Peace fructifies the arts, trade, and
> industry, [but] also develops those states of mind called selfish-
> ness, pessimism, nihilism, egoism' . . . [war can] restore the
> lofty virtues that seem to be fading, raise their spirit, and give
> them new heart.[21]

War was the ultimate test, and it also served to make good women and men even better and the strong, stronger; it served to make young people hard like steel and to forge national solidarity. War allegedly bestowed energy on individuals as well as on peoples, it rejuvenated the "races," revived entire societies, regenerated moral existence, etc. The elite had to be brutal, merciless, and bellicose, preached Nietzsche, and to show itself ready to sacrifice "enormous human masses" in wars without the slightest remorse — which is precisely what would come to pass in 1914–1918. In the society of which Nietzsche dreamed, war was just as essential as slavery. It was only through war, he believed, that Europe could lift itself out of the mud of decadence and decay in order to step boldly into a heroic and glorious future.[22]

"Never before has war received so much homage at the lips of men," complained the Polish-English writer Joseph Conrad in 1905, "and reigned with less disputed sway in their minds."[23] It was not the "little" people, however, but the elite who excitedly guzzled the soup of Nietzschean ideology and pseudo-scientific Social Darwinism. "The cult of war was an elite, not a plebeian, affair," insists Arno Mayer, "[because] there was no spontaneous clamor for war among the presumably aggressive and bloodthirsty masses." And, he added:

> Darwinian and Nietzschean thought . . . became immensely
> meaningful and valuable to the elites engaged in reaffirming
> their dominance . . . Indeed, they became a central component
> not only of the Weltanschauung but also of the persuasive
> belief system of the ruling and governing classes.[24]

The Belgian historian Sophie de Schaepdrijver also recognizes that Nietzschean belligerence "had not only infected Germany, [but] the *Belle Époque* elites of all of Europe." The young Winston Churchill was typical of the British elite. He was "really fascinated by war" which he considered "the normal occupation of man . . . war — with gardening"! In 1914, when the Great War broke out, Churchill would be ecstatic and declare that war was "glorious and delicious." In any event, it was not the working class and the rest of the lower orders, supposedly the *classes dangereuses*, but the openly belligerent ruling elite that revealed itself to be "Europe's most formidable *classe dangereuse*," as Arno Mayer has put it.[25] Theodore Roosevelt, president of the United States from 1901 to 1909, was equally fond of war. He was described on one occasion as

> gush[ing] over war as the ideal condition of human society,
> for the manly strenuousness . . . and treat[ing] peace as a
> condition of blubberlike and swollen ignobility, fit only for
> huckstering weaklings . . ."[26]

The Nietzschean concept of war was adopted most enthusiastically by the elite because that concept was directed primarily against socialism and its revolutionary aspirations, because war could be useful in the elite's struggle against the rise of the masses, and because of its opposition to the democratization process.[27] Even at the time of the French Revolution, the faction known as the Girondins — revolutionaries of the upper-middle class type and therefore (relatively) conservative — and, later, the Directoire and Napoleon, had made use of the instrument of war to prevent a radicalization of the revolution within France at the hands of radical revolutionaries such as Robespierre and his fellow Jacobins. An international war, a conflict against exterior enemies, was deemed indispensable for the purpose of avoiding civil war, a conflict among the French themselves; this is what one of the leaders of the Girondins, Jacques Pierre Brissot, had declared at the time.[28] Also, in the middle of the nineteenth century, Alexis de Tocqueville, who had carefully studied the French Revolution, drew attention to the fact that war could serve to "neutralize social conflicts." That opinion was shared by the famous cultural historian Jakob

94

Burckhardt, a contemporary of Nietzsche, whom he knew well and whose distaste for democracy and socialism he shared. In his widely read book, *Weltgeschichtliche Betrachtungen* (Reflections on World History), posthumously published in 1905, Burckhardt tipped his hat to the Greek philosopher Heraclitus for having stated that "war is the mother of all good things." With respect to all the good things that would presumably flow from the cornucopia of war, at least from the viewpoint of the haute bourgeoisie, the aforementioned sociologist Vilfredo Pareto, a supporter and even theoretician of elite rule, revealed himself equally optimistic. He explained that a war might not be able to prevent socialism forever, but for a minimum of half a century. War would put an end to "an emancipatory process that had been going on for a century"; war would serve to "slow down, and even roll back, the revolutionary movement." According to the German admiral Alfred von Tirpitz, militarism and war were necessary as antidotes to "the propagation of Marxism and political radicalism among the popular masses." He viewed the Roman god of war Mars as the perfect ally against Marx! The European (and American) elite, which felt increasingly threatened by the rise of the labour movement and of socialism, believed that it could use war as a kind of life vest that would allow it to survive the democratic deluge. In this sense, it is true that war was "a profoundly conservative activity," directed "against the Idea of Progress," as the American historian (and World War II veteran) Paul Fussell has written.[29]

As far as the elite was concerned, war could and would be a cure for the great ailment that affected not only the socialists, but the workers and the lower orders in general. With their demands for higher wages and other benefits, the labouring masses had presumably revealed themselves to be overly materialistic, egoistic, even hedonistic. War, inevitably accompanied by privations and hardship, would purge them of this materialism and infuse them with asceticism. War would teach the socialists and workers in general to be satisfied with less and to accept their lot in life instead of making all sorts of extravagant demands. Military service and war were also considered — for example by the many French army commanders who had perused the book by Le Bon — as a means to transform the popular crowd (*foule*), supposedly undisciplined and therefore untrustworthy and dangerous, into disciplined, malleable, and servile "troops" (*troupe*).[30]

It is highly ironic that the nobility and the haute bourgeoisie, living in the lap of luxury and obsessed with the accumulation of ever-greater riches, felt entitled to preach the virtues of asceticism to the labouring masses; however, it must be acknowledged that the elite's intellectual devotees of Mars were convinced that typically bourgeois deficiencies could likewise be cured by a dose of martial medicine, for example mediocrity, sentimentality, and complacency. War, associated with adventure and heroism, would transform the overly docile and timid burgher — the *Spießburger* or *Spießer*, as they said in German — into a proud, bold, and joyous hero. "Nietzsche's influence," writes de Schaepdrijver,

> *had caused many to long for a more heroic existence . . . The elites of the Belle Époque in all of Europe experienced an urge for ruthless action of any kind, for a merciless battle that would put an end to this boring bourgeois existence full of conventions and compromises.*[31]

This viewpoint was shared by the great German general and field marshal (as well as count) Helmuth von Moltke, for thirty years the chief of staff of the Prussian army, known as "Moltke the Elder" to avoid confusion with his nephew Helmuth von Moltke, "Moltke the Younger," who was to be commander-in-chief of the German Army in 1914. In 1880, Moltke senior wrote the following in a letter:

> *Perpetual peace is a dream — and not even a beautiful dream — and war is an integral part of God's ordering of the universe. In war, man's noblest virtues come into play: courage and renunciation, fidelity to duty and a readiness for sacrifice that does not stop at giving up life itself. Without war, the world would be swamped in materialism.*

War, it was said, not only amounted to an edifying spiritual experience but was also a kind of sport and therefore quite enjoyable. In a book published in 1903, based on his experiences during colonial wars, entitled *Modern*

Warfare: Or, How Our Soldiers Fight, Brigadier General Sir Frederick Gordon
Guggisberg wrote the following:

> *An army . . . tries to work together in a battle . . . in much*
> *the same way as a football team plays together in a match . . .*
> *The army fights for the good of its country as the team plays*
> *for the honour of the school . . . Exceptionally gallant charges*
> *and heroic defences correspond to brilliant runs and fine*
> *tackling.*[32]

Perhaps it was these lines that inspired a British officer, Wilfred Nevill, of
the Eight East Surrey Regiment, on July 1, 1916, to give the signal for attack
by kicking a soccer ball toward the German lines. The *Daily Mail* would
celebrate this exploit with this poem:

> *On through the hail of slaughter,*
> *Where gallant comrades fall,*
> *Where blood is poured like water,*
> *They drive the trickling ball.*
> *The fear of death before them,*
> *Is but an empty name;*
> *True to the the land that bore them,*
> *The Surreys played the game.*[33]

War, then, was supposedly good for everyone, and therefore desirable.
War was expected to function as a catharsis: it would cause a wind of fresh
air to blow through the musty old dwelling that Europe had become. Of
war, one expected "deliverance from vulgarity, constraint, and convention."
War was associated with "liberation and freedom."[34] It could not come
too soon. "How I long for the Great War," wrote the English conservative
Catholic writer Hilaire Belloc, "it will sweep Europe like a broom." The
German writers known as pre-Expressionists similarly imagined that war
would bring deliverance from the prison of a sick society and a sad and
boring era. One of them, Georg Heym, openly longed for the occurrence of
some thrilling event that would put an end to "this idle, greasy, and sticky

peace."[35] The year 1914 would finally bring the hoped-for relief from this *taedium vitae*, associated with all sorts of illusions about war.

The association of war with liberation also appeared in the work of an Italian intellectual, Giovanni Gentile, who would later describe himself as "the philosopher of [Italian] fascism." He glorified war as "the suffering through which the human soul is purified and responds to the call of its destiny."[36] Other transalpine admirers of war and violence were the painters and other members of a cultural movement that became known as Futurism. This movement was supposedly "avant-garde," but it was definitely not progressive in the political or social sense of the term. Arno Mayer has described the Futurists as "allied with conservative forces," who

> *distanced themselves from socialists and workers, the political*
> *vanguard of political progress. Instead, they trusted in extreme*
> *Italian nationalism, imperialism, and war to clear the ground*
> *for the machine age and culture, regardless of the human,*
> *social, and political cost. Inspired by Nietzsche . . . the*
> *Futurists denied equality, opposed the leveling of society, and*
> *believed in an aristocracy of the spirit and the arts.*[37]

One might think that Mayer exaggerates somewhat, but in the "Manifesto of the Futurists," published in 1909, the author, the famous writer Filippo Tommaso Marinetti, shouted from the rooftops that

> *we [the Futurists] want to glorify war, the world's only*
> *hygiene, as well as militarism, patriotism, the destructive*
> *gesture of freedom-bringers, beautiful ideas worth dying for,*
> *and scorn for women.*[38]

(The Futurists despised women because they associated them with pacifism, just as they associated men with bellicism; we will return to this theme later on.) Vorticism, an avant-garde artistic current born in England in 1912, promoted similar ideas. In 1914, just before the war broke out, one of its proponents, the painter and writer Wyndham Lewis, a Nietzschean, urged his friends not to "miss a war, if one is going."[39]

In 1914, the wishes of the Nietzscheans were to be granted. Countless young men would go to war voluntarily, convinced that by "undergoing [their] baptism [of war]" they would achieve "manhood," as a German soldier, a member of the Danish minority in the region of Schleswig-Holstein, put it in 1914. One of his comrades, another German of Danish origin, confided to his journal in typically Nietzschean terms that he went to war "to strengthen [his] character, to strengthen it in power and will, in habits, custom and earnestness."[40]

A major advantage that war was expected to bring was undoubtedly the fact that in wartime the rules of the game of democracy — and of the allegedly inefficient parliamentary system that was associated with it — were deemed to be useless, and would therefore have to be abandoned in favour of the authoritarian power relations and strict discipline featured in armies. Was it not evident that in wartime, commanders had to give orders and subordinates had to obey unconditionally? Of discussion and of input from below, of criticism — in other words, of democracy of any kind — there could no longer be any question. And it went without saying that the commanders would be the traditional, natural, or God-appointed leaders of society, in other words, the existing elite — the *aristoi*, to use Nietzschean terminology — held to have emerged "organically."[41] In times of war, the political had to be subordinated to the military; it followed that the high army commanders — consisting virtually everywhere, as we have seen, of members of the nobility and, to some extent, the upper-middle class — would run the show. War thus provided the elite with an opportunity to suspend the process of democratization and halt the rise of the masses, at least temporarily, but hopefully permanently. War would make it possible to restore, within private organizations and in society in general, the supposedly natural and healthy power relations that had been undermined by the rise of democracy but had been preserved in the army, a system in which a small number, an elite, gives orders and a large number, the masses, obey.[42]

For the elite, war would also be an occasion to realize its own supposedly innate potential for leadership, to demonstrate excellence as political and military leaders, and to display heroism. It was hoped that the authoritarianism and discipline associated with war would similary transform the undisciplined, restless, and dangerous masses of workers and other proletarians into a multi-tude of servile and agreeable underlings. War would function as the "school of the nation" in general, but above all it would restore tranquility and discipline among the lower orders. The proletarians needed to be cured of their demo-cratic and revolutionary illness, caused by "judeo-socialist" propaganda, and intrigue, according to elitist types such as the infamous German nationalist Heinrich Class, and for this illness war happened to be the ultimate remedy. War was to function as a "wake-up call" for "all the good elements of the people" and would thus inaugurate a national renaissance.

The elite, then, viewed war as an instrument for the control of the popular masses. This is precisely what was implied in Churchill's aforementioned remarks comparing war to gardening. In both cases, the aim was to control, to tame. Gardening was about the control of luxuriant plants, the taming of nature. War was about the control of society, about the taming of people in general and of the undisciplined, unruly — and dangerous — working class in particular. In the case of gardening, one must sometimes be prepared to prune, and to prune deeply, thus improving quality at the expense of quan-tity. The Nietzschean elite, which also worshipped older, but still influential intellectual idols such as Malthus, was convinced that waging war would involve an analogous kind of pruning. The inevitably high losses war causes among the rank-and-file constituted not only an inevitable and even neces-sary Malthusian "positive check" on the population, but could also be justi-fied as a quantitative cut that improved the quality. The popular masses were simply too plentiful. It was a crowd that, for the good of society as a whole, needed to be culled from time to time. Was it not a fact that culling made it possible to improve the quality of a breed of cows, deer, etc.? It was not a coincidence that during the Great War, hundreds of thousands of ordinary soldiers, consisting overwhelmingly of peasants and workers, would be sent headlong into certain death by their own generals. Virtually without excep-tion, the latter were members of the Nietzschean and Social-Darwinist prewar elite, steeped in bellicism and contempt of death. Contempt of death means not fearing death, and indeed, the elite did not fear the death of proletarians they loathed, over whom they exercised total power, and whose lives they would waste so lightheartedly during the Great War, as the German historian Hermann Glaser has observed.[43] With respect to this culling of their ranks, certain proletarians were in fact convinced that these seemingly senseless massacres reflected a desire on the part of their generals to reduce the ranks of the workers and thus to make the fearsome masses less "massive" and less frightful. During one of the many strikes Paris witnessed in June 1919, a striker, reflecting on the Great War, declared that

> This war was wanted by the bourgeoisie, the industrial
> capitalists, and the leaders of all the countries [involved in the
> war]. They observed the swelling of the ranks of the proletarian
> organisations and they feared for their coffers. And so they
> found a solution: eliminating workers by means of war.[44]

The elite expected the war not only to function as a cure for the distemper of the masses, associated with socialism, but also to give birth to a new form of solidarity, a nonsocialist and even antisocialist solidarity. War was supposed to spawn a "war socialism," that is, a spiritual instead of materialist socialism; a national instead of an international socialism; a German, French, or British socialism instead of a Marxist and therefore "Jewish" socialism. Mars, the god of war, was expected to become the patron saint of a new kind of society, a society without class antagonisms. It was in this sense that — even if it ended in defeat — war would be "great and wonderful," as the renowned German sociologist Max Weber believed. His conviction was shared by the writer Thomas Mann who, in a famous book, *Reflections of an Unpolitical Man*, published in 1918, would sing the praises of what he called the "warrior ideology." This was the conservative concept of a new community, a product of the war, different as day and night from socialist and liberal societal notions. War was expected to be the instrument that would make it possible to integrate the masses into the existing society, and thus to put an end to the social problems and the class struggle.[45]

War was supposed to unite the entire people and integrate all classes into the established order, to the advantage of the elite. Conversely, war would divide the "proletarians of all countries," who had been uniting under the auspices of socialism to the disadvantage of the elite. In the struggle against socialist internationalism, war was considered to be the ultimate weapon, the most effective instrument in the strategy of "divide and conquer."

CHAPTER 6

IMPERIALIST FRIENDS AND FOES ON THE ROAD TO A GREAT WAR

The imperialist rivalries heat up as a result of the rapidly increasing importance of new raw materials such as rubber and oil. War becomes more and more likely and ultimately inevitable. The German Empire urgently wants to acquire "a place in the sun" via territorial expansion in Eastern Europe, increasing the risk of confrontation with Russia and Great Britain. In the United States too, the elite feels that war is a perfectly fine means to achieve imperialist objectives . . .

Around the turn of the century, relations between the great imperialist powers changed dramatically — and most dangerously. In the early nineteenth century, after the common victory over Napoleon, Russia, the most autocratic state at the time, together with the Habsburg Empire and Prussia, the embryo of the unified Germany that was to be created in 1871, founded the "Holy Alliance," and long remained a reliable partner of these two other empires and bastions of the *ancien régime*. But in 1892, to the consternation of Berlin and Vienna, arch-conservative Russia actually concluded an unlikely political and military alliance with France, the daughter of the Revolution and in many ways the most democratic major country in Europe. Germany henceforth faced the prospect of having to fight on two fronts in case of war. Its army's high command therefore developed a plan that purported to solve the dilemma of a two-front war, namely the famous

Schlieffen Plan, named after the chief of staff of the German Army from 1891 to 1906, Count Alfred von Schlieffen. This plan called for a rapid and lethal push into France via the territory of neutral Belgium.[1] Another result was that the majority of Germans, including the social democrats, now considered their country as a beleaguered fortress, pushed onto the defensive by jealous enemies, above all the czar's empire, a backward dictatorship compared to Germany itself, which boasted an electoral system based on universal suffrage, as well as an elaborate array of Bismarckian social services, making it appear to be the world's most progressive country. It was at least partly on account of this newfangled "russophobia" that the majority of Germany's socialists would go to war voluntarily and even enthusiastically in 1914.

Germany had traditionally enjoyed excellent relations with Great Britain, where the royal throne had actually been occupied for centuries by scions of German dynasties. And were the "Anglo-Saxon" British not descendants of Saxons and other Germanic migrants, and therefore close relations — "cousins" was the term often used in this context — of the Germans within the great "Aryan" race and the "Nordic" and/or "Teutonic" family? ("Why do you wage war against your cousins?," a German officer asked a British colleague whom he had taken prisoner somewhere in the North of France in August 1914.) The notion that the British and the Germans were the only genuinely "white" races in Europe, superior to the French, the Russians, and everyone else, and consequently ought to be in solidarity, was still embraced by elitist circles in Albion as well as Germany on the eve of the Great War.[2] At the end of the nineteenth and in the early twentieth century, however, this relationship deteriorated relatively quickly, for reasons that will soon be discussed. Conversely, the British rather suddenly reconciled themselves with their traditional enemy, the French, with whom an informal (and rather vaguely formulated) alliance was concluded in 1904, the celebrated Entente Cordiale. Shortly afterward, Great Britain and Russia patched up their differences. And so a French-British-Russian grand alliance would see the light of day in 1907, to be known as the Triple Entente. In the meantime, Italy had started to cosy up with Germany and Austria-Hungary, and this partnership received the name of Triple Alliance. The core of this Triple Alliance, the tandem of the empires of the Hohenzollerns and the

Habsburgs, was also to be referred to as the Central Powers. A veritable diplomatic revolution, a *"renversement des alliances,"* thus occurred within a few years. The constantly growing hostility between the two blocks was to lead inexorably, via a number of crises, to the Great War. While this system of alliances helped to make the First World War possible, it is undoubtedly wrong to argue, as some historians have done, that the alliance system constituted the direct *cause* of the great conflict.

"Natural" or "historic" sympathies did not play a role in this diplomatic revolution, and certainly not in the birth of the Triple Entente. As we have already seen, a considerable number of the British despised the French as an inferior race and a deadly enemy since the time of the Hundred Years' War. And in France there was little love for either England or Russia, a seemingly schizophrenic land consisting, on the one hand, of snooty and reactionary aristocrats and, on the other hand, of backward and semibarbarian kulaks. As for the Russian elite, it sympathized with its aristocratic homologues in Germany and the Danube Monarchy and looked down on the bourgeois commoners who ruled the ungodly French *republic* and flirted with Russia's francophile and restless Polish minority. The British elite, finally, regarded itself as a class elevated far above Albion's own proletarians; even so, it considered the British people in general to be infinitely superior to all other peoples and certainly to the Russians. (During the Great war, a British nurse sent to Russia was convinced that the people over there were an inferior lot, so that the British — "superior to all other peoples and cultures" — had stumbled into the war "on the wrong side"; she felt that it would probably have been good for the Russians to be exposed for a few years to German rule.)[3]

The powers involved were imperialist powers, and it was material interests, interests that were close to the hearts of imperialists, that had caused the surprising *renversement des alliances*. From the perspective of imperialism, what mattered above all were control over raw materials, markets for industrial products, opportunities for investment, and cheap labour. These were the things needed by the "national economy" of each great power — that is to say by its industrialists and bankers, in other words, its capitalists. One needed these things, or at least believed one needed them, in order to be able to compete and prosper in a Social-Darwinist world with only two options, to survive or to perish. The riches appropriated outside of Europe and the United States had to serve to make the rich of the wealthy imperialist countries even richer — but also to enable them to throw a few crumbs to the poor denizens of their countries in order to appease the latter, as we have already seen.

With their new partners, London, Paris, and Saint Petersburg believed they had much better prospects for success in the ruthless imperialist rat race than with their former friends. Great Britain, for example, had for many decades considered France to be its main imperialist rival, and in 1898 it had almost come to blows with the French on account of a dispute over some real estate on the banks of the Nile in distant Sudan. But in the 1880s and 1890s, "German industry took off like a rocket" and the German Empire started to eclipse Great Britain in the field of economic and particularly industrial performance. The British elite now feared that if things continued this way, Germany would soon dominate the world, not only economically but also politically.[4] It remained possible to take some military initiative to prevent things from going that far, but one had to act soon, because Germany was constructing a powerful navy that threatened to neutralize Albion's great military trump, the Royal Navy's hegemony at sea. Also, Germany possessed a land army that was much more numerous and powerful than that of Great Britain. In order to undertake any kind of military action against Germany, London thus urgently needed militarily powerful allies. It is for this reason that Britain approached France, Germany's arch-enemy, as well as Russia: the combined military might of this duo was believed capable of crushing the German Moloch — even without major assistance from the British.

In the meantime, most colonial conflicts with France had been resolved via an "honest" division of the territorial loot. In Southeast Asia, for example, the French had taken possession of "Indochina," the combination of Vietnam, Laos, and Cambodia, while the British pocketed Malaysia; between these two regions, Siam (or Thailand) was allowed to remain independent as a kind of buffer state. The French and British thus each appropriated their own source of a raw material that was rapidly gaining in importance with the advent of the automobile, namely rubber. (Southeast-Asian rubber, harvested by ridiculously cheap colonial labour, would generate fabulous profits for firms such as Michelin and Dunlop.) Germany felt sadly disadvantaged in this respect. Its industry, in contrast to British industry, was not focused solely on the production of coal and steel, conjured up by names such as Krupp and Thyssen, but also on that of petrochemicals, whereby names such as Bayer, BASF, and Hoechst come to mind, firms that would merge in 1925 to form a trust known as IG Farben. These gigantic and influential enterprises required colossal amounts of rubber as well as oil and were therefore in favour of an imperialist policy purporting to provide Germany with (more) colonies — if necessary, via war.

Great Britain had a mighty navy but, since it had no compulsory military service, had only a relatively small land force, which was dispersed across the entire globe. Scheduled for intervention on the European continent, the British Expeditionary Force (BEF) consisted of approximately 80,000 professional soldiers, fewer in number than the Belgian army, but very well armed with Vickers machine guns and Lee-Enfield rifles, *inter alia*. But compared to the gigantic armies of Germany, Russia, and France, the BEF was a mere dwarf.[5] An armed conflict with the German rival would require millions of soldiers, but this "cannon fodder" could be provided by the French and the Russians. Just as Paris counted on Russian help in case of war against Germany, London counted on French help, and indirectly also on Russian.

As early as 1905, when the ink of the signatures on the Entente Cordiale was barely dry, Admiral Sir John Fisher, First Sea Lord (i.e., the minister in charge of the Royal Navy) *and* supreme commander of the Royal Navy, wrote enthusiastically to Lord Lansdowne, the Minister of Foreign Affairs, that the British had to take immediate advantage of the opportunity offered by a diplomatic crisis about Morocco to go to war against Germany, because the French were now allies of the British:

> *This seems a golden opportunity for fighting the Germans*
> *in alliance with the French . . . We could have the German*
> *Fleet, the Kiel Canal [linking the North Sea and the Baltic],*
> *and Schleswig-Holstein within a fortnight.*

Undoubtedly to Fisher's great regret, this Moroccan crisis did not lead to war, nor did a second crisis over this North-African country in 1911, or

other, similar, opportunities. Fisher and other high-ranking British personalities wanted war not for democracy and freedom and such, but to further
the interests of Great Britain as an imperialist power. In February 1911,
Fisher expressed great concern over the expectation that by the summer of
1914 the Kiel Canal would have been widened sufficiently to allow even
the biggest and most modern German battleships to slip quickly from the
Baltic to the North Sea and vice versa: he felt that military action had to be
taken before that fateful hour were to strike.[6] In the early summer of 1914,
London would finally take advantage of yet another crisis, in reality no
more than a minor event in the distant Balkan Peninsula, to unleash the
dogs of war.

Not that long before, Russia, like France, had loomed as a great and
dangerous rival of Great Britain, particularly with respect to the Middle East
and Central Asia — including Afghanistan, a sensitive buffer zone between
British India and the Russian possessions to its north. The British called
this rivalry "the Great Game." But after its defeat in the war of 1904–1905
against Japan, the empire of the czars ceased to represent a major menace to British imperialism. It became possible to patch up old differences
with respect to Persia, namely by means of a division of that theoretically independent country, in reality a semi-colony, into two spheres of
influence. Russia and Great Britain thus gained access to yet another raw
material that was becoming important at the time: petroleum. To Russia,
the alliance with the British offered the advantage that London henceforth
tolerated what it had hitherto considered to be anathema, namely Russian
ambitions with respect to Constantinople and the Dardanelles at the
expense of the Ottomans.

During the 1890s it became apparent that for military as well as commercial shipping, oil was a far more efficient form of fuel than coal. The
British had started to convert their ships, and their example was soon followed by the Germans and other seafaring nations. Constructing new ships
was relatively easy (though very expensive), but acquiring large and reliable amounts of oil was a trickier task. At that time, the United States was
the world's foremost producer of oil, and at first Great Britain, the world's
greatest maritime power, relied on the US for this fuel. This was a most
unpleasant situation since Albion and its former transatlantic colony were

hardly the best of friends; in fact, they were rivals in the imperialist rat race and found themselves often at loggerheads over issues such as influence in Latin America. The British were therefore keenly looking out for alternative sources of oil. The deal with Russia with respect to Persia was helpful in this respect. It was in this context that the Anglo-Iranian Oil Company was founded, now known as British Petroleum (BP). Great Britain developed an interest in the Middle East, a strategically important region that straddled the route from Europe to British India and bordered on yet another important British possession, Egypt, with its Suez Canal. On the eve of the Great War, however, Great Britain still relied on foreign sources for its oil, of which 65 per cent came from the US and 20 per cent from Russia.[7]

It was during the first decade of the twentieth century that significant deposits of oil were discovered in Mesopotamia, more specifically in present-day Kuwait and in the region around the city of Mosul. Mesopotamia, destined to become Iraq after the First World War,[8] still belonged to the Ottoman Empire, but the European powers had made it a habit to help themselves to pieces of its periphery — such as Libya and Egypt — in order to turn them into "protectorates." By 1899, the British had already snatched oil-rich Kuwait, proclaimed it a protectorate, and were to transform it in 1914 into a supposedly independent emirate; the local oil could thus start to flow unperturbed toward Albion's shores.

With a navy such as that of the British, however, one could never have too much oil. And so Lady Britannia, determined to remain "Sovereign of the Seven Seas," turned her attention to Mosul, situated deep in Mesopotamia's interior. But here a problem presented itself: since 1908, the year when in Istanbul the so-called Young Turks had come to power, the Ottoman Empire had sought a rapprochement with Germany. And the two countries were planning the construction of a railway that would link Istanbul with Baghdad, the Mesopotamian metropolis, situated close to Mosul. Complemented by a track through the Balkans, this project could theoretically create a railway connection from Berlin by way of "Byzantium" (Istanbul) to Baghdad. The British thus faced the prospect that, sooner or later, barrels full of oil from Mosul might start to roll toward Germany for the benefit of its military and commercial fleets — and of its modern and high-flying petrochemical industry — unless, of course, the

British could find a way to lay their own hands on that petroleum. On the eve of the Great War, the Germans would display a willingness to work out a compromise and to collaborate with the British with respect to their railway project, if only because Germany alone could not finance the scheme. But London preferred to look for ways to obtain exclusive control over the oil of Mesopotamia.

It was in this context that British foreign policy switched from its traditionally pro-Ottoman and anti-Russian stance — demonstrated not that long ago during the Crimean War — to a course that was pro-Russian and anti-Ottoman — and therefore simultaneously anti-German. From then on, oil and the oil-rich regions of the Middle East constituted a factor of prime importance in the calculus of the political and military leaders of a country whose navy, and therefore whose power and prosperity, depended increasingly on the new fuel.[9]

Great Britain sought to put spikes in the wheels of the German-Ottoman railway project and discovered possibilities for that in two regions, the Balkans and Mesopotamia itself. On Europe's southeastern peninsula, Serbia started to benefit from British sympathy. That little country functioned as a source of inspiration and support for the South-Slav minorities of the Danube Monarchy and was therefore an enemy of that empire and of its German ally. Serbia straddled the planned railway line from Berlin to Istanbul and was therefore in a position to help thwart the project. During the Balkan Wars of 1912–1913, in which the Ottoman Empire lost a sizeable part of its European territories, London observed with satisfaction how the Serbs appropriated more real estate, namely Kosovo and Macedonia.[10]

London also girded itself to bring Mesopotamia under direct or indirect British control, if necessary via armed intervention. As early as 1911, plans were made to occupy the strategically important city of Basra in case of war against the Ottomans, to be used as a springboard for the conquest of Mesopotamia. When the Great War broke out in 1914, the British proved ready to invade the Middle East from both Egypt and India; the objective was Baghdad, to be reached either via Basra and the Tigris River or from Egypt, via Jerusalem and Damascus. The famous Lawrence of Arabia would not suddenly appear out of nowhere: he was merely one of the numerous Brits who, during the years leading up to 1914, had been carefully selected and trained to "defend" their country's interests — mostly with respect to oil — in the Middle East.

The British aspirations with respect to the Middle East and its oil prove that it is not true that, on the eve of the Great War, "the tensions caused by imperialism seemed to be subsiding [because] there was not much left to divide up in Africa, the Pacific or Asia," as Margaret MacMillan has written only recently.[11] Such statements imply that imperialist rivalries were not a significant factor in the origins of the Great War. To this it can be replied — as the French historian Annie Lacroix-Riz has recently done so effectively — that the "hungry" imperialist powers, above all Germany, which felt disadvantaged compared to "satisfied" powers such as Great Britain, were not prepared to put up with the status quo, but aggressively pursued a redistribution of existing colonial possessions. As Lacroix-Riz emphasizes, the colonial prizes had already been allotted, but they could be re-allotted: there had been a *partage*, but there could be *repartages*.[12] That such *repartages*, or redistributions, were possible but also unlikely to be achieved peacefully, was demonstrated by the case of former Spanish colonies like the Philippines, Cuba, and Puerto Rico, which were transformed into satrapies of America's "informal empire" as a result of the Spanish-American War of 1898. Moreover, a considerable part of the world did in fact remain available for direct or indirect annexation as colonies or protectorates, or for economic penetration combined with American-style "neocolonial" status. The competition between the imperialist vultures was and remained very likely to lead to conflicts and wars, including a general war. It almost came to such a conflagration in 1911 when, to the great chagrin of Germany, France turned Morocco into a protectorate.

The case of Morocco shows how even supposedly satisfied imperialist powers such as France and Great Britain were never truly satisfied — just as immensely rich people never feel that they have enough riches — but continued to look for ways to aggrandize their colonial possessions, no matter how fat their colonial portfolio already was, even at the risk of unleashing war. This is why the Armageddon that was to erupt in 1914 was recently described by a journalist of *The Guardian* as "a savage industrial slaughter perpetrated by a gang of predatory imperial powers, locked in a deadly struggle to capture and carve up territories, markets and resources."[13]

The widely anticipated collapse of the Ottoman Empire — or, at the very least, the continuing redistribution of morsels of its vast territory — had certainly whetted the appetite of the competing imperialist powers that would go to war against each other in 1914, and this was unquestionably one of the factors that caused the First World War. "The war erupted directly from the fight for imperial dominance in the Balkans," wrote the aforementioned journalist of *The Guardian*, and it was a matter of acquiring "pickings from the crumbling Ottoman Empire." In those days London, just like Berlin, St. Petersburg, etc., also had their keen gaze fixed on China, where there was still an awful lot of potential for acquisitions — as is actually acknowledged by MacMillan herself who, elsewhere in her book, refers to the possibility of "a serious scramble for China,"[14] similar to the earlier race to grab chunks of Africa. In the Far East, the great powers also jockeyed for advantages vis-à-vis imperialist competitors, thus contributing to rising tensions between them. Among those powers there was one non-European nation, Japan, which would actually become involved in the Great War on account of its interests in China. And one of the reasons why the United States would enter the war in 1917 was the desire to be present when the victorious imperialist powers would carve up China, economically if not territorially, as everybody expected. With its victory over Russia in 1905, the "land of the rising sun" had revealed itself to be an imperialist power, the only "non-Western" member of the restricted club of imperialists. Like all other imperialist powers, Japan was henceforth eagerly and uninhibitedly eying territories featuring important raw materials, potential markets, and cheap labour. The war that broke out in Europe in 1914 provided Japan with a golden opportunity in this sense. On September 23 of that year, Tokyo declared war on Germany for the simple reason that this permitted Japan to take over the German mini-colony (or "concession") in China, the Bay of Kiao-Chau (or Kiao-Chao), as well as Germany's island colonies in the Northern Pacific. In the case of Japan, we accept it as obvious that the country went to war in order to achieve imperialist objectives, but in the case of the Western imperialist powers, we continue to be told that in 1914 arms were taken up solely to defend liberty and democracy.

Let us now examine things from the perspective of Germany. The unification of that country into a single state had taken place only shortly before, in 1871. The fruit of that achievement was hardly an ordinary country, but rather a great and powerful empire, a *Kaiserreich*, or *Reich* for short, a successor to the prestigious German empire of the Middle Ages known as the Holy Roman Empire and associated with names such as Emperor Barbarossa. The new German *Reich*, founded in 1871, was also the precursor of the infamous "Third Reich" of Adolf Hitler. Despite its power, by the 1870s and 1880s it was already too late for Germany to participate successfully in the great scramble for colonies in Africa and elsewhere. In fact, Germany could consider itself lucky that it was still able to acquire a handful of colonies, for example Tanganyika (or "German East Africa"), "German Southwest Africa," now Namibia, and a handful of islands in the distant Pacific. But those hardly amounted to major prizes, certainly not in comparison to the Congo, a huge region bursting with rubber and copper that was pocketed by minuscule Belgium. With respect to access to sources of vital raw materials, the rapidly growing industry of Germany thus found itself very much disadvantaged in comparison to its British and French rivals. For a great power with the most developed petrochemical industry, it was a source of considerable frustration that it did not have colonies full of rubber and petroleum. Not just rubber and oil, but many other vital raw materials such as copper had to be imported by Germany and therefore purchased at comparatively high rates, which meant that the finished products of German industry were more expensive and thus less competitive on international markets.

This imbalance between extremely high industrial productivity and relatively restricted markets demanded a solution and, in the eyes of numerous German industrialists (and other members of the country's elite), the only genuine solution was a war that would give the German Empire what it was entitled to and — to formulate it in Social-Darwinist terms — what was necessary for its survival: colonies overseas, and territories within Europe as well. The expansionist and aggressive foreign policy of the German Empire in the years leading up to 1914 did indeed pursue the objective of turning Germany into a world power, and Emperor Wilhelm II was the figurehead of this policy, which went down in history under the label of *Weltpolitik*, "policy on a worldwide scale," a term that was merely a euphemism for what was in fact an imperialist policy. In any event, Imanuel Geiss, an authority in the field of the history of Germany before and during the First World War, has emphasized that this "worldwide policy" was one of the factors "that made war inevitable."[15]

There were perhaps no more major regions on earth that could be colonized directly by an imperialist power, but the existing colonies could certainly be *redistributed*, and in Berlin they dreamed of pinching the colonies of small states such as Belgium and Portugal. (And in Great Britain a faction within the elite, consisting mostly of industrialists and bankers with connections to Germany, was in fact willing to appease the Reich; not with a single square mile of their own Empire, of course, but with the gift of Belgian or Portugese overseas possessions.) Nevertheless, it was above all within Europe itself that opportunities seemed to exist for Germany. All sorts of raw materials as well as plenty of cheap agricultural products were to be had in the endless space of Europe's east and southeast, and control over the great southeast-European Balkan peninsula could also serve as a bridge to the Ottoman Empire and its oil-rich regions in the Middle East. It is in this context that the grandiose project of the Berlin-Byzantium-Baghdad railway was born, a project that set off alarm bells in London; and it was also in this context that Berlin started to share Vienna's antipathy for Serbia, an inconvenient roadblock in the middle of the Balkans. In Berlin they dreamed that Europe's east — all the way to the oil fields of the Caucasus! — would become for Germany what India already was for Great Britain and what the famous Wild West was for the United States, namely, a gigantic colony whose raw materials, agricultural products, and the cheap labour of its numerous, supposedly racially inferior but solidly built inhabitants, would be available unconditionally to the metropolis; in addition, to that distant region one would be able to ship Germany's restless and potentially dangerous demographic surplus. For illustration we can cite a pamphlet that was produced in 1894 by the Pan-German League (*Alldeutsche Verband*), a nationalist, racist, militarist, and expansionist lobby in the service of the Reich's *Weltpolitik*:

> *The very ancient Drang nach Osten ["urge to push to the east"] must be revived. We must acquire land in the east and southeast, so that the Germanic race may spread its*

wings there, even if that means putting an end to the useless
existence of minor and inferior nations such as the Czechs,
the Slovenes, and the Slovaks. Thus shall arise, all the way to
the confines of Asia Minor, thanks to German colonisation,
industry, and intelligence, a gigantic German economic
zone.[16]

Hitler's infamous fantasies with respect to "living space" (*Lebensraum*), which he was to reveal in the 1920s in *Mein Kampf* and to put into practice during the Second World War, saw the light under those circumstances. In this respect too, Hitler was not an anomaly at all, but a typical product of his time and space, and of the imperialism of that time and space.

Western Europe, more developed industrially and more densely populated than Europe's east, was seen primarily as a market for the finished products of German industry. Even so, leaders of the German steel industry did not hide their great interest in the French region around the towns of Briey and Longwy. That area — situated close to the border with Belgium and Luxembourg as well as the part of Lorraine that had been annexed by Germany in 1871 — featured rich deposits of high-quality iron ore. Without this ore, claimed some spokesmen of German industry, the German steel industry was condemned to death, at least in the long run. It was also believed that Germany's *Volkswirtschaft*, its national economy, would profit greatly from the annexation of Belgium with its great seaport, Antwerp, its coal regions, etc. And together with Belgium its colony, the Congo, would of course fall into the hands of the Reich; rich in minerals such as copper, the Congo was considered a perfect "complementary zone" (*Ergänzungszone*) for the highly industrialized Reich. Certain German imperialists even dreamed of acquiring the Netherlands as well as Belgium. (Whether the acquisition of the Low Countries would involve direct annexation or a combination of formal political independence and economic dependence on Germany was a matter of debate among the experts within the German elite.) In any event, in one way or another, virtually all of Europe was to be integrated into a "greater economic space" (*Großraumwirtschaft*) under German control, and this would provide a definitive solution to Germany's problems. The Reich would finally be able to take its rightful place next to Britain, the US, etc. in the restricted circle of the great imperialist powers and thus to occupy the "place in the sun" (*Platz an der Sonne*, to use a favourite expression of Emperor Wilhelm II) to which it believed it was entitled.

It was obvious that Germany's ambitions in the east could not be realized without serious conflict with Russia, and the German aspirations with respect to the Balkans risked causing problems with Serbia. That little country was already at loggerheads with the Reich's biggest and best friend, Austria-Hungary, but it was supported by Russia and benefited from the sympathy of the French and the British. The Russians were also very annoyed by Germany's planned penetration of the Balkan peninsula in the direction of Istanbul, especially via its railway project; they were almost certainly willing to go to war if necessary to deny Germany direct or indirect control of the Bosporus and the Dardanelles.[17]

According to the Social-Darwinist concepts fashionable at the time, the growing antagonism between Germany and the Danube Monarchy on the one hand, and Russia and Serbia on the other, loomed like a conflict between two irreconcilable "races," the Germanic and Slavic races, a conflict that was predestined to end with the triumph of the superior race and the defeat of the inferior race.[18] The head of the supreme command of the German Army, Helmuth von Moltke, wrote in 1913 in a letter to his Austro-Hungarian homologue, Franz Conrad von Hötzendorf, that the unavoidable European war would be a war "between Teutons and Slavs." (A few hours before his suicide in his bunker in Berlin, in April 1945, Hitler, who had absorbed this kind of thinking in his youth, came to the logical Social-Darwinist conclusion that the stronger Slav race — in the form of the Soviets — had triumphed over the weaker Germans, so that the latter deserved their defeat.)[19]

As for the German ambitions in Western Europe and Belgium in particular, these obviously ran counter to the traditional interests of the British. At least as far back as the time of Napoleon, London had not wanted to see a major power ensconced in Antwerp and along the Flemish coast — and certainly not Germany, long a great power on land but now, with an increasingly impressive navy, also a menace at sea. With Antwerp, Germany would not only have at its disposal a "pistol aimed at England," as Napoleon had described the city on the Scheldt River, but also one of the world's greatest seaports. This would have made Germany's international trade far less dependent on the services of British ports, sea lanes, and shipping, the principal source of revenue of British commerce.[20] (Seen from this perspective, the project of a railway from Berlin to Baghdad was also a thorn in the British side because such an overland connection constituted a threat to its very lucrative navigation via the Suez Canal.)

In this context, the risk of war against France hardly played a role, because in Berlin it was taken for granted that a war against the Gallic neighbour would have to be fought sooner or later. The real and imaginary interests and needs of Germany as a great industrial and imperialist power thus pushed the country increasingly rapidly, via an aggressive foreign policy, toward a war that would inevitably be a confrontation between blocs of great powers and therefore a major war, a "Great War." But this raised no great concerns within the political, military, economic, and intellectual circles of the elite of the military giant that Germany had already been for quite some time. To the contrary, among the industrialists, bankers, generals, politicians, and other members of the Reich's establishment, only some rare birds did not wish for a war; most of them preferred a war *as soon as possible*, and many were even in favour of deliberately unleashing a war; they were partisans of a *preventive* war. This outspoken bellicism was of course justified by means of Social-Darwinist and Nietzschean arguments. To contemporary racists and Social Darwinists, it seemed that a final showdown between Germans and Gauls was as inevitable as the preordained ultimate confrontation between Germans and Slavs. An armed clash with the British "cousins" also appeared ineluctable: was the rising new Germany not the new Rome, predestined to settle accounts once and for all with the British Carthage? Both nations considered themselves to be superior "Aryans" but, as the German economist and sociologist Werner Sombart would explain in his book *Händler und Helden* ("Merchants and Heroes"), published in 1915, they had two totally different "souls." The Germans, he said, were a people chosen by God, a "people of heroes," while the British were merely a people of "merchants," or worse, "peddlers," and their country nothing more than a kind of "department store."[21]

Of course the German elite also featured less bellicist members, but among them there prevailed the fatalist feeling that war was simply inevitable.[22] The flame of this sentiment was actually fanned from above, for example, in the book *Das Volk im Waffen* ("The Nation in Arms"), published in 1887 but a bestseller for many, many years. The author was a general, Colmar von der Goltz, who would be responsible for all kinds of atrocities committed by the Germans on Belgian civilians in 1914. In this opus, one could read the following:

> *It is necessary to make it clear to ourselves and to the children growing up around us, whom we have to train, that a time of rest has not yet come, that the prediction of a final struggle for the existence and the greatness of Germany is not a mere fancy of ambitious fools, but that it will come one day, inevitably, with full fury.[23]*

It was on account of their imperialist interests, then, that the elites of Great Britain as well as Germany ardently wished for war, and the same can be said for the other imperialist countries. Let us also examine the case of the United States, a country that we are supposed to believe was, or at least strove to be, a champion of peace, with a predilection for "isolationism." In reality, the United States was itself a product of war, namely of the American War of Independence of 1775–1783, which was in reality a war between two great powers, Britain and France. It was a kind of omen that the American state was born under the sign of Mars, the god of war: throughout the nineteenth century the Americans never really ceased to wage war, for example, in a new clash with the British (1812–1815), a confrontation with Mexico (1846–1848), a particularly bloody civil war (1861–1865), and an armed conflict with Spain (1898), not to mention the extremely brutal, even genocidal "Indian Wars," in reality a long string of one-sided massacres.

Like Germany, the United States metamorphosed over the course of the nineteenth century into a great industrial power that developed the familiar imperialist taste for markets, raw materials, etc. As a consequence, it systematically continued to pursue a territorial expansion that had already started very early on, relying on the familiar instrument of war. The so-called Wild West was "won" (i.e., conquered); the Mexican neighbour — traditionally despised as a half-Indian, half-Mediterranean bastard, and Catholic to boot — was robbed of vast territories; Hawaii was annexed; and Cuba, Puerto Rico, and the Philippines were placed under direct or indirect control. And all of that was presumably possible — at least according to the then very widespread belief in "Manifest Destiny" — because God had wanted it. Millions of people, generally of red or brown skin or other non-Nordic and therefore supposedly inferior types, lost their lives in the process, but that presented no problem. What did matter was that after the defeat of the quasi-aristocracy of the Southern, slaveholding plantation owners in the War of Secession, the American elite, henceforth consisting almost exclusively of industrialists based in the great industrial centres of the northeast of the country, profited most handsomely from these wars of conquest, which yielded plenty of raw materials, cheap agricultural products, new investment opportunities, etc.[24]

Another bonus for the elite was the fact that the new regions in the Wild West, "cleansed" of the native "redskins," could absorb the potentially dangerous excess population of the heavily industrialized and urbanized northeast and thus function as a kind of safety valve that alleviated the social pressure tending to build up in New York, Boston, Philadelphia, etc. The wars against the Indians thus made it possible to maintain a measure of social peace within the Yankee heartland, a task that was far from easy even under these conditions, because in the United States too, the popular "masses" revealed themselves all too frequently to be recalcitrant and seditious. In fact, the American state experienced social problems and unrest from the very start, for example, even in the years immediately after independence, in the form of the so-called Whiskey Rebellion of the 1790s.[25]

The case of the United States clearly illustrates the way in which imperialism — "social imperialism" à la Cecil Rhodes — seemed able to resolve the social problems of industrialized countries *without hurting the interests of the elite*, as socialism, an alternative solution, certainly threatened to do. Though it required war, this was considered to be normal and even a good thing, because in the United States too, the elite had embraced Social Darwinism and Nietzschean philosophy. In any event, war had been good for the American elite and, conversely, the American elite had developed a great deal of enthusiasm for war. With respect to the short but victorious armed conflict against Spain in 1898, one of the members of the US elite, Secretary of State John Hay, proclaimed it to have been "a splendid little war." But the most famous partisan of imperialism, expansionism, and war in the years leading up to 1914 was undoubtedly Theodore Roosevelt, president from 1901 to 1909. This "Teddy" — after whom the "teddy bear" was named — was a fanatic racist, convinced that, in the struggle for life, the "Nordic" and presumably superior Americans were predestined to triumph over the inferior Spaniards and Mexicans, and of course also over the "redskins" of whom countless other Americans at that time felt that "the only good Indian was a dead Indian." In 1897, one year before the war against Spain, he confided to a friend that he "should welcome almost any war, for I think this country needs one."[26]

With war, then, the American elite had only positive experiences, excellent experiences even, and continued to look for new opportunities. In 1914 an opportunity did arise, but the American people were unfortunately not in a mood to intervene in a conflict that erupted in Europe. It would take another three years — and require an enormous amount of propaganda and social pressure[27] — before the elite, personified by the president, seemingly an angel of peace, would manage to drag the country into the Great War and reap the fruits thereof. We will soon return to the theme of the entry of the United States into the First World War.

The extravagant imperialist ambitions of all the great powers and the merciless rivalries between them caused the elites of all countries to become more and more bellicose — and war to become more and more likely. Imperialism had begotten wars from the very start, but so far these wars had always been relatively limited conflicts, mostly colonial, that virtually without exception had been brief and victorious. But now, in the beginning of the twentieth century, the rapids of their worsening rivalries caused the great imperialist powers to drift inexorably toward the Niagara of large-scale war. And indeed, the war that was to break out in 1914 would be a conflict between two antagonistic blocs of imperialist powers that were the products of the *renversement des alliances* of the beginning of the twentieth century. And it would not be a minor war, limited and glorious, taking place in distant lands, but a major war, catastrophic and incredibly traumatic, fought in the western-European cradle of imperialism. From this "Great War," the great imperialist powers would not emerge without great damage.

CHAPTER 7
BOURGEOISIE, ARISTOCRACY, CHURCH, AND SOCIALISTS CONFRONT WAR AND REVOLUTION

Of an apparently unavoidable Great War, the industrial bourgeoisie expects considerable economic advantages. But the other pillars of the elite, the nobility and the church, also entertain high hopes with respect to the coming war. The socialist parties remain revolutionary in theory, but in reality they believe increasingly in an evolution toward socialism, and embrace "reformism." Many of them simultaneously abandon internationalism in favour of a socially tinted nationalism known as "social chauvinism" . . .

The primordial aim of imperialism was the conquest (or at least the indirect control) of regions where important raw materials were to be found, where the metropolis could find a market for its industrial products, and where the inhabitants could be used (or rather, exploited) as cheap labour. Within the imperialist powers, the industrialists were the paramount beneficiaries of these bonuses of imperialism — and of the wars associated with it — as they derived greater profits from new markets, raw materials, etc. Imperialism and its wars also involved considerable costs, of course, but those were mostly "externalized" as economists say; that is, not borne by the entrepreneurs and firms involved but taken over by the state. In other words, the costs of imperialism were *socialized*, while the benefits were *privatized*. Even today, the costs generated by imperialist wars such as those waged in Iraq and Afghanistan are socialized, while the profits produced by those wars are privatized for the benefit of oil trusts, arms dealers, and providers of all sorts of military and paramilitary services.

That the capitalists profited from imperialism, that imperialism was a phenomenon associated with capitalism, a manifestation of an increasingly rapidly developing capitalist system, and that capitalism was therefore responsible, via imperialism, for the numerous colonial wars and for the Great War that would break out in 1914, was acknowledged only too well by countless contemporary observers and commentators. As Jean Jaurès already declared in 1895, "capitalism carries war within itself just like the thundercloud carries the storm." Jaurès was a convinced anticapitalist, of course, but many of the members of the bourgeois and aristocratic elite were also keenly aware of the link between war and their economic interests, and occasionally acknowledged this. General Haig, for example, who would command the British Army from 1915 until the end of the war, declared on one occasion that he was not "ashamed of the wars fought to open up the markets of the world to our traders."[1] One of the British "traders" who had thus been able to sell their products all over the world was of course Haig's own Scottish family, which had become fabulously rich by selling whisky.

While in all the imperialist countries there were countless industrialists and bankers who favoured a "bellicose economic expansionism," it is also true that many capitalists — and possibly even a majority — appreciated the advantages of peace and the inconveniences of war and were therefore not warmongers at all, as Eric Hobsbawm has emphasized. But this observation has wrongly caused the conservative British historian Niall Ferguson to jump to the conclusion that the interests of capitalists did not play a role in the eruption of the Great War in 1914. One must also take into account that, like so many other people, countless capitalists displayed an *ambivalent* attitude with respect to war. This means that, on the one hand, they feared certain consequences of war but, on the other hand, they expected certain advantages from it, even considerable advantages. That a war would have unpleasant aspects was something the majority of industrialists and bankers, even the most bellicose among them, realized only too well; however, as members of the elite they also had reason to believe that the unpleasantness would be experienced mostly by others — and of course mostly by the simple soldiers to whom the nasty jobs of killing and dying were traditionally entrusted. At the same time, war brought the acquisition of colonies, markets, raw materials, and similar advantages. And we should not forget that the armament programs eagerly launched by the great powers to prepare for the coming conflict were a cornucopia for the "military-industrial complexes" that were developing rapidly in each country. The armaments race generated major orders and profits for industry and finance, and for that reason the tandem of industry and finance favoured armament.[2]

In many different ways, "the development of capitalism inevitably pushed the world in the direction of state rivalry, imperialist expansion, conflict and war," adds Hobsbawm.[3] In comparison to the catastrophic development of the capitalist *system* in its imperialist mode, the fact that numerous *individuals* among the industrialists and bankers privately cherished peace is ultimately only of marginal importance and does not permit the conclusion that capitalism did not lead to the Great War. It would be equally fallacious to note that quite a few Nazis were personally not anti-Semitic — and even claimed to have Jewish friends, which was true in some cases — and thus jump to the conclusion that Nazism was not really anti-Semitic, or that Nazism did not play a role in the origins of the Holocaust.

Imperialism and the wars associated with it favoured not only the capitalist interests of the upper-middle class, but also those of that other segment of the contemporary elite, namely the nobility. First, as we have already seen, this nobility had invested heavily in capitalist activities such as mining, a branch of industry with a great interest in overseas regions rich in minerals. The British and Dutch royal families had thus acquired enormous portfolios of shares in firms that were prospecting for oil all over the world, such as Shell, so they profited handsomely from imperialist expansion and learned not to worry much about the wars this involved. With this in mind, we are not surprised that in 2003 Great Britain and the Netherlands proved eager to join the "coalition of the willing" organized by the America of George W. Bush for the purpose of conquering the oil fields of Iraq.

Second, the nobility was traditionally a class of large landowners. It is therefore only natural that the men of the *ancien régime* welcomed the territorial acquisitions that imperialism systematically sought to achieve by means of war. In noble families, the eldest son traditionally inherited not only the title, but the family's entire patrimony. New colonies overseas or — in the case of Germany and the Danube Monarchy — in Eastern Europe could function as "lands of unlimited possibilities" where the younger sons could acquire domains of their own and lord it over natives who were to serve as underpaid peasants or domestic servants, just as the crusades had provided "castles in Spain" to junior aristocrats during the Middle Ages, lionized by the Romanticists. When in early 1918 it seemed likely that much of Eastern Europe would fall under the rule of the German Empire, numerous German and Austro-Hungarian princes (such as the Duke of Urach) eagerly sought to acquire a royal title or crown in Lithuania, Ukraine, or Finland; even much later, during the Second World War, German generals with a noble background dreamed of acquiring some "knightly domain" (*Rittergut*), that is, a tract of land associated with a noble title, in Ukraine or elsewhere in Eastern Europe.[4] Adventurous young scions of noble families could also embark on prestigious careers as officers in conquering colonial armies or as high-ranking officials in the administration of colonial territories. The highest functions in the colonies, for example that of Viceroy of British India or Governor-General of Canada, were reserved almost exclusively for the marquesses, counts, and other members of illustrious families.

For all these reasons, imperialist projects also received the support of a disproportionately high percentage of politicians, diplomats, and high-ranking state bureaucrats of noble origin. In those days, as in the Middle Ages, the power and prestige of a country were still associated with the size of its territory, so that territorial expansion seemed important, desirable, and — in the Social-Darwinist context — even necessary. The monarchy in particular, the form of government which still prevailed and in which the nobility had always felt at home, considered "ownership of large territories — empire — a critical measure of virility and grandeur."[5]

It was only in countries where the nobility no longer exerted much power — and that was practically the case only in the United States — that not much importance was attached to formal annexations of territories, and where one sought instead to acquire control of the raw materials, markets, and labour of other countries by indirect means; for example by the installation of so-called *comprador* regimes, generally unpopular and therefore dictatorial in nature. Thus was inaugurated, on the other side of the Atlantic, the passage from colonialism to neocolonialism, a form of colonialism that was more discreet but every bit as real, to which the European powers would only switch after the Second World War.

That other pillar of the *ancien régime*, the Catholic Church, also saw bread in imperialist territorial conquests, whether associated with wars or not. As in the case of the nobility, the church looked back with nostalgia to the "good old days" of the Middle Ages, when nearly everybody in Europe was Christian and it was possible to convince, or rather to coerce, masses of "infidels" in peripheral regions conquered by the brave crusaders to convert to the one and only true faith. With imperialism, the Church was given the opportunity — at least in Catholic countries such France and Belgium — to set forth once more to spread the gospel that way, all over the world but above all in Africa, a "dark" continent seemingly ready to receive the "light" of Christianity. For capitalists, imperialism signified the conquest of raw materials, markets, and cheap labour all over the world; for the Church, it meant the conquest of souls in all four corners of the world.

The conversion of masses of Africans and "natives" of other continents compensated for the losses Christianity had been suffering in Europe itself as a result of the rise of liberal free-thinking and socialist atheism. With its missionary work in Africa and elsewhere, the Church rendered an important service not only to itself but also to imperialism, namely by "socializing" the denizens of the colonies; that is, by integrating them into the colonial order. The Church profited from the conquests of imperialism, and imperialism profited from the missionary efforts of the Church in the conquered territories. This missionary work was to become an important task for the Church. It would give rise to the emergence of specialists in the matter, in the form of new orders such as the White Fathers (*Pères Blancs*) and the Congregation of the Immaculate Heart of Mary (a.k.a. Scheut Missionaries), two pillars of French and Belgian colonialism, respectively.

That imperialism involved wars, and that the ambitions and rivalries of the imperialist powers increased the likelihood of a Great War, did not seem to be a problem as far as the Church was concerned. It was hoped that the ordeal of war would cause the people to rediscover God and to return to the bosom of the Church. War was considered as a sort of trial and a form of expiation of the sins, as a part of God's unfathomable plans. It was not a coincidence that the Church was then keenly endorsing the cult of the (profusely bleeding) Sacred Heart of Jesus. This "dolorist" cult was promoted with extra zeal in France, anticlerical and even atheist since the Revolution. The construction of the gigantic Basilica of the Sacred Heart on top of the hill of Montmartre, for centuries one of the sacred sites of French Catholicism, for example, purported to ask forgiveness and expiate all sorts of "sins" allegedly committed by France in the course of the preceding decades, such as the Paris Commune of 1871 and the separation of church and state in 1905. This sanctuary was to be inaugurated in 1914, just in time to receive the masses who would in fact return to God on account of the war.

Contemporary France also witnessed the promotion of the cult of Joan of Arc, who was glorified simultaneously as a heroine of the fatherland and of the Christian faith, as the personification of all the medieval virtues praised by Romanticism, as a chaste virgin and a pious woman, but also as a brave warrior and, of course, a martyr. With the cult of the Maid of Orleans, the church aimed, not without success, to regain favour in the eyes of the leaders of the French Republic, men who were admittedly mostly anticlerical, but who were also conservative and nationalist, and to win back as many souls as possible in a France that, before the Revolution, had been considered the "eldest daughter of the church." The right wing of the French political spectrum would in fact adopt Joan of Arc as an icon, and she has remained an icon until the present time, as reflected in an annual demonstration of the extreme-right Front National, on May 1 no less, around her gilded statue on the Place des Pyramides in Paris.[6]

The fact that in France, in the years before 1914, the Catholic Church systematically presented war as desirable and necessary in many respects, and above all as a form of expiation and purification, also found a reflection in the reaction of a nun, Anne-Marie Worm, who, in August 1914, on learning that war had broken out, prayed as follows:

Lord, what happiness and grace have you bestowed on me!
Who would have believed, only one month ago, that war and
famine would descend on us! . . . My soul rejoices already
when thinking of all the glory you will harvest on account of
the suffering and death that will expiate the guilty passions of
the sinners.[7]

Not only the Catholic Church, but all the Christian churches, the Anglican one in Great Britain, the Lutheran Church in Germany, and the Orthodox Church in Russia, believed that they would derive major advantages from a Great War. This was all too obvious when, during the summer of 1914, war broke out. High prelates as well as lowly parish pastors of all the churches immediately proclaimed themselves in favour of a war they described as a holy war, a crusade, and they assured the believers that "God was on their side." To cite a few sarcastic lines from the famous song by Bob Dylan.

Oh the First World War, boys
It closed out its fate
The reason for fighting
I never got straight.
But I learned to accept it,
Accept it with pride.
For you don't count the dead
When God's on your side.[8]

We have already emphasized that the aristocratic-bourgeois elite had enjoyed great success with its antidemocratic strategy, consisting of repression as well as reforms, plus nationalism, militarism, racism, imperialism, and all sorts of tricks intended to neutralize or at least limit the effects of democratization. The great majority of the popular masses, whose supposedly irresistible rise had loomed so threatening, had in fact revealed themselves to be attached to traditional values such as king, fatherland, church, and religion. Where the lower orders had the vote, they generally handed it to conservative, clerical, agrarian, or nationalist parties; and they remained

127

deaf to the siren call of socialism. This was the case for the overwhelming majority of the peasants and country folk in general, of the major part of the petty bourgeoisie, and of countless workers who opted to join Christian parties, trade unions, and cooperatives. In short, the popular masses had meekly allowed themselves to be integrated into the established order and had adopted, as Arno Mayer has written, "the sacred values of the elites." Those who voted for socialist parties and/or joined them as members always remained a minority — a not insignificant minority, and a militant minority, certainly, but a minority nonetheless.

Moreover, the revolutionary danger incarnated by the socialists in the beginning of the twentieth century was far less real than it had been earlier. The majority of the socialist parties remained revolutionary in theory, but were no longer so in practice. Paraphrasing what Mark Twain famously said about the music of Richard Wagner, that it was "better than it sounds," one could say that the socialists' revolutionary talk was "not as bad as it sounded," that they were not nearly as revolutionary as they pretended to be. In reality, the socialists, or at least most of them, had allowed themselves to be integrated into the semi-feudal, semi-capitalist social-economic order. How had this become possible?

First, the lot of a considerable part of Western Europe's working class, or at least of the working class in the imperialist countries of Western Europe, had improved perceptibly during the final decades of the nineteenth century. This was due in part to the kind of social legislation introduced by politicians such as Bismarck, and also to social imperialism. As we have seen, imperialism was a system whereby riches squeezed out of the colonies flowed to Europe (and the United States) in order to increase the riches of the wealthy denizens of the metropolis; but a small part of these riches was in fact used to alleviate the lot of the labouring masses (and of the proletariat in general) in Europe and the US.

Consequently, poverty in Europe did not worsen. In other words, there was no continuing "pauperization" (or "immiseration"), which, according to Marx, would sooner or later drive the proletariat into the arms of the revolution. To the contrary, the situation of the workers continued to improve, so much so that there emerged within the working class a so-called "labour aristocracy." A revolution no longer appeared to be necessary, since it looked as if a happy future awaited the proletarians within the existing system. Many socialists convinced themselves of this, including many leaders of socialist parties. These parties thus ceased to believe in, and work for, the revolution. Most of them followed the lead of the great German socialist party, the SPD, described by one of its leaders, Karl Kautsky, as "a revolutionary party that does not want to hear any talk of revolution."[9]

For the higher wages, the improved working conditions, and the social services which improved the lives of the workers, the socialists gave credit not to the capitalists, but to the seemingly neutral, benevolent, and well-intentioned *state* in which they lived. The socialist workers thus also identified more and more with this state. In other words, the theoretically *internationalist* socialists became increasingly receptive to the gospel of *nationalism*, which was already being propagated via the schools, churches, the media, and the military service. A constantly growing number of social-democratic leaders such as Gustav Noske, for example, proclaimed loudly that they adhered to the "principle of nationality" and declared themselves ready to "defend the German Empire if it would become the victim of a war of aggression." This nationalist tendency within Germany's social democracy and European socialism in general became known as "social patriotism" or "social chauvinism."[10]

A second factor that contributed to the integration of the socialists into the established order and to the unspoken abandonment of the revolutionary idea by the majority of the socialists was the electoral success of their parties in countries such as Germany, France, and Belgium. Thanks to the widening of the suffrage, more and more socialists entered the parliaments in order to work there for even more political reforms and social programs. These included further extensions of the right to vote, with as ultimate objective nothing less than universal suffrage. The latter was long viewed as the *nec plus ultra* of democratization, as a substitute for revolution, as the gate to the nirvana of a socialist future.

Why destroy an existing system by means of a potentially bloody revolution when, within this same system, an open road invites us to advance gradually and peacefully to socialism? The struggle for reforms within the existing system thus received priority over the revolutionary struggle for an alternative system. For the same reason the socialists became more and more attached to the state that made the improvements possible; in other words, to their country, their nation. The socialists admittedly did not embrace jingoism, but they certainly adopted a more nationalist stance — and became less internationalist in the process. In France, for example, the socialists were revolutionaries, not in the Marxist sense — they were only "lightly Marxist," writes the historian Michel Winock — but in the tradition of the French Revolution of 1789. Men like Jaurès and Millerand rejected nonpacific and nonconstitutional means — that is, revolutionary, Marxist means — of creating a socialist society, but "steered socialism along democratic, parliamentary channels, [and] considered the [existing French] republic as an adequate instrument for achieving socialism."[11] The summer of 1914 would show how far the process of the rise of nationalism and the concomitant decline of internationalism had gone within the socialist movement: it was with great enthusiasm that the majority of socialists went to war for their own country. Apparently, they had totally forgotten the ideal of international solidarity of the proletarians; but during the war that ideal was to rear its head again.

Electoral successes also produced increasingly big, complex, and bureaucratic socialist parties, as well as an elite of party leaders who were quite frequently of bourgeois origin. Many of them entered the parliaments, where they learned to hobnob with politicians of lower- or upper-middle class and even aristocratic origin. Thus there was born within the socialist parties a kind of "oligarchy." (The famous "iron law of oligarchy," formulated in 1911 by the German sociologist Robert Michels in a study of political parties, was actually based on a study of the membership of the SPD.) The members of this socialist oligarchy, even more so than the rank-and-file, would concentrate on reforms within the existing order, instead of the overthrow of this order, and they internalized, at least to a certain extent, the ethos of this order and convinced themselves that it was possible to reach the socialist future via an *evolutionary* rather than a *revolutionary* path. In historical circumstances that were very different from those of the time of Marx, a revolution was no longer necessary and no longer desirable — or so they thought.

Thus was born socialist "reformism," whose intellectual godfather and great champion was a German social democrat, Eduard Bernstein.[12] Within each socialist party, however, rose a determined opposition to this reform-ism by "orthodox" Marxists who continued to believe in revolution; for example, the Polish-German Rosa Luxemburg and, above all, a Russian, Vladimir Ulianov, nicknamed "Lenin." And so the socialist movement would fall victim to a kind of "great schism" during and immediately after the traumatic events of the Great War and the success of the revolution in Russia and its failure in Germany, events in which Lenin and Luxemburg would play an important role. The revisionist or reformist variety of socialism would spawn modern social democracy, also known simply as "socialism," while after the Great War revolutionary socialism would be called "communism."

In any event, in the early twentieth century, under the leadership of reformists, socialism became less "dogmatic" and more "pragmatic," more "businesslike," so to speak. A good example was provided by Belgium's big socialist party, led by Emile Vandervelde, a personality of "well-to-do" background, a scion of a "good family," namely a "radical, anticlerical, intellectually enlightened milieu [in Brussels]." In Germany too, the revisionists prevailed, if not in theory then certainly in practice. "On paper," wrote the American historian Barbara Tuchman, "the largest Socialist bloc in Europe maintained fidelity to Marx . . . while the facts of Revision con-tinued to flourish."[13]

The leaders of the SPD revealed themselves to be just as "pragmatic" as Vandervelde and pursued political and social reforms in the style of Bismarck. The American historian Gabriel Kolko has written that they "reached a tacit consensus with Germany's rulers regarding their relation-ship to existing authority and their share in managing power." In France, socialism was dominated by the great personality of Jean Jaurès, a con-vinced reformist and pragmatist. As for the British Labour Party, it had never been genuinely socialist, so it had never inscribed the revolution in its program. In any event, its leaders were also pragmatists; in other words, mesmerized by reforms within the existing order. Kolko has described them rather uncharitably as "ambitious careerists . . . committed to operating within the existing power structure."[14]

Henceforth, the socialists were revolutionary and internationalist mostly in theory. In practice, they became increasingly "evolutionary" — as well as nationalist, attached to the "fatherland" more than to their class; in other words, they had become "social chauvinists." With the socialists of other countries and even more so with those of countries that happened to be rivals or enemies of their own country, they felt less and less solidarity. And vis-à-vis the dark-skinned inhabitants of the distant colonies of the "fatherland," there was no solidarity at all. The socialists — or at least some of them — may have been anti-imperialists in word, but not at all in deed.

In Germany, Great Britain, Belgium, and all the other imperialist countries, the higher wages and new social services that were henceforth the focus of socialist activism depended on success in the rat race between imperialist powers. The workers profited from imperialism, and the socialists were therefore partisans of imperialism. In spite of its theoretical hostility to the idea of colonialism, the SPD, de facto reformist, supported the German government in its quest for the colonies for which the Reich presumably had such a great need. It was not a coincidence that Bernstein, the most famous of reformists, was also a champion of German imperialism. He favoured Cecil Rhodes–style social imperialism or, as one can also say, "imperialist socialism" (*Imperialsozialismus*). Emile Vandervelde, the Moses of Belgium's socialist tribe, likewise revealed himself to be an "imperialist socialist"; he supported the acquisition of the Congo as a colony for Belgium. The French socialists were admittedly opposed to the excesses of their country's colonialism, and they argued in favour of a more humanitarian form of colonialism, but they were not genuinely hostile to colonialism and did not advocate terminating it.[15]

Officially, the socialists were opposed to imperialism, but they did nothing, or precious little, to encourage or support the resistance of colonial peoples, and even less to help organize it. The communists, on the other hand, would do so. After the Great War and the Russian Revolution, Lenin proved to be one of the rare prewar socialists to display an interest in the fate of the denizens of the colonies — and to appreciate their revolutionary potential. "Internationally," observed Eric Hobsbawm with great accuracy, "socialism before 1914 remained overwhelmingly a movement of Europeans and white emigrants or their descendants. Colonialism remained marginal to their interests."[16]

The egalitarian sentiment and the solidarity of the socialists in the

United States similarly remained limited to their white comrades. There was generally no question of solidarity with black workers and other poor and oppressed blacks — usually dismissed as "niggers." The majority of America's socialists (and trade unionists) were hardly less hostile to blacks than the American elite and middle class.[17] "Proletarians of all countries, unite!" remained the slogan of socialism, but there was no question of union or even solidarity with the dark-skinned, black, yellow, or other masses in the colonies. Clearly, by allowing themselves to be integrated into the existing order, the majority of socialists — but certainly not all of them — not only absorbed its nationalism but also, at least in part, its racism. (After the Great War and the Russian Revolution, the American Communist Party was "to place racial justice and equality at the top of its agenda and to seek, and ultimately win, sympathy among African Americans.")[18]

Socialism was no longer revolutionary and internationalist, and had therefore ceased to constitute a threat to the established political and social-economic order or to the elite that had constructed that order and profited from it. But was that really so? Had the danger truly been exorcized once and for all? The elite had good reason to doubt it.

CHAPTER 8
FEAR AND TENSIONS IN THE *BELLE ÉPOQUE*

The elite is convinced that the revolutionary danger is increasing rapidly, and also feels threatened by the revolutionary plans of ethnic minorities, by the designs of feminists, and by the perceived menace of hordes of "inferior" races such as the Chinese, the "yellow peril" . . .

According to certain historians, for example Arno Mayer, the revolutionary threat in Europe was actually quite limited, perhaps even nonexistent, during the years that preceded the Great War. It is certainly legitimate to question the magnitude of that danger, but a slightly different, though very important, question is this: How great did the revolutionary danger *appear* from the viewpoint of the aristocratic-bourgeois elite? The answer is that during the *Belle Époque* this danger *seemed* to be increasing rapidly, so much so that action was urgently required to avert a threatening catastrophe. And war seemed to provide the solution.

An entire constellation of factors made it appear that the danger of revolution, as well as the danger of an evolution toward socialism via the electoral path, in other words, the risk associated with the democratization process, *seemed* to be growing rapidly. First, while it is a fact that the majority of socialist parties were no longer revolutionary, the elite was hardly aware of this, because the socialists, while overwhelmingly reformist, continued to speak a revolutionary language. "Until the war," writes Hobsbawm, "the[se] parties remained pure and uncompromising," at least "on the face of it." The socialists were admittedly not yet digging up stones to erect barricades, but it looked imminent that via elections they would soon come to power and thus be able to achieve their revolutionary goals, bringing about the "great transformation." Even the workers' parties that had never been truly revolutionary, such as the British Labour Party, were suspected of secretly working for the revolution. In any event, the adversaries of socialism were firmly convinced that the socialists "wanted a social revolution [and] that their activities implied one." The revolutionary intentions of the socialist tribe were seemingly also affirmed by the massive annual demonstrations on May 1. These were a scary spectacle in the eyes of good burghers, "a kind of annual rehearsal of revolution."[1]

Second, within every socialist party, even the most reformist ones, there was a radical wing of orthodox Marxist men and women who continued to believe in, and work for, the revolution. They rejected political action within the framework of the established order, and championed revolution in the heroic tradition of 1789, 1830, 1848, and 1871, possibly in a new guise, such as the general strike. The latter was seen as a potential catalyst of revolution, at least by the partisans of the "revolutionary syndicalism" that was very fashionable at the time, a movement whose theory had been worked out by Georges in a book, *Réflexions sur la violence* (*Reflections on Violence*), published in 1906. The United States had its own variety of revolutionary syndicalists, namely the Wobblies, as they used to call the members of the radical union Industrial Workers of the World (IWW). Yet another apostle of the revolutionary gospel was the French socialist Gustave Hervé, who petrified the bourgeois of his country with declarations like this:

> *We recognize only one war, civil war, social war, class war,*
> *the only kind of war that today, in twentieth-century Europe,*
> *can produce some benefit for the exploited of all countries.*[2]

Third, even the most reformist socialist parties remained a thorn in the side of the aristocratic and bourgeois establishment, for in those years they came across as more aggressive and dangerous than ever before. The so-called *Belle Époque* was in reality a "beautiful era" only for the rich. For ordinary people it was far from beautiful, but featured problems such as unemployment, high prices and low wages, alcoholism, delinquency, and flagrant poverty, especially for the denizens squeezed together in bleak working-class districts, but also for small farmers and other country folk. After 1900, Europe's working class found itself increasingly under pressure, mainly on account of rising prices, and countless plebeians sought salvation in emigration to the New World; no less than 5 per cent of the British population emigrated between 1900 and 1914.[3] But emigration hardly improved the situation within Europe. The growing tensions and conflicts reflected new and — from the perspective of the elite — extravagant demands on the part of the workers, including the eight-hour workday, and were punctuated by countless strikes, even general strikes, considered by many to be harbingers of revolution.

After 1900, and especially after the Russian Revolution of 1905, "waves of working-class agitation" swept over the industrialized countries and continued until that fateful moment in 1914 when war broke out. Major strikes took place in Marseille and Barcelona (1909), Genoa, Trieste, Amsterdam, and Dublin (1913), Belfast (1907), Newcastle and Liverpool (1911), London and the Welsh coal fields (1910–1911 and 1912), etc. In France, the *Belle Époque* was "a time of great strikes," writes Michel Winock, a historian specializing in that era.[4] "We are on the road to revolution!," lamented certain Parisian periodicals. The situation was hardly different in Germany. In 1910, that country experienced a wave of strikes and demonstrations orchestrated by the SPD, and certain conservative publications concluded that the country was dealing with a kind of rehearsal for the revolution. The last years before the Great War witnessed a veritable orgy of strikes, especially in Great Britain, where the period from 1910 to 1914 has been described as "the great unrest," as years "pregnant with revolutionary change." Russia also experienced an "explosive industrial discord," especially on the eve of the war. During the first half of 1914, 1.4 million workers went on strike. Violence characterized many strikes; for example, those that affected the goldmines along the Lena River in Siberia, where more than two hundred people were killed when troops opened fire on demonstrating strikers. In July 1914, after the assassination in Sarajevo and only a couple of weeks before the beginning of the war, a gigantic strike took place in St. Petersburg involving fifty thousand workers. All this social unrest gave countless members of the Russian elite the unpleasant feeling of "living on a volcano." A nobleman vented this pessimistic mood as follows:

> *We are about to witness things the world has not seen since*
> *the Barbarian invasions. A barbarous era will soon start and*
> *will last for decades.*

For the elite, these strikes were particularly traumatic, because they affected not only economically but also militarily important and sensitive sectors, such as mining, harbours, and last but not least, the railways. The work stoppages thus threatened the very infrastructure on which depended the wealth and the power — including the military power — of nations big and small. Particularly traumatic also was the fact that many of these strikes ended up being successful, so that the owners of factories and mines and/ or the state authorities had to make more and more concessions. In Great Britain, for example, the government was forced to introduce a minimum wage in certain industrial sectors. One of the reasons for this indulgence was that it seemed that one could no longer automatically count on the loyalty of the troops that were traditionally used to teach manners to strikers. In 1907, a mutiny erupted in a regiment of the French Army that had been sent to the Languedoc in order to put down a strike by local vintners. The international elite observed keenly how, a few years later, in 1910, the French government reacted to a general strike by temporarily mobilizing fifty thousand railway workers into the army![5] Subjecting them to military discipline neutralized the revolutionary potential of the strikers. This conjured up the possibility of neutralizing the revolutionary potential of all workers by drafting them. In peacetime, this was of course unthinkable; but during a war, it would certainly be feasible. In 1914, it would come to that. In all belligerent countries, the proletarians would be stuffed into uniforms and delivered to the army in order to be taught how to obey instead of dreaming of that great and abominable collective disobedience, the social revolution.

Together with trade unions, even the most reformist of socialist parties (and workers' parties such as Britain's Labour) played an active role in labour agitation, for they were the champions of the workers and of the lower orders in general. And so, on the occasion of elections, they were rewarded by more and more votes, handed to them not only by the proletarians, but also by the petty bourgeois and the peasants who, during the *Belle Époque*, were likewise experiencing hard times. And these parties also increasingly served as magnets for the votes of all sorts of outsiders; for example, the Protestants in France, the Finns in the Russian Empire, and the Jews just about everywhere.

In Great Britain, the elections of 1906 amounted to a major breakthrough for Labour, interpreted by some contemporaries as an "omen of radical social change."[6] In the general elections of 1912 in Germany, the SPD obtained no less than 4.25 million votes out of a total of 12 million, compared to the 3 million the party had won in 1907. The social democrats moved up in the Reichstag from 43 to 110 representatives, and one of their leaders, August Bebel, came ever so close to becoming that body's chairman. Alarm bells started to ring in the salons of the Reich's elite, because the progress made by the SPD now seemed irresistible. It seemed as if it was only a matter of time before this party would rally the majority of the people behind itself and would therefore be able to "break the chains of the feudal-capitalist state." In Italy, it had been deemed necessary to introduce universal suffrage in 1912, and the results of that reform were far less radical than many had feared. Still, for the country's elite it was most disconcerting that during the elections of 1913 the socialists managed to grab fifty-two seats in the Parliament, considerably more than the thirty-two they had held before. Even in the United States, a country in which virtually everybody wrongly believes that socialism never had a chance, the socialists flourished. Their candidate, Eugene Debs, obtained more than four hundred thousand votes during the presidential elections of 1908, and no less than nine hundred thousand in 1912. There too, red lights started to flash in the salons and boardrooms of the elite. The American establishment, writes Gabriel Kolko, felt threatened by "agrarian discontent, violence and strikes, a Populist movement, the rise of a Socialist Party that seemed, for a time, to have an unlimited growth potential."[7] As for France, already in 1908 a conservative journalist and politician, Charles Benoist, lamented in an article published by the prestigious right-wing periodical *Revue des Deux Mondes* that universal suffrage would sooner or later bring about, by legal means, a "social transformation," in other words, a revolution. In May 1914, only a few months before the outbreak of the Great War, the result of the general elections seemed to confirm his fears, because the socialists managed to increase their number of seats in the National Assembly, the lower house of the French parliament, from 75 to 102.[8]

On the eve of the Great War, the socialist parties could thus look forward to even greater gains. Their leaders, members, and sympathizers felt "a sentiment of excitement, of admirable hope, of the historical ineluctability of their triumph." The trade unions, socialist or not, such as France's big *Confédération generale du travail* (CGT), more militant than ever before, similarly prospered during the *Belle Époque* thanks to the countless strikes they organized and often saw crowned with success. An ever-growing number of workers flocked to the unions. During the five years that preceded the start of the Great War, for example, the British trade unions managed to double their membership. In 1914, the British and German unions each counted approximately three million members, the French unions approximately one million. The strikes they sponsored seemed to many to be revolutionary in nature, especially those that became violent; and of a general strike countless workers hoped, and countless bourgeois feared, that it would set fire to the fuse of the revolutionary powder keg.[9]

All this meant that the socialists, no matter how reformist they were, loomed increasingly like a major menace to the elite. The revolutionary danger seemed to increase by the day; the door could be kicked in any time. The French historian Fernand Braudel, sometimes lionized as the greatest historian of the twentieth century, a conservative man who grew up during the *Belle Époque* in a rural, bourgeois, and nationalist milieu, appeared to voice the contemporary elite's sentiment when, in the 1960s, he wrote in one of his books that "in 1914, the West was ripe to become socialist, socialism was poised to take power, ready to construct a new Europe."[10] Nevertheless, in Western Europe the revolutionary danger, incarnated by the socialist parties, was in reality not nearly as great as the nobility and the bourgeoisie — and Braudel, half a century later — sincerely believed. This is why Arno Mayer was able to write that the elite was "overfearful of socialism," that it "overperceived [the] dangers to their overprivileged positions" and simply "overreacted."[11]

The situation was ambivalent, unclear, extremely uncertain. On the one hand, the elite had no great reason to worry but, on the other hand, its worries were not entirely unfounded. And it was precisely that uncertainty that was so traumatic. It was maddening: the masses would perhaps never gather in front of the gate, but they might also knock it down at any moment! The tension was becoming unbearable, and there was an urgent need for deliverance. In the summer of 1914, the war would bring this deliverance.

It must also be taken into account that, at least in parts of Europe, the revolutionary danger not only *seemed* to be increasing. In much of Southern and eastern Europe, the revolutionary danger was in fact increasing rapidly. In contrast to the "West" referred to by Braudel, the socialist parties over there were sticking to their revolutionary guns, as Hobsbawm has remarked:

> There was in Europe a vast semi-circular belt of poverty
> and unrest in which revolution actually was on the agenda,
> and — at least in one part of it — actually [would] break
> out. It stretched from Spain through large parts of Italy, via
> the Balkan Peninsula into the Russian Empire. Revolution
> migrated from Western to Eastern Europe in [that] period.[12]

One of the reasons for this development was undoubtedly the fact that in the south and in the east of Europe, in contrast to western Europe and Great Britain, the social "blessings" of imperialism were nonexistent or minimal, so neither a "workers' aristocracy" in general nor a quasi-bourgeois "oligarchy" of socialist leaders existed there, who could have allowed themselves to be integrated into the existing system, thus causing socialist reformism to bloom. Another equally important reason was that the elite of the countries in those parts of Europe — such as the Russian nobility, conservative and counterrevolutionary from the start — successfully resisted any attempts to widen the suffrage and/or to introduce social reforms *à la* Bismarck. The socialist parties of these countries could therefore not score any electoral successes and could in some cases not even legally exist. And so the socialists of Southern and Eastern Europe could not be integrated into the established order to the same extent as their western-European comrades. They did not increasingly identify with their state and their country, and they did not embrace nationalism or racism to an appreciable extent. The result was that they would not allow themselves to be swept up by the maelstrom of patriotic enthusiasm that would submerge Europe's popular masses, including the socialists, in the summer of 1914, and drag them into the war.[13]

Everybody knew that the revolutionary danger was considerable in Russia, that Russia was "ripe" for revolution. In 1905, after the humiliating defeat in the war against Japan, a revolution had even taken place, but it had been repressed. According to a specialist in Russian history, the country remained "stuck in a crisis situation that did not cease to get worse and would drag on until the outbreak of war, in 1914."[14] In Italy too, revolution was in the air. The big and popular socialist party there rid itself of its reformists and remained resolutely revolutionary, internationalist, and therefore opposed to war. At the same time, the country was almost constantly rocked by peasant revolts in Sicily and elsewhere, by demonstrations and riots in the great industrial centres, and by strikes involving hundreds of thousands of workers. In June 1914, only weeks before the onset of the Great War, many Italian cities were the scene of impressive antimilitarist demonstrations and even uprisings.[15]

The spectre of social revolution haunted Southern and Eastern Europe, terrorizing the nobility and the bourgeoisie. But yet another factor fanned the elite's fear of revolution. The many European countries that happened to be multi-ethnic and multilingual were also threatened by the menace of *national* revolutions or radical changes brought about by elections. There were movements for independence or at least some form of autonomy for the Irish in Great Britain, the Flemings in Belgium, the Slavs in the Danube Monarchy, the Poles in Russia, the Armenians in the Ottoman Empire, etc. In this realm too, as in the case of the social question, the elite had admittedly managed to neutralize the problem, at least to a certain extent, via concessions and reforms — alternating with occasional severe repression. The national movements of the minorities had thus also been integrated to a large extent into the existing order.

The danger of national revolutions, like that of social revolutions, was thus not really all that great during the *Belle Époque*. Like the majority of the socialist parties, most parties of nationalist movements had relatively modest objectives and programs. As in the case of the socialist parties, however, all national movements included at least some marginal radicals who pursued nothing less than revolutionary change. An example was provided by the zealots of the secret society known as the Black Hand, active among the South-Slav minorities of Austria-Hungary. In this field too, no real solution was anywhere in sight, and problems continued to fester, sometimes in tandem with social problems. The elite was consequently gripped by a great fear, undoubtedly somewhat exaggerated but certainly not without foundation. Furthermore, the main loci of this kind of agitation happened to be the extreme west and southeast of Europe, namely Ireland and the Balkans, which created the impression that the entire continent was threatened by the menace of national revolutions.

As if the partly real and partly imaginary danger emanating from social and national movements did not suffice, the established political and social-economic order was also tormented in another way. The existing order, which was very much a *patriarchal*, sexually repressed order, also confronted a rapidly expanding movement in favour of the emancipation of women in general and of the vote for women in particular. The British elite was hard-pressed in this respect, namely by an offensive of the famous suffragettes, the militant members of an organization founded in 1903, the Women's Social and Political Union (WSPU). These extremely activist suffragettes were not only associated with the demand of the right to vote for women, but also with a sexual revolution, with pacifism, and even with socialism. As in the case of the socialists, the feminists gained more and more support among the women of Britain and benefited increasingly from the sympathy of male compatriots. It thus seemed likely that they would achieve their "satanic" objectives sooner or later. On the eve of the Great War, in early 1914, writes Hobsbawm, "women were on the verge of a massive victory in the long struggle for equal citizen rights, symbolized by the vote."[16]

One of the fatal consequences of an emancipation of women, according to many members of the British elite, among them the famous writer Rudyard Kipling, would be that Great Britain would cease to be a truly virile nation and thus become militarily impotent, unable to wage war, and consequently doomed to disappear from the ranks of the great powers. (Such fears were entertained in other countries too, and it was for this reason that the very bellicose Italian Futurists were also anti-feminists, as has already been mentioned.) For the Tories, the political representatives of the nobility, and for the British establishment in general, aristocratic as well as upper-middle class, conservative as well as liberal, already harassed by socialists and Irish nationalists, their world seemed ready to implode, unless means were found to put a stop to all this nonsense.[17]

For the purpose of neutralizing the feminist danger and thus to save Albion from the menace of "demasculinization," war loomed as a potentially powerful instrument. Was war not an eminently masculine occupation and, as such, a perfect means to marginalize women and send them back into their own sphere, referred to in Germany as *Kinder, Kirche, und Küche*, "children, church, and kitchen"? In this respect too, the Great War would fall short of expectations, because it would cause millions of women to exchange the kitchen for a factory or other workplace and thus to discover a new world: in Russia approximately six thousand women would even voluntarily join the men at the front, fighting in special all-female units.[18] And after the war young women in short skirts would be seen in the bars of the great cities, listening to jazz music and dancing the Charleston, sometimes even with black men!

Finally, the masses of black, yellow, and other "coloured," supposedly inferior inhabitants of the colonies and all other parts of the world loomed more and more seditious and menacing. In Mexico, for example, a revolution erupted in 1910, displaying not only liberal characteristics but also socialist and even anarchist tendencies. And in Southwest Africa, the tribe of the Hereros rose up in 1904 against its German colonial masters. Berlin sent troops that caused such a massacre among the unarmed as well as armed "natives" that historians have likened this bloody repression to a genuine genocide.[19] (During their invasion of Belgium in 1914, the Germans would go to work in similar fashion, though on a much smaller scale, to the great horror of public opinion; on the other hand, hardly any white men made a fuss about the atrocities perpetrated on the Hereros, certainly not in the United States, where the bestial lynching of blacks was practically a daily occurrence.)

143

In those years, countless contemporary Europeans and Americans fretted about the "yellow peril," and saw their worst fears confirmed by events such as the nationalist revolt of the Boxers of 1899–1901, the surprising victory of Japan in its war against Russia in 1905, and of course the Xinhai Revolution in China in 1911. The latter saw the end of the Qing Dynasty, which had been particularly sycophantic vis-à-vis the Western powers, and the advent of a republic headed by a popular nationalist politician who was far less servile to the "West," Sun Yat-Sen. The widespread "yellow peril" paranoia was simultaneously reflected and promoted by books such as the best-seller published in France in 1905, *L'Invasion jaune* ("The Yellow Invasion"), written by Émile Driant under the *nom de plume* of "Capitaine Danrit"; in this story, the western world is the target of a surprise attack by a gigantic Sino-Japanese army. (The French sensitivity with respect to the "yellow peril" undoubtedly had something to do with the fact that the revolution in China inspired *indépendantisme* among the Vietnamese and other denizens of the colony the French called "Indochina.")[20] In Britain, *The War in the Air*, published in 1908 by H.G. Wells, described how China and Japan wage war on the entire world. And in 1914, in an opus entitled *The Unparalleled Invasion,* Jack London had China attempting to conquer the world — but fortunately this evil scheme is spoiled by the "West" by means of merciless biological warfare: China is sprinkled with bombs stuffed with pathogens of the plague, cholera, and similar diseases, so that only a few surviving "yellow people" are left to be massacred by invading armies. The book concludes with a happy end, namely the ethnic "purification" of China and its "American-style" colonization by immigrants from western countries.

CHAPTER 9
REACTIONARY AND BELLICOSE POLICIES

The tension becomes unbearable, and the elite becomes more and more convinced that only war is the definitive solution of the social problem — and of many other problems. There seem to be only two options, revolution or war, and the decision will be made soon. Revolution must be avoided at all cost, so the ruling classes of the great powers deliberately pursue a reactionary policy leading to war . . .

Confronted with partly real and partly imaginary mortal dangers, the elite decided to play hardball. They were less and less inclined to make concessions vis-à-vis socialism, the rise of democracy in general, the national movements of ethnic and linguistic minorities, embryonic *indépendantiste* movements in the colonies, pacifism, feminism, etc. But the social problem and the revolutionary danger associated with it were perceived as the greatest of all threats.

The elite adopted an increasingly reactionary, that is, counterrevolutionary attitude, as socialism appeared to be gaining ground and revolution seemed to be *ante portas*. It was urgent to prevent the revolution in all countries where it appeared to threaten; in other words, everywhere in Europe. And in Western and Central Europe, it was also deemed necessary to put a stop to the accelerating democratization process, a process that was feared would lead to revolution via an electoral triumph of the socialists. This was obviously not an easy task; moreover, it was an intrinsically contradictory task because, as we have seen, the process of democratization had in fact reduced the revolutionary danger. In any event, it was believed that draconian antidemocratic and counterrevolutionary measures, and probably violence, were required in order to successfully combat democracy and revolution. In *Belle Époque* Europe, writes Hobsbawm,

> *Contemporaries . . . had the sense . . . of society trembling as*
> *under seismic shocks before greater earthquakes. These were*
> *years when wisps of violence hung in the air over the Ritz*
> *hotels and country houses.*[1]

More than enough concessions had been made; too many compromises had been agreed to. What was urgently needed was a satisfactory and definitive solution to the social problem, namely a total liquidation of socialism and democracy. And a definitive solution had to be found rapidly, because the barbarians were at the gates: further indecision could be fatal. The fear continued to grow; the tension became less and less bearable. So what stratagem could solve the problem quickly and definitively? To the contemporary elites of all countries in Europe, not only Germany, but also France, Russia, Great Britain, etc., the answer was clear: war.[2] As Arno Mayer has written,

> *[the] grande peur among the notables fostered the presumption*
> *of war as a general prophylaxis . . . the old ruling and*
> *governing classes . . . meant to resolve Europe's crisis in their*
> *own interest, if need be by induced war.*[3]

During the last few years before the Great War, most if not all of the great powers thus embarked on a consistently antidemocratic, antisocialist, counterrevolutionary, militaristic, ultra-nationalist (and often anti-Semitic) domestic policy as well as an aggressive and even risky foreign policy. The elite was henceforth actively looking for an opportunity, for a pretext, for the right moment, to go to war. Let us examine the situation in the major countries.

In 1910–1911, writes Mayer, Germany was "in the grip of an ultra-conservative resurgence." With aggressive and highly risky foreign policy, Emperor Wilhelm II and "his" government aimed to resolve the domestic problems in general, and above all to combat the perceived socialist danger — domestically as well as internationally. In this context, Imanuel Geiss has spoken of "[Germany's] self-imposed role as bastion against revolution and democracy."[4] This policy produced the famous second Moroccan Crisis of 1911, also known as the Agadir Crisis, which brought the Reich to the brink of war against France. In the meantime, the army high command considered the possibility of a preventive war against France and/ or Russia. Such a step had already been envisaged in 1905, at the time of the Russian-Japanese War, which had seemed a golden opportunity, and it had also been recommended in 1909 by the retired General von Schlieffen in an article entitled *"Der Krieg in der Gegenwart"* ("Contemporary War"). Not only the military, but also more and more political leaders felt that war was inevitable and saw much to be gained from a preventive war. As the German chancellor at the time, Bethmann-Hollweg, remarked in June 1914, such a step could be expected to bring about "an improvement of the domestic situation, namely in a conservative direction." Germany's military commanders, writes Max Hastings, "believed that war offered a prospect of reversing the social-democratic tide which they deemed a threat to national greatness as well as to their own authority." Emperor Wilhelm II saw things the same way, and gave the order to better prepare the German people for the coming war.[5]

Another symptom of the ultraconservative upsurge and attendant war-mongering was the agitation orchestrated by the National Association against Social Democracy (*Reichsverband gegen die Sozialdemokratie*), a lobby that had been founded in 1904 by leading members of the Conservative and National Liberal Parties, the great bastions of the Reich's aristocratic and upper-middle class elite, respectively. It was not a coincidence that these gentlemen sought to achieve their objective, the annihilation of the social-democratic movement, by means of propaganda for a blatantly nationalist, militarist, and expansionist policy. But such a policy was not to the liking of the majority of the German people and, as we have already seen, the Reichstag elections of 1912 produced a great victory for Germany's socialists. This greatly alarmed the elite, and under the auspices of none other than the Kronprinz, Friedrich-Wilhelm of Prussia, a coup d'état was considered. (Even earlier, Wilhelm II had already thought of carrying out a coup that would rid him of inconveniences such as the free press, universal male suffrage, elections, and the Reichstag itself.)[6] It was the intention, via drastic measures such as the suspension of the constitution and of freedom of the press, to eliminate the socialists politically, to forestall the revolution they were supposedly planning, and to put an end to the process of democratization; this added up to a restoration of the absolutist monarchy of the "good old days" before the French Revolution.[7] But these plans did not come to fruition. Many German aristocrats and burghers were henceforth convinced that antisocialist, counterrevolutionary, and antidemocratic salvation could only come from a war. On the eve of the Great War, writes the British historian Max Hastings,

> German leaders were acutely sensitive to their enemy within.
> A key factor in Berlin's . . . decision to fight [i.e., go to war
> in 1914] had been a desire to crush the perceived domestic
> socialist menace, by achieving a conspicuous triumph over
> Germany's foreign foes.

Just like its German counterpart, the Austro-Hungarian elite believed itself to be besieged by social as well as national movements and potential revolutions, and tilted toward a military solution to the problems.[8] Blasius Schemua, chief of staff of the army and precursor in this position of the more (in)famous Conrad von Hötzendorff, was partisan of an aggressive foreign policy; he hoped that this would lead to war, and that war would teach the country's citizens, or at least its lower orders, to abandon their "crass materialism," thus inaugurating a "new, more heroic age" for the Habsburg Empire. The worsening internal problems caused the emperor in March 1914 to do what Wilhelm II had not dared to do: he suspended the parliament, known as the Reichsrat, as it had been the scene of too many quarrels between Germans, Czechs, Hungarians, etc. The imperial government now ruled the old-fashioned way, by decree from above.[9] But a permanent solution had to be found. And so, writes Arno Mayer, "The military [leaders of the country] proposed to induce war to reinvigorate and strengthen the primacy of the Austro-German ruling and governing class for an indeterminate but tolerable future." At any rate, if the high command pressed for war as part of an aristocratic reaction, it did so to bolster the regime at home and not to secure foreign-policy goals.[10] Shortly before the outbreak of the Great War, the commander-in-chief of the army, Conrad von Hötzendorff is alleged to have exclaimed: "May God offer us a war!"

According to Eric Hobsbawm, it was "labour unrest and the electoral advance of Social Democracy [i.e., the socialists] that made [the] ruling elites [of Europe] keen to defuse trouble at home with success abroad." The Danube Monarchy was certainly no exception to this general rule. There too, to use Hobsbawm's words, "there were plenty of conservatives . . . [who] thought that a war was needed to get the old order back on its feet."[11] But the multi-ethnic empire of the Habsburgs was tormented not only by social problems and a corresponding fear of socialism and social revolution, but also by the problem presented by nationalist movements of its minorities, above all the South Slavs. In this respect too, the elite deliberately opted for repression, the kind of repression that involved a considerable risk of war. Indeed, a hard line vis-à-vis the South-Slav minority went hand-in-hand with an aggressive policy toward Serbia, the partly real and partly imaginary source of inspiration of South-Slav nationalism in the Habsburg lands. From the viewpoint of Vienna, Serbia was a Balkan version of the small kingdom of Piedmont in northern Italy. With the help of a great power, France, that dwarf had managed to dispossess the Habsburgs of Milan in the 1860s, thus metamorphosing into a great new nation, modern Italy. Vienna was determined to avoid an encore of this kind of scenario, a nightmare in which the Serbian gremlin, aided by a major power, Russia, might transform into a great South-Slav state. It is an irony of history that a "Yugoslavia," that is, a vast "Land of the South Slavs," would in fact arise from a war that was supposed to abort such a project.

The Austro-Hungarian elite was particularly perturbed that Serbia had emerged from the Balkan Wars of 1912–1913 with greater territory and enhanced prestige. It was decided that the time had come to settle accounts once and for all with this pesky little neighbour. Obviously, that meant war, even a major war, because Russia was very likely to become involved, and thus Germany and France as well. But the attitude of the Austro-Hungarian generals revealed a "reckless insouciance," as Max Hastings has written. The heir to the throne, Franz-Ferdinand, was one of the arch-conservative fanatics of the empire's establishment who favoured a hard-line approach that was simultaneously authoritarian, reactionary, and bellicose. (On the other hand, he favoured good relations with Russia, whose autocratic system he proclaimed to be a "model worthy of admiration.") He despised the South Slavs in general and the Serbs in particular, whom he referred to as "pigs." It is therefore hardly surprising that he attracted the attention of the fanatic fringe among the South-Slav nationalists who would assassinate him in Sarajevo on June 28, 1914. This murder would provide men like von Hötzendorff with the excuse they needed to unleash the kind of war they had been longing for — just like their counterparts in Germany, Russia, and elsewhere.[12]

The France of the Third Republic, undoubtedly the most democratic of Europe's great powers, was the incarnation of progress and of the promotion of the ideas of "liberty, equality, and fraternity," at least in theory. Still, the country's social pyramid hardly differed from that of Germany, Great Britain, and other countries that had remained more feudal and conservative. Its achievements in the realm of social services were less impressive than those of Germany, admittedly a more conservative and authoritarian state.[13] In the Gallic republic, the bourgeoisie set the tone, and even the petty bourgeoisie was allowed to say a word, but the nobility — entrenched in the high ranks of the army and the state bureaucracy — continued to play a role that should not be underestimated. Officially, the nation remained loyal to the revolutionary tradition of 1789, but the elite, including the bourgeoisie, traumatized by the Commune and fearful of socialism and revolution, became increasingly conservative, antidemocratic, reactionary, and consequently more chauvinist and bellicose. Germany, the country that had humiliated France in 1870–1871 and had deprived it of Alsace and the northern part of Lorraine, was of course viewed as the great enemy.

In France, the *Belle Époque* witnessed a resurgence of chauvinism, associated with "revanchist" anti-German warmongering, allegedly particularly so among young people. In a kind of public opinion poll, organized a few years before the start of the Great War by "Agathon," the collective pseudonym of Henri Massis and Alfred de Tarde, one could read the following:

> War! That word has suddenly acquired a certain prestige. It
> is a young, new word, radiating the kind of attraction that
> an age-old warmongering instinct has revived in the hearts
> of men. Young people see in it all the beauty they long for,
> the beauty that is missing in their daily lives. For them, war
> signifies above all the triumph of the noblest human virtues,
> virtues that they appreciate the most: the energy, self-control,
> self-sacrifice for the sake of a cause that is greater than
> ourselves.[14]

The writer Charles Péguy was one of the (relatively) young men who embraced this heady combination of nationalism and bellicosity and therefore felt nothing but contempt for pacifists and socialists such as Jaurès. Péguy would be killed in 1914.

The culture of war, reflected in the enthusiasm for war or belief in the ineluctability of war, hung in the air in *Belle-Époque* France. It was also illustrated by the election of Raymond Poincaré as president of the Republic in January 1913: an outspoken anti-German and "revanchist" nationalist. Under his auspices, a three-year compulsory military service was introduced in 1913, which purported not only to better prepare the country for war against Germany, but also to better integrate the workers and other proletarians into the existing order and thus keep them under control. War seemed the best way to achieve this aim, particularly after the success of the socialists in the elections of the spring of 1914, which "had greatly traumatized the propertied class." War was wanted because it was expected to conjure up a common objective for all Frenchmen; it was expected to unite all Frenchmen, regardless of class.[15] The Belgian ambassador in Paris at the time expressed his fear that the "nationalist, jingoistic and chauvinist [sic] politics" pursued by Poincaré and his ilk constituted "the greatest peril for peace in today's Europe."[16]

The Third Republic was still very anticlerical at the beginning of the twentieth century; but, motivated by its fear of socialism that was not only revolutionary but also atheist, the bourgeois elite sought a rapprochement with the Catholic Church. This institution was historically associated with the nobility and the monarchy, remained a pillar of the *ancien régime* and a counterrevolutionary bastion of conservatism, and did not disapprove of war. The Church responded to the overture by promoting the cult of the Sacred Heart, Saint Theresa of Lisieux, and of course Joan of Arc, who became the figurehead of contemporary French "super-patriotism." Many intellectuals also recommended war as a kind of crusade for the ideals of the French Revolution.[17] As far as the French aristocracy was concerned, it was expected that war would furnish "an occasion for redemption and regeneration, an opportunity to reveal the superior qualities that justify the existence of an elite" and "open up the prospect of refounding its social authority after the war."[18]

In Russia too, the nearly exclusively aristocratic elite viewed war as a prophylaxis against social revolution. After the defeat in the war against Japan and the revolution of 1905 that had followed it, reforms had been enacted under the auspices of Piotr Stolypin, prime minister from 1906 to 1911. But those reforms brought no solution to the enormous social problems, and the country remained extremely restless. The czar had agreed to the reforms only reluctantly and looked for ways to arrest, and preferably roll back entirely, this democratizing trend. And the nobility was shocked and traumatized by the plans, ultimately aborted, of the reformers who called for a redistribution of landed property, the *sine qua non* of the wealth and power of this class and of its ally, the Orthodox Church. After the assassination of Stolypin in 1911, possibly (but not certainly) organized by reactionary elements, the government switched to a reactionary, militarist, and bellicose path, which was expected to lead to a revitalization and strengthening of the established order. The army, already gigantic, was increased in size and, more importantly, modernized, and Russia started to construct new railway lines that were clearly intended to facilitate a more rapid mobilization of the troops.[19]

Of course, this would make Berlin very nervous and increase the risk of war, but the feudal elite expected many good things from a war, including a "consolidation of the *ancien régime*, a system based on absolutism and on the power of the nobility." In 1909, a Russian general suggested to an Austrian diplomat that his country urgently needed a war "in order to strengthen czarism." In Russia too, then, it was essentially internal problems, and above all social problems, that pushed the country toward the abyss of war. The czarist establishment had in mind a "liberating" war but — like many other contemporary warmongers — it was also prone to occasional misgivings. This was particularly understandable in view of the 1905 defeat against Japan. This time, however, Mother Russia had a powerful ally on its side in the person of Marianne, the French Republic, so a triumph was guaranteed. Police reports warning about the possibility, in case of unexpected setbacks, of a renewed flaring up of the revolution, were simply ignored.[20]

The possibility that war might lead to revolution had been raised for quite some time by the socialists. Friedrich Engels had already predicted that, as a result of a great war, "the traditional old regimes might collapse" and "royal crowns might roll into the gutter by the dozens." The German socialist August Bebel and his French colleague Jean Jaurès cried from the rooftops that "war would serve first and foremost to suffocate progressive liberalism and the labour movement," but that this kind of war, consciously prepared by the ruling classes, was a risky business, a gamble or — to use the words of Jaurès — "a murderous roll of the dice." Their conclusion: such a war would bring about all sorts of atrocities and "would have catastrophic consequences even for the ruling classes." But little or no attention was paid to these socialist Cassandras. Even so, within all countries there was indeed a handful of members of the elite — the German chancellor Bethmann-Hollweg, for example — who had their doubts and feared that the coming war might engender undesirable and even catastrophic results.[21]

In Great Britain, the situation was very different, but there too, the elite felt that only a war would offer a radical and definitive solution to its problems. These problems were incarnated by the Irish nationalists, socialist or not, who stubbornly fought for the independence of their country, and also by the socialist revolutionaries, admittedly rather few in number, of England, Scotland, and Wales. The British elite feared "the working class in general," wrote the English historian T.A. Jackson in his voluminous history of Ireland, "and, in particular, a combination of the English workers and the Irish nationalists." The conservatives of the British upper class, the

Tories, and especially the "Anglo-Irish" gentry of great landowners, became more and more reactionary because they wanted Ireland to remain British and because they were simultaneously "terrified," as Arthur Marwick has written, "by the sinister shadows of socialism they imagined flickering all around them."[22]

Particularly frustrating for these Tories was the fact that the progress of democratization increasingly threatened their traditional privileges and powers. After a particularly painful defeat in the parliamentary elections of 1906, their representatives had to watch powerless from the opposition benches while a government of presumably "radical" Liberals led by men like Herbert Henry Asquith and David Lloyd George, and supported by the Labour Party, introduced all sorts of reforms during the years that followed, especially immediately before the outbreak of war in 1914. The privileges of the House of Lords, for example, a bastion of Toryism, were drastically curtailed, and social legislature was promulgated, including a law introducing a minimum salary in certain sectors of industry. Preparations were made for the granting of a certain amount of autonomy to Ireland in the form of a system that became known as "Home Rule." The Tories — many of whom owned land in Ireland — were outraged, and quite a few of them became convinced that only a coup d'état could stop this attack on their traditional privileges. Some were convinced that the Asquith Cabinet was full of socialists. The leader of the Tories, Bonar Law, accused the government of nothing less than planning the revolution, and in the army, another bastion of Toryism, it almost came to a mutiny by conservative officers, who clearly benefited from the sympathy of King George V. In Ireland, the conservative opposition to Home Rule, concentrated in the province of Ulster in the north of the country, threatened to produce a civil war, something that was avoided only by the outbreak of the First World War in 1914.[23]

In the case of Great Britain, an international Great War did indeed bring a solution to the domestic problems, or at least to the problem posed by Irish nationalism. (But of course it was not a genuine, definitive solution: "The Irish problem had been refrigerated, not liquidated," writes a specialist in Irish history, Nuala C. Johnson. "Nothing had been solved and all was still to play for.") The British elite would be very grateful to Mars, the god of war, and it was with great satisfaction that it watched the Protestant

Ulstermen and the overwhelmingly Catholic Irish nationalists volunteer immediately to defend the common British fatherland! The outbreak of war also rid Britain of its social problems. Many contemporary observers were convinced that war against Germany prevented a "violent confrontation between the workers, the employers, and the British government." This opinion was shared by Lloyd George, who would later write in his memoirs that, without the war, the country would have certainly experienced a "hot autumn" on the social level in 1914.[24]

During the years immediately preceding the outbreak of the Great War, not only politicians but many other influential and conservative Brits became convinced that a European war would solve their country's problems. A war might have its unpleasant aspects, but in the final analysis it would benefit the country enormously. The famous writer Sir Arthur Conan Doyle let his hero, Sherlock Holmes, explain the situation on the eve of the Great War to his assistant, Watson, as follows:

> There's an east wind coming . . . such a wind as never blew
> on England yet. It will be cold and bitter, Watson, and a good
> many of us may wither before its blast. But it's God's own
> wind, none the less, and a cleaner, better, stronger land will
> lie in the sunshine when the storm has cleared.

During the First World War, Arthur Conan Doyle contributed to making anti-German propaganda. He considered war "a healthy purgative, a purification by fire." [25]

The great good that could be expected from the coming "cold and bitter wind" of war was of course the elimination of the danger emanating from socialists and Irish nationalists, and the land would be "cleaner, better, and stronger" when the God-given established order was no longer questioned and threatened. Lord Frederick Roberts, a general who had covered himself in glory, as the saying goes, during the wars in India and South Africa, praised war as the only effective antidote against "the great human rottenness that is rife in our industrial cities." And another famous conservative personality, Basil Thomson, "an ambitious, deeply conservative former colonial official" who had become the boss of Scotland Yard, confided to a friend that "unless there were a European War to divert the current, we [are] heading for something very like revolution." An officer of the British Army wrote in a letter that "a good and great war was necessary to stop all this socialist nonsense and unrest among the working class." This longing for war, writes the historian Arthur Marwick, reflected the desire to relieve Britain's "essentially undemocratic [societal] fabric" of the "intense strain from forces of democracy, nationalism and economic discontent."[26]

While war was praised to the skies, it was fashionable to be contemptuous of peace. "Peace may and has ruined many a nationality with its surfeit of everything except those tonics of suffering and deprivation," was a comment published in the *Daily Mail* in 1912, echoing John Ruskin's aforementioned remarks about the supposed disadvantages of peace.[27] Contempt for peace went hand-in-hand with fear and hatred of pacifism. Referring to the elite of Europe in general, including the British elite, Margaret MacMillan writes that

> *the widespread public sentiment in favor of peace further*
> *alarmed many of those in positions of authority, statesmen or*
> *the military for example, who felt that war was a necessary*
> *part of international relations and that pacifism would*
> *undercut their ability to use force. And conservatives saw in*
> *pacifism a challenge to the old order.*[28]

The era of peace was presumably a bad time, to which war could and should put an end; conversely, war promised to inaugurate good times. The lower-class Brits who absorbed and internalized this argument — mostly thanks to mass media such as the *Daily Mail* — would realize, as soldiers during the Great War, what a lie that had been. They would provide a sarcastic comment on it while passing each other on their way to and from the trenches, by shouting: "Enjoy the war, boys, peace will be awful!"

At least symbolically, 1906 may be identified as the year in which the signal was given in Great Britain to start a propaganda campaign in favour of war, more precisely in favour of war against the country that had only recently become an adversary, namely Germany. It was then that the *Daily Mail*, property — just like *The Times*, at least as of 1908 — of a particularly jingoist and bellicose press baron, Alfred Harmsworth, a.k.a. Viscount (and therefore Lord) Northcliffe, "declared war on Germany." Via his widely read newspaper, he launched a systematic campaign in favour of armed conflict with this country, a former friend and still a "Nordic cousin." Of Northcliffe, it was later claimed that "after the Kaiser, he did more than anyone else to unleash the war." In the course of the following years, the suspicion of the presence on Albion's soil of German spies and saboteurs — often presumed to be disguised as waiters! — and of a German invasion would be conjured up in countless articles in the *Daily Mail* and in all sorts of books. A huge success was accorded a book by the popular author William Le Queux, *The Invasion of 1910*, in which Britain is swamped by German troops, while the British socialists display their lack of patriotism by demonstrating against the war. This reflected the logic of elite thinking: the socialists (as well as trade unionists, middle-class pacifists, suffragettes, etc.) were for peace and against war because they were hostile to the established order; the "ladies and gentlemen" of the established order, on the other hand, were for war precisely because they loathed socialism, the emancipation of women, and similar threats to the existing order.[29]

Another representative of the British elite who was actively involved in the quasi-hysterical campaign in favour of war against Germany was the aforementioned Lord Roberts. In 1908, he proclaimed that Great Britain teemed with German spies and that Teutonic troops were poised to invade the land. Another notorious Germanophobe was the Foreign Secretary of the Asquith cabinet, Viscount Edward Grey. Under his auspices, British diplomacy developed a stubborn "Teutophobia," aiming at a kind of "encirclement" of Germany in collaboration with France and Russia. In any event, British public opinion was thus systematically prepared to expect a war against Germany at any moment. For this kind of war against "Teutonic cousins," a Social-Darwinist rationale was proposed by yet another member of the British establishment, the biologist Sir Peter Chalmers Mitchell, secretary of the London Zoological Society. It was precisely on account of their relatedness and similarity that these two superior races were predestined to compete and ultimately do battle against each other in a war that would see the triumph of one and the demise of the other:

Were every German to be wiped out tomorrow, there is no
English trade, no English pursuit that would not immediately
expand. Were every Englishman to be wiped out tomorrow,
the Germans would gain in proportion. Here is the first great
racial struggle of the future, here are two growing nations
pressing against each other, man to man all over the world.
One or the other has to go, one or the other will go.[30]

In Italy too, the elite eagerly cranked out warmongering propaganda in the hope that the domestic social problems in general and the revolutionary menace in particular would evaporate at the dawn of war. There was great concern after the introduction of universal suffrage in 1912. This reluctantly conceded reform initially seemed to throw the gate wide open to revolutionary change. In reality, these fears were unfounded, because the electoral system favoured the countryside where, under the influence of the Church, the population remained very conservative and voted accordingly. But the unrest continued in the cities, and the spectre of revolutionary socialism kept haunting the land. The elite reacted with an antidemocratic, antisocialist, counterrevolutionary, chauvinist, militarist, expansionist, and inevitably bellicose offensive. The Nietzschean poet Gabriele D'Annunzio, for example, beat the drum for colonial expansion in Africa and war against "inferior" peoples. But the most extravagant form of warmongering was that of the aforementioned Italian Futurists, "allies of the conservative forces" who, in 1913, launched a noisy campaign in favour of the "liberation" of the Italian subjects of the Danube Monarchy.[31] Nevertheless, Italy's warmongers would have to wait a little longer than their counterparts elsewhere in Europe before their dream came true, because their country would not go to war until 1915.

During the years leading up to 1914, countless people, especially members of the establishment, imagined themselves to be witnessing a race between war and revolution, a sprint whose outcome could be decided at any time. Which one of the two was going to win? The elite feared revolution and therefore prayed for war.

From the viewpoint of Europe's elite, history had been moving in the wrong direction, as democratization was making progress and the revolution appeared to be approaching rapidly. A change of course, a U-turn, was urgently required. The bourgeoisie wanted to return to the era before 1848 and 1871, the years when the working class and other proletarians had become truly troublesome. As far as the nobility was concerned, it preferred to go all the way back to the "good old days" of the *ancien régime*, the era before the French Revolution. In order to put a definitive end to the execrable process of democratization, the clock had to be turned back to that Age of Aquarius before the fateful year 1789, that is, to the time when, as far as class relations were concerned, the planets had been perfectly aligned.

The nobility and the Church believed and hoped fervently that a Great War could annul the changes introduced in 1789, since they had both suffered hard knocks in that year and had lost still more of their feathers in the course of the revolution-ridden nineteenth century. They did not seek to merely avoid further losses, but hoped to recuperate much of the terrain they had already conceded. Within the European elite, it was thus above all the nobility, supported by the Church, that revealed itself in the years before 1914 to be the great champion of a purposeful and relentless anti-democratic, antisocialist, and counterrevolutionary policy that did not stay clear of war, but instead deliberately pursued it.

The nobility had been on the defensive, but now it moved to the offensive. In this context, historians have spoken of an "aristocratic reaction" comparable to a very similar offensive by the nobility in France on the eve of the 1789 French Revolution.[32] "With the maintenance of the status quo as their minimum objective," writes Arno Mayer, these conservative elements "pressed for the material and spiritual renewal of the *ancien régime*, to be fostered and tested in the ordeal of war in a Darwinian sense."[33] It was characteristic that the reactionary nobility contemptuously dismissed all efforts brought to bear by some less irreconcilable representatives of the elite — such as Asquith in Great Britain, Bethmann-Hollweg in Germany, and Stolypin in Russia — to achieve more compromises, introduce new reforms, etc. Mayer also emphasizes the fact that the aristocracy benefited from the unconditional support of the church it happened to be associated with, for example the Anglican Church in Britain, the Catholic Church in Austria, and the Orthodox Church in Russia, which all made propaganda of their own in favour of war. In Russia, for example, the Orthodox Church "became increasingly inflexible and ideologically aggressive, . . . blessed pogrom banners, . . . [and collaborated with] reactionary and conservative [political] formations." And we have already seen that in France the Catholic Church contributed eagerly to the bellicose offensive.[34]

As for the Anglican Church in Britain, it promoted the idea that the people had turned their backs to God and had become overly materialist, egoistic, and even hedonistic, so God would send a war not only to punish them but to accord them a chance to make amends by means of heroic conduct. Was it not spelled out clearly in the Bible (Hebrews 9:22) that "without the shedding of blood there is no forgiveness of sins"? This mentality found an almost triumphalist reflection in a poem, "Without Shedding of Blood" by Geoffrey Howard, published in early 1915, about six months into the war, and featuring these lines:

> Lord, for the years of ease and vice,
> For hearts unmanned and souls decayed,
> Thou has required a sacrifice —
> A bitter and a bloody price —
> And lo! the price is paid
>
> . . . .
>
> The sword Thou has demanded, Lord:
> And, now, behold the sword![35]

The war that would erupt in 1914 thus amounted to a kind of counter-revolutionary offensive undertaken by the nobility with the support of the clergy. But the partner of the nobility within the establishment, the bourgeoisie, likewise happened to be interested in a war that purported to bring a return to better times. As we have seen, this class had been traumatized by the revolutions of 1848 and 1871 and had renounced its "classical" liberal ideas, which had been progressive and revolutionary for their time. Out of fear of democracy, socialism, and revolution it had joined the nobility in the counterrevolutionary camp and adopted its conservative ethos. The economic interests of the bourgeois industrialists and bankers had also become closely intertwined with those of the nobility. Consequently, writes Mayer, the "capitalist bourgeoisie" was "ready and willing if not eager, to serve as quartermaster for this perilous enterprise [i.e. war]," and he adds:

> The magnates of movable wealth calculated that the requisites
> of warfare would intensify the ancien régime's need for the
> 'economic services of capitalism.' Like their senior partners, the
> bourgeois did not shy away from what they too knew would
> be absolute war, confident that it would be a forcing house
> for the expansion of industry, finance, and commerce and an
> improvement of their status and power.[36]

The great majority of Europe's petty bourgeois, many of whom flocked to the banners of socialism during the difficult years of the *Belle Époque,* was not bellicose like the elite. Like the majority of the workers, an indeterminate but certainly fair number of the lower-middle class was inclined toward pacifism. And the peasantry in general may be assumed to have seen no advantages but many disadvantages in war. The "lower orders" were thus mostly in favour of peace. "The cult of war was an elite, not a plebeian, affair," affirms Arno Mayer. On the other hand, in their fear of proletarization, numerous petty bourgeois, mimicking the haute bourgeoisie, opposed not only socialism, but even the liberal-democratic ideas of 1789 and thus became counterrevolutionary and bellicose. A factor in this development was that the "cult of war" was zealously and effectively promoted by the schools and by the Christian churches.[37] Once again, the case of Hitler can serve as an illustration. This petty bourgeois son of a relatively well-to-do Austrian customs officer[38] was an arch-counterrevolutionary in the sense that he was hostile not only to socialism, and later to the bolshevism of the Russian Revolution of 1917, but also to the liberal ideas and democratic practices introduced by the French Revolution of 1789. And in the years leading up to 1914, he too expected counterrevolutionary salvation from a war. Hitler has been identified in a photo taken in Munich in the middle of a crowd, enthusiastically celebrating the news of the outbreak of war.

The upper-middle class and a part of the lower-middle class were just as bellicose as the nobility. But in most European countries, the nobility was still the ruling and governing class and therefore capable of "pushing the red button." It was the nobility that happened to have the most to gain from a war and therefore wanted war the most. Arno Mayer explains this as follows:

> The governors of the major powers, all but a few of them thoroughly nobilitarian, marched over the precipice of war with their eyes wide open, with calculating heads, and exempt from mass pressures . . . They were men of high social standing, education, and wealth, determined to maintain an idealized world of yesterday . . . Under the aegis of the scepter and the miter, the old elites, unrestrained by the bourgeoisie, systematically prepared their drive for retrogression, to be executed with what they considered irresistible armies. They . . . were ready to crash into the past not only with swords and cavalry charges but also with the artillery and railroads of the modern world that besieged them.[39]

The longing for war was of course based on the belief in the certainty of victory, even though a handful of intellectuals — Max Weber, for example — thought that even a losing war might have a salutary effect. One was certain of victory because one had, or believed oneself to have, an invincible army as well as eminently powerful allies. In the years leading up to 1914, all the great powers, with the sole exception of Great Britain, disposed of huge standing armies thanks to the introduction of a long compulsory military service. The military might of Germany increased to 760,000 men, and its Austro-Hungarian ally kept approximately half a million in uniform. But that was relatively little in comparison to France, whose army, owing to an extra-long military service of three years (introduced in 1913), could assemble an armed force of 800,000 men, plus a colonial army of 160,000, or, with Russia, featuring an army of around one and a half million soldiers. It goes without saying that military expenditures beat all previous records, and that was one of the reasons why it was increasingly deemed desirable not to delay going to war for too long.[40] Armament involved a financial bloodletting that was unaffordable in the long run; it was an enormous kind of "investment" that had to produce "dividends" as soon as possible.

It was not only because the revolution seemed to be *ante portas*, then, that some wished that a war would break out as soon as possible. In France, many thought that it would be better to go to war while the country had a more numerous army than the German enemy; indeed, if Germany, with its much bigger population, likewise lengthened its military service, a window of opportunity might close for good. In all countries where the nobility still controlled the army, bigger armies were wanted in order to be able to wage war successfully; but, on the other hand, it was feared that this would require recruiting more commoners as officers, so that the aristocrats might eventually lose their quasi-monopolistic control over the military forces. In Germany, the high army command was afraid that the increasingly higher percentage of recruits from a social-democrat background might sooner or later cause the army to stop being useful as an "instrument of class hegemony" — as Friedrich Engels had hoped. It was also for such reasons that elites everywhere felt that their armies ought to be sent to war as soon as possible.[41]

The certainty of victory stemmed at least partly from the knowledge of having one or more powerful allies. But in this respect too, things could change suddenly, so that it made sense to start a war as soon as an opportunity arose. France, for example, could only expect a victory against Germany if Russia stayed loyally on its side. But the alliance of the democratic republic with the czar's autocratic empire happened to be a rather unnatural arrangement, predestined to end sooner or later, possibly on account of the role of the numerous arch-conservative Russian aristocrats who had little genuine sympathy for a Gallic republic they found much too democratic — and atheist to boot. And did one not have to take into account the possibility that the next czar might not be as much of a francophile as Nicholas II? Moreover, in Russia everything could change overnight on account of a revolution like the one that had shaken the country in 1905. In the years before 1914, countless Europeans expected that a revolution would soon break out again in Russia. It was also far from certain that the Entente Cordiale that was recently concluded with the British might last forever. So it is hardly surprising that the French generals let it be known to President Poincaré — already a convinced *revanchard* — that they preferred to go to war sooner rather than later.[42] In London too, it was realized that one could not count forever on the French and Russian allies within the Triple Entente. It was therefore preferable to act soon if one wanted to prevent the Germans from implementing their plans with respect to a big navy and a railway from Berlin to Baghdad and thus lay their greedy hands on the oil of Mesopotamia. To avoid such a scenario, a war was probably unavoidable, and for this war Albion needed allies with huge land armies.

Another source of confidence in victory was the detailed but much too rigid[43] war plans that had been concocted by the high command of each major power. In this respect sudden changes of circumstances could likewise spoil everything and cause the prospect of victory to evaporate, so that it would no longer be possible to win the war of which the elite expected so many good things. The German Schlieffen Plan called for a rapid settling of accounts with France while Russia was still busy mobilizing its army, a cumbersome and slow process. But, during the years leading up to 1914, the czarist empire not only modernized its army but also constructed new "strategic" railways. Berlin now had to take into account that, in case of war, a titanic Russian army could attack Germany much sooner than in the past. In this case the seemingly brilliant Schlieffen Plan, key to victory, might have to be tossed into the wastebasket. The German generals calculated that this critical point could be reached as early as 1916 and by 1917 at the latest, so that wars fought later would inevitably lead to defeat, and for that reason they urged the Kaiser and his government to go to war as soon as possible. "We are ready," explained the commander-in-chief, von Moltke junior. "The sooner we will have war, the better it will be for us!" Numerous generals and politicians actually felt that advantage should have been taken of opportunities to go to war that had arisen recently, such as the Agadir Crisis.[44] When in the summer of 1914 a far less serious crisis — an assassination in the Bosnian backwater of Sarajevo — provided yet another opportunity to unleash the dogs of war, it would not be wasted. In 1914, Germany did finally "jump through the closing window of opportunity," to paraphrase the words of an American historian, Adam Levine-Weinberg.[45] But the same can be said about Germany's ally, Austria-Hungary, and also about Germany's enemies, namely France, Russia, and Great Britain. Without exception, they had all been watching eagerly for a pretext to go to war, and believed that they could not afford the luxury of missing the opportunity.

PART TWO
THE GREAT CLASS WAR,
1914–1918

CHAPTER 10
AUGUST 1914: ENTHUSIASM AND RESIGNATION (1)

The assassination in Sarajevo — basically a rather unimportant event — does not constitute a genuine casus belli. *But it provides the elite with the pretext it needs to unleash the kind of war it has ardently desired for a long time. The proletarians are shocked and depressed, rather than enthusiastic, but report for war meekly, without protesting, to the great satisfaction of their "betters" . . .*

On June 28, 1914, the Austro-Hungarian heir to the throne, Franz-Ferdinand, and his wife Sophie were assassinated. This happened in Sarajevo, capital of Bosnia-Herzegovina, a region inhabited by South Slavs, that had belonged for centuries to the Ottoman Empire but had been annexed only shortly before — in 1908 — by the Danube Monarchy, to the great irritation of Serbia. (Franz-Ferdinand's visit to this city was therefore not a good idea. Even the date for the visit had been poorly chosen: June 28 is the anniversary of the legendary Battle of Kosovo of 1389 and a sacred day for Serbian nationalists.) The perpetrator was a certain Gavrilo Princip, a South-Slav nationalist and allegedly an admirer of Nietzsche. *Nomen est omen*, "a name is an omen," said the Romans, and Gavrilo is the Slav form of Gabriel, the name of the archangel of the annunciation, meaning "messenger" or "herald."[1]

With his terrorist act, Princip did in fact announce the Great War. But that certainly does not mean that the assassination in Sarajevo was the *cause* of this war, as we have all too often been told. Similar assassinations had already taken place earlier; for example, in 1881, 1894, 1898, and 1901, when Russia's Czar Alexander II, French President Sadi Carnot, Austro-Hungarian Empress Elisabeth (better known as "Sissi"), and American President William McKinley had been killed by anarchists, and nobody had seen any of these as a reason to unleash a war. The infamous murder in Sarajevo did not constitute a true *reason* for going to war. It was "a sensation of the kind to which Europe was accustomed. It passed without causing undue alarm."[2] But the event provided the perfect *pretext* for unleashing the war the European elite had desired for quite some time. The elite believed that it had to take advantage of the opportunity, because later might be too late.

In Vienna, it was felt that a war against Serbia would serve to eliminate once and for all the social problems as well as the problem of South Slav nationalism. Such a war was wanted badly, and this is why an ultimatum was drafted that was known to be unacceptable to the Serbian government, whose culpability in the affair has remained unclear and controversial to this very day.[3] Vienna wanted to be certain that the ultimatum would be rejected, since such a reaction was needed to justify a declaration of war. The ultimatum was therefore prepared slowly and meticulously and was only sent on July 23, four weeks after the fact. The Austro-Hungarian ambassador who handed it to the Serbian government actually left Belgrade immediately, convinced that the answer could only be negative and that Vienna would therefore have the *casus belli* it had been looking for.[4] Vienna was in fact so determined to go to war that it was not taken into account that Belgrade actually accepted virtually all the demands contained in the ultimatum. The latter "could be interpreted only as a deliberate attempt to provoke war," was the conclusion drawn by *Vorwärts*, the newspaper of the German socialists.[5]

In its eagerness to rush to war, Vienna received the *nihil obstat* of its German ally. In Berlin, Serbia was viewed as an obstacle to the projected railroad to Baghdad. The fact that in this tense situation German support for the Danube Monarchy would almost certainly mean war against Russia, protector of Serbia, and therefore also against France, did not appear to be a problem. To the contrary: as we have seen, many of Germany's high-ranking political and military leaders believed that they could not afford to wait much longer before marching to war. In Berlin as well as Vienna, there were of course personalities within the elite, including Emperor Wilhelm II and the Austro-Hungarian Duke Tisza,[6] who got cold feet at the last moment and who wondered if war was really the best option at that time, or if it was perhaps wiser to wait a little longer. In the end, however, those among the warmongers who urged immediate action won the day. A similar scenario unfolded in St. Petersburg, where only after some hesitation was it decided to take advantage of the opportunity to go to war. In France, the government received a German declaration of war before its members had a chance to discuss whether the time was ripe for war or not. But it is highly unlikely that the doubting Thomases would have prevailed because, with Russia onside, President Poincaré and the army high command were poised to go for Germany's jugular at last. In Paris too, time was believed to be running out, so that action had to be taken forthwith.

Here is a concise chronology of the principal facts of the summer of 1914:

- June 28: Assassination in Sarajevo.
- July 23: Austro-Hungarian ultimatum delivered to Serbia.
- July 25: Serbia refuses to accept all the terms of the ultimatum.
- July 28: Austria-Hungary declares war on Serbia.
- July 29: Partial mobilization in Russia.
- July 30: General mobilization in Russia.
- July 31: Germany proclaims the country in danger of war.
- August 2: German ultimatum delivered to Belgium.
- August 3: Germany declares war on Russia and France; Belgium rejects the German ultimatum of August 2.
- August 4: Germany invades Belgium; Great Britain declares war on Germany.

The last power to cut the Gordian knot was Great Britain. It was actually inevitable that that country would also go to war, on the side, of course, of its French and Russian partners. The terms of its alliance did not formally require London to do so, a fact that permitted Berlin to hope for British neutrality. But the British government and the high command of the country's army had concluded secret agreements with Paris — known to the British side as WF, "With France" — that contained a de facto obligation to come to the aid of France. "Britain's decision to intervene," writes Niall Ferguson, "was the result of secret planning by her generals and diplomats." And, like everywhere else, within the British elite there were numerous men of influence and power — including Churchill — who keenly desired war and were convinced that the right hour had struck. They expected that the war would solve the social problems as well as the Irish question and would spoil the German scheme of a railway to Baghdad. A war would make it possible to eliminate a dangerous rival and bring Mesopotamian oil under the exclusive control of Britain, but none of this could be publicly acknowledged. What was urgently needed was an excuse that would be acceptable to the Parliament and to a British public that was not particularly jingoistic and actually rather pacifistic; many Britons even sympathized more with their German "cousins" than with the Russians and Serbians, who were Slavs and therefore supposedly inferior peoples. Germany's violation of Belgian neutrality brought relief, because it provided London with the alibi it needed. "The [German] assault on Belgium came as a heaven-sent deliverance to [the Asquith] government," writes Max Hastings. "The perceived martyrdom of King Albert and his people rallied to the cause of war millions of British people who had hitherto opposed it."[7]

Officially, then, it was on behalf of "gallant little Belgium" that Great Britain declared war on Germany on August 4, 1914. In Berlin, this decision was perceived as pure hypocrisy, and not without reason. The Germans felt betrayed by "perfidious Albion" and they hoped that "God would punish England" (*Gott strafe Engeland*). It was a slogan that, like his equally famous "Hymn of Hate against England" (*Hassgesang gegen England*), was written in a fit of patriotism by the Jewish-German poet Ernst Lissauer, who would later regret this blast of creativity.[8] But the British convinced themselves that they only went to war to save little Belgium from the clutches of the Teutonic brute, as appears from these lines of a popular song of 1914, "Keep the Home Fires Burning":

Over seas there came a pleading,
'Help a Nation in distress!'
And we gave our glorious laddies,
Honor made us do no less.
For no gallant Son of Freedom
To a tyrant's yoke should bend,
And a noble heart must answer
To the sacred call of 'Friend!'

In reality, however, Great Britain was not really attached to the Belgian neutrality guaranteed by London in the so-called *Treaty of the XXIV Articles* of 1839, and could and would surely have found a pretext for ignoring Germany's aggression if it might have found it convenient to do so. A number of cabinet ministers, including Churchill, were allegedly prepared to close their eyes to a German march into France via Belgium, at least if it stayed away from the seaport of Antwerp. Moreover, the British were apparently ready to move into Belgium themselves if the Germans had not done so first.[9] During the days leading up to the British declaration of war on Germany, all sorts of rumours were circulating in London about an impending violation of this neutrality by the British themselves, causing some discomfort in the Belgian embassy. The British were certainly not overly fastidious with respect to violations of the neutrality of other countries. They would demonstrate this in the fall of 1914, when they would move troops through the territory of neutral China in order to attack the German concession in the Bay of Kiao-Chao (with the city of Qingdao or Tsingtao) in cooperation with the Japanese.[10] It is thus not without reason that the German chancellor, von Bethmann-Hollweg, found it incomprehensible that Great Britain went to war on account of a "mere scrap of paper" (*Fetzen Papier*), as he is said to have put it, signed in 1839.

And so it finally came to the war that had long been the object of the fond desires and high expectations of the ruling and governing classes of all great powers. These classes experienced the outbreak of war as a deliverance after years of almost intolerable tension, and they heaved a sigh of relief. The coming of the war, writes Eric Hobsbawm,

was widely felt as a release and a relief . . . Like a
thunderstorm it broke the heavy closeness of expectation and
cleared the air . . . After a long wait in the auditorium, it
meant the opening of the curtain on a great and exciting
historical drama in which the audience found itself to be the
actors. It meant decision.[11]

When he learned the news, the famous Field Marshal Lord Horatio Herbert Kitchener declared laconically that "it is better to have an end of the uncertainty."[12] And a young Briton "from a good family," Rupert Brooke, who would later be well known as an antiwar poet, expressed his enthusiasm in these verses:

Now, God be thanked Who has matched us with His hour,
And caught our youth, and wakened us from sleeping,
With hand made sure, clear eye, and sharpened power,
To turn, as swimmers into cleanness leaping,
Glad from a world grown old and cold and weary.[13]

In Russia too, where 1914 had been a year of tensions and unprecedented social conflicts, the outbreak of war abroad, like a *deus ex machina*, brought peace at home. "The social malaise, which had been growing relentlessly, suddenly evaporated when war broke out," writes the historian Hans Rogger, "what had seemed impossible in peacetime became reality in the wink of an eye." The elite, and the upper classes in general, welcomed the war as a deliverance from the "meanness and narrow mindedness of spirit," a "spiritual awakening," the "end of a moral crisis," an opportunity for Mother Russia to "reclaim its true Russian and Slav identity," and so forth.[14]

The relief was just as great in Germany. The famous writer Thomas Mann, very much a member of the upper-middle class, gave vent to his relief as follows:

The world of peace, which has now collapsed with such
shattering thunder — did we not all of us have enough of

it? Was it not foul in all its comfort? Did it not fester and
stink with the decomposition of civilization? Morally and
psychologically I felt the necessity of this catastrophe and that
feeling of cleansing, of elevation and liberation which filled
me, when what one had thought impossible really happened.[15]

And in the streets of Berlin many burghers congratulated each other for "being over the hurdle."[16] In *Mein Kampf,* Hitler was to describe about ten years later what the feeling was like in Munich when the news arrived that war had broken out: "[The war] was not forced on the masses . . . no, it was desired by the whole people. People wanted at length to put an end to the general uncertainty." And he personally experienced the coming of war as "a release from the painful feelings of my youth," so he "fell down on [his] knees and thanked Heaven from an overflowing heart for granting [him] the good fortune of being permitted to live at this time."[17] Despite what Hitler believed, it was not "the whole people" that was relieved and overjoyed, but primarily the members of the country's aristocratic and bourgeois elite, that is, the ruling and governing classes of all of Germany, and indeed of all countries that were drawing the sword, and also of a part of the lower-middle class of which Hitler himself was a representative specimen. The war that had broken out was the war they had wanted, the war that would dissipate the spectre of revolution, the war to stop and even roll back the democratization process.

The war that was being welcomed with open arms by the elite was of course a war between countries, a war in which a vertical obstacle, the "wall" of the frontline, separated countries, including their upper as well as their lower classes, and was therefore a kind of "vertical" war. But it was simultaneously a "horizontal" war, a conflict in which a horizontal rampart segregated "those above" from "those below" within each belligerent country, the superior classes from the lower orders. Seen from "above," the lower classes, especially the workers and other proletarians, incarnated the great problems that were presumably going to be resolved by the war that had just started. They were the "dangerous classes," the threatening "masses" that had been incited for decades by the socialists and had therefore shown themselves to be restless and seditious; via the process of democratization, they had already made too much progress, and sooner or later they were likely to overthrow the established order via a revolution, just as the Barbarians had destroyed the Roman Empire. From the perspective of the elite, the war was a war against democracy, against socialism, against revolution, against internationalism (linked to socialism) — and against pacifism, directed against war itself.

It is thus hardly surprising that the very first victim of this war was the great French socialist leader Jean Jaurès, assassinated in Paris on July 31, 1914. That the Great War, evidently a war between countries, would also be a war between classes, was reflected in the fact that its very first victim was a socialist who also happened to be a beacon of internationalism, antimilitarism, and pacifism, who was assassinated by a fanatical French nationalist, and in the fact that the first victim on the French side was a Frenchman brought down by a French bullet.[18] In a famous song entitled *"Pourquoi ont-ils tué Jaurès?,"* the late Jacques Brel asked why Jaurès had been killed.[19] The answer is that it was because he attempted *in extremis* to prevent a war in which the elite, not only of France, but also of Germany, Russia, etc., had invested such high hopes.

In the eyes of the European elite, the time of peace had been a miserable time, and the time of war that was now dawning could only be a good time. The outbreak of war was certainly a moment of great illusions, of the *Grande Illusion*, to cite the title of a classic movie on the First World War, produced by Jean Renoir in 1937. One of these illusions was that the war would be a short one, although a handful of military and political Cassandras, including Lord Kitchener, did in fact predict that the war would be long. "The soldiers would be back for the wine harvest" was the widespread belief in France. "Home before the leaves come down" (*Zurück bevor die Blätter fallen*), they said in Germany. In Great Britain they were a little less optimistic, but believed nonetheless that it would all be over soon; the troops were supposed to be "home before Christmas."

Naive ideas also prevailed with respect to the nature of the war. With the precedent of recent colonial wars fresh in their minds (at least as reported in the press), most people expected that the war would cause the soldiers little hardship, but would bring plenty of travel, adventure, perhaps romance, and certainly glory, lots of it. Those rare birds who might actually perish for the fatherland, hit by a bullet in the chest and dying an instant and painless death, would enter Valhalla to the triumphant sound of trumpets. The public, and even countless military experts, did not take into account how murderous modern armaments really were, such as the machine guns that had already existed for quite a few decades. It was thought that the war would resemble the recent Balkan Wars, conflicts that had been brief and limited in terms of casualties, and in which the cavalry had still played its traditional important role. "On the [European] continent, there had been no war between the Great Powers since 1871," writes the American historian Paul Fussell. "No man in the prime of his life knew what war was like. All imagined that it would be an affair of great marches and great battles, quickly decided."[20] His colleague Gabriel Kolko, likewise an American, notes that "romantic militarist illusions left generals everywhere utterly oblivious to the nature of warfare in the machine age."[21]

The war would in fact reveal itself to be a modern, industrial war, but in the summer of 1914 Europeans pictured a kind of medieval conflict. This was reflected in the "essentially feudal language" that would be used to describe the Great War in antiseptic and euphemistic terms until the bitter end of the conflict, as Paul Fussell has observed. The British were the champions in this kind of verbal delicacy. The soldiers did not form ordinary armies, but a "host," and were semantically glorified as "warriors"; without exception, they were not only "brave" but "gallant" and generally "plucky," even when danger lurked everywhere, not only ordinary danger, but the solemn "peril." The enemy whom we needed to "vanquish" was not merely the enemy, he was the sinister "foe" or, even worse, the almost monstrous "foeman." On the battlefield, our brave men were never killed, they "fell" on the "field of honour." Even the worst military catastrophes and cases of cowardice were thus semantically covered in dignity and glory and transformed into glorious happenings. Our soldiers were always "staunch," our officers "cool," without a single exception. Everything they undertook was "magnificent and splendid." To our officers, nothing was ever horrible, but merely occasionally "darned unpleasant" or sometimes even "rather nasty," etc. Consciously or not, such language served to mask the reality of modern warfare. The First World War, writes Paul Fussell, "was perhaps the first time in history that official policy produced events so shocking, bizarre, and stomach-turning that the events had to be tidied up for presentation to a highly literate mass population." Even today, the authorities and the media use similar euphemistic language. For example, it was never stated that our soldiers in Afghanistan had been "killed," but merely that they "died" after an explosion or an exchange of fire with the Taliban.[22]

Just about everybody was confident in victory and believed that this triumph would bring eternal glory to the fatherland in addition to a considerable enlargement of its own territory or portfolio of colonial real estate. Even in minuscule Belgium, about to be crushed under the boots of the German Moloch, countless burghers were convinced that, with Britain and France as allies, victory was certain. In a book about his experiences as a soldier in 1914, *Namen 1914*, the Flemish writer Ernest Claes related how the good folks in Brussels looked forward to seeing their country's postwar borders stretch all the way to the Rhine. And so, in that magnificent, even idyllic summer of 1914, they went to war with an apparently universal enthusiasm, with beaming faces and, as they said in France, "with flowers in the barrels of their rifles" (*la fleur au fusil*). Preceded by marching bands, acclaimed by women and men waving flags, and followed by children, the recruits streamed out of the armouries and marched to the stations; there they boarded trains on whose sides graffiti scribbled with chalk proclaimed that they were heading to the enemy capital: *"Auf nach Paris!,"* or *"À Berlin!"*

We now know that the bellicose enthusiasm of the summer of 1914 was far less widespread than had been generally believed. "The photographs of cheering crowds in the great capitals are misleading," writes Margaret MacMillan in her book about the outbreak of war in 1914. "The coming of war took most Europeans by surprise and their initial reaction was disbelief and shock." The lower classes were not nearly as enthusiastic as the elite, and the villages and small towns in the countryside far less than capitals like Berlin and Paris.[23] But the big cities, where patriotic citizens loudly welcomed the war and where the authorities stimulated the enthusiasm with marching bands and displays of flags, enjoyed by far the most attention from the journalists and photographers. And the political and military leaders were only too happy to send the reports and images of enthusiasm around the world.

A considerable part of the lower-middle class and the great majority of workers and peasants had never been bellicose. They did not share the elite's illusions with respect to war, and they worried about the hardships the war was certain to cause them. In France, "still essentially rural," the country-side reacted "with surprise and consternation" when war was declared. In Russia, "only a minority displayed patriotic ardour and nationalist fury," writes the French historian Alexandre Sumpf, while "the majority wavered between concern and resignation," and the countryside displayed far less appetite for the war than the cities. The state of mind among the Russian peasantry has been described elsewhere as "profound stupefaction," "down-cast fatalism," and "passive obedience." For the peasants, it was particularly traumatic to have go to war at harvest time, when the sight of wheat fields, shining like gold in the August sun, symbolized, as a French author Jean Rouaud has written, "the kept promise of daily bread"; it was an image, he continues, that did not conjure up war but had been associated with "peace, ever since men learned to work the land and to expect from it on a certain date the pleasure of a full belly."[24] From France to distant Serbia and Russia, the peasants did not know how the crops would be harvested now that they and their sons would march off to distant battlefields and the army would come to take away their horses and carts. (Being separated from the familiar companion, the horse, was particularly traumatic for the peasants; in France alone, no less than 730,000 horses were requisitioned in August 1914.) The despondency of English peasants was echoed in the following lines of the poem "August 1914," by John Masefield:

> The harvest not yet won, the empty bin,
> The friendly horses taken from the stalls,
> The fallow on the hill not yet brought in,
> The cracks unplastered in the leaking walls.

> Yet heard the news, and went discouraged home,
> And brooded by the fire with heavy mind,
> With such dumb loving of the Berkshire loam
> As breaks the dumb hearts of the English kind.

> Then sadly rose and left the well-loved Downs.[25]

Among Europe's lower orders in general, there was also talk of "discontent," "angry grumbling," and "critical murmurs" with respect to the "bosses" who were considered to be responsible for the war. Workers everywhere asked themselves how their families would survive on the meagre soldier's pay that would replace their wages for an indefinite period of time. In many cities, for example in London, Frankfurt, and Hamburg, whatever frivolity may have been displayed during the first hours and days soon gave way to a serious and even sombre mood, particularly in working-class districts such as London's East End and the Berlin district of Moabit. Germany's "mass of workers and employees" was reported to remain "very reserved toward the warlike atmosphere." Via a drawing entitled *The Declaration of War* (*Die Kriegserklärung*), the German expressionist painter Max Beckmann dramatically conveyed the consternation of ordinary German citizens. In St. Petersburg, whose German name would be changed on August 18, 1914, to the Russian Petrograd, also meaning "City of Peter [the Great]," many suspected that the scenes of enthusiasm that drew the attention of the media were far from spontaneous, but were probably orchestrated by the authorities, and that countless participants had received money or alcohol for their "work." The ambassador of a neutral country, Spain, observed that the recruits who marched through the city looked rather "quiet and downcast."[26]

Among the departing troops, all too numerous were those who were reluctant to leave their family, their workplace, their village — and had the feeling that they might never return. This type of foreboding is evoked in a poem, "Departure" (*Abschied*), written by Alfred Lichtenstein, a German who would be killed on September 25, 1914, somewhere in northern France:

Wir ziehn zum Krieg. Der Tod ist unser Kitt.	*We go to war. Death is on our side.*
O, heulte mir doch die Geliebte nit.	*I wish my love would stop crying.*
Was liegt an mir. Ich gehe gerne ein.	*I myself do not matter, I go happily.*
Die Mutter weint. Man muß aus Eisen sein.	*My mother cries. One needs to be made of steel.*
Die Sonne fällt zum Horizont hinab.	*The sun disappears behind the horizon*

Bald wirft man mich ins milde Massengrab.	*Soon they will throw us into a welcoming mass grave.*
Am Himmel brennt das brave Abendrot.	*The nice red glare of evening burns in the sky.*
Vielleicht bin ich in dreizehn Tagen tot.	*In a fortnight I will perhaps be dead.*

"In spite of intense pedagogical efforts and a semi-artificial, semi-spontaneous enthusiasm, the desire to go and die in war did not exist at all," is what two historians have written with respect to the German soldiers who marched off to war in the summer of 1914, and the same could be said about their counterparts in the Allied camp.[27] Everywhere, however, the soldiers were imbued with a sincere love of their fatherland and a sense of duty. And they believed — or wanted to believe — what they had been told by their social superiors, namely that the war would be short, require few sacrifices, and would end with victory, thus opening the gate to a better world.

Not only the ordinary *soldiers*, but also the *civilians* of modest origin displayed precious little enthusiasm for the war. During the final days of peace, impressive numbers of them expressed their pacifism and anti-militarism in antiwar demonstrations sponsored by socialist parties, trade unions, and pacifist associations. Between July 26 and 31 such demonstrations took place just about everywhere in Germany, even along the Unter den Linden avenue in the heart of the capital, and on July 27 a wave of demonstrations swept over France. During a final meeting of Europe's leading socialists such as Jean Jaurès, the German Hugo Haase, and Britain's Keir Hardie, on July 29 in Brussels, a crowd of more than seven thousand sang the "*Internationale*" and shouted "War against the war!" In London, on August 2 and 4, great crowds joined protest marches organized by unions and leftist parties, and flocked to an antiwar rally with speakers such as Labour leaders Keir Hardie, Arthur Henderson, and Ramsay MacDonald; and there was talk of organizing a general strike in case it came to war. The Independent Labour Party, founded by Keir Hardie, published a declaration in which one could read that "across the roar of guns, we send sympathy and greeting to the German socialists, [who] are no enemies of ours, but faithful friends," and Sylvia Pankhurst, a well-known suffragette with socialist sympathies, signed an open letter to the women of Germany and Austria-Hungary, imploring them "not to forget that our very anguish unites us . . . and that we must all urge that peace be made." But this truly awesome opposition to the war melted like snow under the sun when, in all countries, the working-class parties and unions pronounced themselves in favour of the war and nationalist feelings triumphed. In Great Britain and elsewhere, writes Arthur Marwick, "the second week of August 1914 presented a picture of unity and enthusiasm for the war."[28]

In that summer of 1914, the plebeians went to war without enthusiasm, obedient and docile. The numerous peasants among them, often illiterate or semi-illiterate, had long been "conditioned to be submissive and blindly obedient to traditional leaders."[29] (In this context, a French historian has emphasized his country's peasants' "culture of obedience" and their "pre-disposition to obey and to accept hierarchical relations, the duty to give every effort and make any sacrifice, and to accept your fate — the main qualities that would be required of soldiers in the Great War.")[30]

For the elite, it was an enormous source of satisfaction to see the members of the lower orders march off to war so acquiescently, shepherded by officers of a higher social background, blessed by bishops and priests, and determined to perform their "patriotic" duty. Similarly, the ethnic and linguistic minorities revealed themselves to be surprisingly docile; for example, the Czechs in the Danube Monarchy, the Irish in Great Britain, the Danish and Polish minorities in Germany, and the Flemings in Belgium. Even the colonies witnessed a wave of enthusiasm and support for the war. In India, for example, "recruitment exceed[ed] all expectations" and "over two million Indian combatants and support staff would eventually serve overseas"; in French Indochina, the war likewise generated exhilaration.[31] Statistically, the number of cases of refusal to serve and desertion proved to be insignificant. In France, the authorities were thus most pleasantly surprised that far fewer men refused to report than they had expected. It had been calculated that between 5 per cent and 13 per cent of the draftees would not report or would desert, but ultimately that number turned out to be only 1 per cent. "Servilely," noted the socialist soldier Louis Barthas in his diary, "everybody hurried to have their freedom curtailed and to submit to the yoke of militarism."

The authorities also did not experience any of the troubles from the side of the pacifist, antimilitarist, internationalist, and supposedly revolutionary socialists. Some units of the British Army were not immediately deployed because it was feared that they might be needed for "home defence," that is, for the repression of "potential troubles on the part of the working class."[32] In France, after the assassination of Jean Jaurès, the government expected all sorts of troubles and therefore kept two cavalry regiments ready for intervention in Paris instead of sending them to the front as originally planned, but no troubles broke out. The French general mobilization went smoothly, much more so than had been expected. Consequently, it proved unnecessary to proceed with the preventive arrest of some 2,500 socialists, anarchists, and union leaders suspected of revolutionary intentions, men of whom the police had drawn up a list, the famous "Carnet B." The decision not to proceed with the roundup, taken on August 1, the day after Jaurès's assassination, simultaneously reflected the authorities' fear of the potentially unpleasant and even revolutionary blowback that might be generated by such a draconian measure; and such a "decapitation" of the working class movement, depriving it of an essentially moderate leadership, might indeed have produced a chaotic and even explosive situation.[33] (It is said that certain elements on the extreme right of the political spectrum were very unhappy about this. They had in fact hoped that the authorities would take advantage of the opportunity offered by the outbreak of war to "annihilate once and for all the workers' movement, breaking the back of "a movement whose rapid rise had ruined their serenity.")[34]

Also impressive was the number of men of all classes who came forward voluntarily to join the army. The most spectacular case was of course that of Great Britain, where a compulsory military service did not exist. During the first eight weeks of the war, between ten thousand and thirty thousand volunteers responded daily to the "call" (or the "summons"), amounting to a total of approximately 750,000 men. By the end of 1914, more than 1.2 million men had already voluntarily reported for duty. Between August 1914 and June 1915, a total of approximately two million men would join, forming a new army that, in honour of Secretary of State Lord Kitchener, was to be called "Kitchener's Army." But the lower orders revealed themselves to be distinctly less enthusiastic for armed service than the middle class. "Members of the working class . . . showed less zeal than the better-off," writes Adam Hochschild, and "volunteer[ed] for the army at a noticeably lower rate than professionals and white-collar workers."[35] Nevertheless, the authorities and the patriciate were also pleasantly surprised by the positive response of the plebeians. It had actually been feared that the quarrel with Germany might leave the workers cold, that the latter might have felt that things would not be worse for them if Germany won the war. (There were also great regional differences: the Irish were less keen than the Scots to fight for "king and country.")[36] Even in countries where military service was compulsory, numerous young men came forward voluntarily. Belgium in general and Brussels in particular were swamped by "waves of patriotic enthusiasm," and countless volunteers reported to the army, to the great pride of their parents, "to go and fight for the fatherland."[37]

CHAPTER 11

AUGUST 1914: ENTHUSIASM AND RESIGNATION (2)

Why do the plebeians go to war so meekly? Because they have been indoctrinated to do so in an extremely effective fashion by the school and the church, or compelled by compulsory military service. Powerful propaganda cranked out by the state and the press and pressure from the side of women, friends, village notables, and employers also plays an important role. Last but not least, the socialist leaders drop their internationalism, reveal themselves to be apostles of the "nationalist faith," and enjoin the workers to perform their patriotic duty . . .

How can we explain the fact that, after a powerful but brief antiwar outburst, "those below," the workers and the plebeians in general, who, in contrast to "those above," had nothing to gain and much to lose from war, jumped on the bellicose bandwagon after all? How was the commodity called war "sold" to the people? How were nationalistic and patriotic values inculcated into the lower orders sufficiently to motivate them to march into battle, if not enthusiastically then at least willingly or obediently?

Historians often emphasize the importance of the socializing role played by primary and secondary schools ever since the introduction of compulsory schooling some decades earlier. Respect and obedience vis-à-vis the authorities and loyalty and love for the fatherland were systematically drilled into youthful and receptive brains by the teachers. It is hardly surprising that in Erich Maria Remarque's famous pacifist novel, *All Quiet on the Western Front*, the patriotic professor who had incited the students to volunteer for the service was portrayed as a jingoist and militarist scoundrel. In France also, enthusiasm for the war had been promoted in the schools. The same can be said about Great Britain, but there the very elitist "public" schools are said to have served as the most effective centres for the indoctrination of jingoism and militarism.[1]

The gospel of patriotism and bellicosity was preached from the church pulpits as well. In all European countries, the Christian churches constituted a solid "pillar" of the establishment, whose nationalism, militarism, and bellicosity they shared. The churches thus sang with tenor voices in the mighty prowar choir. In Russia, the Orthodox clergy went out of its way to justify the war, promote the mobilization, rationalize killing, and guarantee victory. As for Britain, it is very likely that the believers who volunteered for military service were strongly encouraged by the declarations of the prelates of the Anglican Church. Those revealed themselves enchanted that their government had heeded "a call coming from heaven" and declared war on Germany, a step that they qualified as "brilliant," "magnificent," and "divine." One of them declared that "we will fight, not for the honour of our country, but for the honour of our God." And the Bishop of London proclaimed that the war "was the greatest fight ever fought for the Christian faith." Other Anglican prelates announced loudly that the British went to battle for "the principles of Christianity," that the Germans — who themselves proclaimed to have God on their side with the slogan *"Gott mit uns"* — were "the enemies of God," that "all those who would fall in the course of this war will be martyrs" and "will certainly go to heaven." The archbishop of York declared that the objective of the war was "the destruction of German militarism."

In Germany, the Catholic and Lutheran churches supported the war as much as the Anglican Church did on the other side of the Channel, praising it to the sky, so to speak, as a *bellum justum*, a "just war," a war "for God" and "against the Antichrist," and so forth. The Bishop of Freiburg declared that the war was a means by which God wanted to test the believers, and he assured his flock that the war "would heal the wounds of the German people and bring forth a new [German] race, filled with respect for God, sense of duty, and fraternal love"; war, he continued, obviously alluding to the country's socialists, would "give birth to a new [spiritual] order and put an end to godless culture and atheist politics." In France too, the faithful were encouraged by bishops and priests to perform their patriotic duty. They were assured, as Jean-Yves Le Naour has written, that the war was a "crusade," a conflict between "civilization and barbarism, right and might, good and evil." The church, noted Barthas with a *soupçon* of sarcasm, "prayed ardently for victory and elevated the soldier who lost his life to the rank of martyr; he was promised paradise, and thus this inhuman war was transformed into something sacred and divine." For this propagandistic service, Barthas continued sarcastically, the Church was rewarded by the "anticlerical and free-thinking republic" with "permission for regimental bands to enliven religious ceremonies." "Not since the wars of religion of the seventeenth century, and perhaps even the Crusades," concludes the Canadian historian Modris Eksteins, "had [Christian] men of the cloth encouraged killing for the greater glory of God with such enthusiasm."[2]

Nationalist enthusiasm and the readiness to give one's life for the country were also energetically promoted by mayors, lawyers, physicians, and other notables; that is, prominent and influential personalities who still enjoyed much prestige at the time in the villages and small towns all over Europe. In Britain, country squires went after their tenants and other villagers, as is illustrated in these biting lines of a poem by Siegfried Sassoon, entitled "Memorial Tablet":

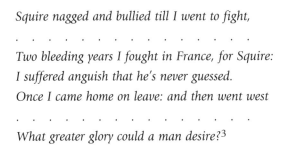

Squire nagged and bullied till I went to fight,

. . . .

Two bleeding years I fought in France, for Squire:
I suffered anguish that he's never guessed.
Once I came home on leave: and then went west

. . . .

What greater glory could a man desire?[3]

A particularly important factor in the patriotism of the ordinary citizens was the compulsory military service which, in France, Germany, Russia, and elsewhere, amounted to a veritable nationalist and militarist type of brainwashing to which even young men from a socialist background were not immune. During their long military service, the soldiers were taught to obey unconditionally, and this was certainly not only the case in Prussia and elsewhere in Germany, where the people are said to have had a "subject mentality" (*Untertanenmentalität*) for centuries, presumably even since the time of Luther. The events of 1914 offered the famous German linguist von Wilamowitz-Moellendorff an opportunity to emphasize the link between military service and a submission mentality:

> *Never before have the public authorities intervened so*
> *profoundly in the existence of the people with all sorts of*
> *orders, and never before have those authorities found the*
> *public so spontaneously ready to obey. This is due to our*
> *military education: it has taught those who give orders a sense*
> *of responsibility, and in those who must obey it has inculcated*
> *the understanding that it is absolutely necessary to obey.*[4]

It happened to be precisely in July 1914 that Heinrich Mann finished a novel that was predestined to cause quite a stir when it was published after some delay, namely in the final year of the war: *Der Untertan,* meaning "the subject," though the English translation is *Man of Straw.* It describes how, in the Kaiser's Germany, the school and the army had imbued young men with nationalism, discipline, and obedience and had thus transformed the Reich into a country of docile "subjects." But it was not only in Germany, but wherever the military service existed, writes Arno Mayer, that the army functioned as a "formidable instrument of socialization."[5]

The high number of volunteers in Britain was was also due to pressure from women and friends. From the very first days of the war, women of the "better" classes crisscrossed London and most other towns in order to offer young men in civilian clothes a white feather, an ancient symbol of cowardice. And women such as the famous Jessie Pope wrote poems and songs in which they expressed their contempt for men who hesitated to join the army and, conversely, their admiration for those who volunteered for service. A good example is the poem "The Call," in which a lady addresses a plebeian as follows:

Who's for the trench
Are you, my laddie?
Who'll follow French
Will you, my laddie?
Who's fretting to begin,
Who's going out to win?
And who wants to save his skin
Do you, my laddie?

. . . .

Who'll earn the Empire's thanks
Will you, my laddie?
Who'll swell the victor's ranks
Will you, my laddie?
When that procession comes,
Banners and rolling drums
Who'll stand and bite his thumbs
Will you, my laddie?

Other songs of this kind were "Your King and Country Want You", a sort of updated version of the medieval summons to fight for your feudal overlord, and the particularly popular "Keep the Home Fires Burning." In many towns and villages an important role was played by peer-group pressure, which resulted in groups of neighbours, work colleagues, members of football clubs, etc., reporting together for duty, thus forming what would be called "pals battalions."[6] Wilfred Owen also refers to pressure from friends and females in one of his poems, "Disabled":

It was after football, when he'd drunk a peg,
He thought he'd better join. He wonders why

. . . .

Someone had said he'd look a god in kilts.
That's why; and maybe, too, to please his Meg,
Aye, that was it, to please the giddy jilts,
He asked to join. He didn't have to beg;
Smiling they wrote his lie; aged nineteen years.[7]

It is clear that under those circumstances, numerous so-called volunteers did not really depart voluntarily for the war. Many of them, moreover, were motivated far less by patriotism than by purely economic motives. It has to be taken into account that in Britain the outbreak of war was accompanied by a financial and economic crisis, whereby countless businesses closed their doors permanently or at least temporarily. Military service thus suddenly appeared as a less unattractive option for the countless wage-earners who found themselves out of work. Some firms deliberately laid off members of their personnel in order to force them to report for duty. Aristocrats did the same with their domestic staff, and countless employers let it be known that after the war they would not hire anyone who had not served in the army. The government made a contribution of its own to the inflation of the number of "volunteers" by asking charitable institutions to refuse assistance to needy men who were deemed to be fit enough to play soldier. In any event, countless volunteers were motivated by the prospect of earning an admittedly meagre but regular income in the form of the King's shilling. The Jewish poet and painter Isaac Rosenberg, for example, permanently short of cash on account of his Bohemian lifestyle, reported for duty not out of patriotism, which he actually despised, but because the army promised that half of his pay would be sent to his needy mother.[8] Even in relatively prosperous Canada, countless men volunteered "out of desperation, so they could escape poverty, menial, mind-numbing jobs, or [in the case of many of the country's "boy soldiers"] the hell-hole of an orphanage or foster home." "I would get a dollar and ten cents a day — good money," recalled a Canadian soldier much later, "on the farm I was only getting fifty cents a day."[9] Yet another determinant of the high number of volunteers was the need experienced by foreign residents to demonstrate their loyalty to their adopted fatherland — and/or to avoid the potentially extremely unpleasant consequences of being suspected of being a spy, which included being lynched. It was this calculus that caused a Polish resident of France named Guglielmo Apollinare de Kostrowitzky, a famous poet, to report for duty and to successfully apply for French citizenship, after which he became known as Guillaume Apollinaire.[10]

Finally, one cannot underestimate the enormous weight of the propaganda for military service, waged systematically and relentlessly. One of the instruments used was the well-known poster on which a finger-pointing Lord Kitchener enjoined Britons to fight "for King and Country," as if in the early twentieth century the man in the street, like a medieval vassal, owed military service and loyalty unto death to his regal overlord. But at that time the *Zeitgeist* was still impregnated by Romanticism with its idealization of the Middle Ages, and Kitchener's appeal met with considerable success. The influence of Romanticism and its fixation on the Middle Ages can also be recognized in the language used to exhort men to go to war. The war was proclaimed to be a "crusade," the "Mongols" or other "Barbarians" had to be prevented from ruining our civilization; like Joan of Arc, one had to save the fatherland in its hour of danger, etc. In September 1914, *The Times* published a poem of this kind, wrung out of the pen of none other than Rudyard Kipling; its title was "For All We Have And Are":

> *For all we have and are,*
> *For all our children's fate,*
> *Stand up and take the war,*
> *The Hun is at the gate!*[11]

Under the influence of Romanticism, Britons thus threw themselves into the first great war of the industrial age with a medieval mindset.

The popular press also helped to recruit plebeian volunteers with a "drum-beating" form of journalism eulogizing war as "the great adventure," a "jolly good time," and, in this poem, published in an English newspaper, as "The Game," a kind of sport:

> *Come, join the ranks of our hero sons*
> *In the wider field of fame,*
> *Where the God of Right will watch the fight,*
> *And referee the game.*[12]

Enthusiasm for military service was zealously promoted by periodicals in general, and by jingoist newspapers like *John Bull* and the *Daily Mail* in particular. Their readers, of whom the majority "had been accepting all their life that if something was printed in the newspapers, then it was true,"[13] learned that the soldiers just loved the war, visited France much as tourists would, enjoyed the fresh country air, were fed very well, and, of course, suffered only minor losses. In these papers, one could read of the war in France and Belgium that "the open-air life, the regular and plenteous feeding, the exercise, and the freedom from care and responsibility, keep the soldiers extraordinarily fit and contented."[14] War correspondents tried hard to encourage prospective volunteers with reports such as the one claiming that dead British soldiers looked much better and more dignified than non-British dead. Finally, one particular argument aimed to disarm, so to speak, Britain's numerous pacifists, summarized in the slogan that this war was "The war that will end war": it was concocted by H.G. Wells, a socialist.[15]

If workers and the lower orders in general went to war meekly or, as in the case of Britain, reported for duty with more or less enthusiasm, that was also due to a great extent to the attitude of the leaders of socialist and other workers' parties. Many if not most of these parties were members of the Second International, and during the meetings of this organization — such as the Basel Congress of 1912 — they had once more formally promised that they would not fight against each other in case a war was unleashed by the capitalists or anyone else. They would observe Marx's admonition: the proletarians of all countries did not have a fatherland to fight for, but were all members of one class, and would be fraternally united. If war broke out, the workers would react with a general strike or with an undefined "uprising." As late as July 29, 1914, French, German, and other socialists, including Jaurès, gathered in Brussels in order to decide how, in case of war, they would live up to their promise, but sadly the meeting failed to produce any concrete agreements.[16] (But this demonstration of socialist internationalism — and the concomitant attempt to prevent war *in extremis* — infuriated the antisocialist nationalists, and it was not a coincidence that Jaurès was assassinated by one of them immediately after his return from Brussels.)

When war broke out, the socialist leaders were offered an opportunity to transform their internationalist words into deeds. All eyes were fixed on Germany's SPD, whose approval was needed in the Reichstag for the extraordinary credit the government required to go to war. As late as July 25, the party had spoken out against "belligerent intervention" and had pointed an accusing finger at the "power lust of the Austrian[-Hungarian] ruling group and the imperialistic profit-interests." And during the following days, the German socialists had helped to organize the antiwar demonstrations that have already been mentioned. But on August 1, the war was a *fait accompli*. And two days later, the 111 SPD Reichstag members met to discuss the situation and decide whether or not they would vote in favour of the war budget and the special war measures proposed by the imperial government. Only fourteen of them opposed giving the seal of approval, among them Rosa Luxemburg, Karl Liebknecht, Franz Mehring, and Hugo Haase; a few days earlier, the latter had met with Jaurès in Brussels. In order to maintain the unanimity the SPD traditionally displayed in the Reichstag, however, the dissenters agreed to vote with the majority. And thus it happened that the following day, August 4, the socialist deputies, "caught up in the orgy of emotion," as the Canadian historian Modris Eksteins has written, "rallied to the nationalist cause." They approved the war credits in the Reichstag, and the SPD leadership urged the party's rank-and-file not to live up to internationalist principles, but to perform their patriotic duty.[17] The German socialists rationalized their anti-internationalist decision by referring to the presumably purely defensive character of a war in which their fatherland was set upon by a cabal of spiteful enemies, above all Russia. And was Russia not the most backward and autocratic country in Europe, the land of czarist dictatorship? Would a victory of czarism not undo all the progress recently made by the working class under socialist auspices in Germany and elsewhere in Europe? Had Friedrich Engels not already warned that Russia was the great nemesis of the socialists?[18]

An even more important factor was the fact that, in the course of the decades preceding 1914, the social democrats in general, and their leaders in particular, had been seduced by political reforms and social legislation and thus become integrated into Germany's established order. They had thus internalized a German nationalism that was admittedly far from fanatical, but nonetheless solid, a "love of the fatherland," and a loyalty vis-à-vis a German state that had brought them a somewhat better existence. Other than this "social patriotism," countless socialist leaders, probably even the majority, had also embraced revisionism à la Bernstein, and had thus not only taken leave from the internationalist idea, but from the revolutionary idea. Simultaneously, they had developed an appreciation of the cornucopia of imperialism, which showered raw materials and other advantages on Germany's *Volkswirtschaft* and thus helped to raise the standard of living of the workers. As parliamentarians, moreover, the social-democratic leaders had become most respectable citizens. This SPD "oligarchy" feared that internationalist action in the nation's hour of danger might spark a revolution that could possibly spoil everything; that is, wipe out not only the gains made by the workers, but also, and perhaps more importantly, their own privileges. And so these socialist oligarchs convinced themselves painlessly that revolution was undesirable, that a defeat of their own country — coupled with a triumph of czarism — would be catastrophic, and that the socialist cause would profit from a German victory.

Thanks to the victory of German imperialism in its colonial wars, the lot of German workers had improved, so it could be expected that another triumph of German imperialism, this time in a great Armageddon on European soil — followed by the appropriation of new sources of raw materials, markets, etc. — would yield even greater benefits.[19] Such was the social-imperialist argument used on August 3 in the Reichstag by Bernstein in order to help convince the SPD deputies to vote in favour of the war: doing so meant that henceforth a "bridge of gold" would unite the SPD and the German state. (It is therefore hardly surprising that later, in the course of the war, the SPD would never seriously oppose the annexations of territory in France, Belgium, and elsewhere, proposed by Germany's nationalists and militarists.)

Yet another determinant in the decision to approve the war credits was the not-unfounded fear that otherwise the army might arrest the leaders of the SPD, dissolve the party, confiscate its assets, etc. It was actually for this reason that as early as August 2, the trade unions promised not to organize any strikes for the duration of the conflict and would not try to modify existing wage agreements between them and the employers. They promised to limit their activities for the time to assistance to the unemployed and various forms of support for the war effort. This decision certainly influenced the attitude of the SPD in the Reichstag.[20] The leaders of the SPD and the unions had good reasons to worry about the potential for such repression of their organizations. In a single blow, it could have destroyed virtually everything the German working-class movement had achieved in the course of the previous half-century, and for the SPD oligarchs it would have meant the sad end of relatively comfortable, prestigious, and even well-paid careers, and perhaps even imprisonment. By collaborating kindly with the government, on the other hand, the leaders of the party and the unions believed that they could not only maintain but even increase the portfolio of benefits to their constituency and to themselves.

In France, after the assassination of Jaurès, the authorities briefly held their breath. Would this cowardly deed provoke a violent, perhaps even revolutionary response on the part of the socialists? The reply came the next day, when the Socialist party let it be known that it would not ask its members to demonstrate or protest in any way; to the contrary, they appealled for a defense of the fatherland against German imperialism. The CGT, a presumably revolutionary union, did the same thing. The supposedly internationalist socialists of France thus likewise revealed themselves to be social chauvinists, and they, too, easily came up with excuses; the democratic French republic, daughter of the glorious 1789 Revolution, had to be defended against an authoritarian and militarist Germany. And was it not obvious that it was the German socialists who had "betrayed" the cause of internationalism, who had allowed themselves to be "corrupted by the Kaiser," who had conspired with the Prussian militarists? Now was not the time to make a revolution: the war itself would be revolutionary, at least if it led to the defeat of Germany and the installation there of a French-style republic instead of a feudal empire.

Henri Barbusse, who would later become famous as the author of a very antimilitaristic book, *Under Fire* (*Le feu*), but who had just volunteered for service, wrote on August 9 in a letter to *L'Humanité*, the Socialist party's newspaper, founded by Jaurès, that the war would be a "social war," a battle against the great enemies of social progress, namely "militarism and imperialism, the sword, the boot, and the crown." The victory of France would liberate the peoples of Europe, mark the advent of eternal peace, etc. The French socialists appeared to want nothing less than victory. They were champions of "war until victory" or "war until the very end," to use the literal translation of the French expression *la guerre jusqu'au bout*. The French partisans of war until the bitter end, mostly conservative, nationalist, and right-wing citizens, but henceforth also including most (but not all) socialists, would now be known as *jusqu'au-boutistes*, a term that could be translated as "hawks" or "hardliners." In any event, the attitude of the socialists did not differ much, if at all, from that of the most chauvinist Frenchmen. But the socialists convinced themselves that this war was a special case, that it would be the "last of the last wars," *la dernière des dernières guerres* or, as some would later put it, rather cynically, *la der des der*.[21]

Like their German counterparts, the French trade unions, including the CGT, agreed to collaborate docilely with the state and the employers for the duration of the war, not to make any demands, and not to go on strike. Instead, they would focus on charitable work such as assistance to the families of members who were called up to the colours and to widows and orphans of soldiers.[22] As for Great Britain, there too, most of the unions agreed to conclude an "industrial truce," putting a sudden end to the "great social agitation" that had been ravaging Britain. Plans for a general strike in November were cancelled, and union leaders travelled around the country to encourage the rank-and-file not to strike but to volunteer for the army. "By collaborating with the Government," writes Arthur Marwick, "the national trade union leaders, in effect, stepped aside from their role of protecting special working-class interests."[23] In Belgium, the socialists used the same rationales as their French and German comrades to justify the fact that they too rallied behind the flag and unanimously approved the war credits in parliament. Emile Vandervelde declared that the war was "a holy war for justice, liberty, and civilization, for the right of peoples to self-determination."[24] However, this "holy war" would reveal itself to be an orgy of cruelty and inhumanity. Friedrich Engels had once commented that the future held two options, socialism or barbarism, as Rosa Luxemburg would remind her readers in an antiwar tract in 1916, the "Junius Pamphlet." When in the summer of 1914 socialism withdrew from the contest, so to speak, it helped open the gate to its horrible alternative, the barbarism of an unprecedented war.

It was only in Russia that a handful of socialist deputies in the parliament, the Duma, voted against the war credits: five Bolsheviks, six Mensheviks, and ten Trudoviks, the latter including Alexander Kerensky. On the other hand, quite a few socialists, anarchists, and other well-known revolutionary Russians came out in favour of the war against "German militarism," among them Peter Kropotkin and George Plekhanov, who revealed themselves to be "social chauvinists." Their pro-war stance, the notion that socialists had to defend Mother Russia, became known as "defensism." Its binary opposite, the antiwar strategy promoted by Lenin, to be discussed later, would therefore become known — rather incongruously — as "defeatism."[25] In any event, the left-wing members of the Duma constituted the exception to the general rule that when the war started the socialists rallied behind the governments of their countries. A kind of social and political harmony thus suddenly descended on all countries, a tranquillity that became known in Germany as the *Burgfrieden*, "peace within the [beleaguered] fortress." The term referred to a practice dating back to the romanticized Middle Ages, as was the phrase used in Belgium, *trêve de Dieu* ("the Truce of God," *Pax Dei* in Latin). In France, the social truce became known as the *union sacrée* or "sacred union" after Prime Minister René Viviani euphorically declared on August 4 in the National Assembly that "in this war France will be defended heroically by all its sons, whose sacred union cannot be broken by anything or anybody."

Since political and social developments during the years leading up to 1914 had been particularly favourable to the socialist political parties (to the great dismay of the elite), and since in Britain and many other countries it seemed, in this hot summer of 1914, that smouldering social troubles might be the prelude to a "hot autumn," possibly producing a revolutionary tempest, it amounted to a massive concession on the part of the leaders of socialist parties and unions that they consented to a "sacred union." It is thus hardly surprising that they were rewarded, ostensibly generously, by the grateful elite, namely with a number of ministerial appointments and other prestigious positions within the coalition governments that were set up in many belligerent countries; coalition governments that nonetheless remained firmly under establishment control. The importance of these appointments was mostly, if not exclusively, symbolic. They purported to signal the goodwill of the elite, but they served mainly to impress the popular masses, to integrate them even more into the existing order, and, last but not least, to legitimate the war in the eyes of the plebs. But such gestures were only made when and where the elite judged it necessary, or at least useful, to do so. This happened to be the case in countries where the political democratization process had already made considerable progress, as in France, but not in authoritarian Germany[26] — even though the Reich's socialists revealed themselves to be particularly obsequious vis-à-vis the elite — and certainly not in absolutist Russia, where the opinions of workers and peasants counted for naught.

In France, a number of socialists and union leaders were co-opted into the *union sacrée* government; for example, Marcel Sembat, who would become minister of public works, and Jules Guesde who, as minister of state, was merely asked to join the government *honoris causa*. Before the war, Guesde had actually been the incarnation *par excellence* of revolutionary and internationalist socialism in France and in this sense he had been a major antagonist of the similarly internationalist but revisionist Jaurès. In practice, Guesde had no say, but his appointment had considerable symbolic value: he was a magnificent socialist scalp ostentatiously dangling from the belt of the elite on the warpath. Much the same can be said about the Belgian socialist head man, Emile Vandevelde, who was enlisted as minister of state in a Belgian government that would spend the war in a comfortable but mostly inert exile in Le Havre. Those socialist leaders who became ministers would exert precious little influence on the policies of the governments of which they were graciously allowed to become members; their appointments were most useful for their personal career and prestige, but for the socialist rank-and-file and for the plebs in general, they made no difference. The few socialist ministers or high-ranking government officials who actually did accomplish anything were those who tried hard to promote the interests of the elite. As example we can cite the case of Albert Thomas, a revisionist French socialist. At first he became a government bureaucrat who devoted his considerable talents to the cause of increasing the production of munitions and weapons; later, as minister of armament, he focused on making workers toil with discipline, zeal, and without complaining or making demands, and thus on keeping the capitalist system functioning as smoothly and profitably as possible. Thomas became the symbol of the collaboration, for the sake of victory, of the trio of state, capital, and labour. This "class collaboration" was the antithesis of the classical Marxian concept of "class struggle," and it amounted to an extreme kind of socialist reformism. With his commitment to the cause of victory for his country, Thomas also symbolized the binary opposite of socialist internationalism, namely the social chauvinism that had made its appearance shortly before the outbreak of the war in the context of socialist reformism. Thomas and the other reformist and social-chauvinist socialists were convinced that class collaboration served the interests of the French workers; however, this system favoured the industrialists, and first and foremost the big industrialists. We will later see that they were the ones who had the most reason to be appreciative of the wartime collaboration of classes, which would not be the case for the majority of the workers.[27]

The "wild beasts of the political forest," as Hobsbawm has sarcastically described Europe's contemporary socialist leaders,[28] were from then on as pets in a cage, to the great satisfaction and advantage of the aristocratic and bourgeois elite — but also to their own advantage and satisfaction. Indeed, in the context of the suspension of politics, their importance and prestige increased, as the elite ostensibly no longer despised but actually appreciated them and treated them as partners. Of Marcel Sembat, who had been a colleague of Jaurès with solid pacifist credentials, a socialist public servant remarked that numerous comrades had been surprised and disappointed that he had been willing to join the government, but that he himself was "thrilled to be a minister and proud as a peacock with his high title."[29]

Even at lower levels, socialist leaders were henceforth treated with more respect and given opportunities to enjoy a measure of power and prestige. In Germany, not a single socialist was admitted to the *sanctum sanctorum* of the Reich government, but in exchange for their eager collaboration with the authorities, the leaders of the SPD and the unions were now virtually pampered by the government and even treated with respect by the higher ranks of the military, who had always been their archenemies.[30] Members of the social-democratic leadership, such as Philipp Scheidemann, experienced "a genuine pleasure . . . in being invited to discuss matters on an equal footing with the ministers of state," writes the historian Carl Schorske. And the fact that, on occasions such as visits to the troops at the front, SPD Reichstag representatives were occasionally fussed over by high-ranking army officers, something that had been unthinkable before the war, "heightened the feeling of being in the club" on the part of these social-democratic oligarchs. In this manner, the socialist and union leaders were drawn "psychologically closer to the ruling group." (From his exile in

Switzerland, Lenin remarked, sarcastically but certainly not inaccurately, that the war had provided the elite with an opportunity "to co-opt the opportunists within the socialist movement and to incorporate them into the existing social-economic order.")

Recognition by the country's ruling and governing class was often complemented by minor concessions, generally of a purely symbolic nature, such as permission for the recruits in the armouries to read the socialist newspaper *Vorwärts*, which was censored anyway. All of that served to enhance the leaders' authority and prestige within the SPD and the unions. Furthermore, the "oligarchic" elite of these organizations benefited from the fact that, in the context of the sacred union, political life — especially political life of the democratic variety, involving input from below — was suspended, obviously to the advantage of the elite, and this was the case in the political parties and trade unions as much as in the country in general. This in turn reinforced the reformist and social-patriotic tendencies within these organizations. The SPD became less democratic and its leaders became more authoritarian and less tolerant with respect to the "left-wing" and pacifist opposition directed by personalities such as Luxemburg and Liebknecht.[31] Even so, everywhere there were also socialists, leaders as well as ordinary party members, who remained faithful to the revolutionary and internationalist ideas and to the attendant pacifism. These women and men refused to support the war, and so did countless nonsocialist pacifists. "From the beginning," writes Adam Hochschild, "tens of thousands of people on both sides recognized the war for the catastrophe it was . . . and they spoke out." Among the best-known personalities of this kind were Rosa Luxemburg and Karl Liebknecht of the SPD, Pierre Monatte of the French CGT, the American socialist Eugene Debs, Keir Hardie of the Independent Labour Party (ILP) ("one of Britain's remaining fortresses of resistance of working-class internationalism"), the suffragette Sylvia Pankhurst, and the famous philosopher Bertrand Russell, who would later also oppose the war in Vietnam. In spite of its defeat in the summer of 1914, British pacifism remained a thorn in the side of the nation's establishment.[32]

To the nonreformist, internationalist, and revolutionary minority within European socialism also belonged a certain Vladimir Ilitch Ulyanov, better known by his nickname, "Lenin." Lenin was a member of the Russian

Social-Democratic Labour Party (RSDLP) and served as leader of the party wing known as the Bolsheviks. The RSDLP was outlawed in Russia, and when the war broke out Lenin was living in exile in Switzerland. He sharply condemned the war in September 1914 as

> *a bourgeois, imperialist and dynastic war, a struggle for*
> *markets and for the freedom to loot foreign countries . . .*
> *an attempt to suppress the revolutionary movement of the*
> *proletariat and democracy in the individual countries, a desire*
> *to deceive, disunite, and slaughter the proletarians of all*
> *countries by setting the wage slaves of one nation against those*
> *of another so as to benefit the bourgeoisie.*[33]

Since it had proved impossible to prevent the war, Lenin developed a new socialist strategy, the aforementioned "defeatism," which took into account the changed circumstances yet remained faithful to internationalism and the revolutionary idea. He argued that a victory of one's own country meant a victory of its established order and would thus solidify this order to the disadvantage of the proletarians. For this reason, true socialists should not rush to defend the "fatherland" as the reformists did; they ought to take advantage of the situation to jumpstart the revolution and thus achieve the victory not of the fatherland in an imperialist war, but of the proletariat in a social war, in a class war. It was with this strategy of "revolutionary defeatism," writes Gabriel Kolko, that Lenin revealed himself to be "the only European socialist leader who unequivocally damned the war and the imperialist claims of all nations." His principled stance — or, as Kolko puts it, "the purity of his opposition" to the war — would gain Lenin a growing number of partisans, not only within the RSDLP, but within the socialist movement of Europe in general, as the evolution of the war would rob a steadily increasing number of socialists of the illusions of the summer of 1914.[34] Lenin proceeded to practise what he preached, as he instructed the Bolsheviks to go to work on behalf of the revolutionary cause. As early as the fall of 1914, reports by the Russian secret police indicated that clandestine cells of Bolsheviks were spreading defeatist propaganda among troops heading for the front.[35]

In the summer of 1914 Europe's proletarians and other plebeians marched off to the killing fields, without enthusiasm but persuaded by their "betters" to do their duty on behalf of the beloved fatherland, overwhelmed by massive propaganda, but not without sadness, regret, fear, and a foreboding of mutilation and death. These mixed feelings are conjured up powerfully in a poem by Charles Ducal, Belgium's "poet of the fatherland" (poet laureate) for 2014-2015, entitled *"Soldaat 1914,"* "Soldier 1914":

De hamer van de taal heeft zijn schedel gekraakt
en alle kamers ingenomen. Het is nog zijn hoofd,
maar wordt nu bewoond door iets groters.
In de keuken wordt proviand klaargemaakt
voor zijn aandeel in armen en benen.
In de woonkamer schept het dagblad het kwaad.

The hammer of language cracked his skull
And invaded all its rooms. It is still his head,
But is now inhabited by something larger.
In the kitchen they prepare the provisions
For his contribution in arms and legs.
In the lounge evil is hatched by the newspaper.

Zo wordt de wil langzaam losgepraat
van have en goed en ingesnoerd
in het uniform van de plicht.

The aspirations are thus diverted
From home and family and packed
Into the uniform of duty.

Een oeroud instinct wordt uit de mottenzak
boven gehaald en gelucht. Er zitten gaten in,
allicht van angst, maar die kunnen gedicht.

From the mothproof bag an ancient instinct
Is retrieved and aired out. Sure it has holes,
Caused by fear, but they can be patched.

Hoofdletters vullen ze in,
geven de dood zijn onsterfelijke zin.
Zijn dood, niettemin.

Capitalized words bestow death
with immortal sense.
His death, nonetheless.[36]

CHAPTER 12
THE END OF POLITICS

When war breaks out, the elite is delighted, and understandably so: strikes and other social troubles suddenly come to an end, the revolutionary threat goes up in smoke, and the political and social-economic position of the still-dominant combination of nobility and upper-middle class is "frozen." The democratization process, previously seemingly irresistible, is brought to a standstill and even rolled back; and it proves possible to undo many of the social gains made by the working class before the war . . .

In the years leading up to 1914, the elite was tormented by fear and uncertainty. A race seemed to be on between war and revolution, and it was feared that revolution might triumph. Whether the revolutionary danger really existed or not is hardly important. Much more important was the fact that within aristocratic and bourgeois circles the conviction prevailed that this danger was real and acute. Thus we can understand the relief and enthusiasm for the war that welled up within the European elite in the summer of 1914: war had won the race, war had eliminated the revolution. In the novel *Demian* (1919), the German writer Hermann Hesse has the titular character say the following when war breaks out: "So it won't be the end of the world, no earthquake, no revolution, but war. People will love it!"[1]

The aforementioned French historian Fernand Braudel described a state of mind rather than a historical reality when, during the 1960s, he wrote that "in 1914, the West stood on the threshold of war, but also of socialism.

Socialism was poised to grab power and to construct a new Europe . . . But, within a matter of a few days or even a few hours, the outbreak of war destroyed this hope."[2] The socialists, at least those of Western and Central Europe, were certainly not poised to grab power in 1914. But aristocratic and bourgeois families like Braudel's certainly feared revolution and were delighted that the advent of war dissipated the spectre of revolution. Braudel was wrong: in 1914, it was not the hope for revolution that vanished on the proletarian side, it was the fear of revolution that evaporated on the side of the elite.[3]

The elite was relieved first and foremost because war abroad produced peace at home. The outbreak of an international conflict instantly neutralized domestic social conflicts. War banished the revolution and metamorphosed the restless and combatant proletarians into compliant citizens. "We no longer have a rabble," exulted a commentator in Germany, who added that, thanks to the war, all Germans were suddenly "spiritual aristocrats."[4] Emperor Wilhelm II was enraptured when he learned that the social democrats had approved the war credits; in other words, that within the SPD nationalism had checkmated internationalism and that the revolution had been struck from the socialist program. Overjoyed, he declared that "henceforth [he] no longer knew political parties, but only Germans." It was in almost identical terms that the president of the French National Assembly declared that in this illustrious institution "there were no longer adversaries but only Frenchmen."[5] A similar atmosphere reigned in Vienna. It found a reflection in the following remarks made by Stefan Zweig, who would later become a famous pacifist, at the moment when his country, Austria-Hungary, was about to go to war:

> From now on, hundreds of thousands of persons experience a feeling they have never known in peacetime, namely that they belonged to one great nation . . . Each individual was henceforth purified of any form of egoism. All differences of class, of religion, and of language had been swept away by a grandiose feeling of fraternity.[6]

When the war broke out, many other German and Austro-Hungarian artists and writers vented their relief and enthusiasm: Hermann Hesse, for example, and Franz Marc, Rainer Maria Rilke with his poem *"Fünf Gesänge"* ("Five Songs"), and the expressionist sculptor Ernst Barlach (who like Zweig would soon convert to pacifism) with his statue entitled *Der Rächer*, "The Avenger."[7]

In Russia, the members of the Duma saluted the outbreak of war with enthusiasm, because it engendered within the country an unprecedented kind of unity that

> *opened the door to a lasting collaboration and a mutual trust*
> *[among Russians] . . . The war brought the nation to its*
> *senses. What had seemed impossible in times of peace had*
> *become reality.*[8]

The prelates of the Christian churches were equally jubilant, for the summer of 1914 indeed appeared to fulfil their fondest hopes. All countries experienced an explosion of piety. Niall Ferguson emphasizes that "the outbreak of the war saw an upsurge in religious observance in nearly all the combatant countries . . . people were seized by religious fervour . . . the people have come [back] to God."[9] Huge crowds assembled in Berlin in front of the imperial palace and burst out in song, alternating patriotic anthems with Lutheran hymns. Ecumenical ceremonies were attended by massive numbers of Catholics and Protestants, who heard preachers declare that the Germans would be "loyal until death" to their Kaiser and "feared God and nothing else in the entire world."[10] Such exuberance caused a young Hamburg woman from an upper-middle class background to conclude that "our people has rediscovered God," and some German ecclesiastics declared that the war had transformed their country into a kind of "kingdom of God on earth." "The light of the star of faith," exulted a Jesuit, "enlightens us in the darkness of the night of war." Of German soldiers, it was reported that they prayed a lot. Another Jesuit had the impression that

> *The entire country has become a church. The men take*
> *communion in the railway stations, in the armouries, in*
> *the cafés, under trees, in the bushes . . . It is wonderful*

how religiosity has exploded among our troops. The officers themselves ask us to celebrate mass in the fields . . . Everybody is praying with the rosary in hand.

In France, "the war provoked a wave of unrest that caused big crowds to come and kneel down in front of the altars," "the churches were full, the candles did not cease to burn, and the confessionals were taken by storm," and the cult of the Sacred Heart as well as pilgrimages to Lourdes flourished as never before. A well-known prelate, Monsignor Baudrillart, noted this with great satisfaction and opined that

in spite of the sacrifices and the suffering, we witness felicitous events, events which I had actually expected for a long time . . . France has rediscovered its strength, and I think the country could not have been reborn other than by a war that will purify and unite our people.

Overjoyed, the Church praised "the return to God of the popular masses as well as the soldiers," a phenomenon that was described as a "return to the altars," a "return to God," and a "religious awakening." The French army chaplains were ecstatic. They reported that countless soldiers resorted to prayer, went to mass, took communion, and accepted and wore the scapulars that were offered to them. "It makes us smile," one of them commented triumphantly, "we who have always believed in God." The soldiers "displayed a hunger for God, a thirst for God," exclaimed a colleague. One of the countless French soldiers who rushed to the altars in 1914 was the poet Apollinaire, who went to mass often and made a contribution of his own to the "sanctification of the war" by devoting a poem to Joan of Arc, imploring her to "throw the Germans out of Alsace."[11]

In that summer of 1914, emperors and kings, princes of the church, aristocrats, and solid burghers like Stefan Zweig exulted, and many petty bourgeois exulted together with them, including that as-yet-unknown Austrian, Adolf Hitler. The revolutionary danger had vanished, but that was not the only reason for exulting. The sacred union, *Burgfrieden,* or whatever it was called — amounted to a moratorium of the political and social hostilities at home, presumably a precondition for victory in the war abroad. This truce also had important implications with respect to the political and social-economic situation within each country. It heralded the end of politics, at least for the duration of the war, and the end of politics meant the end of the process of democratization, the end of the progress that democracy had been making. The war, and the sacred union that was associated with it, gave the elite an opportunity to stop, and even to roll back, a historical democratization process that had hitherto appeared to be irresistible.

In spite of the democratizing concessions that it had previously been necessary to make in most countries, in the summer of 1914 the traditional elite, whether noble or upper-middle class, was still firmly in power. Everywhere governments were formed by parties that represented the elite, even though here and there one had to put up with parliaments with sizeable contingents of socialists or other pesky plebeian politicians. (Even after its spectacular electoral victory of 1912, which made it Germany's biggest party, the SPD still had little or nothing to say and proved unable to achieve any important item in its program; in France too, recent electoral successes had not brought the socialists any real power.) Moreover, the parliaments, or at least the lower chambers of the parliaments, virtually the sole state institutions in which the plebeians enjoyed a modest kind of representation thanks to hard-fought extensions of the suffrage, were not the only locus of state power, far from it. In the other centres of power, such as the unelected upper chambers of the parliaments, the army, and the upper levels of the state bureaucracy, the elite was and remained solidly entrenched, and there the plebs enjoyed no input whatsoever.

Even in Europe's most democratic country, France, the elite — consisting essentially of the haute bourgeoisie with the aristocracy as junior partner — still held enormous power, even though it represented only a tiny demographic minority. With 30 to 40 per cent of the deputies and a quasi-monopoly on the upper levels of the state administration, the diplomatic service, the judiciary, the high command of the army, etc., writes the French historian Michel Winock, the elite "largely controlled the state apparatus," and this in spite of the recent rise of the "new social layers," the working class and the petty bourgeoisie. On the eve of the Great War, concludes Winock, the haute bourgeoisie — and the elite in general — was still the ruling as well as governing class, the class which, in addition to the "essential wealth" also controlled the "fundamental powers."[12]

It was this conservative status quo that was frozen, thanks to the outbreak of war and the accompanying "end of politics." In the case of France, the historian François Bouloc estimates that the sacred union "clearly gave the advantage to those who had an interest in the survival of the established order."[13] And with respect to Germany as well as France, the British historian Max Hastings writes that the "political reconciliation" which the Reich's *Burgfrieden* and the French *union sacrée* happened to be, "was interpreted as a triumph for the political right, reflecting the eclipse of the socialists who had opposed belligerence." Just about everywhere, the established political order favoured not only the nobility but also the industrial bourgeoisie, that is, the capitalists, so the sacred union also worked to their advantage. By accepting the moratorium on domestic strife, the socialists and union leaders accepted and legitimated for the duration of the war the existing social-economic relations, which in spite of previously made concessions still favoured the employers. With respect to the case of France, Bouloc writes that the "dominant situation of the *patronat* [i.e. employers]" was and remained solid.[14]

Thanks to the war, everything remained as it was, and for an indeterminate period of time there would be no question of further progress in the direction of democracy. In addition, the state of war offered the elite an opportunity to further strengthen its already exceptionally high degree of control over the state apparatus, and thus to dismantle, either openly or covertly, the modest measure of democracy that already existed. In other words, the war made it possible not only to arrest but even to "roll back" the process of political and social democratization

With respect to Germany, the American historian Carl E. Schorske has written that the government immediately "gave itself a dictatorial right to decide all military, political and economic questions," but this type of thing happened in all the belligerent countries. It was explained that the situation required it, and that after the (supposedly short) war all would revert to normal. Better still, the authorities hinted at a postwar return to even greater democracy, to a "new orientation" in politics, but such promises remained particularly vague.[15] Not only in Germany, but also in France and Great Britain, the governments in place — and especially the small cabinets that would crystallize within these governments — would arrogate more and more power, so that by 1917 at the latest they would form de facto dictatorships overseen by politicians such as Clemenceau and Lloyd George. In any event, in most belligerent countries elections were no longer held, and in the existing parliaments the governments had little or nothing to fear in terms of opposition, especially since everywhere the socialists, in spite of great electoral successes, were and remained a minority, a minority that had abandoned its role of opposition within the framework of the sacred union. During the entire war, the Belgian parliament, exiled in France, did not even bother to meet. In Russia, the Duma, impotent under any circumstances, proposed of its own volition to suspend its activities for the duration of the war: only a handful of Bolshevik and Menshevik members vainly opposed this move. (The Duma would in fact continue to meet occasionally, but would have little or no influence on the imperial government; it would only emerge from its coma with the outbreak of the revolution in 1917.)[16]

The existing governments arranged for the docile members of parliament to vote for enabling laws that handed the ministers wide-ranging powers, or else simply proclaimed a state of siege. In either case, the result was that all sorts of decisions could henceforth be taken without parliamentary approval. In Great Britain, which was far from being a democratic country in 1914, the so-called *Defence of the Realm Act* (DORA) was passed on August 8, 1914, without the traditional preliminary debate. This law allowed the government to censor at will, to limit the freedom of the press, to have homes searched, and to take all sorts of other undemocratic measures. These powers would in fact be used eagerly to silence "undesirable political opinions" in general and to take steps against socialists, pacifists, suffragettes, Irish nationalists, and other "nonconformists" who had long been a thorn in the side of the British establishment. In the course of the Great War — presumably the war for democracy! — Great Britain would thus degenerate into "a kind of police state." The conservative British historian Niall Ferguson, who observed this, also quotes a periodical, *The Nation*, which in May 1916 deplored that "the country which went out to defend liberty is losing its own liberties one by one."[17] Ferguson reaches the conclusion that "the suppression of dissent" on the "Home Front" was clearly, in Great Britain as in all other belligerent countries, a major objective of the government.[18]

The British government also saw fit to use its DORA powers to improve the uncouth mentality, manners, and habits of the country's plebeians. It was, for example, believed possible and necessary to raise the supposedly low level of patriotism of the lower orders by requiring cinemas and theatres to play the national anthem before or after every show. And the pubs, where the plebs regularly went to quench their thirst, were forced to serve beer of a lower alcohol level and to close for a number of hours in the day, in the afternoon and evenings as early as 10:00 p.m.; this regulation was to remain in place until 1988. The upper class was convinced that alcoholism was not a symptom of poverty and misery but, to the contrary, one of the main causes of social problems — thus implicitly absolving itself of any responsibility. (After the war, the same tortuous reasoning would inspire America's Prohibition laws, in effect from 1920 to 1933.) It was felt that visits to the pub impacted negatively on the discipline and zeal of workers, so that "a great service was rendered to the working class by not quite suppressing temptation [in the form of the pub] entirely, yet by limiting it." In order to increase workplace productivity and lower accident rates, the government also simply closed many pubs, especially those located close to munitions factories and armouries. The measures taken within the context of this "war against the pubs" revealed themselves particularly unpopular. In any event, as the famous British historian A.J.P. Taylor has written, via such measures, "the state established a hold over its citizens which, though relaxed in peacetime, was never to be removed and which the Second World War was again to increase."[19]

In Canada also, at the time still a British "dominion," that is, an autonomous but not independent member of the British Empire, the government endowed itself with great powers via the *War Measures Act* of August 22, 1914. Here too, it was the intention to keep an eye on the potentially troublesome plebeians and, if necessary, to take muscular action against them, from the fact that the planned measures were not only applicable in case of "war and invasion," but also "real or feared insurrection." The government gave itself the right to censor arbitrarily, to arrest and/or deport persons, to take over the systems of communication and transport, to regulate economic activities, to confiscate property, and, not surprisingly, to prohibit strikes for the duration of the war. With this law, which gave the government "a seemingly unlimited and unchecked capacity for repression," the Canadians lost "much of the partial liberty [they] once enjoyed," at least if we may believe the Canadian pacifist F.J. Dixon. According to certain historians, however, the *War Measures Act* was applied "with remarkable restraint." In any event, it is certain that on the basis of this law countless ordinary Canadian citizens who hailed from enemy countries such as Austria-Hungary were deprived of their property and civil rights and interned. And in 1917 and 1918, the law would also be invoked to persecute socialists, pacifists and, of course, Bolshevists. (After the Russian Revolution, the *War Measures Act* would be made even more repressive, e.g., by the addition of a prohibition on joining socialist or communist organizations.) In Canada, this law remains in the statutes today. In 1970, during the so-called October Crisis, Prime Minister Pierre Elliott Trudeau used the *War Measures Act* to deploy troops against Quebec separatists. In Britain too, the government would continue after the Great War to use its powers under DORA, mostly as a handy weapon to deal with social troubles; DORA would be invoked above all to break strikes, for example in 1921, 1926, 1948, 1949, 1955, 1966, and even later.[20]

In Germany, Austria-Hungary, and France, the governments that were in place in 1914 similarly consolidated and aggrandized their powers by means of a de facto suspension of parliamentary activity — virtually the only form of *democratic* political activity — and the proclamation of a state of siege. In France, shortly after the outbreak of the war, the government declared a state of siege, thus giving itself the means to govern by decree for an undetermined period of time. (The state of siege would only be lifted on October 12, 1919.) Under those circumstances, parliamentary elections became redundant and were no longer held. The country's ordinary citizens, who were called upon to go to war to defend democracy and liberty, were thus deprived of many of their own liberties and democratic rights, and found themselves "excluded from the political arena, even more so than in the past." On August 5, 1914, France also witnessed the introduction of a particularly severe form of censorship, symbolized by an old woman manipulating big scissors and referred to as "Anastasia."

It is noteworthy that all these measures were based to a large extent on laws dating back to 1849 and 1878, in other words to the "good old days" before the democratization process had accelerated significantly on account of the emergence of socialist parties. The new measures that could be introduced thanks to the war, then, did not just freeze the status quo of 1914, but entailed a kind of return to the more authoritarian times and systems of the past.[21] As far as the elite was concerned, the wheel of history had reversed itself and was turning again in the "right" direction. At the same time, the elite seized the opportunity offered by the war to transfer even more authority to its traditional power bastions, still virtually unsullied by democratization in 1914. The paramount beneficiary of this process was the army, whose generals and top commanders were typically aristocrats and, to a lesser extent, members of the upper-middle class. In any event, the army was an institution that had remained hermetically closed to outsiders such as politicians and especially members of parliaments, commoners for whom the generals felt nothing but contempt, especially when they turned out to be socialists and other representatives of the lower orders. (The British general Haig, for example, and quite a few of his colleagues would despise Prime Minister Lloyd George as the product of the dreaded democratization process, as "that mass man.")[22] With the outbreak of war, and above all thanks to the state of siege proclaimed virtually everywhere, the army suddenly benefited from an enormous increase in authority, also in purely civilian matters. In Britain, for example, violations of government decisions based on DORA could now cause one to be dragged in front of special *military* tribunals. This happened to Keir Hardie, the pacifist leader of the ILP.

In France also, the army received broad powers of a nonmilitary nature; for example, the power to suspend periodicals. And the commander-in-chief, Joseph Joffre, may well have become known as "papa Joffre" because, when the war started, he acquired the same kind of "patriarchal" — and, according to certain historians, quasidictatorial — powers over all Frenchmen that every *pater familias* had exercised over his own family during the prewar *Belle Époque*. The French army commanders relished the power they had now that it was war, the more so since, not so long before, at the time of the Dreyfus Affair, they had lost some of the authority and prestige they had traditionally enjoyed to the advantage of the detested politicians in the parliament. And so they no longer bothered to dissimulate their contempt for the civil authorities as they had had to do before the war. Conversely, the government ministers displayed the greatest respect for the generals, who had suddenly acquired "the status of infallible Gods of Thunder in all the warring nations." In 1915, when Italy entered the war, the army's commander-in-chief, Luigi Cadorna, was to become "the undisputed boss of Italy during twenty-nine months," with powers over life and death, as the Italian historian Angelo Del Boca has written.[23]

As for Germany, when the war started the army was already accountable exclusively to the person of the Kaiser and in no way to the Reichstag. Even so, its powers were immediately enlarged. Symptomatic of this was the fact that it was an officer of the army high command, and not Chancellor Bethmann-Hollweg, who drafted the declaration by which Emperor Wilhelm II announced the war to his people. And within the framework of the general mobilization, Germany's regional military authorities received the power to "limit individual liberties, confiscate property, censor periodicals, inspect the mail, and arrest dissidents" — and also, just as in Britain, to prohibit the sale of alcohol and to close pubs. These were exactly the kinds of advantages that the elite — not only in Germany, but elsewhere too — had expected of the war. In the course of the war, the high army command's powers over German civilians were to become so vast that historians have described the situation as a military dictatorship, a "silent" dictatorship whose protagonists were the generals Paul von Hindenburg and above all Erich Ludendorff. During the last years of the war, Ludendorff would be the most powerful man in Germany. "In practice," writes Niall Ferguson, "Ludendorff came to be the sole master of German strategy, and much else besides."[24]

It is also symptomatic that all the territories conquered by Germany would be administered by the army, while the Reichstag — with its social-democratic deputies and other representatives elected on the basis of universal suffrage — provided no input whatsoever. Occupied Belgium was governed by a military "viceroy," a nobleman of course, Baron (*Freiherr*) Moritz von Bissing. He acted very much as a governor might have acted in an African colony, that is, benefiting from unlimited authority. Like all

German generals, von Bissing was accountable only to the Kaiser and not at all to the Reichstag. Occupied Belgium would thus degenerate into a kind of "police state"; it became a country subjected to a terror regime. But it was primarily the people of the lower orders who paid the price, because the Belgian nobility was treated with respect and benevolence by German officers, who were described by the American envoy Brand Whitlock as "incredible snobs."[25]

Belgium was ruled over by the Germans in a most authoritarian fashion, that is, in the same manner that Germany itself had been ruled before the onset of the democratization process and Bismarck's introduction of universal suffrage (a little like France had been ruled by its absolutist kings before the revolution of 1789). It was this authoritarian system in the style of the *ancien régime* that the *Kronprinz* had briefly dreamed of restoring via a coup d'état in 1913, and it was this system that the German elite — especially the feudal element within this elite — hoped to be able to resuscitate thanks to the war. Viewed in this light, the experiment in occupied Belgium provided a bitter foretaste of what Germany itself could expect in case of a victorious outcome of the war.

The state bureaucracy, consisting of officials that were not elected but appointed — on the basis of their social origin, high education, and devotion to the established order — was another power bastion of the elite within which even more power was discreetly stashed away as soon as the war started. It is noteworthy that among the institutions that benefited from this stratagem were the embryonic secret services which, in countries such as the US, would later evolve in close collaboration with the army into a kind of state within the state, a "security establishment." Britain witnessed the birth of the Secret Service Bureau, later to be known as MI-6 (Military Intelligence, Section 6). It would collaborate closely with the aforementioned Basil Thomson of Scotland Yard as well as the military authorities in the hunt for real or imaginary spies and other subversive elements. Thomson acted as the spider in the centre of this shadowy bureaucratic web. He was an arch-conservative representative of the elite, in reality far less eager to catch German spies than domestic "enemies" such as suffragettes, Irish nationalists, and, last but not least, socialists.

In other belligerent countries too, secret services were established and made use of spies, informants, and even agents provocateurs in order to combat socialists, pacifists, and other dissidents. In France, for example, employers and the prefects of districts such Le Tarn and l'Aveyron hired infiltrators, known as *mouchards*, or "snitches," to spy on the unions. In Germany use was made of what were called *V-Leute*, with the V referring to the term *Vertrauensperson*, "trusted person" or *Verbindungsperson*, "liaison agent." It has been said that this approach was a prime illustration of the "power needs of the rulers." It was a means to involve not only the army, but the entire population in the gargantuan effort, and to use all available methods, as was required to win the war. (In 1919 in Munich, Hitler would be put to work as a *V-Mann* by nationalist officers of the German army.) In Germany there also gradually emerged the theory and practice of what would be called "total war" (*totaler Krieg*), "people's war" (*Volkskrieg*), and/or "war for existence" (*Existenzkrieg*).[26]

The development here described amounted, at least *grosso modo*, to a return to forms of political and social systems Europe had known before the start of the process of democratization. The outbreak of the war, writes the Italian historian of democracy, Luciano Canfora, produced the "shelving" (*accantonamento*) of democracy. Even worse, the war would lead to the appearance of more or less formal forms of dictatorship such as those of Clemenceau, Lloyd George, and Ludendorff, in reality variants of totalitarian systems. As the Italian historian and philosopher Domenico Losurdo has noted, it was during the First World War that numerous features of systems we call totalitarian (and usually associate with fascism and communism), made their first appearance; for example, the use of military tribunals, executions, censorship, intensive control of the population via espionage, shameless propaganda, witch hunts against spies, and even concentration camps for certain ethnic groups. The Great War, writes Losurdo, was the catalyst of the emergence of systems that would be called "totalism" at first, and later "totalitarianism," which many experts in the field as well as historians such as Emil Nolte prefer to blame on the Bolsheviks, whose nasty example was then presumably followed by Nazism and other forms of fascism.[27]

Not only in Germany, but in all belligerent countries, the war would become a "total war," a "people's war," a war in which it was expected that all individuals and classes would make a contribution to the massive effort and the huge sacrifices required to win. But nowhere was the war either "total" or an affair of the "people" in the sense that the lower classes provided the slightest bit of input into the *management* of the war, that is, in the political, military, social, or economic decision-making with respect to the war. In military matters, ordinary people enjoyed no influence whatsoever. On the political level, the possibility of a minor amount of input "from below" was aborted by the suspension of parliamentary activity. And, by joining the sacred union, the socialist parties as well as the trade unions had given carte blanche to the elite, ensconced more solidly in all power centres of the state than ever before, to make decisions as it pleased with respect to social and economic policy for the duration of the war — presumably for the benefit of all, it goes without saying. (The British historian John H. Horne has noted that the role of socialist parties and trade unions as "advocates of economic and social change" was suspended in 1914 for an indefinite period of time.)[28] It was the intention that everything — wages, working conditions, etc. — would remain unchanged. For the duration of the war, a truce would be observed in the class conflict that had characterized the prewar years. Later, after the common victory over the exterior enemy, the conflict against the interior enemy, the class enemy, could be resumed, presumably with greater chances for success — or so they convinced themselves in the camp of the socialist and trade union leaders.

Ordinary citizens such as workers, peasants, and craftsmen had nothing to say in how the war was run; conversely, the elite decided everything. In all the belligerent states — even in the most "feudal" ones such as Germany, the Danube Monarchy, and Russia, where the nobility continued to be the governing class par excellence — the industrialists, and above all the big industrialists, that other half of the Siamese twin of the elite, did provide considerable input into the way in which the war was managed. The war would soon reveal itself to be an industrial war, and the industrialists would be needed to ensure that it produced a triumph. They were the experts in industrial production; they would be needed to run the increasingly important economic side of a "total war." They soon emerged as the experts in war management, experts compared to whom state bureaucrats trained in classics at Göttingen or Oxford loomed as hapless dilettantes.[29]

216

In all countries, the governments (and army commanders) continued as before to draw up economic plans, but they increasingly did so in collaboration with representatives of industry, represented by personalities such as Walther Rathenau in Germany, or associations such as the association of employers in the steel industry of France known as *Comité des Forges* or, in Germany, the War Committee of German Industry (*Kriegsausschuß der deutschen Industrie*). In all belligerent countries, this collaboration between state and industry, which according to Niall Ferguson was better synchronised in Germany than in France and Britain, spawned a kind of "state capitalism" in which production was left in the hands of the private sector. On both sides it was considered only normal that the latter would continue to earn profits. This attitude was reflected in the slogan, ascribed to Winston Churchill, according to which even during war it had to be "business as usual!"[30] In any event, the industrialists were expected to help win the war by boosting production, which meant making their employees work harder. But this did not necessarily involve paying them more, because it was crucial to maintain or increase profits. And a golden opportunity to increase worker productivity while keeping wages low, thus increasing profits, was of course created by the promise, made by socialists and trade unionists, not to strike for the duration of the war.

The sacred union amounted to a kind of armistice in the class conflict that had been raging virtually everywhere in Europe until the summer of 1914. But this armistice turned out to be a very one-sided affair. Indeed, from the very start of the war, the employers in all belligerent countries, with the collaboration of the far from neutral state, proceeded to make their employees work harder and longer for wages that remained frozen and in some cases for lower wages, and to suspend, de facto if not de jure, the hard-won rights of the unions. Wages and work hours were no longer discussed, everything was fixed by ministerial *diktat*, whereby the desiderata of the industrialists were of much greater weight than the needs of the anonymous working masses, whose formerly pesky representatives were no longer involved at all in the decision-making processes. From this perspective, the situation was the worst in Russia where, from the very start of the war, workers lost the very modest protections and social rights they had been able to achieve only shortly before. The state gave the employers

217

carte blanche to deal as they pleased with their employees, for example by introducing longer working hours, forcing women and children to work also at night, and using the dreaded weapon of the lockout. "In the name of the defence of the fatherland," writes Alexandre Sumpf, "the [Russian] workers were forced to accept deplorable working conditions without any type of material or even symbolic compensations."[31] In Germany, within the context of the state of siege, the local military authorities suspended all sorts of existing regulations for the protection of the workers, regulations that employers had been forced to introduce before the war, for example with respect to dangerous work and work at night.

In Britain also, the tandem of state and industry conjured up all sorts of ways to violate the rights of unions, no matter how docile and accommodating the latter revealed themselves to be. In France, the employers were able, with the help of the state, to regain ground they had lost before the war on account of pressure from the side of socialists and unions. In numerous French enterprises, for example, the system of "hourly wages" was replaced by the ancient system of "piece wages," typical of the miserable working conditions of the nineteenth-century sweatshops. (The system of "piece wages" was the favoured wage system within the capitalist mode of production, as Marx had already emphasized.) Where the unions opposed such regressive measures, the employers could count on the iron hand of the state to nip protests and strikes in the bud. The repressive arsenal also included censorship of publications and the prohibition of assemblies and demonstrations. Workers who dared to lay down their tools in spite of an official moratorium on strikes, or participated in any other form of working-class agitation, and the workers who, for whatever reason, were denounced by their employers, were promptly drafted into the army, which was a method already used in France in 1910 on the occasion of a railway strike.[32] "The sum of all the concessions made by the workers," combined with the "weakening of the trade unions," writes the French historian François Bouloc, "was also a 'war profit' achieved by the employers, and certainly not one of the least."[33]

The outbreak of war initially spawned an economic crisis accompanied by an increase in unemployment, but all too soon it became clear that the war might last a long time and that victory would require an enormous industrial effort. It followed that industry started to run on all cylinders and that the demand for workers increased; a high percentage of them were demobilized in order to go to work in the factories, above all the munitions factories. In order to prevent the workers from profiting, at the expense of their employers, from the increased demand for labour, which would normally have pushed wages to higher levels, the liberty of movement of the workers was restricted in Germany as well as in France. In order to keep the labour supply sufficiently high and thus to prevent the "play" of supply and demand on the supposedly free labour market from causing wages to rise, women were recruited in massive numbers in all belligerent countries and forced labour was also used where possible. In Germany, for example, thanks to the mobilization of more than five million women workers and the forced labour of Belgian civilians as well as Allied prisoners of war, it proved possible to maintain the total manpower stock until 1918 at virtually the same level as in 1914. Britain and France also mobilized women and, at the end of the war, they would represent between 35 and 40 per cent of the labour force.[34]

The two partners of the Entente Cordiale could not recruit forced labour in territories occupied by their armies, as Germany could do in Belgium and the occupied north of France. On the other hand, they could help themselves to an inexhaustible supply of the ridiculously cheap labour represented by the "coolies" traditionally recruited in India and China to perform dangerous and/or dirty work for the colonial bosses. (The large-scale use of coolies had started about a hundred years earlier, namely after slavery had been abolished in Britain for all sorts of reasons that had nothing to do with philanthropy; the coolie system amounted to a kind of "camouflaged slavery.")[35] In the course of the Great War, coolies would be used to evacuate corpses, clear up ruins, dig trenches, construct military cemeteries, etc. The use of coolies also served to maintain wages at low levels, and it is regrettable but understandable that French and British workers did not cherish warm feelings toward these underpaid and badly treated colonial labourers.

The circumstances described here caused wages to decline from the very first few days of the war, though not at the same rate in all countries and all economic sectors. From 1916–1917, wages would start to rise again here and there, but very slowly, for reasons that will soon be discussed. In spite of this comeback, however, at the end of the war real wages would still be below the levels of 1914; in France, for example, about 15 to 20 per cent below 1914. While nominal wages did rise during the war, they never rose as fast as prices. Among ordinary people, complaints about the "high cost of living" (la vie chère) never ceased to be heard.[36] From the start of the war, prices rose rapidly, and between 1914 and 1916 they would augment by approximately 50 per cent. In Russia, by 1916 prices were twice as high as in 1914 and three times as high as in 1913. After 1916, prices in France and in Britain continued to climb and, at the end of the war, they were twice as high as in 1914. But inflation was even higher in Germany, where in 1918 prices would be four times as high as in 1914.[37]

Determinants of rising prices in all countries at war were factors such shortages of virtually all products; the monetary expansion by which governments sought to facilitate paying back the loans they used (instead of increasing taxation) to finance the war; and of course the considerably greater profits made by the producers, ranging from big industrialists and landowners to small farmers. The price of consumer goods rose particularly sharply, by far the most in Germany and in Austria-Hungary, which were subjected to a naval blockade.[38] In any event, virtually nowhere did nominal wages keep pace with the rise of prices. The result was a decline in the standard of living and growing misery among ordinary citizens, especially among the workers. In France, the government was keenly aware of the people's revolutionary tradition — and the precedent of the Paris Commune — and introduced a relatively generous system of assistance to families of soldiers as well as a moratorium on housing rents. The British government turned out to be less charitable and limited itself to introducing a relatively modest assistance to wives of soldiers as well as pensions for war widows. In the Central Powers, the social situation was much worse, and hunger ravaged the ranks of the lower orders. In Germany and the Danube Monarchy, bread and other foodstuffs had to be rationed as early as 1915; the same measures would only be taken in France in 1917 and in Britain in 1918.[39]

And so it happened that the costs and misery of a war that was neither short nor triumphant, but would last many years, were borne mostly by the same lower classes who also generously provided the necessary cannon fodder. In the meantime, thanks to the moratorium on political and union action, industrialists such as Krupp and Citroën could report gargantuan profits. It would not be long before the workers would become aware of this and start to grumble that "the profits of the war go to the imperialists" while "the proletarians massacre each other for a cause that is not theirs." The notorious term "war profiteers" originated in this context.[40] In France in particular, the land not only of liberty but also equality, the proletarians deeply resented that the weight of the war was shared extremely unequally by the citizenry.

Discontent thus mounted irresistibly among the workers, and not only in France. But for the time being the leaders of socialist parties and unions stuck to the sacred union and refused to organize strikes or protests. They did negotiate with representatives of the state and the employers in the (generally vain) hope of concluding advantageous agreements about wages, working conditions, etc. In France, for example, "tripartite" commissions were set up for this purpose, but they did not achieve much. Having deprived themselves of the strike weapon, the socialists and union leaders always negotiated from an extremely weak position; and the state was not an honest broker, but sided resolutely with the employers, so the contest was always one of "two against one." The workers resisted in their own way, namely by working slowly and less productively, by frequently claiming to be sick, by changing jobs frequently where this proved possible. The employers and the authorities reacted by introducing stricter controls and threatening all sorts of punishments, including sending workers back to the front.[41]

In France, the authorities noted a "rise of discontent" among the workers, and in Germany too, the mood of the workers was worsening rapidly in view of the increasing misery. This growing restlessness within the rank-and-file would force the labour unions of all belligerent countries to abandon the sacred union, either officially or unofficially, to dig up the war hatchet, to authorize and even initiate strikes again, and thus return to the class struggle that their antagonists had never really abandoned.

In its opening stages, during the summer and early fall of 1914, the war seemed likely to provide the aristocratic-bourgeois elite with an unprecedented success, and even a definitive triumph, against its adversary in the class struggle, in other words, a victory in the great domestic conflict. Moreover, the war, which nobody believed might end in defeat, initially appeared certain to realize the elite's boldest imperialist dreams, including territorial gains in Europe and/or overseas. The elite could dream the most extravagant dreams because the socialists, who traditionally opposed the imperialist ambitions of the nobility and of the haute bourgeoisie, had abandoned the battlefield, so to speak, within the framework of the sacred union. Thanks to the war, the nobility and the upper-middle class were thus free to pursue even their most grandiose ambitions; however, the "agrarian" nobility and especially the "industrial" upper-middle class were not monolithic blocs, but mosaics of "factions" that sometimes competed keenly among themselves. These factions entertained ambitions that were sometimes extreme and sometimes rather modest, that would change with the ups and downs of the fortunes of war, and were consequently often contradictory and conflicting in nature. In each country, the state sought to defend and promote the interests of the elite *in general* and was therefore unable to satisfy all demands formulated by the lobbies representing all the factions of the elite. The case of Germany is well known: initially militarily successful, it managed to occupy much enemy territory and seemed to have victory within reach, which awakened enormous appetites on the side of the elite. Moreover, Germany was underprivileged with respect to colonies and therefore extremely ambitious to conquer territories in Europe as well as overseas. Finally, historians happen to be most familiar with the case of Germany, whose archives were cracked open after World War II, and whose exposed ambitions of 1914 received a great deal of publicity at the time of the controversy generated by the work of historian Fritz Fischer.

From the very start of the war, the German chancellor von Bethmann-Hollweg was besieged by various lobbies of the elite, who presented the most extravagant desiderata. His background was partly aristocratic and partly upper-middle class, so both pillars of the German establishment counted on his understanding and sympathy. But it is understandable that Bethmann-Hollweg had to reject the majority of the demands presented to him, and that he thus made a lot of enemies, which would ultimately cost him his job.

We already know what kind of imperialist ambitions motivated the

German nobility. As large landowners, they dreamed above all of great territorial acquisitions, especially in Eastern Europe. But for the nobility the war also proved to be an opportunity to undo "1789." And so we can understand that some German aristocrats proposed to take advantage of the expected victory to restore the Bourbon Monarchy in France, just as had been done in 1814–1815 after the victory over Napoleon. It was also planned to erect vassal states in parts of eastern and southern Europe that would not be annexed directly by Germany; these of course were expected to be monarchies, with as crowned heads junior members of Germany's leading noble families.[42] Far better known, however, are the objectives formulated by Germany's leading industrialists and bankers. In their case too, all sorts of territorial acquisitions in Europe and elsewhere were featured on the lists of desiderata. In the fall of 1914, for example, a group of German industrialists asked the economist Hermann Schumacher to draw up a list of demands that was handed to van Bethmann-Hollweg on November 17, 1914. It proposed the annexation of Belgium and of the French region around Longwy and Briey. These war aims coincided harmoniously with the ambitions of the aristocratic army commanders, who wished to annex bits and pieces of Belgium and France, such as Liège with its forts and the Flemish coast and harbours, on account of their strategic importance.

The government itself became more or less ambitious with the fluctuating military successes of the German army. One had not gone to war with a detailed blueprint for conquest, but rather with a vague but very real appetite for an extension of territory and influence, including the direct annexation of, or establishment of protectorates over, small states, the establishment of vassal states (preferably but not necessarily under German dynasties), the creation of free-trade zones dominated by the Reich, etc. Big dreams were dreamed and much was wanted, but exactly what would be achieved was ultimately to be determined by the successful outcome of the war. Bethmann-Hollweg himself proposed a tentative program of war aims — his famous "September program" (Septemberprogramm) — that was only slightly less ambitious than the war objectives of the most fanatic German nationalists and most voracious industrialists such as August Thyssen, who despised the chancellor as a "wimp."[43]

When the war broke out in 1914, however, the Germans were certainly not the only ones to display an enormous imperialist appetite. In comparison to Germany, Britain, France, and even Belgium had plenty of colonies, but that did not prevent this trio from descending like vultures on German colonies all over the world, especially in Africa. The British and the French invaded Cameroon, a German possession, but its conquest proved less of a sinecure than expected; the German resistance would only cease in February 1916 with the fall of the fort of Mora. As far as the Japanese were concerned, they already demanded in August 1914 that the Germans turn over their concession in China, Qingdao. With respect to imperialist ambitions, British deeds were much clearer than their words. The petroleum of the Middle East was one of the objects of their desires, so it is hardly surprising that in Mesopotamia, as Peter Englund has noted, gently understating London's ambitions in the region,

> British operations . . . began immediately after the outbreak
> of war, even before the Ottoman Empire had sided with the
> Central Powers: their original purpose was the very limited one
> [sic] of securing the oilfields down on the coast.[44]

Neither the German, nor the French, nor the British socialists protested against such initiatives, which demonstrated all too clearly the imperialist character of the war. But they probably hoped that in the long run, after the completion of these projects, some crumbs would fall off the table for the benefit of the plebeians, just as had already been the case with prewar "social-imperialist" projects. It is not unlikely that the elites of the countries involved saw things just as Cecil Rhodes had earlier and believed that imperialist conquests might appease the proletarians and serve to integrate them into the established order.

CHAPTER 13
GENTLEMEN AND PLEBEIANS ON THE WAR PATH

The armies of all belligerent countries have a very pronounced "class character." The simple soldiers are almost exclusively plebeians, mostly peasants. The officers belong to the "better" classes, and a disproportionately high number of generals are aristocrats. The armies reflect not only the class structure but also the class relations of Europe in the so-called Belle Époque . . .

Influenced by nationalism, still heavily permeated by racism and Social Darwinism, countless contemporaries perceived the war that broke out in the summer of 1914 as a "racial war" between Germans and Slavs, between superior Latin nations and barbarian *Boches*, etc. But it makes a lot more sense to define this war, which was of course a conventional war between countries, as a war between classes. The years leading up to 1914 had witnessed a bitter class struggle just about everywhere, and after the outbreak of war this struggle continued to rage unabatedly with the same stakes as before, namely wages, work hours, political and social reforms, etc., and with the same weapons, including strikes, censorship, and so forth.

In other words, the struggle continued for and against the emancipation of the plebeians, for and against democracy. In the framework of the famous sacred union, only the socialist and union leaders, champions of the plebs, had laid down their arms in the illusory hope that after the war the struggle could be resumed under more favourable conditions. The elite, on the other hand, took advantage of the opportunity offered by the sacred union to move onto the offensive, hoping not only to consolidate its position but even to regain political and social terrain lost before the war in the context of the democratization process.

We have already seen that the elite had promoted the *militarization* of society, that is, had worked to reconstruct society on the military model, treating people as one treats soldiers in an army. In an army, the officers, a small number of superior individuals, give orders, and the "subordinates," the inferior "masses," have to obey unconditionally. It had been that way since time immemorial in the armies of the great powers, which, with the sole exception of the British army, were in fact gigantic organizations consisting of millions of members, and so it was in the summer of 1914. In all countries, the elite had managed to shelter the army from "contamination" by the democratization process and to preserve it as an exclusive bastion of elite power, characterized by perfectly hierarchical power relations that reflected each country`s social hierarchy, and by iron discipline. Was such an institution not something magnificent, a model to be emulated by society in general? Let us examine what the great armies of 1914 looked like and how they functioned.

As the American historian Gabriel Kolko has emphasized, all armies, even the most democratic one, the French army, displayed a pronounced "class character." And a German historian, Martin Hobohm, writes that the "classification" within the army's hierarchical pyramid conformed to the social layers of the population."[1] At the bottom of the pyramid, one could find the simple citizens, the little people, the peasants, workers, artisans, members of the working class and the lower-middle class, in other words, the plebeians of the "industrial underclass or rural peasantry," as the British historian Max Hastings has written. They served massively as "foot soldiers" in the infantry, the "weapon" that would suffer the highest losses during the war.

Since factory workers would have to be demobilized to go to work in the factories, the peasantry was everywhere overrepresented among the ordinary soldiers. The Russian army consisted of three-quarters peasants, many of them illiterate, who had no idea why they were supposed to go to war.

In France, the peasantry was overrepresented in the infantry, whose ranks would be decimated. And so a disproportionately high number of peasants would lose their lives, allegedly approximately 673,000, as illustrated by the long lists of names of the "fallen" inscribed on the war memorials one can find even in the smallest villages of France. "It is the countryside," writes a French historian, "that paid the heaviest tribute to the war."[2]

The sergeants and other noncommissioned officers (NCOs) were everywhere from a slightly higher social background. Typically, they were white-collar workers, low-level bureaucrats, or teachers. The officers came primarily from the upper-middle class. They were recruited among the members of the liberal professions, businessmen, intellectuals, and the "educated social classes." They were often people who in civil life had the habit of dealing with subordinates and giving orders. In France, where the army — in spite of presumably democratizing reforms introduced in the wake of the Dreyfus Affair — had remained a bastion of the elite, the officers were generally of bourgeois origin, often of a provincial background, and known for their conservative, right-wing, essentially monarchist and clerical convictions. As for the army high command, during the Great War it would continue to be dominated by royalist and clerical personalities who had studied under the Jesuits, such as de Castelnau and Foch.[3] They had little or no sympathy or respect for the plebeians who were their subordinates and to whom, during the socially turbulent prewar years, they had often needed to teach lessons on the occasion of strikes and demonstrations. Even when they developed a measure of sympathy for their underlings — as in the case of Colonel Dax in *Paths of Glory*, a lawyer by profession — they looked down on them in the same way they had done in civil life. This found a reflection in the French officers' paternalist habit of calling their men "kids" (*[mes] petits*), "children" (*[mes] enfants*), or "little guys" (*petits gars*), and of addressing them with the traditional haughty "my man" (*[mon] petit bonhomme*), using the familiar *tu* while the men used the respectful *vous*. The German generals and other officers also frequently addressed their men with "my children," which was not appreciated by the soldiers. In the Belgian army, many soldiers expressed resentment at being called "children" and being treated accordingly. On one occasion one of them loudly asked: "Why do they treat us like children, while we fight like men for our country?"[4]

The British army traditionally featured a strict apartheid between the officers and the "other ranks" or simply "the men," in other words, the ordinary soldiers, but also the NCOs, and this apartheid corresponded neatly with the segregation that prevailed in British society between the nobility and the upper-middle class and the urban and rural plebeians among whom the NCOs and simple soldiers were recruited. Until 1871 the upper class enjoyed a total monopoly over the officer corps because a commission still had to be paid for. In 1914 this was no longer the case, but the officers were very poorly paid, so that it was impossible to become an officer unless one has alternative, "independent," or "private" sources of income, preferably the rents paid by tenant farmers. Consequently, the British army officers were virtually without exception genuine gentlemen, that is, aristocrats or members of the upper-middle class, who formed a most exclusive coterie, with "status conferred by birth and education." Of an officer, it was automatically assumed that he was also a gentleman, and gentlemen who joined the army automatically became officers. During the war, members of the lower orders would occasionally be promoted to the rank of officer, thus becoming "temporary gentlemen"; being allowed to sip gin and tonic in the company of their "betters" in clubs strictly reserved for officers, they would simultaneously adopt the language, manners, and of course the way of thinking of the upper class. In the course of the Great War, on account of the high losses suffered by the officer corps, an increasing number of members of the "*polloi*," including many men who would not normally have been considered to be "officer material," would in fact become "temporary gentlemen."[5] While members of the lower orders might occasionally become officers, military regulations strictly prohibited "any negro or person of colour" from doing so.[6]

In addition, one did not advance on the basis of talent or merit but via recommendations by influential fellow gentlemen. It is thus hardly surprising that a British officer would report for duty in his private car, accompanied by a personal servant, a "batman," sarcastically referred to by Australian soldiers as a "bumbrusher," who polished his boots, helped him to shave, etc. Sometimes the officer also brought an assistant to look after his horse and to cook and serve his meals, a personal secretary, and in some cases a woman, not necessarily his wife, and not necessarily an upper-class woman or "lady." In the French army too, the officers often enjoyed the services of a batman, known in French as *une ordonnance*. An officer described his *ordonnance* as follows:

> *He carried my belongings whenever we went to the trenches,*
> *including a little wooden box full of books that I called my*
> *library. He slept on the straw, under my bed, like a good*
> *guard dog, he looked after all my little needs, accompanied me*
> *on all my rounds.*[7]

In the British army, the ordinary soldiers were known as Tommies. The nickname Tommy Atkins, or more generally just Tommy, had been used to refer to British soldiers as early as the eighteenth century, but was to become universally known and used during the Great War. It amounted to a semantic reflection of the way the gentlemen of the officer corps looked down on their plebeian underlings. "Tommy" referred to a male servant, whatever his real name may have been; female servants were similarly referred to as "Betty." The British army's upper-class types, incidentally, were known as "Nigels," "Ruperts," or "Rodneys."[8] The soldiers of the other armies also had nicknames. For the German soldiers, known as the *Boches* to the French, the British used the names Fritz and Jerry, and sometimes Alleyman, a bastardization of the French word for German, *Allemand*, but with a distinct pejorative flavour, namely that of "denizen of an alley." The term alley conjured up the dark alleys of working-class districts in Britain's big cities as well as the trenches of the battlefields of northern France and Belgium. As far as the French were concerned, an American soldier was a Sammy, a name that was undoubtedly inspired by Uncle Sam; the Americans did not like this nickname, probably because it conjured up black Americans, and they preferred to be called Yankees or Yanks. Collectively, the men of the American Expeditionary Force (AEF) were also referred to as Doughboys, a term that had originated during the American-Mexican War of 1846–1848, but whose significance is unclear. As for the Australians, they were known as the Diggers.[9]

In contrast to their British colleagues, the officers of the armies of the

Empire's dominions were generally not of upper-class background. The reason for that was that over there, especially in Australia, originally a penal colony, there existed no upper class that might have automatically yielded officers. The officers of what were known as the "colonials" were thus usually men of a modest, even lower-class background who had worked their way up through the ranks, and this produced a kind of egalitarianism between officers, NCOs, and ordinary soldiers. The British officers were shocked when they saw how an Australian colleague might be addressed by his subordinates with his first name instead of the respectful "Sir." Conversely, the Australian soldiers detested the British officers.[10]

Countless British officers had been educated in Britain's elitist and very expensive public schools. (During the recruitment of officers, it was often made very clear that priority would be given to graduates of these schools, benefiting from a "good appearance and address.")[11] Homoerotic relationships, platonic or not, often flourished among the students of these schools, relationships in which typically one of the senior boys, or a teacher, developed a "crush" on a younger student. During the war, officers frequently experienced similar sentiments vis-à-vis subordinates, preferably handsome young men, "fair-haired or (better) golden-haired," and tried to find ways to keep them in their company. For soldiers, this could prove to be a way to exchange the hardships of the trenches for a sinecure at a relatively safe distance from the front. A British officer later provided this testimony:

> My personal runners and servants were usually chosen for their looks; indeed this tendency in war to have the prettiest soldiers about one was observable in many other officers; whether they took more advantage than I dared of this close, homogeneous, almost paternal relationship I do not know.[12]

The paternalism displayed by British officers vis-à-vis ordinary soldiers, more or less tinged with homoeroticism, was reflected in the terminology used while speaking to subordinates. Normally, the soldiers were addressed with the term "men." Socially, this parlance was in fact far from neutral, as the men were supposed to respond with the respectful "sir," but sexually, it was definitely neutral. If an officer entertained warm feelings toward his men, he addressed them as "boys"; and "lads" was used in the case of particularly warm feelings toward subordinates who were "potential lovers."[13]

While in all countries the plebeians were recruited as simple soldiers in the infantry, the aristocrats, traditionally associated with the horse, a supposedly "noble" animal, converged in 1914 to the cavalry to serve as officers, as they had always done. This was of course the case in the empires of the Hohenzollerns, the Habsburgs, and the Romanovs, but things were no different in republican France. In France, being able to ride a horse was a requirement for officers, so that most ordinary Frenchmen did not need to apply. (Of the Jews, it was said that they could not ride a horse, so that they could not become officers; if a Jew like Dreyfus did manage to become an officer, it was automatically assumed that he was a crypto-German!) In Britain, the officers were not only poorly paid, but in the cavalry officers had to pay out of their own pocket for the high cost of keeping a horse, joining a polo club, etc., so that only members of the elite qualified.[14]

In virtually all the armies of the world, the generals and other superior officers, and certainly the members of the high command, belonged to the nobility or, at the very least, to the upper levels of the haute bourgeoisie. There had never been any question of democratization of the high ranks of the military apparatus. In most countries, ancient feudal conditions continued to prevail in this respect; in other words, the nobility was all-powerful. In the German Reich, for example, the generals and the field marshals were almost exclusively gentlemen of noble origin, and above all Prussian aristocrats sporting names starting with "von." In view of the recent quantitative expansion of the army, however, there were simply not enough aristocrats to meet the rising demand for officers, and consequently more and more representatives of the upper-middle class had to be admitted. In Germany too, a career as an officer was prestigious but required an independent income, and a promotion was only feasible for those who completely internalized the aristocratic ethos. Consequently, Jews and any citizens nurturing social-democratic sympathies were nowhere in sight. The situation was hardly different in the Danube Monarchy or Russia. There too, the officer corps — and the summit of the military hierarchy in particular — generally represented the feudal element in its most concentrated form and the top commanders were aristocratic scions of old families of large landowners. In

1914, 90 per cent of all Russian generals were aristocrats.[15] In Britain, the highest level of the military hierarchy was accessible only via the elevator of social connections and recommendations by persons of great power and influence. The result was that the quasi-totality of British generals belonged to the upper class. Traditionally, moreover, it was officers of the most aristocratic weapon, the cavalry, who ascended to the high army command. It would not be a coincidence that the commanders-in-chief of the British army during the Great War, French and Haig, were both cavalry men.

In comparison with the British generals, without exception gentlemen of high degree, the milieu of the French generals loomed like a nest of plebeian sparrows. In the early stages of the war, General John French wrote in a letter addressed to Lord Kitchener, the Minister of War, that he found his French colleagues to be "a low lot, and [that] one always had to remember the class these French generals mostly come from."[16] Despite this, the French generals also came from virtually exclusively elitist backgrounds, and in many cases from the nobility. (Of noble origin were, for example, the generals de Castelnau, de Langle de Cary, Franchet d'Espèrey, de Trentinian, de Maud'huy, and de Villaret.) But it is true that the summit of the French military hierarchy was not quite as 24-carat upper-class as the British high command. In any event, the French generals did not seem to experience any difficulty interacting with the exclusively aristocratic homologues of their Russian ally, who apparently turned out to be a little less snooty than the British generals who we are now supposed to believe fought for democracy.

Arno Mayer has described as follows the situation in the high levels of the European armies:

> With few exceptions, the topmost generals were of high birth,
> and those who were of common lineage had long since adopted
> the ethos, mentality, and carriage of the exalted world in
> which they had risen . . . Within these long-standing military
> establishments all officers, regardless of social origin and class
> identification, embraced the traditional social, religious, and
> cultural outlook. As they moved up in the hierarchy, officers
> also acknowledged their conservative or reactionary political

valuations . . . There was little if any chance for officers of
overtly liberal or democratic persuasion to reach a high rank,
since deviants from the conservative norm were discreetly
screened out.[17]

It is therefore hardly surprising that in all belligerent countries, the generals looked down on the plebeians with sentiments that varied from indifference to contempt, and that they felt nothing but repulsion for pacifists, socialists, trade union leaders, liberal politicians who did not share their own reactionary opinions — and for democracy, including its most modest manifestations. This was certainly the case in Germany, in Austria-Hungary, and in Russia, but also in Britain, and even in republican France, where one of the reactionary generals was a certain Philippe Pétain, who would later, with Hitler's assistance, install in France a dictatorship inspired by ideas and institutions predating the revolution of 1789.[18]

CHAPTER 14
FALL 1914: DISILLUSION

During the fall of 1914 the enthusiasm of August, which had not been as great as generally believed, gradually evaporates in all countries, to be replaced by disappointment, despondency, and disillusion. Determinants of this development are unexpected military setbacks, unprecedented losses, and the fact that the war drags on without end in sight instead of finishing quickly and triumphantly. War propaganda, no matter how aggressive, cannot remedy the situation . . .

As far as the elite was concerned, the war had started in the summer of 1914 under particularly favourable auspices. On the "home front," the sacred union put an end to social agitation. And on the military front, the situation was initially nothing less than wonderful. The armies featured perfectly hierarchical relations. Power was safely concentrated in the hands of the elite. The popular masses, whose rise had earlier inspired so much fear, were now under control. There they were, admittedly in huge numbers, but uniformed and neatly lined up in rows, docile as lambs and ready to receive and implement whatever orders they might receive from their "superiors." It was a unique opportunity to teach the plebeians discipline, morality, and respect for their superiors, and to transform a seditious and dangerous "mass" into a malleable human material. The Social-Darwinist baptism of fire in war would cause them to shed their presumed socialist materialism or petty-bourgeois mediocrity and cause them to be reborn as disciplined, ascetic, and patriotic subjects of some crowned head or, as in the case of France, as loyal citizens of the republic.

It soon became obvious, however, that the war was not at all as it had been imagined. It was not a romantic adventure or a kind of sport; it was not a simple matter of marching off to battle, coming face-to-face with the enemy, attacking him with the bayonet, and emerging victorious from the encounter. Many had not taken into account the murderous nature of modern weapons, above all machine guns and artillery, which caused veritable bloodbaths. Of all wounds, mortal or not, inflicted during the Great War, approximately 60 per cent would be caused by artillery fire, 34 per cent by bullets, and only 0.3 per cent by close-range weapons such as the bayonet. Experiencing combat thus generally meant being fired at by cannon, "coming under fire," and participating in combat for the first time became known as a "baptism of fire."[1] Tens of thousands of soldiers perished without having seen the enemy, mowed down or cut to pieces by bullets or shells fired from kilometres away. (The German field artillery had a range of fourteen kilometres and could fire with great precision, thanks to information received from observers in airplanes.) As for committing acts of heroism, there were very few opportunities for such a thing, as the heroes fell like flies together with the cowards, without the least semblance of glory, on the so-called "fields of honour" stretching from the Flemish coast to the distant Carpathian Mountains. "This way of waging war is horribly sad and monotonous," wrote a member of the French army, who continued:

> There is no life, no enthusiasm. Artillery duels of which we are powerless witnesses. Suffering losses without really fighting, when shells suddenly rain down on us. Stinking carcasses of horses, the cries of the wounded all night long, death, mud, blood . . . This is not what I had dreamed of.[2]

"The age-old myths of military heroism and the more recent projections of national pride had collided with the bare face of war as technology and industrialization," writes the author of a study of war and virility.[3]

On all sides, the losses were enormous, but above all on the side of the French, whose red caps and trousers and blue jackets proved to be wonderful targets for German machine guns and rifles. Conversely, in the bright light of August and the clouds of dust, the French soldiers could hardly see the approaching Germans, camouflaged in field-grey (*feldgrau*) uniforms, until they were about fifty metres in front of them. The British troops were also better camouflaged, namely in khaki ("khaki" being an Indian word meaning "tissue"). The Austro-Hungarian troops wore grey uniforms, like the Germans, the Russians were camouflaged in brown. The Belgians initially wore blue uniforms, but moved to khaki in 1915. It was likewise in 1915 that the French switched to camouflaged gear in the shape of "horizon-blue" uniforms.

The French suffered almost 300,000 killed or wounded during the first month of the war. In this context, August 22 was the blackest day of the war, on which the French army suffered more losses than any other army before or since: 27,000 killed, plus wounded, captured, and missing in action. The total of French casualties — that is, the combination of men killed, wounded, missing, or taken prisoner — from August to the end of December 1914 amounted to more than one million, including approximately half a million men killed. The French generals tended to order massive numbers of their soldiers to attack the Germans, who were not only armed with machine guns and field artillery, but were also sheltered in deep trenches, something the French would long consider to be an unchivalrous way to fight; but trenches were a military innovation that would be associated forever with the memory of the Great War.[4]

Within the framework of the Schlieffen Plan, however, the Germans also had to attack frequently, and so they too suffered grievous losses, even at the hands of the small and insignificant Belgian army. In what would be called the Battle of the Silver Helmets, for instance, fought at Haelen on August 12, considered as "the very last cavalry charge, sword in hand, in Western Europe," the Germans suffered nearly one thousand casualties, mostly proud cavalrymen wearing shiny steel helmets, hence the name. Even earlier, the German attack against the Belgian forts of Liège had been repulsed with considerable losses, and the conquest of that city was to cost the Germans no less than 5,300 men killed and wounded. The Germans not only found it necessary to bring in their biggest artillery pieces, Krupp's infamous "Big Berthas," but also, starting on August 5, to send Zeppelins to drop bombs on Liège, which cost the lives of nine civilians; it was the "first aerial bombardment of a city in history." The achievement of the Belgians in defending Liège was celebrated as a victory in Brussels and in Paris, where the Rue de Berlin was rebaptized Rue de Liège and where a delicacy combining coffee with ice cream and whipped cream, Viennese Coffee, would promptly become *Café Liégeois*. On the other side of the Channel, the myth of "brave [or gallant] little Belgium" was born in this context. Conversely, the Germans showed themselves particularly vindictive about the unexpected trouble the Belgians had caused them. They blamed their losses on the action of *francs-tireurs*, armed civilians, who had allegedly attacked their soldiers, and they took revenge by inaugurating a policy of *Schrecklichkeit*; that is, a ruthless and systematic terrorization of the civilian population, consisting of executing innocent burghers, burning down houses, etc. (German historians now explain that certain Belgian army units, notably those of the Civil Guard, wore uniforms that did not look very military, for example featuring shiny top hats, thus creating the impression that these men were armed civilians.)[5] Vis-à-vis small but intrepid Belgium, the mighty German Reich conducted itself like a landowning aristocrat punishing an insufficiently respectful tenant farmer. Here is a comment by a Belgian historian, de Schaepdrijver:

> *A proletarian who did not know his place: Belgium was exactly*
> *that in the eyes of many members of the German officer caste*
> *. . . The latter were a generation of young aristocrats who*
> *considered themselves the armed vanguard of the German*
> *Empire. On the road of their noble mission they had run into*
> *an inconvenient obstacle, namely the insignificant little petty-*
> *bourgeois neighbour, and it had been necessary to teach him a*
> *lesson.*[6]

By the end of the year, approximately one million Germans had either been killed, wounded, reported missing, or taken prisoner; there was hardly a family left in Germany or France that had not suffered some loss. The Austro-Hungarian army received particularly heavy blows at the hands of the Russians and Serbians, against whom Vienna had gone to war so frivolously. It had already begun badly in early August 1914, when an offensive against Serbia, a seemingly light-weight opponent, was repulsed with heavy losses. In September, the armies of the Habsburgs and the Romanovs administered a bloodletting to each other in Galicia that was as savage as it was useless. By October, the soldiers of Emperor Franz-Joseph were "exhausted and low-spirited"; they were only able to "defend [their own] positions and empty their weapons into the brown [uniforms] of attacking Russians." The new recruits who left for the front no longer displayed the slightest trace of enthusiasm; to the contrary, "on their faces, one could read the desperation." Numerous soldiers — and officers — found an excuse for leaving the front; they feigned symptoms of diseases such as cholera, which claimed many real victims on the eastern front on account of inferior food and deplorable hygienic conditions. Finally, countless soldiers belonging to the Czech, Polish, and other minorities deserted or defected to the Russians. (This malaise inspired the famous satirical novel by the Czech Jaroslav Hasek, *The Good Soldier Svejk*.)[7]

By Christmas 1914, the total losses of the Danube Monarchy already surpassed one million, even 1.27 million according to some sources. Of the 450,000 soldiers who had attacked Serbia, more than 273,000 became casualties. But the Serbians themselves had also suffered enormous losses, namely a total of 163,000 men, including 69,000 killed. Of all the belligerent countries, Serbia would suffer the highest comparative losses in 1914–18: 20 per cent of the population would perish. As for the Russians, their losses were as catastrophic as those of the French, especially after the bloody defeats suffered in September 1914 on the East Prussian battlefields of Tannenberg and the Masurian Lakes. There the generals ordered their men to attack in dense formations in the hope of forcing the German defenders to throw in the towel. This caused a newfangled problem on the German side: their machine gunners' field of vision was blocked by mountains of dead and wounded Russians.[8] (As a historian Solzhenitsyn is hopelessly unreliable, but his description of these events in his book *August 1914* is a literary masterpiece.)

The British also suffered heavy losses, for example during the battle fought at Mons, where, on August 23 and 24, 1914, they first encountered the Germans, and the Battle of Le Cateau of August 26, 1914. In Le Cateau, they registered approximately 5,000 casualties, including 700 men killed — more than the British would suffer on D-Day in Normandy in 1944!

— and 2,500 men were taken prisoner. During the retreat from Mons to the Marne, the British suffered 15,000 casualties, and more heavy losses would be endured during the fighting in Flanders in October-November.[9] Approximately one third of the BEF, a professional army of around 80,000 men that was sent to the continent to help stop the German advance across Belgium into France, were reportedly out of action by the end of the year. The Belgian army likewise took a beating during the early stages of the war. About half of the total of 26,000 men who would be killed during the Great War had already perished in 1914.[10] These unexpectedly high losses demoralized the troops of all belligerent countries. Two German historians who have studied letters written by soldiers at the time come to the conclusion that after their "baptism of fire" the soldiers' illusions were shattered and that any enthusiasm they had entertained had gone up in smoke.[11]

The high losses were also due to the prodigality displayed by the generals of all armies with respect to the lives of the plebeians the soldiers happened to be. The generals were not particularly perturbed by the long lists of casualties. Like many other members of the elite, they viewed war as a Malthusian means to cull popular masses that were too numerous anyway. They appeared to believe that plebeian "raw material" needed to be used in copious amounts in order for them, the warlords, to be able to produce victory, and that this human material was in any event virtually inexhaustible. They were "not likely to be particularly sparing of [plebeian] lives," as Arno Mayer has put it.[12] Russian soldiers who had survived the disastrous Battle of Tannenberg complained that their commanders had "acted as if they had at their disposal such millions of men 'that it does not matter how many are thrown to their deaths.'"[13] Haig, commander-in-chief of the British army as of the end of 1915, and other British generals were in fact disappointed and upset when, during an attack, there were relatively few casualties. This was because they believed, as a matter of principle, that the German losses were always higher. (Adam Hochschild cites the case of a British general who, during a supper, proved particularly upbeat because his division had lost a total of 11,000 men during the last months.) But Haig hardly ever visited the wounded because, according to his son, that made him sick. In any event, he managed to convince himself that the wounded were unfailingly "confident, cheery and full of pluck."[14] That the officers found soldiers' lives cheap was also reflected in the fact that it was not unusual for artillery officers to refuse to provide support for the infantry: it was felt to be irresponsible to waste precious shells and to wear out guns in order to save the lives of a bunch of peasants and workers. Incidentally, the artillery all too often fired so carelessly — though not intentionally — that the soldiers often fell victim to what is now euphemistically called "friendly fire." According to Barthas, in 1916, near Verdun, shells fired by the French artillery thus regularly made "numerous victims in our own ranks." A total of 75,000 French soldiers allegedly became casualties of "friendly fire." Finally, it often happened that the artillery shelled its own infantrymen to force them forward during an attack. This happened in Champagne in February 1915, where a general by the name of Géraud Réveilhac gave such an order.[15]

Of particularly low value, in the view of the generals, were the lives of the representatives of the "coloured" peoples who were put at their disposal in the form of colonial troops. This was the case on the side of the British and the French, who recruited soldiers from possessions such as Senegal, Morocco, Algeria, and India. Of these kinds of "primitive peoples," whom it was believed there were just too many on earth, the French general Mangin — a major advocate of the use of colonial troops — stated for example that "life for them is not very important and they are happy to spill their young blood abundantly." As for the British, they preferred to recruit members of colonial ethnic groups which they believed they recognized as "warrior races," such as the Gurkhas from Nepal. And so colonial troops were squandered abundantly, although historians still argue whether the losses of colonial troops were above average or not.[16]

It is generally recognized, on the other hand, that officers, the representatives of the superior classes, suffered disproportionately high losses. There were many reasons for this, some more important than others. During the attacks that proved so deadly, the officers were supposed to be leading their men, and generally they were taller than the plebeian recruits, if only because the elite enjoyed a much better diet. In most armies, also, the officers wore more colourful uniforms than the men; they sometimes looked like "bullfinches," as the Belgian soldiers called their officers, and during the early, mobile stages of the war, the officers frequently appeared on horseback, and the French officers wore white gloves. During an attack, they thus presented an easily recognizable target for the enemy and suffered the consequences. Many officers actually participated in attacks with great courage and even enthusiasm because, as aristocratic or bourgeois members of the elite, they tended to be deeply imbued by romantic notions of heroism and chivalry. The plebeians in uniform, on the other hand, understood all too quickly that they had nothing to gain from this war and therefore had no reason to "give their lives," as the saying goes. Finally, the high mortality of the officers was also due to the disproportionately high rate of suicides: a large number of officers did in fact consider suicide as the only solution to the dilemma presented by their role as intermediaries between their subordinates, whom they knew personally and whose lives they wanted to save but could not if they hoped to produce the military successes their own superiors, the generals and high army commanders, expected from them.[17]

Other than the huge losses, other factors played roles in the great disillusion that overcame the soldiers in the fall of 1914, soldiers who had gone to war in August without enthusiasm but ready to do their duty and confident of victory. First, a large number of them witnessed all sorts of atrocities committed on prisoners of war or civilians — the latter particularly in Belgium, in Serbia, and in the Armenian province of the Ottoman Empire. It is generally known what the Germans wrought in Belgium: a total of 5,500 civilians killed, many deported to Germany, and many houses and even entire cities, such as Louvain, burned to the ground. Less known is that the Austro-Hungarian troops committed similar atrocities, but on a much larger scale. Their victims were Serbian civilians, of whom 3,500 were killed during the two weeks after the start of hostilities. In the autumn of 1914, a Hungarian journalist, Josef Diner-Denes, reported on the "racial war" (*Rassenkrieg*) being waged by the Habsburg authorities: countless South-Slav civilians suspected of pro-Serb sympathies were arrested, crammed into concentration camps, or deported, and tens of thousands of Serbs were executed as "traitors." It was a "systematic policy of extermination" that contributed mightily to the enormous aforementioned Serbian losses during the Great War. A second factor that undermined the morale of the soldiers was the fact that the war did not end in great triumph after a few months, as promised. Even in September 1914, and by December at the latest, the soldiers understood that the war could last a long time and that, for an indefinite period, there would be no question of returning home.[18]

A similar collapse of morale affected the civilians on what would become known as the home front. There too, the outbreak of war in August 1914 was greeted with far less enthusiasm than we have long believed. Nevertheless, high expectations had flared up, and everywhere people had allowed themselves to be convinced that the war would be short and triumphant, that it would bear all sorts of magnificent fruits, even for ordinary people, and that it would lead to the dawn of a better world. But the optimism of August had to give way sooner or later to disappointment and disillusion. The reasons for this were mostly the same as in the case of the soldiers. While in all countries the public was very poorly informed by the authorities and the media about the situation on the front, and while triumphant announcements alternated with nasty tidings and false rumours abounded, the civilians came to understand pretty soon that the military operations were not going according to plan and that heavy losses were involved.

In Germany, the burghers were initially delighted to learn of the rapid advances made in the west, but all too soon unpleasant news arrived from the east, where, on August 20, the Russians crushed German troops at the Battle of Gumbinnen and, according to certain reports, proceeded to "rape and pillage" their way into East Prussia. Suddenly, bad news arrived from France, where the Battle of the Marne had resulted in a major setback for Germany. Conversely, great German victories were unexpectedly pulled out of a hat on the eastern front, namely at Tannenberg and in the Mazurian Lake District. Most depressing, however, was the fact that virtually all cities witnessed the arrival from both east and west of trains full of "silent, bleeding men." German poets, painters, and other artists who witnessed such scenes or who were themselves on the front — Max Beckmann, Ernst Ludwig Kirchner, and Ernst Toller, for example — began in the fall of 1914 to "reconsider their initial enthusiasm [for the war]" and to express their "disenchantment" in their productions, as Ernst Piper puts it.

In the meantime, German morale received a blow through the announcement of a victory of the Royal Navy in the Battle of Heligoland, fought on August 28, 1914. This event showcased the supremacy at sea of the British, forced the German navy to hole up in its ports, and made the Germans fear that their coast might be exposed to bombardments by the Royal Navy and even landings by British troops. Some Germans came to the conclusion that their fatherland could not possibly win a war against Brittania, mistress of the seven seas, and her allies. The authorities responded in October 1914 to the sagging morale by introducing severe censorship, prohibiting discussion of military setbacks in the press; expressing criticism of the country's military and political leaders; and questioning the government's war aims.[19]

The British public had only a very vague notion of the development of the war. Journalists were kept away from the front so the newspapers did not have much to report, but that did not prevent their articles from being "unfailingly cheerful." Reports, occasionally accurate but mostly false, of Russian victories in East Prussia engendered a euphoria that soon gave way to depression as bad news started to come in about the situation in Belgium and France, accompanied by rumours about high British losses there; these rumours were all too soon confirmed by the arrival of trains full of wounded men. The British public thus began to understand that the war was not the sinecure that had been expected, and some representatives of the elite feared, as Max Hastings has written, that one could not continue to motivate "the socially and politically disaffected 'lower orders'" in favour of a war that had been wanted by their superiors of the upper classes. It was feared that "many of our working men may think that, if Germany wins, they will be no worse off than they are now." It was also bad for British morale that on November 1, 1914, during the Battle of Coronel, fought off the Chilean coast, a squadron of the proud Royal Navy was sent to the bottom of the sea by German ships commanded by Count Maximilian von Spee. And on December 16, 1914, German warships were able to shell the coastal towns of Scarborough, Hartlepool, and Whitby, and were able to do so with impunity.[20]

In France, Joffre, at that time virtual dictator of the country, did not permit publication of the heavy losses suffered by his troops. From the very start of the war, he dropped "the veil of secrecy on military operations." Even the prime minister was hardly aware of what was going on at the front. The French public knew little or nothing about the losses suffered by their troops; however, it soon began to transpire that the war was not going well and that the casualties were mounting rapidly. In France too, a telltale sign was the arrival in many cities of tens of thousands of wounded. The French public had already been developing an uneasy feeling when truly shocking news arrived on August 28: on that day it was officially announced that heavy fighting ranged "from the Somme to the Vosges," in other words, deep in French territory. Instead of being able to rejoice in good progress in the direction of Berlin, as had been imagined at the start of the war, another siege of Paris loomed, just as in the "terrible year" of 1870–71. Correctly interpreted as bad portents were the facts that German planes overflew the capital and that on August 30 the government departed for the safety of distant Bordeaux, an example that was followed by many well-to-do Parisian *citoyens*. "Unrest, nervousness, even panic and stupor dominated [in France] in the days before the Battle of the Marne," writes the French historian Annette Becker. However, thanks to the "miracle of the Marne" a catastrophe would be averted, but the the illusions of the early days of the war had definitely been dissipated, for good.[21] The soldier Barthas, who left for the front fairly late, in October 1914, noted the following:

> *There were no happy crowds, full of enthusiasm, like those*
> *that had gathered when the first soldiers departed [in early*
> *August]. No flowers, no blown kisses, no loud applause.*
> *Gone was the short, invigorating, joyous war that had been*
> *announced by the newspapers. The Germans had invaded*
> *France, winter stood at the door, the war promised to be long*
> *and its outcome painful . . . The women dried their tears.*
> *Everybody was sombre and remained silent. The people took*
> *off their hats, as if a bunch of men condemned to death were*
> *marching past.*[22]

Disenchantment also made its appearance in Austria-Hungary and in Russia, countries that had suffered particularly heavy losses and where the population soon came to regard the war as nothing less than a catastrophe. Sigmund Freud, who had joyfully welcomed the conflict, wrote toward the end of 1914 that "these [were] wretched times, this war, which impoverishes as much in spirit as in material goods."[23]

In Russia, in the summer of 1914, the people had gone to war willingly and dutifully, but their "patriotic intoxication," as a German-American historian hyperbolically calls it, "was hardly profound and was not to last very long, especially among the popular masses who had to carry most of the burdens of the war." The war revealed itself to be

> *an insupportable burden for the millions of desperate subjects*
> *of the empire, thrown into the jaws of war with little or no*
> *understanding of, or sympathy for, its objectives . . . The*
> *people of Emperor Nicholas was asked to suffer and die,*
> *not for some noble ideal, but simply because their emperor*
> *demanded it.*[24]

It goes without saying that the disillusion was greatest among the citizens who were themselves directly victimized by the war; for example, seeing their relatives or friends killed, taken hostage, or deported; having their homes destroyed by artillery, looted, or burned down; having to flee far from their homes, etc. But disillusion also set in when it was not possible to deny — as all too many Germans preferred to do — that their own troops committed all sorts of atrocities. The Austrians and Hungarians knew only too well that their soldiers were guilty of nasty crimes whose victims were the Serbian minorities in Bosnia and elsewhere in the empire. Pictures of executions of men and women were publicized by the authorities in the hope of inhibiting acts of resistance, so everybody knew what was going on. While some subjects of Emperor Franz-Joseph undoubtedly felt that the Serbians merited such harsh treatment, "a growing number of [his] subjects recoiled in disgust from the horrors for which [their] gilded warriors were responsible."[25]

Everywhere in Europe, during the years leading up to 1914 and even in the summer of 1914, people had nourished huge illusions with respect to a war that was expected, and even wanted, by many. But instead of relief, deliverance, a rebirth, or other good things that had been hoped for, the war produced a never-before-seen bloodbath and unprecedented misery. This disillusion was reflected in the poem "The Use of War" by the Englishman H.F. Constantine:

When the dark cloud of war burst on the stricken world,
Men said, to solace others and themselves, that from this evil
Good would come; that warring mankind, ennobled by
endeavour
And the hardships and dangers of the war, would come
To a higher level of thought and action. But has that been?[26]

The war brought none of the expected good things but plenty of unexpected bad things, including the prospect of defeat, something that had appeared unthinkable in the summer of 1914.

Secrecy and censorship could not solve the problems. A cold shower of bad news caused the morale of the general population to drop dramatically in all belligerent countries — probably a little earlier and faster within the lands of the Entente, a little later and more slowly in the Central Powers. The authorities therefore deemed it necessary to move to a new, qualitatively higher level of censorship and propaganda. It was openly recognized that the war was a great ordeal, but that there was no alternative, that one had to persevere and hold on until the end — and that a final victory was certain in spite of setbacks.

And so, at the initiative of governments but with the eager collaboration of all sorts of private organizations and personalities, and above all the media, a mighty propaganda machine started to run on all cylinders. A certain number of aspects of this propaganda deserve our attention. First, the defeats of a country's own troops, or those of its allies, were covered by the mantle of silence or, better still, transformed into victories. "The home front never knew with any precision how the war was progressing," writes Modris Eksteins. "Defeats were presented as victories . . . truth became falsehood, falsehood truth . . . Denied factual knowledge, people naturally turned inward. Myths, some of astounding magnitude, were spawned."[27]

The archetypical example of this phenomenon was the transubstantiation of the Battle of Mons, fought on August 23-24, 1914, into a mighty myth. It was an engagement during which the BEF managed to briefly halt the seemingly irresistible German advance, though at the cost of considerable losses. In the British newspapers, this skirmish was fêted as a genuine triumph, made possible by the miraculous intervention of a knight sent from heaven, Saint George, the protector of England, according to some accounts accompanied by angels or, better still, the ghosts of the legendary archers who had turned the tide in favour of England during the medieval battles of Crécy and Agincourt.[28]

Second, everything possible was done to convince the public that this war had not been wanted by "us," but had been unleashed by our enemy, and that it was certain that God was on our side. A struggle was taking place between good and evil, between civilization and barbarism, between our superior and their inferior race. It was a matter of triumphing or perishing. Leaders such as Lloyd George began to present the war in this context as a clash between democracy and dictatorship.[29] In reality, the opposite had happened: the ruling classes had wanted war and had expected that it would stop and reverse the march of democracy.

Third, "we" fought honourably, like medieval knights, while the enemy not only failed to fight chivalrously but committed all sorts of atrocities on peaceful and innocent civilians, including defenceless women and children. Our side fought to put an end to this barbarism. If we did not fight this good fight, if we did not achieve victory in this horrible war, we would all fall victim to such heinous crimes and end up perishing. In this context, the atrocites committed by the Germans in Belgium provided excellent grist for the mill of allied, and particularly of British, propaganda. During their invasion of Belgium (and northern France), the Germans did indeed commit all sorts of atrocities. But in the British press these abominations were exaggerated greatly and supplemented with pure inventions; for example, with stories (and illustrations) of babies nailed to church doors with bayonets. On the German side, on the other hand, the blame was placed on the Belgians themselves, presumably a "savage," "immature" (*unreif*), and "abominable" (*abscheulich*) "race," and in particular on Belgian *francs-tireurs*, who allegedly fired at German soldiers from their houses, and to Belgian women who cut out the eyes of defenceless wounded German soldiers, castrated them, and stole their belongings: did such villainy not deserve to be punished severely?[30]

A fourth theme of the propaganda consisted in assurance that, while the war had admittedly failed to bring good things, a victory certainly would. After the final victory all would be well, and it would only be at that glorious moment that the war would reveal itself as "one of the happiest events in our history." In the meantime, obviously, everybody had to grin and bear it a little longer and do whatever was possible to help achieve the triumphant end to the war.[31]

In the field of war propaganda, the British were the champions. This is understandable, because the British public had always displayed a rather critical attitude toward the war, and pacifists were more numerous and influential across the Channel than in France, Germany, or Russia. Under considerable unwanted antiwar pressure, the British government felt it necessary to establish a special War Propaganda Bureau. As collaborators it recruited all sorts of eminent representatives of the country's intellectual, literary, and journalistic elite, personalities of the calibre of Thomas Hardy, Arthur Conan Doyle, G.K. Chesterton, and H.G. Wells. To them was entrusted the task of eulogizing the war and stimulating enthusiasm for it among a British public that was presumably insufficiently well informed; this was done, *inter alia*, by press stories about the German atrocities in Belgium. Conversely, all forms of pacifism — and of its close associate, socialism — were fought tooth and nail. This was done with particularly great zeal by personalities such as Rudyard Kipling, who condemned pacifists as "human rubbish." Kipling publicly aired his contempt for the Germans, naturally, but also for the Jews, the Irish, and the leaders and members of the trade unions, whom he accused of laziness.

Bellicose propaganda was also mass-produced by the British media in general and in particular by the many newspapers owned by the press magnate Lord Northcliffe, such as the *Daily Mail* and eventually also *The Times*, papers that exercised great influence on the "the classes and the masses," that is, on the upper class as well as the lower orders of the British population. Another famous war propagandist was the aforementioned Horatio Bottomley, owner and publisher of the jingoist journal *John Bull*. He cursed the Germans, referring to them as "Germhuns" — a nasty but potent combination of "germs" and "Huns" — and expressed the desire "to see Germany wiped from the map of the world," so that Britain and France might share its colonies. Bottomley also fired poisoned journalistic arrows at leaders of the Labour Party who opposed the war, such as Keir Hardie and Ramsay MacDonald, whom he accused of nothing less than high treason.[32]

The Great War had been a project concocted by the elite. The elite had expected great advantages from the war, and in the summer of 1914 it seemed that this hope would be fulfilled. But the elite started to worry when, already at the end of the summer and throughout the fall of 1914, the tide of enthusiasm for war proved to be receding rapidly. Not surprisingly, then, it was the elite which tried very hard to restore the sagging morale by means of aggressive bellicose propaganda. The war propaganda was orchestrated from above, but it was aimed first and foremost at the lower orders of society. From the perspective of the elite, the war would bear the expected fruits only if it ended with a victory, and in order to achieve victory the plebeians had to provide the necessary bodies, the necessary cannon fodder. ("The war is for the benefit of the rich," sang the German soldiers, "but the poor have to provide the corpses.")[33] One of the major advantages the elite had expected of the war was the integration of the proletarians into the existing order, thus eliminating the menace — from the viewpoint of the elite — of democratization, socialism, and revolution. If the lower orders — the *classes dangereuses* — turned against the war, this menace would in all likelihood become even greater, with potentially catastrophic consequences.

It was therefore not only logical that, via the media and other private channels, the elite orchestrated and financed war propaganda, and that this pro-war, antipacifist propaganda was simultaneously antidemocratic, antisocialist and anti-union. In Britain, the press barons were particularly active in this field, and a certain number of pro-war organizations, some of them masquerading as workers' associations, such as the British Workers' League, were founded and generously financed by capitalists such as Alfred Milner and Waldorf Astor.

Everywhere, the elite waged systematic and massive propaganda to combat the rising apathy, scepticism, cynicism, and/or pessimism of the public with respect to the war. But the results of these efforts were ambiguous. On the one hand, countless burghers believed much of what was dished out to to them; in Britain, for example, many even believed the fairytale of the angelic appearances during the Battle of Mons. A factor that should not be underestimated is, of course, wishful thinking. People were starved for good news and many desperately wanted to believe that at Mons the British had inflicted a painful defeat on the Germans, that the Russians were steamrolling toward Berlin, that hundreds of thousands of Cossacks had landed somewhere in Scotland and were on their way to lend a helping hand to the allies fighting in France, etc.[34]

It was also helpful that much propaganda lore contained at least some nuggets of truth. The grossly exaggerated stories about German *Schrecklichkeit* in Belgium were credible because the Germans had indeed conducted themselves sadistically there. Moreover, the British public *expected* the Germans to commit atrocities because, in the years preceding 1914, a number of books had been published about fictitious Prussian invasions of Albion, during which great quantities of innocent blood were spilled. That soldiers were capable of bayoneting babies and cutting off people's hands was also believable because it was not long before that the British media had published reports — many of them truthful — of similar bestial acts, committed in the Congo by colonial troops acting on behalf King Leopold II . . . of Belgium![35]

Conversely, a large part of the public in Britain and other countries at war revealed itself sceptical with respect to the flood of bellicose propaganda emanating from the government, the media, the churches, etc. Even more critically inclined were the soldiers who were exposed to the sometimes ridiculous propaganda via newspapers and letters. Much of this propaganda failed to convince, and the soldiers resented the reports about fictitious victories, the supposedly excellent morale of the men at the front, the delicious food served to them, etc. The men despised this kind of "stuffing of skulls" (*bourrage de crâne*), as the French called it, and they also had nothing but contempt for the authorities and the journalists — especially those of the so-called "yellow press" that cranked out this kind of propaganda — and also for the many civilians who believed these stories. They also hated "to-the-end-ism" (*jusqu'au-boutisme*), the appeal to fight "to the end" in spite of the huge losses in order to achieve the questionable objectives for which the war was being fought.[36]

The soldiers were also particularly embittered vis-à-vis prelates and other ecclesiastics who had glorified the war as a "crusade" and who had welcomed it enthusiastically. Not only in France, but in many other countries, the "return to the altars" was never more than a superficial and ambivalent phenomenon. It is true that soldiers and civilians prayed a lot and went to church frequently during the summer of 1914. But nonreligious factors also played a role in this; for example, in the case of soldiers, coercion. German soldiers were often simply ordered to attend Catholic or Protestant services. The same thing happened on the side of the Austro-Hungarians, and of the Russians, where forced attendance at Orthodox services was the rule. Even the soldiers of the theoretically anticlerical French Republic were occasionally officially or unofficially forced to attend religious ceremonies, sometimes musically accompanied by military bands, ceremonies that were considered "ridiculous and irrational" by soldiers such as Barthas.[37] The ordinary British soldiers were generally not very devout and considerably less religious than their officers,[38] but they were often coerced to participate in religious ceremonies and church parades. The lyrics of a popular contemporary soldiers' song, "When this Bloody (or Lousy) War is Over," suggested that one of the things the men looked forward to at war's end was "no more church parades on Sundays."

Fear and hope also played a role. Faith, notes the French historian Frédéric Rousseau, makes it possible to "tolerate the intolerable"; people prayed for fear of death, and "fear caused religious devotion to blossom" is his conclusion. He refers in this context to the case of the Alsatian Dominik (Dominique) Richert, a soldier in the German army, a man whose piety, like that of countless other soldiers, "had been revived by the war." (Richert has left us his war diary, published under the title *Beste Gelegenheit zum Sterben: Meine Erlebnisse im Kriege 1914–1918.*) It was not a coincidence that masses attracted large crowds on the eve of an attack, when the prospect of meeting one's creator was particularly great; perhaps there was no creator, but one just never knows. It is for the same reason that in *Paths of Glory* an agnostic soldier allows himself to be convinced by the chaplain to confess and to pray before being executed. And countless soldiers went to church to please their wives, mothers, or grandmothers. Others considered going to church an opportunity to make eyes at women. In addition, wearing a scapular might imply less a deep Christian devotion than vulgar superstition: whether a scapular or a rabbit's foot did not make much difference as long as it brought luck.

Many members of the military attended religious ceremonies not on account of religious impulses, but because it was a way to strengthen one's membership in a community, to reinforce the ties of friendship and solidarity among the comrades. (It is with the same intention, and not to cause rain to fall, that members of the Hopi nation perform their famous rain dance, as the great American sociologist Robert K. Merton has explained.) Participating in a mass tended to satisfy a psychological rather than a religious need: by their presence, the soldiers proclaimed and reinforced their membership in a community, a "community of suffering."

The famous "return to the altars" turned out to be a fleeting phenomenon, one that went up in smoke as soon as it became evident that the war would not be short. Very soon a countercurrent developed, and even during the summer of 1914 the flame of religious fervour was flickering among soldiers as well as civilians — not coincidentally at the same time as the fires of "patriotic enthusiasm," that had presumably burned so brightly in the early days of the war, were dying down. French army chaplains, earlier so enthusiastic but already disappointed as fall set in, started to bemoan the "religious indifference of the great majority of the French people."[39]

The British soldiers, convinced Anglicans (at least in theory), certainly proved to be less religious than their German, Russian, and French counterparts. But they too, in August 1914, had been seduced by the unctuous phrases of their prelates. And they too, during the fall of that same year, displayed more and more disappointment and resentment vis-à-vis the Anglican authorities. The latter tried in vain to explain that God's ways are unfathomable and that one had to suffer patiently and wait for him to finally decide to let justice triumph. The churchmen attempted to convey this message to the faithful in need of consolation by promoting a hymn by William Cowper, an eighteenth-century poet, entitled "God Moves in a Mysterious Way":

> His purposes will ripen fast,
> Unfolding every hour;
> The bud may have a bitter taste,
> But sweet will be the flower.[40]

But such responses could not prevent cynicism from mounting in the ranks of the British soldiers. The journalist Charles Edward Montague described the situation as follows:

> In the first weeks of the war, most of the flock had too simply
> taken on trust all that its pastors and masters had said [about
> the war] . . . Later, they were out to believe little or nothing
> — except that in the lump pastors and masters were frauds.[41]

In the autumn of 1914, a poem by Harold Begbie, "War Exalts," provided a particularly biting comment on the ecclesiastical message that the war amounted to a kind of crusade purporting to purify humanity, as countless prelates had sought to assure the faithful:

> War exalts and cleanses: it lifts man from the mud!
> Ask God what he thinks of a bayonet and dripping blood.
>
> By war the brave are tested, and cowards are disgraced!
> Show God his own image shrapnel'd into paste.
>
> Fight till tyrants perish, slay till brutes are mild!
> Then go wash the blood off and try to face your child.[42]

The war brought many combatants to the conclusion that God did not care about his human creatures and the awful things they did to each other. "God He takes no sort of heed. / This is a bloody mess indeed," is how the well-known English composer and poet Ivor Gurney put it succinctly in a famous verse of his, in "The Target." And some concluded that there simply was no God; the feminist and pacifist author Vera Brittain, for example, in the poem "August, 1914," alluding to the pre-1914 notion that war would bring people back to God:

> God said, "Men have forgotten Me:
> The souls that sleep shall wake again,
> And blinded eyes be taught to see."

So since redemption comes through pain
He smote the earth with chastening rod,
And brought destruction's lurid reign:

But where His desolation trod
The people in their agony
Despairing cried, "There is no God."[43]

War propaganda was in many ways counterproductive. The majority of the soldiers and a large part of the civilians started to doubt everything the authorities and the media told them, so that they refused to believe not only the lies, exaggerations, and distortions, but even truthful information. What also had a negative effect was "the baroque language and spurious religiosity with which it was marketed." The public felt that it had been fooled and cheated, and was offended. "A lasting revulsion emerged among some of the audience, who felt that they had been duped," writes Max Hastings of the people of Britain. And so, more and more antiwar voices started to be heard, critical of the war, its objectives, the way the war was being waged by the military and political authorities, and even of the allies. In October 1914, for example, the British periodical *New Statesman* reported that the public displayed increasing hostility to the alliance with autocratic Russia; mention was also made of "suggestions . . . that the war was deliberately started by reactionary forces to avoid social reforms," which certainly contained a major kernel of truth. The British elite was shocked that the public did not appear to attach much credit to the official reason for the country's entry into the war, namely the defence of "gallant little Belgium." One of the cabinet members, Lloyd George, deemed it necessary to conjure up new factors, and explained that the war was a crusade against militarism.

A considerable and growing part of the popular masses was progressively "radicalizing," as Gabriel Kolko has put it, in all belligerent countries, and behaving less credulous, and also less respectful, toward the elite that was understood to have wanted this war. "Quite early in the war, there were signs [in Britain] of a trend which became progressively more pronounced," notes Max Hastings, "namely a decline of social deference, to the dismay of its former beneficiaries."[44] The crude bellicose propaganda was supposed to serve as an antidote to pacifism, but in this respect it could also be dysfunctional, as was the case in Germany. In the summer of 1914, the pacifists there had remained silent in contrast to their comparatively numerous and noisy counterparts in Britain, and they had believed what they were told by the authorities, namely that for Germany the war would be purely defensive. But when, in the fall of 1914, it became known that the aristocratic and especially industrial elites entertained plans for large-scale expansion, pacifism reared its head. Increasingly, the demand was heard to put an end to what propaganda could not prevent from being unmasked as a war of conquest and a senseless bloodbath. A formal pacifist lobby was established, the *Bund neues Vaterland* or "League for a New Fatherland." On the far side of the Rhine, pacifism was associated with democracy and socialism, and the desire for peace went hand-in-hand with the demand for reforms, reforms in the sense of parliamentary democracy but also more radical forms of democratization; in other words, demands for the kinds of political and social changes that the German elite had hoped to eliminate via the instrument of war. It was with such reforms in mind that bourgeois pacifists started to collaborate with reformist social-democratic leaders such as Bernstein. This alarmed the elite and above all the military authorities, who proceeded to drastically censor all pacifist publications.[45]

In the meantime, the mighty fortress of the *Burgfrieden* was beginning to crumble. Within the SPD, the radicals of the "Rosa [Luxemburg] Group" who in August had only reluctantly voted for the war credits, became increasingly recalcitrant and less and less inclined to conform to party discipline. The feminist Clara Zetkin was one of this group; in November 1914, she called on all socialist women to agitate against the war and for peace. (In March 1915, Zetkin would organize an international conference of female socialists in Bern, capital of neutral Switzerland.) On December 2, 1914, the Reichstag had to approve war credits a second time, and this time Liebknecht voted against. He took advantage of the opportunity to explain that "the war was an imperialist war . . . an attempt to demoralize and destroy a workers' movement that had been growing rapidly." At the end of 1914, together with Rosa Luxemburg, Clara Zetkin, and other radical social-democrats, he founded the Spartacist League (*Spartakusbund*) and started to publish the "Spartacus Letters," pamphlets in which one could read that "the real enemy can be found within the country." And so, in spite of his parliamentary immunity, Liebknecht would be arrested and sent to the eastern front. He refused to fight and was made to perform all sorts of forced labour, including burying the dead. On account of his poor health, he was freed in the fall of 1915, but he would be arrested again in 1916, and this time he would be convicted and imprisoned for "treason."[46]

CHAPTER 15
FRIENDS AND ENEMIES

In all the armies there exists a strict apartheid between the officers, representatives of the upper class, and their subordinates, almost exclusively proletarians and other members of the lower orders. The majority of the officers look down on the simple soldiers with contempt and treat them accordingly. Conversely, they are despised as enemies by the soldiers. The official "foe," on the other hand, is not considered by many of the men to be a genuine enemy. This is illustrated by meetings and fraternizations between allied and German soldiers, of which the famous "Christmas truce" of December 1914 is merely the most spectacular example . . .

We generally think of a war as a "black-and-white" affair, with ourselves and our allies on one side and the enemies on the other. The Great War certainly seems to fit into this mould. A frontline neatly separated us and our allies, the "good guys," from the "bad guys" on the other side, mostly the Germans but also the Austro-Hungarians and the Turks, people about whom we knew precious little. The movie *Paths of Glory* includes an episode somewhere on the western front, from the viewpoint of French troops. As spectators, we identify spontaneously with these *poilus*; they are our friends. Bad guys also appear in the movie, but they are not Germans: in the entire film, not a single Boche is to be seen. It is only at the very end that a German person appears on the screen, but it is a young woman, and there is nothing hostile about her.[1] Nevertheless, the film certainly features "bad guys," in other words, enemies. They are the French high-ranking officers, the generals, who, via a senseless offensive operation, send countless *poilus* to their deaths and, afterwards, order four of them to be shot for alleged cowardice.

The soldiers who went to war in August 1914 learned all too soon who their real enemies were. As suggested in Kubrick's film, these were not the Germans, Russians, French, or British or whoever else it was that they were ordered to attack, but their own superiors, and above all their own officers, generals, and members of the high army command. The majority of the soldiers did not have many opportunities to see or hear the official enemy, but with their own officers they were in constant contact, and generally that proved to be a most disagreeable experience. The recruits discovered immediately that most of the officers looked down on them and treated them accordingly — which all too often meant mistreating them. And this was certainly not only in the Russian army, which essentially consisted of aristocratic officers and masses of poor and illiterate peasants as ordinary soldiers. In that army, the officers just did not bother to dissimulate their disdain for their subordinates; they "behaved toward their men like country landlords among serfs," and they often had them whipped by Cossacks. In the British army, things were not all that different. Representatives of the country's elite who served as officers — such as Cyril Asquith, son of the prime minister — described the war contemptuously as "fighting barbarians in the company of bores and bounders." The attitude of one British officer, nicknamed "Buffalo Bill" by his men, appears to have been typical; a soldier wrote about him after the war that "he treated all the men the same way — like dirt." The British poet Isaac Rosenberg, who served during the war as a simple soldier, composed beautiful poems about life at the front, and died in 1918, wrote to an acquaintance that "the army is the most detestable invention on this earth" and that "nobody but a private in the army knows what it is to be a slave." French soldiers likewise sometimes compared their predicament to a kind of slavery. For German officers, socializing with subordinates was strictly *verboten*, since the high command felt that familiarity could undermine the authority of the superior ranks. In any event, most officers considered ordinary soldiers as *Untermenschen* and mistreated them at will. An American war correspondent in Belgium witnessed a German officer using his riding crop to slap the face of a guard who had not saluted him quickly enough. Consequently, hatred toward the officer "caste" was widespread among the German soldiers. After the war, Kurt Tucholsky described the "enormous anger of the soldiers" toward their superiors, chests covered with medals, who forced them to kill and to be killed.[2] It was simply nowhere possible, writes Gabriel Kolko, "that noble and educated officers could coexist easily with their underlings" and treat them with more respect than they had done in peacetime; and so it happened that "degrading incidents" occurred all too frequently. In all armies, at the start of the war, there existed a strict apartheid between the officers, gentlemen of high social origin, and the men, essentially peasants, workers, and petty bourgeois. The French historian Frédéric Rousseau writes that there loomed "a gap between the ordinary men, including the NCOs, and the officers."[3]

It already started badly when trains left London, Paris, Berlin, and other cities with soldiers packed into "cattle cars" while their superiors were comfortably seated in first- or second-class compartments. An eyewitness described the situation as British troops were being transported by train from London's Victoria Station toward France:

> *There were six [trains] side by side at the departure platforms.*
> *Into five of them piled a great crowd of men with bulging*
> *packs on their backs to sit five a side in badly lit compartments*
> *. . . In sharp contrast the sixth train was brightly lit: it*
> *had two dining cars and all the carriages were first class.*
> *Obsequious myrmidons . . . guided red-hatted and red-tabbed*
> *officers to their reserved seats. It was nearly 6:30 and the*
> *waiters in the dining cars were already taking orders for drinks*
> *. . . This demonstration of privilege was to rankle in the minds*
> *of the soldiers . . . and to survive in the national memory for*
> *the next half century.*[4]

Across the Channel, things continued in the same fashion. During the train journey from Channel ports such as Étaples to the front, the officers enjoyed comfort and even luxury. In the poem "Any Soldier To His Son," the poet George Willis described how things were for a simple soldier like himself:

I learned to ride as soldiers ride from Etaps [i.e. Étaples] to the Line, For days and nights in cattle trucks, packed in like droves of swine.[5]

The war would certainly not reveal itself to be a classy affair, but from the very start it was definitely a class affair, a demonstration of class distinctions, a manifestation of the British class system. Of the delights of the British class system, Australian soldiers, mostly inclined toward egalitarianism, already tasted a sample when, in November 1914, they embarked on ships that were to take them to war-torn Europe. On board, the officers enjoyed what one of them admitted to be "literally living in luxury"; they were accommodated in first-class cabins equipped with private facilities, they were served meals "better than could be had in the best Melbourne hotel," and they were treated to orchestra music. The "other ranks," however, slept on the deck. In the Royal Navy, officers did indeed enjoy "considerable comfort," as gentlemen were deemed entitled to do. As for the ordinary sailors, they received enough to eat, but on board many ships "the conditions were almost as harsh as those of Nelson's era."[6]

To the elite, the war provided an opportunity to show the proletarians who was the boss, to teach them some good manners, such as respect and blind obedience toward their superiors, and also to punish them a little — or a lot? — because during the turbulent years that had preceded the war they had not displayed sufficient respect to their social "betters." Indeed, in all the armies that went to war in the summer of 1914, the officers, representatives of the elite, made it a habit to harass and humiliate their subordinates as much as possible, a treatment the Germans called *schickanieren*, which would eventually make its way into English as "[inflicting] chickenshit." Just about everywhere, the subordinates had to suffer "unremitting abuse from haughty superiors" and "frequent humiliations."[7] The Tommies complained about the arrogant attitude of their officers and the often absurd "rules and brutal routine" constantly inflicted on them, of the iron discipline to which they were subjected, and to the way in which they were ceaselessly ordered to march and exercise according to the whims of the officers.

It was not without reason that the British found their officers "more arrogant and oppressive" than those of the French. In the "republican" French army, the officers did indeed have to be somewhat more circumspect and treat the men with a bit more respect. Conversely, the French soldiers were more inclined to consider themselves the "equals" of their officers. From a British point of view, the French were virtually obsessed by a "mania," a "rage" for equality. Even the most proletarian French soldiers expected a measure of respect from their superiors. This reflected the fact that France, daughter of the Great Revolution of 1789 — and the revolutions of 1830, 1848, and 1871! — was more egalitarian and democratic than the still largely "feudal" British kingdom. Nonetheless, on the French side too, the officers and the ordinary soldiers lived in two very different worlds; for example, with respect to ways of thinking and talking. The French officers also left for the front by train, ensconced in first-class compartments, while the ordinary soldiers rode in "cattle cars" (*wagons à bestiaux*). And the French officers also frequently revealed themselves haughty toward their subordinates and ready to abuse them. The philosopher and pacifist journalist Alain (Émile Chartier) even felt that "between a simple soldier and a captain there existed a gulf wider than that between a serf and a lord."[8] The soldier Barthas likewise complained regularly in his journal about all sorts of mistreatments inflicted by superiors. As for the armies of the most authoritarian powers, namely Germany, Austria-Hungary, and Russia, the ordinary soldiers were all too often humiliated and mistreated, even physically, for the slightest peccadillo.

It bothered the soldiers a lot that they hardly received any information from their officers about what was going on and what the generals were planning. During the retreat in the north of France, somewhere in the vicinity of the town of Saint-Quentin, a British sergeant complained that "all ranks are much depressed owing to . . . the total absence of any information," so that "we appear to be simply driven blindly back." "We know absolutely nothing," wrote a French *poilu* around the same time, in August 1914, in his diary. "We receive no letters and see no newspapers . . . we march stupidly, silently, like slaves of the god of war."[9]

It is said that the French soldiers in general complained bitterly about the "state of ignorance in which they were systematically kept by the high command." In the French army there was a kind of "embargo on information";

it was pervaded by a "culture of silence." Often the men had no idea where they were, where they were marching to, or if their efforts were crowned with success or not; they knew nothing and could understand nothing. The fact that "a blind obedience was imposed on them" caused all sorts of anxieties and triggered "crazy rumours" as well as "a feeling of insecurity." The men felt "abused, dominated, cheated," and hated it. But that was part of the way in which their superiors took advantage of the war to lord it over them as they had not been able to do before the war. The "masters of information are the masters *tout court.*" The historian who wrote this, Frédéric Rousseau, adds the following remark:

> *The prison of silence that prevents the soldiers from knowing anything at all about the world outside of their unit turns them into inferior beings, into immature adults, puerile people; like children, they were not entrusted with the slightest responsibility, they are taken to unknown destinations, and have no idea about when, how, why, etc. . . . They become children, a gigantic flock of sheep. They are transformed into brute beasts.* [10]

The German soldiers were also frustrated because they were very poorly informed by their officers, if at all. "Knowledge is power" and not knowing therefore amounted to powerlessness. [11]

The elite clearly wanted to take advantage of the opportunity offered by the war to demonstrate its superiority with respect to the plebeians and to teach them not to ask difficult questions or want to know too much — as the socialists among them, in particular, inspired by Marx, had learned to do. Was it not because the proletarians had learned too much, under the influence of socialism, that they had become so critical and rebellious before the war? And, conversely, were not the peasants and the poor in general in the "good old days" of the *ancien régime* so docile because they had been kept in ignorance, thanks to a large extent to the efforts of the church? The less the ordinary soldiers knew, the better, and in 1914 the proletarians in uniform were expected to obey blindly and silently. They did not need information; their superiors knew what they were doing and did not have to explain anything. It was war now, and the motto was: obey and shut up!

Quite a few historians believe that in this respect the war did indeed largely function as planned and did cause not only the soldiers, but also the civilians, to cease to think critically or question the orders and information coming down from above. The war presumably turned most people into more credulous and obedient *subjects* as the political and military authorities censored, withheld or manipulated information, and disseminated gross lies as well as half-truths. It amounted to a kind of totalitarian control — a kind of Orwellian *1984 avant la lettre*! The Canadian historian Modris Eksteins remarks, not without reason, that "men found it difficult to assemble a coherent picture of the war as a whole . . . Most went through the war like blind men." Eksteins errs, however, when he adds that "men stopped asking questions, they ceased to interpret" and "[their] earlier élan gave way to resignation and stoicism."[12] We will soon see that, in all belligerent countries, the soldiers did not remain apathetic and inactive. To the contrary, they became more and more disgruntled, restless, critical, and ultimately rebellious. Eventually, by 1917, not a small part of them would even metamorphose into genuine revolutionaries.

Once they had disembarked from the train, the ordinary soldiers had to cover great distances on foot, so that they were often totally exhausted when actual combat commenced. But the officers rode on horseback, or were transported in automobiles, supplied and chauffeured by rich young men who were allowed to perform their military service that way.[13] This bothered the rest of the men, of course, especially when officers drove by in automobiles while even wounded soldiers had to walk for miles before they could be taken care of.[14] When the British paused during a march, the officers would rest separately, generally on the left side of the road, while the men gathered on the right. The British officers also spoke a type of English, sometimes referred to as "the Queen's English" or "Oxford English," that differed greatly from that of their subordinates, which was often London "Cockney" or some other less refined and prestigious variant of the language of Shakespeare.

In the others armies too, a linguistic gap separated officers from soldiers. Countless French *poilus* came from the south of the country, the Midi, and spoke Occitan, virtually incomprehensible to their northern officers. In the Belgian army, the officers generally used French, while the majority of the ordinary soldiers, the *piottes*, happened to be Flemish. (But it is not true that the soldiers did not understand the orders they were given and were therefore killed in large numbers. Even on the Belgian side, it was above all a "social fault line" that separated the men from their superiors; because of specifically Belgian circumstances, even in Flanders the upper class spoke mostly French.)[15] A more serious problem affected the army of the Danube Monarchy, where the Czech, Slovak, Polish, and other soldiers often hardly understood a word of the German spoken by the great majority of the officers. (More than 75 per cent of the officers were German, representing three times the percentage of Germans in the total population of the Habsburg Empire.) Similarly, the men of the colonial units, consisting of Senegalese, Moroccans, Indians, etc., often did not understand a word of the French or English of their superiors. The wedge between officers and "other ranks" could be linguistic, or ethnic, or a combination of the two. In the Irish units of the British army, the ordinary soldiers were virtually without exception people of low social origin who spoke either Irish (or Gaelic Irish), or Hibernian English, that is, English with a strong Irish accent; but the officers were almost exclusively English *gentlemen* who looked down their racist noses on their supposedly inferior "Celtic" subordinates.

Europe's elite had hoped, and even confidently expected, that to its own considerable advantage the war would *integrate* the proletarians, the ethnic-linguistic minorities, and even the colonial subjects — and the pesky suffragettes and other feminists — into the established political and social-economic order. Immediately after the outbreak of war, in August 1914, it seemed that this enticing scenario was becoming reality. But the degrading way in which the plebeian, ethnic, and colonial subjects in uniform were treated by the generals and other officers — the representatives of the elite in the army — soon produced the opposite effect and *extegrated* the lower orders and outsiders, in other words, turned them even more against the established order and against the elite. The aforementioned historian T.A. Jackson has remarked in this context that the way the officers treated the Irish soldiers in the British army drove the latter into the arms of radical republicanism and caused them to ardently desire nothing less than total independence of their country — as opposed to the measure of autonomy conjured up by the Home Rule formula. An early symptom of this development was the fact that the flood of Irish volunteers ebbed considerably in the course of 1915, to run completely dry in the fateful year of 1916, about which more will be said later.[16]

We have already seen that the officers were transported much more comfortably than their subordinates. In contrast to their superiors, the soldiers also often did not receive enough water to wash or shave. As illustration, the admittedly somewhat extreme case can be cited of an Austro-Hungarian unit that spent a night of October 1914 in a dilapidated building somewhere in the Carpathians. While the soldiers slept closely packed together on the floor, a high-ranking aristocratic officer was ensconced comfortably in a separate room and disposed of pyjamas, shaving gear, and even a portable rubber bathtub featuring his family's coat of arms. Other than markedly better food, the officers also received weapons of superior quality. In the Russian and Serbian armies, it happened frequently that some recruits received no weapons whatsoever and that, in case of an attack, they were told to pick up the rifles of killed comrades![17] It also happened that French officers occasionally received visits from their wives or girlfriends in the vicinity of the frontline. Officially, this was not permitted, but it proved possible if these women were disguised as Red Cross nurses. Such privileges for the officers antagonized the ordinary soldiers. It was one more example of the de facto inequality that separated the *poilus* from their superiors, even in the army of the theoretically egalitarian French Republic.[18]

Wounded officers were treated much better than wounded soldiers. In Russia, hospital trains operated behind the frontline, trains in which daughters of wealthy families went to take care of (preferably young and handsome) officers with wounds above the belt; these trains happened to be particularly active in the slipstream of elite regiments, "whose officers were likely to come from the most eligible layer of St. Petersburg society." Similarly, ladies of the British aristocracy organized and financed private ambulances to assist well-born wounded. And wealthy British personalities, such as Lady Ridley, a relative of Churchill, founded private hospitals for officers in upscale districts of London.[19] And all belligerent countries provided superior treatment to the officers among their prisoners. In POW-camps in Canada, for example, the men were "divided by ethnicity and by class," with "German officers and their civilian equivalents" — the latter presumably German residents of upper-class background — being "first-class internees."[20] In death too, an apartheid divided the upper-class officers from the plebeian "other ranks," as the officers received far better and more dignified treatment. In Britain, relatives of fallen officers were notified by telegram, while families of ordinary soldiers received a card by mail. On the "rolls of honour" of the dead published in newspapers such as *The Times*, the names of officers appeared in bigger letters than those of soldiers and NCOs. Moreover, officers received a decent burial, involving an individual coffin, flowers and wreaths, and a ceremony, while soldiers were summarily dispatched into common graves. Thus looked — and functioned — the army of which it continues to be claimed today, for example by Britain's Prime Minister Cameron on the occasion of the 100th anniversary of the outbreak of war in 1914, that it went to war for *democracy*. The French also buried officers and men separately, at least during the early stages of the war, but after a few months only officers of high rank, captains or above, continued to "enjoy" this privilege. The Germans and the Russians also used to stuff ordinary dead soldiers into mass graves, while officers received individual burial places.[21]

To this class distinction in death, the German journalist and writer Kurt Tucholsky would allude after the war in a poem entitled *"Drei Minuten Gehör!"* ("Three Minutes of Attention!"):

Und noch im Massengrab wat ihr die Schweine,	*Even in the mass graves, you were still just swine,*
Die Offiziere lagen alleine!	*But the officers, they rested alone!*
Ihr waret des Todes billige Ware . . .	*You were death's cheap merchandise . . .*
So ging das vier lange, blutige Jahre.[22]	*So it went for four long, bloody years.*

What bothered the soldiers the most, however, was the fact that countless officers all too often drove their men forward while they themselves remained behind in the relative safety of the rear. The German soldiers, for example, frequently complained that their officers remained under cover while they were forced to attack. The British troops also felt that all too often their superiors remained safely in the rear, or were quick to withdraw to safety. During the Battle of Le Cateau, a superior British officer suddenly withdrew from the fighting, not wounded but visibly shellshocked and demoralized, explaining that he was "just going back for a while," presumably to find a toilet. But "humble rankers" who attempted anything similar were threatened by pistol-toting officers and sent back to the front; if they failed to obey, they were shot on the spot. According to Kolko, "examples of commanding officers remaining safely so far behind the lines as to be useless [were] legion."[23] In the course of the fighting in December 1914, the French soldier Barthas witnessed a similar situation:

> *The colonel stayed with the reserve battalion, the major stayed with the reserve company, the captain stayed with the support troops, and the group commander stayed with the group, far behind the lines. Only the corporal had to personally lead his men. The sergeants followed in closed ranks in order to force laggards to continue to march forward and, if necessary, to discreetly shoot them with the revolver.*[24]

Especially in the early stages of the war, numerous representatives of the upper classes simply never showed up in the danger zones. In most belligerent countries, a disproportionately high number of aristocrats were assigned to the cavalry. Many cavalrymen belonging to the British nobility, for example, remained at a considerable distance from the frontlines. They waited, they said, for the infantry to smash a hole in the German lines, through which they could then gallop forward to pursue and finish off the fleeing enemy. In the meantime, they passed the time hunting foxes and hares and organizing races and horse shows.[25]

The cowardice displayed by many, though certainly not all, of their officers caused bad blood and protests among the soldiers. "The men even dared to say that we were commanded by assassins and butchers and that the general and the colonel should have led us in person instead of remaining in the safety of the rear," noted Barthas; and he added that many men threatened "simply to stop obeying orders." Of the soldiers, it was expected that they would "fight and, if necessary, die," writes Gabriel Kolko, "remaining obedient to those leaders and the ruling classes who had so blithely embarked upon the war," but "the soldiers began to refuse to march unquestioningly to their possible deaths." For the type of "soldiers' strike" to which Barthas already alluded in 1914, the time was not yet ripe; to see that happen in the French army, one would have to wait until 1917.

The French soldiers despised the officers, nicknamed *galonnards*, "men with stripes," whom they considered to be cowards. Conversely, they had a lot of respect and sometimes even a deep affection for officers who, during bombardments or combat, conducted themselves courageously; in the eyes of the *poilus*, these were the true leaders or *chefs*. It was no different on the German side.[26]

All too numerous were the officers who were despised as cowards by their subordinates, but the latter were powerless to do anything about it. Conversely, the officers were always ready to punish severely any real or imaginary form of cowardice or other deficiency in their men. Countless cases of this occurred in the French and British armies in August 1914, during the murderous "Battle of the Frontiers" and the long ensuing retreat to the banks of the Marne River. As a result of the gigantic losses suffered, disorder, decline of discipline, and even panic developed in which soldiers attempted to save their lives by fleeing or, voluntarily or not, found themselves isolated from their units. Thus they were found guilty of some form of desertion. In his diary, the French military policeman (*gendarme*) Jules Allard referred to the numerous "stragglers" (*traînards*) they had to deal with at the time, and he described the situation as an "epidemic of fugitives [*fuyards*]."[27]

In all such cases the officers administered severe punishments, including summary executions. In the French army, such executions were officially authorized by the high command on August 3 *"pour encourager les autres."* "Expiatory ceremonies" was what these executions were called by General Pétain, who thus betrayed his Catholic-dolorist mentality. A well-known case is that of the "martyrs of Vingré": six *poilus*, drawn by lot, were shot on December 4, 1914, by order of General Étienne de Villar after their unit had pulled back without express authorization to do so during a German attack. This was intended to make the men understand clearly that it was important to obey unconditionally and "to help them to recover their taste for combat." On December 15, near the village of Zillebeke in Flanders, a company of Algerian *tirailleurs* of the French army was made to suffer the punishment of decimation — that is, the execution of every tenth man — because they had refused to attack. Such decimations also took place elsewhere, for example, for fraternizing with the enemy.

Yet another case of arbitrary executions of soldiers was that of the "Four Corporals of Souain," which provided inspiration for the book by Humphrey Cobb, *Paths of Glory*, and thus the film of the same title. The execution of these men, in February 1915, in the village of Souain-Perthes-lès-Hurlus, just to the north of Châlons-en-Champagne, was ordered by General Géraud Réveilhac. He did it in order to exact revenge for the failure of a senseless attack he had ordered without any consideration for the lives of his men, at one point even having given an order (which was not obeyed) for the artillery to fire on his French troops in an attempt to push them forward. In the film, Réveilhac is presented as "General Paul Mireau" and is interpreted brilliantly by the actor George Macready.

It is hardly surprising that the commanders sometimes took advantage of an execution done "as an example" to get rid of soldiers known to be socialists, anarchists, union leaders, etc. An example is that of three members of the CGT trade union who were executed on April 20, 1915, in Flirey, near Toul. Known radical elements of this type were also often posted by their superiors in particularly dangerous places, or charged with missions fraught with high risks. In some cases, French soldiers were also shot for minor transgressions, such as stealing a chicken. Arguably more justifiable was a case witnessed in November 1914 by a British nurse: the execution of a young Frenchman who, in a state of drunkenness, had threatened an officer with a revolver. On the side of the British, the very first execution for desertion took place as early as the Battle of Mons; the victim was a boy of seventeen who had fled and sought refuge in a barn.[28]

In the course of the Great War, the British would condemn slightly more than three thousand of their own soldiers to death, mostly for desertion, but also for cowardice, mutiny, and similar transgressions. Of those who were thus condemned, between 200 and 250 were actually executed, though some sources claim that figure was as high as 361. The victims were overwhelmingly ordinary soldiers; twenty-five of them were Canadians, twenty-two Irish, and five New Zealanders. In the Indian units of the British army executions also took place, but the number is unknown. We know that it already started in the autumn of 1914, when Indian troops, newly arrived in France, suffered heavy losses, and were also traumatized by "the shock of the discovery of mechanized warfare" and the cold weather. A number of men reported to the infirmaries with self-inflicted wounds, and their British commanding officer had five of them shot "for cowardice."

The French executed more than six hundred of their own soldiers, the Belgians thirteen, the Germans "merely" forty-eight. In the Italian army there were numerous executions, allegedly no less than 750. One hundred and twenty-nine Australians, including 119 deserters, were condemned to death, but no death sentences were actually carried out. The Americans condemned twenty-four of their men to death, but likewise failed to carry out the sentences. The Bulgarian army witnessed up to 2,500 death sentences, of which about 800 were carried out.[29]

For minor offences, the British officers often applied what was called Field Punishment Number One, which had been introduced in 1881. In the course of the First World War, the British army would register no less than 60,210 condemnations to "F.P. No. 1." This punishment consisted in having the condemned man tied to a tree or a wagon wheel for up to two hours per day and sometimes for a total of twenty-one days, with the arms outstretched and the legs tied together, so that the punishment was nicknamed the "crucifixion." It was a painful and humiliating experience that became the symbol of the "Christ-like" suffering of the British soldiers, who were said to "suffer like Jesus." This comparison — of the soldier with Jesus, of the front with Golgotha — was evoked in numerous poems, for example by Wilfred Owen. The British soldiers and citizens also projected this notion on the German enemy, who was claimed to crucify Belgian civilians and allied soldiers — for some reason usually Canadians. The crucifixes with "suffering Christs" that one encountered frequently along the country roads of Flanders presumably played a role in the fabrication of this myth.[30]

The same sort of punishment also existed in the German army, where the victims were often tied to a tree, and in the Italian army. Sadistic Italian officers sometimes placed the victim in view of the enemy. In the Austro-Hungarian forces, severe forms of punishment were liberally administered from the very first days of the war, for offences such as discarding one's rifle, drunkenness, and self-mutilation. These happened very frequently because countless recruits belonged to the Empire's Slav minorities, who resented having to go to war on behalf of the hated Habsburgs and who sympathized with the Serbian and Russian enemies of their own superiors. The range of punishments included being whipped, hanged, shot, and — in order to save expensive bullets — executed by bayonet.[31]

It was primarily the high-ranking officers, the generals, and the members of the general staff, all of them rarely if ever seen on the frontline but leading lives of security and comfort, who were the object of the ordinary soldiers' contempt. The British soldiers hated the officers of the general staff, who could easily be recognized by a red badge the men referred to as the "the red badge of funk." ("Funk" being slang for "shirking.") The staff members were generally "scions of wealthy and aristocratic houses," and the Tommies "desired their death intensely."[32] In *Paths of Glory*, the role of a French staff officer, a polished young man of upper-class background and the perfect antithesis of the plebeian and rather crude ordinary soldiers, is performed admirably by the actor Richard Anderson.[33]

From the very beginning of the war, a more or less bitter antagonism toward officers in general welled up among the majority of ordinary soldiers. (This did not mean that the men could not develop a great deal of respect and even a deep affection for brave individual superiors who cared for their subordinates — types conjured up by Colonel Dax in *Paths of Glory*.) This was the case in all the armies, including the Belgian forces. "Do you know that the soldiers do not respect their officers, but despise and detest them?" wrote a *piotte*, as the Belgian soldiers were nicknamed, to a family member. And the fact that the men considered their officers as enemies was also reflected in this poem, entitled *"Le révolté," "The rebel,"* written by Georges Haumont, a Belgian who had volunteered for military service:

Il est soldat contre la guerre	*He is a soldier, but he is against the war*
Il obéit, mais à demi.	*He obeys, but only reluctantly.*
Le chef est son grand ennemi	*The boss is his main enemy*
Et l'ordre donné l'exaspère.	*And the orders he receives infuriate him.*

In the French army too, countless soldiers were of the opinion that "our superior [*notre maître*, literally, "our master"] is our enemy."[34]

Before the war, the proletarians had been the class enemies of the noble and bourgeois elite. During the war, this hostility crystallized and intensified in the form of an antagonism between ordinary soldiers and officers. And so it transpired that the war did not provide a resolution to the class struggle, as the elite had hoped. To the contrary, this struggle would worsen over the course of the war. Conversely, the elite had also hoped that the war would undermine the international solidarity preached by the socialists. At the start of the war this proved to be the case, for in early August 1914 the socialist leaders of all belligerent countries suddenly switched from internationalism to social chauvinism and urged their followers to go to war for the fatherland and against the proletarians of other countries. But as it became clear during the fall of 1914 that the supposed "war in defence of the fatherland" was in reality a bloody imperialist project, the uniformed proletarians started to re-embrace proletarian internationalism.

In this context, it is worth citing a comment from the memoirs of the English writer J.B. Priestley, who acquired a "class conscience" as a result of his experiences as a soldier in the Great War, especially because of the way in which the officers treated their subordinates:

> *The British command specialised in throwing men away for nothing. The tradition of an upper class . . . killed most of my friends as surely as if those cavalry generals had come out of the chateaux with polo mallets and beaten our brains out. Call this class prejudice, if you like, so long as you remember . . . that I went into that war without any such prejudice, free of any class feeling.*[35]

The ordinary soldiers developed more and more antipathy and even hatred toward their own officers. Simultaneously, they started to empathize and even sympathize for the men facing them on the far side of the no man's land. The official enemy — the Germans, Russians, French, whatever — was demonized by the authorities, but the soldiers had little or nothing against them. In many cases, they hardly knew the people they were supposed to hate and kill. Furthermore, they soon found out that they had much in common with "the enemy," first and above all a lower-class social background, and, second, the same exposure to danger, misery, and abuse at the hands of their superiors.

The men learned in many ways that the official enemy was in fact not the real enemy, that the soldiers on the other side were human beings just like themselves. This lesson could be learned, for example, by reading letters and looking at pictures found on, or taken from, prisoners. The contempt for the "other," deliberately fabricated by the military and political superiors, thus soon gave way to mutual respect and the feeling "that we are all the same," for a "reciprocal respect and even sympathy." In January 1915, a French *poilu* commented as follows on letters he had found on a prisoner: "The same as on our side. The misery, the desperation, the longing for peace, the monstrous stupidity of this whole thing. The Germans are just as unhappy as we are. They are just as miserable as us."[36]

This kind of lesson was also learned by physical meetings with the enemy: obviously not hand-to-hand combat, which was actually far less frequent than we have tended to believe, but encounters with prisoners of war. Of German captives, a British officer reported that "they were pleasant chaps, who generally behaved like gentlemen."[37] And in 1916 a Scottish soldier, Joseph Lee, expressed his pity and sympathy for German prisoners poetically as follows:

> *When first I saw you in the curious street,*
> *Like some platoon of soldier ghosts in grey,*
> *My mad impulse was all to smite and slay,*
> *To spit upon you — tread you 'neath my feet.*
> *But when I saw how each sad soul did greet*
> *My gaze with no sign of defiant frown,*

. . . .

I knew that we had suffered each as other,
And could have grasped your hand and cried, "My brother!"[38]

Sympathy for German prisoners was also reflected in the poem "Liedholz," written by the British officer Herbert Read. He may have been an officer, but he happened to be a convinced anarchist. Read captured a German named Liedholz, and even before they reached the British trenches, "the barriers of formal hostility were taken away," to use the words of a literary commentator:

Before we reached our wire
He told me he had a wife and three children.
In the dug-out we gave him a whiskey.

. . . .

In broken French we discussed
Beethoven, Nietzsche and the International.[39]

In *Memoirs of an Infantry Officer*, published in 1930, Siegfried Sassoon was to write that, during the war, the Germans were generally hated by British citizens, but not, or certainly far less, by British soldiers. He himself, he added, "had nothing against them."[40] Countless French soldiers likewise failed to develop feelings of hatred with respect to their German "neighbours on the other side." "We don't hate the Germans," wrote a *poilu* in a letter that was intercepted by the censors. The French soldier Barthas soon felt sympathy for the German prisoners he escorted on a train travelling from the front to a camp somewhere in southern France, and who were verbally abused by civilians in railway stations. He and his comrades shared the wine and the grapes received from those same civilians with their prisoners in a gesture of camaraderie. "Those who have seen the dreadful realities of war," observes Max Hastings, "recoiled from displays of chauvinism." The soldiers loathed the civilians, journalists, and politicians who could or would not understand their miserable fate. Conversely, they found it impossible to hate a so-called enemy who shared their misery. "The soldiers of the rival armies felt a far stronger sense of community with each other than with their peoples at home," writes Hastings.[41]

The "no man's land" that separated the armies revealed itself to be less wide than the gap that separated the soldiers from the officers of these armies. During the late summer and fall of 1914, two different wars had thus actually started to ravage Europe. First, a highly visible "vertical" war, a conflict between groups of countries, in which all uniformed men of the one side were enemies of all uniformed men on the other side. Second, below the surface, so to speak, a "horizontal" war, an explosion of class conflict, in which the officers of each army were the enemies of their own subordinates, while a high degree of solidarity united the ordinary soldiers of both sides. In the first war, a "vertical" geographic (or topographic) front-line separated friend and foe. In the second war, a "horizontal" social gap separated the antagonists.

In the autumn of 1914, when on the western front the "war of move-ment" petered out and gave way to a "stationary war," the soldiers dis-covered that their enemies were human beings just like themselves, with whom they happened to have a lot in common. They were overwhelmingly of a lower-class origin and they all experienced an urgent need to curb the mutual massacre as much as possible. Practices emerged that have been described as "live-and-let-live." For example, the soldiers often deliberately refrained from firing their weapons, especially during mealtimes, hoping that the enemy would do the same, as usually turned out to be the case. When at one time, during such a pause, a mortar did suddenly get fired, a German voice loudly offered apologies to the British Tommies, which prevented an escalation of the firing. When specific orders arrived from "above" to open fire, the men often deliberately aimed too high, and the enemy did the same. The artillerists also frequently opened fire at the same time of the day, aiming at the same target, in order to give the enemy a chance to withdraw to a safe area.

Quiet sectors thus came into being along the front, areas where the casu-alty rate was noticeably lower than elsewhere. In the vicinity of Ypres, the British and Germans thus agreed to let the men on both sides sit on the parapet of their muddy and frequently flooded trenches, in full view of each other, in order to stay dry. Yet another form of "live-and-let-live" consisted in the conclusion of unofficial ceasefires, unauthorized by the superiors, after heavy fighting, which allowed both sides to evacuate the wounded and bury the dead. Those opportunities were often used to start a conversation and to exchange small presents such as tobacco and insignia; in other words, to "fraternize." Occasionally this even involved visits to the trenches on the other side of the no man's land! A German soldier later remembered such a pause in the fighting in France toward the end of November 1914: "French and German soldiers walked around, fully visible in the bright daylight. Nobody fired their weapons. It was said that some brave men even visited the enemy trenches." The same soldier related how even later, for example in February 1915, "it was silently agreed to leave each other in peace as much as possible." And a French *poilu*, Gervais Morillon, described in a letter how on December 12, 1914

> Frenchmen and Germans shook hands after unarmed
> Germans came out of their trenches, waving a white flag . . .
> We reciprocated, and we visited each other's trenches and
> exchanged cigars and cigarettes, while a few hundred meters
> farther they were shooting at each other.

In some sectors, such fraternizations developed into an almost daily routine. In the area of the town of Pont-à-Mousson, French as well as German soldiers started in November 1914 to fetch water daily at the Fountain of Father Hilarion (*Fontaine du Père Hilarion*), a spring situated in a ravine in the middle of no man's land. Normally, they took turns to go there, and no shots were fired while water was being collected, but it frequently came to meetings and conversations. According to a report that appears to refer to that site, Frenchmen and Germans exchanged "bread, cheese, and wine," ate together, showed each other pictures of wives and children, amused themselves together, sang songs, played the accordion. That sociability abruptly ended when, on December 7, heavy fighting erupted in the area.

The soldiers were supposed to hate each other, but something very different actually happened: on both sides many men, though admittedly not all, developed a considerable measure of empathy for, and solidarity with, their counterparts on the other side of the no man's land. The outbreak of war had produced an explosion of nationalism and had dealt a heavy blow to the ideal of internationalist solidarity among proletarians, exactly as the elite had hoped. But it now appeared that the vagaries of war caused the uniformed proletarians to rediscover and re-appreciate internationalist solidarity.

The military elite did not approve. Of the war it was indeed expected that it would bury internationalism once and for all instead of resurrecting it. According to Adam Hochschild, such an "outburst of spontaneous solidarity among ordinary, working-class soldiers . . . outraged higher-ups and militarists on both sides."

The ordinary soldiers were keenly aware that their superiors had their reasons for execrating all forms of "live-and-let-live," even though it sometimes proved possible to persuade or even force them to participate, as we will see later. It is therefore understandable that these activities tended to occur when the officers were not present, which was often the case in the dangerous front lines. The fraternizations were immediately aborted whenever it was signalled that officers were on their way. Barthas describes such an occurrence in the Champagne region in the summer of 1916. The French had to inform the German soldiers with whom they were socializing that their officers had become suspicious, so that they had to suspend the sociability. "The Germans were deeply moved and thanked us cordially. Before they disappeared behind their sandbags, one of them lifted his hand and called out: 'Frenchmen, Germans, soldiers, we are all comrades!' Then he made a fist: 'But the officers, NO.'" Barthas commented as follows: "God! That German was right. One should not generalize, but the majority of the officers were morally farther removed from us than those poor devils of German soldiers who are being dragged against their will to the same slaughterhouse."

The officers did indeed abominate any arrangements reflecting solidarity between their own subordinates and the "enemy." Charles de Gaulle, for example, the progeny of a Catholic bourgeois family in Lille, a young officer during the First World War, condemned every form of "live-and-let-live" as *"lamentable."* But there were also many ordinary soldiers who did not approve of such gatherings, since they had internalized the elite's nationalist and militarist ethos and thus genuinely hated the enemy. Hitler was one of them.

The authorities condemned and prohibited all forms of fraternization and "live-and-let-live" in general. The officers sometimes put snipers to work when they suspected that fraternizations "threatened" to take place. But the spontaneous truces and fraternizations also reflected the need of *all* warriors to maintain and display a semblance of humanity even in the middle of an unprecedentedly bestial war, which explains why officers too sometimes chose to participate. The French soldier Gervais Morillon described how an officer walked at the head of a group of Germans who came out of their trenches. Sometimes superiors with a rank as high as that of colonel decided to participate.[42]

The fact that fraternizations were officially strictly prohibited apparently made them even more fascinating and appealing to soldiers. It is probably thus that we can interpret a myth that enjoyed an inordinate amount of success among soldiers of both sides throughout the war. Countless men were convinced that, somewhere in the no man's land, in abandoned trenches and preferably deep under the ground, thus beyond the reach of projectiles and officers, beastlike deserters of all armies dwelled together in a kind of permanent state of fraternization. By night they would rob the dead and wounded, seek food, etc. They became such a threat to the troops that eventually the army brass ordered them to be exterminated with gas.

This myth was a potent cocktail of many ingredients. It amounted to a modern version of the medieval theme of the simultaneously feared and admired "wild man." But it was also a commentary of the soldiers on their own beastly existence in the trenches and a fantasy about disobedience. Last but not least, it vaguely reflected the soldiers' solidarity with the men on the other side of the no man's land, combined with the ardent desire to wave a not-so-fond farewell to their own superiors and the miserable war. "An anti-establishment smell was attached to this myth," writes Tim Cook. It was "a form of disobedience." Indeed, the generals could try to prohibit fraternization in the real world, but they proved powerless in the face of such mythical fraternization — this clearly to the satisfaction of the soldiers who wished to believe in this myth.[43]

In any event, the authorities were also unable to prevent the wave of fraternizations that took place on Christmas Day, 1914. In the vicinity of Ypres, the sector of the western front that was held from

September-October of that year by the British and became known to them as "Flanders' Fields," it started on Christmas Eve. The Germans decorated trees near their trenches with burning candles and started to sing Christmas songs such as *Stille Nacht,*" "Silent Night." The British reacted by lighting bonfires and singing English Christmas carols. Then the soldiers on both sides started to loudly call out Christmas wishes. The Germans arranged to deliver a chocolate tart to the British, accompanied by an invitation to conclude a truce. Shortly thereafter soldiers crawled out of their trenches in order to fraternize in the no man's land and in each other's trenches. That sort of thing continued on Christmas Day itself, and in some sectors even on Boxing Day. Presents such as tobacco, whisky, and cigars were exchanged, and the two sides helped each other to bury the dead. In the no man's land a soccer game was also played, which the British claimed to have won. (It was no coincidence that the game played was soccer, very much a working-class pastime, as opposed to tennis, golf, or rugby, the sports preferred by "gentlemen.") An English soldier wrote in a letter that this was "the most remarkable Christmas" he had ever experienced, and that he "had had the pleasure to shake hands with numerous Germans . . . to smoke together and to enjoy a friendly chat." A favourite conversation topic was the madness of a war of which both sides had had more than enough.[44]

Between the British and the Germans the unofficial Christmas truce affected virtually the entire front of approximately forty kilometres along which they faced each other. In some sectors of that front the truce dragged on until New Year's Day. Some historians claim that the Anglo-German fraternizations of the end of December 1914 were nothing less than "massive."[45] But on Christmas Day, similar truces and fraternizations also occurred between the Germans and the French. Barthas confided to his diary that, in their sector, the morning of Christmas witnessed "singing and shouting and the firing of flares" and that no shots were fired. And it is known that *poilus* met *Boches* to sing together and to exchange tobacco, cognac, postcards, newspapers, and other presents in the vicinity of Soissons and in villages of Picardy such as Cappy and Foucaucourt. A *poilu* later remembered that

> The Boches *signaled us and indicated that they wanted to talk*
> *to us. I approached to three or four meters from their trench*
> *in order to talk to three of them who had surfaced . . . They*
> *asked that we would refrain all day and night from shooting*
> *and said that they themselves would not fire one single shot.*
> *They had enough of the war, they said, they were married and*
> *had nothing against the French, only against the English. They*
> *gave me a box of cigars and a package of cigarettes, and I gave*
> *them a copy of [the magazine] Le Petit Parisien in exchange*
> *for a German newspaper. Then I withdrew to the French*
> *trench, where many men were keen to try my German tobacco.*
> *Our neighbours on the other side kept their word, even better*
> *than we did. Not even one single rifle shot was fired.*[46]

There were many other sites along the front where groups of French soldiers visited the German trenches to enjoy a drink, or where Germans came to offer cigars to the *Franzosen*. Christmas carols were performed in both languages, for example *"Minuit chrétien"* and *"O Tannenbaum."*[47] Belgians and Germans, who faced each other in the lowlands of the Yser River estuary, allegedly also fraternized on Christmas 1914. The Germans agreed to mail letters from Belgian soldiers to family members in occupied Belgium. At the eastern front it also came to fraternizations. The Russians met their Austro-Hungarian enemies in the no man's land in Galicia and exchanged the usual tobacco, but also schnapps, bread, and meat.[48]

The superiors were far from enchanted with the Christmas truces, but could not prevent them. On the British side an officer rushed to the scene with this intention, apparently from the safety of the rear, but he arrived too late: his men had already started to socialize with Germans in the no man's land. He could only resign himself to the *fait accompli*. He himself and a handful of other officers ended up joining their subordinates and went to greet the German officers. One of the latter ordered beer to be fetched for everyone, and the officers courteously drank to each others' health. A British officer reciprocated by treating those present with pieces of a traditional English plum pudding. It was finally agreed that the unofficial truce would last until midnight, and that all would have to be back in their own trenches by then. The "damage" done by the fraternizations, at least from the viewpoint of the superiors, was thus limited somewhat, at least in that sector.

The higher the rank of the superiors, the less they liked this strange Christmas idyll. The British commander-in-chief, General French, who on Christmas Day enjoyed a gourmet dinner featuring turtle soup, with as *digestif* a brandy from 1820 offered by the Rothschilds, issued a specific order to nip in the bud any future attempts to fraternize. One year later, the artillery would be made to fire into no man's land all day, starting on Christmas Eve, in order to prevent any meetings there; however, it proved impossible to prevent fraternizations from occuring here and there and from time to time.

In the 1980s, the strange events of Christmas 1914 inspired the song "Christmas in the Trenches, 1914," written and set to music by the American folksinger John McCutcheon. It features the following lines:

> 'T was Christmas in the trenches where the frost so bitter hung,
> The frozen fields of France were still, no Christmas song was sung,
> Our families back in England were toasting us that day,
> Their brave and glorious lads so far away.
>
> .   .   .   .
>
> 'There's someone coming towards us!' the front-line sentry cried
> All sights were fixed on one lone figure coming from their side
> His truce flag, like a Christmas star, shone on that plain so bright
> As he bravely strode unarmed into the night.
> Soon one by one on either side walked into No Man's land
> With neither gun nor bayonet we met there hand to hand
> We shared some secret brandy and we wished each other well
> And in a flare-lit soccer game we gave 'em hell.
> We traded chocolates, cigarettes, and photographs from home
> These sons and fathers far away from families of their own

Young Sanders played his squeeze box and they had a violin
This curious and unlikely band of men.

. . . .

'T was Christmas in the trenches, where the frost so bitter hung
The frozen fields of France were warmed as songs of peace were sung
For the walls they'd kept between us to exact the work of war
Had been crumbled and were gone for evermore.
My name is Francis Tolliver, in Liverpool I dwell
Each Christmas come since World War I I've learned its lessons well
That the ones who call the shots won't be among the dead and lame
And on each end of the rifle we're the same.[49]

CHAPTER 16
MILITARIA 1914: ABORTED PLANS

August 1914: All armies go to war brimming with confidence. The commanders proceed to implement the plans that are supposed to guarantee success, such as Plan XVII of the French and the famous Schlieffen Plan of the Germans. But none of the planned scenarios become reality and everywhere the war degenerates into an unforeseen stationary conflict. In the meantime, the flames of war also flare up in the Middle East and in Africa. A conflict that had started in Europe thus becomes a genuine world war . . .

Almost everybody had been convinced that the war would be a short and glorious affair, in which cavalrymen and foot soldiers would overwhelm the enemy with sabre and bayonet, win epic victories on behalf of the beloved fatherland, and return triumphantly by Christmas to a homeland purified and reborn in the Nietzschean ordeal of war.

At first it looked as if this scenario would become reality. Inspired by the military philosophy of all-out attack, *l'attaque à outrance*, itself influenced by the then very popular philosophy of Henri Bergson with its *élan vital* or "vital force," the French, under Generalissimo Joffre, immediately proceeded to implement their Plan XVII. This plan called for massive attacks, piercing the German positions, and marching irresistibly toward Berlin. Initially, some successes were scored in Alsace, the province that, following defeat in the war of 1870–71, had been lost to Germany together with the northern half of Lorraine. These regions, known together as "Alsace-Lorraine," were the major territorial objects of desire of the "revanchism" of French nationalists. However, the Germans responded with nasty counterattacks, and the French troops were pushed back and forced onto the defensive. Things would even get worse.

On the German side too, all went well at first. The famous Schlieffen Plan foresaw an encirclement of the bulk of the French army by means of a push through neutral Belgium. That this might provide the British government with the much-desired pretext to declare war on Germany was deemed to be unimportant. In comparison to the gargantuan armies of Germany, France, and Russia, the BEF was indeed only a "contemptible little" force, as Emperor Wilhelm II — or was it Chancellor Bethmann-Hollweg? — is supposed to have declared, though today most historians suspect that this was an invention of British propaganda. In any event, the Belgian resistance turned out to be somewhat more tenacious than Berlin had expected from the "chocolate soldiers" of this little country. (The high command of the German army had actually hoped that the Belgian government would limit itself to a formal protest or put up only a symbolic resistance.) The conquest of the ring of fortresses circling the border city of Liège, for example, dragged on from August 4 to 16. Still, their resistance did not significantly slow down the progress of the massive German army units, which according to an American war correspondent slid through the Belgian countryside "like monstrous grey-green serpents."[1] The Belgian army withdrew behind its national "refuge," Antwerp, surrounded by fortresses, while the BEF and the French army, which had entered Belgium and made it as far as the towns of Mons and Charleroi, were pushed back toward Paris. The Germans had to leave behind an army corps to keep an eye on Antwerp. In addition, the German commander-in-chief, von Moltke, transferred some troops to East Prussia in order to help halt the Russian invasion there, an operation that would succeed with the victories of Tannenberg and the Masurian Lakes. This transfusion weakened the German right wing, whose men and horses were in any event exhausted by fast, long marches of sometimes up to fifty kilometres per day. For the progress of these troops, writes de Schaepdrijver, "a totally unrealistic calendar had been fixed, which, moreover, had been plunged into confusion on account of the unexpected Belgian resistance." The Belgians had also sabotaged their railways, which were therefore useless to the Germans.[2]

The German progress would grind to a halt in early September when Joffre ordered the French, with British support, to counterattack, which produced victory in the crucial Battle of the Marne. In clerical circles, where it was hoped that thanks to the war the country would return to the bosom of Christianity, this "miracle on the Marne" was not credited to the soldiers or to the commander-in-chief, Joffre, nor to General Gallieni, who had had the idea of transporting troops to the front in Parisian taxis, but to Joan of Arc, or to the supposedly very Francophile Virgin Mary, or to Saint Genevieve, patron saint of the French capital, who in her own lifetime had saved the city from the clutches of Attila and his Huns. The Sacred Heart of Jesus also received a fair share of the credit: surely it was not a coincidence that the Teutonic hordes were driven back at the moment when, so to speak, they could perceive the *Basilique du Sacré-Cœur* on top of the hill of Montmartre! Just like the British flights of fancy about ghosts intervening during the Battle of Mons, such fables were typical of the revival of religiosity at the start of the war, a revival that was accompanied by "a boom of prophecies and appearances" and happened to be "strongly tinted by magic and superstition."[3] A German historian, Herfried Münkler, attributes the success of the French and British in the Battle of the Marne at least partly to the fact that von Moltke had not only found it necessary to transfer troops to East Prussia but also to leave troops behind to besiege Antwerp, where a few Belgian sorties caused "considerable unrest" (*erhebliche Unruhe*) to the Germans. "In the Battle of the Marne," he writes, "the outcome was favourable to the French not only thanks to the unexpectedly early advance of the Russians in East Prussia but also thanks to the tenacity of the Belgians in Antwerp."[4]

The Germans were repulsed to the north, but only as far as the Aisne River. The two camps subsequently attempted repeatedly to turn the enemy's flank, which produced the so-called "race to the sea," with the German aim being the capture of Channel ports such as Calais and Boulogne. In late September and early October, heavy fighting raged in northern France, for example in the vicinity of the town of Albert in Picardy, in the province of Artois, and in and around Armentières, a municipality hugging the Belgian border.[5] In the meantime, in the early days of October, the Belgian army managed to extricate itself from Antwerp and withdraw in good order along the Dutch frontier to the coast, where they were to make a stand again behind the Yser River. There they linked up with French and British troops who had been pushing northward in the context of the "race to the sea." Together, they managed to repel repeated German attacks. The exhausted and demoralized Belgians were saved, almost as miraculously as the French on the Marne, when two bright local men, Karel Cogge and Hendrik Geeraert, came up with the idea of flooding the Yser Plain by opening the locks at Nieuwpoort. It took a few days, but by October 29 the flooding was a *fait accompli* and the Belgians could finally get some rest behind a wall of water and mud. Of the Belgian army that had started the war, less than half the soldiers were left, and perhaps only one third: according to some sources, 70,000 men out of an original total of almost 200,000, according to others, 52,000 out of 117,500. Psychologically, it turned out to be a major advantage that for the rest of the war an admittedly minuscule part of Belgium remained beyond the reach of the Germans, and that the Belgian army could ensconce itself in its own territory along an "Yser Front" destined to acquire mythical proportions. For the rest of the war, the Germans could inflict only relatively little damage on the Belgians. Conversely, the water also prevented the Belgian troops from participating in any offensives, for example those launched in 1915 by the French and the British, which also prevented more heavy losses. Joffre did ask for Belgian participation in his offensives, but King Albert stubbornly refused. On the other hand, diseases such as typhoid, typhus, pneumonia, influenza, and dysentery — proliferating on account of factors such as cold, water pollution, mud and dirt, mosquitoes, rats, and fleas — took the lives of many Belgians and would ultimately be responsible for about one-third of the approximately twenty thousand subjects of King Albert who "fell" on the Yser Front.[6]

During the Battle of the Yser and even later, heavy fighting also raged in the vicinity of the city of Ypres between the Germans on the one hand and the French and British on the other. This episode went down in history as the "First Battle of Ypres." On the German side, it was an ultimate attempt to break through in the direction of the French Channel ports. They threw into battle some inexperienced reserve units, including regiments of university students who had volunteered for service in August. But on

November 10, during an attack in the village of Langemarck, the rookies of these "children's regiments," attacking in dense formations, allegedly while belting patriotic songs, were mowed down by the thousands by the "Emma-Gees," as the British called their Lewis machine guns. In Germany this drama engendered the "Langemarck Myth" trumpeting the heroism of German students and young men in general. The formation of this myth, writes the historian Herfried Münkler, came down to an effort on the part of the "elite of the Reich, after the failure of the Schlieffen Plan, to prepare the country's patriotic bourgeois and petty-bourgeois middle class for making the great sacrifices required to win the war in the long run and thus to save the established order."[7] The fighting around the town of Ypres, which was completely destroyed, petered out toward the end of November 1914. The optimistic war plans that were supposed to have been implemented lay in the wastebasket. The "war of movement" was over, the "stationary war" or "trench warfare" started — and would last much longer than anybody could have foreseen.

Much the same thing happened on the other side of Europe. On August 12, in the Balkan Peninsula, Austro-Hungarian troops attacked Serbia from their positions in Bosnia. The idea was to quickly teach that pesky little country a painful lesson. But the attackers were repulsed with heavy losses and took revenge by massacring Serbian civilians, as well as Bosnians who were rightly or wrongly suspected of sympathizing with Serbia. A second attempt in November led to the temporary occupation of Belgrade, but the Serbians counterattacked again, and one month later all troops were back at the positions they had occupied when the war had started. The situation would hardly change for another year. The Serbians' successful resistance — the first victory of the war for the Entente! — made a great impression on allies such as Britain. There it was deemed necessary to rebaptize the small Balkan nation from Servia, a word that conjured up the term serf, to Serbia.

One of the numerous errors committed by the high command of the army of the Danube Monarchy was to launch simultaneous offensives against Russia and Serbia instead of concentrating forces against the most dangerous enemy, Russia, and settling accounts with Serbia later. Against the Russians, the fighting took place primarily on the far side of the Carpathians, in the region of Galicia. The results were disastrous, but the

Russians did not fare any better, so the year 1914 concluded with a kind of tie, unsatisfactory to both sides, who found themselves bottled up in purely defensive positions.

The bulk of the Russian army was supposed to invade Germany's province of East Prussia as soon as possible after the outbreak of war. This is exactly what happened, even sooner than the Germans expected. The Russian invasion already started on August 12, but the two armies involved were surprisingly easily cut to pieces by the Germans in the Battles of Tannenberg (August 26–30) and the Masurian Lakes (September 8–13). The factors that determined this double fiasco include the lack of collaboration between the commanders of the invading Russian armies, the transfer of German troops from the west (which would facilitate the success of the allies in the Battle of the Marne), and the supposedly brilliant tactics of the German commanders, von Hindenburg and Ludendorff. But the real brain on the German side was actually a far less renowned officer, Max Hoffmann.[8] Of the German heroes in this episode, von Hindenburg was by far the least deserving, but he was a nobleman, a Prussian Junker, and that was why he was assigned the role of commander-in-chief, thus becoming the celebrated saviour of Germany. Ludendorff and Hoffmann, on the other hand, were personalities of bourgeois background, who were therefore given less recognition than they deserved. That is how things worked, on the social and political level, in a German Reich that was still anchored in the *ancien régime* and permeated by feudal values, which could also be said of the contemporary Habsburg Empire, Russia, and Britain. The success of the Germans in East Prussia ruined the Russian aspirations in that region; however, the Germans continued to have their hands full on the eastern front, and consequently found it impossible to move onto the offensive there. In Eastern Europe too, the "war of movement" had come to a halt.

The fall of 1914 also witnessed the entry into the war of the Ottoman Empire. For a long time, the Ottomans had been friends of the German Reich, and as early as July 30, 1914, barely a few days after the Danube Monarchy declared war on Serbia, Istanbul secretly concluded a treaty with Berlin. It was directed against Russia, the Ottomans' greatest and potentially most dangerous enemy, an enemy who was generally known to desire to reconquer Constantinople, former capital of the Byzantine Empire, for Christianity, and to lust for control of the straits linking the Black and Mediterranean Seas. Conversely, the rulers in Istanbul dreamed of regaining Russian territories in the Caucasus that were inhabited predominantly by Muslims and had once belonged to the Ottoman Empire. Difficulties also developed with the British as the Ottomans increasingly made it clear that they sympathized with the Central Powers. In Istanbul, power was actually in the hands, de facto if not de jure, of the Germanophile "Young Turks" and their leader, Enver Pacha, who served simultaneously as minister of war and commander-in-chief of the army. In late October/early November, the Gordian knot was cut and in a matter of a few days the Ottoman Empire on the one hand, and the Russians, the French, and the British on the other, officially declared war on each other. It started on October 22, when Enver Pacha ordered the shelling of Russian positions on the coast of the Black Sea. The Ottoman Empire, whose supreme ruler or sultan also bore the title of caliph, thus claiming leadership over all Muslims, proclaimed *jihad*, holy war, on the Entente on November 11, 1914. This meant that the flames of the Great War raging in Europe now also engulfed Asia, and there too unfolded the familiar scenario of failed offensives followed by equally ineffective counteroffensives, a stabilization of the front, high losses on all sides, and unheard-of atrocities inflicted on innocent civilians. By order of Enver Pacha, the Ottoman troops almost immediately launched an offensive against the Russians in the Caucasus, even though winter was at the door. In the Battle of Sarikamis, fought at the end of December 1914 and beginning of January 1915, the attackers were thrown back with heavy losses. (It is against this backdrop that the infamous Armenian holocaust would be orchestrated later in 1915.) In the meantime, in Mesopotamia, the Ottomans faced an invasion by British troops, consisting mostly of Indian soldiers.[9]

We have already seen how the British had been interested for some time in this oil-rich region and were determined to bring it under their control. So it is hardly surprising that they made their appearance there when the Ottoman Empire was still officially neutral, namely at the end of September 1914. On September 29, some British naval vessels already showed up at the mouth of the Chott-el-Arab, the confluence of the Tigris and the Euphrates. Very early in the morning of November 6, the morning after the British declaration of war on the Ottoman Empire, British-Indian troops disembarked there to conquer the virtually undefended town of Al Faw, or Fao. Hence they pushed on to the town of Basra, situated about one hundred kilometres inland, which was taken on November 22. The British commanders received formal orders to protect the oil refineries, storage tanks, pipelines, and related infrastructure, even those that happened to lie on the other side of the nearby border with Persia, which amounted to a violation of that country's neutrality. Oil was what was really at stake here, a raw material of the utmost importance to the British, as the Ottomans had apparently not realized; otherwise they would have expected this British attack and defended the region much better than they did.[10]

Along the Chott-el-Arab and the Tigris, the British advanced without problems to Ctesiphon, a town situated less than forty kilometres from Baghdad. But there Ottoman troops suddenly put up a spirited resistance, and the attackers were repulsed. The British-Indian army withdrew to the locality of Kut-el-Amara, where it was bottled up and would be besieged from early December 1914 until its capitulation at the end of April 1916. According to some historians, it was "the most inglorious surrender in British military history." In Mesopotamia too, then, the early stages of the war produced the failure of plans and offensives and the transition from a war of movement to stationary warfare. And this episode too reflected the incompetence and the elitist mentality of all too many aristocratic commanders, in this case of the British commander, Sir Charles Townshend. After his capitulation, Townshend departed to await the end of the war as a privileged POW, living in relative luxury on an island of the Sea of Marmara. The fact that thousands of his men, British as well as Indians, were imprisoned in abominable conditions and died like flies of hunger and disease, he allegedly found rather "amusing," and later he could never understand why some of his friends and colleagues reproached him for such a trifle. Incidentally, one can understand why numerous Indian POWs would be persuaded by the Ottomans to go and fight against the British along the Afghanistan and Persian frontiers, hoping that a victory of the Central Powers might yield independence for India. The ramifications of a war that had started in Europe started to make themselves felt in deepest Asia.[11]

Already, in its opening stages, the Great War revealed itself as a "world war," namely when, in August 1914, the British and the French invaded Germany's African colonies from their own possessions on that continent. The British had already decided to do this on August 5, barely one day after their declaration of war on Germany. From a purely military point of view, this initiative could not be decisive, but we should not forget that the war was an imperialist war in which the stakes were sources of raw materials, exclusive markets, etc. In those days, Africa was already a kind of promised land in this sense, and therefore a prize of utmost importance. The British "hunters of raw materials" revealed themselves to be indecently keen to take advantage of the opportunity offered by the war in order to amass territorial loot at the expense of Germany, and yet another factor played a role in this: the British wanted to avoid the possibility of German possessions in Africa being appropriated exclusively by countries such as France and Belgium. These countries were allies in the war raging in Europe, of course, but on the other hand — and this was very important in the long run — they too were imperialist "hunters of raw materials" and therefore competitors in the worldwide arena of imperialism.

A counterproductive aspect of this ruthlessly imperialist approach was the fact that, as the German governor of Togo put it, the Europeans "presented to the Africans the spectacle of white men fighting amongst themselves," something that — again, in the long run — was likely to have nefarious consequences for colonialism. In any event, in the month of August, Togo was already invaded and conquered without much difficulty by troops based in neighbouring British and French colonies. Things went far less smoothly in Cameroon, a German possession that was attacked from Nigeria and French Equatorial Africa. The dense jungle, the huge distances, and the difficult communications, especially in the territory's interior, in addition to the diseases, caused considerable losses among all combatants — and among the blacks who served as porters. It was not until February 1916 that the German resistance there would come to an end, making the Allies the masters of the entire country.

The German colony of Southwest Africa, now Namibia, bordered on South Africa, which, since the Boer War of 1899–1902 and the foundation in 1910 of the Union of South Africa, constituted an autonomous part of the British Empire. But the term "autonomous" applied exclusively to the white population, since the blacks had no say; all the power, all the wealth — especially in the shape of raw materials such as gold and diamonds — remained in the hands of an elite composed of settlers of distant Dutch and more recent British origin. (The "alliance of gold and corn," in other words, the partnership between the British mine owners and the Boers or "farmers," who represented agriculture, was the equivalent of the "symbiosis" of bourgeois industrialists and aristocratic large landowners in Europe; in the first case, the necessary cheap labour was provided by the South African blacks, in the second case, by Europe's white proletarians.)[12]

London decided that German Southwest Africa had to be conquered from South Africa, by the South Africans; however, that provoked considerable discontent among the "Afrikaners" or Boers who, during the Boer War, had benefited from German sympathy and support and who also considered themselves close ethnic relations of the Germans. The situation even triggered an outright revolt, and it was only after this revolt had been repressed that it became possible, in the spring of 1915, to embark on the conquest of the land that was later to become Namibia. The South African troops were commanded by generals such as Jan Christiaan Smuts, who would later also play an important military and political role in Britain itself. The Germans put up little resistance and capitulated at the end of May.

After Southwest Africa came the turn of the last German possession on the "black continent," German East Africa. (After the Great War, this part of Africa, transformed into a British mandate, would be called Tanganyika, and after achieving its independence and uniting with Zanzibar and Pemba, in 1964, would become Tanzania.) The hostilities would start in the fall of 1915, when an attempt to disembark British-Indian troops was repulsed. It was only in 1916 that the major part of that German colony would be conquered by British troops commanded by Smuts. Nevertheless, the German commander, Colonel (later General) Paul von Lettow-Vorbeck, would successfully pursue a kind of guerrilla warfare, capitulating only a few days after the armistice of November 11, 1918. On account of this exploit, he would be fêted as a great hero in his fatherland. Less uplifting was the fact that the war in East Africa cost the lives of approximately ten thousand soldiers and a hundred thousand porters, the latter exclusively blacks who, in contrast to the colonial soldiers recruited by the Germans, the famous Ascaris, were mostly recruited by force. Ascari, incidentally, is a Swahili word meaning "soldier."

The conquest of German East Africa also involved Belgian troops who, from bases in the Congo, conquered the German territories of Rwanda and Burundi and, in September 1916, pushed farther to the southeast, reaching the town of Tabora in German East Africa. After the war, the victors would share the spoils of the former German colonial possessions. They would not take them over as ordinary colonies, but as "mandate territories" of the League of Nations, which made little or no difference. The British and the French helped themselves to the best morsels, and Belgium pocketed Rwanda-Burundi as a reward for its efforts. In many ways, the First World War thus functioned as the last phase of the "scramble for Africa."[13] Even so, many historians continue to insist that the First World War had nothing to do with imperialist rivalries.

On the other side of the world too, there were German possessions that, thanks to the war, loomed like ripe fruits, ready to be picked by an eager imperialist rival — but which one? Japan revealed its interest in the matter by declaring war on the German Reich on August 23, 1914. Shortly thereafter, it attacked the German "concession" in China, Qingdao, besieged it, and conquered it on November 7. The British provided some military assistance, far less to be of service to Japan than in order to have a better say in the expected postwar slicing up of the huge and mouth-watering Chinese "pie." As for Germany's island colonies in the Pacific, they were divided more or less "honestly" by the Japanese and the British, allies militarily, but also keen competitors in the imperialist scramble for territories. The archipelagos of the North Pacific, i.e., the Marianas, Carolinas, and Marshall Islands, were occupied by Japan. To the south of the Equator, the Samoa Islands and New Guinea were occupied on behalf of the British Empire by the New Zealanders and Australians. Nowhere did the Germans put up serious resistance. Preoccupied by a war that was not going well on their own continent, the British and other European powers temporarily displayed less interest in China. Tokyo took full advantage of this opportunity and made some aggressive moves.[14] Japan's objective was nothing less than total economic and (direct or indirect) political domination of its big neighbour. After the Great War too, Japan was to pursue that ambition systematically and ruthlessly. The imperialist great power that would be the most perturbed by this, however, would not be Britain, but the United States, against whom Japan would eventually go to war, in 1941.

CHAPTER 17

HUMAN MOLES IN THE "LOVELY LAND OF WAR"

Except in its opening and closing stages, the Great War is a "stationary war," to be associated forever with concepts such as trenches, no man's land, and barbed wire — the great attractions of what an English war poet sarcastically called the "lovely land of war." The soldiers' existence is miserable beyond belief, and millions of them are doomed to die a horrible death or be grievously mutilated . . .

In Western Europe, by the onset of the winter of 1914–1915, the "war of movement" had given way to a "stationary war" or "war of attrition." The front line ran for a distance of approximately 750 kilometres from the Alsatian village of Pfetterhouse, located on the French-Swiss border just to the west of the city of Basel, to Lombartzijde, a Flemish village nestled between dunes and low-lying farmland (known locally as "polders") just to the north of the mouth of the Yser River. At the end of 1914, on the side of the allies, the French occupied nearly seven hundred kilometres of front, the British a little more than thirty, and the Belgians between twenty and twenty-five. In Pfetterhouse, the right sleeve of the "man of the extreme right" (*homme à l'extrême droite*) touched a Swiss border marker, at least figuratively speaking. That was kilometre zero of the "western front." War raged to the left of this *poilu*; to his right, starting in the territory of the Swiss village of Bonfol, peace and quiet prevailed. On the coast of the North Sea, in Lombartzijde, the "man of the extreme left" (*l'homme à l'extrême gauche*) stood on guard behind a wall of barbed wire that stretched from the dunes into the salty sea water. German deserters allegedly sometimes swam around the wire at night to surrender.[1]

Normally, on each side of the no man's land there were at least three lines of zigzagging trenches, supplemented by equally zigzagging "saps," utility trenches connecting the lines and sometimes jutting out into no man's land, to be used for observation purposes or to launch attacks. The western front thus counted a total of approximately forty thousand kilometres of trenches, just about the same distance as the circumference of the earth! Guillaume Apollinaire described it as "a hollow Great Wall of China." "Theoretically," observed Paul Fussell, "it would have been possible to walk [through the trenches] from Belgium to Switzerland entirely below ground."[2] The trenches were sometimes shallow, sometimes very deep, and could be extremely narrow or very wide. They were often reinforced by means of sandbags, wooden boards, etc. In order to reinforce their trenches, especially in the waterlogged Flanders' Fields, the British would import a monthly total of a quarter million empty sandbags to the front by boat from England, beginning in early 1915; by May 1915 that already amounted to a total of six million bags. At the bottom of the trenches, "duckboards" were often laid to facilitate moving around. When they were not available, as happened frequently, the soldiers stood with their feet in the water or mud, especially in the lowlands of Flanders' Fields. In this case the men soon started to suffer from a previously unknown syndrome, whereby their feet swelled, became infected, and sometimes withered away entirely. Cases of "trench foot" were first reported in December 1914 by a British nurse employed in a hospital in the Flemish town of Veurne; she wrote that it was

> . . . *a baffling ailment which is afflicting soldiers who have spent a long time in waterlogged trenches: their feet become cold, swollen, numb and bluish — sometimes affecting them so badly that amputation is the only solution.*[3]

Between the two curtains of trenches there was a strip of land, sometimes narrow and sometimes wide, known as no man's land. To attack, one had to cross this space, but, in order to make that task extra difficult for the enemy, both sides had installed a barrier of barbed wire in front of their own trenches. The no man's land was littered with debris of weapons and other equipment, unburied corpses of men and carcasses of animals, unexploded shells, and ruins of buildings. Mutilated trees and shell holes large and small, often filled with stinking mud and water, completed this sad picture, conjured up vividly by the English poetess Mary Borden as "the twisting field where bones of men stick through the tortured mud" in a poem entitled "Unidentified."[4] In his poem "Any Soldier to His Son," the British war poet George Willis produced the following description of what he sarcastically called the "lovely land of war" — the no man's land and the trenches:

> So I learned to live and lump it in the lovely land of war,
> Where all the face of nature seems a monstrous septic sore,
> Where the bowels of the earth hang open, like the guts of
> something slain;
> And the rot and wreck of everything are churned and churned
> again;
> Where all is done in darkness and where all is still in day,
> Where living men are buried and the dead unburied lay;
> Where men inhabit holes like rats, and only rats live there
> Where cottage stood and castle once in days before the war;
> Where endless files of soldiers thread the everlasting way,
> By endless miles of duckboards, through endless walls of clay;
> Where life is one hard labour, and a soldier gets his rest
> When they leave him in the daisies with a puncture in his
> chest;
> Where still the lark in summer pours her warble from the
> skies,
> And underneath, unheeding, lie the blank, upstaring eyes.[5]

It was after the Battle of the Marne and the "race to the sea" that the armies dug in from Switzerland to the North Sea coast. The Germans now hoped to win the war on the eastern front, so they adopted a purely defensive posture in the west. For the purpose of entrenching themselves, they chose the most advantageous positions, preferably hilltops and other forms of high ground. As they found themselves deep in French and Belgian territory, a few square miles did not matter much, and they were therefore quite willing to withdraw to wherever they could find favourable positions to dig their trenches. (The high ground also offered the advantage that their trenches were more easily drained, so that trench foot was less of a problem.) Moreover, the Germans were ready to stay for a long time in the same place, which meant that they took the trouble to dig in deeply and solidly. Abundant use was made of concrete in order to construct bunkers here and there, as well as fortified shelters, called "dugouts" in English, which made the defences even stronger and provided relative safety and comfort for the men. These bunkers often reached a depth of ten metres underground; they were equipped with steel doors, complete with a doorbell, wooden floors, stairs, kitchens, electric lighting, water reservoirs, toilets, mirrors, and all sorts of furniture; they sometimes had bedrooms with as many as sixteen bunk beds.

The contrast with the French trenches was striking. The French were eager to chase the *Boches* out of their country as fast as possible and were therefore compelled to adopt an attacking strategy. Consequently, there was no question of digging in deeply; the trenches were only there to provide a temporary (and therefore very basic) shelter between offensives. It was simply never the intention to remain long in the same place, so the *poilus* were never given an opportunity to make themselves safe and relatively comfortable in their trenches. Their superiors did not want them to start thinking defensively. The flame of the much-praised offensive spirit had to keep burning; the men should not think that their next offensive might not succeed. Compared to the Germans, the French combatants never enjoyed the slightest comfort in the trenches. Even in 1916, in the vicinity of Verdun, Barthas and his comrades "never even had a simple sheet of corrugated iron or even a wooden board to protect themselves against the rain between two tours of duty," even though they found themselves "in a sector of the front that had been stable for a year." "The military upper caste considered the situation . . . as temporary," added Barthas. "Things could change from one day to the next, and it was therefore not permitted to try to improve the lot of the soldiers in the trenches."

Moreover, the French trenches always had to be dug as close as possible to the German lines, so that in case of attack one would not have to cross an unduly wide no man's land. That meant that the French trenches were usually to be found on the low ground, in a valley where they — or at least their lines — were easily visible to the Germans on the high ground, including the German artillery observers. Other disadvantages were the abundance of mud and water in the lower positions, and the fact that, in case of an attack, one had to climb. This kind of predicament is conjured up in the film *Paths of Glory,* in which the French soldiers suffer huge losses while attacking a German position on the high ground, called the "ant hill." When, at the cost of high losses, the French sometimes did manage to drive the Germans out of their most advanced positions, the latter simply withdrew to the next hillside, so it was back to "square one." An example is the particularly murderous 1915 conquest of the hill of Notre-Dame-de-Lorette, situated near Arras; when this height was finally taken by the French, the Germans drew back to the far side of the next valley and entrenched themselves on top of the hillside of Vimy.[6]

Compared to those of the Germans, the British trenches were also "wet, cold, smelly, and thoroughly squalid." Here too, the offensive mentality played an important role. A Tommy left the following testimonial:

> The whole conduct of our trench warfare seemed to be based
> on the concept that we, the British, were not stopping in the
> trenches for long, but were tarrying awhile on the way to
> Berlin and that very soon we would be chasing Jerry across
> country. The result, in the long term, meant that we lived
> a mean and impoverished sort of existence in lousy scratch
> holes.[7]

The Tommies could only dream of bunkers such as those of the Germans. They had to settle for "funk-holes" dug into the inner walls of the trenches, rarely large or deep, and usually with just enough space for one or two soldiers. Sections of trenches were baptized with names of streets and squares in London or elsewhere that conjured up luxury, prestige, and fun, such as "Piccadilly" or "Regent Street." The enemy positions received less prestigious names, but they reflected the reality that life there was slightly better, for example, "Pilsen Lane" and "Pint Trench." Other names were more realistic: "Dead Man's Alley" and "Hellfire Corner."

The British spent the winter of 1914–1915 and the rest of the war in Flanders and in the north of France, where they often hit groundwater when digging even fairly shallow trenches, and where the rains came down from the heavens with great regularity, to the despair of the soldiers. The latter convinced themselves that the Germans could make it rain whenever they wanted, and that they had invented a system to make the water flow to the British lines. The Tommies, who were aware of the relative comfort of the German trenches, also imagined that their adversaries enjoyed the company of women. As many of them were tenant farmers used to renting land from aristocratic landowners, some were also convinced that their government paid rent to the French for the use of the real estate that the trenches happened to be![8]

The Irish poet and actor Cyril Morton Horne described the soldiers in a poem, "The Moles," written in 1915, as "human moles."[9] And indeed, for years on end, hundreds of thousands of men did live underground like moles in a stinking labyrinth of narrow and crooked corridors, between two walls of dirt, with high above their heads a sky that was all too often grey, but sometimes tantalizingly blue. Only the sky made them realize that they were not holed up in a long and narrow kind of mass grave.[10] And so it is not surprising that the birds flying and singing high above their heads played an important role in the life of the combatants. Larks in particular appealed to the imagination of the British soldiers, while the Germans were mesmerized by nightingales. This was not a coincidence: in the British literary tradition back to Chaucer and Shakespeare, the lark, with its appearance and its song, announces the dawn and therefore, symbolically, a new life, as well as "passage from Earth to Heaven and from Heaven to Earth," in other words, the link between life and death, which was of course particularly fragile at the front. And the German fascination for the nightingale had a lot to do with the fact that for them this songbird conjured up foreboding, above all a presentiment of death, but also a sign of spring and of love, in other words, of the life to which one was so attached, of the joy of life to which one aspired so passionately; and the *Nachtigall* also bespoke the loved ones who, for the denizens of the trenches, were as far away and as untouchable as the birds circling and singing high in the sky.[11]

Larks make an appearance in the famous poem written by a Canadian officer, John McCrae, entitled "In Flanders' Fields," even though there they play only a secondary role in comparison to the red poppies:

> *In Flanders' fields the poppies blow*
> *Between the crosses, row on row,*
> *That mark our place; and in the sky*
> *The larks, still bravely singing, fly*
> *Scarce heard amid the guns below.*[12]

The soldiers lived below ground and, other than their comrades, they never saw a human being. One could occasionally look at the other side through a periscope, but in most cases no sign of life was visible, neither in no man's land nor at the enemy lines beyond. One saw virtually nothing and no one, but one could smell all the more, namely, a repulsive stench. Indeed, countless corpses of men and horses were lying around unburied near the trenches, and it even happened that parts of bodies were integrated in the walls and parapets of the trenches. Paul Fussell writes that

> *The stench of rotten flesh was over everything, hardly repressed*
> *by the chloride of lime sprinkled on particularly offensive sites.*
> *Dead horses and dead men — and parts of both — were*
> *sometimes not buried for months and often simply became*
> *an element of parapets and trench walls. You could smell the*
> *front line miles before you could see it.*[13]

The stench not only of cadavers, but also of excrement, was part and parcel of life in a system of trenches that had become one huge open sewer, a modern-day *cloaca maxima*. Admittedly there were latrines, and it goes without saying that the very class-conscious British had separate privies for officers and ordinary soldiers; however, the latrines were often hit by shells, which caused the contents to be scattered over a large area. It also did not help that diarrhoea was pandemic, producing situations such as the one described in detail by Barthas:

> *For a soldier who had to go, it was a horrible prospect having to clamber to the large shellhole that functioned as our latrine. It was always postponed until the very last moment, in spite of truly horrible spasms. One of our comrades in the latrine was startled by a sudden burst of gunfire and, terrified, fell back on his behind. In order to avoid such misfortunes, some men used sardine- or corned-beef tins, so they did not have to leave their hideout. One pour soul even sacrificed his mess tin [gamelle] for this purpose.*[14]

Bits and pieces of horse carcasses might also rain down occasionally on the soldiers on account of explosions.[15] And the cadavers of horses reportedly smelled even worse than those of human beings. In any event, the "human moles" had no choice but to learn to live with the stench. They got used to the odour, as is illustrated by the following two lines from George Willis's aforementioned "Any Soldier To His Son":

> *I learned to sleep by snatches on the firestep of a trench,*
> *And to eat my breakfast mixed with mud and Fritz's heavy stench.*

If the soldiers of all armies smoked a lot, pipes as well as cigars and cigarettes, it was to calm their nerves and forget their hunger, but most of all to mask the omnipresent and insupportable stench of corpses and excrement.[16]

The generals and other high-ranking officers who occasionally visited the trenches were not used to the odours that prevailed there, and were disgusted by the stench and the sight of excrement. But they did not get any sympathy from the ordinary soldiers who had to live permanently in such nasty circumstances. This lack of sympathy oozes out of the text of a humorous song that was very popular among the Tommies, "That Shit Shute":

The General inspecting the trenches
Exclaimed with a horrified shout,
'I refuse to inspect a division
Which leaves excreta about'

But nobody took any notice
No one was prepared to refute
That the presence of shit was congenial
Compared with the presence of Shute

And certain responsible critics
Made haste to reply to his words
Observing his staff of advisers
Consisted entirely of turds

For shit may be shot at odd corners
And paper supplied there to suit
But shit would be shot without mourners
If someone shot that shit Shute.[17]

A typical day in the trenches started before the first rays of sunlight pierced through the darkness of night, which, during the summer, meant around 4:30 a.m. Everybody had to appear fully equipped, weapon in hand, as if an attack were imminent. The British called this routine "stand-to," or "standing to arms." The Tommies, like the French, stared in the direction of the rising sun, saw the first larks, and wondered if they would survive the coming day and if they would ever return home and reunite with their loved ones. On the other side of no man's land, the Germans' gaze chased the fleeing night and their ears strained to hear the nightingales' finales, conjuring up life and loved ones. Then came the order to "stand down," followed by permission for the men to have breakfast. In certain British units, rum was served on this occasion, two spoonfuls per person, to add to tea or to drink separately. The distribution of rum was a much-prized ceremony. And before an attack the Tommies received a more generous ration than usual. After an attack by the British, an odour not only of corpses and excrement but also of rum floated throughout the no man's land.

During the day, there was work to be done. The majority of the soldiers were peasants or industrial workers, very much used to hard work. And their bosses — the officers — liked to order them to perform all sorts of tasks, feeling that it had to be that way, and observed keenly to see that the work was done properly. They also felt that it was necessary to keep the soldiers permanently occupied in order to prevent boredom and keep morale high. Trenches had to be dug, enlarged, strengthened, or repaired after a bombardment. The weapons had to be cleaned and the uniforms and boots made to look as good as possible under the circumstances. The men were subjected to frequent inspections, and there was a constant need for soldiers to perform guard duty. That was a risky business because of the snipers lurking on the other side. The enemy positions and the no man's land had to be watched at all times, preferably via periscopes. When the chores (called *corvées* by the French) were finished, or in between chores, one was allowed some free time to write letters, delouse oneself or comrades, and sleep as much as possible. The latter was necessary because most work had to be performed at night. A rather large part of the "leaden routine of war work" was in fact done in the dark, as de Schaepdrijver writes, for example "digging, carrying away dirt, filling sandbags, laying barbed wire, putting down duckboards"; and it was also at night that munitions and other equipment had to be brought in, that water had to be pumped out of the trenches, that patrols were sent into the no man's land, etc.

The daily routine ended in the evening with the same stand-to ritual as in the morning. This time, the Germans eyed the sun setting in the west, and the British, French, and Belgians observed the approaching night; everyone looked out longingly for larks and nightingales.[18] The atmosphere of such a stand-to is conjured up in a poem penned in 1914 by Laurence Binyon, "For the Fallen," in verses that are still recited during British World War I commemorations:

> They shall grow not old, as we that are left grow old:
> Age shall not weary them, nor the years condemn.
> At the going down of the sun and in the morning
> We will remember them.[19]

The soldiers often spent days on end in the dangerous advanced lines, bordering on the no man's land and sometimes awfully close to the German trenches. "Suicide ditch" is what the British called their very first line of trenches. But from time to time the units were relieved and transferred to the rear, where they could take a break in a camp, a hamlet, or a village at a relatively safe distance from the front. Receiving a permit to go home and visit the family was an exception, and it was of course out of the question for the majority of the Belgians and many of the men from northern France, whose villages or towns of origin were occupied by the Germans. The same applied to the "colonial" soldiers from Senegal, India, and elsewhere. The Belgian soldiers normally spent four days in the first lines, followed by another four days in the rear to perform all sorts of jobs; finally, they were allowed four days of "rest," but that also often involved doing work and exercising at the whim of their superiors. In any event, it was then possible to relax somewhat, for example by playing cards and of course visiting taverns and brothels.

How was the food at the front? The answer: not bad at all in theory, but in practice far from satisfactory. Perhaps surprisingly, the British were the most spoiled in this respect. A soldier's daily ration might include a decent amount of bread, fresh or canned meat, fresh or dried vegetables, some bacon and cheese, and small quantities of tea, sugar, and jam. For the majority of the Tommies, that was more and better food than at home in peacetime! It was extremely rare that fresh meat arrived in the trenches, however, and in general one had to settle for canned beef, "corned-beef," known in the soldier's lingo as "bully beef." (It seems that the term bully had nothing to do with bulls, but was derived from the French word *bouilli*, "boiled," which is how the British traditionally like to have meat prepared.) But the bully beef was actually rather tasty, and the Germans loved it. The Tommies knew this and were understandably proud of it, as it was probably the first and last time in history that British food was held in high esteem by foreigners. They sometimes offered cans of bully beef to German POWs as a gesture of generosity, solidarity, and Christian charity, as appears from these lines of the poem "On the Somme," from the pen of soldier Claude Penrose:

And when they brought their captives back, hungry and
downhearted,
They called them 'Fritz' and slapped their backs, and, all with
one accord,
They shared with them what food they'd left from when the
long day started,
And gave them smokes and bully to the glory of the Lord.[20]

The daily ration of the French consisted in theory of "750 grams of bread, one pound of fresh meat, an ounce of rice or dried vegetables, salt, sugar, some form of fat, instant coffee, one litre of wine, and twenty grams of tobacco." Precious little of this regularly reached the men in the trenches though, and the *poilus* were generally unhappy with the food they ended up with. In May 1915, a soldier complained, for example, that in the evening the men only got to eat *singe*, "monkey," that is, canned meat with pota-toes, smothered in a "hopelessly unappetizing sauce." The monotony of the rations annoyed the soldiers of all armies, but those who had enough money could buy food in nearby shops or farms, where — for high prices — tasty treats were available such as butter, chocolate, and jam. It was occasionally possible to exchange food with allied troops stationed nearby. Barthas relates how this was done by the British and the French in May 1915, somewhere in Artois:

Because in their trenches they only received biscuits and
canned food, they came to us to ask for pieces of bread and to
lick the leftovers in our casseroles. In exchange, we received
tobacco and cigarettes, of which they had plenty.

The French, on the other hand, had great quantities of wine, and much of it found its way into the thirsty throats of the Tommies. It was at that time that the English term "plonk," meaning inferior wine, originated; it was derived from the French (*vin*) *blanc*, "white wine." The *poilus* drank an awful lot of wine: wine was "their God," it made them "forget their misery," it was "their best friend"! The military authorities displayed remarkable gen-erosity in this respect: in the summer of 1914 the French soldiers received a daily ration of a quarter of a litre, but by 1917 the daily allowance had risen to one full litre. Enormous quantities of alcohol were in fact consumed in all the armies. As mentioned, the Tommies regularly got rum for breakfast. Elsewhere, in addition to wine or rum, the men occasionally received gin or brandy. The reason for this generosity on the part of the military authorities was simple, writes a historian: the soldiers needed this kind of "doping" to be able to fight and tolerate the stress of combat in general. The alcohol, he continues, "provided a remedy against fear," served "as a kind of shield," and made the killing easier. Attacks were unthinkable without some alcohol first being served to the combatants. The superiors themselves also needed alcohol in order to function; British officers consumed one to two bottles of whisky per day. And of course this alcohol abuse caused serious problems, including fights, insubordination, etc.[21]

As far as sustenance was concerned, the German soldiers were much worse off than the British and the French, and during the course of the war their situation would not improve; to the contrary. Even at an early stage, the men were complaining about the poor quantity as well as quality of the food. On the eastern front, in September–October 1915, the situation was so bad that the soldiers were virtually starving and talked about defecting to the enemy in the hope of receiving some food there. The soldiers of Germany's ally in the east, the Danube Monarchy, were even worse off, and often virtually perished of starvation. It was common for them to sell some of their equipment and clothes for some food and drink, and they frequently begged civilians for something to eat. On the Russian side, the situation was no better.[22]

In the trenches, at least some got lots to eat: the rats. The soldiers hated these omnipresent, dirty, and aggressive pests, who were particularly big and fat because they feasted on the corpses of men and horses, and they constantly bothered the men when they tried to get some sleep. Against this plague the British used Jack Russells and other terriers, or any available dogs, known as "ratters"; cats were also used for this purpose. Likewise well-fed, mostly at the expense of the soldiers themselves, were the insects and the vermin that infested the frontlines. Barthas described the plague represented by the flies:

> *Thousands of voracious flies descended on the corpses. All*
> *these horrible flies of the mass graves of Lorette, swarming out*
> *far behind the frontline, they disgusted and sickened us. They*
> *crawled into the wine bottles, the mess tins, and kitchen pots*
> *and never ceased to buzz around us. Looking for prey, they*
> *moved from the dead to the living, and vice versa.*

A similar constant nuisance were lice and fleas. Referring to those pests, Barthas wrote the following in his diary:

> *Our main occupation was hunting for lice. They descended*
> *on us by the thousands. We found them everywhere in our*
> *clothes. Some were white, some black, some grey, and some*
> *had a cross on their back, like crusaders. Some were tiny, and*
> *some were big as grains of wheat. This vermin multiplied like*
> *crazy and feasted on our skin . . . To get rid of them, some*
> *men sprayed petroleum on themselves every evening, others*
> *rubbed themselves with camphor or any kind of insecticide.*
> *Nothing helped. When you had killed ten of them, one*
> *hundred took their place.*

Equally bothersome were the fleas. A Canadian soldier complained that "we are alive with vermin and sit picking at ourselves like baboons. It is months since we have been out of our clothes." The Tommies also grumbled loudly about the problem of the fleas. Hunting for fleas was known to them as "reading your shirt." And it was in this context that in 1915 the English term "lousy" originated.[23] In "Any Soldier to His Son," George Willis had the following to say about fleas:

> *I learned to hunt for vermin in the lining of my shirt,*
> *To crack them with my finger-nail and feel the beggars spurt;*
> *I learned to catch and crack them by the dozen and the score*
> *And to hunt my shirt tomorrow and to find as many more.*[24]

Another war poet who found inspiration in the hunt for fleas and lice was Isaac Rosenberg. In a poem entitled "The Immortals" one can read the following:

I killed them, but they would not die.

. . . .

In vain — for faster than I slew
They rose more cruel than before.

I killed and killed with slaughter mad;
I killed till all my strength was gone.
And still they rose to torture me,
For devils only die in fun.

I used to think the devil hid
In women's smiles and wine's carouse.
I called him Satan, Balzebub.
But now I call him, dirty louse.[25]

The winter cold and summer heat, the dampness, vermin, lack of hygiene, and many other inconveniences caused all sorts of diseases. Among the most common of those were tuberculosis, heart problems, diarrhoea, throat infections, bronchitis, dysentery, and of course also venereal diseases. But from the military medical doctors, officers of the "better" classes, the simple soldiers could not expect much sympathy, if any. The physicians all too often revealed themselves to be haughty and arrogant and assumed that the diseases of which one complained were unimportant or feigned. In order to be sent to an infirmary or field hospital, one had to be near death. It was even risky to report sick, because the superiors were quick to suspect that this was motivated by cowardice or shirking of duty and ready to mete out appropriate punishment.[26] Countless men did indeed feign some sort of disease in order to escape, even temporarily, the hell of the trenches.

In the trenches, there were no proper shelters to accommodate all soldiers. All too often, the men had to sleep out in the open, in winter as well as in summer. Consequently, they suffered from the heat in the summer and the cold and dampness for much of the rest of the year. Many men froze to death in the trenches; for example, British soldiers in the vicinity of Ypres during the winter of 1916–1917. It was also difficult to find a spot where one could lie down. Mostly, one tried to sleep while sitting on a bench or leaning against the wall of the trench. It was quite a treat to be able to crawl into a funk-hole or a dugout; only the Germans were better off in this respect, as we have seen. Being able to sleep, and to sleep well, was a great pleasure, and one that was all too rare. ("During the last four days here in the trenches, I was not even able to sleep for eight hours," a British soldier wrote to his father in September 1915.) Sleep not only brought men the necessary rest after long and exhausting marches, hard labour, or hours of guard duty, but also represented a kind of escape from the horrible reality of their existence in the trenches. The Tommies called sleeping "being Murphyized," or "lying in the arms of Murphy." Murphy was a typically Irish and therefore proletarian name, but the saying was inspired by the very similar name of Morpheus, the god of sleep and dreams. The expression thus reflected the fact that sleep had the same effect as morphine.[27]

In all armies, the officers benefited from relatively comfortable accommodations. Even in the presumably egalitarian French army, the officers were "more equal" in this respect: in the trenches, they usually had some sort of shelter featuring basic amenities such as a small table and a lamp, where they could regularly enjoy a minimum of comfort and privacy, read a newspaper, or simply be alone. In the film *Paths of Glory*, Colonel Dax (Kirk Douglas) inhabits such a hideout.[28] Barthas reports how, near the Artesian village of Neuville-Saint-Vaast, in the fall of 1915,

> *the captain was holed up in a hideout of at least twelve steps deep. He was seated behind a little table and was quietly playing some card game . . . Next to him, a little stove diffused a pleasant heat. A batman served him tea. What a difference with our fate!*

But the officers did even better at a more or less safe distance from the first lines, where the men were put up in abandoned and often partly ruined homes and barns. Barthas describes the situation in the village of Vermelles in January 1915:

*Not a single house was left intact. The least damaged ones
were requisitioned by the gentlemen senior officers, those
that were half destroyed became the property of their lesser
colleagues, such as lieutenants, and those with collapsed roofs
and a few missing floors became the home of our company.*[29]

This kind of discrimination, with the officers typically sleeping in beds
and they themselves on straw or simply on the cold ground, infuriated the
men. What annoyed them even more was that they also convinced themselves that their superiors enjoyed female company in their accommodations, something of which they could only dream. And much irritation was
provoked by the fact that the officers ate considerably better. In the Austro-
Hungarian army, where the ordinary soldiers frequently starved, the officers enjoyed "more calories than the entire company — wine and cake, also
cigarettes and cigars." The officer who acknowledged this added that "such
inequality was revolting. In trenches where we were all obviously equals
in the face of death." But more typical for an officer, or at least a general,
was a comment by the commander of the Austro-Hungarian troops on the
Serbian front, General Oskar Potiorek. When it was reported to him that his
men did not have enough to eat, he replied that "making war means going
hungry." The Austro-Hungarian soldiers would indeed "go hungry," very
hungry, until the end of the war. As late as February 1916, an officer on the
Serbian front reported that the men only received one-third of the normal
food rations, with only one lump of bread every four days, while "the staff
officers' mess [continued to] serve the usual four-course dinners."[30]

Similarly, in spite of being reasonably well fed, the British soldiers complained that the officers received more and better sustenance. This found an
echo in these lines of a popular soldiers' song, "Tell Me Now":

I don't know why we feeds so pore,
Tell me, oh, tell me now.
I don't know why we feeds so pore,
When the officer men eats so awful much more,
Tell me, oh, tell me now.[31]

During meals, a strict apartheid was observed between the officers and their subordinates. A member of the Canadian forces, which during the Great War served as a corps within the British army, described a typical scene:

> *It was a French home that had escaped damage with the exception of losing one corner of its roof, and was now an officers' mess. They were having lunch. A table was spread with a white cloth. On it were real dishes, a bowl of roses, tall bottles with expensive labels. The officers were in slacks, clean clothed and their batmen hovered about arranging seats for them. It was too much for us to watch. We went out front and saw the men lined up for their meal. They carried dirty mess tins and were issued with a ladlefull of greasy mulligan in the tin tops, and weak-looking tea. They sat around the ruins and ate, wherever they could squat, without speaking, hurriedly, as if they hated the business. Some emptied part of their issue on the ground and scrubbed their mess tins with bits of sandbags as they shambled off to where they slept.*[32]

In contrast to the soldiers, the officers could also wash and shave regularly. All too often, the ordinary soldiers had no water and, if they wanted to shave, had to do so with coffee or even wine. (It was probably the sight of many unshaven men that generated the French slang for ordinary soldier, *poilu*, meaning "hairy," probably in 1915.)[33] The soldiers were so dirty that it tended to depress them. Paul Fussell cites a British soldier on the Gallipoli front, who candidly admitted that "we were all lousy and couldn't stop shitting because we had caught dysentery. We wept, not because we were frightened, but because we were so dirty."[34] Similarly, the term by which the German soldiers frequently referred to themselves, "front-line swine" (*Frontschweine*), was an allusion to their filthy appearance.

The social distance between the upper-class officers and their plebeian underlings also revealed itself during card games, a form of sociability. The French officers played poker or bridge among themselves, while the men played a far less classy but very popular game, belote.[35] Among themselves, the officers could feel at ease, socially speaking, but not in the company of their subordinates, and the reverse was also true. The soldiers formed small, tightly knit groups of comrades, "little families," as Barthas wrote, "where everybody felt comfortable and where an atmosphere of affection, solidarity, and mutual trust prevailed," but "from which the officers and even NCOs were excluded."[36] And that was in the relatively egalitarian French army, where the officers were less snooty than in the British, German, and Russian forces.

The officers also benefited from all sorts of other more or less important privileges that angered the men. For example, the officers were the first to receive equipment suitable for trench warfare. Barthas told how in 1917 a small number of real raincoats and rubber boots were finally issued to the troops, something that would have been particularly welcome to soldiers in the advanced lines; but, he continued,

> . . . the officers, sergeants, and their orderlies descended on
> the boots like a flock of ravens on a prey. And all of that under
> the approving gaze of the captain, who had set the shameful
> example himself.

The officers also enjoyed first choice when it came to looting abandoned homes in the vicinity of the frontline. A German soldier reported how, in the French village of Cuy, near Noyon, the troops took all sorts of furniture and other equipment out of the houses to use in their bunkers and elsewhere in the trenches. "First, the officers appropriated whatever they liked, and it was only afterwards that the men got their turn." The French officers frequently received small parcels from relatives and friends, containing presents, tobacco, cigars, and all sorts of goodies; the ordinary soldiers rarely if ever received such gifts, because the shipping rates were very high. Some upper-class officers had delicacies sent to them that their plebeian underlings had never seen, such as dried figs and dates, lobsters, and even a complete Marseille-style fish stew known as *bouillabaisse*! As for the British officers, they ordered cigars, coffee, tea, biscuits, and other types of ambrosia directly from prestigious London sources such as Fortnum & Mason.[37]

The soldiers were also disgusted by the fact that their superiors were all too often able to avoid the dangers of trench warfare. The higher the grade, the further from the front line, seemed to be the rule of thumb. This system prevailed among the Germans and the British, less so among the French. A German soldier on the eastern front thus wrote in the fall of 1915 that "they hardly ever saw the officers," that "they revealed themselves only by sending us written orders, which usually involved some kind of prohibition." Another soldier complained that his commanding officer rarely showed up in the trenches, that he preferred to stay safely in his casemate; "he even relieved himself in his underground bunker, namely by using an old steel helmet which his orderly had to empty outside."[38] It also bothered the men that after heavy fighting the officers received the lion's share of the honours. The German soldiers expressed their feelings about this in the following short verse:

Auf vorne klatscht der Kugelregen,	*Bullets rain down on those exposed up front,*
Auf hinten fällt der Ordenssegen.	*Honours shower those sheltered in the rear.*[39]

Generally speaking, the soldiers did not like their own, or any, officers, but despised and sometimes even hated them passionately. The news of the death of unloved officers was usually met with indifference and contempt. And soldiers sometimes — often? — shot their own officers, something for which opportunities presented themselves regularly in trench warfare. Later, the killing of officers would become fairly common, for example among the American soldiers in the Vietnam War, where this was called "fragging." During the First World War, the US military courts dealt with about 370 cases of violence perpetrated on officers, but it is estimated that barely 10 per cent of such acts ended up before a court-martial.

The German army featured a particularly high number of snobbish "gentlemen officers" of lofty social background who insulted, humiliated, and mistreated their men. Their chances of being killed by subordinates remained high throughout the war. The Alsatian Dominik Richert mentions the case of a lieutenant who, during an attack, had shot wavering soldiers and was eventually killed by a bullet fired into his back by one of his own men.[40] Barthas relates how during the offensive on the Somme of summer 1916, he and his comrades "had found the corpse of a German officer near a trench . . . his head was covered with blood, and next to him lay a blood-stained shovel. We concluded that his own men had eliminated him." Barthas opined that this had happened because the officer had refused to surrender.[41] The contempt and hatred of the soldiers for their officers was proportionate to the rank of the officer, and the most detested were the generals and colonels. During the entire duration of the war, this military *crème de la crème* was generally to be found ensconced in some comfortable hotel or even a château at a safe distance from the front — like the castle, featuring fine furniture and rugs, in which the generals sojourn in *Paths of Glory*.[42] That in a modern war the commanders cannot personally lead their troops as in Napoleon's time, was obvious, and the majority of soldiers understood this very well, but it did offend them that these high-ranking gentlemen, representatives of the "better classes" and often aristocrats, enjoyed all sorts of luxuries and could live virtually the same privileged life they had been used to before the war, while on account of the war the proletarian soldiers suffered even greater misery than they had known in peacetime.

The example was set by German Emperor Wilhelm II, who installed himself in Spa, like Karlsbad and Baden-Baden one of the prewar playgrounds of the elite, associated with delicious food, music, leisure, and the good life in general. But then again, he was the supreme commander (*oberster Kriegsherr*), and the majority of generals had to settle for somewhat less luxurious and prestigious quarters. Still, they too located comfortable and pleasant accommodations, usually in some castle, hotel, or villa. After the Battle of the Marne, General Joffre installed his headquarters in the deluxe Hôtel du Grand Condé, situated in the aristocratic town of Chantilly, a little to the north of Paris; he himself resided in a pleasant villa nearby. The headquarters of John French, the commander-in-chief of the BEF, changed frequently at first as the British withdrew from Mons to the Marne and then moved north into Flanders' Fields. But it rankled the Tommies that he and his entourage always managed to enjoy fine suppers, served by lovely young women, while an orchestra provided musical accompaniment. French was particularly fond of feminine company and some of his own colleagues felt that there were "too many prostitutes" hanging around his headquarters! French also liked to zip over to Paris for dinner in the Ritz Hotel, where, just as in the nearby deluxe restaurant Maxim's, senior officers dined daily — often in charming (but paid) feminine company. Of the generals in their distant and comfortable, even luxurious headquarters, the ordinary soldiers — not exactly teetotallers themselves! — generally felt that they drank too much.[43]

From their lofty chateaux and hotels, the generals and other staff officers also looked down, almost literally and certainly symbolically, on the ordinary soldiers in the trenches; at least, that is how the latter saw things. Barthas felt that way after a visit to a general in a castle in the village of Titre in April 1916:

> The entrance hall, the corridors, the staircases, it all shone,
> perfectly waxed and polished; carpets covered the floors.
> Servants, batmen, chamber maids, they all gave me a dirty
> look, as if they were saying: what is this lousy Poilu doing
> here? And they looked with great contempt at my boots, which
> left dirty, muddy tracks on the floor and on the rugs.[44]

The men were convinced that the staff officers had no idea what their miserable existence was like at the front, in the trenches. "[They] had heard of the trenches, yes," writes Fussell, "but as [London's upscale] West End hears of the East End — a nasty place where common people lived." And Lloyd George was to declare after the war that "the distance between the castles [i.e. the generals] and the trenches was as great as that between the stars of the firmament and the deepest caves here on earth." Admittedly, the generals sometimes came to inspect the trenches, but only when it was calm at the front. General Haig allegedly never visited the trenches, not even once. And it was precisely because they had no clue how things really were at the front that the staff officers could spout all sorts of nonsense that the ordinary soldiers perceived as insults. "No soldier who has fought ever entirely overcomes his disrespect for the Staff," emphasizes Fussell, and he cites a poem by Robert Graves, "The Persian Version," containing this "mimicry of complacent Staff rhetoric":

Despite a strong defence and adverse weather
All arms combined magnificently together.[45]

The men were exasperated by the fact that stupid ignorance made it possible for "the army commanders, ensconced in warm and dry quarters, to consistently emphasize the need to maintain an offensive spirit, to keep aggressive instincts honed for the coming decisive battles," and to repeatedly order "spirited attacks."[46] The soldiers' hatred and contempt of the generals was voiced as follows by a famous war poet, Siegfried Sassoon, in "The General":

> *'Good-morning; good-morning!' the General said*
> *When we met him last week on the way to the line.*
> *Now the soldiers he smiled at are most of 'em dead,*
> *And we're cursing his staff for incompetent swine.*[47]

Again and again, the soldiers had to pay a high price with their blood for what they felt to be the idiocies of the generals. And they felt that the headquarters were full of shirkers or *embusqués*, as they were called in French; *embusqués*, meaning something like "those in hiding." The Germans saw those shirkers as the binary alternative of their own fate as "front swine" and called them *Etappenschweine*, "swine of the rear." Barthas had this to say about the despised *embusqués*:

> *In the command posts of the majors and captains we noticed*
> *more and more young and strong men who generally had ill-*
> *defined positions as messengers, orderlies, signalers, tailors,*
> *barbers, etc. They fussed over and waited on the officers,*
> *the new lords of the twentieth century. In return, they were*
> *allowed to escape the first circle of the new hell of Dante: the*
> *trenches.*[48]

Countless ordinary soldiers wondered how they themselves could escape the hell of the trenches. A number of possibilities did in fact exist; for example, self-mutilation, preferably in the form of a wound to the hand.

Feigning a disease might also serve as a way out of the trenches, at least temporarily. But we know that the military physicians happened to be particularly suspicious and that this stratagem involved the risk of being considered a coward and treated accordingly. And yet, numerous were those who tried that route, and the number of attempts increased over time. Barthas relates how the *poilus* tried all sorts of tricks "to catch a fever or to cause a pulmonary wheeze, to make fluid appear in eyes or ears, even at the risk of becoming blind or deaf." Some men had themselves injected with products that triggered symptoms of jaundice, or arranged to infect small wounds in order to be hospitalised for some time. The soldiers also visited bordellos in the hope of getting a venereal disease. In keeping with the law of supply and demand, one had to pay a supplement for the services of prostitutes infected with syphilis![49]

Something of which every soldier dreamed was the kind of light injury that was also serious enough to result in being sent for as long as possible to a hospital far from the frontlines. The British called this a "Blighty wound," a wound resulting in being sent for treatment to "Blighty," that is, England. (The term "Blighty" was the English version of the Hindi term *bilayati*, meaning "European" in general and "English" or "British" in particular.)[50] The French called this kind of injury *la fine blessure*, "the delicate injury," while the Germans used the expression *Tangoschuß*, *Heimschuß*, or *Heimatschuß*, "tango- or home-shot," i.e., a wound that served as a permit to go home, to the *Heimat*. In the poem *"Gebet vor der Schlacht"* ("Prayer before the Battle"), Alfred Lichtenstein vented his desire for such a *Heimatschuß*:

Aber muß ich doch dran glauben,	*But when my time will come,*
Laß mich nicht zu schwer verwunden.	*Let it not be a serious injury.*
Schick mir einen leichten Beinschuß,	*Make it a light wound in the leg,*
Eine kleine Armverletzung,	*A little something on the arm perhaps,*
Daß ich als ein Held zurückkehr,	*So that I can go home as a hero,*
Der etwas erzählen kann.[51]	*And tell them some tall tale.*

Surrendering was yet another way to escape the trenches, but that too was a risky stratagem, because both sides sometimes executed both prisoners of war and wounded enemy soldiers to avoid possible trouble, which also happened because, in the heat of battle, the well-ventilated fire of hatred for the official enemy could flare up. Having seen comrades killed or injured, the combatants were not always inclined to be charitable, or even deal correctly, with prisoners. Even so, countless soldiers decided to run the risk, and collective surrenders were likewise a common occurrence from the beginning until the end of the Great War. It was above all in the Austro-Hungarian army that collective capitulations took place, especially during the Russian Brusilov Offensive in 1915, when the Russians bagged 380,000 prisoners. On the side of the Germans, the fall of 1918 would witness a veritable epidemic of surrenders both individual and collective. In any event, massive numbers of soldiers ended up surrendering. After only one year of war, the Germans had already bagged more than one million allied POWs. The British would end up with a total of 328,000 German prisoners, and the Russians just over one million Germans and about two million Austro-Hungarians — more than 2.7 million, according to Alexandre Sumpf. At the end of the war, a total of anywhere from seven million to nine million soldiers would find themselves prisoners. Practically none ever tried to escape; being a POW was no sinecure, but it was paradise compared to the hell from which surrender had allowed them to find deliverance. The great majority of prisoners were quite content to wait patiently for the end of the war and of their detention.[52]

Death constituted a particularly radical form of escape from the hell of trench warfare. It was what the *poilus* called *la grande permission*, "the big furlough."[53] This option was, not seldom, chosen by officers, as we have already seen, but also by ordinary soldiers.[54] Siegfried Sassoon devoted a poem to the suicide of a young soldier, "Suicide in the Trenches," and he ends it with a reference to the hell from which this act of desperation offered deliverance:

> I knew a simple soldier boy
> Who grinned at life in empty joy,
> Slept soundly through the lonesome dark,
> And whistled early with the lark.

In winter trenches, cowed and glum,
With crumps and lice and lack of rum,
He put a bullet through his brain.
No one spoke of him again.

You smug-faced crowds with kindling eye
Who cheer when soldier lads march by,
Sneak home and pray you'll never know
The hell where youth and laughter go.[55]

To the overwhelming majority of officers and soldiers who would not survive the Great War, however, in total approximately ten million men, death brought escape from hell without having been invited. During the opening stages of the war in the summer of 1914, the titanic battles of Verdun and the Somme, etc., hundreds of thousands perished. But even on ordinary days, when all was quiet on the front, many men were killed. On the western front, the two sides sacrificed a daily average of 2,250 dead — of whom 800 to 900 were French — and nearly 5,000 injured, for a total of approximately 7,000 "casualties," that is, the total of dead, injured, missing in action, and POWs. Calculated over the entire duration of the war, the British alone suffered 1,500 casualties daily, of whom it is assumed that approximately 50 per cent were killed. Even on the calmest days, hundreds, even thousands of men died. "Wastage" is what the British high command called it.[56]

The chances of being released from the trenches by the Grim Reaper, then, were very high. Conversely, an infantryman's chances of survival in the trenches were low. It has been calculated that the British soldiers had close to a 60 per cent chance of becoming a casualty, and of that number about one third were likely to be killed. The risks were even greater for the French *poilus*. But the majority of the men managed to convince themselves that somehow they would survive. This sentiment was reflected in the words of a song that was very popular with the British troops, "The Bells of Hell":

The Bells of Hell go ting-a-ling-a-ling, for you but not for me.
And the little devils have a sing-a-ling-a-ling, for you but not
for me.

Oh death where is thy sting-a-ling-a-ling, oh grave thy victory?
The Bells of Hell go ting-a-ling-a-ling, for you but not for me.[57]

In any event, death did bring deliverance from a miserable existence to many soldiers, and in this sense at least death was "welcome," as was suggested by a British officer, Captain R.C.G. Dartford, in a 1916 poem entitled "Welcome Death":

When you've been dead beat, and had to go on
While others died; when our turn to be gone
Is overdue; when you're pushed ahead
('Go on till you die' is all they said),
Then die — and you're glad to be dead.[58]

Another English war poet, Alec de Candole, saw death as "an everlasting rest [he] oft yearn[ed] for," and he added

. . . I find not death a curse
Better than life perchance, at least not worse.[59]

The theme of death as liberation was also featured in a German soldiers' song, *"Bald, allzubalde,"* "Soon, all too soon":

Einsam im Walde blüht wohl ein Blümlein rot,	*A lonely red flower blooms in the forest,*
bald, allzubald bin ich tot,	*Soon, all too soon, I will be dead,*
bald, allzubalde.	*Soon, all too soon.*
Fleugt wo ein Stückchen Blei, nimmt mir mein Sorgen.	*A piece of lead takes away my worries.*
Mir ist halt einerlei: heut oder morgen.[60]	*It does not matter to me: today or tomorrow.*

In Hollywood war movies, the soldiers tend to die of a bullet in the chest, and they drop dead instantly — except, of course, if it is a bad guy who needs a moment to make a confession, or a hero who still needs the time to give a last kiss to his tearful beauty. But the majority of combatants who were killed in the Great War were not carried off in a flash by the angel of death, even though this is what the authorities or comrades liked to tell the bereaved. In reality, a speedy demise was a privilege allowed only to a lucky minority. For the others, death was accompanied by hellish suffering and an agony lasting many hours, even days; for example, hanging in the barbed wire or lying stuck in the mud of a shell hole somewhere in no man's land. The lamentations of the dying were a veritable torture for their powerless comrades, and also for their enemies in nearby trenches, who realized of course that a similar nasty fate was perhaps reserved for them.

The overwhelming majority of injuries received by the soldiers did not belong to the coveted category of Blighty wound, but were painful and ended all too often in death. The survival chances of the wounded were low because of the still relatively primitive state of medical care at the time, combined with the indifference of all too many medical doctors and members of the medical services in general. The injured French had one chance in four of dying, British and Germans one chance out of seven. The situation was considerably worse on the Eastern front, especially on the side of the Russians and the Serbians.[61] Grave injuries were a nightmare for the soldiers when they did not eventually lead to a liberating death. It often meant that the injured were left horribly and permanently mutilated. Each army produced thousands, if not tens of thousands of cases of what was called *gueules cassées* ("smashed faces") by the French, and *Menschen ohne Gesicht* ("faceless people") or, in the case of missing arms or legs, *Korbmenschen* ("men in baskets") by the Germans. Numerous were those who, after being subjected to crude forms of plastic surgery, considered their fate worse than death and refused to return home or even to receive the visit of relatives, because they did not want to traumatize loved ones with their hideous appearance. And so they were stashed away until the end of their days in special institutions, called *Geheimlazaretten* or "secret hospitals" in German, from which, for obvious reasons, all mirrors were removed. France would end up with slightly less than ten thousand cases of *gueules cassées*.[62]

Even more than death itself, the soldiers dreaded an injury that might bring about a slow death or a permanent mutilation. In comparison to such a fate, a rapid crossing of the bar loomed like a blessing.[63] This opinion oozed out of the following stanza of Cyril Morton Horne's aforementioned poem, "The Moles":

> *And this is our Fate: when the Gods are kind*
> *Our existence shall simply cease —*
> *A sniper's bullet — a trench that's mined —*
> *Godspeed, and a quick release![64]*

The writer died "somewhere in France" on January 27, 1916, while he was trying to help a wounded comrade get out of the no man's land. When he was poised to return safely and his comrades were about to cheer him for his courage, he was mortally wounded by shrapnel from a shell exploding above him. Let us hope that he was killed instantly and thus rewarded for his gallantry with the "quick release" conjured up in his poem.

To countless Tommies, and the combatants of the Great War in general, death brought not only deliverance from the misery of trench warfare, but also of the social misery that the lives of all too many of them were saturated with, a condition which would not change significantly, in Britain and elsewhere, until after the war — but certainly not thanks to the war! — as we will soon see. In a poem entitled "Armistice Day, 1921," by English war poet Edward Shanks, the dead were happy. Indeed, where they dwelled, there was no misery, no poverty, and no exorbitant rent had to be paid. They did not experience hunger and could truly be free. In other words, where they dwelled it was as different as day and night from the British fatherland they had left behind and for which they had presumably "given" their lives.

> *Mourn not for us. Our better luck*
> *At least has given us peace and rest.*
> *We struggled when our moment struck*
> *But now we understand that death knew best.*
>
> . . . .
>
> *We, out of all, have had our pay,*
> *There is no poverty where we lie;*

The graveyard has no quarter-day,
The space is narrow but the rent not high.

No empty stomach here is found;
Unless some cheated worm complain
You hear no grumbling underground:
Oh, never, never wish us back again!

Mourn not for us, but rather we
Will meet upon this solemn day
And in our greater liberty
Keep silent for you, a little while, and pray.[65]

Finally, a word about an expression often seen on monuments and heard in the official discourse whenever the subject arises of those "fallen" in the Great War, namely that they "gave their life" for "us," for "humanity," for "liberty," etc. May it suffice to refer to a comment offered by someone who was there, the French soldier Louis Barthas:

And in the villages they are already talking about erecting
monuments to the glory of the victims of this great massacre
or, as the jingoists say, to "honour those who freely offered
their life." As if those poor souls had an alternative . . . Oh!
If only the dead of this war could rise from their graves. They
would smash these hypocritical monuments, for those who
erected them are the ones who sacrificed them mercilessly.[66]

CHAPTER 18
MILITARIA 1915: THE GREAT OFFENSIVES

In 1915, the French and British launch a number of large-scale offensives on the western front, hoping to pierce the German lines and thus to win the war. But in trench warfare the defenders, equipped with modern weapons such as machine guns, enjoy the advantage. On the battlefields of Neuve-Chapelle, Loos, Notre-Dame-de-Lorette, and elsewhere in Artois and Champagne, the attacking poilus and Tommies thus perish by the hundreds of thousands, but the Germans too suffer huge losses . . .

Toward the end of 1914, the Germans entrenched themselves in strong defensive positions on the western front in order to be able to transfer troops to the east. There, with the help of their Austro-Hungarian ally, they hoped to defeat the Russians in the spring of 1915 and thus to win the war. Conversely, the French and the British believed that in the same spring of 1915 they would finally be able to finish the job started with their success at the Battle of the Marne, namely driving the Germans out of France and Belgium. They realized that the German defences were very strong but they believed that via concentrated attacks they would be able to pierce the enemy lines, so that the cavalry could pour through the gaps, roll up the German lines, and thus open the way for a triumphant march to Berlin.

It started with a British and French offensive in the north of France in the spring of 1915. On March 10, the British tried to break through the German lines in the vicinity of the village of Neuve-Chapelle, just to the south of Armentiers. They made some progress, but their advance petered out after three days. The forty thousand men involved in the attack suffered about twelve thousand casualties, including more than four thousand Indian troops. Like the generals at the time, today historians of what has been called the "drum-and-trumpet school [of historiography]" continue to rationalize this affair by claiming that the German enemy as well as the French ally were impressed by the unexpectedly good performance of British forces they had supposedly underestimated. The English war poet H.W. Garrod, on the other hand, did not seek any excuses. He offered the following laconic comment in a short poem entitled "Epitaph: Neuve Chapelle":

> *Tell them at home, there's nothing here to hide:*
> *We took our orders, asked no questions, died.*[1]

While the British were recovering from their experience at Neuve-Chapelle, the Germans suddenly delivered a major surprise. On April 22, in the vicinity of Ypres, Franco-Algerian and Canadian troops were subjected to the very first attack involving poison gas. They suffered considerable losses and a gap briefly opened up in the allied lines. But with the help of improvised gas masks, "handkerchiefs soaked in water or urine," the Canadians succeeded in halting the German advance. The allies were fortunate that the Germans had underestimated the potential of their new weapon and did not have the reserves necessary to take full advantage of the surprise. The Germans continued their gas attacks for a few more days, but it was in vain. Soon after the first gas attack, the gas mask was invented by a Newfoundland medical doctor serving in the British army, Cluny Macpherson; his prototype was a German helmet to which he added a canvas hood with eyepieces and a breathing tube.[2]

On May 9, 1915, the French tried their luck in Artois, to the northwest of Arras, in the vicinity of the pilgrimage centre of Notre-Dame-de-Lorette, situated on top of a hill. In the fall of 1914, there had already been heavy fighting with as objective possession of this "hill of death." The hilltop was taken after forty days of intense combat, and this "victory" cost the deaths of more than a hundred thousand men. The Germans withdrew to the next line of high ground, Vimy Ridge, which could not be conquered in spite of repeated attacks. (It would only be in 1917 that the Canadians took the height.) So the French had as little success as the British with their attempt to break through the German lines.[3] In May-June 1915, Barthas participated in the Battle of Lorette. "Notre-Dame-de-Lorette, a sinister name," he wrote,

> . . . *conjuring up sites of horror and fear, dreary forests, hollow roads, heights and ravines taken and retaken twenty times; [an area] where, for months on end, day and night, throats were cut, people never ceased to be massacred, making this corner of the earth a veritable human slaughterhouse.*

Today, the hill of Notre-Dame-de-Lorette is crowned by a gigantic military necropolis. A general lies fraternally buried there among the graves of tens of thousands of *poilus*. At the time the ordinary French soldiers had little good to say about their generals, who planned these kind of offensives. Barthas claims that, time and again, the *poilus* "left for the trenches without protesting or complaining," but he himself larded his account with an unflattering reference to the "stupid generals" and their obsession with offensives and attacks.[4] He also refers to a famous comment by Joffre, justifying the bloody offensives he launched in 1915:

> *"I nibble away at them slowly," said fat old Joffre. A sentence that was celebrated by the fawning press like a rare pearl. But this useless bloody offensive would continue for many months.*[5]

Thousands of lives were wasted in these attacks but, from the viewpoint of the commanders, they were merely the lives of common people, of peasants and workers, and of course also of black- or brown-skinned Africans of whom there was an overabundance anyway. With these Senegalese, Algerians, or Moroccans, one could plug the holes in the ranks of the common soldiery, and they were perfect for being used in the first waves of an attack. And was it not said that they loved fighting? In 1915, many of these colonials perished in the vicinity of Arras, in often cold and damp northern France, far from their sunny, warm homelands.

During the summer of 1915 no large-scale offensives took place, but fighting occurred daily and heavy losses were suffered on both sides. In the vicinity of Ypres, an average of three hundred British soldiers died each day.[6] The French and Germans made each other's lives miserable in the area of Pont-à-Mousson, especially in the Bois-le-Prêtre, called *Priesterwald* in German. Heavy fighting had already been taking place there since September 1914, but reached a particularly violent climax in July 1915. This battle, during which the Germans used gas again and also introduced flame-throwers, inspired a famous French song, written by Lucien Boyer, "Au Bois-le-Prêtre."[7]

The large-scale offensives resumed in the autumn. Artois was again a theatre of operations, and so was Champagne. The commanders were hoping for a breakthrough, but again the attacks failed miserably. The attackers — and, considerably less so, the defenders — suffered enormous losses. On September 26, near the village of Loos, the British launched a major offensive. In order to surprise the enemy, artillery was barely used before the zero hour, so that the German positions did not suffer much damage and their barbed wire remained mostly intact. Gas was used by the British, but the poisoned clouds drifted back to their own lines and allegedly caused more losses there than among the Germans. The British attackers crossed the no man's land "as if it were a parade ground" and they were mowed down in large numbers by the "meat grinders" (*Fleischhackmaschinen*) or "sewing machines" (*Nähmschinen*), as the Germans called their machine guns, as usual ensconced in positions on the high ground. "Ye nae had a chance," was the commentary of a survivor, a Scotsman. The Germans themselves were shocked by the carnage they had been able to cause. According to Adam Hochschild, more than eight thousand of the ten thousand Tommies in the first wave became casualties; it was "a blatant, needless massacre," he writes, "initiated by generals with a near-criminal disregard for the conditions their men faced."[8]

For the British, the Battle of Loos would finish with a total of sixty-two thousand men killed, wounded, missing, or taken prisoner. The seventeen-year-old son of Rudyard Kipling was one of those who lost their lives. But the British generals congratulated themselves for the fact that their men had faced death with so much discipline and style, having done exactly as they had been ordered to do. It was precisely this kind of conduct, blind obedience to their "superiors" — or "betters," as one also used to say — that the British elite had expected the war to instill in the plebs. One of the generals reported proudly that the attack had not succeeded, but that the men had obeyed orders so well that some of them had *almost* made it to the German trenches, because "one could see their corpses hanging in the German wire." It was perhaps this remark that inspired the sarcastic song "Hanging On The Old Barbed Wire," which was disapproved of by officers but proved very popular among ordinary soldiers:

> *If you want the old battalion,*
> *We know where they are, we know where they are,*
> *We know where they are,*
> *If you want the old battalion, we know where they are,*
> *They're hanging on the old barbed wire,*
> *We've seen them, we've seen them,*
> *Hanging on the old barbed wire,*
> *We've seen them, we've seen them,*
> *Hanging on the old barbed wire.*
>
> .　.　.　.　.　.　.　.　.
>
> *If you want to find the General*
> *He's pinning another medal on his chest*
>
> .　.　.　.　.　.　.　.
>
> *If you want to find the Colonel*
> *He's sitting in comfort stuffing his bloody gut.*[9]

The Battle of Loos also inspired a number of literary works in Britain, among them the celebrated war memoirs of the poet and writer Robert Graves, *Goodbye to All That*.

The high-ranking officers were very happy with the conduct of their men, but far less so with that of their colleagues. The military prima donnas competed keenly for promotions and prestige, and the slightest error or weakness of a rival was exploited in order to advance one's own career.

General Haig had his eye on the supreme command of the BEF from the start, and he ruthlessly took advantage of the fiasco at Loos to discredit his boss, John French, via friends in high places in London. He achieved his goal in December 1915, when French was recalled and Haig himself took over as surpremo of the BEF. But for the Tommies this would not mean that they would suffer fewer losses; to the contrary.[10]

In the meantime, in Champagne, the French had launched an offensive. Here too, it was hoped that a breakthrough might be achieved, and hordes of cavalrymen were kept ready to pour through the gap the infantry was supposed to open up in the German lines. It started on September 22 with a preliminary artillery bombardment that was to last no less than three days. On September 25, the infantry followed with a general attack, and there would be intense fighting until the end of October, then sporadic combat here and there. On October 9 the curtain came down on this particular martial play. The German lines had been rolled back three to four kilometres, but they had not been pierced. The losses on the French side were enormous: more than twenty-seven thousand men killed, almost a hundred thousand injured, and fifty-three thousand taken prisoner. The Germans had suffered far fewer casualties.[11] The *poilus* had had enough. Already in September, during the fighting in the area of Neuville-Saint-Vaast, that is, at the foot of Vimy Ridge, the men of Barthas's unit had protested loudly against orders to advance. To a written order to attack, sent by a major ensconced in the rear, the soldiers reacted by crying loudly, "We will not attack!"[12] Nineteen-fifteen would be the deadliest year of the war for the French, after 1914 that is, at least as far as the number killed was concerned, namely 320,000. In 1914, 360,000 *poilus* had been killed, and this over a period of only five months. The number of dead for the years 1916, 1917, and 1918 was 270,000, 145,000, and 250,000, respectively. In total, more than 1.3 million Frenchmen would die for the fatherland — an unprecedented bloodletting, especially if one considers that in 1914 France had 39 million inhabitants.[13]

The French losses would have been even higher if, in the summer 1915, they had not started to issue the men with uniforms in "horizon-blue" colour, more suitable for camouflage purposes, and with steel helmets instead of the traditional caps, which served to reduce the number of head injuries.

These were a common occurrence in trench warfare, as shells exploded frequently and sent shrapnel flying all around. (It was actually in order to treat head wounds more easily, and not because of the lice, that they also started to cut the soldiers' hair extremely short.) The French helmet was called the "Adrian helmet" after its (presumed) inventor, Louis Auguste Adrian. Later, the Belgian soldiers would also be equipped with this type of helmet, and so would the Russians, Romanians, Italians, and Serbians. In October–November 1915, the British likewise adopted a steel type of headgear, the "Brodie helmet," so named because it had been developed by a certain John Leopold Brodie. But it had other names as well, including the "shrapnel helmet" and the "Tommy helmet." The ordinary soldiers called it their "tin hat," while the officers, gentlemen who, in their own country, never left home without a bowler hat on the head, preferred the term "battle bowler." The Germans laughed at this "salad bowl" (*Salatschüssel*) on the head of the Tommies, and at first all soldiers found the new steel helmets to look rather ridiculous. (And Apollinaire found the new Adrian helmet to be "a mistake, artistically speaking.") The Canadians started to use the Brodie helmet in March 1916, and later it was also issued to the American soldiers. The Germans responded to the appearance of the Adrian helmet by producing their famous *Stahlhelm*, "steel helmet," which was first tested on the front in December 1915. From the end of January 1916 it was mass-produced and supplied to the troops just in time for the Battle of Verdun. Until then, the Germans had continued to use the famous "spiked helmet" (*Pickelhaube*) they had gone to war with in 1914 and which dated from the 1840s. It was unsuitable for trench warfare because it was made of leather and therefore offered inadequate protection against shrapnel; and the spike attracted the unwanted attention of snipers.[14]

The large-scale Franco-British offensives of 1915 brought minimal gains and maximum losses. By the end of that year, only a little more than twenty of the approximately fifty thousand square kilometres — or 8 out of 19,500 square miles — of France and Belgium occupied by the Germans at the start of the year had been retaken.[15] But the losses had been huge, especially among the attackers, the British and French. It appeared that in trench warfare the defence, taking full advantage of weapons such as machine guns and barbed wire, enjoyed a major advantage. The high losses were due not only to the great offensives and attacks in general, but also to the fighting in between, and to artillery bombardments that could rain down on any given sector of the front for hours. This system, defined as "a particular method of delivering massed artillery fire . . . along one or more lines that can be from a few hundred to several thousand yards long," was introduced during the winter of 1914–1915 and became known as the "barrage." It terrified the infantrymen, as Erich Maria Remarque relates in *All Quiet on the Western Front*. Those who survived such hellish bombardments often ended up with a case of what became known as "shell-shock," a syndrome first officially mentioned by the British medical authorities in 1915. Today, this condition is called "post-traumatic stress disorder." A typical case has been described by Gabriel Kolko as follows:

> *The soldier lost control of his nervous system, beginning most commonly with a violent pounding of the heart, an intensely nervous stomach, then trembling and a cold sweat, a weakening of the legs, and, ultimately, for a minority, a loss of control over their urination and bowels . . . [Others symptoms were] uncontrollable weeping, a loss of hearing, and failure to obey orders.*

Failure to obey orders was of course a mortal sin from the perspective of the military authorities, and it was primarily on account of this symptom that they had no sympathy whatsoever for the affected soldiers. (In *Paths of Glory*, a soldier is slapped in the face for this reason by a general on an inspection of the trenches.) This kind of psychological injury was not recognized and its symptoms were interpreted as signs of cowardice. Soldiers were sometimes shot under these circumstances. Others received prison sentences, were sent into penal battalions, or received "therapy" with electric shocks and returned to the front as soon as possible. Between 1914 and 1918, approximately eighty thousand cases of shell-shock were reported in the British army. Shell-shock also affected the higher ranks, but in their case the problem was euphemistically identified — in typical "officer-speak" — and whitewashed as "neurasthenia."[16]

As for the use of poison gas, it is not clear whether this new weapon made many or relatively few victims. According to the conventional view, the effect of gas was devastating. Between April 1915 and July 1917, gas allegedly caused nearly two thousand dead and twenty-two thousand injured among the British. Later, the Germans introduced an even more deadly type of gas, namely mustard gas, thus called on account of its smell, but also known as yperite, after the Flemish city of Ypres, where it was first used. This gas is said to have been responsible for 4,000 dead and 160,000 injured. On the eastern front too, the Germans used gas. Among the Russians, it reportedly killed 56,000 men and wounded 425,000. On the other hand, it can be argued that gas was an intrinsically inefficient weapon. It was relatively easy to protect oneself against it, so that after the introduction of gas masks this new weapon caused relatively few victims. A fairly large percentage of the injured did survive. Only 2 to 3 per cent of those gassed on the Western front died. (Hitler was one of those who survived being gassed.) Wounds inflicted by conventional weapons such as bullets and shrapnel were ten to twelve times deadlier. Chemical weapons reportedly accounted for less than 1 per cent of all battle fatalities during the Great War. The damage caused was also very limited in comparison to the amount of gas that needed to be used. It required an average of one tonne of gas to eliminate one soldier. On account of this, and also because it made the life of soldiers extremely uncomfortable, gas would hardly be used anymore after the Great War.

The reason the use of gas was widely condemned was mostly psychological, if we may believe the historian Trevor Wilson. According to traditional, romantic notions about warfare, victory was supposed to go to the most courageous. But with the use of gas, courage was useless, and death did not result from the manipulation of a bladed weapon such as a sword or bayonet, but came unseen, or hidden in clouds of fog, blown in by the wind. The same thing may be said of the machine gun — the "coffee mill" (moulin à café), as the French soldiers called it, while the bayonet was known as the la fourchette, "the fork," or le cure-dents, "the toothpick" — and the cannon, likewise weapons that sowed death and destruction from a distance. Modern warfare heralded the end of the romantic idea of war, endemic among the virtually exclusively aristocratic gentlemen of the supreme command, and among high-ranking officers in general. In this type of warfare, the cavalry, their favourite weapon, turned out to be almost totally useless. It was powerless against machine guns and artillery, and gas was a weapon that they did not know, had not expected, did not know how to use, and against which they could not defend. The generals were disgusted by the use of gas, obviously not because it was a particularly deadly or cruel weapon (since they were enthusiastic about the equally cruel sword and bayonet), but because it was so unchivalrous. They simply had not expected that war would be fought with such weapons.[17]

The British generals were said to be "bewildered," and found this kind of warfare "peculiar." Lord Kitchener declared that, "This is not war!" From the British point of view, gas certainly also symbolized Germany's advanced petrochemical industry; it was this industrial branch which, during the years before 1914, had been the dynamo of a new industrial revolution that had permitted the Reich to overtake Britain with its "old" industry, still based mostly on steam, coal, steel, and textiles. (Incidentally, in Germany poison gas was produced primarily by the well-known firm of Bayer, managed by Carl Duisberg, who was also known as the father of the scheme to deport workers from occupied Belgium to Germany.) Finally, in the eyes of the nobility of all belligerent countries, gas also conjured up the superiority of new, industrial forms of warfare in which they had no expertise, and thus also, at least indirectly, the technological superiority of the nobility's partner — but also rival! — within the elite, namely the industrial upper-middle class, producers of all sorts of things new and unfamiliar.

Other new and particularly deadly and cruel weapons were introduced in 1915. The flame-thrower, for example, was first used, again by the crafty Germans, in July 1915 in the Flemish village of Hooge and in the Bois-le-Prêtre. (With the use of flame-throwers, the expression "being under fire" acquired an additional and macabre meaning.) Another new form of warfare consisted in bombing targets, civilian as well as military, from flying machines such as airplanes and Zeppelins. The Germans thus attacked London and other British targets from the air with incendiary bombs launched from dirigibles, starting in May 1915. These bombardments would result in a total of 1,400 dead and 3,400 injured. Yet another new weapon that started to play an increasingly important role in 1915 was the U-boat, the German submarine, and this form of warfare too was considered "cowardly" and "non-British." The problem was that the proud Royal Navy was relatively powerless vis-à-vis this martial novelty. In 1915, German submarines managed to sink 227 ships of the British Merchant Navy.[18]

CHAPTER 19
FROM THE DOLOMITES TO THE DARDANELLES

In 1915, countless allied lives, mainly Australian and New Zealander, are wasted in a vain attempt to advance toward Istanbul via the Gallipoli Peninsula and thus to knock the Ottoman Empire out of the war. In the meantime, the Ottomans also have to confront the Russians, and it is in this context that the Armenians become the victims of a veritable genocide. Italy enters the conflict on the side of the Entente, but suffers heavy losses. Bulgaria, on the other hand, joins the Central Powers and thus a new front opens up deep in the Balkan Peninsula . . .

In the spring of 1915, the military leadership of the Entente believed it would be possible to win the war via an offensive strategy purporting to pierce the German positions on the western front. But a number of generals as well as political leaders in Paris and London doubted that this strategy would work and started to look for other options. One of the sceptics was Winston Churchill, who was at the time First Lord of the Admiralty; in other words, the cabinet minister in charge of the Royal Navy — not to be confused with its military chief, known as the First Sea Lord, a position occupied as of October 1914 by the aforementioned John Fisher.

Churchill conjured up a plan to attack the Ottoman Empire, supposedly the weak link in the chain of the Central Powers. The idea was to capture Istanbul and thus open a passage to the Black Sea via the Bosporus. This would have created a connection by sea to the Russian ally, who needed to be supplied with all sorts of equipment. It might thus also become possible to finish off the Ottomans, cause neighbouring countries such as Bulgaria and Romania to join the war on the side of the Entente, and perhaps even to march all the way to Vienna via the Balkans.

The plan was implemented. Things got going in February–March 1915 with attempts by ships of the British and French navies to squeeze through the Dardanelles, but they were repulsed by the Ottoman defenders, who proved to have been greatly underestimated. The latter had not only laid mines, but also made excellent use of the artillery in their coastline fortresses. It was therefore decided to land British and French forces, supplemented by troops newly arrived via Egypt from Australia and New Zealand, the men of the Australian and New Zealand Army Corps, the Anzacs. The landings started on April 25 on the coast of the Gallipoli Peninsula, which stretches between the Aegean Sea and the Dardanelles. The men managed to disembark, but could not penetrate far inland and had to settle for a handful of bridgeheads with names such as Anzac Cove and Suvla Bay. The Ottomans had expected the landings and were well prepared; they were also led by competent officers, Germans as well as Turks, including Mustafa Kemal and Otto Liman von Sanders. (After the war, the former would become the founder of the modern Turkish Republic and earn the nickname of Ataturk, "father of the Turks.") An initiative that purported to resolve the problem of the stalemate on the front in France and Belgium thus produced the same kind of stationary warfare as on the western front. And here too, the two sides tried in vain, and at the price of countless human lives, to break through the enemy lines.

Bulgaria's entry into the war on the side of the Central Powers in October 1914 created an overland connection between Germany and the Ottoman Empire. Shortly thereafter, the Turks at Gallipoli started to shell the allied positions with heavy guns and even airplanes that were being delivered to them by the Germans. For the British and the French, the situation became untenable, and it was decided to repatriate the troops. This kind of evacuation is far from easy, so it had to be carried out carefully and slowly. By late December 1915 and early January 1916, the job was done at the price of remarkably low losses. But the landings and the ensuing fighting at Gallipoli had demanded a heavy tribute in men and resources.[1]

337

In Australia and New Zealand, "Gallipoli" is a name that, like "Flanders' Fields" for the British and "Verdun" for the French, conjures up the horrors of the First World War. And Anzac Day is a national "remembrance day" similar to November 11, but it is celebrated on the anniversary of the landings in Gallipoli, i.e., on April 25. A moving musical commemoration of the Gallipoli tragedy is the song "And The Band Played Waltzing Matilda," written in 1971 by the Scottish-Australian Eric Bogle. The song was inspired by "Waltzing Matilda," a famous Australian ballad that has become a kind of unofficial national anthem. Bogle's creation is a denunciation of all forms of jingoism and militarism.[2] Here is a sample of the lyrics:

> *How well I remember that terrible day*
> *How the blood stained the sand and the water*
> *And how in that hell that they called Suvla Bay We were*
> *butchered like lambs at the slaughter*
> *Johnny Turk he was ready, he primed himself well*
> *He chased us with bullets, he rained us with shells*
> *And in five minutes flat he'd blown us all to hell*
> *Nearly blew us right back to Australia*
> *But the band played Waltzing Matilda*
> *As we stopped to bury our slain*
> *We buried ours and the Turks buried theirs*
> *Then we started all over again.*

For the Ottomans, who had also suffered considerable losses, the Battle of Gallipoli was a success; however, they were less fortunate on the other side of the Anatolian Peninsula, where their offensive against the Russians had come to a standstill between the end of 1914 and early 1915, namely during the Battle of Sarikamis. For this reason, retribution was exacted, as had already happened in Belgium and in Serbia, from civilians suspected of sympathizing with the enemy, of spying, of acting as *francs-tireurs*, etc. These civilians were above all the Armenians, an ethnic as well as religious minority in the Ottoman Empire, who were believed to be sympathizing with the Russians. There was some reason for this, since for years the Russians had been inciting them against the Ottomans, just as the Ottomans had been inciting the Muslims within the czar's empire against their Christian rulers. Consequently, the Istanbul authorities had abandoned their traditional relative tolerance already well before 1914 in favour of repression of their Armenian and Greek Christian minorities.

A number of factors caused this repression of the Armenians to degenerate in 1915 into systematic atrocities, surpassing by far what the Germans had wrought in Belgium and the Austrians in Serbia, eventually culminating in what is now widely considered a genuine genocide that claimed between a million and 1.2 million victims.[3] First, many Armenians fought as soldiers, officers, and even generals, in the Russian army, some against the Germans and Austrians, but mostly on the Caucasian front against the Ottomans. A number of Russian army units consisted entirely of Armenian volunteers, some of whom had come from the Ottoman Empire. One battalion of these volunteers made an important contribution to the Russian success in the Battle of Sarikamis. Second, the Russians openly declared that they sought the support of the Armenian inhabitants of the Ottoman Empire and promised to establish an exclusively Armenian and, of course, Christian state. Czar Nicholas II personally alluded to such plans during a visit to the Caucasian front on December 30, 1914. It may be assumed that notes were made of all this in Istanbul and that the Ottoman authorities thus became even more likely to consider their Armenian minority as a dangerous "fifth column" in the service of the Russian enemy. Third, the fighting against the Russians took place in the eastern stretches of Anatolia, home to numerous Armenians, where Armenian partisans were in fact active. This "Armenian Militia," known as the *Fedayi*, was born at the end of the nineteenth century, when the Ottomans started to persecute the Christian minorities, loot Armenian villages and massacre their inhabitants, mainly in the east of Anatolia. The *Fedayi* hit back hard, for example with assassination attempts, acts of sabotage, and attacks on Muslim villages. Their main objective was autonomy or, better still, total independence for Armenia. In April 1915, a Venezuelan serving voluntarily as an officer in the Ottoman army noted in his diary that his unit had to deal not only with Armenian battalions of the Russian army but also with Armenian partisans.[4] A fourth factor was the need to find scapegoats, a need felt primarily by Enver Pacha, orchestrator of the offensive that ended with the catastrophe of Sarikamis.

He blamed the fiasco on the Armenian inhabitants of this eastern Anatolian region, which gave the green light for an orgy of systematic deportations and massacres of hitherto unseen brutality that was rationalized as a form of self-defence. But to the Venezuelan eyewitness there was no doubt: this was not a spontaneous program, but "a thoroughly planned operation conceived at the centre." It is not possible to provide details here of the horrible story of what the Armenians themselves call the "great crime," but it should be noted that this massacre, often referred to as the first genocide of the twentieth century, took place in the framework of the even greater massacre that was the Great War. Although many people had expected all sorts of wonderful things from the war, in reality a Pandora's box was thrown open, releasing all sorts of unprecedented atrocities and horrors.[5]

We already know that the Great War did not "break out" suddenly and unexpectedly, but had been wanted for quite some time by the elite of the European countries, was considered inevitable, was carefully prepared, and, finally, was unleashed cold-bloodedly — with as *pretext* an assassination in Sarajevo that was not a real *casus belli*. The elite *wanted* the war and prepared for it in order to resolve the huge social problem once and for all to their satisfaction; that is, to chase away the spectre of revolution and to arrest the process of democratization. At the same time, it was the intention to achieve objectives of an economic nature, that is, imperialist objectives, namely to conquer territories that could yield raw materials and labour cheaply, provide ample investment opportunities, and function as exclusive markets for the finished products of the metropolis. And in these mostly distant lands one could also get rid of many restless and potentially dangerous elements of the lower classes. It was precisely these kind of factors which, in the spring of 1915, caused Italy's elite to lead their country, in cold blood and with open eyes, into the war, even though the overwhelming majority of the population wanted nothing to do with the bloody conflict raging to the north of the Alps.

In 1914, the Italian elite still found itself firmly in the saddle, but it had two major reasons for concern. First, imperialist motives played an important role: the elite realized that one of the two European sets of allies, either the Entente or the Central powers, would lose the war. The losers' colonies, and even some of their own territory, were likely to become available, and these spoils would be pocketed only by countries that were among the victors, not by those that had only been spectators. Moreover, the gentlemen at the top of Italy's social pyramid, apparently infected by a case of megalomania, believed rather naively that their country's support would cause one of the two sides to win the war. If Italy stayed on the sidelines, it would surely gain nothing, but an investment in war seemed to guarantee major dividends — at least, that is what a growing number of decision-makers within the transalpine elite started to believe. It only remained to decide which allies would be the lucky beneficiaries of Italy's favours.

From the Central Powers, the club of which Italy had been a member before the war, one could expect territorial presents at the expense of France and Britain, such as Nice (*Nizza* in Italian), originally an Italian city, the birthplace of Garibaldi no less, that had been part of France only since the 1860s. Conversely, an alliance with the French and the British opened up prospects for the "liberation" of Italian-speaking regions of Austria-Hungary, such as Trentino and Trieste — morsels, just like Nice, of what was called *Italia irredenta*, "unliberated Italy" — and the Dalmatian Coast, where places like *Spalato* (Split) were inhabited by considerable numbers of Italians. From the Entente, one could also expect to receive as gifts bits and pieces of the huge Ottoman Empire. It was only shortly before, in 1912, that Italy had grabbed a piece of that empire, namely Libya. This time Italian thoughts focused on the Aegean coast of Anatolia, especially the area around Izmir, and even on the Anatolian interior; for example, Cappadocia.

It was the Italian nationalists who clamoured loudly for territorial conquest via war, presumably to "liberate" fellow Italians languishing on the wrong side of supposedly artificial borders and to fulfill Italy's destiny, namely to become a great empire like the Roman Empire of old. But behind this jingoist façade there lurked industrialists such as Alberto Pirelli of the tire company bearing his name and the automobile tycoon Giovanni Agnelli of Fiat. They expected to derive the familiar advantages from imperialist territorial extensions, so it was not a coincidence that their list of desiderata included regions such as Anatolia, not an "unliberated Italy" by any stretch of the imagination, but rich in minerals. War also promised the industrialists an instant maximization of profits through the sale of uniforms, ammunition, weapons, and other martial equipment. Similarly, like their counterparts elsewhere, the aristocratic and other large landowners saw opportunities in territorial expansion in regions far and near. It might become possible, for example, to get rid of Sicily's and Calabria's surplus rural proletariat by shipping them to Anatolia to colonize that land at the expense of the "natives."

It was for those reasons that the country's elite, on whose behalf the government functioned as a kind of executive committee, decided to go to war. But against whom, and on whose side? Negotiations were engaged in with both sides, and finally it was decided to opt for an alliance with the Entente, because London and Paris promised more than Berlin and Vienna were able or willing to do. On April 26, 1915, a secret treaty was concluded in London, and on May 24 Italy declared war on the Central Powers. In the case of Italy, just as in the case of Japan, the entry into the war was thus obviously "motivated by imperialist ambitions," as Max Hastings has observed. This is not 100 per cent correct, however, because the elite also had aspirations of a social-political nature, namely the ardent desire to halt and roll back democratization. The war the Italian elite wanted was not only a war of imperialist expansion, but also a war against democracy, against socialism, against revolution. The Italian elite was extremely worried about the fact that, thanks to the universal suffrage (for men only) introduced in 1912, the socialists had been able to achieve much progress during the elections of 1913. These socialists continued to talk about revolution, and the revolution had seemed to be close to breaking out in June 1914, during the so-called "red week," characterized by a wave of strikes and riots. And it seemed likely that very soon a major electoral victory might allow Italy's revolutionary socialists to come to power and overthrow the established order. Such a scenario had to be prevented at any price, and war, believed to be a potent antidote to revolution, looked like a small price to pay. Italy's "bloc of industrialists and landlords," writes Michael Parenti, believed that "war [would] bring [not only] bigger markets abroad [but also] civic discipline at home"; these gentlemen, he continues, "saw war as a way of promoting compliance and obedience on the labour front and . . . [were convinced that] war 'would permit the hierarchal reorganization of class relations.'" From the viewpoint of the country's elite, the situation in

Italy resembled that in France, Germany, etc., in 1914: it seemed that the choice was between war and revolution, and that by opting for war one could prevent revolution. It was "war or revolution," declared the Italian interventionists, "war on the frontiers [against an exterior enemy] or war in our own country [against an interior enemy]." It is therefore only logical that the decision to go to war reflected a lack of democracy and the elite's hostility vis-à-vis democracy. Everything happened in the greatest secrecy, without any information being dispensed to the members of Parliament, and war was declared in spite of the opposition expressed clearly by a parliamentary majority. Public opinion was likewise overwhelmingly opposed to the war. Most Italians wanted nothing to do with war, and certainly not with a seemingly absurd war against countries that had only recently been allies, and on the side of countries that had been considered enemies. "Public opinion was definitely against the war," writes the French historian Marc Ferro, but "the leaders had no intention to keep the country out of the war." In fact, the Italian declaration of war amounted to a kind of coup d'état carried out by the elite and orchestrated by the king of Italy in person, Victor Emmanuel III, the prime minister, Antonio Salandra, and the minister of foreign affairs, Sidney Sonnino. In the other countries, for example in France and in Germany, the elite went to war in order to be able to put a stop to democratization. In Italy, one can say that the elite had already arrested the democratization process before war was declared — or that it arrested democratization, that it had to eliminate democracy, in order to be able to go to war. But these are details of minor importance, because the consequences were essentially the same. The essence was that in Italy too, as in all belligerent countries, parliamentary life, reflecting a modest measure of democracy, was suspended for the duration of the war to the advantage of an elite that continued to monopolize all other power centres of the state. And, just as in all other belligerent countries, the transalpine elite also profited from the occasion to drastically limit the modest rights the trade unions had won before the war. Longer work hours were introduced, the right to strike was cancelled, workers could no longer change employers without permission, etc. In order to prevent social conflicts, committees of employers and union leaders were established, but if the union leaders were allowed some input de jure, they had no de facto influence whatsoever.[6]

In Italy too, however, all sorts of unexpected problems arose. A "sacred union" could not be summoned forth, because in contrast to their comrades in Germany, France, Belgium, and elsewhere, the Italian socialists spoke out courageously against the war. Italy's socialist party was the only socialist party to refuse to approve war credits, and it maintained its opposition to the war from the beginning until the end. The Italian socialists, or at least the majority of them, remained loyal to the principle of international solidarity. They declared the war to be a crime, and they appealed to the proletarians not to go to war against the proletarians of other countries. In other words, they found themselves on the same wavelength as Lenin.

Benito Mussolini, editor of the socialist newspaper *Avanti*, but in reality not a socialist at all, at first also spoke out against the war. But a few months later he broke with the socialists in order to found his own newspaper in which he zealously proceeded to make prowar and jingoist propaganda. He also founded a nationalist, extreme right-wing party of his own, the "Fasci of Revolutionary Action" (*Fasci d'Azione Rivoluzionario*), which would receive financial support from armaments firms and other corporations; its members, known as *fascisti*, "fascists," would become mortal enemies of socialists, pacifists, and such. (The phenomenon of fascism is clearly not to be explained as a reaction to the Russian Revolution, as was done by Ernst Nolte and other historians, but originated earlier, namely in the context of the Great World War.)[7]

One of the major reasons the proletarians of France, Britain, Germany, etc. had gone to war so willingly in 1914 was that the socialist leaders had encouraged them to do so. In 1915, the Italian proletarians did not go to war meekly, but reluctantly and grudgingly, at least partly because their socialist leaders condemned the war. On the other hand, Italy's peasants and workers, who would have to provide the bulk of the cannon fodder, did not need socialist leaders to understand that they had nothing to gain and everything to lose. Italy was born as a modern nation state only in the 1860s, and countless citizens did not yet identify fully with this state. Between 1860 and 1914, it still proved necessary for the state to "make Italians" (*fare Italiani*), as they used to say sarcastically at the time, in the entire country. The people's loyalty went out first and foremost to their home, village, and region, their *paese* ("village" or "land"), and the people there were their *paesani*, their "compatriots." With the inhabitants of Lombardy, for example, the Sicilians had little or nothing in common. The majority of Italians were not yet Italians; they cared little where exactly the borders of their country were situated somewhere in the damp and foggy regions to the north, and they did not feel the slightest desire to leave their sunny *paese* in order to fight and die for the glory of the so-called father- land. They knew what was happening on the front in France and elsewhere and therefore did not believe what their "superiors" tried to tell them, namely that this war would be short, glorious, and triumphant. Among the recruits, consequently, no enthusiasm whatsoever was to be noticed. An Italo-American volunteer, who had just disembarked in Italy and travelled by train to the front, eagerly looking forward to martial adventure, was called a fool and a donkey by soldiers who accompanied him; it was the fault of imbeciles like him, he was told, that the war might last a long time.[8]

From the very start, the morale of the Italian soldiers was particularly low. The officers sought to remedy the situation by imposing an incredibly harsh, even draconian discipline. Severe punishment was meted out even for the slightest peccadillo, and in the course of the war 6 per cent of the men would be punished for some transgression, but that did not resolve the problem. Desertion was common, even though it carried the death pen- alty. Officially, no less than 4,028 death sentences would be pronounced, a large part *in absentia*, as the perpetrators had managed to flee. In total, 750 Italian soldiers would be executed during the war: 66 in 1915, 167 in 1916, and 359, that is, more than half, in the catastrophic year 1917; but it is acknowledged that numerous executions also took place without the benefit of a formal trial. In addition, more than fifteen thousand men were condemned to prison sentences for violations of military discipline. Some of the convicted were still in jail in 1945, at the end of the Second World War! In order to discourage their soldiers from surrendering too easily, Italy's political and military authorities made use of a particularly barbarous stratagem: they announced that they would not contribute financially, via the International Red Cross, to the care of their prisoners of war, as other countries did. To be taken prisoner, voluntarily or not, was considered to be a "sin against the fatherland." The result was that tens of thousands of Italian POWs would die of starvation and cold in camps in Austria.[9]

Among the Italians too, a wide gulf separated the ordinary soldiers from their officers. The Italian officers were privileged with respect to accommodation and food, and the Italian generals likewise wasted thousands of lives in attacks against strong enemy positions. In October 1915, the aforementioned Italo-American volunteer witnessed on the front how officers emerged from their solid bunker after a breakfast including hot chocolate, toast, and even wine. They went to the observation post to watch an attack from a safe distance and remained unperturbed as wave after wave of their men was mowed down by Austro-Hungarian machine guns. The volunteer was sickened by the indifference displayed by the officers.[10]

In the spring of 1915 the Italian elite hoped what the French and British elites had hoped in the summer of 1914; that the war would be short and victorious. And, again like their French and British colleagues on the western front, the Italian generals expected that success would come by means of an offensive strategy. But on the Italian front, just as on the western front, the defenders, in this case the troops of the Danube Monarchy, enjoyed all the advantages, including the high ground, barriers of barbed wire, and weapons such as machine guns and artillery, against which the attackers proved to be extremely vulnerable. The Italian commander-in-chief, field marshal Luigi Cadorna, scion of a prestigious aristocratic family from Piedmont, believed that after the troubles experienced in 1914 the Austro-Hungarian soldiers would be weak and demoralized. And so, starting in June 1915, he ordered attack after attack against enemy positions along the River Isonzo. He dreamed of a quick breakthrough, followed by the capture of Trieste and a march toward Vienna, but the Italian attackers suffered terrible losses and did not advance an inch. By the end of 1915 they were still as far away from Vienna as in the spring. Cadorna did not seem to care about his army's huge losses. It is therefore not surprising that the Italian soldiers despised and hated him profoundly. "Our real enemy was not the Austrian, but Cadorna," an Italian war veteran would later tell his son.[11] (Cadorna was certainly not the only member of the Italian elite who, exactly like Haig in Britain, viewed things through Malthusian glasses and therefore found it advantageous that the plebeian "masses" were culled by the means of war; the journalist and poet Giovanni Papini, for example, who would later associate himself with Mussolini, declared that "there were too many people in this world, the pot of the [human] masses is threatening to boil over, and the morons multiply too fast." He drew the conclusion that "there are simply too many among us who are absolutely useless and redundant.")[12]

The fighting along the Isonzo Front, especially in the vicinity of the small town of Gorizia, is conjured up in the song "*O Gorizia tu sei maledetta*" ("O Gorizia, you cursed town"). This song is still popular in Italy, and is considered a musical symbol of the country's antimilitarist tradition. It seems that it was already very popular among the Italian soldiers of the Great War itself, but singing it then could cause a man to be accused of defeatism and executed. This is easy enough to understand, because the lyrics point an accusing finger not only at generals such as Cadorna, who sent their men to a certain death, but also at the other "gentlemen officers" (*signori ufficiali*) who are denounced as "cowards," "murderers," and "traitors."[13] Here are a few verses of this powerful song:

La mattina del cinque di agosto	*On August five, in the morning*
si muovevano le truppe italiane	*The Italian soldiers set off*
per Gorizia, le terre lontane	*For Gorizia, a town far away*
e dolente ognun si partì.	*And they were all sad to leave.*
Sotto l'acqua che cadeva a rovescio	*While the rain came pouring down*
grandinavano le palle nemiche	*They faced a hail of enemy bullets*
su quei monti, colline e gran valli	*In those mountains, hills, and valleys*
si moriva dicendo così:	*They died with these words on their lips:*
O Gorizia, tu sei maledetta	*O Gorizia, town cursed by*
per ogni cuore che sente coscienza;	*Everyone with a heart and a conscience;*
dolorosa ci fu la partenza	*Leaving was painful enough*
e il ritorno per molti non fu.	*And most of them never returned.*
O vigliacchi, che voi ve ne state	*You cowards, who stayed safely*
con le mogli sui letti di lana,	*In bed with your wives,*

schernitori di noi carne umana,	*Laughing at us, meat for the*
questa guerra ci insegna a punir.	*slaughter,*
	For this war you have to be punished.
Voi chiamate il campo d'onore	*You call 'field of honour'*
questa terra di là dai confini,	*That land over there on the border,*
qui si muore gridando: assassini,	*Those who die cry out: murderers,*
maledetti sarete un dì.	*The day of reckoning will come.*
Traditori, signori ufficiali	*Gentlemen officers, you are traitors,*
voi la guerra l'avete voluta	*You have wanted this war*
scannatori di carne venduta	*You are butchers selling human meat*
e rovina della gioventù.	*You are the ruin of Italy's youth.*

In the spring of 1915, the Germans and Austro-Hungarians launched a major offensive against the Russians. On the eastern front, which was two to three times as long as its western counterpart, there was never an uninterrupted frontline with strongly defended enemy positions that needed to be pierced, as was the case on the western front and in Italy. Under these conditions, the Germans managed to achieve a progress of many hundreds of kilometres in regions of the Russian Empire that are now part of Poland, Belarus, Lithuania, and Latvia. They advanced as far as Riga and Minsk. In this case it was the defenders who suffered heavy losses, namely more than one million dead, wounded, or taken prisoner in six months, amounting to an average of 7,500 casualties per day.

The morale of the Russian troops had already declined strongly in 1914, and now, during what would become known as "the great retreat," during which Russia abandoned Poland, Lithuania, and much of Belarus, things were getting even worse. This was reflected in countless desertions. "Defeatist" propaganda by the Bolsheviks also played a role. Fraternizations, above all with Austro-Hungarian soldiers, were common. As in the case of the Italian army, the officers reacted by imposing even harsher discipline and by introducing severe punishment, including flogging. The civilians living in the affected regions also suffered terribly, especially since during their long retreat the Russians resorted to the "scorched earth" tactic, destroying homes and dragging along with them not only millions of willing refugees but also reluctant civilians who would have preferred to stay. The latter included Jews, ethnic Germans, and Poles, people whom the Russians believed might otherwise be of service to the Germans. Czar Nicholas II, meanwhile, took over as commander-in-chief of the army. He ensconced himself in a sumptuous headquarters, obviously at a safe distance from the front, and moved around in a luxurious Rolls-Royce. As a strategist he was useless, and he was unable to persuade the god of war, Mars, to bestow his favours on the Russians. In any event, as a French expert in Russian history, Alexandre Sumpf, has written, the war, which had initially been welcomed with considerable patriotic enthusiasm, "was henceforth associated by all social layers of the population with negative connotations," "pessimism gripped the land," and "the social tensions, which had momentarily subsided, reappeared with increasing violence." And by the fall of 1915, the formerly generally adored czar was despised by many if not most Russians. Another fateful consequence of Russia's military misfortunes of 1915 and the miseries associated with the "great retreat" was that they encouraged, and in some cases even engendered, nationalist aspirations in the Polish, Latvian, and other western regions of the czar's empire.[14]

Starting in the spring of 1915, the Austro-Hungarians had to focus on the new front in Italy, but in the fall the wind suddenly turned in their favour in the conflict against Serbia. On October 14, Bulgaria, hitherto a neutral country, declared war on Serbia and invaded its neighbour from the east, which facilitated an irruption into Serbia by Austro-Hungarian and German troops from the west. Serbia was soon completely overrun by its enemies. Bulgaria had gone to war for reasons similar to those of Italy, and equally cynically. The Entente as well as the Central Powers had first been approached in order to find out what loot Sofia might carry off in exchange for its contribution to victory. The Bulgarian government finally opted for an alliance with Berlin and Vienna. This choice involved war against Serbia and thus opened up the prospect of regaining territory — mainly present-day Macedonia — lost to that hated neighbour as a result of the Second Balkan War, fought in 1913. Another determinant was the spectacular progress made in the summer of 1915 by the Germans at the expense of

Russia, seemingly a portent of a victory by the Central Powers. As in the case of Italy, however, not only imperialist objectives but also antidemocratic and counterrevolutionary considerations played a role in the calculus of the Bulgarian elite. In that Balkan country too, the elite had been confronted with all sorts of political and social problems during the years before 1914. The socialists and Agrarian Party, champions respectively of workers and peasants, had won important electoral victories and the proletarian "interior enemy" thus seemed to be poised to grab power soon. In this case also, the elite expected salvation from a short and triumphant war against an exterior enemy.

Paris and London were deeply involved in the intrigues that preceded Bulgaria's entry into the war, intrigues that also brought up the issue of a possible entry into the conflict by Greece. In that country, the elite was divided in this respect, a situation that was reflected in the disagreement between the Germanophile King Constantine I, who happened to be married to a sister of Emperor Wilhelm II, and the prime minister, Eleftherios Venizelos, who favoured the Entente. This disagreement degenerated into a virtual civil war. The British and the French cut the Gordian knot by landing troops in the vicinity of Thessaloniki in October 1915, which amounted to a flagrant violation of Greek neutrality. The objective was to lend a helping hand to the Serbians, but Bulgaria's entry into the war made it impossible to link up with them. The latter could not be saved by operations from the bridgehead around Thessaloniki. However, what was left of the Serbian army managed to escape via Albania to the Adriatic coast during the winter of 1915–1916, albeit at the cost of heavy losses. The Serbians reached the Greek island of Corfu, and were transferred from there to the front near Thessaloniki, where they joined the French and British troops. Of the 250,000 men who had started this adventure, only 140,000 arrived at the coast.[15]

Stationary warfare involving the familiar systems of trenches would thus develop along the Greco-Bulgarian border, just to the north of Thessaloniki, and last for many years. There the Bulgarians confronted the allied forces of the "army of the Orient," so called because in those days the Balkans were still considered to be the "Near East" and therefore to be part of the "Orient" (and the train that crossed the peninsula on its way to Istanbul was called the Orient Express). On the Macedonian front, no murderous offensives were ever launched, but the Serbian, British, and French soldiers were tormented by cold and heat, mud, insects, etc., so much so that the British would refer to the area as "Muckedonia." There were relatively few casualties, but diseases — above all malaria and dengue fever — exacted a heavy tribute.

As for Greece, that country would officially remain neutral, even though trenches crisscrossed its northern reaches. But the allies schemed to have King Constantine abdicate in favour of his son Alexander, and so Venizelos would eventually — in the spring of 1917 — emerge as the winner from the "national schism" and arrange for Greece to officially enter the war on the side of the Entente. Venizelos hoped that this would cause his country to be rewarded generously after the expected allied victory at the expense of Bulgaria and the Ottoman Empire. His dreams of territorial expansion included making a Greek city again of Constantinople, the former capital of the Byzantine Empire, conquered in 1453 by the Turks and known ever since as Istanbul. This "great idea" (*megali idea*) was the fond hope not only of Venizelos, but of countless other Greek nationalists. And on account of the weakness of the Ottoman Empire — and of the small Balkan countries that were Greece's neighbours — this dream could actually be considered to be realistic. Venizelos hoped to metamorphose the small Hellenic nation into a new edition of the Byzantine Empire, not only with Constantinople again as its capital, but also with Orthodox Christianity again as its state religion. In Greece too, then, the nationalist elite, imbued by the spirit of Romanticism, hoped to achieve a "great leap backward" in the direction of the Middle Ages, a return that was to be made possible thanks to war. It was a megalomaniac and imperialist dream that first dragged Greece into the miserable Great War and, afterwards, into a disastrous conflict against Turkey, thus transforming a dream into a nightmare.[16]

CHAPTER 20

TIRED OF WAR

The soldiers of all the armies are tired of the war. They dream of being able to go home, even if this means that their country will not win. They hate the politicians, their military superiors, the journalists, and the "jusqu'au-boutiste" civilians. Why do they stay on the front? Not because of love of the fatherland, but because they are coerced to do so, because of a sense of duty, and above all because they do not want to let down their comrades. Among many civilians too, there is no longer any enthusiasm for this miserable war . . .

In the fall of 1915, the soldiers of all belligerent countries shed their last illusions with respect to the war, as the trees were shedding their leaves. In the spring they had still hoped that the war would be decided that same year, and that the fatherland would emerge victorious. High expectations were placed on the huge offensives planned in the headquarters, and the men could still be persuaded to make heavy sacrifices. But the offensives caused hitherto-unseen bloodbaths and brought none of the hoped-for results. Among the combatants there now arose a despair that got worse as offensive after offensive turned into a fiasco or, even if successful, as in the case of the German advance in the east, failed to bring an end to a murderous conflict that had already raged for an entire year. Among the French infantrymen, of whom hundreds of thousands had died in 1914 and more again in 1915, the conviction grew that the war would never end, that they were dealing with a new "Hundred Years' War."[1] Numerous British soldiers likewise became convinced that the war would never end, that henceforth war, and not peace, would constitute the norm of human existence.

"Rare birds" were those soldiers who still attached some credit to the fine words that had warmed their patriotic hearts in the summer of 1914. Now most had only contempt for the official discourse with respect to the war, a discourse that in French became known as *bourrage de crâne*, the "stuffing of skulls." The "great patriotic words" of the officers, Barthas confided to his diary in the summer of 1915, "fail to arouse even the slightest enthusiasm among us." And two French historians, André Loez and Nicolas Mariot, emphasize that the *poilus* no longer felt any conscious patriotism and no longer agreed with the patriotic talk of their superiors. The love of *la patrie* was melting like snow in the sun, together with the confidence in victory. Whether France recuperated Alsace, which had been the fervent hope of many in the summer of 1914, or not, did not matter at all anymore for the majority of the men. Similarly, to the British soldiers the objectives for which they had gone to war in 1914 had totally lost their importance. Whether "brave little Belgium" was liberated from the claws of the German brute or not left the majority of Tommies utterly cold, even though they were supposed to be fighting for this noble objective. "They say it's all for little Belgium, so cheer up, says I: but wait til I gets hold of little Belgium," was the cynical comment made by a British soldier in a letter to a friend.[2] Even the outcome of the war was no longer important to most combatants; they had had enough of the fighting, the killing and being killed, the misery of the entire war.[3]

Most soldiers wished only for one thing, namely the end to this misery, a return to peace. More and more graffiti reflected the men's longing for peace. Peace meant being able to go home, to return to the family, the village, and the familiar world, being able to live a normal, peaceful existence again. "I ceased to think of all but one thing," a French soldier wrote to his wife, "and that is: the END, going home for good."[4] On the British side a song became very popular at that time, "I Want to Go Home":

> I want to go home, I want to go home.
> I don't want to go in the trenches no more,
> Where whizzbangs and shrapnel they whistle and roar.

Take me over the sea, where the Alleyman [German] can't get
at me.
Oh my, I don't want to die, I want to go home.

. . . .

Take me over the sea, where the snipers they can't get at me.
Oh my, I don't want to die, I want to go home.[5]

The peasants, a majority among the *poilus*, longed to return to their village, and they were even prepared to pay for this privilege "with the most humiliating defeat of their own fatherland," as an appalled officer remarked in January 1915. But all soldiers wanted to return to their village, home, *paese*, or *Heimat*, and the sooner the better. The peasants wanted to see their fields again, their vineyards, their cows.[6] And *all* the men dreamed of being able to return for good to the woman or women they had left behind, their wife, mother, daughter, sister. If the half-happy, half-sad song *"La Madelon"* was able to become what was probably the most popular song of the war in France, it is undoubtedly because "Madelon" — diminutive for Madeleine, "little Madeleine" — conjured up the beloved "village girl" (*payse*) waiting for the soldier's return to his village (*pays*), his "little fatherland" that was so much more important than that "big fatherland," France:

Nous avons tous au pays une payse	*We all have in our village a girl*
Qui nous attend et que l'on épousera	*waiting for us to marry her*
Mais elle est loin, bien trop loin pour qu'on lui dise	*But she is far, too far for us to tell her*
Ce qu'on fera quand la classe rentrera	*What we will do when we will return*
En comptant les jours on soupire	*We count the days and sigh*
Et quand le temps nous semble long	*And when we get terribly bored*
Tout ce qu'on ne peut pas lui dire	*Everything we can't tell her*
On va le dire à Madelon	*We'll go and tell dear Madelon*
On l'embrasse dans les coins. Elle dit 'veux-tu finir . . .'	*We steal a kiss from her in the corner. She says 'stop it . . .'*
On s' figure que c'est l'autre, ça nous fait bien plaisir.	*But we imagine it's our village girl and that gives us great pleasure.*[7]

Rather similar to *"La Madelon"* was the very popular old German song *"Der Treuer Husar,"* "The Faithful Hussar," the story of a soldier whose fiancée becomes ill and dies while he is fighting abroad. At the end of the film *Paths of Glory*, this song, performed by a young German woman, brings tears to the eyes of rugged *poilus*, who realize that the *Boches*, just like them, long to return to their own "Madelon in the distant heimat."[8]

If one had offered the soldiers of any army the choice between "carrying on" with the war or to simply return home, even if the latter choice would have meant that they would later not be considered heroes and that the fatherland might perhaps end up on the losing end and gain neither territory nor glory, there can be no doubt that perhaps as many as 99 per cent of the men would have packed their bag immediately. This sentiment was expressed succinctly but powerfully, with a *soupçon* of sarcasm, by a British soldier endowed with some poetic talent. The verse started in the pompous style of the official — and therefore elitist — English discourse with respect to the war, but ended with a pithy plebeian parlance:

> *Though we observe the Higher law*
> *And though we have our quarrel just,*
> *Were I permitted to withdraw*
> *You wouldn't see my arse for dust.*[9]

The Alsatian Dominik Richert was convinced that not a single one of his comrades would have remained voluntarily on the front if given an opportunity to "return to safety and live a decent life, as behooves a human being."[10] Not a single soldier genuinely felt like being a hero or being considered one. In this respect, Barthas provided a comment about an impending attack of his unit in the fall of 1916:

> *The men in the muddy trenches, exhausted and hungry,*
> *grumblingly received the order to attack. Many of them left*
> *the lines on the pretext of having been buried by explosions of*
> *shells, of being sick, of having frozen feet. They did not care if*
> *these excuses would be accepted or not . . . Not everybody can*
> *be a hero.*

355

This did not mean that the men were not capable, either collectively or individually, of displaying heroic conduct. A soldier might risk his own life, for example, trying to save a wounded comrade trapped in the no man's land. And groups of soldiers often risked death in order to perform their duty or to avoid abandoning comrades; more will be said later about this type of motivation. But no heroic deeds were to be expected from the men for the sake of the king or emperor, for the sake of Alsace-Lorraine in the case of the French, or for abstract concepts such as the fatherland, "liberty and justice," and such — and certainly not for a token of approval, words of praise, or a decoration from the military or other authorities. The majority of the soldiers did not care at all for such kudos. Barthas describes how he and his comrades reacted when their unit was suddenly showered with praise:

> It rained congratulations and honors for a few days. The
> general of the division, the general of the brigade, the colonel,
> everybody had a mouth full of compliments. They extolled our
> courage, our bravery, and our indestructible energy. It was
> utterly ludicrous.[11]

The ardent longing for peace and for a return home went hand-in-hand with a mixture of contempt and hatred for all those who wanted to keep the men at the front in order to fight "until the end," in other words, for those whom the *poilus* called the *jusqu'au-boutistes*. And these included the political leaders who were held responsible, first for having caused the war, and then for perpetuating it, such as President Poincaré, who was utterly detested by the *poilus*.[12] Also included were the military superiors as well as the so-called "warriors of the pen," that is, the journalists of the arch-patriotic, so-called "yellow" press. The Belgian soldiers, for example, "abhorred the official rhetoric of the journal of the Belgian army," called the *leugenbode* or "messenger of lies" by the Flemish and the *bourreur de crânes* or "skull stuffer" by the French-speaking Walloons. Among the Belgian combatants too, there was nothing left in 1915 of the enthusiasm of the summer of 1914; they only thing they wanted was peace.[13] A British soldier, George Willis, voiced a widespread sentiment among his comrades when, in the poem "Any Soldier to His Son," he cursed the journalists of the bellicose yellow press with these verses:

> *May a thousand chats from Belgium crawl under their fingers*
> *as they write;*
> *May they dream they're not exempted till they faint with*
> *mortal fright;*
> *May the fattest rats in Dickebusch race over them in bed;*
> *May the lies they've written choke them like a gas cloud till*
> *they're dead;*
> *May the horror and the torture and the things they never tell*
> *(For they only write to order) be reserved for them in hell!*[14]

The soldiers of all armies felt increasingly bitter toward superiors whom they had regarded with respect before the war, particularly teachers, professors, and men of the cloth, who had encouraged them in the summer of 1914 to go fight. In *All Quiet on the Western Front*, the hero has some unflattering, critical words to say about the professor who persuaded him and his friends to report voluntarily to join the army and go to war.

The soldiers were bitter but, even more so, disappointed by the attitude of the civilians on the home front. The latter seemed convinced that with a little extra effort it would be possible to finish off the enemy, and they were apparently also unable to understand how horrible conditions at the front really were. Civilians appeared to swallow whatever the authorities and the "yellow press" told them and, conversely, the soldiers found it simply impossible — and for many reasons also undesirable — to convey to them the truly "unspeakable" verity of the war. (In their adaptation of Jerome Kern's poem "They Didn't Believe Me," the Tommies make it clear that "when they ask us, how dangerous it was, / Oh, we'll never tell them, no, we'll never tell them.") In any event, the officers censored the soldiers' letters, so that the latter complained that they were "muzzled" and therefore limited themselves to writing banalities. A gigantic fissure thus separated the soldiers from the civilians. Those two constituted "two worlds that did not understand each other."[15]

As far as the British were concerned, "two distinct Britains" thus emerged, as Paul Fussell has written: "the soldiers and sailors who had fought . . . and the Rest [sic], including the government." The Tommies felt alienated from the ordinary citizens, "from everyone back in England." In this context, Fussell cites the journalist and writer Philip Gibbs, who explained that the men

> *hated the smiling women in the streets. They loathed the old men . . . They desired that profiteers should die by poison-gas. They prayed God to get the Germans to send Zeppelins to England — to make the people know what war meant.*[16]

The civilians could not possibly understand the soldiers. But could anybody? The answer to this question was affirmative: there were indeed human beings who could understand the soldiers, namely the soldiers on the other side of the no man's land. That too was one of the reasons why the combatants felt a certain measure of sympathy and solidarity vis-à-vis the men designated as "the enemy" by the military and political authorities. On the Somme, during the summer of 1916, Barthas wrote for example that he and his comrades "felt compassion for the *Boches* who suffered the same misery and dangers." This sympathy and solidarity were also reflected in the aforementioned fraternizations and in the "live-and-let-live" arrangements. Such sentiments were also conveyed by the language used by the British soldiers, who liked to add the term "old" to familiar things for which they felt a measure of affection. The German soldiers — but not the officers — were also "old" in this sense and, since the nickname for the Germans was Jerry, reference was constantly made to "old Jerry." The French similarly alluded to the Germans as "our neighbours," more precisely, *nos voisins d'en face*, that is, "our neighbours across the street."[17]

After the experiences of Christmas 1914, the fraternizations and "live-and-let-live" arrangements were strictly prohibited, which the soldiers deeply regretted. On May 1, 1915, countless soldiers on both sides dreamed of fraternizing, but it proved impossible, and the same thing happened at Christmas 1915. In order to prevent such meetings, the generals had the artillery fire into the no man's land. And a British sergeant was allegedly shot when, in spite of such orders, he set out to fraternize. "Who could still dream of social equality, of universal fraternization," sighed Barthas, "when everything around was so sombre? We were stuck in the iron grip, in the straitjacket, of militarism."[18]

In secret, however, the fraternizations and "live-and-let-live" arrangements continued. Barthas gives an example from the winter of 1915–1916 in the vicinity of the Artesian village of Neuville-Saint-Vaast, near Vimy:

> *The following day, 10 December, the soldiers had to get out of the trenches in many places in order to avoid drowning; the Germans had to do the same thing, and the result was an unusual sight: two armies facing each other without a shot being fired. The community of suffering brought the hearts together, caused the hatred to melt and sympathy to blossom between people who were very different, enemies even . . . French and Germans looked at each other and saw that they were all similar. They smiled at each other, talked to each other, shook hands, even embraced each other, they shared tobacco, coffee, or wine. If only we had spoken the same language! . . . A German giant of a man stood up and gave a speech which only the Germans understood but whose meaning was clear to all of us, because he broke his rifle on a tree trunk in an expression of anger. Everybody applauded and we sang the* Internationale.

Soldiers singing the *"Internationale,"* the song of the working class of all countries before the war and the musical symbol of the solidarity of the world's proletarians, was something the officers found abominable, because it reflected the soldiers' desire to fraternize — as well as their aversion to patriotic discourse. Barthas alludes to an incident in a village behind lines, where the soldiers

> *. . . took to protesting, and wandered through the village singing the* Internationale. *That will always remain the song of the poor and oppressed, giving voice to their hope as well as despair . . . Our big bosses were furious. What would happen if, may God forbid, the soldiers refused to kill each other?*

> *Would the war not grind to a halt? Our artillery received the order to fire on all unauthorized gatherings that were reported and to kill Germans and French alike, just like they killed wild animals in the Roman amphitheatres that were intelligent enough to refuse to devour each other . . . When the first line had been repaired as much as possible, it was declared punishable by execution to get out of the trenches and to socialize with the Germans in any way.*

In spite of this prohibition, the soldiers continued to fraternize. Barthas described the situation in a quiet sector of the front, in Champagne, in the summer of 1916, when the *poilus* found themselves in trenches at a short distance from the Germans:

> *It was almost possible to stretch out your arm and shake hands with them . . . All was calm. Some smoked, others preferred to read, others were chatting without lowering their voices . . . while the Germans just as casually coughed, talked, and hummed . . . [Sometimes] the French and German sentries sat on top of the parapet of their trench and quietly smoked a pipe and occasionally even came out to get some fresh air and have a chat with their 'neighbours.' At each changing of the guard, these same customs and habits were maintained. The Germans behaved in the same way . . . Sometimes we exchanged gifts: packages with French army tobacco, which they smoked in their big German pipes, and delicious cigarettes 'Made in Germany' that arrived in our French position. We also gave each other buttons, newspapers, and bread. It was a strange affair: commerce and collusion with the enemy. The patriots and super-patriots would have been appalled.*

According to Barthas, this kind of thing happened frequently. It provided ample proof, he commented, that "this awful war had been unleashed against the will of the people." He also wondered if "these gestures of fraternity implied a revolutionary protest against the terrible fate that causes people to fight other people even though they have no reason at all to hate each other."

Barthas cited more cases of fraternizations and understandings between French and Germans. In early 1917, in the region known as the Main de Massiges, the French field kitchens were set up close to the trenches, and were barely camouflaged. The Germans had also installed theirs close to their positions. "On account of mutual tolerance and common interest, the two sides let the cooks work undisturbed." Barthas relates how, later in 1917, engineers dug tunnels under the German lines in order to explode mines. But there was an "unspoken agreement" to set off the explosions

> . . . each time between two and six in the morning. The
> result was that, each night, ten minutes before ten, the two
> sides withdrew the sentries from the first lines. At six in the
> morning, they quietly slipped back to their positions. There
> were also far fewer casualties because on both sides the sacred
> patriotic fire had died down. The war had been going on for
> too long.[19]

Between the British and the Germans too, fraternizations continued after Christmas 1914, as exemplified by the fact that, as late as December 1917, British officers were still worried that the men might take advantage of the Yuletide opportunity to contact the enemy. And in January 1918, in the vicinity of Cambrai, an officer had to break up a fraternization that had already started. As a true gentleman, he went to explain courteously to a German colleague that "we cannot accept the invitation." Even so, for a few brief moments, cigars and cigarettes were exchanged before the two officers saluted each other and withdrew with their men into their own trenches. On the eastern front, fraternizations likewise continued. On the occasion of Easter 1916, Russians and Austrians got together in the no man's land. They not only exchanged small presents, but music played by a Russian military band provided a festive ambiance. And in 1917 and 1918, the eastern front would witness a veritable orgy of fraternizations.[20]

The ordinary peasants and workers who constituted the overwhelming majority of the soldiers became increasingly aware that their "superiors," that is, those who looked down on them from the apex of the social pyramid, had wanted this war and profited from it, while they themselves, who had not wanted the war, were saddled with its costs. In addition to their detested officers and especially generals, the men directed the arrows of their ire at two types of civil representatives of the elite. First, those who managed to stay away from the front, the *embusqués*. Those were often scions of elite families who had not been called to arms or who were allowed to perform their military service at a safe distance from the trenches; for example, as staff in some headquarters, driver of some general, etc. In all the belligerent countries — but especially in Russia, apparently — such a sinecure or an exemption of service was relatively easy to obtain for people of superior social rank, who boasted a better education, good manners, excellent contacts, etc. Another object of the hatred of the soldiers was the war profiteers, above all the big industrialists who earned fortunes by producing weapons and other martial equipment, but also the merchants who managed to fill their pockets by doing business on the black market. Soldiers on leave in Paris, London, Berlin, or St. Petersburg could see this type of individual having a great time in cafés and restaurants along the big boulevards, which made the men's miserable existence in the trenches even more intolerable and increased their resentment.

The war revealed to the soldiers the great and growing inequality of the social system of the fatherland for which they were making such great sacrifices, not only the inequality of wealth, but also the inequality in the face of danger and death. The poor had to suffer, fight, and die so that the rich could enjoy the good life and become even richer; that was the conclusion arrived at by the soldiers. "We only fight for the profits of the fat wallets," was the acidic comment of a German soldier, "and whatever else they would like us to believe is nonsense." Barthas gave voice to similar sentiments on the part of the *poilus*. "One thing is certain," he wrote, "with every offensive, the munitions manufacturers become richer . . . Anatole France was right when he stated that 'people think they die for the fatherland, but in reality they die for the industrialists'."[21]

The soldiers of all armies vented their frustration, anger, and disgust with

362

respect to a war that increasingly revealed itself to be a blessing for a few, but a curse for too many. When asked why they were in the trenches, the Tommies now responded with the popular song "We're Here," sung to the melancholic tune of Robert Burns's "Auld Lang Syne:"

We're here because
We're here because
We're here because we're here.
We're here because
We're here because
We're here because we're here.[22]

With this song, the British made it abundantly clear that they could not think of one single sensible reason for waging war. So why, in this case, did they, and the soldiers of the other armies, for that matter, continue to fight? Many historians have pondered this question and here are the main factors they have put forward.

First, the soldiers were *coerced* to wage war. Escaping from the trenches was basically impossible, because an iron discipline prevailed in each army, and "desertion" carried the death penalty. Anyone trying to flee risked being shot on the spot by an officer or, if he made it to the rear, being arrested by the military police, a.k.a. "battle police," which meant being court-martialed, with high odds of being condemned to death. Remaining in the trenches carried the risk of being killed or wounded, but he who deserted was virtually certain to die. "The prospect of being tied to a post to be shot," a French soldier wrote in a letter intercepted by the censors, "keeps us from leaving immediately," and he added that "it is only out of fear of being shot that we stay at the front."[23] A German soldier explained candidly that he and his "scared and desperate" comrades certainly did not keep on fighting out of "bravery and such" — virtues whose existence he actually doubted — but that they "were motivated by nothing other than the terrible discipline and the coercion that sent us to our death."[24] And in the summer of 1915 Barthas confided to his diary that he and his companions "tolerated it all with stoicism and without complaining," but certainly not

. . . out of love for the fatherland . . . or to defend the peoples'
right to self-determination or to ensure that this war would be
the last war. It was very simple, we were coerced, we were the
helpless victims of a merciless fate. We all knew that at the
slightest attempt, no matter how minor, to rebel, we would be
ground up by the horrible teeth of a gigantic cogwheel.[25]

Secondly, a sense of honour and duty kept the men at their posts. What dishonour it would have been for the family and the entire village if a man failed to do his duty and, above all, if he were branded a coward and possibly executed on account of desertion! What would the women think of such a man? The fear of losing the respect of one's own wife or mother, which played an important role in this context, was reflected in the lamentation of an Italian soldier who had to surrender to the Austrians in December 1917, during the catastrophic Battle of Caporetto: "What will our mamma say?!"[26] Being a soldier was also considered to be a kind of profession, a trade, a job that needed to be done, and the men felt the duty to do that job properly.

A third reason, and perhaps the most important one of all, was the feeling of solidarity vis-à-vis the comrades, whom one could not leave in the lurch and whose esteem and friendship one did not want to lose. "It's for them, it's for the comrades," wrote a *poilu*,

that we hang in there. In order not to abandon them, In order
to remember the comrades who already fell. So that they did
not die in vain . . . And also, very simply, very ordinarily, in
order to preserve our own dignity: the others keep an eye on
us, and their faces are like a mirror that is held in front of
each one of us.[27]

The main factors, then, were "the moral pressure exerted on each one of us by the comrades," the "esprit de corps, the solidarity, the camaraderie," the "sense of duty," the need "not to lose the esteem and affection of the comrades." Anyone who did not observe this "masculine code of honour" was excluded from the community, making life unbearable for him. One did not shirk one's duty; one remained at the front "for the buddies."[28]

364

And so the great majority of the soldiers accepted their fate, powerlessly and fatalistically. Of the French *poilus* it was reported that a "great resignation" had enveloped them. When asked why they were in the trenches, the answer was straightforward: "We are here because we are not allowed to be anywhere else."[29]

Among the civilians, the morale likewise deteriorated because no end to the war was in sight and because the war increasingly demonstrated the social inequality, that is, the class difference, vis-à-vis death and misery. In France, in the course of the year 1915, the civilians complained more and more about the steep rise in prices since the beginning of the war, and they cursed the speculators whom they blamed for this. The morale of French civilians also suffered a blow when information began to arrive about the executions of soldiers, for example in the area of Arras in June 1915.[30] And the public learned about the enormous losses France had suffered in 1914 and continued to suffer in 1915. An aversion thus arose to what became known as *la boucherie*, "the slaughter," or *la tuerie*, "the killing." Even in the relatively few proletarian circles where, in the summer of 1914, there had been some enthusiasm for the war, for example among the Parisian socialists, the conviction gained ground that it would be better to end the massacre by means of negotiations. In the ranks of the French socialists who had rallied to the "sacred union" in 1914, there emerged a minority that rejected this arrangement and started to view the war through critical eyes. These "minority socialists" loudly condemned the party leaders who had joined the government, allowed themselves to be dominated there by the bourgeois politicians, and thus had revealed themselves too passive and all too ready to make concessions.[31]

The workers became more and more unhappy about the *union sacrée*, because they could experience daily how the employers took advantage of that arrangement to lower their wages and/or lengthen their work hours, even introducing work on Sundays, all of this presumably in the name of the war effort. They complained that "the mentality of the bosses was even worse than that of the Germans," that "only the bosses, the industrialists, profited from the war and that the working class was the war's greatest victim." Even union leaders began to display hostility toward the *union sacrée*. In Paris, one of them declared that "capitalism is and remains our major enemy . . . The bosses take advantage of the situation to lower wages and sack workers . . . The capitalists profit from the war." The majority of the leaders and members of the unions in Paris sooner or later became totally convinced that "the capitalists" had provoked the war, were the real "warmongers." The reason given was that the war allowed the capitalists to realize even bigger profits than in peacetime and to violate the workers' rights with impunity. A Parisian trade union member hit the nail on the head when he expressed the opinion that "the capitalists had unleashed this catastrophe [the war] because they were alarmed by the growth of the labour movement" and had decided that war would dissipate their worries. In any event, the unionists concluded that "war was not in the interest of the workers," that "those who did not realize this allowed themselves to be massacred for a cause that was not theirs," and that the workers wearing a uniform "were doing their duty not in order to save the fatherland, because workers have no fatherland, but to defend the strongboxes of the capitalists." More and more Parisian union members spoke out in favour of peace at any price, even at the price of a military defeat. And more and more of them felt that the French government was just as much to blame as the German one for the war.[32]

Within the socialist parties and the trade unions, not only in France but in all the belligerent countries, minorities emerged in the course of 1915 that were resolutely against the war, wanted to return to socialist internationalism, and began to appreciate and embrace the "defeatist" viewpoint of Lenin and the Bolsheviks. Representatives of these minorities met between September 5 and 8, 1915 in the village of Zimmerwald in Switzerland. Lenin and Trotsky were among the participants. But the Zimmerwald Conference produced nothing more than an appeal to the peoples of Europe to struggle for peace, for international fraternity, for socialism. A second socialist conference of this nature would be held in Kienthal, likewise in Switzerland, from April 24 to 30, 1916, but again nothing more was yielded than pious declarations. But the two meetings illustrated how within trade unions and socialist parties opposition to the war was increasing, as was discontent with the *union sacrée* policy.

In Germany too, the year 1915 witnessed a decline of civilian morale, above all among the proletarians, who realized more and more that "the sacrifices were not shared equally and that a rich elite profited from the war." Like their French counterparts, the leaders of the Reich's socialists were confronted with a vocal and growing minority, led by Karl Liebknecht, that was disgruntled by the *Burgfrieden* and felt, not without reason, that measures such as the state of siege and censorship operated to the advantage of the elite and to the disadvantage of the plebeians. These radical socialists condemned the war in general as an imperialist undertaking, and in May 1915 they launched an audacious, provocative slogan: "The real enemy is to be found in our own country!"[33] In Russia, the war increasingly revealed the sharp social dichotomy between the very poor popular masses, from whom enormous sacrifices were required, and the rich elite, whose aristocratic and bourgeois members knew how to shelter themselves from the misery of war and, in all too many cases, even profited from it, as Maxim Gorki bitterly remarked in August 1915. The populace suffered all sorts of shortages and lacked even the most essential food, while expensive restaurants were bursting with "well-dressed people gorging themselves on copious quantities of food and alcohol to the accompaniment of an orchestra." This is how a British nurse, who was working as a volunteer in Russia and witnessed this state of affairs, put it. She commented grimly that "these contrasts existed earlier, of course, but the war has made them more acute, more glaring and, morally speaking, more offensive."[34]

As for the British workers, they too were increasingly unhappy with the way in which the industrialists and employers in general profited from the war while they themselves were forced to tighten their belts. The trade unions were no longer willing to put up with wages being frozen while companies made considerable profits, and during the year 1915 they organized numerous strikes to achieve wage increases. No less than three million workdays were thus lost in that year. These figures, writes the British historian Max Hastings, "emphasize the depth and bitterness of Britain's social divisions," divisions that had been veiled at the start of the war, but which the war itself had gradually and mercilessly exposed.[35] The growing malaise among Britain's citizens was reflected in the ebbing of the wave of men volunteering to join the army. In the spring of 1915, the number of volunteers began to drop noticeably from its previous monthly average of approximately one hundred thousand. It was therefore deemed necessary, in May of that year, to increase the age limit from thirty-eight to forty years. (In the Dominion of Canada, in response to a similar decline in the number of volunteers, observed as early as January 1915, the minimum standards for height were lowered, the need for a married man to have his wife's permission was waived, and candidates under the official minimum age of eighteen were increasingly enrolled; no less than twenty thousand of these "boy soldiers" would be sent to Europe.) But the situation hardly improved, and an inquiry carried out the following summer showed that millions of capable men failed to report for duty, so that the government had to consider introducing conscription. In October 1915, Lord Edward Stanley, the seventeenth Count Derby, an eminent representative of the country's elite, was appointed director of the recruitment office. He launched the famous "Derby Scheme," by means of which pressure was exerted on young and not-so-young men to report "voluntarily," and therefore presumably honourably, before compulsory military service would be introduced, which would induce them into the army in a less honourable fashion.[36] All this shows that in Albion the initial enthusiasm for the war had cooled off considerably. It is also telling that in 1915 no more ladies were to be seen distributing white feathers. All too many British women had already had to sacrifice a husband or son to the god Mars, and many others feared for the lives of men who were doing their bit at the front — why, and how much longer? That this disenchantment was widespread found a reflection in the huge success in Britain of a pacifist song born in the US in 1915. Its title alone spoke volumes: "I Didn't Raise My Boy to Be a Soldier."

> *Ten million soldiers to the war have gone,*
> *Who may never return again.*
> *Ten million mothers' hearts must break*
> *For the ones who died in vain.*
> *Head bowed down in sorrow*
> *In her lonely years,*
> *I heard a mother murmur thro' her tears:*
> *I didn't raise my boy to be a soldier,*
> *I brought him up to be my pride and joy,*
> *Who dares to place a musket on his shoulder,*

To shoot some other mother's darling boy?
Let nations arbitrate their future troubles,
It's time to lay the sword and gun away,
There'd be no war today,
If mothers all would say,
"I didn't raise my boy to be a soldier."[37]

What is remarkable in the lyrics of this song is the appeal to all nations to lay down "the sword and gun" and to settle their differences by means of "arbitration." Indeed, in 1915, leading personalities in all belligerent as well as many neutral countries began to argue in favour of ending the war by means of negotiations. The US president, Woodrow Wilson, for example, sent his chief foreign policy advisor, Colonel Edward M. House, to Europe in an attempt to get peace talks started; however, both sides stuck stubbornly — and literally — to their guns. It is remarkable also that the song mentions ten million mothers whose "hearts must break": the Great War would indeed cause the death of approximately ten million soldiers.

In all the belligerent countries, the authorities worried more and more about the slumping morale of civilians as well as soldiers, and remedies were sought, war propaganda cranked out even more grimly than before. It was in this context that on May 3, 1915, in the vicinity of Ypres, a Canadian officer, Lieutenant-Colonel John McCrae, known as a keen supporter of the British Empire (of which his country was still a dominion) and of the war, was inspired to write a poem in which he urged the men to carry on with their task in spite of all the hardship. This composition, entitled "In Flanders' Fields," was destined to become famous all over the world, presumably on account of its potent description of poppies floating in a sea of crosses marking the tombs of the dead, and also of larks singing, high above the heads of the trench-bound combatants, in spite of the rumble of the guns:

In Flanders' fields the poppies blow
Between the crosses, row on row,
That mark our place; and in the sky
The larks, still bravely singing, fly

Scarce heard amid the guns below.

We are the Dead. Short days ago
We lived, felt dawn, saw sunset glow,
Loved and were loved, and now we lie,
In Flanders' fields.

Take up our quarrel with the foe:
To you from failing hands we throw
The torch; be yours to hold it high.
If ye break faith with us who die,
We shall not sleep, though poppies grow
In Flanders' fields.[38]

In his brilliant book on the Great War, Paul Fussell has critically dissected this poem. He denounces it as an almost "vicious and stupid" but particularly powerful and effective literary instrument of war propaganda, of what the French called *jusqu'au-boutisme,* in which the line "take up our quarrel with the foe" naturally jumps to the fore. The poem was indeed potent and effective, because it evoked images the denizens of the trenches were familiar with and found appealing, such as they sky stretching high above their heads, the dawn and sunset they observed keenly every single day, the mesmerizing larks, untouchable high in the sky, the blissful "mock-death" (Fussell) of the sleep they cherished so much — and the red poppies, traditionally associated not only with sleep, dreams, and oblivion, but also with love, blood, and martyrdom. (To the British soldier and poet Isaac Rosenberg too, the poppies were a strong symbol in the sense of blood and sacrifice; in his poem "Break of Day in the Trenches," he wrote that "the roots" of the poppies "are in man's veins.")[39]

It was not a coincidence that poppies flowered abundantly in Flanders' Fields in the spring of 1915. Normally, the minuscule seeds of this flower penetrate deep into the earth in order to wait there, sometimes for years, for the soil to be upturned for some reason, and thus exposed to the sunlight and warmth they suddenly germinate. With the digging of miles of trenches and the explosion of tens if not hundreds of thousands of shells starting in the fall of 1914, the conditions were created for an unprecedented burgeoning of poppies the following spring in that corner of Belgium, of course most spectacularly so in the immediate vicinity of the trenches and in the pockmarked no man's land.[40] With its poppies, McCrae's poem thus certainly catered to the sensibilities of the Canadian and British soldiers. Even more effective as a tool of motivation was the fact that the poem loomed like an appeal emanating from the fallen comrades, rather than from officialdom, including officers like McCrae himself. It insinuated in a particularly subtle way that *not* to persevere in "our [sic] quarrel with the foe" would have amounted to a kind of treason, a gross shattering of the chain of solidarity that bound the men together — the living as well as the dead! Not holding "high the torch" thus became unthinkable, as it would have meant betraying the dead comrades. Such disloyalty would have prevented the latter from finding rest in an eternal sleep, even though they were cradled by a lovely landscape bursting with soporific blossoms:

> If ye break faith with us who die,
> We shall not sleep, though poppies grow
> In Flanders' fields.

Such a *jusqu'au-boutiste* poem could hardly fail to find favour with military and political authorities keen to find ways to motivate the men, with the media, and thus with the public. McCrae received heaps of letters and telegrams congratulating and praising him. "In Flanders' Fields" was published on December 6, 1915 in the satirical but nationalist British magazine *Punch* and thus embarked on a career as one of the most celebrated and cited literary products of the Great War. The reason was not its literary merits, nor was it because ordinary soldiers liked it, which does not seem to have been the case at all. It became famous because it would be used systematically, year after year, to make propaganda in favour of the war and against pacifism, in favour of the sale of war bonds, of the recruitment of volunteers all over the British Empire and later, in 1917, in the United States — and in Canada, again in 1917, in favour of the introduction of conscription, a measure that met with much opposition, especially in the province of Quebec.[41] Even today, the red poppy is associated not only with remembrance, but with nationalism and militarism, which is why on occasions such as Remembrance Day pacifists have turned to wearing an alternative, white poppy.

The poppy also made an appearance in a very different literary and musical creation of 1915, but one of a strongly antimilitarist nature, namely the aforementioned French song inspired by the bloody fighting in the infamous forest known as Bois-le-Prêtre, in Lorraine. In this chanson the red poppy is an analogue of the futile medals bestowed on the fallen *poilus*:

Si, du canon bravant l'écho,	*If the sun dares to ignore the gunfire,*
Le soleil y risque un bécot,	*And comes to bless us with a little kiss,*
On peut voir le coquelicot	*Red poppies all around us*
Partout renaître . . .	*Spring to life again . . .*
Car, dans un geste de semeur,	*It is God who, like a sower,*
Dieu, pour chaque Poilu qui meurt,	*Generously casts decorations*
Jette des légions d'honour	*One for every soldier*
Au Bois-le-Prêtre!	*Who dies in Bois-le-Prêtre!*

CHAPTER 21
MILITARIA 1916: MATERIEL AND HUMAN MATERIAL

If men armed with rifles and bayonets cannot open a gap in defensive lines, perhaps it can be done by simply obliterating the enemy in his trenches by means of massive shelling by the artillery. This is the unsubtle idea behind the infamous "attrition battles" fought in 1916 and associated with the names of generals such as von Falkenhayn, Pétain, and Haig. The Germans called these battles Materialschlachten, *an allusion to the huge amounts of materiel, or war equipment, that were involved. However, an unprecedented amount of "human material" was also used — and pulverized — in those titanic battles of 1916, and in France and Britain as well as in Germany their names — Verdun and the Somme — continue to conjure up the horrors of the Great War . . .*

Nineteen sixteen was the third year of the war. It had been preceded by two years of death and misery, and it would be followed by two more horrible years. Nineteen sixteen was the midpoint of the Great War and in many respects also its nadir, as it featured unprecedented massacres, above all in the vicinity of Verdun and in the *département* of France named after the River Somme. Near Verdun, General Erich von Falkenhayn, who had taken over from von Moltke as Germany's supreme commander after the Battle of the Marne, concentrated the greatest collection of cannons the world had ever seen. He knew that the French would want to defend this small but historically important town, where the famous Verdun Treaty had been signed in 843, to the last man if necessary. He therefore intended to shell the French positions so intensively and so long with his artillery that eventually there would be virtually nothing left of the defending *poilus*, so that Paris would be obliged to throw in the towel. Von Falkenhayn was convinced that he could thus win the war; that is, by means of what he baptized a *Materialschlacht*, a "battle of materiel," a form of warfare in which German materiel, more specifically artillery, would slowly but surely grind down the French infantry with its incessant bombardment.

The French would indeed suffer catastrophic losses in the defence of Verdun. But the Germans also took a terrible beating during the many months the fighting dragged on, namely from February 21 until early December 1916. Finally, the battle — or, more accurately, the slaughter — of Verdun ended in a macabre kind of tie. The French suffered the greatest losses, but kept the city; von Falkenhayn did not manage to overcome their resistance and failed to win the war with his strategy. In any event, the result of this "battle of materiel" — in which a total of sixty million shells were fired, amounting to six per square metre[1] — was catastrophic for the "human materiel" involved on both sides. (Men were henceforth considered to be just another type of materiel, of cheap materiel, a "raw material" necessary for the massive production of death.)[2] Between 163,000 and 221,000 French soldiers, as well as 143,000 German soldiers lost their lives, were taken prisoner, or were reported missing; 320,000 French and 500,000 Germans were wounded, for a grand total of a little more than one million casualties. (According to Niall Ferguson, the French suffered 377,000 and the Germans 337,000 casualties.) In any event, hundreds of thousands of men perished in what the French called the "hell" of Verdun. Verdun has also been described as a "meat grinder," through which 259 of the 330 units of French infantry had to pass, whereby the survival chances of each *poilu* were minimal. According to a report of June 1916, that is, in the heat of the battle, of every one hundred men who went to Verdun, only thirty returned unscathed.

Other than artillery and "human material," yet another kind of materiel was involved, namely trucks. For months on end, only one road was available, the one from Bar-le-Duc, to send men and supplies to the front around Verdun. Along this *voie sacrée* or "sacred road," as it became known, thousands of trucks rolled both ways, day and night, bringing in men and ammunition, food, etc., and taking out the wounded. (Additional good were transported via a little railway line running parallel to the road.) It has been calculated that one truck passed every fourteen seconds, amounting to a total of 250 trucks per hour! Without this link, the French would not have been able to hold their lines around Verdun. On the other hand, the two sides also relied on some old-fashioned materiel, carrier pigeons and dogs, for example, in order to stay in touch with the combatants in the first lines. A particularly "heroic" French pigeon, called "Cher Ami," was stuffed after its death and may now be admired in the Smithsonian Institution in Washington.[3]

Nineteen sixteen was also the year of the infamous Battle of the Somme, a second massacre in which hundreds of thousands of men lost their lives, this time mostly British and Germans, but also French. This battle was not fought along the river named Somme, which meanders lazily from east to west through northern France, thus crossing the frontline, which in this area ran from the southeast to the northwest. The name referred to the French administrative district or *département* where this battle took place and which was itself named after the river. This *département* corresponds more or less to the ancient province of Picardy, whose capital city is Amiens. Most of the fighting took place to the east of Amiens, between the small town of Albert, which was held by the allies, and the towns of Bapaume and Péronne, both situated behind the German lines.

This area, which had been a particularly calm sector of the front, had been occupied for some time on the allied side by British troops. Many of the men holding it now were newcomers to the war, inexperienced recruits who had arrived in France only shortly before. They were not professional soldiers like the men of the BEF, but volunteers who had joined the forces in 1914 and 1915 and who were therefore collectively known as "Kitchener's Army," for they had heeded the latter's famous summons to fight for king and country. The great majority of these troops were from Britain itself, that is, from England, Scotland, and Wales, as well as Ireland.

In contrast to the Battle of Verdun, the Battle of the Somme was not an offensive launched by the Germans, but by the allies, more in particular the

British, even though French forces would also be involved. The objective was to reduce the pressure exerted on Verdun by the Germans. But Haig, the British commander-in-chief, who directed the operation, viewed it as an opportunity to do what his predecessor, French, had been unable to achieve in 1915, namely, to pierce through the German lines and thus win the war. He spoke optimistically of the offensive he planned as the "Great Push Forward" or, short and sweet, the "Big Push." Haig was now in charge and was convinced that God had chosen him personally to guide the British to victory. (Of his offensive, he would later say that he "felt that every step in [his] plan had been taken with the Divine help.") Haig dreamed of a battle in the style of the supposedly good old days, perhaps not the Middle Ages, but those of the Napoleonic Wars, during which foot soldiers, with the aid of artillery, blew a hole in the enemy lines, through which the cavalry, the favourite weapon of the nobility — and of Haig too — could charge in a decisive move, rolling up enemy lines and harvesting the glory of victory. Haig had allegedly persuaded himself that "the ability of bullets to stop horses was greatly exaggerated"; maybe that is only a legend, but it does illustrate his unquestioned confidence in the huge potential of warriors on horseback. Conversely, he had a rather low opinion of machine guns, an opinion typical for the British aristocracy and elite in general. How could a weapon mass-produced by workers in some anonymous factory and manipulated by any proletarian be superior to an aristocrat high on the "noble" animal that was his horse?[4]

Haig and his colleagues were perfectly conscious of the fact that there would be numerous casualties among the infantrymen who would attack first, but that did not present much of a problem. The men of "Kitchener's Army" were extremely numerous and overwhelmingly of modest origin. They were the kind of people of which Britain was overpopulated anyway, so that — seen from the elite perspective — the country would benefit from seeing their ranks thinned out somewhat. Moreover, the planned offensive was perceived as an excellent opportunity to inculcate some discipline and *class* into these proletarians. The latter received instructions to move to the attack in good order, like schoolchildren, nicely lined up, in order to progress slowly and unswervingly through the no man's land, erect and dignified, just the way their superiors liked to see it. Finally, in order to make this a fine and enjoyable show for the superiors watching from a safe distance, the attack was scheduled to take place in full daylight. From the experiences of 1914 and 1915, however, Haig had learned that artillery was also important, even very important. And so, like von Falkenhayn at Verdun, the British commander-in-chief assembled a colossal quantity of guns, allegedly approximately 1,600 pieces. With the help of this arsenal, he intended to bomb the German lines so thoroughly that during the attack the advancing British troops would only have to liquidate the rare surviv-ors. The German positions would be shelled for no less than five days, during which time about one and a half million projectiles would be fired.

The offensive got under way on July 1, 1916. The weather was described as "divine," but that day would turn out to be the darkest in the history of the British army. At exactly 7:30, the order was given to the Tommies to "go over the top" or "jump the bags," as exiting the trenches was called, and move forward through no man's land as they had been told, the British way: disciplined and dignified, marching slowly, body upright, shoulder to shoulder. In the case of the Surrey Regiment, someone kicked a soccer ball in the direction of the German trenches when the attack began. To the still-inexperienced Tommies, all of this created the impression that the situation was under control, that all would be well. Moreover, the officers had assured the men that, after days of shelling, not much would be left of the German positions and their defenders.

The composure and discipline of the soldiers made an excellent impres-sion on the generals. Their feelings were reflected in these lines of a poem entitled "On the Somme," in which Charles Penrose, an officer who wit-nessed the attack, described in a half-serious, half-sarcastic way how well the scenario unfolded on that morning of July 1:

> *All across the No Man's land and through the ruined wiring,*
> *Each officer that led them, with a walking-cane for sword,*
> *Cared not a button though the foeman went on firing*
> *While they dribbled over footballs to the glory of the Lord.*[5]

But Haig had not foreseen that so many Germans, ensconced in solid tunnels and bunkers as much as ten metres deep under the ground, would be able to survive the hellish bombardement. As soon as the artillery ceased to fire, the Germans realized that the attack was imminent, so they rushed out of their shelters with their machine guns. They could not believe their eyes when they saw thousands and thousands of British soldiers approaching through no man's land, slowly, erect, in neat lines. Countless Tommies were mowed down in very little time on that fateful morning. The preliminary shelling, no matter how impressive, had also been far less effective than expected for another reason. The British shells were of mediocre quality, and no less than one-quarter of all projectiles fired appeared to be "duds" that did not explode. Whose fault was that? Perhaps the manufacturers, who earned fortunes by producing ammunition, and who sought to increase their gains by using material of lower quality? As far as Haig was concerned, however, there could be no doubt. The culprits were the British factory workers whom he believed to "have too many holidays and too much to drink." "A notable argument," remarks Adam Hochschild, "for someone whose family fortune was based on whisky." Haig suggested in a letter to his wife that it would be a good idea to "take and shoot two or three of them" so that "the 'Drink habit' would cease."[6]

And so the first waves of British attackers were mowed down, one after the other, by the German machine guns. Still, the Tommies kept moving forward. This was the case, even late in the day, for the Newfoundland Regiment, one of the rare British units involved in the battle that was not from Britain itself. (At the time, the great island in the northwest Atlantic was not yet part of Canada, as it is today, but was still a separate British colony.) In the vicinity of the village of Beaumont-Hamel, 684 of the 752 Newfoundlanders involved fell victim to the machine guns of Germans of whom they never even saw one single specimen. But what British general would worry about the loss of a few hundred fishermen, miners, and others workers from a distant and insignificant part of the glorious Empire? On this fateful July 1 — later to become a "Remembrance Day" in Newfoundland — the British army lost more men than ever before in one single day: 60,000 casualties on a total of 110,000 men who participated in the attack. The German losses allegedly amounted to 8,000 men. The thousands of cavalrymen kept in readiness by Haig waited in vain for the signal to move forward, as the hoped-for breach in the German lines never materialized.[7]

The British generals were of course disappointed that the attack had not produced the desired result. But they were most satisfied with the way in which the men had followed orders and conducted themselves in such a dignified manner. "Where today we might see mindless killing," writes Adam Hochschild, "many of those who presided over the war's battles saw only nobility and heroism." And with respect to the bloodbath of July 1, 1916, he quotes the report of a general:

> Not a man shirked going through the extremely heavy barrage,
> or facing the machine-gun and rifle fire that finally wiped
> them out . . . He saw the lines which advanced in such
> admirable order melting away under the fire. Yet not a man
> wavered, broke the ranks, or attempted to come back. He
> has never seen, indeed could never have imagined, such a
> magnificent display of gallantry, discipline and determination.
> The report that he had had from the very few survivors of this
> marvellous advance bear out what he saw with his own eyes,
> viz, that hardly a man of ours got to the German front line.[8]

Two days after the attack, when Haig received a report stating that the losses amounted to forty thousand men — while in reality they were much higher! — he remarked coolly that "this cannot be considered severe, in view of the numbers engaged, and the length of front attacked." He found that even such high losses were not very important in the big scheme of things. The death of thousands of soldiers did not cause him any headaches. "We lament too much over death," he stoically commented on one occasion, "we should regard it as a change to another room." And he added:

> The nation must be taught to bear losses . . . [and] to see
> heavy casualty lists for what may appear to the uninitiated to
> be insufficient object[s] . . . Three years of war and the loss of
> one-tenth of the manhood of the nation is not too great a price
> to pay in so great a cause.[9]

Incidentally, Haig avoided all direct contact with the ordinary soldiers whom he sacrificed so lavishly on the altar of the Moloch of war. He alleg-edly never even once ventured into the trenches. And whenever he did come face-to-face with a soldier, he addressed him as aristocrats had done since time immemorial, namely with a condescending "my man," to which the subordinate was supposed to respond with a respectful "sir."[10]

The opinion of the generals was echoed by the media in Britain. A war correspondent over there reported that, "on balance, [it had been] a good day for England and France. It is a day of promise in this war." And the *Daily Mirror* of November 22, 1916 even justified and glorified the demise of tens of thousands of men with the following description of a dead Tommy:

> *Even as he lies on the field, he looks more quietly faithful,*
> *more simply steadfast than others. He looks especially modest*
> *and gentlemanly too, as if he had taken care while he died*
> *that there should be no parade in his bearing, no heroics in his*
> *posture.*

The soldiers themselves, however, saw things in a different light. The Somme offensive, Haig's "Big Push," was referred to by the men as "the Great Fuck-Up," a term that would eventually also designate the war in general. It was a term with a double edge, reflecting not only the soldiers' contempt for the generals' incompetence, but also their perception of being terribly abused by Haig and their other superiors. The latter point, or some-thing very similar, was also conveyed by the German soldiers when they called the war a *Schwindel*: a "fraud," "scam," or "racket."[11]

The Battle of the Somme started catastrophically on July 1, 1916, and would drag on until November of that same year, demanding many more victims in the process. The allies would register minimal territorial gains, but more important was undoubtedly the fact that Haig's scheme had pro-vided some much-needed relief for the beleaguered French around Verdun. In any event, as at Verdun, the losses were enormous. The British suf-fered losses totalling approximately a half-million men, including at least 125,000 killed, while the French registered 200,000 casualties. The German losses amounted to about a half-million men. To all the forces involved in it, the bloody affair at the Somme cost more than one million killed, wounded, missing in action, and prisoners of war.[12]

The Battle of the Somme provided inspiration for a song that would become a huge hit in Britain, "Roses of Picardy," written by a lawyer and famous songwriter, Frederick E. Weatherley. The province of Picardy, more or less the territorial equivalent of the Département of the Somme and therefore the theatre of the great battle, is not known for its roses: those flowers functioned as the powerful symbol of the blood that was spilled in that region, much as the poppies did for Flanders' Fields. Moreover, as Paul Fussell has noted, roses are closely connected to England and are a symbol of loyalty to the British fatherland. In this song, loyalty to the homeland is closely associated with loyalty to the loved one:[13]

> Roses are shining in Picardy
> In the hush of the silver dew
> Roses are flowering in Picardy
> But there's never a rose like you
> And the roses will die with the summer time
> And our roads may be far apart
> But there's one rose that dies not in Picardy
> 'T is the rose that I keep in my heart.

"Roses of Picardy" is a beautiful song that was very effective in conjuring up the atmosphere in Britain during and after the Battle of the Somme. But the horror and absurdity of the battle in general and the attack of July 1 in particular are conveyed even more strikingly in the poem "After the 'Offensive'" by Theo Van Beek, an artillery officer:

> Waves of strong men
> That will surge not again,
> Scattered and riven
> You lie, and you rot;
> What have you not given?
> And what — have you got?[14]

During the Battle of the Somme, the British attacked toward the east, and on July 1, 1916, they died by the thousands as they marched through no man's land toward the rising sun. And yet it appears to be around that time that, in order to refer to being killed or dying in general, the Tommies started to use the expression "going west," seemingly inspired by the ancient association of the cardinal point of the setting sun with the underworld and death. (Other expressions with a similar meaning were "going under" and "being knocked out.") It was while marching to the east, literally so, that tens of thousands of soldiers "went west," figuratively speaking.

In the poem "From *Sed Miles*" — meaning something like "excerpt from the latin poem *Sed Miles* "[dying] like a soldier" —, A.E. Tomlinson asked why, in the Battle of the Somme, so many Tommies had to go west. He gave a sarcastic answer: for the glory of the British Empire, in order to cause even more parts of the world to be painted in the red colour indicating British possessions on the famous maps produced by the firm Bartholomew:

> *But when West you go,*
> *It's nice to know*
> *You've done your bit*
> *In spite of it;*
> *And Blighty's name*
> *And Blighty's fame*
> *Will find in your*
> *Demise, manure,*
> *To sprout and spread*
> *Till English red*
> *Is the favourite hue*
> *For Bartholomew.*[15]

For the British soldiers, however, the affair on the Somme, and thus the entire summer of 1916, marked a turning point. They no longer believed that the war would be over by the following year. "The soldiers still marched dutifully to the front," writes Adam Hochschild, "but no longer sang." They now radiated "a kind of dogged cynicism, a disbelief that any battle could make a difference."[16] How could this war ever come to an end, if even a huge offensive failed to change the deadlock? Toward the end of 1916, a British officer calculated that, based on the progress made since the beginning of the war in the trenches, it might take the British 180 years to reach the Rhine. Another officer was of the opinion that "God knows how long [the war] will be at this rate" and that "none of us will ever see its end and children still at school will have to take it over." After a visit to General Haig, George Bernard Shaw wrote that the commander-in-chief had left him with the impression that the war could last another thirty years and that Haig seemed determined to carry on leading the British army until his superannuation. As 1916, the *annus horribilis* of the massacres of Verdun and the Somme, drew to a close, not only countless British but also French and German soldiers started to feel that the war would never end, that war had become "the permanent condition of mankind." Many Tommies were convinced that it would be war for the rest of their lives, and they cynically told each other that "the first seven years will be the worst." One of those "neverendians" was the poet Robert Graves, who was to write later that "we held two irreconcilable beliefs: that the war would never end and that we would win it."[17]

The idea of an endless war is not that outlandish. The Vietnam War, too, appeared for a long time to be endless; and is the present so-called War on Terror not only a universal but also a permanent form of warfare? Having spent more than two years in a murderous conflict that was supposed to have been short and glorious, the combatants had plenty of reasons to believe that they might never see it end. Even if the war did someday come to an end, asked some of them cynically, would their officers be kind enough to let them know? Not to worry, was the answer in a soldier's joke, we will find out that the war is over when they fire four black flares at midnight!

The small town of Albert, in the heart of Picardy, was nicknamed "Bert" by the British. "Bert" was (and is) not exactly a place of great beauty and interest, but functioned as a hub to the soldiers who took part in the Battle of the Somme, just as Ypres did for the British in Flanders' Fields. And the road from Amiens to Albert was the only one that could be used to transfer men and materiel to and from the front, resembling in this respect the road from Poperinge to Ypres in the "Ypres Pocket" — and, in the case of the French in Verdun, the famous "sacred road." The men who trekked to Albert via this sinister road could already perceive from far away the great local attraction: a gilded statue of the Virgin Mary that had been hit by a shell and remained for years dangling precariously from its base on top of the high belltower of the local church. The Tommies called her the Lady of the Limp. They were convinced that the war would end when the statue detached from its base and came crashing down to the ground. The Germans also believed this and their gunners tried again and again to shoot the statue down, but in vain. In the spring of 1918, when "Bert" fell in the hands of the Germans, it was the turn of the British artillery to take aim at the Madonna of Albert. In April 1918, she finally did come down, hit by a British projectile. A little more than six months later, the war finally came to an end.[18]

Verdun and the Somme constituted the "highlights" of the program of battles in the year 1916, but elsewhere there also occurred actions that deserve our attention. On May 31 and June 1, for example, the only major naval battle of the Great War was fought in the waters of the North Sea, off the coast of Denmark's Jutland Peninsula, which is why the event entered history as the Battle of Jutland. It was a confrontation between the British Royal Navy and the German war fleet, and the two adversaries withdrew after having inflicted relatively heavy losses on each other. The British lost 6,784 men; the Germans less than half that, 3,039. The Germans lost fewer men and sank more British ships, which enabled them to claim victory. And in Germany the battle was duly celebrated as a triumph; even after the end of the Second World War, it was still considered a victory by the Germans. Conversely, the British public was shocked that their powerful Royal Navy, while not defeated, had certainly suffered a setback, and some newspapers proclaimed the Germans to be the victors. But it gradually became clear that the Germans had minimised their own losses, and that what mattered was not only the number of ships sunk and lives lost, but also the result of the encounter. The German fleet's attempt to deprive the Royal Navy of control of the North Sea had in fact ended in failure because, after the battle, the German ships withdrew to their ports in order to inactively await the end of the war. The British thus remained the masters of the North Sea and were able to prevent the deployment of German ships. They could also continue to prevent the food and raw materials that Germany badly needed in order to wage war on land from reaching the Reich via neutral ships and neutral ports in, for example, the Netherlands. This British blockade was undoubtedly one of the determinants of Germany's ultimate defeat. Conversely, one can say that Germany could *perhaps* have won the war if its fleet had triumphed in the Battle of Jutland, thus preventing the blockade. In this sense, the Battle of Jutland constituted a victory, unspectacular but very important, for the British. As far as British public opinion was concerned, the disappointing result of the Jutland encounter soon evaporated as the media started to report good news, albeit mostly false, from the western front after the start of the Battle of the Somme on July 1, 1916.[19]

On the Oriental Front, the combatants did not remain inactive either in 1916. The major event of the year over there was a large-scale offensive orchestrated by the Russian general Brussilov, an offensive that lasted from early June to the end of September. It took place in the western reaches of what is now the Ukraine, for example in the vicinity of the city of Lviv, then better known under its German name, Lemberg. Initially, all went well. After an intensive preliminary bombardment by the artillery, the Russian infantry moved to the attack, the Austro-Hungarian lines were pierced, and the Russians were thus able to advance along a long stretch of the front and bag a few hundreds of thousands of prisoners. The troops of the Habsburg Empire deserted in large numbers, not only individually but also collectively. Regiments consisting of Czechs and other Slav minorities, in particular, crossed over in their entirety to the Russians. But then German reinforcements started to arrive by train and launched counterattacks. After weeks of fighting, the two sides became exhausted and the military operations degenerated again into a stationary type of warfare. In the meantime, Romania, impressed by Brusilov's initial success, had declared war on the Central Powers. Like their counterparts in Italy and Bulgaria, Romania's leaders were motivated by the prospect of being on the winning side and thus being able to achieve territorial gains. However, the Romanians soon came close to being overwhelmed by Bulgarian, Austro-Hungarian, and German troops. Brussilov had to come to their assistance, but in vain, because by December 1916, the Germans entered Bucharest and Romania was de facto knocked out of the war. An armistice would be negotiated in December 1917 and a peace treaty would be signed in Bucharest on April 21, 1918. (Germany was thus able to lay its hands on the country's oil fields.) In any event, the Brusilov offensive thus petered out. But by drawing German troops to the eastern front, it had provided some relief to the French in Verdun. And it had delivered a nasty blow to the Danube Monarchy, a blow from which that empire would never recover. Afterwards, the Habsburg Empire proved virtually incapable of waging war without German assistance.[20]

CHAPTER 22
DISGRUNTLED SOLDIERS AND CIVILIANS

In the course of the year 1916 it becomes increasingly evident that soldiers as well as civilians are disgruntled and restless. The workers and other plebeians are experiencing great difficulties on account of low wages and high prices. Their fate contrasts dramatically — and provocatively — with the good life of the war profiteers and the embusqués, that is, all those who manage to avoid serving at the front. Not only the proletarians, but also the ethnic minorities have had enough, as is demonstrated spectacularly by the Easter Rising in Dublin . . .

In 1914, the peasants, petty bourgeois, and workers of all countries had obediently gone to war to the great satisfaction of the aristocratic, bourgeois, and ecclesiastical elite that had wanted the war, had unleashed it, and had expected a lot from it — not least the metamorphosis of the plebeian masses into a retinue as meek and malleable as the serfs of the Middle Ages, the era glorified by Romanticism. From this point of view, however, the war would reveal itself to be rather dysfunctional; the plebeians lost a great deal of whatever respect, confidence, and credulity they had displayed vis-à-vis the nobility in general, and especially the haughty but incompetent generals who "butchered" their own soldiers by the tens of thousands, but also the crowned heads who were deemed responsible for the war, as well as the prelates who had praised the war as a crusade and an expiation of sins. And the lower orders manifested more and more hostility to, and contempt for, the industrialists and bankers who profited shamelessly from the war. In other words, the war made the "little" people — in uniform or not — more recalcitrant, restless, seditious, and therefore more dangerous to the elite than ever before.

It was in the course of the year 1916 that this became obvious. In August of that year, a British nurse working on the oriental front near Thessaloniki expressed the unrest and fear that arose in the elite:

> The war began as an attempt to preserve Europe exactly as
> it was, to uphold the status quo, but it is now changing the
> continent in a more sweeping way than anyone could have
> imagined in their worst nightmares.

And she blamed "those in power . . . [who] have unleashed uniquely uncontrollable forces: extreme nationalism, social revolution, religious hatred."[1]

The morale of the soldiers who served as cannon fodder during the big battles of 1916 descended to a nadir. The fall of 1914 had been the time of disillusion, and 1915 had been the year of war weariness and despair; 1916 witnessed the emergence of the first symptoms of discontent, disaffection, and even sedition. On the walls of houses in a devastated village in occupied northern France, for example, German soldiers had scribbled in big letters the following graffiti:

> Let us stop the killing, we want peace . . . No heroic death
> for us! . . . Those who praise dying as a hero should go to the
> front themselves . . . To hell with the officers, they are dogs
> and scoundrels!

More and more German soldiers had had enough of the war and longed for peace. It had been like that for some time already, but in 1916 the horrors of Verdun and the Somme released an unprecedented wave of longing for peace (*Friedenssehnsucht*), not only among Germany's soldiers but also its civilians. It is said that the British offensive on the Somme, in particular, dealt a heavy blow to the Germans' morale; it was then that the men in field grey first started to desert or surrender in significant numbers. (The British took no less than eleven thousand German prisoners during the first two weeks of the battle.) And it was also in 1916 that the "front pigs" started to point an accusing finger at those whom they considered responsible for the bloodbath, namely "the capitalists," including those of their own country. In August 1916, a high-ranking government official thus reported that

> . . . for months already, not a single letter [from soldiers on the front] arrives without containing an urgent demand for peace . . . In the army the conviction is widespread that the war drags on only because it is in the interest of the capitalists.[2]

The following verse, entitled *"Der Krieg ist für die Reichen,"* "War is for the Rich," became particularly popular among the ordinary German soldiers:

Wir kämpfen nicht für Vaterland,	*We do not fight for fatherland,*
Wir kämpfen nicht für Gott,	*We do not fight for God,*
Wir kämpfen für die reichen Leut',	*We fight for the rich people,*
Die Armen schießt man tot.	*The poor simply get shot.*

A slightly different version was as follows:

Wir kämpfen nicht für Vaterland	*We do not fight for fatherland,*
und nicht für deutsche Ehre,	*And not for German honour,*
Wir sterben für den Unverstand	*We die for absurdities*
und für die Millionäre![3]	*And for the millionaires!*

In the German army, the dissatisfaction, the restlessness, and the hostility of the men toward their military superiors and the aristocratic and bourgeois elite in general were increasing dramatically. In an attempt to relieve the pressure, the authorities proceeded to reduce the most glaring, and therefore most provocative, privileges of the "gentlemen officers." By March 1916, for example, the high command of the fleet at Wilhelmshaven arranged to remove all luxurious features from the officers' cabins. The fact that these cabins were "furnished like upper-class homes, with oriental rugs, padded leather armchairs and original art" and that the officers bene-fited from excellent food and drink and enjoyed regular and long furloughs, had long been a thorn in the side of the ordinary sailors who had to live in Spartan conditions; the sailor who has left us a testimony about this saw it as a demonstration of "the class system." At the same time, the officers started to wear their pistols, because they feared possible explosions of the "growing sense of frustration among the crew."[4]

The German civilians likewise displayed a growing war weariness in 1916. In that year the Reich already counted at least six relatively large and active pacifist organizations. Some were bourgeois, others were proletarian and cultivated relations with the SPD, especially its radical faction, the cir-cle around Karl Liebknecht, although in early 1916 the latter was excluded from the party, which, faithful to the idea of the *Burgfrieden*, continued to support the war. On May 1, in Berlin, Liebknecht led a demonstration against the war and in favour of peace. He was arrested, but no less than fifty thousand workers in the Berlin ammunition factories went on strike in protest against this measure. In the Reichstag, a commission was charged with studying the possibility of peace negotiations; in 1917, this would produce a resolution in favour of them.

The rise of pacifism triggered a counteroffensive by diehard militarists, rep-resentatives of the political, military, and social elite who rejected any kind of peace initiative and continued to see promise in the war. They kept dreaming of a victory that would realize their objectives, namely the consolidation of the established social and political order and an imperialist expansion both within Europe and overseas. In order to achieve that goal, not only the exter-nal enemy had to be tackled ruthlessly, for example via unlimited submarine warfare, but also the domestic enemy, that is, the pacifists and the radical socialists. Nobody personified the latter better than Karl Liebknecht, Rosa Luxemburg, and Franz Mehring, the pacifist and socialist hard core who were targeted with weapons such as censorship and arrest on account of alleged "treasonous activities." During the spring and summer of 1916, the socialist-pacifist trio thus spent considerable time behind bars, but that sparked protests in the shape of demonstrations and strikes. The war was obviously causing German society to be increasingly polarized.[5]

In addition, the Germans were suffering the consequences of the British naval blockade. Like every other industrialized country, the Reich had long been importing foodstuffs from abroad, and this was now becoming very difficult, if not impossible. Domestic agriculture had become largely dependent on imported fertilizer, which was also becoming very scarce. (But Germany could compensate at least partly for this shortage by introducing new chemical fertilizers — like poison gas, a specialty of the country's big petrochemical corporations such as BASF; it is estimated that this enabled the Reich to continue to wage war for at least one extra year.)[6] The result was a growing food shortage, with concomitant high prices. In working-class families, pork disappeared from the diet. This was a traumatic development, not only for the stomachs but also for the minds of the German workers for whom, in the years before 1914, the consumption of pork — mostly in the form of sausages — had represented a remarkable achievement of the labour movement, a veritable "symbol of progress and social integration." Conversely, the disappearance of pork from the proletarian table loomed not only as "a calorific loss, but also a serious form of social regress."[7]

The prices of more basic staples such as bread, potatoes, and milk rose sharply, so that the lower orders were exposed to hunger, especially in the cities. During the winter of 1916–1917, countless Germans had to make do without bread or potatoes and settle for turnips — *Steckrüben*, also sarcastically referred to as "Hindenburg turnips." This sparked hunger riots and demonstrations against the high cost of living, and caused even more of the Reich's burghers to long for an end to the war that had brought on all that misery. The shortages inspired the following verse:

Im Jahre 1916 und 17,	*In the years 1916 and 17,*
Do war'ne Erpelsnot,	*There was a potato shortage,*
Do schlogen seck die Wiewer	*The women beat each other*
Öm enen Erpel tot.	*To death for a potato.*[8]

Among Germany's soldiers and civilians a song became popular in which it was sarcastically asked if "Michael" — code name for the average German

— could possibly wish for something more than all the good things one enjoyed in the beloved Reich, such as machine guns and cannons. This song, *"Mein Michel was willst du noch mehr?"* ("Michael, What More Could You Possibly Want?") featured the following lines, referring to the contemporary scarcities:

Du hast Kohlrüben und Eicheln,	*You have plenty of turnips and*
und frägst du nach and'rem Begehr,	*acorns,*
so darfst du am Bauche dich	*And if you want anything more,*
streicheln,	*You can simply rub your belly,*
Mein Michel, was willst du noch	*Dear Michael, what more could you*
mehr?	*possibly want?*[9]

On account of the food scarcities, the high prices, and the rationing, life became increasingly difficult for the lower orders. In the context of the *Burgfrieden*, wages had been frozen at the levels of 1914; however, pressure from below forced the trade unions to demand higher wages and to back up these claims by means of strikes if necessary. The authorities reacted by imposing stricter controls on workers and by forcing civilians into the labour force. Such measures further increased the plebeians' hatred of the Reich's elite and the war.[10] The widespread disenchantment of the German plebs also rose on account of the fact that high prices and undernourishment went hand-in-hand with a general deterioration of the people's health, particularly higher infant and child mortality, and increased criminality. With respect to Germany, it should also be mentioned that the social-economic problems there caused the Reich's authorities to proceed with a systematic and ruthless exploitation of the occupied territories, especially northern France and Belgium, producing there an even greater misery than in Germany itself.[11]

The countries of the Entente were not being strangled by a naval blockade, so they could import virtually anything from anywhere in the world, including from their many colonies, and thus they did not suffer from food shortages, as Germany did. And yet, in the Entente countries too, the war revealed itself in many ways to be a much nastier experience for the lower than for the higher classes, so that discontent and unrest were rife in the lower levels of the social hierarchy. In France prices rose, real wages decreased, and the plebeians complained more and more about the high cost of living. The authorities did their best to provide the people — and the inhabitants of Paris in particular — with sufficient food, especially bread, at relatively low prices; they remembered the revolution of 1789, when the high price of bread drove the Parisians into the arms of the revolution.[12] As good patriots, the French were willing to make sacrifices, but what bothered them was that during the course of the war many of their bourgeois "superiors," especially industrialists and merchants, seemed to do better than ever before. In July 1916, the hotels on the coast were full of rich customers who were enjoying the good life, and in Paris — often referred to by the *poilus* as *Paname*, "Panama," in other words, an exotic but distant realm — the expensive restaurants did a wonderful business. Maxim's was always full of high-ranking army officers and rich bourgeois, often accompanied by prostitutes, and champagne and other pricey booze was flowing freely. Strolling along the boulevards were countless *nouveaux riches,* businessmen who had earned fortunes thanks to army contracts and black-market dealings. Their female companions were dressed extravagantly and even provocatively in fashionable outfits bedecked with jewelry. This contrasted greatly with the soldiers — often decorated amputees — who roamed the same boulevards while begging, selling postcards, or singing patriotic songs in order to earn some spending money.[13]

The biggest war profiteers were usually a little more discreet than the loafers along the boulevards, but everybody knew who they were: the country's big industrialists, whose enormous earnings were subjected only in theory to windfall taxes introduced by a law of July 1, 1916. This law was not rigorously enforced, and it was transgressed on a large scale. An example was provided by Monsieur Schneider, the big arms manufacturer of Le Creusot, also known as the French Krupp. By supplying guns and other weapons to the army, his firm enjoyed a profit boom, but he reported to the taxman only a fraction — allegedly one-eighth — of the real earnings. Another arms producer, Hotchkiss, specializing in machine guns, likewise raked in unprecedented profits: officially, they rose from 861,000 francs in 1913 to 14 million francs in 1917.[14] The law on windfall profits hardly benefited the state treasury. The French historian who draws attention to this, Jean-Baptiste Duroselle, emphasizes that this meant that the costs of the war were shared most unequally: "While such high sacrifices were demanded from the soldiers, one did not dare to make the rich pay." In Germany too, the big corporations realized enormous profits but paid only minimal taxes. Rosa Luxemburg provided a laconic and sarcastic comment: "The proletarians fall, but the dividends rise."[15]

Such details may not have been known to the public, but the workers, peasants, petty bourgeois, and other ordinary Frenchmen were aware enough that, thanks to the war, the big (and even small) capitalists could easily fill their pockets and did not hesitate to do so, while they themselves had to tighten their belts more and more. From the lower orders there arose louder and louder criticism about the phenomenon of war profiteering, especially since profits rose to unprecedented highs while wages remained mostly frozen. Increasing numbers of Frenchmen expressed the opinion that no profits ought to be made at all during the war. In any event, criticizing profits was tantamount to criticizing capitalism, a system in which profits constitute the alpha and omega. Before the war, writes a French historian, François Bouloc, the socialists had criticized capitalism on the basis of their theory and of an empirical analysis of social-economic realities, and in the name of the workers. But during the war, and because of the war, the capitalist system was subjected to criticism not only in the name of the workers, but in the name of the entire people, the entire nation. As a result of the war, continues Bouloc, capitalism was thus increasingly considered as "contrary not only to the egalitarian principles, but to the interests of the entire nation for which the comrades, sons, brothers, husbands and fiancés risk their lives." This situation was fraught with risks for "the social-economic elites" and particularly the industrialists, whose prestige and legitimacy were being jeopardized in the process.[16]

In any event, French workers were no longer willing to settle for low wages while their bosses were making fortunes. Their trade unions came back to life, registered many new members, and as of February-March 1916 strikes broke out again in France. A veritable wave of strikes in May and June of that year has been described by the French historian Jean-Louis Robert as "a formidable expression of class struggle." Moreover, starting in the middle of 1916, the French unions elected more and more militant new leaders who were critical of the sacred union. These "young Turks" openly questioned the war aims of the government and revived the idea of the international solidarity of workers; they demanded not only wage increases and other material improvements but even a general "social trans-formation," in other words, revolutionary societal change.[17] The previously comatose but now born-again unions attracted more members, and by the end of the war they would have double the number of members they had in 1914. The socialists, on the other hand, who remained loyal to the sacred union and continued to collaborate with the government in pursuit of social peace and military victory, lost many members. Their kind of "class collaboration," personified by Albert Thomas, was less and less appreciated by the socialist rank-and-file, and a minority — the *socialistes minoritaires* or "minority socialists" — openly opposed the war and the party's close col-laboration with the government. In 1916 it became increasingly obvious that the French plebs had shed the docility they had displayed in 1914 and were increasingly embracing radical, even revolutionary ideas. The war, which had at first seemingly snuffed out the idea of revolution, as the elite had hoped, was now bringing it back to life.

The war undermined the prestige not only of the war-profiteering indus-trialists, but also that of the high-ranking military, most of them conserva-tive and often clerical gentlemen who had never had much sympathy for the relatively democratic system of the secular Third Republic. In 1914, they had profited from the opportunity to increase their power, and the commander-in-chief, Joffre, had become a kind of de facto dictator. "Papa Joffre" initially enjoyed much confidence and admiration among all classes of the French population, and his blunders of the summer of 1914, mostly due to his commitment to an offensive strategy, were forgiven on account of his near-miraculous success in the Battle of the Marne. But his bright star faded irrevocably when in the course of 1915, and in spite of huge sacrifices in terms of lives of French soldiers, he proved unable to pierce the German lines and thus to conjure up victory for France. Moreover, the media and many politicians criticized him sharply because he ordered so many soldiers to be executed *"pour l'exemple."* Joffre and the other generals were gradually forced to dismount from their high horses and surrender the management of the nation and even of the war to the politicians in the cabinet and the parliament, civilians they despised especially because they were democratically elected.[18] That actually benefited another faction within the French establishment, namely the aforementioned industrialists (and bankers), who were increasingly needed as "experts" in production. On the one hand, those industrialists had to put up with a greater amount of state intervention in their affairs; in other words, a greater dose of *dirigisme*. On the other hand, they could strengthen their position within the state apparatus and increase their political influence; and, thanks to gigantic state orders, more profitable business could be done than ever before. In France, this was certainly the case with members of the *Comité des Forges*, such as the firm of Monsieur Schneider. Corporations thus became more important, more influential, more powerful, and above all richer, not only in France but in all belligerent countries. The war was good for the "accumulation process," and was this not one of the reasons why the industrialists (and bankers) had wanted war? We already know that this shiny coin had another, darker side, however, namely the fact that the big corporations were perceived increasingly by their workers, and by the lower orders in general, as war profiteers.

In Russia also, the situation was worsening quickly in 1916, as soldiers and civilians displayed more and more signs of discontent on account of the huge losses, the obvious incompetence of the generals, the poor quality of the food and medical services, etc. The men received less and less bread to eat, and they hated the lentils they were served instead. Mutinies and less serious cases of insubordination were reported by quite a few units. Civilians were disgruntled mostly because of the shortage and high prices of food staples. Factory workers went on strike again, as they had done in the turbulent time just before the war. As if the situation was not sufficiently alarming, in October 1916 the soldiers refused to fire on strikers. Increasing numbers of young men resisted being drafted into the army. Clearly, the Russian people had had enough of the war the czarist elite had unleashed, or at least helped to unleash, and which it appeared determined to pursue until victory. A German-American expert in Russian history, Hans Rogger, has written that in 1916 it became obvious that "an immense gap separated the mass of ordinary Russian citizens from the respectable classes of society."[19]

As of December 1916, the British government was headed by Lloyd

George, who relied on a small "war cabinet" of no more than seven members. Lloyd George and his team collaborated closely with eminent personalities from the world of business, whom the new prime minister referred to as "men of push and go." In Britain too, the industrialists thus got to provide a growing amount of input into the affairs of government and, more specifically, the management of the war, which was of course much to their advantage. But in Britain too, real and perceived war profiteering sparked more and more protests in the ranks of the lower classes, who were experiencing hard times and were particularly unhappy about the low level of wages and the high cost of rent and life in general. It became all too obvious that the costs imposed by the war were shared unequally, that the folks at the lower end of the social scale, civilians as well as soldiers, were making the greatest contribution to the effort to win a war that had been wanted by the people at the top of the social pyramid.

The "industrial truce" agreed upon in 1914, a moratorium on strikes that clearly favoured the employers at the expense of the employees, had already broken down in 1915. In that year, the unions emerged from the comatose state into which they had slipped in 1914, and strikes broke out again. In total, no less than three million workdays were thus lost in 1915. Lloyd George tried to overcome that problem, on the one hand by formally prohibiting strikes in certain important sectors of industry, e.g., in munitions factories, and, on the other hand, by introducing a minimal surtax on windfall profits. (In virtually all the belligerent countries and even in many neutral countries, pressure from public opinion caused the governments sooner or later to introduce higher taxes on war profits. In general these taxes were rather modest, were not systematically or zealously collected, and avoidance proved all too easy.)[20] But Lloyd George's efforts proved to be a plaster on a wooden leg, because 1916 witnessed a new wave of work stoppages. British workers became increasingly militant, and in the course of the war they would participate in more strikes than their comrades in Germany, France, and Italy.

In the face of this working-class fury, Lloyd George initially opted for repression, e.g., by having the police identify and persecute the "subversive elements," "agitators," and "traitors" who were deemed to be responsible for the strikes. But cooler heads within the British elite realized that repression was a dangerous weapon and that better results could be obtained by making concessions. In the spring of 1916, a cabinet minister, Lord Robert Cecil, publicly warned that the "comfortable classes" could not expect the working class to continue to make sacrifices while they themselves avoided carrying their share of the burdens of war. Cecil and like-minded members of the elite feared that the situation might lead to a general strike, with the potentially revolutionary consequences associated with such a scenario. The government put pressure on the employers, already beleaguered by their own workers, to increase wages. More and more strikes thus concluded with concessions to the strikers, and the wage level rose noticeably. The unions organizing and directing these fruitful strikes were rewarded with an increase of their membership, and by the end of the war total union membership would be twice as high as in 1914. (In Canada union membership also doubled during the war.)[21] This was not something the British elite had expected from a war they had so much looked forward to. Except for a very short time, in August 1914, the war was not making the British people meek and docile, and it did not put an end to the social agitation, as the nation's elite had expected. In fact, the conflict was increasingly producing the opposite of what the aristocratic and bourgeois upper classes had hoped for. Conflict abroad was not stifling, but was stimulating conflict at home.

In 1916, the British elite also experienced a lot of trouble with pacifists such as Bertrand Russell and Edmund Dene Morel of the Union of Democratic Control (UDC), who demanded that peace negotiations be initiated. Other sources of nuisance were suffragettes like Sylvia Pankhurst, who frequently demonstrated on Trafalgar Square together with pacifists; the members of the No-Conscription Fellowship (NCF), who militated against compulsory military service; the countless conscientious objectors; and the radical socialists, admittedly few in number but particularly pesky. Among the latter was William Holliday who, like Liebknecht in Germany, proclaimed that "the real enemy is not to be found at the front, but within the country itself." Against these perceived troublemakers, the government relied on outright repression. Russell, Morel, and many other pacifists and conscientious objectors were treated as traitors to the fatherland and thrown into prison. Against this kind of opponent, the police and secret services also used agents provocateurs.[22]

What traumatized the British elite the most in 1916 was the famous Easter Rising in Ireland. And yet, on that island the war had started so promisingly from the elite's perspective. In August 1914, the Ulstermen and the Irish nationalists had both declared themselves ready to defend the British Empire; the spectre of civil war between champions and enemies of Home Rule or any form of Irish autonomy or independence had thus been evaporated by the advent of international war. But the huge losses suffered at the front and the misery engendered by the war at home, combined with German moral and material support for Irish nationalists, encouraged the radical, republican elements among the Irish nationalists and caused them to start an armed uprising in Dublin during Easter Week 1916. The rebels received little popular support, and the British authorities responded with an iron fist. A state of siege was proclaimed and the insurgents were attacked by forces twenty times their own number. After a week of street fighting, resulting in 400 dead and 2,500 wounded, the uprising was over. The surviving rebels were shot, including the wounded James Connolly, a socialist Irish nationalist and a friend of Keir Hardie. Ireland was subjected to draconian measures such as the arrest of real or suspected sympathizers of the rebels, secret trials, more executions, and imprisonment in concentration camps, a series of quasi-totalitarian measures that were personally approved by prime minister Lloyd George. George Bernard Shaw sourly noted that with their atrocities in Ireland the British matched the horrors committed by the Germans in Belgium. The Irish insurrection of 1916 was the only national uprising in a European country during the Great War; according to the British historian A.J.P. Taylor, this amounted to "an ironic commentary on the British claim to be fighting for liberty."[23]

In 1914, the elite had hoped that the war it was unleashing would not only dispel the danger of *social* but also of *national* revolutions, that is, of revolutions by ethnic minorities such as the Irish and the Scots. In this respect too, the war was a disappointment. "The Easter rising," writes Adam Hochschild, "was a sharp blow to all who hoped that the shared ordeal of war would strengthen the bonds holding together the British Empire."[24] The insurgence in Dublin was doubly traumatic because it featured both a social and a national dimension. Within the British Empire, the Irish constituted a kind of underclass. The British proletariat was largely Irish, and in Ireland itself the elite of landowners and industrialists was an "Anglo-Irish" minority; that is, its members resided in Ireland but were of English origin. The Dublin insurrection, whose objective was an Irish republic, was simultaneously perceived as a kind of proletarian uprising, a social revolution; to Britain's aristocrats and bourgeois burghers, it was a two-headed monster, a combination of social and national revolution.

To the British elite, the Irish rebels loomed like a deadly menace to all they held dear. They saw them as anti-British Irish nationalists, anti-monarchist republicans, Catholics opposed to Protestantism in both its Anglican and Scottish Presbyterian manifestations, mortal socialist enemies of capitalism, and pro-German traitors poised to betray Britannia. A comment about the Easter Rising, typical of elite opinion at the time, was provided by Gilbert Murray, an Oxford professor who blamed what he called "the terror regime" unleashed by the insurgents in Dublin not only on the Irish nationalists of the Sinn Fein movement, but also and above all on the "savages of the Labour Party" and their "criminal [Irish] partisans, friends of the Germans."[25]

Irish nationalism was a colourful mosaic of factions and ideologies. Certain Irish nationalists were willing to settle for a form of autonomy within the monarchical British Empire, while others were convinced republicans; some were ready to use violence in order to achieve their objectives, others preferred to walk the path of nonviolence; some accepted help from the Germans, others refused this kind of assistance; among their number there were socialist radicals who belonged to "the left," while other elements were conservative, even reactionary, and above all clerical, and therefore classified as "right-wing." What they had in common was that they repudiated the established order in Ireland, which was an imported order, a British order. Of the war, the elite had hoped that it would consolidate this British order in Ireland, but after the Easter Rising it was all too obvious that the old order was doomed to disappear from the Emerald Isle. But one question still remained to be answered: what would Ireland's new order look like, and how great would be the damage the British elite would suffer on account of revolutionary changes the war had not prevented but made inevitable?

In 1916 it became obvious not only in Britain but also in Germany,

France, and the other belligerent countries that the war would not yield the fruits that the elite had so confidently expected from it. This was also the experience of the Christian churches, solid pillars of the elite and champions of the *ancien régime* since time immemorial. For them too, the time of disillusion arrived all too soon after that glorious summer of 1914, when the lower orders had returned *en masse* to the altars. In Britain, church attendance declined sharply over the course of the war. The soldiers generally loathed their chaplains, often disrespectfully referred to by American soldiers as "skyscouts" or "holy Joes"; they were embittered that the Anglican clergy had promoted the war with such jingoistic enthusiasm and continued to do so in spite of all the war's horrors and absurdities.[26] A testimony of this is provided by this selection from the text of a soldiers' parody of the famous hymn, "Onward Christian Soldiers":

> *Onward, Christian soldiers! Duty's way is plain;*
> *Slay your Christian neighbours, or by them be slain,*
> *Pulpiteers are spouting effervescent swill,*
> *God above is calling you to rob and rape and kill,*
> *All your acts are sanctified by the Lamb on high;*
> *If you love the Holy Ghost, go murder, pray and die.*
> *Onward, Christian soldiers! Rip and tear and smite!*
> *Let the gentle Jesus bless your dynamite.*
> *Splinter skulls with shrapnel, fertilize the sod;*
> *Folks who do not speak your tongue deserve the curse of*
> *God.*[27]

On account of their patriotic parlance and their appeals to the men to carry on, the Catholic as well as the Protestant clergy in general, but army chaplains in particular, perceived as sidekicks of the officers, were also detested by the German soldiers. The Belgian soldiers likewise turned their backs on religion and the Church. "Church attendance dropped dramatically," writes the Belgian historian de Schaepdrijver. "Already in 1916, the *piottes* failed massively to absolve their Easter obligations . . . evidence of a religious and moral decline was everywhere." The war failed to make the soldiers return to God, as the clergy had hoped; to the contrary, its horrors and misery seemed to provide irrefutable proof that God did not exist, that God was dead, or that He did exist but did not care. The German soldiers were reported to pray less and less, but to swear and to blaspheme more and more. A German soldier, son of a farmer, wrote that:

> The obvious uselessness of prayer and the interminable length
> and incredible cruelty of the war made many doubt the divine
> justice and omniscience and stimulated religious indifference;
> blasphemous statements were frequently heard.[28]

The horrors of war caused countless soldiers not only to deny the existence of God but even to curse God because he had permitted such an atrocity. This kind of sentiment was expressed in a poem by a British writer of Jewish origin, Gilbert Frankau, "The Other Side," written in 1917:

> Men maimed and blinded: men against machines —
> Flesh versus iron, concrete, flame and wire:
> Men choking out their souls in poison-gas:
> Men squelched into the slime by trampling feet:
> Men, disembowelled by guns five miles away,
> Cursing, with their last breath, the living God
> Because he made them, in His image, men . . .[29]

What the war caused to blossom profusely in the minds of the soldiers was not a typically religious concern with an afterlife, but the desire to live and the associated sexual appetite. The human beings conjured up in the latter poem, the denizens of the trenches, were exclusively men, young men who found themselves in the permanent company of death. They dreamed of life and of sex, like eating and drinking a vital need as well as pleasure, and of women. "I love the ladies," sang the Tommies, "I love to be among the girls,"[30] but they were imprisoned in a distant and cold world inhabited only by men. The soldiers at the front were condemned to lead an ascetic life, sexually speaking, like involuntary hermits. They were sexually oppressed and frustrated, sex-starved. A widespread fear among the soldiers was that one might die a virgin. The men were also concerned that spending all this time without sex would make them impotent. Sexual pleasure was sought above all in masturbation and, by some, in homosexual relations. As for relations with women, the majority of the soldiers had such relations all the time — in their dreams. When they were not in the trenches, they did everything to see women. They even went to church in the neighbouring villages in order to stare at girls and young women. ("Avid eyes lusted after them [the women in the church] and the most beautiful among them were greeted with crude compliments," wrote the *poilu* Roland Dorgelès, in his account of the war, *Les Croix de bois*.) And the soldiers' theatres and cabarets in which women performed were extremely popular. *Paths of Glory* ends with a pretty young woman appearing on the stage, to be greeted enthusiastically by a rowdy crowd of *poilus*. Incidentally, in the cabarets and theatres, the officers occupied the front rows, which caused the men to sarcastically remark that "it was only in the trenches that the *poilu* may sit in the front row!"[31]

During the periods when they were not in the trenches, the soldiers went looking for women and sex. Women were not that hard to find, because many of them moved close to the front to find work as laundresses, servants, waitresses — or full- or part-time prostitutes. Some young British women allegedly also travelled to the Channel ports in order to meet soldiers and treat them to sexual services, something they considered "doing their bit for the war." Similarly, in France, young women in the villages close to the front were allegedly often willing "to do their best to help resolve the men's problems." So it was certainly not impossible for soldiers to meet women and have sex. Even so, the majority of the men headed straight for the bordellos where women and sex were readily available for not too much money. But the price reflected the quality, and both were higher in the bordellos reserved for the "gentlemen officers." On the British as well as the German side, bordellos for the soldiers could be recognized by a red light; the establishments for officers featured a blue light. The small town of Béthune, in northern France, had a bordello for the British. Three women ran it, but the demand was so high that often more than 150 Tommies were lining up at the entrance, as if it were a bus stop in London. Business was done very quickly because the urge was generally very great, and physiological deliverance often occurred quickly, even *ante portas*. A sex worker in the bordello *The Black Cat* in Armentiers, having "just saved a battalion from dying of sexual starvation," told a Canadian soldier: "You know, I just put it between my legs, give it a squeeze, and yell 'next'."[32] The average duration of a visit seems to have been ten minutes, but experienced prostitutes such as the one in *The Black Cat* managed to serve an average of eighty men per day.[33]

There were of course plenty of bordellos in Paris, and the soldiers visited them whenever an opportunity presented itself, not only during a furlough, but also on the way to or back from the front. Whenever they went to the French capital for a few days, or even a few hours, the soldiers opted to drop into the bordellos of Pigalle and the many cafés where women of little virtue could be found, rather than visiting the Eiffel Tower or the Louvre, let alone Notre Dame Cathedral or the Sacré Cœur Basilica. During the war, prostitution was big business in Paris. With respect to sex, the French soldiers were privileged there in comparison to their allied comrades, because many patriotic prostitutes became "godmother" of a *poilu* and offered him their services free of charge whenever he visited the capital. The seaport of Le Havre was also well known for its bordellos. There was a street there with establishments in which, in one single year, no less than 171,000 men were "served." London was also renowned for its numerous prostitutes and bordellos catering to soldiers, and some villages in the vicinity of the front had a reputation in this respect. In the Flemish village of Afsnee near Ghent, for example, a tavern unofficially known as *De Veertien Billekes*, "The Fourteen Buttocks," functioned as a magnet for the German military. But for sexual services in occupied Belgium, the German soldiers and officers could also find what they were looking for in cities such as Ghent and Brussels. Ghent had quite a reputation in this respect: it was "the German army's bordello-town."[34]

Ever since the beginning of trench warfare, bordellos had popped up like mushrooms at a relatively safe yet close distance from the frontlines. The military authorities had not only permitted but often even encouraged this, in spite of the objections and even outright opposition of certain political and above all ecclesiastical authorities who preferred to encourage chastity and "self-control." A French historian explains why:

Prostitution behind the lines flourished, and was widely tolerated, even encouraged, by the military authorities in order to provide the men with some sexual relief and thus to boost their morale after all the depressing experiences in the trenches.

On the British side it was felt that the officers, gentlemen of good families, were capable of exercising the necessary self-control, but that this could unfortunately not be expected from the proletarians in uniform that the ordinary soldiers happened to be. If bordellos were not set up for them, so it was argued, the men would undoubtedly seek relief from streetwalkers or from homosexual practices or, worse, rape respectable women. Some British military commanders, including Lord Kitchener, nevertheless preferred a policy of encouraging total sexual abstention.

Contraceptives had already existed for a long time, but were not always available, and the soldiers did not like using them. In this kind of combat, they preferred to fight the old-fashioned way, with an "open visor" or "ungloved fists," so to speak. In France, many prejudices continued to inhibit the use of condoms. The objections might be inspired by religious considerations, and it is hardly surprising that the Catholic chaplains were among the adversaries. But even many nonreligious, anticlerical, free-thinking members of the French elite were opposed to the use of contraceptives. They were haunted by "the spectre of the depopulation of France," of a demographic regression that had started in the early nineteenth century and loomed like a harbinger of the nation's demise as a great power. (It was one of the contradictions of the French elite's predicament at the time: on the one hand, like its British and other counterparts, it wanted to rid the country of its surfeit of proletarians, but, on the other hand, France needed to catch up demographically with Britain and especially Germany in order to preserve its status of great power in the long run.) The British elite also had misgivings about the use of contraceptives: it was feared that making them available and recommending their use would cause the men to think that there was nothing wrong with fornication.

Yet another factor explains why the soldiers often failed to use contraceptives in bordellos. Contracting a venereal disease was a way to escape from the trenches, and so the men were even willing to pay higher prices for the services of infected prostitutes, as we already know. It is thus not surprising that countless cases of gonorrhea, syphilis, and similar diseases infected soldiers of all the armies. In 1917, of all the allied soldiers who visited Paris, 20 per cent allegedly became infected. In 1915, 22 per cent of all Canadian soldiers stationed in France suffered from some sort of venereal ailment. In 1917, 7 per cent of the Belgian soldiers were infected. As for the British army, in that same year a little less than fifty-five thousand men were admitted to hospital for that reason; by the end of the war, three hundred thousand Tommies would have received treatment for this kind of disease; the corresponding number for the French troops in 1914–18 was approximately half a million. Among the Americans who joined the Allies in 1917, a real "epidemic" of venereal diseases broke out in December of that year, involving 40 per cent of the men. The military authorities responded with an aggressive campaign against the bordellos but also in favour of the use of contraceptives. This initiative was supported by the YMCA, which launched all sorts of programs that purported, via sports, theatre, etc., to "to make the men forget their sexuality."

Venereal diseases also ravaged the German army. In occupied Belgium alone, thirty thousand soldiers were allegedly infected in 1915. On the other hand, the "sexual logistics" associated with the bordellos were regulated in draconian fashion by Germany's military authorities. The bordellos were subjected to strict medical controls, the customers were registered, and, during the evening "rush hour" a time limit of ten minutes per visit was enforced. Contraceptives were made available, and the German army thus suffered less from venereal diseases than the allied forces. Another factor that played a role here was the superiority of the Reich's chemical and pharmaceutical industry, which, for example, had developed Salvarsan, the first effective medication against syphilis, just before the outbreak of the war. In addition, the Germans regularly inspected the genitalia of the ordinary soldiers and NCOs, but not of the officers, a check that became known as the "sausage parade."

The soldiers in the trenches dreamed of women. They longed for women, not only their own woman, but (almost) any woman. A British officer declared that "the majority of the soldiers were ready to have sexual relations with any, or almost any, woman."[35] One could say that the soldiers idealized women, but this shiny coin also had a reverse side. The men also often displayed resentment against women *inter alia* because they had not prevented the war and because they did not have to share the misery of the trenches, which they could not even fully understand. Numerous soldiers feared that their own wife or girlfriend was cheating them, playing around with some *embusqué*. This fear found a bittersweet reflection in the words of a song often hummed by the Tommies, "I Wonder Who's Kissing Her Now":

> *I wonder who's kissing her now,*
> *Wonder who's teaching her how,*
> *Wonder who's looking into her eyes*
> *Breathing sighs, telling lies;*
> *I wonder who's buying the wine,*
> *For lips that I used to call mine,*
> *Wonder if she ever tells him of me,*
> *I wonder who's kissing her now.*

"This question of the fidelity of the women," writes a French historian, "permanently tortured many of the men." "Strongly misogynist sentiments" thus welled up among them. The authorities perceived this as an excellent opportunity to limit the modest gains with respect to sexual liberty that women were slowly achieving during the war, for example on account of the fact that many of them were now working outside of the home, in offices and factories. Before the war, European society was still extremely patriarchal, and the elite, who were extremely antifeminist, had felt threatened by the political and sexual emancipation of women, promoted and personified by the British suffragettes; like the presumably avant-garde Futurists, the elite also associated women with pacifism. In this sense too, the Great War provided the elite with an opportunity to halt, and possibly even reverse, an emancipatory trend that threatened its privileges. (In Russia, the Orthodox clergy had taken advantage of the outbreak of the war to exhort women "to be more loving and kind toward their husbands" if God allowed them to return alive!)[36] And so we can understand why the authorities took advantage of the soldiers' frustrations to start spying — on married women above all, but also on women factory workers, not only to control their sexual behaviour but also their conduct in general, and to take repressive measures if deemed necessary. In Germany, for example, police "vice squads" (*Sittenpolizei*) were used for this purpose. Women thus became the victims not only of the sexual desires of the sexually deprived and, indeed, oppressed men in uniform, but also of "a veritable sexual oppression" and of a repression in general.[37]

The growing discontent of civilians and combatants also found an artistic way to express itself. The year 1916 witnessed the birth of an avant-garde artistic movement that may be interpreted as a form of protest against the war: Dadaism, or Dada *tout court*, which saw the light of day in Zurich in that year, at least officially, because it can in fact be argued that the movement had emerged earlier. Dada was born as an artistic expression of disgust with respect to the horrors of a war that did not seem to make sense. It amounted to a kind of "artistic revolt and protest against the traditional beliefs of a pro-war society." The Dadaists "condemned the nationalist and capitalist values that led to the cataclysm of the war" and mounted a spectacular and provocative challenge to the conservative, antisocial, and nationalist bourgeoisie, judged to be responsible for the war. The Dadaist movement established links with radical left-wing groups, and took root in France, Germany, and the United States. Among its leading personalities were George Grosz, Otto Dix, John Heartfield (Helmut Herzfeld), Max Ernst (who, during the war, served in an artillery unit of the German army), André Breton, Paul Éluard, Marcel Duchamp, and Louis Aragon.[38]

CHAPTER 23
MILITARIA 1917: CATASTROPHES AT CAPORETTO AND ELSEWHERE

The particularly turbulent year 1917 brings the Allies a lot of bad news. In an offensive on the Chemin des Dames, the French suffer enormous losses. The Third Battle of Ypres concludes with a Pyrrhic-victory for the British. And the Italian army virtually implodes at Caporetto. In all the belligerent countries, soldiers and civilians have had enough of this awful war, and this leads not only to mutinies in the French army but also to a genuine revolution in Russia . . .

In 1917, the official "vertical" war between countries as well as the unspoken "horizontal" war between classes continued unabatedly. And, as had been the case in 1914, 1915, and 1916, the development of the vertical conflict influenced that of the horizontal, and vice versa. Let us start our overview of the year with a summary of the main events in the war between nations.

On the western front, the spring of 1917 witnessed a bloody new offensive by the French in the hope of piercing the German lines. This attack took place along an ancient road connecting the towns of Soissons and Reims. It was called the Chemin des Dames because, in the eighteenth century, it had often been used by the daughters of King Louis XV, the "ladies [*dames*] of France," while shuttling between the royal palace of Versailles and their own château in Louvois, a village near Reims. The offensive was the brainchild of the new commander-in-chief of the French army, General Robert Nivelle, a fairly young man who, like his predecessor Joffre, was a champion of the strategy of all-out attack. (Nivelle's promotion apparently also had a lot to do with his supposedly "aristocratic" looks; he was "tall, young, of elegant demeanour," and had "a proud, regularly-featured face.") All along the Chemin des Dames, the Germans, as usual, had strongly fortified their positions on the high ground, so that once again the French had to attack from the valley below. The fighting lasted from April 16 to 25, 1917, and hundreds of thousands of Frenchmen were massacred there — much as they had been the year before at Verdun. (The total losses of the French — killed, wounded, and taken prisoner — were reported to total 271,000, of whom 145,000 were killed, against 163,000 on the German side.) But while the unprecedented losses at Verdun had ultimately prevented the Germans from taking the symbolically significant city and thus delivered a victory of sorts, the fighting at the Chemin des Dames revealed itself to be a senseless slaughter, because it produced no positive outcome whatsoever.[1]

Even today, the mere mention of the name Chemin des Dames sends shivers up French spines. More importantly, the *poilus* who served as cannon fodder at the time had made it clear that they were no longer willing to be slaughtered by "butchers" like Nivelle or any other ambitious generals, because mutinies broke out in a number of units. For the moment it should suffice to mention that, in order to support Nivelle's initiative, the British undertook some local actions in their own sector of the western front, especially in the vicinity of Arras, in the hope of diverting the Germans' attention. Some of these attacks took place even before the start of the bloody affair on the Chemin des Dames.

It was in this context that on April 9, 1917, Canadian troops assaulted and conquered the hill or "ridge" of Vimy, located between Arras and Lens. This feat of arms was celebrated as a great victory in Canada, where it continues even today to be considered as a glorious highlight of the nation's history. Some historians and politicians even claim that Canada as an independent country with an identity of its own — as opposed to its earlier status of an autonomous but not independent dominion of the British Empire — was "born" on the battlefield of Vimy. After the war, the hilltop of Vimy would be crowned triumphantly by the Canadians with a gigantic monument that attracts many visitors. It is far too imposing for the relatively modest victory that was won at the usual high cost, but this can be rationalized by the fact that it was erected to honour the role of all Canadians, not only those who fought at Vimy in April 1917, but on all fronts from the beginning to the end of the Great War.[2]

In contrast to Vimy, the monuments that commemorate the fighting along the Chemin des Dames in the spring of 1917 are rather modest. One of them may be found in the village of Craonne, but the massacre of 1917 is conjured up much more touchingly by the lyrics and the music of the pacifist *"Chanson de Craonne"* or "Song of Craonne," created at the time and enormously successful among the *poilus*. It was also known by other names, such as *"Les sacrifiés,"* "The Sacrificial Lambs," a term the soldiers used to refer to themselves, immolated by the tens of thousands on the altar of the Moloch of war. The authorities prohibited the singing of this song — a prohibition that remained in effect until 1974! — and offered a monetary reward, plus an honourable release from the army, to anyone who would reveal the author's identity, but in vain. The authorities' feelings toward the song are understandable in view of lines such as these:

Adieu la vie, adieu l'amour,	*Good-bye to all the women,*
Adieu toutes les femmes	*It's all over now, we've had it for good*
C'est bien fini, c'est pour toujours	
De cette guerre infâme	*With this awful war*
C'est à Craonne sur le plateau	*It's in Craonne up on the plateau*
Qu'on doit laisser sa peau	*That we're leaving our skins,*
Car nous sommes tous des condamnés	*'Cause we've all been sentenced to die.*
Nous sommes les sacrifiés	*We're the ones that they're sacrificing*
C'est malheureux d'voir sur les grands boulevards	*On the grand boulevards it's hard to look At all the rich and powerful whooping it up*
Tous ces gros qui font la foire	
Si pour eux la vie est rose	*For them life is good*
Pour nous c'est pas la même chose	*But for us it's not the same*

Au lieu d'se cacher tous ces embusqués	*Instead of hiding, all these shirkers*
Feraient mieux d'monter aux tranchées	*Would do better to go up to the trenches*
Pour défendre leur bien, car nous	*To defend what they have, because we*
n'avons rien	*have nothing*
Nous autres lespauv' purotins	*All of us poor wretches*
Tous les camarades sont enterrés là	*All our comrades are being buried there*
Pour défendre les biens de ces	*To defend the wealth of these gentlemen*
messieurs là	*here*
Ceux qu'ont le pognon, ceux-là	*Those who have the dough, they'll be*
reviendront	*coming back,*
Car c'est pour eux qu'on crève	*'Cause it's for them that we're dying.*
Mais c'est bien fini, car les troufions	*But it's all over now, 'cause all of the grunts*
Vont tous se mettre en grève	*Are going to go on strike*
Ce s'ra vot' tour messieurs les gros	*It'll be your turn, all you rich and*
D'monter sur le plateau	*powerful gentlemen,*
et si vous voulez faire la guerre	*To go up onto the plateau.*
Payez-la de votre peau.	*And if you want to make war,*
Good-bye to life, good-bye to love,	*Then pay for it with your own skins.*[3]

The British supremo, General Haig, thought he could take advantage of the troubles experienced by the French to try once again to achieve a decisive breakthrough of the German lines. This time he planned an offensive in the vicinity of Ypres, in the infamous Flanders' Fields. Battles had already been fought there in the fall of 1914 and the spring of 1915, so Haig's initiative was to go down in history as the Third Battle of Ypres. It was to be an extremely violent affair.

Haig's new "big push" was prepared very thoroughly. Things got going with a kind of prelude on June 7. The British, who had dug tunnels under the German lines, blew up the enemy positions to the south of Ypres with mines. The explosion was so loud that it could be heard on the other side of the English Channel. The British infantry attacks that followed succeeded in pushing back the German lines by about seven kilometres in the course of a week, which reduced the enemy pressure on Ypres. This so-called Battle of the Mines at Messines (or second Battle of Messines) was also a success in the sense that, for the very first time, there were more men killed on the side of the defending Germans than the attacking Tommies, namely twenty-five thousand versus seventeen thousand. In any event, the result was yet another plentiful harvest for the Grim Reaper. The craters carved into the Flemish soil by the explosion of the mines were to fill gradually with water, thus creating ponds like the one in the village of Wijtschate, known today as the Pool of Peace.

On July 31, the Third Battle of Ypres started officially with a large-scale British attack on German positions to the east and north of the city. Once again, the German defence proved to be particularly resolute. Two factors played important roles. First, in front of their own first lines, on carefully chosen strategic spots within the no man's land, the Germans had constructed small concrete bunkers — nicknamed pillboxes by the British — whence they could mow down attackers with their machine guns even before they reached the first German trenches. Second, the Germans relied increasingly on a new kind of soldier, handpicked, highly motivated, thoroughly trained, and armed to the teeth, especially with machine guns and grenades. These "storm troopers" (*Sturm-* or *Stoßtruppen*) had first made an appearance at the front toward the end of 1915. (And the Russians used a similar type of soldier during the Brussilov Offensive of 1916.) Their specialty was the infiltration of enemy trenches, and it is in this capacity that they would be used massively during the great German offensive in the spring of 1918. But they also performed very well defensively, and it was these storm troopers, ensconced in pillboxes, that would inflict heavy losses on the attacking British and Canadians in the Third Battle of Ypres, for example in the vicinity of the village of Passchendaele, whose surroundings had been transformed by endless rain into a sea of stinking mud. It is not a coincidence that the Tyne Cot Cemetery, the largest British war cemetery in the world, situated at a stone's throw from that village, was constructed on the remains of three German pillboxes. With respect to the storm troopers, it should be noted that they were to serve as model for the brown-shirted militia of Hitler's Nazi party.[4]

After particularly nasty fighting, the Third Battle of Ypres concluded in

November 1917 with the capture of Passchendaele by the Canadians, of whom no less than seventeen thousand were killed or wounded in the course of that action. A British general who subsequently came to inspect that sector of the front could not believe his eyes when he saw how the men had had to advance through the mud and past numerous pillboxes before they had been able to conquer the German positions on the high ground of Passchendaele village. "Good God," he cried out, "did we really order the men to go and fight in *this*?"[5] The British generals had most certainly given such an order, and it had cost the British and Imperial forces a quarter of a million of men killed or wounded. The German lines had been pushed back, but the breakthrough of which Haig had dreamed had never even come close to materializing. That did not prevent Haig from proclaiming loudly that the Third Battle of Ypres had produced a most splendid British triumph.

During the month preceding the start of his offensive in Flanders' Fields, Haig had received orders from above to "dismount" the cavalry and to transfer its men to the infantry. It was the intention to ship the horses via Egypt to the front in Palestine. Over there, in contrast to the western front, the cavalry continued to be useful in the mobile war against the Ottomans. Haig protested and opposed this decision because the cavalry was his favourite weapon, and in spite of the experiences of the Battle of the Somme, he planned to involve the men on horseback in his new offensive, albeit with less ambitious objectives than in the previous year. He was allowed to keep enough cavalry to keep on dreaming of a heroic, and possibly decisive, role for it, and opined that the cavalrymen might be able to take advantage of opportunities created by the infantry, perhaps in cooperation with tanks. Nothing was to come of this, but Haig continued to fantasize about glory for his horsemen until October, when heavy autumn rains soaked the battlefield and made any use of the cavalry chimerical.[6]

In the Austro-Hungarian army, most units of the aristocratic cavalry had already been dissolved in the spring of 1917 on account of their uselessness. A Hungarian officer sadly noted that "the cavalry, the pride of [the] army, the jewel in its military crown, the men with the finest uniforms, is to be wound up," and he concluded that "one more piece of the old Europe is disappearing." The cavalrymen continued to be used only for escorting prisoners of war, for patrols behind the lines, and, of course, for parades. But the officer acknowledged that it had not been possible to use the mounted troops effectively in this modern war, and that all too often great numbers of men and horses had been mowed down by machine guns. Another problem was that the horses ate too much. It was not such mundane economic considerations but "the aesthete and the snobbish side of him" that made this officer bemoan the demise of the cavalry. In the spring of 1918, the majority of the cavalrymen of the French army would likewise have to dismount. They did so all the more reluctantly because they now had to join the humble footsoldiers in the trenches. The latter did not hide their *Schadenfreude*, because for years they had resented the fact that the gentlemen of the cavalry had been able to lead a comparatively safe and leisurely life behind the lines, waiting for the day when they would be able to gallop through a gap in the German defences.[7]

It was in this inglorious fashion that everywhere in Europe — with the exception of the Balkans and a few sectors of the eastern front — the role of the cavalrymen in the Great War was terminated in 1917. The opening stages of the conflict, in August 1914, are still associated with images of the cavalry, more specifically *paintings* of German *uhlans* and French *cuirassiers*, sporting fur hats or shiny helmets and armed with sabre or lance, appearing proudly on the scene as vanguards of armies on the march. In the *photos* taken on the battlefields in 1918, however, the men on horseback are absent and we see infantrymen being transported to the front in trucks or advancing in the no man's land behind tanks, with airplanes circling overhead. And yet the upper classes, especially the nobility, had hoped that their favourite weapon would distinguish itself in this war.

In the fall of 1917, violent fighting occurred not only in Flanders but also on the Isonzo front in Italy. On October 24, in the vicinity of the small town of Caporetto, now situated in Slovenia and known as Kobarid, or Karfreit in German, the Austro-Hungarians suddenly launched an offensive. They were supported by German units transferred from the eastern front, where they were no longer needed for reasons that will be discussed soon. The ensuing battle, which was to last until November 9, has gone down in history as the Battle of Caporetto. The totally surprised Italian defenders were badly mauled. 40,000 of their men were killed or wounded, 300,000 surrendered, and 350,000 fled in a panic, many leaving their weapons behind. Countless soldiers simply returned to their homes. It was the worst defeat in the history of the Italian army, and in the Italian language the name Caporetto is synonymous with humiliating defeat. With the help of French and British troops quickly brought in as reinforcements, the Italians managed to retrench behind the Piave River and thus put a stop to the enemy's progress. The catastrophe of Caporetto caused the dismissal of Luigi Cadorna, who was replaced as commander-in-chief of the army by Armando Diaz. Cadorna himself refused to accept any responsibility and blamed the disaster on the alleged cowardice of his soldiers. The defeat at Caporetto also heralded the end of one of the illusions entertained by Italy's elite when it had decided to go to war, namely the ambition to have Italy join the lofty ranks of Europe's great powers; during the Paris peace talks in 1919 it would be ignored by Britain and France.[8] Caporetto was a catastrophe for the Entente, but the year 1917 ended with more bad news. In the spring of that year a revolution broke out in Russia, catalyzing a momentous series of events. One of the dramatic consequences was that the new leaders in Petrograd decided to get out of the war. On December 15, an armistice was concluded with Germany, and peace negotiations were started in the town of Brest-Litovsk. This opened up the perspective of an end to the fighting on the eastern front and the transfer of German troops from there to the western front, with potentially nasty consequences for the British and French.

In 1917, the war also continued to rage in the Middle East. A new British commander in the region, General Frederick Stanley Maude, succeeded in taking Kut Al Amarna in early 1917. From there he advanced along the Tigris River toward Baghdad, which fell to the British on March 11. There, in a famous proclamation to the people of Mesopotamia — today's Iraq — he used virtually the same hypocritical language that was to roll from the tongue of American president George W. Bush not so long ago, namely that "our armies did not come here as conquerors or as enemies, but as liberators."[9] At the same time, from their base in Egypt, British forces commanded by General Edmund Allenby backed a revolt against the Ottomans in Arabia. This initiative involved a British agent named Thomas Edward Lawrence, whose exploits were to provide inspiration for the blockbuster

Lawrence of Arabia. In order to secure the support of the Arab tribes and their chieftains against the Ottomans and the Germans, the British allowed Lawrence to make all sorts of promises they would later fail to fulfil. As far as London was concerned, the interests and desiderata of the Arab people were of no importance whatsoever. What was important for London was the prospect of military success against the Ottoman enemy — and of course the prospect of control over the oil fields of the Middle East. But the millions of spectators who watched Lawrence do his thing on the silver screen were of course not confronted with such trivialities.

Already in May 1916, the British and French governments, with Russian blessing, had concluded an agreement on how the territorial spoils of the Ottoman Empire in the Middle East were to be shared by the victors: the famous Sykes-Picot Agreement, named after the negotiators, Mark Sykes and Georges Picot. Oil played a primordial role in this arrangement, above all for the British, who had had their eye on the oil wells of Mesopotamia from the very start of the war. The British appropriated Iraq, Kuwait, Palestine, and Jordan, while France was to acquire Syria and Lebanon. With respect to Palestine, the British government gave its blessing to the Zionist plans for a "national home for the Jewish people" in this region via the Balfour Declaration of December 2, 1917; it was piously stipulated that the interests of the existing Palestinian population were to be safeguarded. With this promise, the British government sought to obtain the support of influential members of Britain's Jewish community, including Lord Rothschild, the banker; and it was also intended that the Jewish immigrants in Palestine would function as faithful allies of the British Empire in the Middle East.

In any event, in the course of the year 1917, the British managed to relieve the Ottoman Empire of Palestine, and this conquest culminated in the capture of Jerusalem on December 9, of that year. If, during the Great War, the British fought for democracy, as many still would have us believe, the inhabitants of Palestine did not notice it. General Allenby, who considered himself a "born-again crusader," was to govern the region like a dictator or a "quasi-monarch," that is, in approximately the same ruthless way that von Bissing ruled over occupied Belgium. In August 1918, Allenby would resume his offensive and "liberate" Syria at the expense of the Ottomans. (The Western leaders' condescending attitude toward the locals would also be symbolized by Henri Gouraud, the French general who, upon his arrival in Damascus in 1920, proclaimed the return of the crusaders and the victory of the Cross over the Crescent while kicking the tomb of Saladin.) Incidentally, during these operations in the Middle East, the cavalry remained useful, especially in the pursuit of fleeing Ottoman troops. Damascus and Aleppo fell to the British on October 1 and 25, respectively. The Ottoman Empire would capitulate shortly thereafter, on October 30, 1918, on board a British ship in the port of Mudros, on the Greek island of Lemnos.

The Ottomans were also chased out of Arabia. There too, the British installed a new order, taking into account mainly their own interests, as well as those of a handful of tribal chieftains, the equivalent of Britain's own aristocratic families, who had revealed themselves to be useful wartime partners. The huge homeland of the Arabs was parcelled out and the pieces flipped over to these partners, who turned them into states — such as Saudi Arabia — they could govern as their personal property. The fact that in the Middle East kings and sheiks are still able to rule in an extremely undemocratic, quasi-medieval manner over their subjects is therefore also part of the legacy of the Great War. Not only does this contradict the hypocritical allegation that the British fought for democracy, but it demonstrates that from the perspective of the elite of all belligerent countries, the war represented a "great leap backward"; that is, an attempt to revive, as much as possible (and in the case of Saudi Arabia, to create) the very *undemocratic* conditions of the time before the French Revolution and the democratization process triggered by that revolution. On account of the Great War, much of the Middle East was plunged back into the Middle Ages.[10]

CHAPTER 24

1917: THE YEAR OF TROUBLES

The soldiers of all belligerent countries become rebellious and mutinies break out. On the home front, the restlessness and discontent of undernourished civilians is reflected in countless strikes. On the other hand, the attitude of the political, social-economic and military leaders hardens, as they are determined not to give up until the ambitious objectives for which they have gone to war are realized . . .

Let us examine the morale of soldiers and civilians in the year 1917. Already on New Year's Eve, December 31, 1916, the tone for the coming year was set by Belgian soldiers stationed behind the lines in the Flemish village of Alveringem. Large numbers of *piottes* broke into cafés that had closed on orders from above, and forced the owners to serve them drinks. The gendarmes who tried to intervene were beaten up, shots were fired, and grenades were allegedly thrown in the direction of the widely detested military police. Rumours went around to the effect that "the revolution had broken out among the soldiers of Belgium's third division" and that French troops were poised to restore order and "to open fire, if necessary, on the rebellious men." "We finally settled down," wrote a soldier involved in this affair in his diary, and calm was restored. This brawl was not a genuine mutiny, much less a revolution, but it provided the authorities with an unpleasant foretaste of what soldiers and civilians disgusted by the war had in store for them in the year 1917.[1]

For the Belgian soldiers on the Yser front, it would be a miserable year. The lack of decent food and the shortages in general, the low pay, the length of the war, and the impossibility for the overwhelming majority of the men to visit their families in occupied Belgium during a short furlough, all played a role. There was a strong increase in "war pessimism," "discouragement," "despondency," and "discontent," and the soldiers suffered massively from *le cafard*, "the blues."[2] Protest actions and mini-mutinies (or disorderly brawls such as the one at Alveringem) would occur more and more frequently during 1917. The official numbers of desertions rose from 1,200 in 1916 to 5,630 in 1917, and there were many more cases of collective or individual surrender to the enemy than in previous years. In Belgium it is widely believed that much of this agitation reflected the activities of Flemish nationalists, but historians such as de Schaepdrijver are convinced that these troubles expressed a more general, international war weariness and revulsion against the war. She cites the fact that demonstrating Flemish soldiers were often heard to sing not only the Flemish anthem but also the *"Internationale"* and the *"Marseillaise."* Belgian civilians in France likewise showed signs of restlessness and rebellion. In February 1917, for example, a strike broke out among the workers of a Belgian munitions factory near Le Havre, during which the workers protested against low wages and poor food.[3] This recalcitrance displayed by Belgian soldiers and civilians was indeed a symptom of a general malaise that affected the morale of their counterparts in all belligerent countries in 1917. The Italian journalist, writer, and diplomat Kurt Erich Suckert, better known by his *nom de plume* Curzio Malaparte, was to write:

> *In early 1917, facts reflecting great unrest occurred in all the belligerent armies of Europe. Protests, rebellions, and cases of collective insubordination became increasingly frequent. In France, as in Germany, Austria[-Hungary], Russia, or Italy, the denizens of the trenches displayed signs of war weariness, even black anger. Even the threat of nasty penalties was not enough to put an end to the wave of desertions. Entire units refused to leave for the first lines.*[4]

Let us look at the situation in a few individual countries, beginning with France.

The year 1917 started with a major strike in the firm Panhard-Levassor, in Paris, which forced the government to intervene and to introduce a system of compulsory negotiations and of wage settlements dictated by the authorities. Even so, 1917 would turn out to be a year of labour conflicts, above all in the French capital, and May and June witnessed a veritable "explosion" of strikes involving a surprisingly large number of women; for example, female workers in the munitions factories, known as "*munitionettes*." A relatively quiet summer was followed by a particularly "hot" autumn during which, for a total of three months, not a single day went by in Paris without some strike breaking out. The number of strikes increased from about a hundred in 1916 to 336 in 1917, and the number of strikers went up during the same period from 11,500 to 246,000.[5]

What motivated the strikers primarily was the high cost of living. In the course of 1916, the real income of ordinary Frenchmen had decreased by approximately 10 per cent compared to 1914, and this trend was to continue until the end of the war; in 1918, real wages would be 25 per cent lower than in 1914. Wage increases were thus urgently needed in order to catch up with prices. Another demand of the strikers was the *semaine anglaise* or "English week," that is, a workweek of five and a half days; in other words, with not only Sundays but also Saturday afternoons off. Initially, the strikers did not mention any pacifist or revolutionary objectives but, starting in the spring, that changed. In March, the news of a revolution in Russia reached France, and sparked an explosion of enthusiasm among the Parisian socialists and trade unionists. They expressed great admiration for the supposedly backward Russian people, who had shown themselves capable of starting a genuine revolution while "we, the French, the revolutionary people *par excellence*, support the bourgeois regime without demurring." From then on the strikers increasingly demanded an end to the war as well as political changes. During the strikes in May, red flags were waved, the "*Internationale*" was sung, and one heard cries such as "Long Live Peace!", "No to the War!", "Bring back our Husbands!", and "The Bosses at the Front, Our *Poilus* at Home!" A high-ranking official reported a little later that France had experienced a "turbulent spring," characterized by the same war weariness as in Russia: disobedience, strikes, and demonstrations.[6]

It was primarily in Paris that the workers would not only reveal themselves to be more militant, but also more radical and even revolutionary. They no longer had any faith in the *union sacrée*, the "sacred union," which they now denigrated as the *duperie sacrée*, the "sacred swindle"! Military terminology slipped into the discourse of the workers in general and of the strikers in particular. The factory was more and more referred to as a "battlefield" and there was again talk of "class conflict," as before the war. In this conflict, the workers had their own "war aims," their own dreams of "conquests and annexations." The "English week" was one of these aims, the eight-hour workday was another. Internationalism also made a remarkable comeback among the workers. In Paris, a speaker received enthusiastic applause when he explained that "just like us, our German comrades must fight for an ideal that is not ours . . . the victory we seek is not that of the trenches, but that of the working class and of the Internationale."[7]

While the workers were visibly radicalizing, especially in Paris, a majority within the French socialist party remained committed to the sacred union and prepared to collaborate with the bourgeois parties in order to obtain a final victory for France and her allies. But the "majority socialists" were losing a lot of support among the workers who, following the Russian example, were no longer dissimulating their refusal to support a war they despised and condemned as *la maudite* ("the cursed enterprise"), "the carnage," "the killing." Moreover, the majority socialists were criticized because they were considered "overly conciliatory vis-à-vis the bosses." On account of what was perceived as their "class collaboration" and their "lack of energy and militancy," the socialist leaders were also denigrated by much of the rank-and-file as "cowards," "traitors," and *arrivistes*, "social climbers," leading a pleasant bourgeois life at the expense of the workers. Under these circumstances, the socialist party lost members by the tens of thousands. The contrast was great with the fate of the trade unions, which may not have organized the strikes but nonetheless benefited from them, because the positive outcome of many labour disputes demonstrated the advantages of belonging to a union. The French and especially Parisian trade unions thus gained many new members. By the end of 1917, the unions of the capital were enjoying "a blossoming like they had never known before the war." The elite had hoped that the war would stop and even roll back that form of working-class emancipation, but in this respect too, it produced the opposite effect.[8]

In France, the soldiers had had more than enough of the war for a long time, but 1917 proved to be the year when this war weariness manifested itself most spectacularly, causing huge headaches for the authorities. The massive losses suffered in the offensive of the Chemin des Dames in the spring, combined with the pacifist and revolutionary example set by the soldiers in Russia, triggered a wide range of protest actions on the part of the *poilus*. Units receiving an order to attack or even just to occupy the first lines sometimes bleated like sheep on the way to the slaughterhouse. And the men frequently refused to go over the top when the signal for the attack was given. Barthas reports how officers chose to ignore such insubordination because "they feared to be shot in the back or to have a grenade tossed into their hideout." He also describes how in his sector, in May and in June, "a wind of rebellion," coming from Russia,

> *was blowing through all the regiments . . . When someone started to sing some anti-war protest song, hundreds of mouths would shout "Peace or Revolution! Down with the War!", "Furlough! Furlough!" Some evening — patriots, hold your breath — the "Internationale" was sung thunderously. That really shocked our commanders.*[9]

On another occasion, Barthas opined that the *"Internationale"* was "the heartfelt revolutionary battle cry of the *poilus.*"

Larger and smaller groups of soldiers also organized meetings in an attempt to set up soldiers' councils similar to the "soviets" in revolutionary Russia. Occasionally, the *poilus* still fraternized with the Germans and together they sang the *"Internationale."* Two regiments mutinied and took control over an army barracks. Shots were fired at officers. Other units laid down their weapons, demoted their officers, installed soldiers' councils, hoisted the red flag, took control of trains, and even tried to march on Paris. Between May 20 and June 10, a total of approximately forty thousand men were allegedly involved in anywhere from two hundred and fifty to three hundred demonstrations, drawing as few as a hundred but sometimes as many as two thousand participants. Nineteen seventeen also witnessed the assassination of members of the detested military police, the *gendarmerie,* presumably mostly by deserters.[10]

The reaction from above came in the form of ruthless repression and a hardening of discipline. In total, 3,427 soldiers were punished; 554 death sentences were pronounced, of which fifty-one were carried out. Severe punishments went to 1,381 men; 1,492 were given lighter sanctions. Extremely tough discipline was enforced. "One single subversive word was enough to bring about a court martial," reported Barthas, or being sent to a penal battalion. It was even forbidden to sing *"La Madelon."*[11] The authorities used not only the stick, however, but also the carrot. General Pétain ordered far fewer attacks, allowed more soldiers to go on furlough more frequently, arranged for better food, etc.

The mutinies of 1917 constituted an exception — though admittedly a pretty spectacular one — to the general rule that, from the Great War's beginning to its end, the soldiers of the French army performed their deadly duty obediently, almost apathetically, like machines. "The overwhelming majority of the population" likewise continued to support the war in spite of widespread war weariness and "patriotic pessimism"; at least, in the opinion of the French historian Jean-Jacques Becker. But other historians, such as the American Gabriel Kolko, beg to differ. They estimate that the 1917 mutinies prove that, possibly on account of Russian influence, a kind of "sub- or counter-culture" had developed among the *poilus,* a counterculture characterized by disagreement, by "dissidence" with respect to the official patriotic discourse.[12] The latter opinion certainly seems to be verified by the statistics of convictions for desertion: the French army had known 509 such cases in 1914, 2,433 in 1915, 8,924 in 1916, and no less than 21,174 in 1917! (In 1918, the situation was to improve, as "only" 13,032 men would be convicted for desertion.)[13] In 1917, the mutineers presumably numbered between 59,000 and 88,000 men, and no less than one third of the French army was involved in the mutinies, namely 68 divisions, 128 infantry regiments (including seven "colonial" regiments), 22 battalions of light infantry, and seven artillery regiments. It should not be overlooked that many soldiers who did not participate personally in any mutinies sympathized with their comrades who did. All that seems to confirm that countless *poilus* not only had had enough of the war, but were also no longer keen to perform their duty.

The soldiers' war weariness and even outright opposition to the war, and the general *cafard* or "blues" which affected so many of them, was also reflected in the letters intercepted by the military censors. The soldiers wrote, for example, that they "wished for this war to end as soon as possible," that they "longed for the hour of liberation," that the war was "a disgusting butchery" and a *cochonnerie*, a "swinish bunch of crap," that they "only wanted one thing: peace," that they "had had more than enough of this business," and that they considered their commanders to be "assassins," "a bunch of scoundrels," "sons of bitches," "bandits," and "traitors," to be blamed for the perpetuation of the war. The letters also expressed hatred toward war profiteers, *embusqués*, capitalists, "the big shots," and "the rich," as well as sympathy for the Russians and the desire for a revolution in France. At the end of a show in a cabaret catering to *poilus*, a colonel asked an actress to sing the "*Marseillaise*," but the soldiers prevented her from doing so by whistling loudly and by screaming "Peace!" and "Long Live Russia!"[14]

In Britain too, 1917 was a bad year. In the country itself, on the home front, the atmosphere was more despondent than ever before. The end of the war was nowhere in sight. The population realized more and more that the British army had suffered, and continued to suffer, huge losses in the Somme district, in Flanders' Fields, and elsewhere. An aristocrat came to the conclusion that "we are slowly but surely killing off the best of the male population of these islands." The losses in plebeian lives, on the other hand, did not seem to perturb this gentleman. With respect to food supplies, Britain was far better off than Germany, but shortages nevertheless occurred in coal, for example, for which one had to line up, and some foodstuffs, particularly meat and fat. The German submarines, which sank countless freighters en route to Albion, played an important role in this respect, so rationing had to be introduced. Even worse was the fact that, as in France, wages failed to keep pace with inflation. In the course of the Great War, real wages would decline in Britain by 10 to 20 per cent. As in other countries, it was the ordinary citizens who had to shoulder most of the burdens of the war; in the form of military service, of course, but also in terms of low wages and high prices. It was generally known, meanwhile, that the industrialists achieved colossal profits and prospered on account of the war. According to historian Arthur Marwick, "working-class discontent with high prices and other irritations [sic] brought about by the war reached a peak in 1917." In that year, as in France, considerably more strikes took place than in the previous year and the workers flocked for salvation (or at least relief) to the trade unions, whose membership would increase spectacularly during the war, namely from 4 million in 1914 to 6.5 million in 1918.

The Labour Party continued to collaborate with the government and to support the war, but its rank-and-file was fast becoming much more pacifist and radical. In order to avoid losing many members, like the French socialist party, the leaders of Labour, who had always avoided appearing to be "socialist" before the war, now began to openly identify with socialist objectives such as "the socializing of the means of production, distribution, and commerce." Labour faced tough competition from more radical socialist parties such as the very militant Socialist Labour Party, with its newspaper *The Socialist*, which at a given time reached a circulation of twenty thousand copies and enjoyed a lot of success with antiwar titles such as "You Gave Us War, We Will Give You Revolution." The success of socialism was partly due to the Russian Revolution, which galvanized the British plebeians when news of it arrived. The latter had never cherished warm feelings toward the authoritarian czarist regime, and they acclaimed its fall. As early as March 1917, about twelve thousand persons met in London's Royal Albert Hall to demonstrate their support for the Russian revolutionaries. The pacifist-socialist radicals henceforth attracted much more attention, for example with mass demonstrations in favour of peace, organized on May Day in London and Glasgow, and, in June 1917, with a huge meeting in Leeds of all sorts of left-wing forces, the famous "Great Labour, Socialist, and Democratic Convention." The Leeds meeting not only expressed itself in favour of revolution, but also of independence for Ireland, India, and Egypt. There was even talk of setting up soviets in Britain, but nothing was to come of that.[15]

The British elite must have found all this pretty shocking. It had wanted the war because it had firmly believed that war would function as an antidote to the revolution and other forms of socialist "danger," but in 1917 it became obvious that the war had actually stimulated interest and enthusiasm for socialism in large segments of the population. To the great consternation of the elite, an official, quoted by Adam Hochschild, reported in that year that

> . . . there is scarcely a community or group of persons in England now . . . among whom the principles of socialism and extreme democratic control [sic] are not beginning to be listened to with ever increasing eagerness . . . There is no gathering of working people in the country which is not disposed to regard Capitalism as a proven failure.[16]

The British authorities reacted to the spectacular rise of the "socialist danger" with searches of the homes of leaders and other members of pacifist and socialist organizations, confiscation of their printing presses and pamphlets, interception of their mail, censorship, and the use of agents provocateurs. The fear of the "spectre of revolution" would also force the authorities to make concessions and introduce reforms,[17] but one area in which concessions were out of the question was the war: that chalice's bitter potion had to be drunk to the last drop. In this respect, Prime Minister Lloyd George revealed himself to be a ruthless *jusqu'au-boutiste*. The poet S. Gertrude Ford responded to his bellicose discourse with a poem entitled "A Fight to the Finish," featuring lines such as these:

> *'Fight the year out!' the Warlords said:*
> *What said the dying among the dead?*

> *'To the last man!' cried the profiteers:*
> *What said the poor in the starveling years?*

> *'War is good!' yelled the Jingo-kind:*
> *What said the wounded, the maimed and blind?*

> *'Fight on!' the Armament-kings besought:*

427

Nobody asked what the women thought.
'On!' echoed Hate where the fiends kept trust:
Asked the Church, even, what said Christ?[18]

It was in 1917 that the famous British war poets Siegfried Sassoon and Wilfred Owen began to make their pacifist sentiments loud and clear. In October of that year, Sassoon published "Glory of Women," in which he denounced the bellicosity of the British women who had had harassed young men into volunteering for service and who, in some cases, continued to preach an unthinking patriotism.[19] In the same month, one of the most famous antiwar poems of Wilfred Owen, entitled *"Dulce and Decorum Est,"* was published:

If you could hear, at every jolt, the blood
Come gargling from the froth-corrupted lungs,
Obscene as cancer, bitter as the cud
Of vile, incurable sores on innocent tongues,
My friend, you would not tell with such high zest
To children ardent for some desperate glory,

The old lie: Dulce et decorum est
Pro patria mori.[20]

It was not only on the British islands, but also elsewhere in the vast Empire, that war weariness was now expressed loudly. In May 1917, conscription was introduced in Canada, but the measure met with massive opposition, especially in the province of Quebec. Protests and riots achieved the concession that exemptions could be requested, and huge numbers of potential recruits did indeed request to be exempted, namely 380,000 of a total of 404,000. In Quebec, of a total of 117,000 cases, an overwhelming 115,000 requested an exemption. These statistics reflected a total lack of enthusiasm for the war, especially among the mostly Catholic French Canadians, who felt neither loyalty to the British Empire, in which they had never felt at home, nor sympathy for a supposedly anticlerical French Republic, and who did not cherish the idea of sacrificing their lives in the distant fields of France or Flanders. Thus it became crystal clear in 1917 that in Canada, like everywhere else within the British Empire, countless people were extremely war-weary and no longer supported the war.[21]

Finally, the British soldiers themselves had had more than enough. As early as the fall of 1914, the commanders of the Royal Navy, referred to as "their lordships," had noticed that the initial enthusiasm of the ordinary sailors, the "lower decks," was cooling off, giving way to increasingly profound discontent, to an "alienation between the officers and the men," to complaints with respect to the poor pay and bad food, and to a general unrest. In September 1917, this trend culminated in a mutiny, or at least a serious case of collective disobedience, on HMS *Amphitrite* in Portsmouth. (On account of the inferior fare served to them on board, the crew used to refer to the ship as "am and tripe.") Via reluctantly yielded piecemeal concessions and solemn promises of improvements to be implemented after the war, the unrest in the Royal Navy could be kept under control.[22] As for the soldiers of the land forces, all too many men displayed obvious signs of "a sense of deadly depression"; in other words, they were totally demoralized. They wondered why they had to spend such an awful long time in the trenches and fight against men who asked themselves the same kind of questions and who, just like themselves, would have preferred to return immediately to their homes. These sentiments also surfaced in a previously mentioned song that was then very popular among the Tommies, "Tell Me Now":

> *I don't know why I went to war*
> *Tell me, oh, tell me now. I don't know why I went to war or*
> *What dese folks are fightin' for,*
> *Tell me, oh, tell me now.*

> *I don't know why I totes dis gun,*
> *Tell me, oh, tell me now.*
> *I don't know why I totes dis gun,*
> *'Cause I ain't got nothin' 'gainst de Hun,*
> *Tell me, oh, tell me now.*

> *I hopes dey surely is a God,*

Tell me, oh, tell me now.
I hopes dey surely is a God,
When de grave-digger slaps me in de face wid de sod,
Tell me, oh, tell me now.[23]

Drunkenness and desertion became major problems, and in 1917 not only the French but also the British army had to cope with cases of "collective indiscipline," including mutinies, of which a spectacular outbreak rocked the little French channel port of Étaples, a station on the way to and from the front for many Tommies, in September. The men liked to refer to Étaples as "Eat Apples," "Eatables," or "Staples." In 1917, the town was described by war poet Wilfred Owen in a letter to his mother as "a kind of stable where they keep the beasts before sending them to the slaughter house." It was a dreary and even sad borough, where the Tommies were lodged in armouries. A bridge across the little River Canche linked the locality to nearby Le Touquet. That was another planet, a chic beach resort reserved for officers and consequently off-limits to ordinary soldiers. On September 9, trouble broke out when a soldier, allegedly a New Zealander, attempted to cross the bridge to visit Le Touquet but was prevented from doing so by the military police. This triggered no less than six days of riots and demonstrations involving ten thousand soldiers, some of whom waved red flags. Finally, with the help of loyal troops, the military police managed to restore order. One mutineer was executed "as an example."[24]

The incident at Étaples reflected the fact that in 1914–1918 the British army experienced more and more problems with lack of discipline, unrest, insubordination, and even rebellion among the ordinary soldiers. Consequently, a growing number of military policemen were required. In 1914, when the war started, there was one military policeman for every 3,306 soldiers; when the war ended, there would be eleven times more, namely, one policeman for every 291 soldiers.[25] In Étaples, the Tommies were only a few hours by boat from England, or Blighty. Returning to Blighty as soon as possible, and thus escaping from this awful war, is what all Tommies dreamed of. A huge hit at the time was the song "Back to Dear Old Blighty":

Take me back to dear old Blighty!
Put me on the train for London town!
Take me over there,
Drop me anywhere,
Liverpool, Leeds, or Birmingham, well, I don't care!

Hurry me home to Blighty,
Blighty is the place for me![26]

In no army was the morale of the soldiers as low as it was among the Russians, but nowhere was it better than among the French, British, and Belgian combatants. War weariness reigned supreme, and from the spring of 1917 onward, the influence of the revolutionary events in Russia played an increasingly important role. In Germany, yet another factor had a negative influence, namely the British naval blockade. This strategy caused more and more shortages, which also affected the soldiers, for example in the form of much less bread in their rations, especially after March 1917. The resulting discontent was all the greater because the officers continued to receive plenty of bread and other food. On account of this, but also under the influence of the events in Russia, the mood of the men became rebellious, even revolutionary. "The entire state is nothing but an instrument of capitalism and of the speculators," was the comment of one soldier. And another opined that "we have to do things here like in Russia, so that we get rid of that damned militarism."[27] More and more soldiers developed an antagonism vis-à-vis Germany's traditional class system. A "proletarian" sailor, for example, explained in May 1917 that he had been an "ultra-patriot" in 1914, but that afterwards "restlessness, irritation, and disillusion" had irrevocably infected him, as well as resentment with respect to "the country's fundamental principle, the class system." "The war," he declared,

> *had turned out to be something that few people had foreseen,*
> *let alone wished for, and the existence of the class system was*
> *one of the things the war had revealed; a few years of war*
> *had achieved what dozens of years of socialist and anarchist*

propaganda had been unable to do: they had laid bare the
hypocrisy and the contradictions of the old order.[28]

The year 1917 demonstrated all too clearly that the German soldiers, too, were tired of the war. In that year, the number of cases of desertion, voluntary surrender, and insubordination rose significantly.[29] This war weariness also found expression in a poem which, if found in possession of a soldier, could have cost him fourteen days of detention:

Ich bin Soldat, doch bin ich es nicht gerne;	*I am a soldier, but I dislike being one;*
. . . .	. . . .
Komm ich ins Feld, dan muss ich Brüder morden,	*When I go into action, I must kill my brothers,*
Von denen keiner mir was zu Leid getan.	*Who have never done anything wrong to me.*
Als Krüppel trag ich nachher Band und Orden,	*As an invalid I will be able to show off ribbons and medals,*
Doch schmachtend ruf ich dan: Ich war Soldat!	*And then I will sigh and say: I was a soldier!*[30]

An aforementioned sarcastic song, *"Mein Michel was willst du noch mehr?"*, also became increasingly popular in 1917. One of its verses made it abundantly clear that the soldiers had enough and were not willing to "get killed for the Kaiser":

Du darfst exerzieren, marschieren, am Kasernenhof, kreuz und quer, und dann für den Kaiser krepieren.	*You may exercise and march, Back and forth in the armouries' yard, And then go and get killed for the Kaiser.*
Mein Michel, was willst du noch mehr?	*My dear Michael, what more could you possibly want?*

In 1917, the Italian soldiers were particularly disgruntled and rebellious, and this found its reflection in the attitude of the men toward the officers and the military police, the *carabinieri*. Of the latter, a high number were assassinated, hanged, or stabbed. This episode has been referred to as a veritable "hunt for carabinieri."[31] But in all other armies the military police were likewise detested by the soldiers and sometimes killed. Barthas wrote that "[our soldiers] felt a murderous hatred for the *gendarmes . . .* who never stopped harassing them, spying on them, and disturbing their rest and freedom whenever they left the trenches." He related how in the summer of 1916, in his sector of the front, somewhere in Champagne, two *gendarmes* had been found hanging from a tree. Such cases were allegedly not rare at all.[32]

With respect to the morale of the soldiers in general in the year 1917, Gabriel Kolko sums up the situation as follows:

> *The troops' refusal to obey their superiors totally and blindly*
> *was their most subversive act . . . it was a condition that made*
> *them dangerous even if they were not necessarily political*
> *radicals, and it opened an abyss full of uncertainties . . .*
> *Throughout the last eighteen months of the war, the question*
> *arose as to how, or to whom, soldiers would respond in*
> *giving vent to their deepening alienation and disenchantment*
> *with traditional rulers and their folklore and values . . . A*
> *qualitatively new situation was emerging, and all the latent*
> *social tensions within peacetime societies were brought to a*
> *head under the mounting pressure of suffering and pain.*[33]

Certain countries would survive this traumatic experience without too much damage, others would fall prey to the revolution. But the front-line soldiers would play a crucial role everywhere.

The civilians of the belligerent countries also showed in many ways in 1917 that they were sick and tired of the war, disgruntled, restless, and seditious. They blamed the traditional military, political, and social-economic elite for having wanted the war, for frivolously unleashing it, and for managing it so catastrophically — overwhelmingly at the expense of the lower orders. Everywhere the people were impressed with what was going on in Russia. There the hated old order had been overthrown by soldiers and civilians. Democratic reforms, unprecedented even by Western criteria, had been enacted, and the Russian revolutionaries were poised to withdraw the country from the generally despised war. In this sense, the Russian Revolution, and above all the Bolsheviks' October Revolution, functioned as "the main ray of hope during one of Europe's darkest nights," as Arno Mayer has remarked.[34]

In Germany, the consequences of the British blockade, which only started to be enforced consistently and ruthlessly in that year, were now having a great impact on the population. Food was becoming increasingly hard to come by, and prices were rising sharply. The high cost of food inspired the following verse, a sarcastic criticism of the leaders of a supposedly great and powerful empire who proved unable to feed their own citizens and even their soldiers:

O Deutschland hoch in Ehren,   *O Germany, hallowed fatherland,*
Du kannst dich nicht ernähren.   *Why are you unable to feed*
                                                        yourself?[35]

These lines were featured in a soldiers' song that mercilessly lampooned one of Germany's most patriotic hymns, dating back to approximately 1850, "O Deutschland hoch in Ehren," "O Germany, Hallowed Fatherland," with its *jusqu'au-boutiste* call: "*Haltet aus im Sturmgebraus*" — "Persevere, though the storm is raging!"[36]

Until early 1917, the British had not isolated Germany hermetically from the outside world with their blockade, specifically to avoid antagonizing neutral countries like the Netherlands and above all the United States. But in the spring of that year the US entered the war on the side of the Entente. The noose of the blockade could thus be tightened, so that henceforth it became virtually impossible for Germany to import goods via the Netherlands and Denmark, for example.[37] (And it goes without saying that the blockade also caused huge problems for the Danube Monarchy, where famines broke out, especially in the big cities, Vienna and Budapest. In all belligerent countries, city residents indeed tended to suffer much more than people living in the countryside.)

In Germany, the working class suffered the most as a result of the blockade, because real wages continued to decline. The discontent was great, the more so since on the black market all sorts of things were still available, at high prices of course, so the rich did not starve. "The privileges of the rich and the corrupt are becoming simply intolerable," wrote the French historian Frédéric Rousseau in a comment on this situation.[38] Moreover, everyone knew that, thanks to the war, the Reich's capitalists were making profits as never before. At Krupp, for example, profits rose from 31.6 million marks in 1916 to 79.7 million marks in 1917. Among the other industrial giants who achieved huge profits at the time were the steel producer Stinnes, AEG, the great specialist in electro-technics, and the naval constructor Blohm & Voss, producer of submarines.

The war reinforced German industry's trend toward gigantism and the creation of monopolies, the spectacular emergence of a relatively small elite of giant enterprises that attracted most of the very profitable state orders for the production of war materiel. Conversely, countless small firms could not profit from the war. Many of those thus lost their suppliers or their customers, and saw their benefits decline drastically; and many of them simply disappeared from the scene. This process of monopolization had already started long before the Great War, and it also occurred in the other belligerent countries. In this sense, it is true, as Niall Ferguson has remarked, that during the war the *average* profits of enterprises were not particularly high, but the profits of big firms, of *corporations*, who would henceforth play a determinant role in the development of the capitalist industrial system, were considerable, as Ferguson himself acknowledges.[39]

Class conflict is a multi-faceted phenomenon, as Domenico Losurdo has emphasized. It is not merely a bilateral conflict between "capital" and "labour," as depicted not only by Ferguson but also by Habermas and Dahrendorff, and as even a number of Marxist authors seem to believe, but it also reflects the contradictions between the bourgeoisie and the nobility, between the industrialists of different countries, between the mother countries and the colonies, and, as we have just seen in the case of Germany, between factions within the industrial bourgeoisie, for example, between big and small producers.[40] Not coincidentally, the Great War, a big war as well as an industrial war, favoured the big industrial producers.

The German population was undernourished if not starving, more and more tired of the war, and longed not only for peace but also increasingly for democratic reforms of the Reich's authoritarian and militarist system. Most Germans might not have believed that this system had wanted and deliberately unleashed the war in 1914, and preferred to continue to believe that for their homeland this was a defensive war; but they did believe that, with their overly ambitious war aims, the imperial government and the army's high command, personified by Ludendorff and von Hindenburg, were responsible for drawing out the conflict for so many years. The pressure exercised by the people in favour of peace and reforms thus became huge, even irresistible, in 1917. In the spring, for example, the pacifist and radical social-democratic dissidents left the party to form an "independent" SPD, the "Independent Social-Democratic Party of Germany" (*Unabhängige Sozialdemokratische Partei Deutschlands*, USPD). With its relentless struggle for peace and reforms, this new socialist party soon acquired a considerable following, mostly at the expense, not surprisingly, of the SPD, which remained loyal to the *Burgfrieden*. The Spartacist faction left the SPD to join the USPD. In 1917, the SPD membership was thus reduced to a quarter of its size in 1914.[41]

A number of bourgeois parties now also started to demand peace negotiations and modest political reforms. And so the Kaiser felt coerced to make certain promises, for example, a reform of Prussia's electoral system, an ultraconservative arrangement that strongly favoured the upper classes — the landowning nobility and the industrial bourgeoisie — in comparison to the much more numerous petty bourgeois and proletarian subjects of Wilhelm of Hohenzollern. But the promised reforms were to be implemented only after the victorious end of the war. In any event, on July 19, 1917, the Reichstag approved a resolution in favour of a peace without annexations, to the great displeasure of the Kaiser, Ludendorff, and all the other German *jusqu'au-boutistes*, still numerous at the time. This resolution heralded the end of the *Burgfrieden*, because the SPD as well as a number of liberal and Catholic bourgeois parties were no longer unconditional supporters of a *Siegfrieden*, that is, "peace through victory." But a *Siegfrieden* happened to be the alpha and omega of the program of the military dictatorship of Ludendorf and von Hindenburg, who monopolized power in the Reich from the summer of 1917 onward, more specifically, from July 13, the day the "wimp" Bethmann-Hollweg was forced to resign as chancellor on account of machinations by the *jusq'auboutiste* hard core within the German elite.

Yet another belligerent country in which the great majority of civilians, and especially the lower orders, had enough of carrying most of the burdens of the war and ardently longed for peace was Italy. The war had been unpopular there from the very start. Moreover, compared to the wages, prices were increasing more than in any other country at war, which caused further discontent. In 1918, the wages of Italian factory workers amounted to only 65 per cent of what they had been in 1913, and the wages of agricultural workers had declined even more dramatically. Countless Italian cities were the scene of spontaneous demonstrations against the war, in which the return of the soldiers was demanded; between December 1916 and April 1917, no less than five hundred demonstrations of this type took place, involving tens of thousands of workers and peasants. In August 1917, a workers' revolt in Turin resulted in the deaths of no less than fifty people.[42]

Karl Marx had predicted that the capitalist system would necessarily bring about a "pauperization" or "immiseration" that would inexorably cause the proletariat to overthrow the system via a revolution. During the years preceding the war, however, many had come to believe that he had been wrong in this respect, that life for the proletarians was getting better and that a revolution was therefore useless and impossible; numerous socialists had adopted this point of view and had become "reformists," devotees of evolutionary rather than revolutionary socialism. But now, during and because of a bloody war that required the plebeians to make unprecedented sacrifices and caused hunger and other misery, a very real kind of pauperization with considerable revolutionary potential was indeed materializing. The war, writes Gabriel Kolko, provoked an "increasing immiserization [sic]," and

> *undermined the material welfare of the masses in ways for which there was no precedent in modern European history, taking away from countless millions of them the material incentives to remain committed or, at the worst, acquiescent to ruling classes that had so blithely led them into the conflict's interminable economic maelstrom.*[43]

Paradoxical, but certainly not contradictory, was the role in all this of imperialism, which, on the one hand, had somewhat improved the standard of living of the plebeians in Europe and thus stifled the pauperization trend but which, on the other hand, had helped to provoke the war, an "imperialist" war in many ways; and that war sparked an unprecedented kind of pauperization, which ultimately produced the revolution.

It was the year 1917, writes Kolko, that witnessed "the deepening alienation among the masses" as well as "insecurity among the leaders" and saw the social structure become the object of intense pressures. From the middle of that year, the elites everywhere feared that the war they had unleashed might lead to the destruction of the traditional order, *their* order. The popular masses "failed to endorse a coherent ideological or political alternative to the dominant social systems," continues Kolko, but "their actions nonetheless entailed an unprecedented rejection of the prevailing social orders and functionally opposed the existing ruling classes' politics, institutions, and pretensions," and thus "threatened large parts of Europe's status quo at its moment of greatest weakness."[44] In some countries this status quo was more fragile than in others, and in some countries the pauperization was advancing further than in others, so that the revolutionary potential was greater there than elsewhere. In Russia, it was in early 1917 that the pauperization of soldiers and civilians had already gone so far that the revolution broke out, provoking the collapse of the established order, the czarist system.

While countless soldiers and civilians desperately wanted not only peace but also changes, the attitude of the elite hardened considerably. More than ever before, representative personalities of the nobility and the bourgeoisie revealed themselves determined to do whatever was necessary to win the war in order to be able to reap, at home as well as abroad, the fruits they expected from a triumphant conclusion. In 1917, Germany became a de facto military dictatorship under Ludendorff, who wanted nothing less than total victory. In Britain, Lloyd George ruled via a small "war cabinet" of seven members in quasi-dictatorial or, as Arthur Marwick has written, virtually "totalitarian" fashion. Lloyd George was an outspoken *jusqu'au-boutiste*, who became notorious for hawkish statements such as this negative response to a suggestion that peace talks might be considered: "the fight must be to a finish — to a knockout."[45]

In France, a counteroffensive of the *jusqu'au-boutistes* brought Georges Clemenceau to power in November 1917. His mandate was to ruthlessly pursue the war in spite of the mutinies and all the other problems. In order to do so, Clemenceau saw fit to transform the previously moderately democratic French republic into a kind of dictatorship with undeniably totalitarian characteristics. It was for example forbidden to question and, *a fortiori*, to contradict official military announcements, and "alarmism" became severely punishable; telephone communications were tapped and even ordinary conversations were listened to; the freedoms of assembly and of the press were curtailed; militant socialists and pacifists were arrested and often punished by being sent to the front. In the context of this "brutal repressive policy," the "Tiger" — a nickname Clemenceau had acquired in 1906 on account of his pugnacity — also took particularly drastic action against strikers. Conversely, the strikers and trade unionists in general came to regard Clemenceau as their main enemy, calling him "a threat to the proletariat," "the champion of repression," and even "the assassin."[46] This development in France likewise illustrates how, from the perspective of the elite, the pursuit of victory against the foreign or exterior enemy was inseparable from the pursuit of victory against the domestic or interior enemy; how victory in the vertical war between nations was associated with victory in the horizontal war between classes.

A large percentage of the population wanted peace, even if peace eliminated the prospect of a glorious victory for the fatherland. On the other hand, a not insignificant percentage of the civilians and soldiers had internalized the bellicose ethic of the elite, which continued to be dispensed abundantly via state propaganda, newspapers, schools, pulpits, etc. This meant that they, too — like Clemenceau, Lloyd George, and Ludendorff — could not imagine any outcome other than an unconditional victory of their own country, bringing all the glory and benefits expected from it, even if this meant that much more blood would have to be shed. In 1917, Germany thus witnessed not only the founding of the socialist and pacifist USDP, but also of the nationalist and ultra-bellicose "German Fatherland Party" (*Deutsche Vaterlandspartei*, DVLP). One of its founders was Admiral Tirpitz, and the newborn party was financially baptized most generously by the army's high command. Among the most eminent members of this

antidemocratic and "proto-fascist" party loomed "numerous large landowners, members of the most prestigious liberal professions [*Bildungsbürger*], as
well as industrialists from the Rhineland"; in other words, the "old elites
of the Reich," as the German historian Ernst Piper has put it. The DVLP
supported Ludendorff and worked in favour of a *Siegfrieden*, a "peace via
victory," a.k.a. a "Hindenburg peace." Within merely one year, the party
counted 1.25 million members, thus becoming a mass party of the same
calibre as the SPD. One of the reasons countless civilians, even among the
petty bourgeoisie, were partisans of a *Siegfrieden*, was that they had purchased the bonds by means of which the Reich financed the war, so that
they feared the consequences of a defeat — and even of a peace that would
bring Germany few or even none of the advantages so many of its citizens
had dreamed of in 1914.[47]

The kind of German citizens that found a political home in the
Vaterlandspartei continued to believe that the war was justified and needed
to end with a victory for the Reich, and they found ways to rationalize and
justify the slaughter of hundreds of thousands of their own soldiers. For
example, the death and misery of the war were presented by numerous
intellectuals as something positive, even precious, as the sort of "purification" that many of them had already associated with the outbreak of war in
1914. The philosopher Edmund Husserl thus wrote in November 1917 that

> *Need and death are our educators. For years already, there has
> been nothing exceptional anymore about death . . . Death has
> regained its original sacred right. It is there to remind us of
> eternity [etc.].*

In other words, the war amounted to a healthy and necessary meditation
about death. It was a "spiritual exercise" that permitted the Germans to
escape from the banality of ordinary existence and be confronted with the
real meaning of life. According to Thomas Mann, the proximity of death
deepened our knowledge and ennobled our soul; the war thus promised
to produce "a more noble humanity" (*höhere Menschlichkeit*), as well as "a
certain freedom, reservation, aloofness with respect to life, a distancing-
oneself from life and a capacity to transcend fear and hope . . . and finally,

a victory over death." In the Habsburg Empire, Sigmund Freud had already imagined in 1915 that death was banished from life in peacetime but, conversely, now that people died daily by the thousands, "life was becoming interesting again"; he concluded by paraphrasing the old Latin advice, *si vis pacem, para bellem*, "if you want peace, prepare for war"; *si vis vitam, para mortem*, "if you wish to live, prepare to die."[48]

The Virgin Mary had more success with her apparitions in 1916 and 1917 in the Portuguese village of Fatima. Since 1910, that country had been a liberal and anticlerical republic like France. But Mary's apparitions in Fatima between May and October 1917 aroused enthusiasm among much of the still deeply religious Lusitanian population. This prompted conservative, clerical, and monarchist members of the country's elite, led by Sidónio Pais, to revolt in December 1917 and to replace the republic with an authoritarian regime that would soon give way to a "clerico-fascist" dictatorship under Antonio di Oliveira Salazar.[50] In France, during the Great War, the Virgin Mary, assisted by Claire Ferchaud, was unable to achieve such a success, but a very similar result was to be pulled out of a hat in 1940, when, thanks to the good services of Adolf Hitler, Marshal Pétain would bury the Third Republic in favour of the arch-conservative Vichy regime.

Countless front soldiers had also internalized the conservative, antidemocratic, nationalist, antisocialist, racist, and all too often anti-Semitic, counterrevolutionary, and bellicose ethos of the elite. Those men had learned to glorify brutality, bloodshed, and contempt for death. They cherished the mutual camaraderie and "shared destiny" (*Schicksalgemeinschaft*) of tough guys who had experienced the misery and hardship of the trenches together, thus forging a "community of warriors" or "community of blood" (*kriegerische Gemeinschaft, Blutgemeinschaft*), to use terminology coined by one of them, Ernst Jünger. (Jünger would later write a book about his experiences at the front, entitled *Storm of Steel*.) Thus was born what would be called "socialism of the trenches." It was a way of thinking whose apostles and adepts — emerged mostly from the ranks of the petty bourgeoisie — found to be far superior to the internationalist socialism of the prewar era, which was presumably tainted by its association with pacifists, Jews, and proletarians. (For some members of the petty bourgeoisie, the war actually constituted an opportunity for social climbing. A clerk in a London insurance agency, for example, who would otherwise have been "doomed to a life of insignificance and tedium," managed to rise in the ranks during the war, become an officer, and even marry a lady "who once firmly turned him down"; he had "achieved everything he had ever dreamt of, become the man he always believed he was. And it is the war that made it possible.") At the same time, this type of soldier felt far superior to ordinary burghers with their typical fear of danger and need for security.[51] Robert Graves conjured up this storm trooper mentality in his poem "Two Fusiliers":

> *Show me the two so closely bound*
> *As we, by the wet bond of blood,*
> *By friendship, blossoming from mud,*
> *By death: we faced him, and we found*
> *Beauty in Death,*
> *In dead men breath.*[52]

Hitler and Mussolini are two good examples of soldiers who believed they discovered in their frontline experiences a new form of socialism, and who found inspiration in it for a new type of thinking and acting, later to be known as fascism.

During the year 1917, the "year of troubles," very different camps thus emerged within the population of belligerent countries. First, the pacifists and the radical socialists such as Liebknecht, who wanted an unconditional end to the war but also more or less radical democratic reforms. Second, those who wanted to continue the war to an "honourable" conclusion and who, on the home front, remained loyal to the sacred-union type of arrangement, which served to preserve the status quo. The latter group included liberal and even some "enlightened" conservative elements within the elite, but also the German social-democrats and the majority of the socialists of other countries, for example France. Third, the ultraconservative, reactionary, and protofascist elements, who were determined to win the war in order to realize their country's imperialist objectives and, at home, to halt and even reverse the democratization process and destroy socialism.

CHAPTER 25
THE YANKS ARE COMING!

In 1917, the US government decides, against the will of the great majority of the population, to take the country into the war on the side of the Entente and against Germany. It does not do so on account of attacks by German submarines against ships such as the Lusitania, *which was sunk in 1915, and even less in order to defend the cause of democracy against dictatorship and injustice. It is done because the American elite, like the elite of the European countries in 1914, expects to reap all sorts of advantages from participation in the war: for example, much higher profits and more docile workers, in addition to access to the raw materials and markets of foreign countries . . .*

1917 was not a good year for any of the belligerent countries, but for the members of the Entente it was nothing less than catastrophic. The main reasons for that were the mutinies in the French army, which made the situation on the western front extremely precarious, as well as the revolution in Russia, which raised the spectre of Russia exiting the war, leaving Britain and France bereft of the ally that forced Germany to fight on two fronts. Add to this the fact that civilians as well as soldiers in France and Britain were desperate for peace, and one understands why the political and military authorities in London and Paris had plenty of reasons to be concerned. They had wanted this war and wanted desperately to win it, and to achieve this they needed the support of the population and of all their allies. But in 1917, victory was nowhere in sight, and had never seemed so far away.

And what would happen if the war was not won? The answer was provided by the events in Russia, and it was a grim warning: revolution!

The only ray of hope in 1917, from the viewpoint of the Entente, was that in April of that year the United States declared war on Germany, something Paris and London had fervently been hoping for. It would obviously still take some time before American troops would disembark in Europe to help turn the tide in favour of the Entente, but hope for a final victory was thus revived. For the overwhelming majority of the people of the United States, however, the entry of their country into the war was hardly a wonderful thing. They realized that the war raging in Europe had been a disaster, and that in all belligerent countries civilians as well as soldiers longed for a return to peace. The Europeans wanted to exit this war as soon as possible; why would Americans want to enter it? And why would they have to fight on the side of the British and the French against the Germans? Why not on the side of the Germans against the countries of the Entente? Let us examine the factors that caused many Americans to ask such questions.

For a long time already, the United States had enjoyed good relations with Germany. It was not Germany but Britain that was the traditional enemy and great rival of Uncle Sam. The British were former colonial masters against whom the country's war of independence had been fought during the 1770s, and against whom another armed conflict took place between 1812 and 1815, the so-called War of 1812; and throughout the nineteenth century relations with Britain had remained tense on account of issues such as the border of the US with British North America (which became the Dominion of Canada in 1867); influence and commerce in the Pacific, South America, and the Caribbean; and British sympathy for the South during the American Civil War. (Until the 1930s, in fact, Washington would have plans ready for a possible war against Britain.) The Americans did not regard the British as beloved "Anglo-Saxon" twins. Clearly, many Americans were of English origin and supported Albion and its allies. But the majority of Americans — unlike the elite of the country's northeast, consisting to a large extent of WASPs — were not "Anglo-Saxons" at all but came from all over Europe, with a great many from Ireland and Germany. In 1914, when the war broke out

THE YANKS ARE COMING!

in Europe, Americans of Irish or German origin had good reasons to hope for a German victory and a defeat of Britain. As for France, the Americans who disembarked there in 1917 held banners proclaiming "Lafayette, we are here!", an allusion to the aid the Americans had received from France during their war of independence against Britain, aid that was personified by the Marquis de Lafayette. The slogan suggested that the Americans were now paying back a debt of gratitude to the French; but why had they not rushed to support their old Gallic friend in 1914? In reality, hypothetical gratitude toward the French had nothing to do with the US entry into the war, the more so since many Americans were very religious and had little or no sympathy for a republic that was anticlerical if not atheistic. The Protestant Americans sympathized with Germany, ruled by the Lutheran Hohenzollerns, and Catholic Americans had a soft spot for Austria-Hungary, whose rulers, the Habsburgs, had been the great white knights of Catholicism ever since the time of the Reformation.[1] And Russia? That empire was viewed by many Americans as a bastion of autocratic, old-fashioned monarchism, as the antithesis of the democratic republic the United States was (at least in theory). Numerous Americans such as Jews and Ukrainians were refugees from the Czarist empire who had about the same feelings for Russia as the Irish had for Britain. In the United States, Germany was not the object of rivalry, dislike, or outright hostility.[2] Moreover, many Americans, for example Theodore Roosevelt, considered themselves to belong to the superior "Nordic race" and therefore to be close relatives of the "Aryan" Germans, presumably an equally superior breed. The fact that Germany was hardly a democracy did not constitute a problem for elitist types such as Roosevelt, who looked down on the popular "masses." As for the Americans who did not belong to the elite and did in fact favour democracy, even they had little or nothing against Germany. Indeed, with its social legislation and universal suffrage, the Reich loomed in some ways as more democratic than Britain, for example, and the United States itself. American democracy was indeed a kind of "*Herrenvolk* democracy," that is, a democracy for an ethnic elite, namely the "white man," a system from which Indians and blacks, a large part of the population, were ruthlessly excluded — de facto and/or de jure. This "democracy for the few," as the political scientist and historian

Michael Parenti has called it, featured a kind of apartheid *avant la lettre*, in which blacks were the victims of segregation and lynchings and Indians were cast aside in wretched reservations. In comparison to that, the Reich of Wilhelm II was an egalitarian paradise. President Woodrow Wilson's claim that the US went to war for the sake of democracy, a claim that even today many consider to be sincere, was not only totally false, but even ludicrous. If Wilson had really wanted to do something to promote the cause of democracy, he should have started in his own country, where there was still an awful lot of work to be done.[3]

One can say that in early 1917 the American population was divided with respect to the war. Some Americans — and above all the WASPs and other citizens of English origin — rooted for the Entente, while others sympathized with the Central Powers; and countless Americans probably had no particular opinion about what was going on in distant Europe. But sympathy is one thing, and fighting is something else. Most of the citizens tended to be pacifist or "isolationist," wanted nothing to do with the war raging in Europe, and were against their country becoming involved in it. It is in this context that the song "I Didn't Raise My Boy to Be a Soldier," which originated in 1915 and had already enjoyed a lot of success in Britain, became the musical icon of pacifism in the United States. The song was deeply offensive to those Americans who did favour intervention in the war, the bellicose type of Americans whose figurehead was "Teddy" Roosevelt.[4] The presidential elections of 1916 were won by Wilson, the incumbent. He was perceived as the peace candidate, opposed to America's entry into the war. As happens more often in the case of US presidents, he was to do exactly the opposite of what was expected of him: on April 2, 1917 he persuaded Congress to declare war on Germany, and this decision became official on April 6. Wilson claimed that Western civilization might collapse and mankind perhaps even become extinct if the United States did not intervene in the conflict; with the US involved, he suggested, the war would become a "war for democracy," a "war to end all wars."

It is understandable that many historians have failed to take these Wilsonian declarations seriously and have sought elsewhere for the real reasons that caused America to join the war against the will of the overwhelming majority of its people. Germany is usually blamed for this, namely because in 1917 the Reich responded to the British blockade — and the fiasco of the Battle of Jutland in the previous year — with an escalation of submarine warfare. By means of this strategy, Berlin hoped to be able to force the British to capitulate within six months. From January to April 1917, an enormous tonnage of ships was sent to the bottom of the sea, but from May on, when the British introduced the convoy system, their losses declined drastically. Submarine warfare also antagonized neutral powers, including the United States, and spoiled relations between Washington and Berlin, eventually leading to war. It is in these terms that numerous historians try to explain America's entry into the conflict. In this context the name *Lusitania* is inevitably mentioned. This great British ocean liner left New York for Liverpool but was sunk by a German U-boat, and American citizens were among the victims. Stateside, this fanned the flames of anti-German sentiments. The attack proved to be grist for the mill of the "interventionists," the partisans of entry into the war, and this allegedly led to an American declaration of war on Germany.

The problem with this explanation is that the *Lusitania* had already been sunk on May 7, 1915, that is, no less than two years before Washington went to war. Also, the 1,198 victims included only 128 Americans, the others being British and Canadian. Moreover, the *Lusitania* transported munitions and war materiel, something that, according to prevailing norms of international law, made the ship "fair game" for the Germans to target. (The German consulate in New York had in fact warned potential passengers via newspaper advertisements that this might happen.) Finally, it is likely that the British authorities, including Churchill, had intentionally arranged for the ship to take on ammunition in the hope that it would be attacked by the Germans, thus triggering an American entry into the war. It is understandable that, under such questionable circumstances, the US government failed to take the bait. In early 1917, on account of the intensification of submarine warfare, relations between the United States and Germany were admittedly deteriorating. Even so, it was not for this reason that Wilson declared war in April.[5]

It was not the American people but the American elite — of which Wilson, a former president of Princeton University, was a typical representative — that wanted war; and the war it wanted was a war against Germany.

447

The reason for this is that in 1917 the US elite, like its European counterpart in 1914, expected war to bring considerable advantages, and also help to dodge a major threat. The US was a great imperialist power, different from Britain, France, Russia and Germany in one small but important aspect: the US had developed a new imperialist strategy, later to be known as neocolonialism. This involved acquiring raw materials, markets, sources of cheap labour, and investment opportunities not via direct colonial control of a country, but via an indirect, mostly economic penetration, combined with the establishment, usually with the collaboration of local elites, of preponderant political influence. The US thus no longer used colonies and protectorates to achieve imperialist aims, as the European powers continued to do.

The Great War was a conflict between great imperialist powers. It was clear that the powers that would emerge triumphant from this war would also be the great winners with respect to imperialist interests. And it was equally clear that, as in a lottery, those who did not play could not win. It is highly probable that at the time of its declaration of war on Germany, the US government was aware of a statement made shortly before, on January 12, 1917, by the French Prime Minister, Aristide Briand, had thought about it, and had drawn conclusions from it. Clearly alluding to the United States, Briand had let it be known that "it would be desirable, at the peace conference, to exclude the powers that had not been involved in the war." Was it not obvious that there would be much to gain for those who would in fact be present at this conference? The vast possessions of the losers would be divided: "German" real estate in Africa, the oil-rich regions of the Ottoman Empire, and influence in China were all at stake. (The imperialists had been ogling this gigantic but weak country, determined to be present when more concessions could be carved out of its territory, when rights to exploit its mineral wealth or construct railways there would come up for grabs, and when the green light would be given for other ways to penetrate it economically.) In this respect, Japan had already shown its hand by pocketing the German concession in China. A relatively small country inhabited by members of a presumably inferior race, Japan nonetheless revealed itself as an aggressive and pesky rival of the United States in the Far East. Thanks to their "splendid little war" against Spain, the Americans had been able to establish a foothold in this part of the world in the form of tutelage over the Philippines, a Spanish colony they had "liberated." If the United States stayed out of the war, it would not be present when the Chinese prizes were distributed among the victors, and there loomed a very real danger that Japan might end up monopolizing China economically, so that American businessmen would not find the "open door" there that they were longing for. In any event, stateside it was feared that not only Japan, but also Britain and France — all of them rivals in the "rat race" of imperialism — would take advantage of victory in the war to keep the US out of China and elsewhere. Even a Wikipedia contributor acknowledges this on the topic "American entry into World War I":

> [I]f the Allies had won without [American] help, there was
> a danger they would carve up the world without regard to
> American commercial interests. They were already planning to
> use government subsidies, tariff walls, and controlled markets
> to counter the competition posed by American businessmen.

With his declaration of war on Germany in April 1917, Wilson neatly eliminated this danger. Much later, in the 1930s, an inquiry by the Nye Committee of the American Congress was to come to the conclusion that the country's entry into the war had been motivated by the wish to be present when, after the war, the moment came "to redivide the spoils of empire."[6]

The US went to war in order to achieve imperialist objectives: more specifically, to be able to share in the rich booty that awaited the victors of the slugfest among imperialists that the Great War happened to be. Remaining neutral would not only have meant not profiting from victory but, conversely, running the risk of becoming the object of the imperialist appetite of the victors. In the case of the US, that risk was admittedly virtually nonexistent, but for small neutral countries it was very real. On March 9, 1916, Portugal thus entered the war on the side of the Entente in order to prevent its colonial possessions from being redistributed by the victorious powers. Lisbon was particularly worried about the intentions of the British, who did in fact entertain such thoughts and were therefore allegedly keen to keep Portugal out of the conflict.[7] Its participation in the war, opposed by the great majority of the population, would cost Portugal eight thousand dead, thirteen thousand wounded, and twelve thousand men taken prisoner, and brought the country zero benefits.[8] Other countries were also forced to reflect on the advantages and disadvantages of neutrality. Like the US, the Netherlands could hope that abandoning neutrality might bring advantages. Like Portugal, its government feared that maintaining neutrality would be risky. By rallying to the side of Germany, the Netherlands could perhaps acquire Flanders, the Dutch-speaking part of Belgium, and this possibility was in fact conjured up by Berlin through its ambivalent "Flemish policy" (*Flamenpolitik*) in occupied Belgium. Conversely, remaining neutral meant that after the war the victors might force the Netherlands to cough up some of its colonies or even part of its own territory. During the war and during the Paris Peace Conference, some Belgian politicians actually pursued such a goal — vainly, as it turned out — hoping to annex some Dutch territories.

There was a second reason why war was wanted by the US elite, which consisted almost exclusively of the big industrialists and bankers of the northeast of the country. In the years before 1914, the United States had been hit by a major economic recession. But the war that broke out in Europe generated orders for all sorts of materiel, and on account of this increase in demand, production and profits also increased. Between 1914 and 1917, the nation's industrial production grew by at least 32 per cent, the gross national product by about 20 per cent, and American exports to the belligerent countries rose spectacularly. Agricultural products were also exported, naturally, but it was primarily the big industrialists — the capitalists, to use that terminology — who made fortunes thanks to the war that, to their great advantage and joy, seemed destined to go on indefinitely. It was hardly a source of concern that in that war an average of six thousand men died daily and that countless others were mutilated.[9] What mattered were the profits, and those were fabulous. As illustrated below, one can cite the profits made by a number of big American corporations thanks to the Great War:

Corporation Profits, in millions of dollars

	Before the war	At the end of the war
DuPont	6	58
Bethlehem Steel	6	49
US Steel	105	240
Anaconda	10	34
International Nickel	4	73

Most of the business generated by the war was done with the countries of the Entente. Between 1914 and 1916, US exports to Britain and France increased dramatically, from approximately $800 million to $3 billion. Conversely, because of the British blockade, it became virtually impossible to supply the Central Powers; the volume of American exports to Germany and Austria-Hungary shrunk during the war to an insignificant $1–$2 million. But what counted was that the war revealed itself to be good for business, and in the end it mattered little if the customer was an old friend or an old enemy, a democratic or autocratic country, an "Anglo-Saxon" relative or not.

Still, not all was well. Business was done above all with the British and, to a lesser extent, with the French, and the lion's share of these purchases was based on credits and loans extended to these countries by American banks. In 1917, the US banks had already made a total of $2.3 billion available in this manner. The loans to France alone rose spectacularly during the war, namely from 50 million francs in 1914 to 1.9 billion in 1915, 1.6 in 1916, 7.5 in 1917, 5.3 in 1918, and 9.2 in 1919. Crucial in this context was the role of J.P. Morgan & Co, the bank that was also known as the "House of Morgan." With offices in London and Paris, this Wall Street institution was in an ideal position to finance the transatlantic business, and already in 1915 Morgan was designated as the sole agent for stateside purchases made on behalf of Britain of ammunition, foodstuffs, etc. (The British also made purchases in the US on behalf of their French and Russian allies.) Thus there emerged in the US a kind of "circle of friends" of Morgan, consisting of firms such as DuPont and Remington, which obtained the contracts and were able to make fortunes. Morgan pocketed a 2 per cent commission on this business, which in 1917 alone amounted to a total value of $20 billion. The US thus replaced Britain as the world's financial superpower, New York's Wall Street took over from London's City as financial capital of the world, and the dollar replaced the British pound as the leading currency.[10]

As far as Wall Street was concerned, the war in Europe was a kind of goose that laid golden eggs, and the longer it lasted, the better — as long as the Entente ended up being victorious. In other words, "economic interests placed the United States clearly in the camp of the Allies." The financial collaboration with Britain possibly amounted to a de facto violation of American legislation with respect to neutrality, as some US politicians argued at the time and the aforementioned Nye Committee of Congress would acknowledge in the 1930s. In any event, it is understandable that Germany saw things that way and demonstrated a growing hostility to the United States. Morgan could not have cared less, but in 1916 Wall Street began to worry about the fact that the British debt was becoming extravagant. And in early 1917 the situation became truly worrisome when the revolution in Russia conjured up the spectre of a Russian exit from the war, likely to be followed by a German victory. In this case, Britain might not be able to pay off its debt, which would mean a financial catastrophe for Morgan. It became all too obvious that only an American entry into the war on the side of the British could forestall such a scenario. In March 1917, the US ambassador in London warned Wilson that "the imminent crisis" constituted a grave menace for Morgan and that "a declaration of war on Germany was probably the only way to maintain an excellent commercial situation and to prevent a panic." Naturally, Morgan and the bank's influential circle of friends likewise started to lobby in favour of entry into the war. A few weeks later, in early April 1917, the United States did declare war on the Reich, and so Wall Street had achieved its goal. "Money talks," says an American proverb; in 1917, money talked and President Wilson listened.

Wilson's radical critics were convinced, writes Adam Hochschild, that "the real reason the US was fighting for an Allied victory was to ensure that massive American war loans to Britain and France would be paid back." And by this decision, adds Niall Ferguson, Wilson saved not only Britain and the Entente in general, he also "bailed out" the House of Morgan. The nasty reality of German submarine warfare was invoked to camouflage this indecent truth. Henceforth, Morgan was to make even more money via the sale of war bonds, euphemistically referred to as "Liberty bonds," whose aggregate value would rise to $21 billion by June 1919, when the Versailles Treaty officially put an end to the war.[11]

In contrast to the country's industrial and financial elite, the American people never displayed the slightest enthusiasm for the war. American blacks, in particular, "hesitated to give their support to a project they considered hypocritical." One of them, a resident of the New York district of Harlem, declared that the Germans had never done anything wrong to him, and if they had done so, he forgave them. Alluding to Wilson's slogan to the effect that America went to war for the sake of democracy, some Afro-American leaders asked him publicly "to start by introducing democracy into America itself." Precious few volunteers signed up to go serve as cannon fodder on the other side of the Atlantic. The authorities were hoping for one million volunteers, but only 73,000 men responded to the call. On May 18, a law was therefore passed, the *Selective Service* (or *Selective Draft*) *Act*, which introduced a selective system of compulsory military service, the "draft", making it possible to recruit the required number of soldiers. But the draft faced much opposition, and more than 330,000 men were classified as draft evaders.

It is not surprising that members of the upper classes as well as skilled workers, whose presence in the factories was indispensable, remained mostly exempt from the draft. It was primarily the poor who were targeted because they were considered redundant. As in the case of the armies of the other belligerent countries, ordinary American soldiers came overwhelmingly from the lower classes of the population; they were mostly blacks, recently arrived immigrants, illiterates, and other people with little or no education. Afro-Americans were called up in large numbers, but they were mostly drafted into separate work battalions so that white soldiers would not have to consider them as their equals. In their segregated units the blacks received clothing, food, and accommodation of inferior quality. Of the total of 370,000 Afro-Americans who served in the army, 200,000 went to Europe, but only 40,000 of them received weapons and were permitted to join one of the two black combat divisions. Thus was scraped together an army that presumably went to war to fight for democracy.[12]

That America was going on a crusade for the benefit of democracy and/ or to end all wars is what Wilson wanted the American people and the rest of the world to believe. In order to achieve this aim, an enormous propaganda machine was set up, which would make use of press articles, speakers, Hollywood productions, etc., to convey the Wilsonian message to American households. The headquarters of this machine was the euphemistically named Committee on Public Information (CPI, headed by the presumably "progressive" journalist George Creel). The objective was to make Americans accept and even applaud a war they did not want and from which they would not derive any benefits, but for which they would pay a high price with their blood, their sweat, and their money; in other words, to "fabricate the public's approval or at least agreement." A collaborator of Creel, the journalist Walter Lippmann, called this the "manufacture of consent" — a term that would later be echoed by Noam Chomsky. What needed to be manufactured from scratch, so to speak, was an anti-German sentiment in the American population. It was done by following the example set by the British, that is, by atrocity-mongering, especially by a shameless exaggeration of the atrocities committed by the Germans in 1914 in Belgium.

Creel and his team did an excellent job and the country soon witnessed the blossoming of a veritable anti-German hysteria. Sauerkraut, which was a popular dish in the US at the time, was rebaptized "freedom cabbage," and the disease known as German measles became "liberty measles." Hollywood was persuaded to crank out a collection of propaganda films, for example a blockbuster with the unsubtle title *The Kaiser, the Beast of Berlin*. (Later, other enemies of the US, such as Saddam Hussein and Colonel Kaddafi, would be demonized in the same fashion.) More serious was the fact that Americans of German origin were obliged to wear a distinctive yellow sign and often had their property confiscated, a fate that would later befall the Jews in Nazi Germany.[13] The churches also made propaganda for the war. The Protestant churches, in particular, claimed that the conflict was a "crusade" against imperial Germany. The Catholic Church revealed itself to be slightly less enthusiastic, because the Vatican discreetly sympathized with the Central Powers, especially with the Empire of the Habsburgs, and it did not want to offend the numerous Catholic Americans of Irish and German origin, who supported the Berlin-Vienna axis.[14]

There was yet another reason why the American elite longed for war in 1917. Like the European elites in 1914, the US elite in 1917 was convinced that a war would consolidate its power and prestige, halt and possibly even roll back the trend toward democracy, and finally, liquidate the danger of revolutionary change. Indeed, during the years preceding 1914 the nation's elite had been traumatized by grave social tensions, numerous strikes, and the apparently irresistible rise of the Socialist Party and of the militant trade union IWW. This agitation culminated in April 1914 in the so-called "Ludlow Massacre." A camp of strikers in one of the Rockefellers' coal mines in Ludlow, Colorado, was attacked by troops and more than twenty persons were killed, including wives and children of the strikers. The entire country was up in arms, and in Denver an army unit even refused to intervene against the strikers.

Fortunately, the public's attention would soon be diverted by the fact that President Wilson suddenly found it necessary — on a ludicrous pretext — to shell the Mexican seaport of Vera Cruz and to wage a mini-war against this neighbouring country, where a revolution happened to be taking place. The American historian Howard Zinn feels that this was not a coincidence. He suggests that "patriotic fervor and the military spirit [served to] cover up class struggle," that "guns [were supposed to] divert attention" and that focus on "an external enemy" might "create some national consensus" at home; he concludes that the aggression against Mexico was "an instinctual response of the system for its own survival, to create a unity of fighting purpose among a people torn by internal conflict."[15] The war against Mexico may also be considered to be a class struggle. It was in fact a conflict between two "classes" of countries. It was a conflict that reflected the oppression and exploitation of a poor and powerless country by a powerful and rich country.

Wilson's declaration of war on Germany may similarly be viewed as a stratagem to preserve social peace at home by means of war abroad. Wilson certainly did not opt for war solely for this reason, but he eagerly took advantage of the opportunity offered by the war to repress all forms of radicalism in word and deed — to the advantage of the nation's elite. Wilson, a "democrat" only in the sense that he belonged to the Democratic Party, accomplished this objective in a most undemocratic fashion, namely by awarding himself all sorts of exceptional powers that enabled him to "legally" violate the democratic rights of Americans, and to do so with impunity. May 1917 witnessed the promulgation of the draconian *Espionage Act*, a law that officially purported to combat German espionage, and in 1918 Congress would provide the president with even greater special powers by means of the *Sedition Act*. These laws would remain on the statutes until the summer of 1921, that is, until the United States signed a peace treaty with Germany. Some historians have described these laws as "the country's most repressive legislation" and as "quasi-totalitarian measures." The government was henceforth free to censor, close down periodicals, and arrest and incarcerate people *ad libitum*, on the pretext that the country was at war against a particularly vicious enemy who disposed of all sorts of spies and agents within the US. Those who opposed the war were deemed to oppose America; in other words, to be "un-American." Pacifism and its twin, socialism, were viewed as enemies of "Americanism."

These laws obviously aimed to scare the American people, to motivate them in favour of the war, and to repress antiwar protests, obstruction of the draft, and doubts about the righteousness of the war. Under this legislation, it became a criminal offence to speak in "disloyal" or other negative or condescending terms of the nation's government, flag, or army. It was now risky not to agree with the policies of the Wilson administration. Voicing a moderate criticism of his war, even in the privacy of one's home, might lead to imprisonment. (The *Espionage Act* was to be amended repeatedly after the war, but it was never totally abolished; whistleblower Chelsea [born Bradley] Manning was indicted on the basis of military codes that are themselves based at least in part on this law.)[16]

During the First World War, more than 2,500 Americans were persecuted on the basis of these draconian laws, and about one hundred were convicted and condemned to sentences of ten to twenty years in prison. This is not a large number in comparison to the country's total population, but it is important to consider that the fear of persecution caused Americans to stop thinking and expressing critical thoughts and to adopt instead an unthinking conformism — and this in a country where rugged individual-ism had always been glorified. Countless journalists thus abandoned their earlier "muckraking" practices in favour of autocensorship and a bland but safe regurgitation of government announcements. Too many of America's citizens, previously known to be critically inclined, adopted the habit of swallowing, hook, line, and sinker, whatever their leaders told them and of unthinkingly following whatever orders arrived from above.

The repressive legislation was used selectively, first and foremost against radicals and dissidents of the lower classes, America's own "*classes dan-gereuses*"; in particular Afro-Americans and Jews. But the radicals and dis-sidents *par excellence* were the American socialists, then still numerous and militant, who pursued more or less revolutionary democratic reforms and who were opposed to the war. Like their reformist comrades in Europe, some US socialists revealed themselves to be partisans of the war, but the majority of America's socialists were convinced pacifists, and for this they would pay a heavy price. Their figurehead, Eugene Debs, openly spoke out against the war and encouraged the rank-and-file to follow his example. In June 1918, he would be thrown into prison on the basis of the *Espionage Act*, and the same fate befell hundreds of other socialists who were found guilty of treason, incitement to rebellion, espionage, use of violence, etc.

The big trade unions, for example the American Federation of Labor (AFL), were traditionally allies of Wilson's Democratic Party, and Wilson defended their interests, at least to a certain point, in exchange for their support. Not surprisingly, in 1917 they supported his entry into the war, just as the European unions had supported their governments when they went to war in 1914. The famous union leader Samuel Gompers turned out to be a particularly useful ally to Wilson, and he collaborated closely with Creel and his Commission of Public Information. One trade union failed to warm up to Wilson and his war, however, namely the radical and even revolutionary IWW. Its leader, "Big Bill" Haywood, would be thrown in jail, just like Debs, for daring to criticize the war. The IWW had been a thorn in the side of the US establishment for a long time, so the latter took advan-tage of the war to destroy that nest of revolutionaries via physical attacks on its headquarters, confiscation of documents, arbitrary arrest of many of its leaders and their conviction on the basis of fabricated evidence, etc.[17]

In the US, as in Europe, socialism, or at least its radical, nonreform-ist version, was allied with pacifism. Most socialists were pacifists and a considerable percentage of the pacifists were socialists. But not all pacifists were socialists; there were also countless bourgeois pacifists with political convictions that may be described as progressive or, as they also say in the US, "liberal." Among these bourgeois pacifists were courageous people who openly expressed their opposition to Wilson's war, and in many cases they paid dearly for this, for example by losing their jobs or even their seats in the legislative assembly of a state. Paul Jones, an Episcopalian bishop from Utah, was divested of his high ecclesiastical function because he spoke out against the war. And in the universities, which revealed themselves to be "homes of intolerance," the highly touted academic freedom was de facto suppressed for the duration of the war, and pacifist professors were system-atically removed from their chairs.[18]

The US is supposed to be the land of free enterprise, which means that the state believes, at least in theory, in the benefits of the traditional lib-eral laissez-faire approach and therefore intervenes as little as possible in economic and social life, allowing the private sector to "do its thing." In the context of America's entry into the war, this implied that the repression of pacifists, socialists, union leaders, etc., was "privatized," that is, turned over to individuals and groups favouring the war, and in general these were people who were simultaneously antidemocratic, antisocialist, anti-Semitic, and "anti-Hamitic" (i.e., hostile to blacks) and presented themselves as champions of "Americanism." Prominent among these groups were the American Patriotic League, the Patriotic Order of Sons of America, and the Knights of Liberty, a branch of the Ku Klux Klan. The methods used by these "vigilantes" included denunciations, beatings, tarring and feather-ing, painting houses of pacifists yellow, and lynchings. In particular, these vigilantes targeted "Wobblies" — members of the IWW; one of its leaders, Frank Little, was lynched in Montana in August 1917.[19]

On the western side of the Atlantic Ocean too, a kind of twin war broke out in 1917, consisting of a "vertical" war in which the US as a country confronted another country, Germany, but also a "horizontal" war in which two classes of American society — the elite and the rest of the popu-lation — clashed with each other. In the latter conflict, the elite, directed by Wilson, immediately went on the offensive, namely via repressive laws as well as "vigilantism," and thus it pushed back the plebeian forces much as the Germans had pushed back the French and the British in 1914. But, as in 1914, that early success did not bring the conflict to an end, and we will later see how it developed during the rest of the war. As for the "vertical" war against Germany, the US elite appeared to be in less of a hurry: it would take quite some time, namely until early 1918, before American troops showed up in significant numbers on the western front and started to make their presence felt.

CHAPTER 26

REVOLUTION IN RUSSIA, ON THE WAY TO REVOLUTIONS IN ASIA

In Russia, in early 1917, war weariness and discontent, and hostility toward the czarist regime, reach unprecedented heights. In March, crowds demonstrate in front of the Winter Palace in Petrograd, and the Czar has to abdicate. But a new government, led by Kerensky, continues the war against the will of the overwhelming majority of the population. Lenin and the Bolsheviks, who promote immediate peace as well as profound changes, thus obtain the support they need to come to power during a new revolutionary wave, the October Revolution. On the banks of the Neva River, the Great War thus engenders an event that will truly shake the world . . .

From Russia, a British nurse who worked there reported in February 1917 that the population of the capital, Petrograd, was sick and tired of the war and extremely unhappy. There was talk of riots, sabotage, strikes, inflation, and hunger, and food riots had broken out. The people hated the war, she wrote, and were merciless in their criticism of the authorities, including the czar himself. "So yes, it is a bad winter," was her conclusion.[1] One of the biggest problems was the fact that the cities were not sufficiently supplied with food, resulting in shortages and sky-high prices. The price of food had already doubled between 1914 and 1916, and in 1917 it was three times as high as in 1914. Wages had simultaneously decreased, and in 1917 they only amounted to 50 per cent of the level of 1913. Russia's civilians were hungry, and very disgruntled.[2]

Discontent was also very high among the soldiers. They had already made too many sacrifices, they had enough of the war, and they preferred fraternizing with the Germans and Austro-Hungarians, rather than confronting them in yet another absurd offensive. It was especially among troops that had been earmarked for attacks that the fall of 1916 witnessed numerous cases of desertion and voluntary surrender to the enemy, as well as cases of insubordination and even real mutinies. By early 1917 the Russian army, czarism's "main prop," had become unable to pursue the war, as the soldiers, who had suffered staggering losses — approximately five million killed and wounded since 1914! — were exhausted and rebellious; they wanted peace at any price; they wanted to return home. The soldiers sympathized and collaborated with like-minded civilians, especially the peasants, the workers, and the petty bourgeois. In early 1917, writes Arno Mayer, "the strains of protracted warfare . . . shook and cracked the foundations of the embattled old order, which had been its incubator," and in Russia this would cause "the most unreconstructed of the old regimes [to come] crashing down."[3]

This situation brought forth a revolution in Petrograd. It took place from February 23 to 27, at least according to the ancient Julian calendar that was still in use in Russia at the time; between March 8 and 12 according to the newer Gregorian calendar. (Russia would switch to the Gregorian calendar after the October Revolution.) It started with antiwar demonstrations by civilians and soldiers. Revolutionary slogans were shouted, the *"Internationale"* was sung, and two hundred thousand workers went on strike in the munitions factories. The troops that were ordered to intervene mutinied, joined the demonstrators, and occupied government buildings. Countless officers were shot by their own men. This reflected the hatred felt by most ordinary soldiers, who were mostly peasants, toward their superiors, who were overwhelmingly gentlemen of the upper classes and therefore symbols of the established order that was deemed to be responsible for the war and its misery.[4] An officer visiting Petrograd in March described the events in the Hotel Astoria, "where many of the higher-ranking officers and their families were staying and someone . . . had fired out on passing demonstrators":

The demonstrators had responded with machine-gun fire, after which armed men had stormed the lobby and heavy fighting had broken out amid the crystal chandeliers and mirrored walls. Many officers had been shot or bayoneted to death and the hotel's wine cellar had been looted.

Later on, that same officer had to have himself elected officer by a soldiers' committee of his regiment. He was hardly enchanted with this democratic practice, but considered himself lucky, because in many other units officers were not only not approved that way by their subordinates but some were even killed.[5]

The czar felt obliged to abdicate, and a provisional government took over the reins of power. It was a coalition consisting essentially of bourgeois liberals as well as socialist partisans of democratic reforms. A moderate, in other words reformist, socialist, Alexander Kerensky, became the head of this government. And in the space of very little time a number of major democratic reforms were introduced; for example, the separation of Church and state. It was the prospect of precisely these kind of changes that the Russian elite had hoped to see snuffed out once and for all by the war. It was even judged indispensable to introduce universal suffrage, something that did not even exist yet in Britain.[6] By means of these measures, the reformers hoped to bring the explosive situation under control, but in vain.

The problem was that the Russian civilians and soldiers not only wanted to be rid of the czarist elite that had unleashed the war, but also of the war itself. However, the provisional government decided to continue to wage war on the side of the French and British allies, and in June 1917 Kerensky even ordered a new offensive. The direction of the operations was entrusted to a new commander-in-chief, General Lavr Kornilov. The latter believed that he could restore order in the army by enforcing an iron discipline, and he ordered his officers to be severe vis-à-vis their subordinates and to execute deserters on the spot. But the soldiers proved to be recalcitrant, and deserted or surrendered to the enemy in unprecedentedly large numbers. Between January and August 1917, at least seven hundred thousand Russians deserted! And countless officers who attempted to implement Kornilov's instructions were assassinated by their men. In the meantime, the soldiers had developed the habit of establishing committees, known as "soviets," in which they collectively discussed their problems and took decisions; for example, the decision not to obey orders and not to attack. And the soviets increasingly elected their officers, instead of accepting those appointed by the higher authorities.

Kornilov not only wanted to pursue a war loathed by the ordinary soldiers, but he also revealed himself to be a champion of the old order, someone who was determined to undo the reforms that had just been introduced. However, the war had "pauperized" and traumatized the Russian soldiers, overwhelmingly peasants and workers, to such an extent that these were now extremely eager to obtain nothing less than far-reaching political, social, and economic changes. Kornilov was a rabid counterrevolutionary (or "reactionary"), who disapproved of any kind of reforms, while the great majority of the soldiers and countless civilians longed for revolutionary, or at least very radical, change. In September 1917, Kornilov, disgruntled by Kerensky's reforms, attempted a coup d'état, hoping to restore Russia's *ancien régime*. This caused him to be sacked and imprisoned, but he managed to escape; he would later fight the Bolsheviks, and be killed by them, in the Civil War.

If this Civil War would be extremely brutal, this was due first and foremost to the fact that it was a child of the Great War, which was itself the most brutal war in the history of mankind. Millions of Russians had fought in this war, millions had perished in it or had been wounded, and almost all the "actors" of the Russian Revolution and of the Civil War that followed it had experienced the Great War with its unprecedented atrocities and had been brutalized in the process. In 1917, two million armed deserters were roaming the country, as well as huge numbers of fierce soldiers who for years had had to kill in order not to be killed. With this mentality, they now attacked each other instead of Germans. All this is brilliantly described in a book by Arno Mayer, *The Furies*.[7]

The military and political leaders who had wanted to keep Russia in the war, whether reformists such as Kerensky or reactionaries like Kornilov, enjoyed less and less support from a population that wanted peace at any price and as soon as possible. Conversely, the civilian and military leaders who enjoyed increasing popularity were those who favoured peace via an immediate cessation of the hostilities, to be followed by negotiations aimed at the conclusion of a peace treaty acceptable for all sides. It is not a coincidence that it was precisely, and even only, the most revolutionary political forces in the Russian political arena, namely the Bolsheviks, who led this movement, under Lenin. The latter had returned from exile in Switzerland in April 1917; he had been allowed to travel by way of Germany and German-occupied territories, which allowed Kornilov and others to falsely denounce him as a German agent. As for the rivals of the Bolsheviks in the socialist camp, the Mensheviks, they supported the provisional government and favoured continuation of the war. And so the Bolsheviks, that is, the only political group unconditionally opposed to the war and favourable to peace, enjoyed a rapidly growing popularity among soldiers and civilians. It also helped that they were partisans of popular radical democratic reforms such as redistribution of land in favour of the peasants (and to the disadvantage of the landowning nobility), the eight-hour day, etc. Their ranks swelled spectacularly from barely 20,000 in March to 260,000 in October. It was this massive popular support, combined with the undeniable organizational talent of Lenin, that made it possible for him and his comrades to come to power in what was to become known as the 1917 October Revolution.[8] (According to the Gregorian calendar, this event took place in the night of November 6 to 7, and for this reason the October Revolution was later commemorated in November.)

Lenin immediately undertook whatever was required to provide the Russian people with the peace they craved. Already in early November — the end of October according to the old calendar — he issued a "declaration of peace" in which he invited the governments of all belligerent countries to start peace negotiations immediately. This declaration made a great impression on the war-weary peoples, and the American president, Wilson, found it necessary to respond with his own peace program, the famous "Fourteen Points," which were presented to the world on January 8, 1918. In this document, Wilson tried to make it appear that the Entente, or at least the United States, fought only for democracy and justice. However, the French and British leaders failed to be seduced by his rhetoric, because they were determined to do whatever was necessary to win the war and reap the benefits they expected to flow from victory.

The October Revolution was not the result of a conspiracy or a coup d'état, as many historians have presented things. And this revolution was not the exclusive handiwork of Lenin, as Churchill implied when he stated that it would have been better if Lenin had never been born. In Russia, revolution had been in the air for years when the war broke out in 1914; the war created the conditions that made the revolution possible in February/March 1917, and during the summer and fall of 1917 a new revolution became inevitable. The revolution of February/March of that year had not brought what the overwhelming majority of Russians longed for, namely peace and profound political and social change. Moreover, even the important but still relatively modest democratic achievements of the first half of the year 1917 risked being lost on account of the hopelessly reactionary attitude of military and political leaders such as Kornilov. Thus it cannot be claimed that Lenin and his comrades "made" or "created" the revolution. What can be said is that they saved the revolution by taking over its leadership and determining its further course — an effort in which they enjoyed the support of the majority of the population.[9]

London, Paris, and Washington observed the events in Russia with concern and horror. In those Western capitals, the authorities — still almost exclusively members of the elite and personalities of whom we suppose too readily, but wrongly, that they were democrats — were not very happy with the collapse of the authoritarian czarist regime and with the democratic reforms introduced by Kerensky's provisional government. And they found it abominable that Lenin and his fellow Bolsheviks aimed to *revolutionize* Russia; in other words, that they wanted to democratize the country radically, not only politically but also economically, to the disadvantage of the aristocratic large landowners as well as of the bourgeois industrialists and bankers, the capitalists; that is, of people like themselves.

Moreover, the leaders in London, Paris, and Washington were simply horrified that the Bolsheviks wanted Russia to exit the war. The fact that the great majority of the Russian population supported Lenin because it wanted peace and political as well as economic changes, was of no importance. It is therefore not surprising that, in 1917, the gentlemen ensconced in the Allied halls of power and military headquarters were cheering for Kornilov and that they were sorely disappointed when his reactionary coup d'état failed miserably. It is an absurdity of history, or rather of historiography, or at least of Western historiography, that Lenin, who gave the Russian people the peace and the revolutionary changes wanted by the majority of that people, is usually portrayed as a "dictator," while Western statesmen like Churchill, who wanted to keep the Russians in the war against their will and consequently supported reactionary elements such as Kornilov, are lionized as wonderful democrats.

The handful of Western war correspondents that was present in Russia acknowledged that the Bolsheviks enjoyed massive popular support. But the big newspapers that functioned as mouthpieces of the elite — such as *The Times* — denigrated the Bolsheviks from the very start as fools, criminals, thieves, assassins, and/or blasphemers. "The remedy for Bolshevism," *The Times* proclaimed, "is bullets."[10] The British elite, in particular, displayed great aversion to Bolshevism. Churchill explained that the Bolsheviks were "terrifying baboons" who posed a threat to civilization and that Bolshevism was "a baby that needed to be strangled in its cradle."[11] And the elite added deeds to its words. Britain's Secret Intelligence Service (SIS) sent agents to Russia to support adversaries of Bolshevism like Kornilov and, if possible, to assassinate Lenin; one of them was the writer William Somerset Maugham. Thus arguably began, in the midst of the Great War, the conflict that would later be known as the "Cold War." The Western elite's hatred of Bolshevism flared up even more when Russia's new leaders published the secret agreements that had been concluded by the members of the Entente, such as the Sykes-Picot Agreement with respect to the Middle East. There it was clearly spelled out that the Allies' war aims had nothing to do with democracy or justice but were of a blatantly imperialist nature. The entire world thus learned, for example, that Paris, London, and St. Petersburg had schemed to divide the Ottoman Empire and appropriate its juiciest morsels. The Western elite was also disgusted that the Bolsheviks kept the promises they had made to the Russian people by negotiating an armistice with the Germans. In addition, Lenin and his associates displayed their immorality, at least from the perspective of the elite in London, etc., by repudiating the debts to French and British suppliers, contracted by the czarist government when purchasing all sorts of merchandise; mostly weapons, but also great quantities of champagne. Above all, however, the Bolsheviks were despised because they were held responsible for the kind of social revolution whose spectre had terrorized the elites of all of Europe during the years before 1914; the type of social revolution, in fact, that the Great War was supposed to have chased away forever. This revolution had not only raised its head in Russia, but this revolutionary example also appeared likely to infect other countries. From the viewpoint of the elites of France, Britain, etc., the Russian Revolution henceforth actually constituted an even greater threat to the established order than the German enemy did. There was yet another important reason why the Western elites execrated Bolshevism. Lenin and his companions openly proclaimed their determination to work for the emancipation of all oppressed people, not only the lower classes in Europe itself, but also the colonial peoples of Africa, India, etc.; that is, the millions of black, yellow, and other coloured folks whom their white masters viewed with suspicion and fear. The Bolsheviks made no secret of their solidarity with the oppressed colonial peoples, something that Europe's prewar socialists had never done. Their own successful revolution provided inspiration for the struggle for independence and democratic change in the colonies, and Russia's new rulers promised to support this struggle.

Europe's elite, exemplified by personalities like Churchill who looked down on coloured people and were very much committed to retain their colonial possessions, were horrified. The fact that the Bolsheviks took up the cause not only of the soldiers, peasants, workers, and other socially "underprivileged" elements within their own country and in all of Europe, but also of the supposedly inferior "races" all over the world, engendered within Western elitist circles the Social-Darwinist myth that the emergence of the Bolsheviks and the outbreak of "their" revolution was itself a question of race, a reflection of race conflict. Lenin and the Bolsheviks, it was claimed, were Jews (and/or Mongols, or members of some other presumably inferior race) who, motivated by pure envy or hatred, sought to subvert, in their own country and in the entire world, the perfectly fine established order created by racially as well as socially superior people, an order that reflected the presumably natural hierarchy of individuals and of peoples. The fact that there were quite a few Jews among the Bolsheviks — if only because Jews, oppressed by czarism, had much to gain from revolutionary change in Russia — gave birth to the myth of "Judeo-Bolshevism." This is

the idea that the Russian Revolution was a stratagem concocted by the supposedly inferior Jews to combat the allegedly superior "Aryans" and their
Christian faith as well as political and social-economic established order. It
is in those terms that leading German personalities saw things; for example,
General Wilhelm Groener, who accused the Jews of "pulling the strings"
behind the scenes of the Russian Revolution. Churchill was another early
apostle of this anti-Semitic as well as anti-Bolshevik gospel. In 1919, in the
House of Commons, he alluded to the considerable number of Jews among
the Bolsheviks and averred that in 1917 the Germans, by allowing Lenin to
transit the Reich, had sent to St. Petersburg "a phial containing a culture
of typhoid or cholera," thus hoping to destroy the Christian religion in
Russia. (And in the summer of 1918 the British would have airplanes drop
pamphlets in Russia, in which the Bolsheviks were denigrated as a dangerous bunch of Jews.) The myth of Judeo-Bolshevism was to be propagated
in the United States by Henry Ford, who wrote a rabidly anti-Semitic book
entitled *The International Jew*, and in Germany by a certain Adolf Hitler.
"The process of identifying Judaism as a subversive virus," writes Domenico
Losurdo, "culminated in Nazism," which condemned Judaism as the "ethnic and racial base of the revolutionary disease" and saw only one single
antidote against this disease: "the physical elimination of the Jews."[12]

It is impossible to know with certainty if Russia would have experienced
a revolution without the Great War. But it is very likely that this would have
been the case. Already in 1905, the country had been shaken by a revolution, and between 1905 and 1914 revolution had constantly been in the
air; one felt it coming, one expected it, and within and without Russia a lot
of people hoped for a revolution, because they perceived the existing czarist
order as an anachronism that was doomed to disappear. The Great War that
broke out in 1914 was unleashed by the European elite, and particularly the
Russian elite, in the hope that, with the aid of Mars, the seemingly inevitable revolution might yet be avoided. However, the Great War actually
engendered great revolutions, not only in Russia but later also in Germany.
The Great War, remarks Domenico Losurdo, "was supposed to serve as
antidote to revolution, but it paved the way to revolution."[13]

In Europe's belligerent countries, the war caused increasing misery, discontent, and pauperization, and a concomitant longing for revolutionary

change. This became crystal clear in the catastrophic year 1917, when a revolution did in fact break out in Russia. But the same kind of chain reaction occurred not only in Europe, but also in Europe's overseas possessions. The "mother countries" wanted their colonies to make a considerable contribution to the war effort, for example by coughing up all sorts of vital raw materials, of course, but also by supplying cheap manpower, not only workers, but also soldiers; in other words, what was wanted from the colonies was a plentiful dose of "blood, sweat, and tears."

We have already seen that in Africa tens of thousands of blacks had to serve as soldiers or as porters in order to help their white masters fight the colonial bosses of other Africans, and also that tens of thousands of North Africans and Senegalese were forced by the French to serve as cannon fodder on the western front. The French also (ab)used Indochinese, and particularly Vietnamese, often referred to at the time as "Annamites" or "Tonkinese," depending on their specific region of origin, either as soldiers or as (cheap) labourers. Hundreds of thousands of Africans (including Egyptians) and Indians were deported to Europe by the French and the British in order to fight or perform hard labour in a war that was really of no concern to them and from which they had absolutely nothing to gain. As had been the case since the abolition of slavery, the British recruited a type of forced labourers, known as coolies, not only in their own colonies, for instance India, Fiji, Mauritius, the Seychelles, South Africa, and some Caribbean islands, but also in nominally independent China. Between 1916 and 1918, approximately 140,000 Chinese would be transported to France and Belgium to slave away, mostly in the service of the British, others for the French and the Americans.

For a proverbial song, these labourers from distant lands had to perform hard, dirty, and dangerous work such as loading and unloading ships, build railway lines and — often in the immediate vicinity of the front — dig trenches, construct cemeteries, clear mines and unexploded shells, fill sandbags, carry wounded soldiers to hospitals, bury men and horses, and literally do the dirty laundry. (In 1918, Barthas stayed in a hospital where "the dirty work was done by Annamites," for example, "emptying the spittoons and cleaning the latrines.") These semi- or quasi-slaves normally worked ten hours per day, seven days per week, and were very poorly paid, normally one franc daily. They were provided with poor clothes and shoes and were generally subjected to "deplorable material and human conditions," as they were accommodated in tents or primitive huts in closed camps, located far away from inhabited centres. The authorities did not want them to have contact with civilians. The main reason for this was that contact with women and the concomitant risk of "racial pollution" had to be avoided. It was also deemed necessary to prevent that social contacts with locals might cause these coloured people to imagine that they were the equals of white folks. For the same reasons, the Belgian authorities, exemplified by King Albert himself, did not want black soldiers from the Congo to come and fight on the Yser Front. It was felt that, in view of their supposed sexual appetite and potency, blacks might pose a threat to European women; and the fact of being allowed to fight with — and against — white soldiers might instill undesirable egalitarian ideas into the minds of blacks. Lucas Catherine, author of an interesting book on the First World War in Africa, quotes in this context the British journalist Edmund D. Morel, who expressed fear that "an African soldier who comes to Europe, has shot or bayoneted white men, and who has had sexual relations with white women, might lose his belief in the superiority of the whites." Similar racist phobias inspired the high command of the American army when it enjoined the French military authorities to ensure that Afro-American soldiers under their command had as little contact as possible with white women. The French were also asked not to praise these men too much for their excellent performances, because it was feared that they might get it in their head that they were as good as white folks.

The system of colonial forced labour made it possible to overcome the labour shortages that affected the belligerent countries in Europe, shortages caused by the mobilization of millions of men. At the same time, the wages, which might have risen considerably on account of the "play" of supply and demand, could thus be maintained at low levels. This was keenly realized by the European workers, whose socialist leaders had never made much of an effort to promote solidarity with non-European proletarians, and their contempt and even hatred for these Chinese, Indians, and other foreigners made the latter's miserable sojourn in Europe even more traumatic. (It was allegedly pressure by the trade unions that prevented the British authorities from importing Chinese coolies to work in Britain itself.) Thousands of Chinese lost their lives, not only on account of the hard labour and the poor food and hygiene, but also of diseases such as the Spanish Flu. But the exact number is unknown, probably because such statistics were considered unimportant. Some sources suggest that more than ten thousand men died. In any event, 850 Chinese rest in the British military cemetery of Nolette, in the village of Noyelles-sur-Mer, near Abbeville, which happens to be the biggest Chinese cemetery in France and indeed all of Europe.[14]

The colonies also provided assistance to the "mother country" in the form of soldiers. Hundreds of thousands of Africans fought for France. Depending on their country of origin, they were known as Senegalese or North African infantrymen (*tirailleurs sénégalais, tirailleurs nord-africains*) or simply as "Turcos." A large percentage of them were forcibly recruited to fight for their colonial bosses, and in Algeria, Mali, and elsewhere this provoked protests and even rebellions. A hundred and thirty-five thousand such men were made to fight in Europe, and approximately thirty thousand would be killed there. Regiments of colonial infantrymen were also constituted in Indochina and became known as *tirailleurs vietnamiens*. They enjoyed the honour of participating in the Battle of Verdun. According to some sources, France recruited a total of about eight hundred thousand men in its colonies, of whom seventy-one thousand died. Of all the colonial subjects of the British Empire, it was above all the Indians who had to serve as soldiers, in Mesopotamia and East Africa, for example, but also on the western front in Europe itself. In total, at least one million Indians thus served the British Empire, far from their homeland, during the Great War. Sixty-two thousand of their number lost their lives, and sixty-seven thousand were wounded. A grand total of 74,187 Indian soldiers perished on all fronts during the First World War.[15] A young nationalist poet, Sarojini Naidu, "India's nightingale," devoted a poem to them, "The Gift of India," which includes these moving lines:

> *Gathered like pearls in their alien graves,*
> *Silent they sleep by the Persian waves.*
> *Scattered like shells on Egyptian sands*
> *They lie with pale brow and brave, broken hands.*

They are strewn like blossoms blown down by chance
On the blood-brown meadows of Flanders and France.[16]

In 1914, India had greeted the advent of war with great enthusiasm,
much to the satisfaction of its British rulers. And Indian nationalists such as
Gandhi had contributed to the recruitment of volunteers in the (vain) hope
that, after the generally expected victory, the grateful British would thus
feel obliged to grant the country its independence, or at least autonomy.
However, during the war discontent with respect to British rule increased in
many ways and for many reasons. (And it did not help, of course, that the
Germans incited the Indians against their colonial masters.) The fact that
Britain, a self-proclaimed Christian nation, was at war against the Ottoman
Empire, whose sultan was simultaneously caliph, that is, theoretical leader
of all Muslims, induced many Muslim Indians to conclude that in this
jihad they found themselves on the wrong side, so that they should turn
their back on their Christian masters and rush to the aid of the Ottomans
— and Germans. Other Indians began to dream of independence because
the development of the war revealed the weakness of the British. More and
more Indians hoped that the British would soon have to grant their nation
some form of autonomy, of Home Rule. Some of their leaders, Gandhi, for
example, thought that it would prove possible to achieve certain nationalist objectives without resorting to violence, but others begged to differ and
felt that force would be needed to get rid of the British yoke. During the
war, and especially in 1915, it came to conspiracies, rebellions, and mutinies during which violence was most certainly used, and whose repression
involved even greater violence. This was not only the case in India itself,
but also in Singapore where, in March 1915, a mutiny broke out that ended
with the public execution of forty-seven members of the military who had
been involved.[17]

The spectre of a national revolution in the greatest of their colonial possessions henceforth haunted the British. They hoped to forestall such a
nightmare scenario by promulgating the *Defence of India Act* later in that
year, 1915, an act which permitted the authorities to drastically censor the
press and to lock up dissidents for long periods of time without any kind
of due process. This repressive measure was far from democratic, but we

should not forget that Britain itself was not yet a full-fledged democracy and that in Britain's overseas possessions dark-skinned denizens enjoyed little or no democratic rights. The very modest, embryonic democracy that existed at the time in the British Empire was a democracy for the white man, a *"Herrenvolk* democracy,"* as Domenico Losurdo has called it, alluding to the Nazis' term for "master race," reserved exclusively to the white population of dominions such as Canada. There was still no question of voting rights for the Canadian first nations (a.k.a. "Indians") or for the Australian aboriginals.

In 1917 the British authorities in India were deeply worried about "revolutionary conspiracies" that were reportedly being orchestrated. It was feared that a revolution in India might break out on account of support provided by the Germans, who were known to have been of assistance to the revolutionaries in Russia; for example, by facilitating Lenin's voyage from Switzerland to his homeland. However, developments in India were to be influenced far less by support provided by the soon-to-collapse German Reich, than by the example set by Bolshevik Russia. After the October Revolution, the Indian nationalists were increasingly inspired and encouraged by "the revolutionary cure being pioneered in Russia," as an expert in Indian history has formulated it.[18] Ultimately, it was primarily, though not exclusively, the dialectic of Indian revolutionary pressure and Britain's bloody repression that would force London to resign itself to India becoming an independent nation. For the nonviolence preached by Gandhi, on the other hand, British leaders such as Churchill had nothing but contempt, and via the path of nonviolence the destination of independence would never have been reached.[19]

In the French colony of Indochina too, the war witnessed an increase in discontent with respect to the authoritarian and parasitic colonial regime. The symptoms of this malaise included demonstrations, strikes, and — *inter alia* in the terrible year 1917 — armed rebellions and mutinies minor and major within the colonial police force, the *Garde indigène*, which were brutally repressed with the aid of locally recruited *tirailleurs*. Here too, the circumstance of war paved the way for a national revolution. The French promised reforms, and this made a good impression on some of their colonial subjects. But it was the news of the Russian Revolution, above anything else, that would galvanize workers and intellectuals and make them understand that only revolution would lead to independence. One such worker-cum-intellectual, Ho Chi Minh, would emerge as the leader of an independence movement that would clearly be inspired by the revolutionary events in Russia in general, and the Bolshevik example in particular.[20]

In China also, the war engendered revolutionary conditions. In that huge country, a revolution had already taken place in 1911, and it had metamorphosed the autocratic empire, China's *ancien régime*, into a fairly modern and embryonically democratic republic. But China continued to be abused and humiliated by the Western powers (and by Japan), which enjoyed all sorts of privileges in Shanghai and elsewhere; for example, city districts reserved exclusively for themselves, the famous "concessions," where signs loudly warned that "no dogs or Chinese [were] allowed." Countless Chinese found this situation increasingly intolerable, the more so since the war revealed the relative weakness of the great European powers as well as their internal divisions. It was thanks to unity among themselves that the great Western powers had been able to suppress the nationalist Boxer Rebellion of 1899–1901. Was division not an ideal opportunity for the Chinese nationalists to strike again, this time with much better prospects for success?

In this context, the experiences of the Chinese coolies in France played a rather important role. The government in Beijing had accepted this rather humiliating arrangement in order to curry the great powers' favour, hoping to achieve some diplomatic progress by doing so. In 1917, in order to ingratiate London and Paris, China thus even declared war on Germany. But this flattery was in vain, and at Versailles China's interests would be ignored. Massive numbers of students demonstrated in protest against this affront in Beijing on May 4, 1919, that is, even before the peace treaty was signed. China ultimately refused to sign the Treaty of Versailles. The protests of May 1919 gave birth to the "May 4 Movement," which demanded revolutionary changes. And revolutionary change meant change in the Marxist sense. Indeed, under the influence of the Russian Revolution, orthodox Marxism, that is, revolutionary socialism, became "increasingly attractive to those hungry for change."[21] Many Chinese became acquainted with the ideas of Karl Marx while working in France during the war, and there they also learned about the revolutionary events in Russia. They came to the conclusion a revolution was also possible in China, and that the combination of Marxist theory and Leninist, or Bolshevik, practice demonstrated how things should and could be done. (They drew essentially the same lessons as Ho Chi Minh was doing with respect to Vietnam.) After the war, the Chinese workers left France and returned to China. There they joined the country's new Communist Party (founded, not coincidentally, shortly after the signing of the Treaty of Versailles), and influenced leaders such as Zhou Enlai, Deng Xiaopeng, and even Mao Zedong.[22]

Under the leadership of Mao, China would not only experience a far-reaching domestic revolution, but would also revolutionize its role on the international scene, ridding itself once and for all of the yoke of the foreign powers. Until 1914, China had been a huge country, but a very poor one, whose people were exploited by the traditional local elite, above all the large landowners, China's "feudalists." China was also a particularly weak country, a kind of gigantic pie seemingly predestined to be carved up and divided among the great imperialist powers. If China is today a powerful country, whose population has achieved great progress in terms of well-being and continues to make good progress, even though much work remains to be done and many problems persist, it is thanks to a revolutionary movement that was conceived and born during, and because of, the Great War.

CHAPTER 27

MILITARIA 1918: GERMAN SPRING OFFENSIVE, ALLIED FINAL OFFENSIVE

On March 3, 1918, Germany and Russia sign a peace treaty in Brest-Litovsk. Shortly afterward, on the first day of spring, March 21, the western front witnesses the start of a huge German offensive, directed by Ludendorff. The Allies are in deep trouble, but during the summer they manage to turn the tide and launch a counteroffensive. The Germans are now fast running out of resources and capitulate on November 11 in the railway car that serves as headquarters of Marshal Foch, the Allied commander-in-chief, in the village of Rethondes, near Compiègne . . .

On December 15, 1917, approximately one month after Lenin had made his famous "declaration of peace," the Bolsheviks and the Central Powers concluded an armistice, and on the eastern front the guns fell silent. And on December 22 peace talks were started in the town of Brest-Litovsk, situated in what is now Belarus. (The town is now known as Brest, that is, minus the adjective *Litovsk*, meaning "Lithuanian.")

It was a somewhat bizarre gathering. On the side of the Central Powers, dominated by Germany, there appeared only arch-conservative, reactionary representatives of their country's elite, mostly generals, politicians, and diplomats of aristocratic origin. The Russian delegation, on the other hand, consisted exclusively of revolutionaries of proletarian or petty-bourgeois background, unconditional partisans of the revolution in their country who hoped, moreover, that revolutions would soon also break out in the countries of their interlocutors. The Russians wanted "peace without annexations or indemnities"; in other words, they sought an agreement by which nobody would have to give up territory or make reparation payments. However, the high command of the German army felt that their side was negotiating from a position of strength and formulated extraordinarily harsh demands. These reflected the grandiose imperialist ambitions the political and economic leaders of the Reich had entertained when they started the war in 1914 — a war they had hypocritically presented to the German people as a purely defensive war. These demands included major territorial gains in Eastern Europe, mostly territories that had been part of the Czarist Empire of which revolutionary Russia was the successor state. We have seen that with respect to Europe's eastern regions, including Russia, Germany's political, military and also economic leaders had displayed an enormous territorial appetite in 1914, and now, in early 1918, their representatives in Brest-Litovsk were convinced that they could finally realize these ambitions. But the Bolshevik negotiators, led by Trotsky, rejected the German proposals and quit the talks in protest on February 10, 1918. They explained that the situation amounted to "neither war, nor peace." The Central Powers responded by suspending the armistice, taking up arms again, and ordering their troops to penetrate deeper into Russian territory. Ukraine, Belarus, and the Baltic States were thus occupied in very little time. The Russians had no choice but to return to the negotiating table and ended up having to accept even less favourable conditions, including making considerable financial reparation payments. The Treaty of Brest-Litovsk was signed on March 3, 1918. Russia thus officially exited the Great War — to fall prey, shortly thereafter, to an equally terrible civil war.[1]

To Germany, this treaty offered the enormous advantage of no longer having to fight a war on two fronts. German troops could now be transferred from the eastern to the western front. This involved a total of forty-four divisions, that is, approximately a half-million men. For the very first time since the beginning of the war, the Germans enjoyed a numerical superiority on the western front. Even the arrival of American forces did not make a significant difference, since in early 1918 there were still only a hundred thousand "Yankees" in Europe, and they were inexperienced soldiers. On the western front, everybody now knew that a German offensive was about to be unleashed soon; the only question was when. Many French, British, Belgian, and Italian soldiers, already totally disgusted by the war, therefore feared that the worst was yet to come, now that they confronted virtually the entire German fighting force. Pessimism pervaded their ranks as the inevitable German offensive was coming nearer and an allied victory seemed less likely than ever before. The number of desertions and voluntary surrenders to the enemy increased dramatically. Convictions for attempted desertion or surrender multiplied; in the Belgian army, they rose from a total of 28 in the period from 1914 to 1917 to 190 in 1918, but they were rarely followed by executions. The repression was relatively lenient, writes de Schaepdrijver, because "in spite of all the hierarchy, the Belgian army was essentially a bourgeois army in which there reigned no merciless martial discipline," as in the armies with mostly aristocratic officers such as those of Germany and Britain. In spite of this pessimism, the great majority of the soldiers of the Belgian and other allied armies "carried on," certainly not on account of patriotic sentiments or pure heroism, but rather of "lackluster resignation," a mixture of a sense of duty and fatalism, "stubborn peasant loyalty," and, last but certainly not least, of "solidarity with their fellow soldiers," to avoid leaving their comrades in the lurch.[2] The soldiers hoped that, whatever its outcome might be, the looming German offensive would bring about an end to the war, so that they could finally go home, victorious or not. The song "When This Bloody War Is Over," a reflection of these sentiments, was extremely popular among the British soldiers at the time:

> When this bloody war is over
> Oh, how happy I will be;
> When I get my civvy clothes on
> No more soldiering for me.[3]

The tension also mounted on the side of the Germans, because they knew that time was working against them. Every day, in fact, more Americans were arriving to join their French and British brothers in arms. The Reich was lacking all sorts of products, including crucially important war materiel, so that they had to make do with *Ersatz*, that is, substitute products of poor quality. For example, in order to compensate for the dramatic shortage of fats, the carcasses of horses were shipped from the front to special factories in Germany. In those "carcass-processing plants" (*Kadaververwertungsanstalten*), the carcasses were transformed into glycerin, which could be used to make ammunition, candles, etc. As the German word *Kadaver* conjured up not only animal carcasses but also human corpses, a myth arose in 1917 among the allied soldiers to the effect that the Germans recycled the bodies of dead soldiers in special "corpse factories." It was a macabre comment on the fact that the war had turned out to be an *industrial* war, a kind of factory in which death was mass-produced, in which every day countless living human beings were transmuted into corpses. It is understandable that the Germans — like the British — did not want to see the unused "industrial" potential of dead horses go to waste. Indeed, during the war horses died by the hundreds of thousands. In 1914–1918, there was one horse for every three human combatants, and a total of eight million horses would be killed. The percentage of horses killed was even higher than the corresponding percentage of human combatants. France alone lost about one million animals, amounting to one third of its equine stock, and the result was a shortage that had nasty consequences for the nation's agriculture.[4]

Moreover, German civilians as well as soldiers were undernourished and hungry. They were so disgruntled that it was feared that they would follow Russia's revolutionary example. Already in the beginning of the year, Berlin and other big cities were the scenes of demonstrations and riots as well as strikes. Germany's Austro-Hungarian, Bulgarian, and Ottoman allies, moreover, were increasingly displaying alarming signs of war weariness. An offensive had to be launched as soon as possible in order to achieve the victory that, like a *deus ex machina*, would solve all the problems *in extremis* — or so it was hoped. However, in view of its extravagant demands vis-à-vis the Russians at Brest-Litovsk, the German high command had lost much precious time in Eastern Europe. And the occupation of a gargantuan territory in the European east required that approximately one million men be kept there. These forces would have been very useful for the purpose of compensating for the enormous losses that the offensive on the western front was certain to cause. Finally, on account of the devastation wrought by the war, the occupied regions of Eastern Europe were virtually useless to Germany as sources of raw materials and food that might have served to improve the material and mental condition of Germany's soldiers and civilians.[5]

The famous "spring offensive," the brainchild of Ludendorff, was code-named "Michael," referring to the archangel who slew Lucifer. The idea was that this would be the conclusive contest in which the German, nicknamed "Michael," as we have seen earlier, would defeat the Franco-British Satan. The attack was launched on the first day of the spring, on March 21, 1918, at 4:30 in the morning, after a mammoth artillery bombardment, a "storm of fire and steel," as the German front soldier Ernst Jünger later described it.[6] The "theatre" was a stretch of the front of about sixty kilometres in the same area where the Battle of the Somme had taken place in 1916. The attackers managed to break through the British lines and to make rapid progress. About ten days later they were already more than sixty kilometres from their starting positions. The British lost all the terrain they had conquered at such high cost in 1916, and they suffered huge casualties in the process, allegedly more than one hundred thousand men. On April 12, Haig gave his famous "backs-to-the-wall" order, prohibiting any further withdrawal, no matter how desperate the situation. Many Tommies who wanted to flee or surrender were shot by their officers. In March 1918, a colonel thus ordered the execution on the spot of no less than thirty-eight men of a group of about forty; he later proudly reported that "officers displaying courage and initiative" had to be able to do this kind of thing. Later in that spring as well as in the early summer of 1918, more German attacks followed against the British in Flanders and against the French along the Aisne River in the direction of Paris, and the results were always very similar: the Germans made impressive territorial gains, but the hoped-for big prize, total victory, kept eluding them. As they made progress and carved deep pockets in the Allied lines, the front line became longer, requiring the Germans' resources in manpower and materiel to be dispersed rather than concentrated, making their attacks less forceful, and their increasingly long flanks more vulnerable to Allied counterattacks. Their progress in the direction of Paris was finally halted during the famous "Second Battle of the Marne," also known as the Battle of Reims, between mid-July and early August 1918.[7]

However, it was not the genius of Haig or Foch or the grim determination of the British and French officers that put an end to the progress achieved by the Germans. Nor was it the fact that, beginning on March 26, 1918, all allied forces were placed under the command of one single chief, namely the French General Foch, although this clearly had its advantages.[8] It is more correct to say that the German progress petered out by itself. The German soldiers knew that "Michael" was the offensive of the last chance. The prospects for success of an offensive on the western front had never been so good since the start of the war in 1914, and they knew that the German army had committed all the resources at its disposal on a bet to achieve the offensive's objectives and thus to win the war. It was all or nothing, now or never. Paradoxically, the success of the attack was also responsible for its failure, at least partly. When the German soldiers overran British positions, they noticed that these were bursting with weapons and ammunition as well as stocks of food and drink that they themselves had not seen in years. The officers often tried in vain to incite their men to attack the next British or French line of trenches; the soldiers simply interrupted their advance to feast on canned meat, white bread, etc. Paul Fussell describes such a situation as follows:

> The successful attack ruin[ed] troops. In this way it [was]
> just like defeat . . . The spectacular German advance finally
> stopped largely for this reason: the attackers, deprived of the
> sight of "consumer goods" by years of efficient Allied blockade,
> slowed down and finally halted to get drunk, sleep it off,
> and peer about. The champagne cellars of the Marne proved
> especially tempting . . . By mid-summer it was apparent that
> the German army had destroyed itself by attacking successfully.

Fussell also quotes the report of a German officer who met soldiers returning from the conquered town of Albert:

> [They were] strange figures, which looked very little like soldiers, . . . making their way back out of the town. There were men . . . carrying a bottle of wine under their arm and another one open in their hand . . . Men staggering. Men who could hardly walk.[9]

The losses of momentum of the German offensive permitted the British and French to reorganize, shore up defences, and bring up reserves, many of them American soldiers, of whom more than half a million became available in the spring of 1918; since the end of March 1918, approximately a hundred thousand Yankees had been arriving in France every month. The Americans may not have been the finest soldiers, but they showed up wherever help was needed. That demoralized the Germans, who got the impression that the Allies disposed of unlimited reserves not only in food, weapons, and ammunition, in all sorts of war materiel, but also in men, in "human material." In the meantime, the German attackers themselves also suffered considerable losses: 230,000 men, allegedly, during the first two weeks of the offensive, and at least half a million, and possibly as many as a million, between March and July.[10] These losses, which could not be compensated for, inspired a famous poem by Bertolt Brecht, "Ballade vom toten Soldaten," "The Legend of the Dead Soldier," featuring these sarcastic verses:

Und als der Krieg im vierten Lenz	And when the war, in its fourth spring,
Keinen Ausblick auf Frieden bot	No longer offered any prospects of peace
Da zog der Soldat seine Konsequenz	The soldier drew the logical conclusion
Und starb den Heldentod.	And died a hero's death.[11]

How many more times did the Germans have to attack an allied position before the enemy would capitulate? How could one defeat an enemy who had such inexhaustible reserves of men and equipment?[12] Even the sight of the prisoners they bagged in huge numbers demoralized the Germans. These men looked well-fed and healthy. A Hungarian officer was very impressed when he first encountered American prisoners of war, and commented as follows:

> *Their amazingly good physical condition, the excellent quality*
> *of their uniforms, the heavy leather in their boots, belts*
> *and such, the confident look in their eyes even as prisoners,*
> *made me realise what four years of fighting had done to our*
> *troops.*[13]

However, it was yet another factor that played the most important, and possibly decisive, role in the failure of the German offensive in the spring and summer of 1918. If again and again the Allies succeeded in bringing up the reserves in men and materiel that were needed to slow down and eventually stop the German juggernaut, it was because they disposed of thousands of trucks to do the job. The French — who had already made good use of motorized vehicles earlier, for example taxis to transport troops to the battlefield of the Marne in 1914 and trucks to supply Verdun along *voie sacrée* in 1916 — produced massive numbers of excellent trucks, mostly models designed and built by Renault, a constructor who would produce more than nine thousand of them for the French army during the Great War. The British, who had started the war without one single truck, had fifty-six thousand of them in 1918. On the other hand, as in 1914, the Germans still transported their troops mostly by train, but many sectors of the front, for example the Somme battlefields, were hard to reach that way. In any event, in the immediate vicinity of the front, both sides would continue until the very end of the war to rely heavily on horse-drawn carts to transport equipment. But in this respect too, the Germans were disadvantaged, as they suffered from a serious shortage of draft horses as well as fodder, while the Allies were able to import large numbers of horses and robust mules from overseas, and especially from the US.[14]

The greater mobility of the Allies undoubtedly constituted a major factor in their success. Ludendorff would later declare that the triumph of his adversaries in 1918 had come down to a victory of French trucks over German trains. This triumph can also be similarly described as a victory of the rubber tires of the Allies' vehicles, produced by firms such as Michelin and Dunlop, over the steel wheels of German trains, produced by Krupp. Thus it can also be said that the victory of the Entente against the Central Powers was a victory of the economic system, and particularly the industry, of the Allies, against the economic system of Germany and Austria-Hungary, an economic system that found itself in great difficulty because of the British blockade. "The military and political defeat of Germany," writes the French historian Frédéric Rousseau, "is inseparable from its economic failure."[15] However, the economic superiority of the Allies clearly had a lot to do with the fact that the British and French — and even Belgians and Italians — made use of colonies from which they could fetch whatever they needed to win a modern, industrial war, including rubber, oil, and other raw materials. The Great War happened to be a war between imperialist rivals, in which the great prizes to be won were territories bursting with raw materials and cheap labour, the kind of things that would benefit a country's "national economy," more specifically its industry, and thus make that country more powerful. (In this context one should not underestimate the importance of colonial manpower: it was above all the coolies who repaired and maintained the roads — and even constructed new ones — that were used in the spring and summer of 1918 by the Allies to truck troops to wherever they were needed.)[16] It is therefore hardly a coincidence that the war would be won by the countries that were most richly endowed in this respect, namely the great industrial powers with the most colonies; in other words, that the biggest "imperialisms" — those of the British, the French, and the Americans — defeated a competing imperialism, that of Germany, admittedly an industrial superpower, but underprivileged with respect to colonial possessions. In view of this, it may seem amazing that it took four long years before Germany's defeat was a *fait accompli*. On the other hand, it is also obvious that the advantages of having colonies and therefore access to unlimited supplies of food for soldiers and civilians as well as rubber and similar raw materials could only reveal themselves in the long run, especially since in 1914 the war was not yet the titanic industrial contest which it would gradually reveal itself to be. In 1914, Germany still had a chance to win the war, but by 1918 that chance was already long gone. (Hitler and his generals would draw the conclusion that Germany, in order to win a second edition of the Great War, would have to win it fast, very fast, which is why they were to develop the concept of *Blitzkrieg*, "lightning-fast war," to be followed by *Blitzsieg*, "lightning-fast victory"; this formula worked against Poland and France in 1939–1940, but the spectacular failure of the *Blitzkrieg* in the Soviet Union in 1941 would doom Germany to fight a long, drawn-out war again, a war which, lacking sufficient raw materials such as oil and rubber again, it could not possibly win.)[17]

Rubber was not the only type of raw material the Allies had in abundance, while the Germans lacked it. Another one was oil, for which the increasingly motorized land armies — and rapidly expanding air forces — developed a great appetite. During their final offensive, in the fall of 1918, the Allies would consume 12,000 barrels (of 159 litres each) of oil daily. During a victory dinner on November 21, the British minister of foreign affairs, Lord Curzon, would declare, not without reason, that "the Allied cause had floated to victory upon a wave of oil," and a French senator was to proclaim that "oil had been the blood of victory." A considerable quantity of this oil came from the United States and was supplied by Standard Oil, a firm belonging to the Rockefellers, who made a lot of money in this type of business, just as Renault did by producing the gas-guzzling trucks. (Of all the oil imported by France in 1917, the United States furnished 82.6 per cent and Standard Oil alone 47 per cent; in 1918, the United States furnished 89.4 per cent of the oil imported by the French.) It was therefore only logical that the Allies acquired all sorts of modern, motorized, and oil-consuming war materiel. In 1918, the French had not only phenomenal quantities of trucks, but also a big gas-guzzling fleet of airplanes. And in that same year the French as well as the British also had a considerable number of automobiles equipped with machine guns or cannons, pioneered by the Belgian army in 1914, as well as tanks. The latter were no longer the lumbering, ineffective monsters that had first shown up at the front in 1916, but machines of excellent quality such as the light and mobile Renault FT "baby-tank," considered the "first modern tank in history." On the side of the Germans — whose supposedly brilliant commander-in-chief, Ludendorff, did not believe in the usefulness of tanks — the appearance of these monsters often provoked panic. If the Germans themselves had only very few trucks or tanks, it was also because they did not have sufficient oil for such vehicles — and for their planes; only Rumanian oil was available to them.[18]

The British blockade strangled Germany slowly but surely, and Ludendorff's spring offensive was for the Reich the very last opportunity to win the war. But in spite of spectacular initial successes, the Germans could not overcome the Allies. Sooner or later, the offensive was bound to run out of steam, and this happened in the summer of 1918, more specifically in early August. The Second Battle of the Marne finished at that time with a victory of the French, who admittedly benefited from considerable American aid. Symbolically, however, the day the tide turned was August 8. On that day, the French, British, Canadians, and Americans launched a counterattack and the Germans troops were pushed back systematically. Ludendorff would later describe August 8 as the blackest day in the history of the German army.

In the course of the summer of 1918, Germany's military situation became critical, not only because of the failure of Ludendorff's great offensive, but also because at that time the Reich's allies were likewise experiencing major difficulties. The Austrians, for example, had launched an offensive against the Italians along the Piave River. But on account of the British blockade they suffered from the same problems as the Germans, namely shortages of food and all sorts of materials, and even of horses. In the case of their offensive too, progress made initially soon ground to a halt. The Italians reorganized, counterattacked, and the famous Battle of the Piave, fought between June 15 and 23, 1918, ended with a withdrawal of the Austrians to the positions from which they had started their offensive. They had lost 150,000 men. Desertions began to multiply, and soldiers of the Czech, Croat, and other minorities of the Empire, in particular, increasingly refused to obey orders. The Austro-Hungarian army was barely able to continue the war. And so it was hardly a surprise that it would suffer a catastrophic defeat when, on October 24, 1918, exactly one year after the Battle of Caporetto, the Italians attacked and won a major battle at Vittorio Veneto. This battle ended on November 3 with the armistice of Villa Giusti, near Padua, which witnessed the capitulation of the Austro-Hungarians and the de facto dissolution of their army. The Habsburg Empire ceased to exist and broke up into a number of new states such as Czechoslovakia, officially founded on October 28. The Italian troops, meanwhile, proceeded to occupy all sorts of territories that had been assigned to their country by the 1915 London Treaty with Britain and France; for example Trento, South Tyrol, and Trieste. As far as Germany was concerned, the collapse of its principal ally contributed strongly to its own decision to throw in the towel.[19]

Another German ally, Bulgaria, had already given up earlier. The long war had considerably weakened that country's economy and undermined the morale of its soldiers as well as civilians. In the summer of 1918, riotous protests against the high cost of living and against the war — in which women played an active part — reflected the nation's deteriorating morale. After a defeat at the hands of French and Serbian troops in the Battle of Dobro Polje, on September 15, 1918, the Bulgarian army started to disintegrate and on September 29 an armistice was signed in Thessaloniki. The Bulgarian army had to withdraw from all Greek, Serbian, and Rumanian territory it had occupied during the war. For Berlin, this was yet another heavy blow that contributed to the decision to end the war. The Great War thus ended in some ways in the same Balkan Peninsula where it had started, as Lloyd George remarked. An official peace treaty between Bulgaria and the Allies would be signed on November 27, 1919, in Neuilly-sur-Seine.[20]

The majority of the German soldiers on the western front realized that the war was lost, they wanted to get it over and done with, and go home. And they did not hide their contempt for the political and military leaders who had unleashed the conflict and thus caused so much misery. And they were not willing to lose their lives for a lost cause. The German army began to disintegrate, discipline broke down, and the number of desertions and mass surrenders skyrocketed. Some German historians have described this sutation as a *Kampfstreik*, an undeclared "military strike" or "refusal to fight," a "refusal to carry on with the war."[21] Between mid-July 1918 and the armistice of November 11 of that year, 340,000 Germans surrendered or ran over to the enemy. (The Alsatian Dominik Richert was one of them.) In September 1918, a Tommy witnessed how German POWs laughed and applauded each time a new contingent of prisoners was brought in. Even elite soldiers capitulated in large numbers. Of the

German losses at that time, prisoners represented an unprecedented 70 per cent. The German soldiers now used all kinds of tricks to avoid going to the front, a practice that became known as *Drückebergerei*, "shirking." Many men who were transferred from Eastern Europe to the western front crossed into the neutral Netherlands in order to be able to await there the end of the war as internees. No less than 750,000 German soldiers allegedly deserted at that time; and just about as many were simply reported as "absent" from their unit. The number of deserters hanging around in the capital, Berlin, was estimated by the police to be in the tens of thousands. The epidemic of desertions, mass surrenders, and shirking mushroomed during August and September 1918, so much so that this state of affairs has been described as an "undeclared military strike." And that is certainly how the "front swine" themselves saw things. The soldiers who were leaving the front often insulted men that were marching in the opposite direction, calling them "strike breakers" and *Kriegsverlängerer*, "war prolongers"! The influence of the Russian Revolution in all this became obvious when, in October, the sailors stationed in the port of Kiel mutinied. They refused to obey orders — especially an absurd order for the fleet to undertake a suicidal sortie against the Royal Navy — and set up councils of soldiers and workers; in other words, Russian-style soviets. Similar councils soon emerged all over Germany.[22]

Under these circumstances, it amounted to a miracle that the Germans managed to put up an ordered and relatively effective resistance when their enemies launched a final offensive toward the end of the summer and in the fall of 1918. They had to withdraw, and did so, but slowly and in good order. Until the bitter end, the Great War thus remained the murderous enterprise it had been from the start. During the last five weeks of the war, half a million men were still killed or wounded. Even the very last day saw heavy casualties being inflicted on both sides. Some soldiers "fell" only minutes before the armistice went into effect on November 11 at 11 a.m. On November 10, British and Canadian troops arrived on the outskirts of the Belgian town of Mons, where in August 1914 the British forces had first faced the Germans in a battle. Late at night, a message reached the local commanders. In Rethondes, a hamlet in a forest near Compiègne, where General Foch, supremo of the allied armies, had installed his headquarters, an agreement had been reached with German emissaries to lay down the arms later that same day, namely at 11 a.m. The British poet May Wedderburn Cannan has saluted this long-awaited announcement in a poem entitled "The Armistice":

> *The news came through over the telephone:*
> *All the terms had been signed: the war was won*
> *And all the fighting and the agony,*
> *And all the labour of the years were done.*[23]

At Mons, however, the fighting and agony were not done yet. The men could have enjoyed a leisurely breakfast and waited until 11 before sauntering into the town. However, the Canadian commander, General Arthur Currie, gave the order to take Mons early in the morning, knowing very well that the Germans would resist and that blood would flow. "It was a proud thing," he was to explain later, "that we were able to finish the war there where we began it, and that we, the young [Canadian] whelps of the old [British] lion, were able to take the ground lost in 1914."

But his subordinates saw things quite differently. Two Canadian historians describe their reaction:

> *[They] openly questioned the need to advance any further . . .*
> *None of [them] wanted any part of the Mons show. They were*
> *all grumbling to beat hell. They knew the war was coming to*
> *an end and there was going to be an armistice. 'What the hell*
> *do we have to go any further for?' they grumbled . . . At the*
> *end of the day the men were furious about the losses."*

These losses included George Ellison and George Price, respectively the last Tommy and the last Canadian to "fall" in the Great War; they were killed within minutes before the arms were laid down. They rest in the British-German war cemetery of Saint-Symphorien, a few kilometres outside of Mons, together with John Parr, the very first British soldier to lose his life in the Great War. Hundreds of other British, Germans, and Canadians perished in and around Mons in the early stages and in that war's final minutes. However, the very last soldier to be killed in the Great War was an American of German origin, named Henry Gunther; he fell in the village of Chaumont-devant-Damvillers, situated to the north of Verdun, just one minute before the end.[24] On the last day of the Great War, November 11, 1918, all armies combined suffered 10,944 casualties on the western front, including 2,738 men killed. This was approximately twice the daily average of killed and wounded during 1914–1918. (It was also about 10 per cent more than the total casualties on D-Day, the first day of the landings in Normandy in June 1944.) This bloodshed could have been avoided if the French and allied commander-in-chief, Marshal Foch, had not refused to accept the German negotiators' request to declare a ceasefire as soon as the capitulation was signed in the night, rather than to wait until 11 a.m. In Mons, the disgruntled Canadian soldiers "were exhausted and just wanted a good meal, a hot shower, and a comfortable bed. They were glad the war was over, but for many it was not a cause for celebration because of the many friends they had lost . . ." There were no celebrations other than "some jumping around and things like that," a soldier reported; and it did not help that the commanders ordered a general inspection, causing the men to have to "stand out six hours in the cold rain." With respect to the final minutes of the Great War, a quaint anecdote deserves to be mentioned, even though it may be apocryphal. Shortly before 11 a.m, somewhere on the western front, a German started to fire his machine gun furiously. At precisely 11 he stopped, stood up, took off his helmet, took a bow, and walked quietly to the rear.[25]

CHAPTER 28
REVOLUTION, COUNTERREVOLUTION, AND REFORMS

The war that was supposed to be an antidote to revolution actually produces the revolution. The revolution is smothered in blood in Germany and Hungary, but succeeds in Russia in spite of domestic opposition and foreign intervention. And in many Western European countries revolution can be avoided only via the introduction of major political and social reforms, in other words, by escalating a democratization process that was supposed to have been halted or even rolled back by war . . .

In all belligerent countries, the four long years of war brought about a high degree of "pauperization" among soldiers and civilians, a situation ripe for revolution. But whether a revolution broke out or not depended very much on specific local conditions, such as the rigidity (or flexibility) displayed by the ruling elite and the revolutionary zeal of the socialists and trade unionists. Such factors also determined whether any revolution was successful or not, or if democratic reforms would be sufficient to displace revolutionary change. Let us examine briefly what happened in the principal countries.

On January 27, 1918, a high-ranking French civil servant noted in his diary that "the struggle between the people and their rulers" had produced "a new challenge," namely that

the people are demanding to know why their rulers are forcing
them to fight. It has taken four years for this legitimate desire
to come to the surface. It has already achieved its aim in
Russia. Now it is raising its voice in England. It is beginning
to break out in Austria. We do not know how strong it is in
Germany and France. But the war has entered a new phase: a
conflict between the shepherds and their flocks.[1]

In all the belligerent countries, the "flock" was indeed extremely war-weary, disgruntled, restless, and rebellious, causing the authorities to fear that the situation could degenerate into a real revolution — as in Russia the year before. In France, and especially in Paris, it was the numerous strikes that were a cause of great concern. They were generally short, but often involved violence, and in most cases the strikers achieved their demands. Many strikes were initiated by the unions, and the demands included not only higher wages but also official recognition of the unions and input in the management of firms. It was clearly labour's intention to launch a counteroffensive in the class war that had been waged since 1914, and to undo the gains employers had been able to make thanks to the war and the sacred union. In this context, heavy criticism was directed at the socialist Albert Thomas, a champion of the *union sacrée* and of wartime class collaboration, "a traitor who delivered the proletariat to the capitalists." The strikers also made no secret of their hatred for the war profiteers. They openly expressed themselves in favour of a revolution that was needed "to get rid, once and for all, of the capitalists and the militarists."

The revolutionary model that inspired most of the French strikers was not the Russian Revolution, however, but the French Revolution of 1789. The workers wanted "a new 89," a new edition of France's "Great Revolution." Thus they demonstrated that, in spite of everything, they remained loyal patriots; they were simultaneously revolutionaries and patriots in the Jacobin tradition of the French Republic. Their criticism of the war was contradictory. On the one hand, they declared that the capitalists of all countries were responsible for the war, were profiting from it, and caused it to drag on while "the proletarians had to bear its costs." On the other hand, they remained ready to contribute to the salvation of the fatherland in a war against Germany that was presumably purely defensive. The French (or at least Parisian) strikers of 1918 were *défensistes*, "defensists," and not "defeatists" like Lenin and the Bolsheviks in Russia. The predilection for the French Revolution of 1789 instead of the Russian Revolution of 1917 may also be understood in light of the fact that in the meantime the Bolsheviks had sat down at the negotiating table with the Germans, which opened sinister prospects for France and Russia's other allies. In spite of this, the French strikers were very restrained in their criticism with respect to the Bolsheviks.[2]

It is therefore hardly surprising that the start of the German spring offensive brought an end to the strikes that had shaken Paris during the first months of the year. The "defensist" workers did not want to jeopardize the defence of the fatherland. But the employers and the government took advantage of the opportunity to hit back. Numerous trade union leaders and radical socialists who had played an active role in the strikes were called to arms and shipped to the front, triggering a veritable "massacre [*hécatombe*] of militants." Some trade union leaders were arrested, censorship was reinforced, newspapers were shut down, public meetings prohibited, etc. On account of these measures, Clemenceau became the object of the hatred of the French workers, who cursed him as the "number-one cop [*flic*] in France," the "bastard" (*salaud*), the "assassin of the proletariat," etc.[3] The strikes gradually resumed, especially when the German offensive started to run out of steam. May witnessed a new wave of strikes in the capital, where some one hundred thousand workers laid down their tools between the thirteenth and the eighteenth of the month. This time, the demands included first and foremost higher wages, but also the eight-hour day, the "English week," and supplements for overtime, and in many cases the strikes were successful. Many strikes in Paris also featured strong pacifist notes, typified by slogans such as "War on the War!" and "Long Live Peace!" Many union actions lasted for a long time, involved violence, intervention by the police, and arrests, which reflected "the intensity of the social conflict in Paris," "a resurgence of genuine class warfare," and "hatred of the employers." In any event, the sacred union now appeared to be dead and buried. The strikers openly displayed their admiration for the Russian Revolution and their sympathy for the revolutionary movement that was emerging in Austria-Hungary. A striker asked loudly if "the French working class, which suffered so much during the war, would be the only one to remain inactive?"[4]

The contradiction of the aspirations of the French working class, which pursued two irreconcilable objectives, namely a military triumph *à la* Clemenceau as well as a social victory *à la* Lenin, came to a head during the final months of the war. Patriotic fever and the hope for a military victory rose irresistibly, but pacifism also remained a force, as well as "the idea that only the bourgeoisie has something to win in this war" and the hope for revolutionary change. More and more workers feared that victory would engender "a wave of chauvinism" and might lead to "a triumph of imperialism."[5] From the viewpoint of employers and the government, however, the situation was ambivalent and troubling. The workers seemed willing to support the war effort and to contribute to the final victory, but they also increasingly voiced all sorts of extravagant demands, and many of them obviously strove for a revolution *à la russe*.

The end of the war against Germany on November 11, 1918, did not mean the end of the class conflict raging in France itself. One month after the armistice, on December 12, the country's trade unions collectively presented their demands: to operate freely in all enterprises, to negotiate collective agreements, to have the eight-hour day introduced, and to nationalize certain firms. From the end of 1918 until late in the spring of 1919, Paris was flooded by a new tsunami of work stoppages, for example in the transport sector and in the big Renault factory located in the suburb of Boulogne-Billancourt. In addition to wage increases, also for women, the strikers demanded the eight-hour workday in tandem with the "English week." And they did not hide their sympathy and admiration for the Russian Revolution, expressed in slogans such as "Long Live the Soviets!" and "Long Live Lenin!" This was in striking contrast with the contempt they displayed for their own government, directed by their *bête noire*, Clemenceau, "the henchman of the capitalists." The Parisian strikers accused him of being a dictator and of running an old-style, decadent bourgeois regime, doomed to be replaced soon by a proletarian system of government like the one being forged in Russia by the Bolsheviks. At least some of the strikers, especially the metal workers, undoubtedly aimed to provoke a revolution. If they did not manage to achieve that goal, it was because the majority of the strikers and other workers did not favour a revolution but were happy with far less radical, "pragmatic" results such as higher wages. Moreover, the strikes were not coordinated; what was sorely missing was a central leadership with a "revolutionary drive," in other words, a French Bolshevik party and a Gallic Lenin. Another hindrance was the fact that the strikes were numerous enough in Paris and its suburbs, but relatively rare in the rest of the country. But the factor that ultimately contributed the most to taking the wind out of the sails of the Parisian strikers was a spectacular concession announced by the Clemenceau government on April 23, 1919, namely a law introducing the eight-hour workday. The eight-hour day was an old, radical, and very popular objective of the labour movement. It had already been featured in the program of the First International in the 1860s, and before the war it had constituted one of the most ambitious demands of the French trade unionists and socialists.[6]

On the other side of the Channel, 1917 had been a turbulent year, socially speaking, as we have seen. The British elite had been traumatized by the fear of socialism, republicanism, and revolution. It had responded with merciless repression of anything that smacked of revolution, with home searches, censorship, and the use of agents provocateurs. But the elite also believed it could take the wind out of the revolutionary sails by means of reforms. In early 1918 the government introduced a number of political and social reforms that were quite far-reaching in democratic terms — precisely the kind of reforms the elite had hoped to avoid by means of the war. The major initiative in this sense was the *Representation of the People Act* of February 1918, a widening of the right to vote that caused the number of voters to increase considerably, namely from 7.7 to 21.4 million people. This was achieved by the elimination of property qualifications and by giving the vote to women, albeit only those above thirty years of age. The British historian Arthur Marwick has said of this law that it "brought the country for the first time within an approximation to democracy in the formal sense." The law was certainly not 100 per cent democratic; it did not introduce a system of universal suffrage with "one man [or woman], one vote," but kept in place a form of plural suffrage. Seven per cent of the British population had more than one vote, and not surprisingly these were members of the elite; for example, businessmen whose firms had plants in more than one riding. The urgent need to reduce social tension in the country and thus to banish the revolutionary threat also caused the British elite to push the state to introduce "collectivist social legislation on behalf of the lower sections of the community," notably in the form of a number of laws governing education, public health, and housing.[7] It is virtually certain that none of these democratic reforms would have seen the light of day had the war, or rather the Russian Revolution caused by the war, not aroused an abject fear of revolution in the British elite.

Nevertheless, a kind of quasi-revolutionary situation persisted in the country. Throughout 1918, strikes and demonstrations continued, for example in January and in July–August in London, Manchester, and elsewhere. In total, close to six million workdays would be lost on account of union actions in 1918. The authorities were particularly alarmed because many strikes affected the munitions factories, and because at the end of August even the London police force refused to work. The fact that strikers often waved red flags convinced some that Albion was ripe for a Bolshevik revolution. "Today we are threatened more by Bolshevism than by the *Boches*," declared a general. In spite of the German offensive the government kept a million and a half soldiers in the country to be able to maintain order in case of serious troubles, and lists were prepared of socialists who were to be arrested. The influence of the Russian Revolution — "Bolshiness," as it was sometimes called — was believed to be infecting not only the workers within the country, but also the soldiers at the front. In October 1918, some Australian soldiers mutinied in Flanders. And in the Channel ports of Folkestone and Calais, transit points for countless men on their way to or from the front, the Tommies displayed a disquieting lack of respect for their superiors; for instance, by removing "For Officers Only" signs from the waiting rooms of railway stations. The British soldiers obviously had had enough, not only of the war, but also of the traditional class relations prevailing in their country and its army.

The government of Lloyd George profited from the armistice of November 11 to organize new elections. As expected, the euphoria generated by victory allowed his Liberal-Conservative coalition to triumph on election day, December 14, 1918. The armistice had put an end to the "vertical" war that had pitted Britain against Germany, but not to the "horizontal" war raging between classes within the country, and Lloyd George's electoral success did not put an end to the social unrest. In 1918, six million workdays had been lost due to strikes, but in 1919 this number would balloon to thirty-five million, and the strikes would involve no less than 2.4 million British workers. It was especially in the beginning of the year 1919 that social revolution was in the air. Toward the end of January, strikes in Glasgow and Belfast were accompanied by mass demonstrations with red flags omnipresent, and featuring riots in the streets and intervention by soldiers armed to the teeth, even showing up in tanks. The strikers described their actions as a "socialist revolution," and a spokesman of the authorities claimed they were facing a "Bolshevik insurrection." Lloyd George even considered the possibility of using the air force to bomb the rebellious cities of Glasgow, Liverpool, and Manchester. But the government also had reason to fear that the troops might refuse to repress the strikers and demonstrators. In January 1919, in Folkestone and Calais, a crowd of approximately ten thousand soldiers demanded to be demobilized immediately and councils of soldiers were set up. On January 13, mutinous sailors on the Royal Navy's HMS *Kilbride* hoisted the red flag.

Lloyd George finally found a solution. He negotiated with the mostly reformist, that is, nonrevolutionary, trade union leaders, making a number of important concessions. And the employers, equally desperate to avoid revolution, agreed to raise wages. The revolutionary fever thus began to decline. Even so, social peace would only return to the land toward the end of 1919. In any event, it can be said that in 1918–1919 Britain teetered on the edge of the revolutionary abyss. If it did not come to an actual revolution, it was certainly not for a lack of revolutionaries, because many British civilians and soldiers were in a genuinely revolutionary mood; it was because the great majority of the Labour Party, most of the other socialist parties, and above all the trade unions, were not revolutionaries at all, and were in fact as hostile to social revolution as Lloyd George himself. Gabriel Kolko has observed in this context that in Russia the popular masses wanted radical and even revolutionary changes and the Bolsheviks provided the supply that met this demand, while elsewhere the forces of the left revealed themselves unable or unwilling to take advantage of the unique historical opportunity for revolution brought about by the war.[8]

In any event, the reforms that resulted from this quasi-revolutionary situation distinctly improved the lot of Britain's lower orders compared to the prewar era. Social inequality certainly did not disappear, but it became less great and less "visible." The workers henceforth enjoyed higher wages, shorter work hours, better working conditions, and modest but important advantages of other forms of social legislation. All these good things they owed to the war, at least according to historians such as Arthur Marwick. In reality, they owed these improvements to the revolution that had succeeded in Russia and threatened to break out in Britain. The British lower classes owed these improvements more to Lenin and the Bolsheviks than to Lloyd George, the British Labour Party, or trade unions.[9]

In Britain itself, revolution could be avoided thanks to the hasty introduction of reforms. In most overseas possessions of the British Empire, however, the elite relied on repression to chase away the spectre of revolution, whether of the social or the national variety. In Ireland, for example, the nationalists, who in 1919 proclaimed the Irish Republic, were fought ruthlessly by means of a terrorist militia known as the Black and Tans, of which Churchill was one of the godfathers. But this rearguard battle ended in failure, because in 1921 London was forced to recognize the independence of Ireland, although the north-eastern part of the island, today known as Northern Ireland, was to remain British against the will of the majority of its population but to the advantage of a minority, the local Anglo-Irish elite. In India too, London relied on violence to put a lid on the growing demand for independence, as shown by bloodbaths such as the infamous Amritsar Massacre of April 13, 1919. But repression again proved to be counterproductive, because it persuaded countless Indians that the nonviolent pursuit of some form of autonomy was fruitless and that salvation could only come from a revolutionary struggle for total independence. They would achieve their goal after the Second World War.[10]

In Germany, the situation of the population in 1918 was simply catastrophic. The civilians were starving and malnutrition caused diseases and high mortality rates, especially among children, older people, and women. It is estimated that during the Great War no less than 762,000 Germans died of malnutrition and associated diseases. The most infamous and deadliest of these diseases was of course the "Spanish flu," believed to have caused the death of between twenty million and a hundred million victims worldwide from 1918 to 1919, including four hundred thousand Germans in 1918. (There the illness was originally called the "Flemish flu," undoubtedly because it had been brought to Germany by soldiers coming home from the front in Flanders.[11]) This macabre context of misery and death witnessed an intensification of a polarization that had already become visible in 1917, namely the one between the pacifists with their democratic, radical, and even revolutionary aspirations, and the *jusqu'au-boutistes* with their conservative, authoritarian, and militarist convictions. In 1918, the former were in the ascendant, because the great majority of the people wanted peace even without gains for Germany and also favoured political and social reforms as well as radical and even revolutionary changes such as those formulated by the leaders of the USPD and its radical wing, the Spartacists.[12] Already in January 1918, massive strikes broke out in Berlin, and the strikers' demands included better nutrition, democratic reforms, and an end to the war. After the fiasco of the Ludendorff offensive in the summer of 1918, a revolutionary situation developed in Germany. It reached a high point at the end of October and in early November, when sailors mutinied in Wilhelmshaven and Kiel and installed soldiers' "councils" (*Räte*) modelled after the Russian soviets, while many workers occupied factories. Ludendorff was more or less forced to resign and fled abroad. The Kaiser himself abdicated and departed on November 10 for exile in the Netherlands. Germany's other crowned heads, for example the King of Bavaria, likewise vacated their thrones. Wilhelm II was one of the most prominent European monarchs (and aristocrats in general) who, in 1914, had wanted war and expected wonderful things from it, first and foremost a kind of return to the "good old days" before 1789. When, in the Belgian resort of Spa, he stepped onto the train that was to take him to exile in Holland, he grumbled: "My God, who could ever have thought that it would end this way?" Whose fault was that? The Kaiser immediately answered that question: "The German people are nothing but a bunch of swine."[13]

The army high command, one of the bastions of the German elite, subsequently looked for a way to nip the revolution in the bud. And for this purpose the generals found eager partners in the leaders of the SPD. The latter, long-time reformists, had already distanced themselves from the Bolsheviks in Russia and loathed revolution. From the SPD "oligarchs" the generals obtained *carte blanche* to put down the revolution, even if this involved spilling proletarian blood. In return, the generals permitted the SPD leaders to provide Germany with a democratic political system and to introduce social reforms as well. Such was the essence of the Ebert-Groener agreement, named after the SPD headman Friedrich Ebert and General Wilhelm Groener, who had replaced Ludendorff at the head of the army.

The type of democratic republic — democratic in the bourgeois-liberal sense — that the SPD wanted and the generals loathed but were willing to tolerate, was proclaimed on November 9 from a balcony of the Reichstag by the social-democrat Philipp Scheidemann. (The constitution of this republic would be promulgated in August 1919, in the town of Weimar, which is why Germany would become known as the Weimar Republic.) A few hours later on this same day, however, Karl Liebknecht, standing on a balcony of the former imperial palace, proclaimed that Germany was henceforth a "free socialist republic." What he and the other Spartacists had in mind was a soviet-style republic, inspired by the Bolshevik model. In December 1918, the Spartacist group, now known as the Spartacist League, would metamorphose into the Communist Party of Germany. And in January 1919 it would come to a Spartacist insurrection against the liberal-democratic republic set up by the SPD with the support of the army. In order to put down this rebellion, Groener and Ebert could hardly count on the regular army units; many of those had been dissolved because countless soldiers favoured the revolution. The generals therefore created units of volunteers, recruited among officers and "elite front soldiers," often storm troopers, but also nationalist university students and other volunteers. It was these proto-Nazi "free corps" that would smother the revolutions in Berlin, Munich, and elsewhere in blood; for example, by brutally murdering Liebknecht and Luxemburg in January 1919.[14] But the drama of the revolution in Berlin in January 1919, and of its bloody repression, also demonstrates that the revolutionary momentum in Germany had already mostly dissipated. The main reason for this was the attitude of the SPD, which managed to retain the loyalty of the majority of workers and soldiers. The SPD persuaded them to follow Ebert and his consorts on the path to democratic reform instead of opting for revolution. The revolutionary councils disappeared from the scene as fast as they had appeared, and the genuinely revolutionary socialists were left behind as a minority, to be obliterated rather easily by heavily armed freecorps.[15]

In Germany, the revolution was brutally suppressed, but the bourgeois-liberal democratic system that emerged there in the wake of the Great War, the Weimar Republic, nonetheless represented a major step forward in comparison to the pre-1914 empire. With not only universal suffrage but also proportional representation, ministerial accountability to the legislature, and an impressive array of social achievements (including the eight-hour workday), the "new" Germany revealed itself to be one of the most democratic countries in Europe. Never before had Germany's plebeians made so much political and social progress, never before had it achieved such an impressive measure of emancipation. Unfortunately, the Ebert-Groener agreement, which had made it possible to tame the beast of revolution, also meant that the army remained a bastion of the landowning nobility, and that other nerve centres of power and influence, such as the state bureaucracy, the judiciary, and the universities, remained safely in the hands of the traditional elite. The country's elite thus continued to be extremely powerful; and it continued to despise democracy, including the democratic "Weimar system." The elite had helped to bring about that democratic system, but without the slightest enthusiasm; it had done so only to avoid a revolutionary, Russian-style alternative. Once the revolutionary threat had evaporated, it looked out for an opportunity to reintroduce an authoritarian system such as that of the "good old days" of the *Kaiserzeit,* the "emperor's era." It would achieve that goal in 1933, when Hitler would destroy the Weimar Republic.[16]

In 1918 the formerly powerful and glorious Habsburg Empire similarly fell victim to unrest, riots, rebellion, mutinies, and other problems caused by a war the empire's elite had wanted and unleashed. The year had already started badly, namely with a mutiny of the sailors on about forty naval vessels anchored in the Bay of Cattaro (Kotor), situated on the Adriatic coast of modern Montenegro. The causes included poor food, iron and often absurd discipline, and, unsurprisingly, the example of the Russian Revolution. The mutineers demanded not only better treatment, but also peace and political changes in the democratic sense. With the help of loyal troops, the authorities regained control of the situation after a few days, and heavy sanctions were meted out, including four executions. Shortly after the signing of the Treaty of Brest-Litovsk, however, the problems became even worse when numerous Czechs, Croats, and other members of the ethnic minorities decided to go home and, influenced by the example of the Russian Bolsheviks, demanded peace as well as revolutionary changes. Croatia, which had displayed much pro-Habsburg and pro-war enthusiasm in 1914, increasingly metamorphosed into a hotbed of potentially revolutionary discontent. The Croatians wanted not only separation from Austria-Hungary in order to join Serbia in a new South-Slav state, to be known as Yugoslavia, but also aimed at radical social reforms such as land redistribution at the expense of the large landowners. In army camps in Mostar and elsewhere rebellions broke out, and in the countryside peasants looted the estates of aristocratic landowners. In the fall, Croatian soldiers at the front in Italy mutinied. Emperor Charles I, who had succeeded Franz-Joseph in 1916, hoped it might still be possible to keep his empire together by introducing reforms according a measure of autonomy to various ethnic minorities. This formula conformed to one of Wilson's Fourteen Points, namely the principle of the self-determination of peoples. Charles could thus hope that his plan might be acceptable to the Allies, but the latter made it clear that they would settle for nothing less than complete independence for the Czechs, Croatians, etc. By the end of October, Paris, London, and Washington had already recognized provisional governments for Czechoslovakia and Yugoslavia. On October 29, the Croatian parliament proclaimed the country's independence and its decision to join the new "State of Slovenes, Croatians, and Serbians," which would in turn amalgamate with the Kingdom of Serbia on December 4, 1918 to form the Kingdom of Serbians, Croatians, and Slovenes. Moreover, on October 31, during the so-called "Chrysanthemum Revolution" in Budapest, Hungary declared its own independence in order to become a democratic republic led by a social democrat, Mihály Károlyi; this *fait accompli* was recognized on the same day by Charles. All that was left of the Habsburg Empire at that stage was the German-speaking heartland, Austria, cradle of the dynasty. On November 11, 1918, the day of the German capitulation,

Charles issued an ambiguous manifesto that was not intended as decision to abdicate but was certainly interpreted that way, with the unintended result that the next day the Austrian Republic was proclaimed. The now ex-emperor remained in the country for a few more days, achieving nothing, and would end up leaving for exile in Switzerland on March 23, 1919.[17] In 1914, the Habsburg Empire had gone to war frivolously, in the hope of taming the nationalism of its ethnic minorities and avoiding social and national revolutions as well as other radical political and social changes. Four years of war brought precisely the opposite result: the empire fell, and in the German-speaking Austrian heartland, just as in Germany, a revolution broke out that produced a bourgeois-liberal democracy directed by the social-democrats. It was originally the intention that this small new state, tentatively called "German Austria," would join the new German republic, but this formula was not in the interests of the victorious Allies, who preferred an independent Austria and vetoed union with Germany.

In Vienna, they might possibly have followed the Russian rather than the German example, by proclaiming a soviet-style republic, but it never came to that. In 1919 a soviet republic would in fact be established in Hungary, but it would last only from March 21 to August 1. Its leader was Béla Kun, a kind of Hungarian Lenin. Like Bolshevik Russia, Béla Kun's Hungary became embroiled in a civil war that was the object of foreign intervention, namely when it was invaded by troops from Romania, Czechoslovakia, and Yugoslavia, countries lusting after large portions of Hungarian territory. The hastily reorganized remainders of the Hungarian army, led by Admiral Miklós Horthy — who had taken over the command of the Austro-Hungarian navy after the mutiny at Kotor — would take advantage of the opportunity to bring down Kun and set up a regime with Horthy as dictator. But his official title was "regent," because the conservative leaders of the army, representatives of the *ancien régime*, found a republic to be an overly democratic form of government. They made the country a monarchy again, if only in theory.

When the war came to an end, Italy likewise found itself in a critical political and social situation. There, too, the "vertical" war against foreign enemies was over, but the "horizontal" war continued to rage unabatedly. In Italy, the Moloch of war had demanded the sacrifice of more than one million victims, allegedly 680,000 soldiers and approximately 700,000 civilians. It had ruined the economy, provoked inflation, and caused the wages of factory and agricultural workers to collapse. The proletarians were miserable and disgruntled, and they responded with protests, demonstrations, riots, and strikes. Tens of thousands of men swelled the ranks of the trade unions as well as a socialist party that remained revolutionary in theory even though more and more of its leaders had embraced reformism. The country's elite and the government, monopolized by the elite, began to fear for a Russian-style revolution. Like the British elite in very similar circumstances, it reacted by making important concessions. In the wink of an eye, all sorts of political and social reforms came down the pipe, including an electoral system with proportional representation and the eight-hour workday, and a major land redistribution was promised. Wages were increased, and between 1918 and 1921 the real wages of industrial workers would actually double. The people's hatred of the established order was great, and during the *biennio rosso*, the "two red years," of 1919 and 1920, an Italian Lenin might have taken advantage of the opportunity to unleash a revolution; however, at this critical juncture the leaders of the socialist party did not rise to the occasion. They settled for reforms and waited — in vain, as it turned out — for an opportunity to come to power legally before initiating genuinely revolutionary action.[18]

As for Belgium, the exiled government and King Albert worried about the situation in a country that, in the fall of 1918, was about to be liberated by their troops. King Albert fretted about the possibility of a revolution, since in Brussels a revolutionary situation had arisen when soldiers of the German occupying forces started to set up soviet-style councils and fraternized with Belgian civilians in a "boiling, rebellious atmosphere." In Russia and elsewhere, royal crowns were rolling into the gutter, and "in all of Europe the rulers lost credit among the much-suffering population." It was obvious that considerable political and social reforms were required to avoid the worst. Suddenly, the Belgian elite revealed itself ready to introduce the kind of democratic reforms — including universal suffrage on the basis of "one man, one vote" — that in 1914 it had hoped to avoid thanks to the war. It was socialist politicians, "personalities with whom one could discuss things, certainly no revolutionaries . . . very much committed to the preservation of the social order," who came up with this idea, writes Belgian historian de Schaepdrijver. (Because those socialists believed, just like their Liberal colleagues, that women would tend to vote for the Catholic party, it was decided to give the vote only to men above the presumably mature age of twenty-one.) This democratic innovation was adopted without the theoretically required constitutional amendment. It was also achieved in a very undemocratic fashion, namely during a meeting, in a castle in the village of Loppem, tucked away in the countryside near Bruges, far from the "madding crowd" of Brussels, during a meeting of a very "select company," namely the king himself, his advisors, and a handful of politicians. A new government "of national unity," now including socialists (of the reformist variety, naturally), replaced the government that had spent the war in exile in Le Havre. The first elections based on the new electoral law were to be held in November 1919 and would produce a victory for the socialists, whose party thus became the second biggest in the country and was afterwards to be included regularly in the country's governments, typically consisting of coalitions. After the armistice of November 11, the social and political situation remained unstable for quite some time, and in 1919 a new wave of strikes swept the country. It was therefore judged necessary to complement the political democratization, that is, the electoral reforms, with concessions of a social nature, for example wage increases, a minimum wage, shorter workdays, more efficient health insurance, better pensions, and above all, the eight-hour day. At the same time, higher taxes were imposed on high incomes, inheritances, and especially war profits. This remarkable dose of democratization benefited the organizations that were known to favour them and claimed credit for them, namely the socialist party and the trade unions. Union membership increased considerably in the years after the war, and the socialist party soon had twice as many members as in 1914. The socialist party became respectable and influential in a way that had been unimaginable before the war, but it also became more integrated than ever before in the "new and improved" edition of the established order. In 1914, the Liberal and Catholic elite — or "oligarchy," as de Schaepdrijver calls it — had entertained very different expectations from the war, and its most conservative elements were far from happy with the "coup d'état of Loppem" and the reforms conceived there. But things could have been much worse. In all of Europe, 1918 and the following years saw "Bolshiness" make headway everywhere under the influence of the Russian Revolution, which caused the elite in Belgium to tremble. The elite had been forced to concede a generous dose of democratization, and had done so reluctantly, but it could live with the consequences, something that could not be said of the Bolshevik option. To the defenders of the old order, who feared, even if only momentarily, that the end was near, "anything was better than Bolshevism," as Eric Hobsbawm has written in this context.[19]

In neutral countries such as Switzerland and the Netherlands, too, the Great War had constituted a wonderful opportunity for the elite — the landowning agrarians as well as the industrial-financial bourgeoisie — to enrich itself, for example by supplying foodstuffs or weapons to belligerent neighbours. Conversely, there too the proletarians experienced hard times because wages declined while prices increased, and they became more and more embittered, seditious, and impatient for radical democratic reforms. There too, "the class struggle thus gradually intensified" in the course of the war, leading to a quasi-revolutionary situation by late 1918 and early 1919. This development was characterized by massive strikes (even of the employees of the banks in Zurich!), demonstrations, food riots, and so forth. In Switzerland the socialists and trade union leaders had already established a joint action committee in the town of Olten by the end of 1917, which was denounced by the elite as the "Olten soviet." In the fall of 1918 a revolution and/or a civil war even threatened to break out as a result of a general strike. The Helvetian establishment briefly flirted with the idea of restoring order by setting up a military dictatorship, but ultimately opted to defuse the situation by means of hastily introduced political and social reforms. In the Netherlands the bourgeoisie was likewise haunted by the spectre of revolution, and in November 1918 troops were kept in readiness to intervene against the numerous strikers and demonstrators. In Holland, too, social peace would return only after the introduction of reforms such as the eight-hour workday.[20]

In 1918 and 1919, the fear of a Russian-style revolution also terrorized the elites on the other side of the Atlantic. In the United States, the war had caused discontent among countless people; they wanted not only peace but also more democracy, not only political but also social-economic democracy. The real wages of industrial workers were still very low, and in the factories women and men often had to work twelve and even fourteen hours per day, and six or even seven days per week; work safety was virtually nonexistent and no law had yet challenged the fact that more than two million children were working in factories. The socialists and the unions had a huge following, but the authorities had profited from the war to combat the labour movement via extremely repressive legislation. As Michael Parenti emphasizes, the war was also useful to the elite because it "focused people's attention on the menace of the 'barbarian Huns' of Germany, who supposedly threatened Anglo-American civilization."[21] Many Americans felt sympathy and admiration for the Russian Revolution and its egalitarian objectives. Even members of the middle class reacted positively; for example, the writer Lincoln Steffens and the journalist John Reed with his famous book, *Ten Days that Shook the World*. On the other hand, the US establishment abhorred the Russian Revolution and feared that the revolutionary fire might blow over to the United States. "Lenin and Trotsky are on their way!" proclaimed a headline in *The Wall Street Journal*, then already the reactionary mouthpiece of the nation's industry and finance. President Wilson was not inclined to make concessions. To the contrary: he used and even abused the repressive laws he had introduced earlier in order to intervene ruthlessly against anything that smacked of Bolshevism. Thus it came in the United States to the infamous Red Scare, which involved an extremely brutal way of dealing not only with sympathizers of Bolshevism but also with moderate socialists, other dissenters, anarchists, trade unionists, and their like. But the social unrest did not subside, and hundreds of thousands, even millions of workers went on strike, and in local elections socialist candidates continued to enjoy success. The US elite would continue to be "scared of red." (How this situation evolved later, in the context of the Great Depression and the Second World War, is explained in my book *The Myth of the Good War*.)[22]

The unrest also affected neighbouring Canada, where it culminated in a great strike in Winnipeg in June 1919.[23] And it had a major impact in Latin America, characterized since the arrival of the Spanish conquistadors by flagrant class contradictions and horrible social problems. In January 1919,

Argentina experienced a "tragic week" of strikes and demonstrations that were put down by the police and the army in a particularly brutal and bloody fashion. The authorities blamed the troubles on a "Bolshevik conspiracy." The repression was accompanied by pogroms, because here too there were many who identified Bolshevism — and Marxism and socialism in general — with Judaism in the context of the theory of "Judeo-Bolshevism." In neighbouring Chile, no less than 229 strikes broke out between 1917 and 1921, including nearly 100 in 1919 alone. The small town of Puerto Natales, situated in remote Patagonia, was temporarily taken over by protesting and striking workers; the army intervened, "restored order," as they usually say, and executed some leaders of the rebellion. Mexico, Cuba, and Colombia were similarly shaken by demonstrations, riots, and work stoppages. The elite reacted everywhere with the usual bloody repression. But in Latin America too, "sections of the traditional oligarchies" wisely opted to try to defuse the potentially revolutionary situation by means of concessions, in this case in the form of modest democratic reforms of a social as well as political nature. In countries like Chile, the early 1920s thus witnessed the introduction of fewer work hours, pensions, paid holidays, and other social benefits, and it was obvious that this purported to "prevent unrest among the workers" and to "co-opt labour into the political system." For these improvements in the miserable lot of the Latin-American working class, Lenin and the Bolsheviks deserve much credit. It is generally recognized that, starting in 1917, their example and their influence transformed the traditionally docile proletarians living between the Rio Grande and Cape Horn into a militant host that intimidated the elite and forced it to make previously unthinkable concessions.[24]

All over Europe, the war had brought about a potentially revolutionary situation as early as 1917. In countries where the authorities continued to represent the traditional elite, exactly as had been the case in 1914, they aimed to prevent the realization of this potential by means of repression, concessions, or both. But in the case of Russia, the revolution not only broke out but succeeded, and the Bolsheviks began work on the construction of the world's very first socialist society. It was an experiment for which the elites of the other countries felt no sympathy whatsoever; to the contrary, they fervently hoped that it would soon end in a dismal fiasco.

(It was also a revolutionary experiment that would disappoint numerous sympathizers because the socialist Utopia failed to spring whole, Athena-like, from the brow of the Russian revolutionary Zeus.) In elitist circles in London, Paris, and elsewhere, they were convinced of the ineluctability of the failure of the Bolsheviks' bold experiment but, just to be sure, it was decided to send troops to Russia to support the "white" counterrevolutionaries against the Bolshevik "reds" in a conflict that would become a great, long, and bloody civil war.

A first wave of allied troops arrived in Russia in April 1918, when British and Japanese soldiers disembarked in Vladivostok. They established contact with the "whites," who were already involved in a full-blown war against the Bolsheviks. In total, the British alone would send 40,000 men to Russia. In that same spring of 1918, Churchill, then minister of war, also sent an expeditionary corps to Murmansk, in the north of Russia, in order to support the troops of the "white" General Kolchak, in the hope that this might help to replace the Bolshevik rulers with a government friendly to Britain. Other countries sent smaller contingents of soldiers, including France, the United States (15,000 men), Japan, Italy, Romania, Serbia, and Greece. Using Czech POWs and deserters, the czarist Russians had constituted a Czech Legion of somewhere between 30,000 and 40,000 men in order to fight the Austro-Hungarians during the Great War, but after the Treaty of Brest-Litovsk, this force stayed behind in Russia and it too fought the "reds" on the side of the "whites." In some cases, the allied troops became involved in fighting against the Germans and Ottomans on Russia's frontiers, but it was clear that they had not come for that purpose, but rather to overthrow the Bolshevik regime and to "strangle the Bolshevik baby in its crib," as Churchill so delicately put it. The British in particular also hoped that their presence might make it possible to pocket some attractive bits and pieces of territory of a Russian state that seemed to be falling apart, much like the Ottoman Empire. This explains why a British unit marched from Mesopotamia to the shores of the Caspian Sea, namely to the oil-rich regions around Baku, capital of modern Azerbaijan.[25] Like the Great War itself, the allied intervention in Russia aimed both to fight the revolution and to achieve imperialist objectives.

In Russia, the war had spawned not only conditions favourable to a *social* revolution, but also — at least in some parts of this gigantic country — to *national* revolutions among a number of ethnic minorities. Such national movements had already reared their heads during the war, and they generally belonged to the right-wing, conservative, racist, and anti-Semitic variety of nationalism. Germany's political and military elite recognized close ideological relatives in these movements and potential allies in the war against Russia. (Lenin and the Bolsheviks, on the other hand, were considered useful in the war against Russia, but ideologically these revolutionary Russians were antipodes of Germany's reactionary regime.) The Germans did not support the Finnish, Baltic, Ukrainian, and other nationalists out of ideological sympathy, but because they could be used to weaken Russia; they also did it because they hoped to stamp German satellite states out of the ground in Eastern and Northern Europe, preferably monarchies with as "sovereign" some scion of a German noble family. The Treaty of Brest-Litovsk proved to be an opportunity to create a number of states of this type. From July 11 to November 2, 1918, a German aristocrat named Wilhelm (II) Karl Florestan Gero Crescentius, Duke of Urach and Count of Württemberg, could thus enjoy being King of Lithuania under the name of Mindaugas II. With the armistice of November 11, 1918, Germany was doomed to disappear from the scene in Eastern and Northern Europe and that put an end to the dream of German hegemony over there. However, Article 12 of the armistice authorized German troops to remain in Russia, the Baltic lands, and elsewhere in Eastern Europe as long as the Allies deemed it necessary; in other words, as long as they remained useful for the purpose of fighting the Bolsheviks, which is precisely what the Germans did. In fact, British and French leaders such as Lloyd George and Foch henceforth considered revolutionary Russia as a more dangerous enemy than Germany. The national movements of Balts, Finns, Poles, etc., were now totally embroiled in the Russian Civil War, and the Allies replaced the Germans as their supporters, also militarily speaking, as long as they fought the "reds," rather than the "whites," as they also often did, since much Eastern European real estate, formerly part of the Czarist Empire, was claimed simultaneously by the Russian "whites" and by Polish, Lithuanian, Ukrainian, and other nationalists.

In all the countries emerging from the clouds of dust rising after the collapse of the czarist empire, there were basically two kinds of people. First, workers and peasants and other members of the lower classes, who favoured a *social* revolution, supported the Bolsheviks, and were willing to settle for some sort of autonomy for their own ethnic-linguistic minority within the new multi-ethnic and multi-lingual state — inevitably dominated by its Russian component — that was taking the place of the former czarist empire and would be known as the Soviet Union. Second, the majority, though certainly not all, of the members of the old aristocratic and bourgeois elites and of the petty bourgeoisie, who were against a social revolution and therefore detested and fought the Bolsheviks and wanted nothing less than total independence vis-à-vis the new state being created by the latter. Their nationalism was typical nineteenth-century nationalism, right-wing and conservative, associated with an ethnic group, a language, a religion, and a supposedly glorious past, mostly mythical, that was expected to be reborn thanks to a *national* revolution. Civil wars also erupted between "whites" and "reds" in Finland, Estonia, Ukraine, and elsewhere. If in many cases the "whites" emerged victorious and were able to establish resolutely anti-Bolshevik and anti-Russian states, it was not only because the Bolsheviks would long fight with their backs against the wall in the Russian heartland itself and were therefore rarely able to provide much support for their "red" comrades in the Baltic and elsewhere in the periphery of the former czarist empire, but also because first the Germans and then the Allies — particularly the British — intervened *manu militari* to aid the "whites." At the end of November 1918, for example, a squadron of the Royal Navy, commanded by Admiral Edwyn Alexander-Sinclair (and later by Admiral Walter Cowan) showed up in the Baltic Sea in order to supply the Estonian and Latvian "whites" with weapons and help them to fight their "red" countrymen as well as Bolshevik Russian troops. The British sank a number of ships of the Russian fleet and blockaded the rest of it in its base, Kronstadt. As for Finland, in the spring of 1918 already, German troops had helped the local "whites" to achieve victory and enabled them to proclaim the independence of their country.[26]

It was clearly the intention of the elitist decision-makers in London, Paris, Washington, etc., to also insure victory for the "whites" at the expense of the "reds" in the civil war in Russia itself and thus to abort the Bolshevik enterprise, a large-scale experiment for which too many British, French, American, and other plebeians displayed interest and enthusiasm and which therefore displeased their "betters." In a note addressed to Clemenceau in the spring of 1919, Lloyd George expressed his concern that "the whole of Europe is filled with the spirit of revolution," and he continued by saying that

> *There is a deep sense not only of discontent, but of anger*
> *and revolt, amongst the workmen against the war conditions.*
> *The whole existing order in its political, social and economic*
> *aspects is questioned by the masses of the population from one*
> *end of Europe to the other.*[27]

The Allies' intervention in Russia was counterproductive, however, because foreign support discredited the "white," counterrevolutionary forces in the eyes of countless Russians, who increasingly considered the Bolsheviks as true Russian patriots and therefore supported them. In many ways, the Bolsheviks' *social* revolution was simultaneously a *national* Russian revolution, a struggle for the survival, independence, and dignity of Mother Russia, first against the Germans then against the allied troops who invaded the country from all sides and conducted themselves "as if they were in Central Africa." (Seen from this perspective, the Bolsheviks look very much like the Jacobins of the French Revolution, who had simultaneously fought for the revolution and for France.) It was for this reason that the Bolsheviks could benefit from the support of a large number of bourgeois and even aristocratic nationalists, support that was probably a major determinant of their victory in the civil war against the combination of the "whites" and the Allies. Even the famous general Brussilov, a nobleman, supported the "reds." "The awareness of my duty toward the [Russian] nation," he explained, "caused me to refuse to obey my natural social instincts."[28] In any event, the "whites" were nothing more than "a microcosm of the ruling and governing classes of [Russia's] *ancien régime*

— military officers, landowners, churchmen — with minimal popular support," according to Arno Mayer. They were also corrupt, and a large part of the money the Allies sent them disappeared into their pockets.[29]

If the allied intervention in Russia, sometimes promoted as a "crusade against Bolshevism," was doomed to failure, it was also because it was strongly opposed by countless soldiers and civilians in Britain, France, and elsewhere in the "West." Their slogan was "Hands Off Russia!" The British soldiers who had not been demobilised after the armistice of November 1918 and who were supposed to be shipped off to Russia protested and organized mutinies; for example, in January 1919 in Dover, Calais, and other Channel ports. In that same month Glasgow was hit by a series of strikes whose objectives included forcing the government to abandon its interventionist policy with respect to Russia. In March 1919, Canadian troops rioted in a camp in Ryl, in Wales, causing five men to be killed and twenty-three wounded; later in 1919, similar riots occurred in other army camps. These troubles certainly reflected the soldiers' impatience to be discharged and return home, but they also revealed that all too many of the troops could not be relied on for a tour of duty of indefinite duration in distant Russia. In France, meanwhile, strikers in Paris loudly demanded an end to armed intervention in Russia, and troops that were already in Russia made it clear that they did not want to fight the Bolsheviks, but wanted to return home. In February, March, and April 1919, mutinies and desertions ravaged French troops stationed in the port of Odessa and British forces in the northern district of Murmansk, and some of the British even changed sides and joined the ranks of the Bolsheviks. "Soldiers who had survived Verdun and the Battle of the Marne did not want to go fight in the plains of Russia," was the sour remark made by a French officer. (Among the French mutineers was a Vietnamese, Ton Duc Thang, who, after his return to his homeland, would join the new communist party, founded by Ho Chi Minh, and who would later become president of North Vietnam and then of reunified Vietnam.) In the US contingent, numerous men resorted to self-mutilation in order to seek repatriation. The Allied soldiers sympathized increasingly with the Russian revolutionaries; they were becoming more and more "contaminated" by the Bolshevism they were supposed to be fighting. And so it happened that in the spring of 1919 the French, British, Canadians, Americans, Italians, and other foreign troops had to be ingloriously withdrawn from Russia.[30]

The Western elites turned out to be unable to overcome the Bolsheviks via an armed intervention. They therefore changed course and provided generous political and military support to the new states that emerged from the western territories of the former czarist empire, such as Poland and the Baltic countries. These new states were without exception the products of national revolutions, inspired by reactionary varieties of nationalism, all too often tainted by anti-Semitism; and they were dominated by the survivors of the old elites, including large landowners and generals of aristocratic background, the "national" Christian churches, and the industrialists. With rare exceptions such as Czechoslovakia, they were not democracies at all, but were ruled by authoritarian regimes, usually headed by a high-ranking military man of noble origin, for example Horthy in Hungary, Mannerheim in Finland, and Pilsudski in Poland. The outspoken anti-Bolshevism of these new states was matched only by their anti-Russian sentiment. However, the Bolsheviks managed to recuperate some territories on the periphery of the former czarist empire, for example Ukraine. The outcome of this confusing medley of conflicts was a kind of tie: the Bolsheviks triumphed in Russia and as far west as Ukraine, but anti-Bolshevik, anti-Russian nationalists with great and mutually conflicting territorial ambitions prevailed in areas further west and north, specifically Poland, the Baltic States, and Finland; it was an arrangement that satisfied nobody, but was ultimately accepted by everybody — though clearly only "for the duration."

A *cordon sanitaire* consisting of a string of hostile states was thus erected around revolutionary Russia with the assistance of the Western powers in the hope that it would "isolate Bolshevism within Russia," as Margaret MacMillan has written.[31] For the time being, that was all the West was able to do, but the ambition of putting an end to the revolutionary experiment in Russia sooner or later remained very much alive in London, Paris, and Washington. For a long time, the Western leaders kept hoping that Russia's revolution would collapse by itself, but that failed to happen. Later, during the 1930s, they would hope that Nazi

Germany would take on the task of destroying the revolution in its lair, the Soviet Union; this is why they would allow Hitler to remilitarize Germany and, via the infamous "appeasement policy," encourage him to do so.

CHAPTER 29

VERSAILLES: PEACE OR ARMISTICE?

On June 28, 1919, exactly five years after the assassination in Sarajevo, the signing of the Peace Treaty of Versailles officially terminates the Great War. In reality, this treaty merely inaugurates a long truce that will expire in 1939, when worldwide warfare will resume, lasting until 1945. Many historians now indeed consider the First and Second World Wars as parts one and two of one single conflict, as a kind of twentieth-century edition of the disastrous "Thirty Years' War" of the 1600s, with the years from 1918 to 1939 constituting a long intermission . . .

On a dark night toward the middle of November 1918, a ship bound for the United States encountered an oncoming vessel with all lights blazing, which was unheard of in view of the state of war and the danger represented by submarines. Via light signals, it was asked if perhaps the war was finished. The answer was: "No, it is only an armistice."[1] And indeed, an armistice such as the one signed by military officials at Rethondes did not put an end to the state of war. The state of war officially continued after November 11, 1918, to be terminated only when statesmen would reach an agreement and sign a peace treaty. In the meantime, allied troops entered Germany as conquerors, the Royal Navy continued its blockade of Germany, and in many regions of Eastern Europe fighting continued between withdrawing German troops, the Bolshevik revolutionaries, Polish and Lithuanian nationalists, etc. In France the state of siege, associated with the war, would be lifted only on October 12, 1919.

The peace negotiations took place in Paris. They started on January 18, 1919, and resulted in a treaty signed on June 28 of that same year in the Hall of Mirrors in the Palace of Versailles. The French had decided on that venue in order to obtain some symbolic revenge for the fact that it was from that same room that the German Reich had been proclaimed in January 1871, during the Franco-Prussian War of 1870–1871. The Treaty of Versailles officially ended the war between Germany and the Allies, except for the United States and China, which would sign separate peace treaties with Germany. With the Ottoman Empire and the successor states of the Habsburg Empire, Austria and Hungary, peace treaties would be signed with the former at Sèvres in 1920 and with the latter at Lausanne in 1923.[2]

The main points of the Versailles Treaty demonstrated all too clearly that the war had not been about freedom, justice, democracy, the defence of small countries such as Belgium, or to put an end to warfare and similar concocted rationales; this type of discourse was, and remains even today, only vulgar propaganda. It was all about consolidating and increasing the power and privileges of the elite. At Versailles the elite was admittedly unable, at least for the time being, to undo the unpleasant social outcome of the war, the revolution in Russia and democratic political and social reforms in Britain, France, and elsewhere. On the other hand, the elite had also unleashed the Great War in order to achieve imperialist objectives for the benefit of banks and corporations, and in this respect the war had produced considerable gains (for the winners, of course), which were enshrined at Versailles. The French, British, Japanese, and even the Belgians were confirmed in the possession of Germany's former colonies in Africa and elsewhere, and of the oil-rich parts of the now-defunct Ottoman Empire. Nobody considered the possibility of independence for any of these regions, except under some undemocratic regime that could be counted on to do the bidding of the British or some other Western power, as in the case of Saudi Arabia. There was no question of independence for India, China was not allowed to provide any meaningful input during the Paris talks, and not a single foreign power contemplated giving up its "concessions" in that country.

The socialist English poet W.N. Ewer provided the following sarcastic comment on this kind of imperialist gluttony and on the hypocrisy of the statesmen who made the decisions at Versailles in a poem entitled "No Annexations":

"No annexations?" We agree!
We did not draw the sword for gain,
But to keep little nations free;
And surely, surely, it is plain
That land and loot we must disdain,
Who only fight for liberty.

.   .   .   .

Of course it happens — as we know —
That 'German East' has fertile soil
Where corn and cotton crops will grow,
That Togoland is rich in oil,
That natives can be made to toil
For wages white men count too low,
That many a wealthy diamond mine
Makes South-West Africa a prize,
That river-dam and railway line
(A profitable enterprise)
May make a paying paradise
Of Baghdad and of Palestine.

However, this is by the way;
We do not fight for things like these
But to destroy a despot's sway,
To guard our ancient liberties:
We cannot help it if it please
The Gods to make the process pay.

We cannot help it if our Fate
Decree that war in Freedom's name
Shall handsomely remunerate
Our ruling classes. 'T was the same
In earlier days — we always came
Not to annex, but liberate.[3]

With the Treaty of Versailles, the "ruling classes" were indeed "handsomely remunerated"; at least, those of the powers that emerged victoriously from the war and dictated the terms of the peace.

The armistice of November 11, 1918, had not put an end to the war, and the peace treaty signed at Versailles, as well as the other treaties mentioned here, did not produce a genuine peace. On the side of the losers — and even of the winners — there were those who longed for a *revanche* while the ink on the documents was not yet dry. In fact, nobody was entirely satisfied with any of these treaties, but the least satisfied of all were to be found in Germany, where the once so powerful and ambitious elite had lost many of its feathers, but unfortunately not enough of them to abandon any hope for a military comeback and a revanchist war.

On the side of the winners, too, the desire for revenge and the cupidity of the imperialists, reflected in the terms of the Treaty of Versailles, gave many people the nasty feeling that some of them had already experienced during the war itself, namely that even in case of victory over the German "Huns" there would be no question of real peace, but that a new Great War was likely to erupt again soon between the imperialist powers. In 1915 already, in his poem "War," the writer Joseph Leftwich (or Lefkowitz) had accurately predicted the following:

> *And if we win and crush the Huns,*
> *In twenty years*
> *We must fight their sons,*
> *Who will rise against*
> *Our victory,*
> *Their fathers', their own*
> *Ignominy.*
>
> *And if their Kaiser*
> *We dethrone,*
> *They will his son restore,*
> *or some other one,*
> *If we win by war,*
> *War is force,*
> *And others to war*

Will have recourse.

And through the world
Will rage new war.
Earth, sea and sky
Will wince at his roar.
He will trample down
At every tread,
Millions of men,
Millions of dead.[4]

The armistice of November 1918, which ended the hostilities, did not inaugurate peace, and the peace officially proclaimed at Versailles in 1919 really amounted to a mere armistice, a truce predestined to expire sooner or later with the resumption of open hostilities and the official return of the state of war. That moment would come in 1939, when a new Great War would break out. Historians such as Arno Mayer have therefore spoken of a "Thirty-Years' War" of the twentieth century, waged from 1914 to 1945, but interrupted by an uneasy "armistice" from 1919 to 1939.[5]

While the statesmen were negotiating in Paris in early 1919, the French capital was swept by a wave of strikes. Reports were also arriving daily of strikes, demonstrations, riots, and other expressions of social unrest and rebelliousness from all over Europe and from as far away as Canada. It was also at that time that the Allies were forced to abandon their armed intervention in Russia on account of the widespread opposition of their own soldiers and civilians. The dreaded revolution was seemingly poised to triumph in Russia and to be gaining ground everywhere. Lloyd George, Clemenceau, and their colleagues were in some ways more concerned with finding ways to stop the revolution than with making a real peace. This is the reason Germany was not forced to lay down its weapons and disarm entirely, but was allowed to have its troops fight the Bolsheviks as they withdrew from Eastern Europe, and also to keep an army of 100,000 men, namely to be able to fight Germany's own revolutionaries. In any event, it is understandable that, under these circumstances, the upper-class gentlemen from the Entente countries and Germany gathering in Paris did not want to invite revolutionary Russia's Bolshevik leaders to participate in the talks. Such an invitation would have increased their prestige and would have provided them with an opportunity to fan the flames of the revolutionary fires that were already burning just about everywhere. Not being a party to the Versailles Treaty, the Bolsheviks would eventually conclude a number of peace treaties of their own when the hostilities finally ended in Russia itself and in Eastern Europe, namely with the new states that originated on Russia's western frontier: the Treaties of Tartu with Estonia and Finland (1920), of Moscow with Lithuania (1920), and of Riga with Poland (1921).

In 1919, the social problems of the prewar era had not been solved, and were becoming worse; the social, "horizontal" war between classes, which the elite had unleashed in 1914 at the same time as the political and military "vertical" war between nations, was far from finished. And while the treaty being prepared in Paris, to be signed in Versailles, would put an end, at least temporarily, to the "vertical" war between countries, it would do nothing to terminate the "horizontal" war within the Great War, the class war within the war between countries. The statesmen gathered in Paris solved the problem of the "vertical" war poorly, and the problem of the "horizontal" war, not at all. It is hardly surprising that the Parisian strikers condemned the Versailles Peace Treaty as one concocted "without any input from the proletariat," as an agreement "against the interests of the proletariat," a "treaty of imperialists," "a crime."[6]

PART THREE

THE LONG SHADOW OF
THE GREAT WAR

CHAPTER 30

VIA FASCISM TO A SECOND WORLD WAR, 1918–1945

The European elite, henceforth dominated by the industrial and financial bourgeoisie, is frustrated by the counterproductive outcome of the Great War. After 1918 it seeks again to exorcise the demon of revolution, to arrest and reverse the democratization process, and to achieve major imperialist gains, this time via a new instrument, fascism. German fascism is expected — and encouraged — to destroy the revolution, now incarnated by the Soviet Union, but Germany's resurgence might also threaten the interests of the other imperialist powers. A new "Great War" is thus unleashed, with yet another unexpected and ambiguous result: a victory for the homeland of revolution against German fascism, but also a triumph for the US in the struggle for supremacy among imperialist powers . . .

This book has focused on the "horizontal" rather than the "vertical" war fought in 1914–1918. It has demonstrated that the Great War was also a conflict between classes within each country, rather than just a war between countries. It is therefore legitimate to refer to the Great War as the Great Class War. In some ways, however, this terminology is misleading, because it seems to imply that peace prevailed on the class front before 1914. In reality, this was not the case at all. Class struggle, a war between the classes, or at least the "contemporary" edition of the war between the classes, had been raging in Europe — and increasingly in much of the rest of the world

— since the French Revolution. It had been a latent, smouldering conflict, certainly not imperceptible but spectacularly visible only when it erupted in the form of revolutions, such as those of 1789, 1830, and 1848. In military terms, appropriate if we view the class struggle as a kind of war, these revolutions amounted to offensives launched by the lower classes. These offensives achieved considerable political and social gains of a democratic nature — that is, for the benefit of the majority of the people, the demos — such as the abolition of slavery, the widening of the suffrage, and some social benefits, but they did not achieve the great goal of the socialist champions of the plebeian cause, namely the overthrow of the established semi-feudal, semi-capitalist order. When in 1914 the smouldering class conflict erupted once again, it was in the form of a counteroffensive launched by the upper classes, by the elite, a bold move that manifested itself in the shape of a formal war. It was a large-scale, extremely ambitious counter-offensive, purporting to achieve a total victory over the restless "masses," namely by destroying any prospects of revolutionary change, by arresting and even rolling back the democratization process, undoing the democratic achievements of the nineteenth-century revolutions and perhaps even achieving a "great leap backward" to the good old days of the pre-1789 ancien régime. The objective was a total triumph over the plebeian class enemy, an end to the class struggle, a kind of "final solution" to the great social problems — in the interests of the elite, of course. Using metaphors inspired by the Great War itself, one could say that the elite's scheme was a kind of Schlieffen Plan, purporting to encircle and destroy the forces of the proletarian class enemy, just as the German high command had hoped to do with the French enemy. As in the case of the real Schlieffen Plan, in spite of great initial successes — exemplified by arrangements such as the French "sacred union" and Britain's "industrial truce" — things did not work out as planned. What was supposed to have been a short and trium-phant offensive thus degenerated into a long and miserable social form of "trench warfare."

Pursuing the metaphor inspired by the Great War itself, one might similarly describe the Russian Revolution as the equivalent of the Battle of the Marne, which caused the Schlieffen Plan to be tossed into the wastebasket. This revolution destroyed the elites' ambitious counterrevolutionary and antidemocratic plans of 1914 and forced them to adopt a defensive posture, similar to the Germans' after the Battle of the Marne. But there is definitely no analogy between the Russian Revolution and the victorious counteroffensive launched by the Allies in the summer of 1918. The latter was an initiative that produced victory, eventually putting an end to the "vertical" war between countries. While the curtain thus came down, at least formally, on the "vertical" Great War between countries, via an armistice and a peace treaty, the outcome of the "horizontal" Great War, the "Great Class War," remained uncertain, not only in 1918 but even in 1919. As in the case of the trench warfare that followed the Battle of the Marne, the social conflict within the Great War remained deadlocked even after the signing of the peace treaty of Versailles.

Class struggle, class "war," had not started in 1914, and it did not end in 1918 or 1919. After its spectacular eruption during 1914–1918, the class war that had started with the French Revolution reverted to its earlier latent configuration, in some ways comparable to trench warfare. Entrenched, so to speak, on opposite sides of the great social no man's land, the upper and lower classes, torn between fear of defeat and hope for victory, would henceforth conduct themselves sometimes defensively, and sometimes offensively, sometimes winning and sometimes losing ground. But after 1918/1919, the latent class warfare was qualitatively different, and much more complex, than it had been before 1914. Until 1914, the revolution that had been so loathed by the elite was an abstract concept, of whose practical incarnation the Paris Commune had presumably provided a foretaste. It was a chimera, to be dissipated by war, or so it was hoped. But after the Great War, the revolution found its incarnation in the country that was the product of a great revolution and symbolized the revolution, a new and bigger edition of the Paris Commune: the Soviet Union. Thus, while the class struggle remained a "horizontal" conflict between classes within each country, it now also acquired a "vertical" dimension. The class struggle now *also* became a conflict, a "cold" (and sometimes "hot") kind of war between countries: the single country that was the champion not only of its own but of the international lower classes, and consequently the more or less active sponsor of revolution all over the world, opposed by all other countries, which continued to be dominated by an elite, and were therefore actively involved in counterrevolutionary action at home and abroad. References to this "vertical" dimension of the class struggle, to the international conflict with the Soviet Union, would henceforth obscure its domestic social dimension, the primordial conflict between classes, and would make it possible for champions of radical and revolutionary change to be discredited as unpatriotic agents of a hostile foreign power, much as radicals had been denigrated in the US during the Great War as "un-American" German agents.

In 1919, nothing had been decided; everything was still possible, including successful revolutions in countries other than Russia, as well as victory for the counterrevolution within Russia. The Bolsheviks and their domestic and international sympathizers could still hope that other countries in Europe and throughout the world would follow their example, so that the established order might go down in the flames of a worldwide revolution and give way to the socialist Age of Aquarius. It is in this context of high hopes and expectations that in March 1919 the Third International (or Communist International, a.k.a. Comintern) was founded, with as mandate the promotion of worldwide revolution. And it is likewise in this context that in 1920 a great conference was organized in Baku, purporting to support the colonial peoples — especially in Asia — in their struggle for independence; however, the colonial peoples and the "semi-colonial" Chinese would have to wait until the end of the Second World War to rid themselves of their masters. In other words, for their national revolutions to succeed. The high hopes invested in social revolutions in Europe also remained unfulfilled. None of the other revolutions that broke out before or after the end of the Great War were crowned with success, and so the Russian revolutionaries, henceforth known as communists rather than Bolsheviks, proceeded to focus on the construction of a socialist society in what remained of the former czarist empire, to be known as the Soviet Union. After the death of Lenin, the Soviet communists would concentrate on the construction of "socialism in one country" under Stalin's leadership. (Trotsky's break with Stalin was due to the fact that the former wanted to continue the struggle for worldwide revolution.) The social revolution launched by the Bolsheviks thus merged increasingly with the struggle to resurrect Russia after the traumas caused by the war against Japan and the revolution that followed it, the disastrous Great War, the twin revolutions of 1917, and a nasty civil war.[1] The construction of a socialist society went hand-in-hand with the extremely rapid but far from painless industrialization and modernization of the gigantic country. Russia, in 1914 a generally overestimated but intrinsically still very backward country, thus metamorphosed into a superpower, though that would not become obvious until 1941–1945, when the widely underestimated Soviet Union would triumph over powerful Germany in a titanic war. While this victory was of course facilitated by help from allied nations, it was unquestionably first and foremost the Soviet Union's own handiwork, made possible by an industrial and military power that had been built up in very few years. Whatever one may think of his ruthless "totalitarian" policies, it is an undeniable fact that Stalin had come to power in the 1920s in a country that was backward, beaten, humiliated, internationally quarantined behind a *cordon sanitaire*, and internally divided, but left it behind at his death in 1953 as the world's second most powerful nation. This is something for which even the most anticommunist Russian nationalists tip their hat to him.

Entrenched on the opposite side of the no man's land in the ongoing class war, the European (and US) elite was to be found. We know what kind of ambitions this elite had entertained when it unleashed the Great War, but as Gabriel Kolko has written, "when Europe's leaders unleashed the dragons of war in 1914, they had no prevision whatsoever of its possibly grave, even fatal consequences for the future of their political and ideological world."[2] Their decision to go to war would indeed cause that world to be shaken to its very foundations, and to be damaged and altered dramatically. When the Great War came to an end, the revolution was no longer a chimera but a fact, and many countries witnessed the advent of unprecedented democratic reforms, rather than a roll-back of the modest prewar reforms. The Great War had not become a "great leap backward," but had catapulted Europe, and much of the rest of the world, forward into a more democratic era. Viewed from the perspective of the elite, the twentieth century, which had in some ways started with the Great War, threatened to become the century of democracy: unless, of course, the elite did something to prevent it. And indeed, the elite was not prepared to resign itself to the state of things; it was determined to recuperate the lost ground and, if at all possible, somehow achieve the ambitious counterrevolutionary and antidemocratic objectives it had had in mind in 1914. To understand how the establishment planned to do this, we must first examine how the world of the elite itself had been transformed during, and by, the Great War.

In 1914, the elite that embarked on a counterrevolutionary, antide-mocratic, and antisocialist offensive in the shape of a war consisted of a "symbiosis" of the landowning nobility and the industrial and financial bourgeoisie or upper-middle class. But the offensive was unquestion-ably directed by the nobility, which was still the senior partner within the European establishment. In a European society that had been rapidly modernizing for many decades but nonetheless retained many of its tradi-tional "feudal" features, the nobility enjoyed a quasi-monopoly of political power, a declining but still considerable amount of economic power, and enormous social prestige. The nobility hoped to be able to liquidate the democratic heritage of the French Revolution and reset the clock to the time of the presumably "good old days" of the *ancien régime.*

The upper-middle class or haute bourgeoisie went along with this project of a "great leap backward." This class had benefited in many ways from the French Revolution, but that revolution had produced the idea of equal-ity. Equality before the law was fine, and had been legally enshrined, but social equality was a different kettle of fish. The bourgeoisie had favoured social equality when it implied equality between itself and the nobility, but loathed that same equality when it was interpreted to mean equality between the bourgeoisie and the proletarians and other plebeians. The upper-middle class also went along with the nobility's penchant for war because its bastions were the big enterprises and banks who trusted that war would bring them great profits, for example, via the production of weapons, and achieve great imperialist objectives; and the bourgeoisie also hoped that war would provide a wonderful opportunity to teach good man-ners to the restless workers and other plebeians. It is probably fair to say that the upper-middle class also dreamed of a great leap backward, but to the imaginary "good old days" before 1848, rather than before 1789.

In the summer of 1914, it seemed for a moment that the scheme con-cocted by the nobility and backed by the bourgeoisie would succeed. The subjects of the crowned heads marched meekly toward the battlefields, blessed by the prelates, commanded by aristocrats on high horses, and ready to sacrifice their lives for the glory of the sovereign and the good of the fatherland; and the leaders of the formerly fearsome popular masses, namely the socialists and trade unionists, gave up the class struggle by signing on to arrangements of the *union sacrée* type. But disillusion came all too quickly. The course of the war soon revealed that the generals, mostly members of the nobility, were useless as managers of modern war. Their colourful uniforms, horses, sabres and lances, and above all their attacking strategies were hopelessly out of place in a conflict that was not at all like the crusades and other medieval or even Napoleonic conflicts glorified by the Romanticists, but that revealed itself to be a modern, industrial war. The aristocratic and upper-middle-class officers also became the object of the hatred of the uniformed proletarians because they were so wasteful with the latters' lives. Add to that the fact that in states such as Germany and the Danube Monarchy agriculture, the great speciality and therefore responsibility of the landowning, "agrarian" nobility, proved unable to feed its soldiers and civilians. In short, the war demonstrated that the economy, the military and organizational talents, the weapons, the strategy, the mentality, and ultimately the rule of the nobility belonged to the past and not to the present, let alone the future.

As the setbacks multiplied and the misery increased, the population, civilians as well as soldiers, lost their respect for the monarchs and the aristocratic military and political leaders, became disgruntled, disrespectful, rebellious, and ultimately ready and even eager to overthrow the established order, in many countries still very much a feudal order, via a revolution. The war thus produced exactly the opposite of what the nobility had expected of it: not a return to the glories of the days of old, but the ignominious end of the rule of centuries-old dynasties and the collapse of great and presumably glorious empires, namely the German Reich as well as the Habsburg, Romanov, and Ottoman empires. The German Empire had been a federation of monarchies and city states, and together with Wilhelm II, who had been not only emperor of Germany but also king of Prussia, about twenty other German sovereigns lost their crowns, ranging from the powerful King of Bavaria to Lilliputian rulers such as the Count of Saxony-Coburg-Gotha, some of whose relatives managed to survive the feudal *Götterdämmerung* and still occupy royal thrones today, namely in Britain and Belgium.[3] "The war . . . forever shattered the self-assured, sunlit Europe of . . . emperors waving from open, horse-drawn carriages," writes Adam Hochschild.[4] And in countries in which the monarchy and the nobility, closely associated with the monarchy, did not become the victims of revolutionary change, they had to concede the kind of democratic reforms that in 1914 they had hoped to roll back. These reforms restricted their privileges and power even more than had been done by the limited reforms introduced in the decades preceding 1914. In Britain, for example, universal suffrage was finally introduced in 1918. The Great War heralded the end of the political hegemony the nobility had enjoyed until 1914 but had found insufficient and had hoped to augment via the instrument of war.

On the economic level, too, the nobility lost many of its advantages. The war failed to create opportunities for increasing landed property, as especially the German and Austro-Hungarian aristocrats had hoped, and the social reforms that were introduced at the end of the war included a certain amount of land redistribution to the advantage of the small peasantry and the disadvantage of the large landowners; this was the case even in the new countries in Eastern Europe that were saddled with undemocratic, authoritarian regimes. The elite agreed to these measures in order to prevent the poor peasants from turning to the revolutionary option promoted by the Bolsheviks. "By creating a class of peasant smallholders," writes Mark Mazower, a historian specializing in the Balkan countries and Eastern Europe, "politicians hoped to buy social tranquillity and prevent revolution."[5] After the war, it also became necessary just about everywhere to pay considerably higher wages to the servants and other staff members whose services had been cheap before 1914. And the cost of maintaining chateaux and city mansions skyrocketed after the war.[6] The "good old days" were gone forever for the landowning nobility of the type portrayed in the popular TV series *Downton Abbey*. In the case of aristocrats in countries that had lost the war, such as Germany, the prestige of the army, traditionally a power bastion of the nobility, had suffered a nasty blow. The church, another pillar of the establishment, likewise tied to the nobility, lost much of its influence and prestige on account of its unconditional support for the hated war. The fact that God did not seem to care that human beings massacred each other on a bestial and unprecedented scale caused even more people to turn their backs on the Catholic, Protestant, and Orthodox Churches. The demise of the great empires amounted to a heavy blow to the religions that had been closely associated with them, namely Lutheranism in Prussian-dominated Germany, Catholicism in the Danube Monarchy and South-German states such as Bavaria, Orthodox Christianity in Russia, and Islam in the Ottoman Empire. In the latter empire, the sultan had simultaneously held the title of caliph, that is, successor to the Prophet and head of the worldwide Muslim community. The end of the Ottoman sultanate, a political institution, also signified the end of the caliphate, an important and prestigious institution for the Islamic religion. Finally, the war also ruined the previously unassailable cultural position of the nobility. During and because of the Great War, Romanticism, the cultural movement closely associated with the nobility and the church and their conservative, quasi-medieval ideas, which had glorified and promoted crusades and presumably chivalrous war in general, went out of fashion quickly and irreversibly. The brave knight Ivanhoe could not be a hero in the eyes of civilians and soldiers who had experienced the very unmedieval and extremely unromantic holocaust of the Great War.

Of all the wonderful things the aristocratic component of the elite had dreamed of in 1914, essentially a glorious *"retour en arrière"* to before 1789, nothing had materialized during the Great War. To the contrary, a major share of the power and wealth still enjoyed by the nobility in 1914 was lost; however, after 1918, there remained the hope that, with the help of the army, the church, and above all the financial and industrial bourgeoisie, much of the damage might be repaired and some of the lost ground might be recuperated. Other than in Russia, the nobility had not yet been counted out. Large landownership was no longer the great source of wealth and power it had been in the past, but rental income, derived from such immobile property, remained a considerable source of income for countless aristocratic families. And many aristocrats had invested in mining, industry, and banking. In countries such as Germany, the highest ranks within the army were to remain a quasi-monopoly of the nobility until 1945. (The family of field marshal Gerd von Rundstedt, who orchestrated the Third Reich's final offensive in the Battle of the Bulge, was a member of Prussia's *Uradel* or "old nobility.") In the diplomatic service, too, noble-men would continue to be overrepresented for many more decades. The Christian Churches had lost many of their followers and much of their prestige, but remained nonetheless useful allies of the nobility. After 1918, they continued to be particularly influential in rural regions. Thanks to its wartime patriotism, the Catholic Church even achieved a remarkable come-back in the previously strongly anticlerical French republic. Diplomatic relations between the Vatican and France were restored, and Joan of Arc as well as Marguerite-Marie Alacoque, the nun who had launched the cult of the Sacred Heart in the seventeenth century, were canonized in 1920. Pious prayers and the *"Marseillaise"* could henceforth resonate in harmoni-ous togetherness under the vaults of sanctuaries such as Notre Dame and the Sacré-Cœur and Catholic chapels would appear clinging like barnacles to the hulls of patriotic shrines erected during the 1920s in commemora-tion of the Great War, for example at Verdun. The dream of a rebirth of a Catholic and conservative France, inspired by medieval antecedents, was thus able to live on even in the twentieth century. What remained possible in France remained *a fortiori* possible in many other European countries: there too, nobility and Church, no matter how much damage they had suffered, kept looking out for an opportunity to turn the clock back as far in time as possible.[7] Even so, it is clear that nobility emerged considerably weakened from the Great War.

Other than losers, wars also "create winners . . . among social classes," as Gabriel Kolko has pointed out.[8] And it was the nobility's partner within the elite, the industrial and financial bourgeoisie, that emerged as major winner from the social struggle the Great War had been. In contrast to the plebs, the bankers and the industrialists had profited from the war and accumulated unheard-of riches. For them the war had been a cornucopia, a wonderful experience from the viewpoint of their primordial objective: profit maximization. The Great War had been a modern, industrial war, fought with modern weapons such as cannons, machine guns, poison gas, tanks, airplanes, flame-throwers, trucks, barbed wire, and submarines. All this materiel had been mass-produced in the factories of the industrialists, showering them with gargantuan profits. In all belligerent countries the state had to finance the war effort by borrowing enormous amounts of money, which had caused banks such as J.P. Morgan & Co. to accumulate unprecedented riches. Nowhere, however, had the state attempted to limit the profits in the same way that it limited the wages of workers. And the big corporations and major banks of the victorious imperialist powers could expect to derive considerable advantages from the acquisition of territories inside and outside of Europe that were part of the victors' war booty.[9]

Peter Englund describes the Great War as "an economic competition, a war between factories," in which it gradually became clear that the countries that were the strongest and the best organized on the industrial level were likely if not certain to triumph. The management of the war was therefore increasingly turned over to industrial "experts" such as Walter Rathenau of AEG in Germany and representatives of the *Comité des Forges* in France. In Britain, Lloyd George arranged for high government positions to be occupied by countless businessmen and bankers, with as result a kind of "businessmen's government." The war, unleashed so frivolously in 1914 by the agrarian nobility, revealed itself to be a wonderful opportunity for the industrial and financial bourgeoisie to make money and increase its power. It is a paradox, as Arno Mayer has noted in this context, that "[the agrarians'] cooperati[on] with the captains of industry," required by the war, "contributed . . . to the very modernization that was hastening their eclipse."[10]

The big enterprises — and the big banks closely associated with them — increased their influence on the state during the Great War, and afterwards they would maintain and even further increase that influence. Conversely, the profitable collaboration with the state also implied a greater state influence on industry and banking; in other words, more dirigisme and less laissez-faire. But for the time being that was the only way in which the industrialists could secure the huge state orders (for weapons and such) on which their profitability henceforth depended. Industry itself experienced a trend that had already set in toward the end of the 1800s, namely an increasing intimate collaboration between big firms and big banks in the form of trusts, holdings, and limited companies. Via such "gigantism" the industrialists and bankers aimed to avoid or at least limit the potentially harmful consequences of the all-out competition glorified in classical liberal, laissez-faire theory, and also to better defend their common interests against their workers and other employees.[11]

Compared to the aristocratic agrarians, their partners within the elite, the industrialists revealed themselves to be far better managers of the industrial conflict that the Great War happened to be. And so, in striking contrast to the nobility, they emerged triumphantly from this conflict. Within the elite, the bourgeoisie would henceforth dominate, while the nobility was downgraded to the role of junior partner. The bourgeoisie enjoyed greater economic power than ever before, but henceforth it also enjoyed the lion's share of political power. Arthur Marwick writes that in Britain businessmen had already been "an accepted part of the political elite of Edwardian Britain" (i.e., before 1914, more precisely between 1901 and 1910) but that during the war they had massively penetrated into the nerve centres of political power. Personalities from the world of big business even crowded landowning aristocrats out as leaders of the Conservative Party. During the 1918 elections, the first after the reform of the electoral laws, they carried numerous constituencies, above all in the large cities. This perturbed many aristocrats, who looked down on businessmen as *nouveaux riches* and felt that their very own party was becoming "thoroughly commercialized and vulgarized" on account of the influx of upstart "plutocrats." The British upper class, concludes Marwick, was and remained a "composite class," a symbiosis, consisting of aristocrats and businessmen, "but primacy had slipped from the hands of the landed interest into those of the businessmen."[12] In postwar Germany, too, leading bankers and big industrialists such as Krupp, Siemens, and Thyssen overtook the previously omnipotent aristocratic large landowners in terms of political influence and power. Georg Lukács described the situation as follows in Marxist terms: "After the defeat in the recent war, the alliance between German monopoly capital and the patriciate of the *Junkers* persisted within the military and civil bureaucracy, but monopoly capital took over the leading role in all respects."[13]

This important shuffle within the European elite may be illustrated by means of a small kaleidoscope of images from the Great War. The important personalities associated with August 1914 are the emperors Wilhelm II, Franz-Joseph, and Nicholas II. In pictures and even in old film footage, we see these aristocratic superstars, dressed in magnificent uniforms, chests bedecked with decorations, emerging from their palaces on high horses to ride (symbolically) off into war through admiring and cheering crowds.

The official end of the war, on the other hand, the peace conference in Paris, conjures up gentlemen of a different plumage, namely bourgeois types such as Clemenceau and Wilson. These are soberly dressed in tailcoats and top hats and arrive in automobiles at the very bourgeois Hotel Majestic. With the former, the "long" nineteenth century came to an end; with the latter, the twentieth century got underway, admittedly somewhat belatedly. The opening phase of the Great War also brings to mind images of uhlans and *cuirassiers* with shiny breastplates, heads covered with fur hats or feathered helmets, riding into battle on "noble" steeds, armed with sabres and lances; it seems a flashback to the Napoleonic wars, fought a hundred years earlier. The German spring offensive and the final offensive of the Allies in 1918, on the other hand, is associated with storm troopers in steel helmets, fighting their way forward with machine guns and flame-throwers, with Krupp's big cannons firing at Paris from a distance of more than a hundred kilometres, with tanks, airplanes, and thousands of trucks ferrying troops to the front; the Great War ended as a truly modern war of the twentieth century, not very different from later conflicts such as the Second World War. The symbolic halfway point was July 1, 1916, the beginning of the great *Materialschlacht* in the Somme District. There and then, General Haig oversaw the biggest artillery bombardment in history, but also kept a huge number of horsemen ready in the hope that, as in Napoleon's time, the cavalry might deal the final blow to the enemy.

After the Great War, the bourgeoisie clearly overshadowed the nobility, just as the economy industry (and finance) clearly eclipsed agriculture. Before the war, Europe was still a feudal-capitalist society; after the war, it was overwhelmingly capitalist and remained only minimally feudal. In other words, the "old continent" looked much more like the "new world" of the United States before the war: a thoroughly capitalist society with an elite consisting not exclusively but predominantly of big industrialists and bankers: "capitalists." The US itself, wrongly considered by many historians to be "isolationist," would display an increasing interest in Europe, perhaps not politically, but certainly economically. Its big corporations and banks, for example, invested massively in Germany. And its cultural influence suddenly became huge, with jazz music and Hollywood films taking Europe by storm. When the Great War had started, Americans had been invisible in Europe; but at the end of the war, and especially during the peace conference in Paris, in early 1919, President Wilson became a superstar on the European scene. In short, the Great War launched the "Americanization" of Europe. It is not a coincidence that, after the Great War, on the international level, the French language, associated for centuries with monarchs and diplomats and thus, in a way, with fading-out feudalism, was dethroned by English, the idiom closely connected with business, commerce, and money; in other words, with conquering capitalism.

If, after the Great War, the decline of the nobility was dramatic, it was far from total and irreversible. Conversely, the concomitant triumph of the industrial and financial bourgeoisie was far from perfect. When the war had caused the plebeians to be disillusioned at first, then miserable and progressively more disgruntled and rebellious, finally exploding in strikes, demonstrations, riots, mutinies, and even revolutions, all of this also had very disagreeable consequences for the industrialists and bankers. Their social prestige, for example, did not increase at all in the way their profitability and political power did. The soldiers and workers, whose wages were frozen, cursed them as war profiteers. Moreover, the industrialists and bankers hardly appreciated the fact that more or less radical political and social reforms, such as universal suffrage and the eight-hour day, had to be introduced at the end of the war in order to forestall revolution. They were hardly pleased that here and there it proved necessary to allow socialists, no matter how reformist, to join coalition governments, and that trade unions had to be granted some input into the management of corporations. But by far the most irritating result of the Great War, from a capitalist perspective, was that a revolution had not only broken out but actually succeeded, namely in Russia. This Russian Revolution purported not only to wipe out the old czarist *ancien régime* but also Russia's budding capitalism, which caused considerable losses to the Western capitalists themselves. Indeed, the Bolsheviks did not honour the foreign debts incurred by the czarist regime and ruthlessly nationalized — without compensation — the Russian branch plants and other investments of foreign corporations. During the war, Shell, for example, had made a lot of money, but the Russian Revolution caused it to lose "its" oil wells in the Caucasus, which brought upon Lenin and his comrades the hatred of Henri Deterding, the big boss of Shell. Deterding would later encourage and support Hitler's anti-Soviet ambitions in the hope of recuperating his Caucasian assets. It was also particularly painful for the industrial and financial upper-middle class that it proved impossible to "strangle the Bolshevik baby in its crib" by means of armed intervention in the Russian Civil War, so that the capitalist system henceforth faced unwanted competition from an alternative model that served as a source of inspiration and encouragement for radicals everywhere. First and foremost among these radicals were of course those socialists who, in contrast to the reformist majority, continued to believe in the possibility and even ineluctability of the revolution, sympathized and collaborated with the Russian Bolsheviks, and were increasingly known as "communists."

The revolutionary experiment in Russia also served as example to the exploited and oppressed population of colonies such as India and Vietnam and "semi-colonies" such as China. Before the Great War, the latter, a huge but weak country, had loomed in imperialist eyes as an "Ottoman Empire of the Far East," as a potential Shangri-la of unlimited possibilities for territorial expansion and above all economic penetration. Communists such as Ho Chi Minh and Mao Zedong were all the more detested in London, Paris, and Washington because in the colonies they simultaneously preached social and national revolution. In contrast to the reformist socialists, the Russian Bolsheviks and international communists did not support imperialism but, to the contrary, incited the supposedly inferior yellow-, brown-, or black-skinned peoples against their white colonial masters. This made it easy for the Western elites to conclude that the Bolsheviks themselves were nothing other than a despicable bunch of racially inferior "oriental" or "Asian" bashi-bouzouks, bastards who out of blind hatred wanted to put an end to the supposedly "natural" or "God-given" (and presumably beneficial) worldwide hegemony of the white "Aryans" — "white supremacy," as it was known in the US. The spectre of revolution henceforth haunted the entire world and threatened not only what remained of the *ancien régime* so dear to the hearts of the nobility, but the capitalist — more specifically, imperialist — system built up by the industrialists and bankers. It is clear that the bourgeoisie was not prepared to remain inactive while at home and all over the world its power and privileges were thus threatened. It looked for ways not only to protect what it had acquired but also to recuperate lost ground, specifically in the form of the political and social concessions that had to be made at the end of the Great War in order to forestall revolution. Since the bourgeoisie's junior partner within the elite, the nobility, as well as the Churches associated with the nobility, were likewise looking for ways not only to hold their ground but to recuperate their losses, the elite remained just as eager after 1918 as it had been before 1914 to do battle with the Lucifer of revolution, in the metropolitan countries as well as in the colonies.

Whenever and wherever it proved feasible, the elite ruthlessly repressed revolutionary movements and ensured, via the installation of authoritarian political systems, that hardly any democratic reforms of a political or social nature had to be introduced. This was the case in Hungary, for example, where the revolution led by Béla Kun had to give way to the dictatorship of Admiral Horthy, a figurehead of the Habsburg *ancien régime*. Elsewhere, reforms had to be hurriedly introduced in order to avoid the fearsome revolutionary alternative. In Britain and in Belgium, the elite was thus able to forestall a threatening revolution. In Germany, where revolution did in fact break out, it was ruthlessly repressed; but far-reaching reforms were still enacted, specifically in order to appease the plebs, who would remain restless and potentially revolutionary for some time. In cases like this, the elite could usually count on the collaboration of the reformist socialists; for example, the Belgian socialists and the German social-democrats. Thanks to the reforms, which seemed to be the fruit of their labours, and in spite of the new competition from the communists, the reformist socialists managed to maintain their popularity among the workers and other plebeians. Their electoral successes would lead to participation in coalition governments, and so the reformist socialists became even more integrated into the established order. The same thing happened to the trade unions, which also contributed to the introduction of political and social reforms. Even more than before the Great War, the lower classes gave their support to socialism, and they mostly gave it to reformist socialists or social-democrats, and less to the revolutionary socialists or communists.

In both Western and Central Europe, the working class opted for the path of gradual democratization, for reforms within the established order. But in this established order the elite continued to enjoy the lion's share of power, and it was determined to use that power in order to get rid, sooner or later, of the reforms it had reluctantly allowed. With the exception of the communists, the lower orders that had loomed so threatening before 1914 had been integrated into the established order in much of Europe, but neither the bourgeois nor the aristocratic wing of the elite had any warm feelings for socialists or trade unionists, no matter how accommodating and cooperative they happened to be. To the contrary, they despised them only slightly less than they hated the communists. Once the dark clouds of revolution had blown over, the elite hoped to get rid of the reforms and to roll the democratization process back as far as possible. The bourgeois-aristocratic establishment constituted only a small demographic minority; in a democracy with universal suffrage and proportional representation, its traditional political parties had hardly any prospects of success. The industrialists, bankers, and aristocrats therefore aspired to a return to one of the authoritarian systems that had been the norm before 1914, and they longed to turn back the clock — as they had done in 1914.

Already in 1918 and 1919, experience showed how such a leap backward could be achieved. In Germany, the army commanders had received the green light from the SPD to snuff out the revolution. But the high command did not trust its own troops, because these were infected by the revolutionary virus; it had therefore dissolved most army units and replaced them with bands of volunteers, recruited among reliable officers, fanatic storm troopers, and bourgeois as well as petit-bourgeois nationalist students. Many of these volunteers were soldiers who, during the war, had internalized the ethos of the elite. They believed that in the trenches they had discovered a new and supposedly superior form of socialism. The cocktail of this "socialism of the trenches" included a heavy dose of German nationalism and did not resemble Marxist socialism with its internationalism, allegedly a pernicious invention of the "international people," the Jews, and therefore considered to be a "Jewish" socialism; "trench socialism" was presumably a German, a "national" brand of socialism. Thus were set up the "free corps" that, in Berlin, Munich, and elsewhere, smothered the revolution in blood; for example, by brutally assassinating Karl Liebknecht and Rosa Luxemburg in January 1919. Historians have justifiably described these free corps as "proto-Nazis," because they served as model for the political movement founded by Hitler in Munich, a movement he baptized "national socialism." In any event, the German elite was very impressed by the performance of the free corps. It concluded that similarly brutal action might be useful not only for fighting the revolution but also for rolling back democratization. While the free corps could be used to intimidate and tame the restless workers, the German elite understood and appreciated that such a force might be useful for establishing and maintaining an old- or new-style authoritarian state in which the demographic minority of industrialists, bankers, and landowners would be able to rule and prosper as they could not do within a democracy. Hence the support they already gave at an early stage to the nascent "national socialism" of Adolf Hitler.[14]

The same kind of lesson was also learned by the Italian elite, consisting of industrialists, bankers, large landowners, the royal family, the high army command, and the Vatican. In the years immediately following the end of the Great War, Italy found itself in a state of revolution, but the Italian equivalent of the German free corps, the brutal *squadristi* of the Fascist Party of Benito Mussolini, played an important role in the ultimate repression of the revolutionary movement. Via a so-called "March on Rome," a well-orchestrated charade, the elite hoisted Mussolini into the saddle of political power to do what was expected of him: lower wages, get rid of the embryonic democratic system by abolishing universal suffrage and rolling back social reforms such as the eight-hour day, teach the workers the necessary "discipline" and respect for their superiors, and eliminate the trade unions as well as the socialist and communist parties. The royal dynasty and nobility could thus preserve and even increase their wealth and power, though the latter was now exercised behind the stage of fascist pomp and circumstance. The Vatican received its share of the loot, so to speak, when in 1929 Mussolini concluded the "Lateran Agreements" with the Pope. These put an end to the separation of church and state in Italy and offered the Catholic Church enormous financial and other advantages, including laws prohibiting divorce and a major, if not preponderant, role in the nation's educational system. In Italy Mussolini thus achieved what the European elite had expected of the war in 1914, several steps back in the direction of the *ancien régime,* to the time before the establishment of the Italian state in the 1860s and even before the French Revolution of 1789, when church and state had been separated for the first time. But Mussolini also revealed himself useful to Italy's bankers and industrialists such as Pirelli and Agnelli, because he abolished the recently introduced social legislation, lowered wages, and eliminated workers' parties and unions; and his armament program produced lucrative state orders for their factories. Moreover, his brutal imperialist policy bore fruit in the shape of colonies and vassal states such as Ethiopia and Albania, conquered in 1936 and 1939, respectively: their raw materials, markets, and cheap labour proved most useful to Italy's industrialists. In these colonies the elite could also dump the surfeit of Sicilians who, like other poor, non-Nordic, and therefore "inferior" folks, were not welcome in the United States after the Great War.[15]

The elite of all of Europe was greatly impressed by the antidemocratic labours of the fascist Hercules. In 1926, when a general strike raged in Britain, Churchill was extremely upset with this example of plebeian seditiousness. He proposed to have the striking miners sprayed with machine gun fire and declared in this context that Mussolini, "the Roman genius, the greatest lawgiver among men," "had rendered a service to the whole world" by showing how one should fight subversive forces. Two other representatives of the British elite who did not hide their admiration for Mussolini were Lloyd George and General Haig. After a visit to fascist Italy, the latter proclaimed that "we want someone like that at home at the present time."[16] Mussolini also made a great impression on Germany's industrialists and others members of the country's elite; for example, the conservative and clerical mayor of Cologne at the time, who would later be chancellor of West Germany, Konrad Adenauer.[17] By crushing the revolution, the German free corps had already done useful work for the elite, but the latter remained uncomfortable and unhappy in the Weimar Republic, a state that was much too democratic to its taste. The elite longed for the coming of a fascist messiah in Germany, for a "German Mussolini" who would rid them of this democratic nuisance. This messiah was to make his appearance in 1933 in the person of Adolf Hitler. The *Führer*'s advent would be made possible by the German elite, and their members would expect, and receive, great things from him, not only socially regressive policies but high profits and impressive imperialist conquests. Hitler would also try very hard to realize what was perhaps the fondest dream, not only of the German but also of the international elite, namely the destruction of the Soviet Union; but that project was to end in dismal failure.[18]

A few years after Hitler's advent to power, the elite would also manage, via a nasty civil war, to replace Spain's budding democracy with a semimilitary, semifascist regime led by Francisco Franco. Under his auspices, Spain would rush back in some ways to the medieval era of the "Catholic Kings," Ferdinand and Isabella. It was not inappropriate that one of the features of their coat of arms, the yoke, symbol *par excellence* of oppression, was eagerly adopted by Franco. Portugal, the Baltic states, Finland, and Poland witnessed very similar scenarios. In all these countries, more or less democratic systems had emerged at the end of the Great War. But in the course of the 1920s and 1930s these democracies were dismantled by the large landowners, industrialists, and bankers, usually with the blessing of the Church and the assistance of the army. One by one, they were replaced by authoritarian systems that were congenial to the elite. By the end of the 1930s, only a handful of formally democratic countries would be left in Europe. But in these countries too, the elites worked hard to liquidate the presumably inefficient "parliamentary" systems, and to replace them with authoritarian systems led by "strong men" like Hitler, Horthy, Mussolini, Mannerheim, Pilsudksi, Franco, and other Salazars. Some indiscreet "philofascists" of the elite did not hide their admiration for such regimes and leaders, including Hitler; Lord Halifax was one of them, and so were British bankers such as Montagu Norman of the Bank of England, American industrialists such as Henry Ford, and even members of the British royal family, for example the Prince of Wales, who would briefly occupy the throne as Edward VIII.[19] (Film footage has recently surfaced in which the latter teaches the present Queen Elizabeth II, then a young girl, to perform the Hitler salute.)

The authoritarian and often dictatorial regimes that dominated Europe's political landscape during the interbellum happened to be very much like the political and social-economic systems the elite had hoped to bring about by means of war in 1914. These regimes strongly resembled the brutal regime Germany had imposed on occupied Belgium, but managed to even surpass it in brutality. The Great War had not turned out as the elite had hoped. Still, it was in some ways on account of this war that, virtually everywhere after the revolutionary convulsions of 1917–1919, the process of democratization could be reversed in favour of dictatorships that were agreeable to the elite. Gabriel Kolko even feels that such "authoritarian and repressive movements and regimes became the war's dominant legacy."[20] Some of these authoritarian regimes were led by military men like Franco and Pilsudski, gentlemen who, with an iron hand, steered their country "forward to the past," to a new edition of an *ancien régime* that, as they saw it, had been heroic and glorious, like the Spain of the "Catholic Kings" (and the Inquisition) or the Republic of the Two Nations (a.k.a. the Polish-Lithuanian Union) that once stretched from the Baltic to the Black Sea shores. However, the even more authoritarian regimes that were known as "fascist" (in imitation of the name given by Mussolini to his party) revealed themselves to be better adapted to the modern times of the twentieth century. Hitler's national-socialist regime provided the most striking example of this type of state. The great advantage offered by the fascists, from the perspective of the elite, was that in contrast to the military dictatorships, they managed to attract quite a following among the plebeians — especially among the lower-middle class and the peasants, though far less so among the workers. During elections, the fascist parties harvested large numbers of votes, and this bestowed on their regimes a certain aura of legitimacy. But the fascists never obtained a majority in any free elections, contrary to what we have too often been told. It was only thanks to active support of the elite that Mussolini and Hitler could come to power. The false allegation that Hitler was elected by a majority of Germans is not just a simple error, but consciously serves the purpose of making "the people" in general responsible for his advent to power, thus absolving the elite of any responsibility in the matter.[21]

The military dictators — Horthy, Pilsudski, and Franco, for example — were clearly representatives of the elite, associated with the army, the Church, the nobility, and the highest levels of the bourgeoisie. It was only too evident that their regimes defended and promoted the interests of the elite. Fascist leaders such as Mussolini and Hitler, on the other hand, were not representatives of the elite themselves, but men with roots in the mass of the people, plebeians and even former socialists or front soldiers. They could speak the idiom of the people, and they were excellent demagogues. They were also "populists," that is, politicians who *seemed* to defend the interests of ordinary people against the elite. They masqueraded as socialists, as anticapitalists, and even as revolutionaries, because anticapitalism, socialism, and revolution still enjoyed widespread popularity, and this approach was useful for the purpose of "vote-maximization." In reality, however, they defended the interests and pursued the objectives of the elite and actually did so more effectively than the elite's own representatives could have done: they did away with the trade unions and with the (genuinely) socialist as well as communist parties, and arranged for gargantuan state orders, which, in spite of the great economic crisis of the 1930s, generated unprecedented profits for big corporations. What the fascist and other authoritarian regimes ordered above all, to the great satisfaction of the generals, were weapons and all sorts of other war materiel. Disposing of such an arsenal made it possible for the elites of great powers with authoritarian governments, such as Italy and especially Germany, to dream of unleashing wars aimed at fulfilling grandiose imperialist aspirations. From the viewpoint of the elite, war would again become desirable, as it had been in 1914, but this time it would even become indispensable. Indeed, only via the booty produced by war would it be possible to pay back the huge loans fascists like Mussolini and Hitler had taken out to pay for the military expenditures. Profiting greatly from this business were the big banks, usually those that happened to be partners, or even owners, of the big corporations that made fortunes thanks to the fascist states' armament bonanzas. The wars unleashed by the fascist regimes were thus predestined to be wars of rapine. In light of this we can understand why, in the 1930s, Italy went to war against Ethiopia and Japan — a de facto military dictatorship — against China; and why, under Hitler, Germany rearmed, pursued an extremely aggressive foreign policy, and ultimately unleashed a second Great War.

Like the Great War of 1914–1918, Hitler's war was a "wanted" war. It was wanted not only by Hitler personally but also by Germany's industrialists and bankers, aristocratic large landowners, the high army command, and the rest of the country's establishment.[22] With this war, the Teutonic elite hoped not only to compensate for the losses in terms of colonies and territory within Europe itself, suffered as a result of defeat in the 1914–1918 clash of the imperialist titans; the intention was also, and even foremost, to finally realize the great imperialist ambitions the German industrialists and bankers had already entertained in 1914, as Fritz Fischer has demonstrated in a famous book about Germany's war aims. Germany's elite dreamed of a territorial expansion into the depths of Eastern Europe, especially Russia, a "land of unlimited possibilities" full of fertile soil, all sorts of minerals, including oil, and plenty of cheap labour. This "eastern land" (*Ostland*) was supposed to serve as a giant colony for Germany, exactly as India was for Britain and the "Wild West" had been for the United States. It is clear that the resurgence of great imperialist schemes in Germany was hardly welcome in London and Paris, so the war Hitler and the German elite wanted was likely to mean a new war against Britain and France — or, as one could also say, an end of the "truce" concluded in Versailles in 1919.

Conflicts between imperialist powers do not necessarily have to be settled by war; they can also be resolved by reaching agreements and concluding alliances. As had been the case in 1914, on the eve of the Second World War there were also industrialists, bankers, and politicians in Britain and France who would have preferred to reach an agreement with Hitler's Germany rather than risk a conflict with this powerful rival. They would try vainly to appease Germany with all sorts of concessions at the expense of third parties, for example Czechoslovakia, which, in Munich in 1938, was made to hand over to Hitler its border regions, inhabited by the German-speaking Sudeten. The British prime minister at the time, Neville Chamberlain, was also inclined to reach a settlement with Hitler by offering him all or part of the colonial possessions of Belgium and/or Portugal. It was only natural that this infamous "appeasement policy" appealed above all to the numerous members of French, British, and even American elite who sympathized with Hitler and other fascist dictators, not only because they liked their antidemocratic and socially regressive domestic policies, but also because they believed they could actually derive enormous advantages from an eastward German territorial expansion. Such an expansion, euphemized by the Nazis as an acquisition of "living space" for the German people, implied the obliteration of the Soviet Union, the cradle and homeland of revolution, the construction site of the "countersystem" to capitalism, the source of inspiration and guidance for revolutionaries all over the world. Secretly, but ever so fondly, many members of the Western elites hoped that Hitler might succeed where the Allies themselves had failed, namely when they had had to abandon their armed intervention in the Russian Civil War, aimed at defeating the Bolsheviks. It was hoped that Hitler would destroy the revolution by destroying the country that incarnated it. During the 1930s, as it happened, to the elite of the "Western," that is, capitalist world, the obliteration of the Soviet Union was becoming more desirable than ever before. Under Stalin's leadership, the Bolshevik project launched under Lenin had not only failed to implode, as had so often been predicted, but made enormous economic and social progress — admittedly at the price of great sacrifices — while everywhere else the Great Depression raged and caused unemployment, poverty, and misery. This made countless people believe that they were witnessing the demise of capitalism and the triumph of revolutionary socialism.[23]

And so it is not only because it was also a clash of imperialist titans that the Second World War resembled the First World War, or can be considered to be continuation of that war, an Act II of the Thirty-Years War of the twentieth century: it is also because both world conflicts had a major counterrevolutionary dimension. As in 1914, in 1939 the international elite hoped that the coming war would finish the revolution once and for all, with Hitler cast in the role of "great white hope" of the counterrevolution. But there was a difference: the revolution that needed to be liquidated in 1914 was an abstract idea, a chimera, while the revolution that Hitler was poised to tackle in 1939 was incarnated in a state, the Soviet Union. In any event, at the end of the 1930s it was again not the plebs, but the elite, that wanted war. The old order, which had been the "incubator" of war in 1914 but whose foundations, "as of 1917, shook and cracked," writes Arno Mayer, had enough of its forces survive the war and "recover sufficiently to . . . sponsor fascism [in the 1920s and 1930s] and contribute to the resumption of total war in 1939."[24]

The Second World War was again a very complex phenomenon, a combination of a "vertical" war between countries and a "horizontal" war between classes. It was a contest between, on the one side, the revolution incarnated by the Soviet Union, but also, as we should certainly not forget, by a large part and possibly even the majority of the members of the resistance in the occupied countries, and, on the other side, the counterrevolution incarnated by Nazi Germany and its collaborators and sympathizers in the occupied countries as well as the countries allied with Nazi Germany. But the vagaries of war, which cannot be elucidated here, caused countries with intrinsically counterrevolutionary elites, such as Britain and the US — fierce imperialist rivals of Nazi Germany — to become allies of the revolutionary Soviet Union, according to the motto that "the enemy of my enemy is my friend."

"Vichy France," led by the collaborator regime of Marshal Pétain, incarnated the reactionary aspirations of the French elite, eager to set the clock back to the "good old days" before the Russian Revolution of 1917, the revolutions of the "crazy year," 1848, and even the mother of all modern revolutions, the French Revolution of 1789. The motto of Pétain's France was not the revolutionary "liberty, equality, fraternity," but the ultra-conservative "work, family, fatherland." And it was not a coincidence that the cult of Joan of Arc, a heroine of monarchical France as well as its Siamese twin, the Catholic Church, was zealously promoted by Vichy. Already, in 1914, the French elite had hoped to achieve such a *"retour en arrière"* via a triumphant war against Germany. This great ambition was realized in 1940, but via an ignominious defeat. We now know that this unlikely rout, this "strange defeat," was *wanted*, much as in 1914 war had been wanted: the French elite consciously opted for a military defeat at the hands of Hitler's Germany because that seemed to be the only way it could achieve its counterrevolutionary objectives. In 1934 the elite had tried, but failed, to bring its own "strong man" to power in Paris, namely Marshal Pétain, just as Mussolini and Hitler had earlier been brought to power in Italy and Germany. But defeat against Germany in the spring of 1940 did make it possible to achieve that ambition, and Pétain came to power when the ink on the capitulation document was barely dry. Via a trouncing by an admittedly unloved but ideologically congenial *foreign* enemy, the elite managed to achieve victory against its despised *domestic* enemy, its plebeian class. Not surprisingly, Vichy France would be a paradise for the country's industrialists, bankers, and other members of the elite, many if not all of them eager collaborators, because collaboration was profitable, but a hell for the country's lower orders who, not surprisingly, would be overrepresented in the Resistance.[25]

CHAPTER 31

CLASS WARS FROM 1945 TO THE PRESENT

Like the Great War, the Second War produces a most unsatisfactory outcome for the elite of the "Western" World, namely a triumph of the Soviet homeland of revolution and the resulting need to introduce even more democratic reforms — symbolized by the term "Welfare State" — in many countries, and to grant independence to most colonial possessions. Once again, the elite resorts to war to undo these gains for the revolution and for democracy: the Cold War. This conflict leads to the implosion of the Soviet Union and permits "rolling back" many of the social services of the Welfare State. And the subsequent War on Terror, de facto a permanent and worldwide form of warfare, makes it possible to increasingly limit the rights and freedoms of denizens of the "Western" world — as had already happened during the Great War of 1914–1918 . . .

The First World War had amounted to a large-scale offensive launched by the counterrevolutionary elite in the context of a contemporary class conflict that had started with the French Revolution, but it had produced unexpected and most undesirable results: a great revolution in Russia and a flood of democratic reforms in most Western countries. The Second World War can be interpreted as a similar offensive by the elite. It was not a coincidence that Germany's "crusade against Bolshevism" was joined by volunteers from all over Europe, who departed for the eastern front with the blessing of their political and religious superiors. But this new counter-revolutionary project likewise failed miserably, namely on the battlefields of Moscow and Stalingrad. The military triumph of the Soviet Union was simultaneously a triumph for the revolutionary forces everywhere, and a corresponding nasty defeat for the international counterrevolution. The Soviet Union not only continued to exist but, in spite of titanic sacrifices and huge losses, emerged from the war with considerably increased power and prestige. In Eastern Europe, liberated by the Red Army, and in the eastern part of Germany, revolutionary changes were brought about, under Soviet direction, at the expense of the feudal element, the aristocratic land-owners and the Churches, as well as the capitalist element, the bourgeois big corporations and banks. In France, Britain, and Italy, and in the western part of Germany, the defeat of counterrevolutionary fascism produced a quasi-revolutionary situation which, exactly as at the end of the First World War, made it necessary for the elites to relieve the pressure via major con-cessions in the shape of a new wave of democratic reforms of a political and social nature; and later, during the Cold War, it would be necessary to maintain a high level of popular prosperity in order to be able to compete with the countries of the "communist bloc" with their elaborate systems of social services, including guaranteed employment and free health care and education. In Britain, for example, the plural suffrage was finally abolished, and in Belgium women got the vote; in all Western countries an impressive array of social services was introduced virtually overnight, transforming these countries into what became known as "welfare states," and certain sectors of industry (such as mining) and certain corporations were even nationalized.[1] Commenting on this historically important development, a Belgian university professor, Jan Dumolyn, has emphasized that "the men in power never voluntarily give presents in the form of social benefits," but only when "they feel threatened to such an extent that they make conces-sions in order to avoid the worst." He adds that

> Here in the West, [after the Second World War], the political leaders made important concessions to working people out of fear of the communist East. In order to keep the people quiet and to undermine the attractiveness of socialism on the other

side of the Iron Curtain, important progress was achieved on
the level of social security.²

The victory of the revolution, incarnated by the Soviet Union, over the Nazi-German incarnation of the counterrevolution thus unquestionably also amounted to a victory for political and social-economic democracy in Western Europe. Incidentally, if the United States did not witness the birth of a welfare state in the years following 1945, it was because the American elite did not feel the same need as its European counterparts to compete with the Soviet Union, especially since it had already been forced to introduce high wage levels during the war.³ But in neighbouring Canada the establishment did feel sufficiently insecure and even threatened, so that a welfare state on the British model was introduced there. (However, "almost all initiatives in social welfare legislation ceased" as soon as "the pressure of popular demands abated.")⁴

Equally, and perhaps even more important, was the fact that the victory of the anti-imperialist Soviet Union against Nazi Germany, a seemingly invincible imperialist Goliath, who had hoped to turn Eastern Europe into a huge German colony, a German "India," provided hope and encouragement, and in many cases considerable material support, to communist as well as and other proponents of national revolutions in the colonies. This was a major determinant of the fact that many colonies would be able to achieve independence shortly after the end of the Second World War. When in 1947 the British had to quit India, it was definitely not on account of the nonviolent resistance preached by Gandhi. As Domenico Losurdo has explained in his book on nonviolence, the real reason was that intelligent leaders in London, including Churchill himself, understood only too well that Britain, exhausted by the war, could not, in the long run, keep at bay the mushrooming numbers of freedom fighters who could count on Soviet support. (Neither could Britain count on the support of the US, which speculated that a British withdrawal from the subcontinent would create an "open door" for US products and investments.)⁵ And in Indochina too, the armed revolutionaries benefited from Soviet assistance. There, the French colonial masters had to throw in the towel after a humiliating defeat at Dien Bien Phu. The Americans took over and tried, in a long and bloody war, to repress Vietnam's national revolutionary movement and maintain the colonial system at least in the southern part of the country, but in 1975 they, too, had to acknowledge defeat. Without the victory of the Soviet Union in 1945, these triumphs of anti-imperialist forces in Asia would not have been possible.

In the United States, too, a very important achievement indirectly resulted from the Soviet victory over Nazi Germany: the country's elite finally decided to do something about political and social emancipation for the oppressed Afro-American minority. Even the supposedly super-democratic President Roosevelt had never lifted a finger to end the systematic discrimination and frequent lynchings to which blacks were still exposed at the time of the Second World War, especially in the southern states. It was only in the 1960s, in the context of the Cold War, that the elite consented to a modest emancipation of Afro-Americans; it realized that the system of segregation as it existed in the US itself, combined with US support for the apartheid regime in South Africa, made the US look bad in the eyes of the populations of the then still numerous nonaligned countries. The Soviet Union, on the other hand, was clearly a multi-ethnic country that did not practise discrimination on the basis of skin colour, supported liberation movements in the Third World in word and deed, and was the main enemy of the apartheid regime in South Africa, where, not coincidentally, opponents of apartheid tended to be automatically branded as communists and Soviet agents. Thus embarrassed and pressured, the Americans finally decided to treat their black population like human beings and citizens. It amounted to a democratic achievement for which the Soviet Union deserved, but never received, credit from the theoretically objective Western media; the latter preferred to attribute these important but still fairly basic improvements to presidents such as Kennedy and Johnson — as if sterling magnanimity had suddenly moved a New England patrician and an ultraconservative Texan rancher to go to bat for the black underclass of America.[6]

After the Second World War, Western Europe reached an unprecedentedly high level of political and social-economic democracy. It cannot be denied that this had happened via two major waves of democratization that followed the First and Second World Wars, respectively. In 1914, for example, Britain was not yet a full-fledged political democracy, and not a democracy at all on the social level, as great poverty would continue to prevail there until 1945, disappearing only with the advent of the welfare state.[7] Historians such as Arthur Marwick associate the chronological link with causality, according to the well-known logical fallacy *post hoc, ergo propter hoc,* "after this, therefore because of this." Such historians suggest that this progress was achieved thanks to the preceding wars; it was presumably by means of political and social reforms such as the introduction of universal suffrage and the eight-hour workday that the elite intended to reward the nation's brave soldiers and good civilians for their loyalty, efforts, and sacrifices during the war. That this was not so is demonstrated clearly by the fact that, virtually everywhere, the personalities and political parties most typically representative of the elite openly repudiated these reforms, and, when they proved unable to prevent them, left their implementation to the reformist socialists, so that they themselves would not be associated with them. In Belgium, leading conservatives thus condemned the hasty introduction of reforms in 1918 as the result of a coup d'état, and at the end of the Second World War Churchill and the Tories fought tooth and nail against the plans for democratic reforms: after the war, the British welfare state had to be introduced under the auspices of the Labour Party. It is also striking that the British elite did not bother to reward the huge contributions to victory made by the Empire's Indian subjects. To the contrary, when in the spring of 1919 there were demonstrations in India, in some ways a kind of demand for compensation for the wartime services rendered, the British authorities responded with brutal repression, exemplified by the infamous Amritsar Massacre. As for the very deserving Senegalese and North-African *tirailleurs*, they "were sent back to their homes immediately after the war" to remain what they had been before, namely "subjects, devoid of any political rights," of their French colonial masters. Similarly, the more than one million Afro-American soldiers did not receive any reward whatsoever for their efforts, as many of them had hoped; the American form of apartheid known as segregation, accompanied by lynchings, continued after 1918. Numerous black war veterans would be lynched in the years 1918–1920, sometimes even wearing their uniform.[8] An Afro-American poet and songwriter, Andy Razaf (Andrea Razafkeriefo), gave vent as follows to the deception and bitterness of his people:

With all your talk of justice
And grand Democracy,
The weak are still exploited
And robbed of liberty.[9]

It is also an error to think that the high level of political and particularly social democracy was a spontaneous development of the capitalist system, so that even without wars these advances would have burst forth from a hypothetical cornucopia of capitalism; in other words, the "free market" allegedly produced more democracy and the prosperity associated with the welfare state. According to this kind of thinking, the primordial function of capitalism is the creation of wealth, of which the lion's share goes, supposedly deservedly, to the "entrepreneurial" individuals and firms, while an admittedly lesser but still "fair" part flows more or less automatically to the working folks; the size of this part presumably depending on economic conditions, which determine the volume of the wealth that is created and is therefore available to be shared, and also — as we hear again and again from economists and politicians — of the "productivity" of the workers. But this argument is contradicted by the historic fact that some periods of great economic growth and considerable increases in labour productivity bring little or no improvements in terms of higher wages or social advantages; as examples we can cite the pinnacle of the industrial revolution in the nineteenth century, as well as our own time, which manages to combine high corporate profitability, much of it due to increased labour productivity, with the lower wages and lower social service levels of "austerity."[10] Conversely, the two waves of political and social reforms occurred in Western societies when the end of a great war caused major economic problems and while labour productivity was not on the rise. It is also not realistic to claim that the social and political reforms of the aftermath of two world wars were the fruit of the dedication and zeal of the reformist-socialist (or social-democratic) parties and the trade unions. At the end of the Second World War, for example, the continental socialist parties and trade unions were hardly combative, as they had just emerged shell-shocked from the trauma of years of Nazi occupation. As for Britain, its archetypical welfare state was the spiritual child not of Labourites but of conservative politicians with an elite background, such as Baron William Henry Beveridge, author of the 1942 Beveridge Report, the welfare state's blueprint. It cannot be doubted that it was fear of the revolution that caused the elite, more specifically the more moderate elements within the elite, to introduce the important political and social reforms that, in the years following 1945, blessed Western Europe with more democracy and prosperity than ever before. In 1918, a similar fear had been the consequence of the revolution in Russia, a revolution that briefly threatened to sweep Western Europe; and in 1945 this fear was provoked by the triumph of the Soviet Union over Nazi Germany, a triumph that earned the Soviet Union — and Stalin — enormous prestige all over the world and provided inspiration and moral support for revolutionary elements in Western Europe and elsewhere. In some ways, writes the Canadian political commentator Stephen Gowans, "Stalin forced Western governments to build robust programs of social welfare to maintain the allegiance of their populations." Thus it can be argued that for the relatively high level of democracy and prosperity achieved after 1945, much credit should go to Lenin and Stalin, even though these two Soviet leaders are traditionally depicted in Western media and history books as antidemocratic personalities.[11] Even so, these reforms would not have seen the light of day if the workers and other plebeians of Western Europe had not put enormous pressure on the elite via strikes and demonstrations and thus forced it to make important concessions. In this sense, the two remarkable doses of democracy and social services administered to Western Europe after 1918 and 1945 were the result, as Domenico Losurdo emphasizes, "of a political and social mobilization of the lower classes and therefore of class struggle."[12] These two major steps forward in the direction of the emancipation of the "populace" were indeed the product of a class struggle, of a "class war" waged within the first as well as the second of the world wars of the twentieth century. The elite had wanted and unleashed these wars because it had invested high hopes in them, but in both cases it ended up being sorely disappointed and forced to concede much ground to the forces of revolution and democracy. Not the upper, but the lower classes emerged in some sense victoriously from these two conflicts, which had required huge efforts and sacrifices from them.

As in the aftermath of the Great War, the elite did not resign itself to its setback, but proceeded immediately to make plans to vanquish the revolution and roll back the concessions it had had to make in terms of political and social reforms. Once again, war played a crucial role in these plans, albeit war of a new variety. This new type of war was the Cold War, unleashed virtually as soon as it became obvious that World War II would produce a defeat for counterrevolutionary Germany and a triumph for the Soviet incarnation of the revolution. In the class war of 1914–1918, Britain and France had been in some ways the flagships of the elite, and in the class war of 1939–1945, Nazi Germany may be said to have played that role. But the world conflict of 1939–1945 was also a struggle for supremacy between imperialist powers, and thanks to the crushing defeat of the German candidate for this supremacy, the US emerged in 1945 as the imperialist hegemon. America thus also became the flagship country of counterrevolution, expected by its own, and by the international, elite not only to confront the Soviet Union and revolutionary and anti-imperialist forces worldwide, but also to take the lead in the search for ways to roll back as many as possible of the political and especially the social concessions wherever they had been made. And so it was the US that unleashed the so-called Cold War against the Soviet Union and the forces it was associated with, although it is not unreasonable to argue that the origins of this Cold War can be traced back to the Allied intervention in the Russian Civil War at the end of the Great War.

Ever since the end of the 1861–1865 Civil War, the US elite had been a virtually exclusively bourgeois elite, focused on industry and finance. After 1945, it collaborated closely with junior partners in other Western countries, first and foremost their bourgeois counterparts, that is, the big industrialists and bankers of Britain, France, and above all Germany, locus of major US investments since the 1920s, but also the still predominantly aristocratic large landowners and, last but not least, the prelates of the Catholic Church in general and the Vatican in particular. The collaboration with the Vatican was already extremely close in 1945, especially for the purpose of helping German war criminals, Nazi collaborators, and Croatian, Ukrainian, and other fascists who had kindly rendered anticommunist and anti-Soviet services to escape to South America and elsewhere, including Canada, via the infamous "ratlines."[13] This collaboration between

Washington and the Vatican demonstrates how even in more recent history the elite has remained a symbiosis of the modern industrial and financial upper-middle class and of the *ancien régime* upper class, consisting of the nobility and the Church, united in a common opposition to revolution and democracy. It is symptomatic that this policy had to be carried out stealthily by the US secret services, since it would have shocked and offended the great majority of Americans.

Like the two world wars, the Cold War was simultaneously a "vertical" war between countries and blocs of countries (members of NATO versus those of the Warsaw Pact) and a "horizontal" conflict between classes. For the international elite, headed by Washington, the objective was not so much to achieve victory against a country, but rather to defeat a system, namely the socialist countersystem to capitalism that the Soviets had been constructing since 1917. This system, introduced in Eastern Europe under Soviet auspices after 1945, seemed poised to conquer not only Western Europe but also the rest of the world, even without assistance from the Red Army. The Soviet model of socialism, associated with rapid industrialization and modernization as well as victory over one of the most powerful capitalist countries, Nazi Germany, did indeed exert much attraction in the postwar era, not only in Western and Southern Europe but also in the colonies and semi-colonies of the Western countries. It was therefore less against the Soviet Union as a country than against the Soviet system and the idea of radical socialism or communism, incarnated by the Soviet Union, that the US, on behalf of the international elite, launched an offensive starting in 1945, making use of diplomacy, the CIA, and NATO. The CIA orchestrated against communism an intellectual and cultural offensive in which it enjoyed the collaboration of countless writers, artists, ex-communists, social democrats, and other left-wing personalities. Intellectuals now known to have been "funded and promoted by the CIA" included George Orwell, Isaiah Berlin, Sidney Hook, Daniel Bell, Hannah Arendt, Arthur Koestler, and Raymond Aron.[14] In contrast to revolutionary socialism, or communism, which it feared, the elite merely loathed reformist socialism or social democracy, and it tolerated it and co-opted it as an ally in what could be called, in analogy with "Great Class War," the "Cold Class War." It was for services of this kind that the Belgian socialist Paul-Henri Spaak was rewarded with the position of secretary-general of NATO. In order to win the Cold Class War against the "interior enemy," all means were admissible, including the most mendacious forms of propaganda, the use of agents provocateurs, and even terrorism in the form of "false-flag" attacks, a.k.a. "black operations." It is now well known that in the 1970s and 1980s the CIA and NATO secretly adopted the "strategy of tension." Attacks were carried out and innocent people were killed in order to put the blame on communists and thus to discredit communism, particularly in countries where it was deemed to enjoy too much success, such as Italy. A spectacular example of this was the 1980 bomb attack in the railway station of "red" Bologna, Mecca of Italian communism. In Belgium, too, innocent people were assassinated in the context of this strategy, according to a Swiss specialist in the field, Daniele Ganser.[15]

The elite also resented greatly that Soviet socialism proved to be a source of inspiration and hope for millions of people in the colonies. "Even the mere existence of the Soviet Union," writes the Italian historian Enzo Traverso, "signified an enormous advantage for the colonial peoples in their struggle for liberation and against imperialism."[16] The colonies were part and parcel of the capitalist "free world," which claimed to be the cradle of prosperity and democracy. But at the time these lands were characterized by oppression, exploitation, and extreme poverty. And for their inhabitants there was no question whatsoever of freedom and prosperity, except for an infinitesimal, usually corrupt and kleptocratic comprador elite. Within the colonial framework, the prospects for improvement were non-existent as far as the overwhelming majority of the plebs was concerned. Here, too, practice revealed that the Cold War was a manifestation of class warfare: Washington and the "West" in general defended (semi-)colonial rule as long as possible, and after independence — mostly conceded very reluctantly — they all too often supported dictators, such as Mobutu or Pinochet, who could be counted on to defend the interests of Western banks and corporations in a "neocolonial" context, while they fought tooth and nail against all those, communists or not, who stood for the cause of genuine independence and liberty. If deemed necessary, openly imperialist wars were unleashed in which millions of people lost their lives, as in the case of Vietnam. It is telling that in that country the freedom fighters who fought to emancipate their people and replace colonial rule with democracy were opposed by the troops of a great power that claims to be the champion of liberty and democracy, and that in this war the United States benefited from the unconditional support of the supposedly very democratic and freedom-loving West Germany, or at least of its government; conversely, the freedom fighters were supported by the population as well as the leaders of the supposedly antidemocratic Soviet Union and East Germany, as we are reminded by faded posters of the 1970s in the war museum of Ho Chi Minh-City (Saigon). Luciano Canfora has observed that the support offered by Moscow to countless liberation movements in the Third World cost an enormous amount of money and thus unquestionably contributed to the "implosion" of the Soviet Union.[17] Meanwhile, the ruthless exploitation of the Third World further enriched the United States and other "Western" countries; or rather, their corporate and banking elites. Even today, in spite of the much-vaunted "aid to developing countries," each passing year sees considerably more wealth being transferred from the poor Third World countries to the wealthy Western nations, the former colonial powers, than vice versa.

The Vietnam War was unquestionably a class war. It was not only a conflict between a small elite, exemplified by the South-Vietnamese Diem clan, and the popular masses of the country itself, but also a war between a poor and oppressed "proletarian" country and a big, rich, and mighty neocolonial "capitalist" country. Elsewhere in the Third World the international elite, directed by Washington, fought the forces of democracy, freedom, and emancipation, which were supported by the Soviet Union and communists all over the world. In Congo, in 1960, in order to safeguard US and Belgian interests, the popular leader Patrice Lumumba was assassinated and replaced by a pro-Western dictator, Mobutu Sese Seko. In 1965-1966, in Indonesia, Washington lent a helping hand to the organizers of the massacre of hundreds of thousands of people favourable to communism, or supposed to be so, and helped to bring to power the pro-Western General Suharto, a murderous and kleptocratic dictator with whom lucrative business could be done. In Chile, in 1973, on that other "nine-eleven," General Pinochet received the green light from Washington to assassinate the democratically elected President Salvador Allende; the natural wealth, labour, and market of Chile were thus offered on a silver platter to US and other Western banks and corporations such as ITT. And in South Africa the Americans supported the apartheid regime and fought the activists who opposed this racist system. (The CIA, for example, assisted in the arrest of Nelson Mandela, whose death toward the end of 2013 caused a plethora of hypocritical Western leaders to go and shed crocodile tears in Pretoria for PR purposes.)[18] It is obvious that for the West, the Cold War was no more a war for liberty and democracy than the Great War had been, but was exactly the opposite: a war against democracy and against freedom, particularly against freedom for the people of the Third World. Similarly, like the conflict of 1914–1918, it was also a war with imperialist objectives that had disastrous consequences for the colonies, semi-colonies and ex-colonies that make up the Third World. The Soviet Union had many faults, but with respect to the Third World it must be acknowledged that the Soviet state and the Soviet people supported the cause of liberty and democracy.

Via the "Cold Class War," the Western elite hoped above all to put an end to the revolutionary experiment that had been in progress in the Soviet Union since 1917. In spite of enormous problems, much bloodshed, internal strife, and domestic as well as foreign wars, this experiment had achieved a lot, as reflected in the country's triumph over powerful Nazi Germany, and later, the spectacular success of the Soviet space program. But the Cold War sparked an armament race for which Moscow, in contrast to Washington and the West in general, did not have sufficient financial resources. It has already been mentioned that Soviet support for liberation movements in the Third World depleted Moscow's coffers and thus contributed to the Soviet Union's implosion. But the Soviet Union was also torn by grave internal conflicts, which after the death of Stalin in 1953 sparked a change of course that had nefarious consequences.[19] The result of all this was that in the early 1990s, the Soviet Union collapsed. Thanks to the "Cold Class War," the international elite thus managed to achieve what it had been unable to realize via the two great class wars of 1914–1918 and 1939–1945: victory over the revolution. Ironically, this counterrevolution-ary accomplishment was — and continues to be — attributed to "velvet-" and other "revolutions" that started, at least symbolically, with the fall of the Berlin Wall in 1989 and finished in some way in 1993, when Boris

Yeltsin ordered troops to fire on the Russian Parliament.

In order to realize that these were in reality counterrevolutionary happenings, it is sufficient to ask the question *cui bono?*, "who profited from this?" In other words, "who were the winners?" Beneficiaries from the so-called revolutions in Eastern Europe were certainly the nobility and the Church, the primordial counterrevolutionary elements. During the Great Class War of 1914–1918, their dream of a *retour en arrière* to the *ancien régime* had backfired; and in 1945, they had lost their castles and vast landed properties together with their previously preponderant political power and great social prestige. In the years following 1990, however, not only the noble families of the former German and Austro-Hungarian Empires, but also, and especially, the Catholic Church, were able to recuperate in Eastern (and much of Central) Europe their landed property that had been socialized in 1945. (They could do so thanks to the benevolent collaboration of "democrats" such as Lech Walesa and Vaclav Havel, personalities who were lavishly rewarded for their services.) The result is that the Catholic Church is once again the biggest landowner in Poland, the Czech Republic, and Hungary. To this landlord, the Eastern European plebeians — e.g., Polish tenant farmers and Slovenian stall-keepers on the little market square behind the Cathedral of Ljubljana — now have to pay much higher rents than in the supposedly "bad old days" before 1990. Thanks to Havel and consorts, many former aristocratic landowners, such as the dynasty of the Schwarzenbergs, are back in possession of chateaux and large domains in Eastern Europe and enjoy once again great social prestige and political power, just like in the "good old days" before 1914.[20]

About these kinds of things, not a word was ever said or written in our mainstream media. To the contrary, we were persuaded to believe that Karol Józef Wojtyla, Pope John-Paul II, collaborated with the arch-conservative American President Ronald Reagan and the CIA against the Soviets only in order to restore democracy in Eastern Europe. That the head of the Catholic Church, an eminently undemocratic institution in which the Pope has everything to say, and millions of ordinary priests and believers nothing at all, might be an apostle of the democratic gospel, is an absurd notion. If the Pope really wanted to go to bat for democracy, he could have done so in the Catholic Church itself. That John-Paul II really wanted nothing to do with genuine democracy appears all too clearly from the fact that he condemned "liberation theology" and fought tooth and nail against the courageous champions of this theology — generally ordinary, low-ranking priests and nuns — who promoted democratic change in Latin America, democratic change that was much more needed there than in Eastern Europe. Indeed, in most of Latin America the population has never benefited from free education, medical care, or the many other social services that were taken for granted in communist Poland and elsewhere in Eastern Europe. Of course, in Latin America the Catholic Church had always been a large landowner, whose privileges and wealth — fruits of the bloody conquest of the land by the Spanish conquistadors — might have been erased by a genuine democratization to the advantage of peasants and other proletarians. It is undoubtedly for this reason that the Pope worked hard for change in Eastern Europe but opposed it in Latin America. And the Pope did not even protest when in El Salvador counterrevolutionary partners of his friend Reagan massacred a number of nuns as well as Bishop Romero on account of their democratic convictions. That Wojtyla was not a democrat but a reactionary was likewise demonstrated by the fact that he had cordial relations with dictators such as Pinochet and neofascists such as the Austrian politician Jörg Haider. And he chose to beatify some disreputable, reactionary historical figures, such as the last Habsburg emperor, Charles I, and the philofascist Aloïs Stepinac, archbishop of Zagreb during the Second World War.[21]

It is also highly questionable that the changes in Eastern Europe after 1990 heralded a step forward in the direction of democracy and emancipation of ordinary people. In Poland, for example, since the fall of communism, the separation of Church and state, one of the great achievements of the French Revolution, has existed on paper but not in practice. Citizens who do not happen to be Catholic, as well as homosexuals and feminists, cannot feel at home there. Poland has in some ways returned to the era before the French Revolution when, in just about every country, a specific religion was the religion of the state and there was no question of religious freedom or tolerance.[22] That the leaders of the postcommunist states of Eastern Europe are not particularly enamoured of democracy also appears from the fact that all too many of them are devotees and keen apostles of some extreme right-wing nationalism, associated not only with a specific religion but also with xenophobia, racism, anti-Semitism, and so forth. Furthermore, virtually everywhere these leaders have seen fit to exculpate and glorify the extremely undemocratic and even openly fascist elements that ruled their countries in the 1930s and/or collaborated with the Nazis and committed all sorts of war crimes during the 1940s. This has stimulated the sometimes spectacular rise of neofascist and even, as in Ukraine today, openly neo-Nazi movements. The majority of the population — and certainly the ordinary citizen who was unable to fill his pockets thanks to the "revolutions" of the 1990s — does not feel spoiled in the "new" Poland or Bulgaria. Opinion polls reveal that in countries such as Romania, a majority feels that life was better under communism. A major determinant of this nostalgia is the fact that vital social services such as medical care and education, including higher education, are no longer free of charge or very inexpensive, as they used to be. Conversely, some practices usually associated with nasty nineteenth-century capitalism, such as child labour, have reappeared in countries such as Uzbekistan. The women of Central and Eastern Europe, and of the former Soviet Union, also lost many of the considerable gains they had achieved under communism, for example with respect to employment opportunities, economic independence, affordable childcare, and other social benefits.[23] It is not surprising that countless young people see no decent future for themselves in their Eastern European homeland and leave to try their luck elsewhere. Thus they vote against the new system "with their feet," as they used to say triumphantly, during the Cold War era, of dissidents who left either Europe's communist bloc countries or Cuba.

Other than an "oligarchy" of newborn domestic capitalists, roguish opportunists who took advantage of the "revolutions" to plunder their countries' socialized wealth, and the multinationals that descended like vultures on postcommunist Eastern Europe, the major beneficiaries of the changes in Eastern Europe were the *ancien régime* institutions and personalities who managed to regain much of the terrain they had lost at the end of the two world wars. So it was in the Russian heartland of the former Soviet Union. There the Orthodox Church has made a spectacular comeback, similar to the one achieved by the Catholic Church in Poland. It has recuperated virtually the entire gigantic portfolio of land and buildings it possessed before 1917, and the state has generously financed the restoration of old (and the construction of new) churches at the expense of all taxpayers, Christian or not. The Orthodox Church is once again big, rich, and powerful, and closely associated with the state, exactly as in the "good old days" of the czars. A powerful symbol of this *retour en arrière*, and of the rehabilitation of the *ancien régime*, was the canonization of Czar Nicholas II in August 2000.[24]

If we compare today's Russia and China, we note that in the former country first Yeltsin and then Putin have set the clock back to the time before 1917. For a small elite of oligarchs, that has been a wonderful thing, but for the majority of the people the situation has not improved at all; to the contrary. (The Yeltsin era of the 1990s was catastrophic in this respect, but there has admittedly been considerable improvement in recent years under Putin.) Today, Russia is hardly an exemplary democracy. As a result of the counterrevolution orchestrated by Yeltsin, Russia became again what it had been at the time of the czars: a great power (though not nearly as great as before 1990), ruled autocratically, and featuring a huge social gap between an immensely rich elite and a relatively poor majority. In China, on the other hand, an embryonic "velvet revolution" — in reality a counter-revolution — was nipped in the bud in Tian'anmen Square in 1989. In their own enigmatic way, the Chinese leaders have continued to walk the path of the revolution. Western-style democracy, with presumably free elections, does not exist in China and, like Russia, the country has witnessed the emergence of a small elite of super-rich people. But the latter have not come to power, and their rise has not prevented the undeniable fact that for millions and millions of ordinary Chinese life has also improved enormously and continues to improve even today. Thanks to the revolution inspired by the Russian antecedent of 1917 and orchestrated by Mao along Leninist and Stalinist lines, China has become a great power and an increasingly prosperous land, while before the revolution it was a weak and immensely poor country.[25]

Thanks to the fall of communism in Russia and elsewhere in Eastern Europe, the nobility and above all the clergy have been able to recuperate a large part of the losses they had suffered after the two great eruptions of class war in the twentieth century. Nonetheless, the great winner was the senior partner within the international elite, the bourgeois financiers and industrialists such as George Soros,[26] and the big banks and corporations. The latter are generally American, West-European, or Japanese multinationals. Being a multinational means doing business in all countries and paying taxes in none. The multinationals entered Russia and Eastern Europe triumphantly in order to sell their hamburgers, cola, weapons, and other merchandise; to take over state enterprises for a song; to grab raw materials; to hire highly qualified workers and staff, educated at state expense, at low wages; etc. The great losers in this scheme were the workers and employees of the Western countries: their relatively high wages and favourable working conditions, introduced after 1918 and/or 1945, were henceforth seen to make them "noncompetitive," and the social benefits that had been introduced were now suddenly "unaffordable." Consequently, the wage-earners were told to settle for less, but even when they did agree to have their wages lowered and their benefits "clawed back" in the framework of "austerity" measures, they often saw their jobs disappear in the direction of the low-wage countries of Eastern Europe and the Third World. After the fall of the Berlin Wall, the big West German corporations, which had collaborated so profitably with the Nazis between 1933 and 1945, were allowed to plunder East Germany economically. On the other hand, the West-German workers saw their wages — lowered by the Nazis but increased immediately after 1945 — decline rapidly. And they saw their jobs migrate to former East Germany or Poland — and even farther east, to Third World countries like Thailand, for example, where people are desperate enough to slave away for even lower wages.

The financial and industrial elite of Western Europe managed to profit in yet another way from the implosion of the Soviet Union. Political and social reforms had been introduced hurriedly in the immediate aftermath of the Second World War and in the framework of the Cold War. The political democratization, mainly in the form of a widening of the suffrage, never constituted a serious problem for the elite. With the collaboration of the mainstream media and the big political parties, both tightly controlled by the elite, it was not always easy but virtually never impossible to "fabricate" electoral victories for reliable conservative, liberal, and, if necessary, reformist-socialist (or social-democratic) parties.[27] Thus it proved possible time and again in Western Europe to bring governments to power that could be counted on by the elite to support the established order and to promote its interests at home and abroad. But the social reforms caused more trouble for the elite, because the emergence of the welfare state had restricted, not drastically but certainly to some extent, the possibilities for profit maximization. Neoliberal intellectuals and politicians condemned the welfare state from the very start as a nefarious state intervention in the presumably spontaneous and beneficial operation of the "free market." The end of the Cold War offered the elite a golden opportunity to dismantle the Welfare State and social security schemes in general, a project already launched in the 1980s by the likes of Margaret Thatcher and Ronald Reagan. In the years after 1945, writes the previously quoted Belgian historian Jan Dumolyn,

> the elite had made major concessions to the working
> population out of fear of communism, . . . in order to keep
> people quiet, and to counter the appeal of socialism behind
> the Iron Curtain. And so it is not a coincidence that the social
> services began to be rolled back after the fall of the Berlin
> Wall in 1989. The threat was gone. It was no longer necessary
> to appease the working population.[28]

From the moment it was no longer necessary to compete with the Soviet Union, the elite was free to roll back the social services associated with the welfare state all over Western Europe with impunity. It is still very much focused on this task, clearly in the hope that soon nothing at all will be left of the welfare state. We are witnessing a return to the unbridled, ruthless capitalism of the nineteenth century.

Even during the Cold War, the big corporations could maximize their profits thanks to state orders in the framework of gargantuan armament programs, necessary — we were told — to defend the "free world" against Soviet aggression. NATO organized this "defence" and distributed the lucrative contracts, whose lion's share naturally went to US enterprises, members of the infamous transatlantic military-industrial complex. After the fall of the Berlin Wall, the implosion of the Soviet Union, and the dismantling of the Warsaw Pact, it could no longer be claimed that the West was threatened by the Eastern Bloc. But NATO continued to exist and even expanded, absorbing numerous countries of Eastern Europe that subsequently became buyers of expensive military hardware made in the USA and elsewhere in the West; to raise the necessary funds or comply with conditions attached to loans from Western banks, their governments typically cut back social services dating back to the communist era. An enemy was of course needed against whom this weaponry was supposed to protect us, and after the fall of the Soviet "evil empire" that enemy was briefly Saddam Hussein. But then "terrorism" appeared on the stage like a *deus ex machina*, and a new war, the "War on Terror," rose spectacularly from the ashes of the Cold War. This new, worldwide conflict provided a much-needed rationale for the existence of NATO and for the continuation of the lucrative production and sale of weapons that happens to be the dynamo of the "war economy" of contemporary capitalism in general and of the "Pentagon system" in particular. This "Pentagon system" is also known as "military Keynesianism" or — in analogy to the "welfare state" — the "warfare state"; it emerged in the US at the end of the Second World War as a kind of joint venture of the government and the "military-industrial" corporate complex, and purported to prevent the American economy from sliding back into a Great Depression–style crisis when the Niagara of huge state orders associated with the war threatened to run dry. Thanks to new wars, first the Cold War and then the War on Terror, whose costs are borne by the taxpayers, big corporations have been able to continue to register huge profits by selling all sorts of weapons and other martial materiel.[29]

During the Great War of 1914–1918, countless soldiers believed that the war would never end. With the War on Terror, this nightmare has in some ways become reality. An abstract concept such as "terror" cannot capitulate, and so a war against it can never be won. We are therefore condemned to live for an indefinite period of time in a state of war. The gargantuan profits achieved thanks to armament and war go to the big corporations, but the huge costs are financed by the state via loans, which constitutes an extremely lucrative business for the big banks. The loans cause the national debt to mushroom, but a country's debt is the "property" of all its citizens. This means that the great majority of the population is responsible for the great majority of the debt. Via taxation, the costs of armament and war are thus socialized at the expense of the plebeians, while the profits are privatized to the advantage of the elite, the big corporations and banks, and their shareholders. Since the time of Reagan and Thatcher, big corporations in all Western countries have paid less and less tax, and sometimes no tax at all. On account of this, the state has increasingly found itself in financial difficulty, which means that it has had to rely more on contributions from ordinary citizens, from the plebs. The permanent fiscal crisis that accompanies the permanent War on Terror thus also furnishes a rationale for dismantling the supposedly overly expensive and unaffordable social services in the context of "austerity" programs, and this while wages are being ground down and unemployment and precarity are on the increase, so that solid social services are actually more needed than ever before. (Greece provides a spectacular example of this kind of situation.) The rich are thus rapidly becoming richer, the poor are becoming poorer, and the middle class is becoming less prosperous. Every few years the plebeians are still allowed to vote for one of a range of political parties that only do what the elite wants or permits; but can such a system be called a democracy?

The War on Terror thus also amounts to a class war, to a major offensive of the elite against the plebeians, against emancipation, against democracy. What the elite confidently expects this offensive to yield is the reconquest of terrain it had to give up in the years after 1918 and 1945; in other words, the end of the relatively limited degree of democracy and the relatively high level of social services, known as the welfare state, that emerged in most Western countries at that time. That the War on Terror is a class war is also revealed by the fact that, especially in the US, this war has provided an excuse to restrict even further the citizens' freedom by means of repressive legislation similar to President Wilson's *Espionage Act*. Those Wilsonian statutes were never fully repealed, and were supplemented by George W. Bush with the repressive *Patriot Act*. While such laws often target vaguely defined terrorists, preferably dark-skinned Arabs and other Muslims, virtually every form of unorthodox thinking and acting is thus potentially criminalized. As in Britain in 1914–1919, citizens in Western countries are now systematically bombarded via the media and Hollywood with mendacious propaganda, and are also being spied on and intimidated by their own governments. The plebeians have no influence whatsoever on these governments, not only because the "fabricated" elections are meaningless, but also and especially because virtually all important decisions are made by unelected representatives of the elite. These are entrenched more solidly than ever before in the traditional bastions of the elite within the state apparatus, namely the army and the bureaucracy, particularly the secret services, but also in the bureaucratic labyrinths of supra-national institutions such as the World Trade Organization (WTO). In other words, in the US it is not the elected president — elected, incidentally, in a most undemocratic manner — who wields the most power, but the elitist combination of little-known Pentagon generals and anonymous apparatchiks of the CIA, the NSA, and the FBI, who maintain intimate relations with the country's big corporations and banks. And in countries such as Greece, the cradle of democracy, the democratically elected parliamentarians have almost nothing to say in comparison with the "experts" of the International Monetary Fund (IMF).

Finally, it is obvious that the War on Terror is also an imperialist war, purporting to prevent the denizens of the Third World from determining for themselves things such as the price of oil and other minerals found in their soil. Via the War on Terror the Western elite of big banks and multinational corporations hopes to roll back the modest emancipation achieved by the former colonies in the process of decolonization. It is the intention to achieve unrestricted access to the raw materials, markets, and labour force of these countries. Such a "neocolonial" policy requires the collaboration of authoritarian (and usually corrupt and kleptocratic) regimes that, if deemed necessary, are brought to power via a coup d'état, a "colour revolution," or — not surprisingly — a war, as in the case of Iraq, Afghanistan, and Libya. Quite often, such interventions are simultaneously directed against powers that are perceived to be rivals or even enemies or at least competitors of US and Western imperialism, namely Russia and China. In the past, the existence of the Soviet Union hindered and often even prevented these neocolonial aggressions, but since 1989/1990 the US has been able to bomb and wage war to its heart's content in countries such as the former Yugoslavia, Iraq, Somalia, Libya, Syria, and Afghanistan.

Symptomatic of all of this was the attack by the US and Britain (and some other countries) on Iraq. This brutal aggression was not orchestrated because Saddam Hussein happened to be a dictator, but because he refused to put his country's oil wells unconditionally at the disposal of the big American and British oil trusts, something the present — and equally undemocratic — US-installed comprador-regime in Baghdad certainly does. (The desire to obtain control over the oil of Mesopotamia already played an important role in the British decision to go to war in 1914, as we have seen earlier.) As for the occupation of Afghanistan, that project has served first and foremost to put geostrategic spokes in the wheels of Russia and China. Yet another typical case of neocolonial aggression was NATO's attack on Libya and the bestial lynching of Colonel Kadhafi in 2011. This particularly brutal mugging did not reflect a hypothetical desire to introduce democracy and liberty in that part of North Africa or to achieve other humanitarian objectives, but rather the West's determination to achieve control over Libyan oil and to eliminate Africa's sole welfare state, which is what Kadhafi's country was. NATO's Libyan initiative was to reveal itself as "good business" for the international elite, but a catastrophe for the Libyan population and the large number of other Africans who had found jobs and lived fairly well in Kadhafi's country and who, like the Colonel himself, were brutally murdered by the NATO-sponsored "rebels."

Time and again we hear that a grave economic crisis has been raging all over the world for quite a few years already; however, the elite has been doing very well. The big corporations have been raking in greater "earnings" than ever before, and each year the super-rich become richer still. Worldwide poverty, on the other hand, has not increased and even slightly diminished recently only because of the increasing prosperity of a large section of the huge Chinese population. But in the West the poor are definitely becoming poorer, the middle class finds itself increasingly under pressure, and unrest and discontent are on the rise in that part of the world. This "pauperization" could lead to a potentially revolutionary situation, as in France in 1789 and in Russia in 1917. On the other hand, this situation also provides a fertile breeding ground for the weed of counterrevolutionary, neofascist movements — such as France's Front National — that blame all sorts of scapegoats for the troubles, as in Germany in the 1930s. In the 1930s, those scapegoats were the Jews, simplistically associated with revolution; now it is the Arabs and Muslims in general, equally simplistically associated with terrorism.

We live in an era of discontent, unrest, strikes and demonstrations, assassinations, shameless propaganda and self-censorship in the media, spying even in our own living rooms, intimidation, and oppression, even "black operations" — all of this against a background of seemingly endless warfare. This predicament is similar to the situation on the home front during the Great War of 1914–1918, in whose sinister shadow the history of the "short" twentieth century and the early twenty-first century has unfolded, just as the history of the "long" nineteenth century unfolded in the shadow of the earth-shaking French Revolution. Jean Jaurès was assassinated at the very moment of the eruption of a Great War that, even at the very last minute, he still hoped to prevent. In 1905, he had prophesied that

> From a European war a revolution could spring up . . . But
> it may also result, over a long period, in a crisis of counter-
> revolution, of furious reaction, of exasperated nationalism, of
> stifling dictatorship, of monstrous militarism, a long chain of
> retrograde violence.[30]

Jaurès's prediction has come true. The world in which we live today corresponds in almost every detail to his apocalyptic tableau. We still shiver in the cold shadow of the Great Class War.

ACKNOWLEDGEMENTS

I thank all those who, when I was still a child, awakened in me an interest in the Great War, told me stories about it, accompanied me during visits to battlefields, and helped me to understand that war. I am also grateful to the historians, film producers, poets, singers, and others whose books, films, songs, and poems about 1914–1918 not only opened my eyes, but also my heart. Thanks to all those who encouraged me to write this book and to those who contributed with improvements and corrections to the manuscript; and a very special thanks to my wife, Danielle, for the patience she displayed during the many months when, like a maniac, I hardly bothered with anything other than labouring on this opus. Finally, I thank in advance all those who, during this centenary of the Great War, will not just take another look at that war on television, but who will look at it in "Dali-vision" by reading this book and thus come to understand what 1914–1918 was: a great class war.

ENDNOTES

FOREWORD

1   The lyrics of *Marieke* may be found on this website: http://lyricstranslate.com/en/ marieke-marieke.html.

2   Quoted in Clapham, pp. 22–23.

3   The title of Cobb's book is from a poem by Thomas Gray, written in 1751, "Elegy Written in a Country Churchyard": "The boast of heraldry, the pomp of pow'r,/And all that beauty, all that wealth e'er gave,/Awaits alike th'inevitable hour./The paths of glory lead but to the grave."

4   Scenes from *Paths of Glory*: Night patrol, http://www.bing.com/videos/search?q=sentier s+de+la+gloire&view=detail&mid=93E04D184F6652FD08A493E04D184F6652FD08A 4&first=21; large-scale attack, http://www.bing.com/videos/search?q=paths+of+glory&v iew=detail&mid=48D21FB76B206B43BE3D48D21FB76B206B43BE3D&first=41.

5   Scenes from *Paths of Glory*: the beginning of the movie, with the *"Marseillaise,"* http:// www.tcm.com/mediaroom/video/201211/Paths-of-Glory-Movie-Clip-Opening.html; The German love song at the end: http://www.bing.com/videos/search?q=paths+of+gl ory&view=detail&mid=F91B7C99688CB80A83EFF91B7C99688CB80A83EF&first=81.

6   See the article by Annika Mombauer, "The Fischer Controversy 50 years on: Conference Report."

7   The painting, dating back to the mid-1970s, is actually entitled "Gala contemplating the Mediterranean Sea which, from twenty metres, becomes the portrait of Abraham Lincoln (Homage to Rothko)"; a slightly different version is displayed in the Salvador Dalí Museum in Saint Petersburg, Florida.

8   The French Revolution was certainly not the first class conflict, because class struggle also characterized the history of Antiquity and the Middle Ages. However, the French Revolution was the first important conflict of the modern class struggle, which continues today. It is actually preferable to talk of a "contemporary," rather than "modern" class struggle, since historians tend to employ the term "modern" to refer to the era from 1500 to 1789 or 1800 and designate as "contemporary" the era from 1789/1800 to the present time. On the class struggle in Antiquity, see the book by Arthur Rosenberg, *Demokratie und Klassenkampf im Altertum*; on the class struggle in the Middle Ages, see for example the book by Paul Lafargue, *Les Luttes de classes en Flandre de 1336–1348 et de 1379–1385*.

9   See Pauwels (2007), p. 192.

10   See the study by Maurice Bologne, *L'insurrection prolétarienne de 1830 en Belgique*.

11   Losurdo (2013), p. 27: "La lotta di classe non si presenta quasi mai allo stato puro."

12   The First World War is thus described as "Europe's collective folly" in De Vos, p. 95.

13   *Imperialism, the highest stage of Capitalism* is available online at http://www.marxists. org/archive/lenin/works/1916/imp-hsc.

14   Losurdo (2013), pp. 9–19.

CHAPTER 1

1   "In order to understand the origin and the problems of modern democracy, one must first closely examine the French Revolution," wrote the Italian historian and philosopher Domenico Losurdo. And Luciano Canfora, author of an excellent book on the history of democracy, describes the French Revolution as the "matrix of the entire European history that followed it." See Canfora (2008), p. 30.

2   Mayer (2000), pp. 47–49.

3   Pauwels (2007), pp. 191–98.

4   Rosenberg, pp. 25, 45.

5   See e.g. the article by Jef Verschueren, "Het grote taboe: Braaf Nationalisme, vroeger en nu."

6   De Schaepdrijver, p. 14; Hobsbawm (1994), pp. 20, 137; Kolko (1994), p. 97.

7   See e.g. MacMillan (2013), pp. 35–36.

8   See the book by Maurice Bologne, *L'insurrection prolétarienne de 1830 en Belgique.*

9   Mayer (2010), pp. 178–79.

CHAPTER 2

1   http://www.phrases.org.uk/meanings/254050.html.

2   Blum, p. 420.

3   Quoted in Losurdo (2006b), p. 74.

4   See e.g. Hobsbawm (1979), p. 183; Hobsbawm (1994), p. 84; Stone and Kuznick, pp. xviii-xx.

5   Koch, p. 332.

6   Mayer (2010), p. 133.

7   Losurdo (2013), p. 148.

8   Blum, pp. 422–27.

9   Mayer (2010), pp. 7, 131.

10 Mayer (2010), pp. 97–98.

11 Quoted in Winkler, pp. 51–52. Winkler also cites the liberal German historian Hermann Baumgarten, who wrote in 1866 that "the bourgeois is created to work, not to rule."

12 Poulantzas, pp. 118–19.

13 In general, governments controlled by the nobility took account of the interests of industry, "but nevertheless gave priority to large-scale agriculture," see Mayer (2010), p. 33.

14 Hobsbawm (1994), pp. 34–43.

15 Faulkner (2013), pp. 14–15.

16 Title of a book by Raf Custers.

17 We refer to studies of slavery such as the classic opus by Eric Williams.

18 Faulkner (2013), p. 15.

19   Stone and Kuznick, p. xvii.

20   See e.g. the remarks on the function of uniforms in Germany in Münkler, pp. 64–65.

21   Hobsbawm (1994), p. 305.

22   Quoted in Canfora (2008), p. 162; see also Schorkse, p. 69.

23   Canfora (2006), p. 41; Canfora (2008), p. 163; Mayer (2010), p. 310.

24   Quoted in Canfora (2008), p. 105.

25   See e.g. Eichholtz (1999b), p. 143.

26   "Jingo" seems to be the English version of the Basque word *Jainko*, "God," so "by Jingo" means something like "by Jesus."

27   With respect to France, Le Naour, p. 71, writes that "nationalism gradually penetrated the reactionary and conservative ideology at the end of the 19th century."

28   Mayer (2010), p. 278.

29   Mayer (2010), pp. 210–12, 266; with respect to gold in Wagner operas, see Glaser, p. 20.

30   Mayer (2010), p. 82.

31   Dance scene in *Paths of Glory*: http://www.myspace.com/video/qbrick/paths-of-glory-s26/5306554.

CHAPTER 3

1   Hobsbawm (1994), p. 116.

2   Quoted in Winkler, pp. 67–68.

3   Napoleon's remarks from http://monblog.ch/atheisme/?p=200509301605528.

4   See e.g. Winkler, p. 65.

5   De Schaepdrijver, p. 18; Losurdo (2013), p. 60.

6   Washington as quoted in the article by Richard L. Berke in the *New York Times*.

7   Hastings, pp. 274, 342.

8   Firchow, pp. 158–59; Hastings, pp. 39–40; MacMillan (2013), pp. 397–403; Saint-Fuscien, p. 24.

9   Canfora (2008), pp. 148–51.

CHAPTER 4

1   Rachschmir, p. 15.

2   The term *Volksgenosse* is of course associated with Nazism, but it was already used at the end of the 19th century.

3   See e.g. Firchow, p. 177.

4   Hibberd and Onions, pp. 250–51; Firchow, pp. 105–06, 112–13.

5   Hibberd and Onions, pp. 251–53.

6   Firchow, p. 164.

7   The origin and meaning of the term *Boche* is discussed in Roynette, pp. 20–22.

8   Koch, p. 348.

9   Quoted in Firchow, p. 167.

10   Canfora (2008), p. 235.

11   Hobsbawm (1994), pp. 153, 160.

12   See the article by Kristin Ross.

13   Mayer (2010), p. 300.

14   Jackson, pp. 368–69.

15   Deneckere, pp. 160–63.

16   Losurdo (2013), pp. 18–19; Johnson, p. 20.

17   Losurdo (2013), pp. 156–57.

18   Quoted in Losurdo (2006b), p. 110.

19   Winock, p. 80.

20   Hobsbawm (1994), pp. 70–71. Benjamin Disraeli thus preached that all members of the "privileged and prosperous English people" constituted a "natural aristocracy" towering high above the inferior races, see Losurdo (2010), p. 85.

21   Hobsbawm (1994), p. 81; Losurdo (2013), p. 12.

22   Quoted in Hobsbawm (1994), p. 56; Chamberlain is quoted in Eley, p. 162.

23   Hobsbawm (1994), p. 61: "[To the] advantage of metropolitan ruling classes . . . imperialist policies and propaganda . . . counteracted the growing appeal to the working classes of mass labour movements."

24   Rachschmir, p. 14; Winkler, pp. 62–63; quotations of Rhodes and Wahl in Lenin's book on imperialism, chapter VI.

25   Losurdo (2013), pp. 163–64.

26   Hochschild, p. 110.

27   A remarkable exception to this rule is provided by the case of Napoleon, son of Napoleon III, who was exiled to England after the Franco-Prussian War; in 1879, this "prince impérial" was killed in the Zulu War while serving as an officer in the British Army.

28   See the study by Rosa Amelia Plumelle-Uribe, La Férocité blanche.

29   Hobsbawm (1994), pp. 103–04.

CHAPTER 5

1   Mayer (2010), pp. 247–51.

2   See e.g. the quotation in Cohen and Major, p. 702.

3   Canfora (2006), p. 43.

4   Losurdo (2006a), pp. 311, 337.

5   According to the American sociologist Robert K. Merton, Le Bon was "an apprehensive conservative, worried by the growth of the proletariat with its socialist orientation . . . [displaying] an unremitting hostility to every aspect of socialism." See Le Bon, preface, p. xxxvii. On Langbehn, see Mayer (2010), pp. 292–94.

6   See e.g. Hobsbawm (1994), pp. 85–86.

7   Hobsbawm (1994), pp. 82–83.

8   Saint-Fuscien, p. 40.

9   Mayer (2010), p. 282; see also Koch, "Social Darwinism as a Factor in the 'New Imperialism'."

10   See Hobsbawm (1994), pp. 32, 252, 254; Mayer (2010), p. 285.

11   See e.g. the remarks about "Nordic," "Mediterranean," and other races in Firchow, pp. 21–29.

12   Pauwels (2013), p. 224.

13   Losurdo (2006b), pp. 240–45.

14   Losurdo (2006a), pp. 311–13; Losurdo (2013), p. 41; Lukács, III, pp. 112–24.

15   Mayer (2010), pp. 285–89.

16   Losurdo (2006b), pp. 242–43.

17   Eksteins, p. 90.

18   Firchow, pp. 131–32.

19   Ruskin, p. 70; comments in Firchow, p. 133.

20   Hawkins, pp. 209–10; see also Koch, pp. 343–44.

21   Quoted in Weber, p. 243. See also MacMillan (2013), p. 25.

22   Mayer (2010), pp. 284–89.

23   Quoted in Cohen and Major, p. 702.

24   Mayer (2010), pp. 292–94, 306.

25   Quotations from de Schaepdrijver, p. 44; Fussell, p. 234; Mayer (2010), p. 292; Jablonsky, p. 81.

26   Quoted in Zinn, p. 293.

27   See also Martens, p. 13: "war was also supposed to eliminate the socialist movement, a genuine threat to the existing system."

28   Pauwels (2007), p. 120.

29   Quotations from Losurdo (2006a), p. 283, and (2006b), p. 118; Fussell, pp. 8, 314. See also MacMillan (2013), p. 270.

30   Saint-Fuscien, p. 36.

31   Losurdo (2006b), pp. 118–19; de Schaepdrijver, p. 44.

32   Cohen and Major, pp. 699–700; Koch, p. 341; Rohkrämer, p. 97; Peeters, p. 123. The French poet Guillaume Apollinaire would even describe war as "entertainment for big children," see A. Becker, p. 36.

33   Fussell, pp. 27–28; Breverton, p. 240.

34   Eksteins, pp. 92–93.

35   Beloc as quoted in MacMillan (2013), p. 284; Piper, pp. 99–100. Heym as quoted in Glaser, pp. 198–99.

36   Losurdo (2001), pp. 15–19.

37   Mayer (2010), pp. 208–09.

38   "Italian Futurism." See also the commentary in Canfora (2006), pp. 56–57.

39   Quoted in Ferguson, p. 455.

40   Quoted in Englund, p. 57.

41   Saint-Fuscien, pp. 40–42, 48.

42   Lukács, I, p. 68.

43   Glaser, p. 202.

44   Quoted in Robert, p. 369; for similar opinions of French soldiers, see Nicot, pp. 131–32.

45   Losurdo (2001), pp. 12–15.

CHAPTER 6

1   De Vos, p. 27; Peeters, pp. 57–60.

2   Quoted in Hastings, p. 255; Firchow, pp. 31–33; Geiss, pp. 42, 48; MacMillan (2013), p. 56 ff.

3   Englund, pp. 225–26.

4   Martens, pp. 10–11.

5   Fussell, p. 116.

6   Fisher as quoted in Cohen and Major, pp. 704–05.

7   Engdahl, pp. 27–28; Stone and Kuznick, p. 4.

8   For the origins of the name Iraq, see Pauwels (2008), pp. 230–31.

9   Canali, p. 4 ff.; Engdahl, pp. 23, 28–37; Hochschild, p. 195; Hobsbawm (1994), pp. 317–18.

10   Clark, pp. 355–57.

11   MacMillan (2013), p. 16.

12   Lacroix-Riz (2014), chapter 1.

13   Milne.

14   MacMillan (2013), pp. 16, 50, 271; and on p. 165, one can read that "China, the Ottoman Empire, Persia, all were weak, divided, and apparently ready to be carved up"; could it be expected that this "carving up" would happen peacefully?

15   Geiss, pp. 36, 57.

16   Quoted in Weißbecker, p. 65.

17   Hastings, pp. 12, 16.

18   Losurdo (2006b), p. 164; quotation of A.P. Izvolsky in Cohen and Major, pp. 705–06; Geiss, p. 42.

19   Fischer (1998), p. 33.

20   Losurdo (2006b), p. 154, alluding to the remarks made by Paul M. Kennedy in his book *Rise of the Anglo-German Antagonism*.

21   Piper, p. 236; Münkler, pp. 246–47.

22   *14–18: Mourir pour la patrie*, pp. 50–51.

23   Cohen and Major (2004), p. 700.

24   See e.g. Zinn, pp. 290-313; Stone and Kuznick, pp. xxii–xxxiii.

25   The idea that the availability of land in the Wild West functioned as a safety valve is associated with the historian Frederick Jackson Turner and his "Frontier Thesis," also known as the "Turner Thesis."

26   Quotations from Cohen and Major, p. 617; Zinn, p. 290.

27   Zinn, p. 355; Knightley, p. 122 ff.

CHAPTER 7

1   Quoted in Hochschild, p. 17.

2   Hobsbawm (1994), pp. 307–09.

3   Hobsbawm (1994), p. 316.

4   Ferguson, p. 409; interview of the German historian Stephan Malinowski, quoted in the article of Staas and Ullrich; Müller (2011b), p. 140.

5   Hastings, p. xxix.

6   Le Naour, pp. 27, 41, 78-79, 124-28; Mayer (2010), pp. 223–24. Joan of Arc was beatified in April 1909 by Pope Pius X and she would be canonised by Pope Benedict XV on May 16, 1920. Regarding Montmartre as an ancient and important sanctuary, see Pauwels (2006), pp. 140–41.

7   Le Naour, p. 132.

8   Full text on http://www.bobdylan.com/de/node/26496.

9   Hobsbawm (1994), p. 133; however, historians such as Geoff Eley have argued that "the party [i.e. the SPD] was never *really* revolutionary in the first place." See Eley, p. 173.

10   Schorske, pp. 77–78.

11   Hobsbawm (1994), p. 129; Thomson, p. 49; Winock, p. 280.

12   More on Bernstein and reformism in Schorske, p. 16 ff.

13   De Schaepdrijver, pp. 21–22; Tuchman, p. 508.

14   Kolko (1994), pp. 114, 154–55.

15   Martens, pp. 14-15; Schorske, p. 85; Le Gall, pp. 33-35; Losurdo (2010), pp. 85–86; Losurdo (2013), pp. 114, 146–47.

16   Hobsbawm (1994), p. 72.

17   Zinn, p. 321, 339; Weinstein, pp. 63–74.

18   See the remarks on Mark Solomon's book, *The Cry Was Unity: Communists and African Americans, 1917–1936*, http://books.google.ca/books/about/The_Cry_Was_Unity. html?id=AJDEPnUWQ6EC&redir_esc=y.

CHAPTER 8

1   Hobsbawm (1994), pp. 132, 139; Weber, pp. 114, 241.

2   Weber, p. 126; Winock, pp. 269-73; *14–18: Mourir pour la patrie*, p. 17; Zinn, pp. 322–30.

3   MacMillan (2013), p. 251.

4   Winock, pp. 135–50.

5   Canfora (2006), p. 24; Schorske, pp. 177–80; Horne, pp. 6–9; Hastings, pp. 13, 22–23; Stockton; Rogger (1966), pp. 95, 98–100; Rogger (1983), p. 240; Hobsbawm (1994), pp. 49, 55, 109, 123, 130; Thomson, p. 174; Marwick, p. 32.

6   Hobsbawm (1994), pp. 131, 137–39; Marwick, p. 32.

7   Canfora (2006), pp. 18, 33–36; Tuchman, pp. 534, 537; Hochschild, p. 63; Kolko (1963), p. 285.

8   Winock, p. 122; Bouloc (2008), p. 129.

9   Hobsbawm (1994), pp. 117–18, 130; Hochschild, p. 86; Tuchman, p. 537; Weber, pp. 126–29; Stockton.

10   Braudel, pp. 420–28. See also Canfora (2006), pp. 16–17, and (2008), p. 229.

11   Mayer (2010), pp. 247, 304.

12   Hobsbawm (1994), pp. 134–36.

13   Canfora (2008), pp. 172–73.

14   Lewin, p. 292; Hobsbawm (1994), pp. 294–96, 299.

15   Feldbauer (2008a), pp. 68–71, 78.

16   Hobsbawm (1994), p. 216.

17   Hobsbawm (1994), pp. 216–18; Hochschild, p. 48; Hastings, p. 25.

18   Sumpf (2014), pp. 152–57.

19   Plumelle-Uribe, pp. 122–23.

20   Viên, pp. 160–64.

CHAPTER 9

1   Hobsbawm (1994), p. 109.

2   See e.g. Joll, p. 318.

3   Mayer (2010), pp. 304–05.

4   Mayer (2010), p. 228; Geiss, pp. 36–37.

5   Geiss, pp. 60–72; Hastings, p. 78; MacMillan (2013), pp. 328, 395.

6   MacMillan (2013), p. 130.

7   Canfora (2006), pp. 18, 33–36; Tuchman, pp. 534; Geiss, p. 69.

8   Hobsbawm (1994), pp. 322–24.

9   Hastings, p. 10, 29; MacMillan (2013), pp. 233–37, 334.

10   Mayer (2010), p. 311.

11   Hobsbawm (1994), pp. 322–24.

12   Mazower, pp. 105–06; Mayer (2010), pp. 327–28; Geiss, pp. 72–74; Hastings, pp. xxviii–xxix, 11, 29; MacMillan (2013), pp. 229–31.

13   Bouloc (2008), p. 369.

14   Quoted in Winock, p. 299; see also *14–18: Mourir pour la patrie*, pp. 22–23.

15   Bouloc (2008), p. 371.

16   Quoted in Clark, p. 309.

17   Mayer (2010), pp. 108-09, 223-24, 309; Canfora (2006), pp. 43-44; Losurdo (2001), p. 18.

18   Goujon, p. 52.

19   Tilly, pp. 300-01.

20   Sumpf (2014), pp. 21, 216-17; Rogger (1966), pp. 96-101; Mayer (2010), pp. 29, 312-13; Canfora (2008), pp. 191-201; Hobsbawm (1994), pp. 322-24; Losurdo (2006b), p. 101; MacMillan (2013) pp. 191-93, 334.

21   Mayer (2010), pp. 315-20.

22   Jackson, pp. 370-72; Marwick, pp. 37, 40-43.

23   Marwick, pp. 32, 37, 40-43; Hastings, pp. 21-25, 59-60; Jackson, p. 370 ff.; Mayer (2010), pp. 155-56.

24   Hastings, pp. 96, 112; Johnson, p. 22; Jackson, p. 383; Marwick, pp. 47-48; quotation of Lloyd George from Stockton.

25   Cohen and Major, p. 707; Hochschild, p. 291.

26   Quotations from Englund, p. 284, footnote 6; Hochschild, pp. 70-71; Marwick, pp. 47-48.

27   Hochschild, p. 69.

28   MacMillan (2013), p. 303.

29   MacMillan (2013), pp. 115-18, 132-33; Münkler, p. 75.

30   Firchow, pp. 36-47, 168, quotation from pp. 46-47. See also MacMillan (2013), p. 272; Clark, pp. 160-66, 202-04.

31   Feldbauer (2008a), p. 60.

32   Pauwels (2007), pp. 68-69.

33   Mayer (2010), p. 300.

34   Mayer (2010), pp. 15, 252, 290, 300-03; Losurdo (2006b), pp. 220-21.

35   Quoted in Hibberd and Onions, pp. 72-73.

36   Mayer (2010), p. 323.

37   Mayer (2010), p. 306.

38   Pauwels (2009), p. 23.

39   Mayer (2010), pp. 322-23.

40   See e.g. the remarks concerning Germany in MacMillan (2013), p. 132: in the Reichstag, which needed to authorize the necessary expenditures, not only the social democrats but also the conservatives opposed new taxes purporting to finance an enlargement of the army.

41   Canfora (2008), p. 163; Tuchman, p. 534.

42   Hobsbawm (1994), pp. 322-24; Clark, p. 313.

43   See the remarks in MacMillan (2013), p. 323 ff.

44   Hochschild, p. 83; Geiss, pp. 70-71; Kolko (1994), p. 23. More about the bellicosity of Moltke and other German generals in Hastings, pp. 30-32, and Clark, pp. 327, 332-33.

45   Levine-Weinberg, p. 20.

CHAPTER 10

1   Hochschild, p. 80; Canfora (2006), p. 64; Geiss, pp. 72–78.

2   Tuchman, p. 538; see also Hastings, pp. xxxii–xxxvii: "Most of Europe received the news with equanimity, because acts of terror were so familiar."

3   See e.g. Clark (2012), pp. 47–64.

4   Hochschild, p. 84; Canfora (2006), pp. 66–73.

5   Quoted in Tuchman, p. 538.

6   Canfora (2006), pp. 75–76; Rogger (1983), p. 256.

7   Ferguson, p. 443; Hastings, pp. 37–40, 72, 86–90.

8   Piper, p. 131.

9   Clark, p. 549; Ferguson, p. 443: "If Germany had not violated [Belgian neutrality] in 1914, then Britain would have."

10   Hatton, p. 31; Hochschild, p. 94.

11   Hobsbawm (1994), p. 326.

12   Quoted in Hochschild, p. 96.

13   Hibberd and Onions, p. 38; comment in Firchow, pp. 130–31.

14   Rogger (1966), pp. 112–13.

15   Quoted in Cohen and Major, p. 708; see also Piper (2013), p. 102.

16   Hochschild, pp. 90, 102.

17   Hitler, p. 161.

18   See http://www.youtube.com/watch?v=DzY3UCf2-tk; for the full text of the song, see: http://www.parolesmania.com/paroles_jacques_brel_11660/paroles_jaures_397453.html.

19   For the full French text and an English translation, see http://lyricstranslate.com/en/jaures-jaures.html-0.

20   Fussell, p. 21.

21   Kolko (1994), p. 24.

22   Fussell, pp. 21–22, 178, 181; Braudy, p. 382.

23   MacMillan (2013), p. xxvii; Ulrich, pp. 111–12; Duroselle, pp. 61–62; Clark, pp. 553–54.

24   Sumpf (2014), pp. 38–40; Rouaud, p. 29.

25   Quoted in Clapham, pp. 133–34.

26   Baldin, p. 2; *14–18: Mourir pour la patrie*, p. 54; Guéno and Laplume, p. 9; Rousseau (2006), pp. 34–38; Winock, p. 384; Hastings, pp. 82, 104–07, 118, 121–22; Rogger (1966), pp. 104–08; Ulrich, p. 112.

27   Ulrich and Ziemann, p. 48.

28   Schorske, p. 286; Hochschild, pp. 87–88, 90–91, 100, 107, 128; Marwick, p. 51; Tuchman, pp. 539–40; Hastings, p. 71; Duroselle, pp. 54–55.

29   Mayer (2010), p. 307.

30   Rousseau (2006), p. 62.

31   Keay, p. 470; Hill (2011), pp. 54–56.

32   Hastings, p. 132.

33   Hastings, p. 132; Barthas, p. 26; Hobsbawm (1994), pp. 100, 325; Hochschild, p. 92; Bouloc (2008), p. 131.

34   Bouloc (2008), p. 131.

35   Hochschild, p. 177; Hastings, p. 521.

36   Hobsbawm (1994), pp. 108, 325–26; Ferguson, pp. 198–99, 228–29.

37   Hochschild, p. 177; Hastings, p. 521; Hobsbawm (1994), pp. 108, 325–26; Ferguson, pp. 198–99, 228–29; Horvat, p. 38; de Schaepdrijver, pp. 60, 64.

CHAPTER 11

1   Ferguson, pp. 201–02; Hastings, pp. 420–23; Rousseau (2006), pp. 16–17; MacMillan (2013), p. 277.

2   Sumpf (2014), pp. 45–47; Deschner, pp. 585–87; Firchow, p. 131; Hochschild, pp. 177–78; Hastings, pp. 124, 434; Fischer (1998), pp. 184–89; Barthas, p. 423; Le Naour, pp. 130–31; Eksteins, p. 236; Münkler, pp. 233–36.

3   Hibberd and Onions, p. 260.

4   Quoted in Canfora (2008), pp. 174–75; see also Rousseau (2006), pp. 15–16.

5   Mayer (2010), p. 178. On the role of military service in Germany, see Ulrich, Vogel, and Ziemann, p. 146 ff.

6   See the article by Robinson, "The Pals Battalions in World War One."

7   Quoted in Clapham, pp. 153–54.

8   Ferguson, pp 205–06; Hochschild, pp. 119, 148–51; Hastings, p. 121; Connor, p. 6.

9   Black and Boileau, pp. 62, 74.

10   A. Becker, p. 30 ff.

11   Quoted in Hibberd and Onions, p. 8.

12   Hochschild, pp. 118–19. The full text may be found on this site: http://paperspast.natlib.govt.nz/cgi-bin/paperspast?a=d&d=PBH19150126.2.10.25.7.

13   Knightley, p. 99.

14   Fussell, p. 87.

15   Hochschild, pp. 222–23; Piper, pp. 197–98; Hibberd and Onions, p. x. In August 1914, Wells wrote a number of newspaper articles that were later published under the title The War That Will End War.

16   Tuchman, pp 539–40.

17   Eksteins, p. 63; Schramm, p. 80; Hastings, pp. 66–67; statement of July 25 quoted in Schorske, p. 286.

18   Eksteins, p. 63; Canfora (2008), p. 174.

19   Canfora (2006), pp. 143–44.

20   Tuchman, p. 542; Schorske, pp. 288–89; Piper, pp. 59–60.

21   Robert, pp. 22–30; Barbusse, quoted in Harvey, pp. 171–72. See also Bouloc (2008), pp. 173–75 on the "jusqu'au-boutism" of the socialist minister Albert Thomas.

22   Schorske, p. 289; Boscus, pp. 228–29.

23   Marwick, p. 99; Hochschild, p. 101; Horne, p. 51.

24   Martens, p. 16.

25   Rogger (1983), p. 256.

26   Schramm, pp. 87–88; Piper, p. 410.

27   Bouloc (2008), p. 161 ff; Rousseau (2006), pp. 80–82.

28   Hobsbawm (1994), p. 102.

29   Englund, pp. 60–61.

30   Kolko (1994), pp. 113–14.

31   Schorske, pp. 292–94; Lenin-quotation from Martens, p. 13.

32   Schorske, p. 286; Hochschild, pp. xvi, 87–88, 90–91, 100, 107, 128; Marwick, p. 51; Tuchman, pp. 539–40.

33   http://www.marxists.org/archive/lenin/works/1914/aug/x01.htm.

34   Quotations from Schramm, pp. 75–77, and Kolko (1994), pp. 119–20.

35   Hochschild, p. 117.

36   http://www.dichterdescaderlands.be/info; translation from the Dutch by the author.

CHAPTER 12

1   Quoted in Byrnes. See also Libardi, Orlandi, and Scudiero, pp. 20, 25.

2   Quoted in Canfora (2008), p. 229; see also Canfora (2006), pp. 16–17.

3   Braudel, pp. 420–28.

4   Eksteins, p. 193.

5   Quotations from Hochschild, p. 118, and Tuchman, p. 542.

6   Quoted in Losurdo (2001), pp. 11–12.

7   Libardi, Orlandi, and Scudiero, pp. 27–32; http://rainer-maria-rilke.de/100144fuenfgesaenge.html.

8   Rogger (1983), p. 255.

9   Ferguson, pp. 207–08.

10   Eksteins, pp. 65–66.

11   Deschner, pp. 585–92; Fischer (1998), p. 188; Duroselle, pp. 64–65; Le Naour, pp. 29, 131; Hibberd and Onions, p. xviii; Rousseau (1999), pp. 235–43; Ulrich and Ziemann, p. 109; A. Becker, pp. 106–11.

12   Winock, pp. 132–34.

13   Bouloc (2008), p. 133.

14   Hastings, p. 123; Bouloc (2008), pp. 183–84.

15   Schorske, p. 292; Peeling.

16   Rogger (1966), pp. 110–11; Rogger (1983), pp. 255–56.

17   De Schaepdrijver, p. 65; Hochschild, p. 155; Ferguson, p. 221.

18   Ferguson, p. 215.

19   Fussell, p. 315; Taylor, p. 2.

20   Brown, pp. 104–08.

21   Bouloc (2011), pp. 86–87; Losurdo (2006b), pp. 155–56; Ferguson, pp. 219–21.

22   Wolff, pp. 64–65, 68.

23   Englund, p. 61; Hastings, p. 111; Cazals, p. 43; Duroselle, p. 130 ff.; Del Boca, pp. 134, 146.

24   Hastings, p. 81; Deist (1970), part one, pp. 26–28; Ferguson, p. 288.

25   De Schaepdrijver, pp. 120, 125–26, 130.

26   Boscus, p. 230; Weißbecker, pp. 131, 169; Horne, pp. 58–59.

27   Canfora (2008), p. 223; Losurdo (2006b), pp. 205–08.

28   Horne, p. 42.

29   See e.g. Bouloc (2008), pp. 165–66.

30   Ferguson, pp. 259–63; Bouloc (2008), p. 162.

31   Rogger (1983), pp. 241, 260; Rousseau (2006), p. 89; Sumpf (2014), pp. 132–33.

32   Deist (1970), first part, pp. 26–28; Ferguson, p. 270; "Piece Work"; Marwick, pp. 95, 98–99; Kolko (1994), pp. 108–09; Boscus, pp. 229–31.

33   Bouloc (2008), p. 173.

34   Hastings, p. 417; Ferguson, pp. 267–68; Horne, p. 100; Rousseau (2006), pp. 86–89.

35   Losurdo (2007a), p. 198.

36   Dupeux, pp. 207–08; Duroselle, p. 200; Horne, pp. 91–92.

37   Rousseau (2006), p. 91; Horne, pp. 91–92; Kolko (1994), pp. 88–94, 101, quotation on p. 94; Rogger (1983), p. 260.

38   Ferguson, pp. 320–21, 330.

39   Hastings, pp. 412, 414; Ferguson, pp. 276–77.

40   Marwick, p. 95; Pötzl; Dupeux, p. 203; Boscus, p. 229.

41   Ferguson, p. 270; Boscus, pp. 229–30, 233, 237.

42   Hastings, p. 248.

43   Piper, pp. 80–84.

44   Englund, p. 185.

CHAPTER 13

1   Hobohm, p. 139.

2   Kolko (1994), pp. 126–27; Hastings, p. 208; 14–18: Mourir pour la patrie, p. 164.

3   Le Naour, p. 150; Saint-Fuscien, p. 77.

4   Mayer (2010), pp. 308–09; Lafon, pp. 35, 38–39; Saint-Fuscien, pp. 82–84; Horvat, p. 45.

5   See the article by Laura Root.

6   Breverton, p. 156.

7   Saint-Fuscien, p. 62.

8   Braudy, p. 376; Breverton, p. 300.

9   Roynette, p. 147; Braudy, p. 376; Saint-Fuscien, pp. 62–63; Claisse, p. 167; Breverton, p. 277. About the origin and meaning of the term Yankees, see Pauwels (2008), p. 126.

10   Hochschild, p. 299.

11   Hastings, p. 128.

12   Fussell, pp. 272–75.

13   Fussell, pp. 272–83.

14   Goujon, p. 50; Mayer (2010), p. 185; Hochschild, p. 6; Hastings, p. 170; Braudy, p. 355.

15   Kolko (1994), pp. 46–48; Mayer (2010), pp. 310–11; Sumpf (2014), p. 30.

16   Kolko (1994), pp. 45–46; Hochschild, pp. 6, 104; Hastings, p. 549.

17   Mayer (2010), pp. 178–79.

18   *14–18: mourir pour la patrie*, p. 191.

CHAPTER 14

1   Cazals, pp. 18, 53.

2   Marty, p. 76.

3   Braudy, p. 381.

4   Guéno and Laplume, p. 9; Hastings, pp. xvii, 159–60, 181, 321, 438; Englund, p. 213.

5   Piper, p. 151 ff; Hastings, pp. 161, 164, 183–84; Peeters, pp. 89–90; Münkler, pp. 113–21.

6   Hastings, pp. 161, 164, 183–84; Peeters, pp. 89–90; de Schaepdrijver, pp. 69–72, 91–92.

7   Hastings, p. 497.

8   Knightley, p. 139; Hastings, pp. xviii, 150–55, 497–99, 505, 513–14; Münkler, pp. 176–94.

9   Hastings, pp. 224–25, 236, 257–58, 495, 548; Fussell, p. 179.

10   *14–18: Mourir pour la patrie*, pp. 113–21; Eksteins, p. 100; Ferguson, p. 340; de Schaepdrijver, p. 180.

11   Ulrich and Ziemann, p. 51.

12   Mayer (2010), p. 307.

13   Hastings, p. 282.

14   Quoted in Hochschild, pp. 209–10.

15   Mayer (2010), p. 307; Hochschild, pp. 209–10; Knightley, p. 108; Kolko (1994), p. 128; Barthas, p. 255; Rousseau (1999), p. 103; Breverton, p. 72.

16   Hastings, pp. 180–81; Das (2011a), p. 80; Duroselle, p. 329.

17 Rousseau (1999), p. 207.

18 Hastings, pp. 148–49. Pictures in Friedrich, pp. 138–43; Couliou, p. 63.

19 Englund, p. 65; Hastings, pp. 373–74, 432, 435; Piper, pp. 109–16, 141–44.

20 Hastings, pp. 185–86, 292, 294–95.

21 Hastings, pp. 287, 293; A. Becker, p. 30.

22 Barthas, pp. 47–48.

23 Hastings, p. 541.

24 Rogger (1983), p. 256, quotation from Hastings, p. 508.

25 Mazower, p. 118; Hastings, pp. 148–49, 497.

26 Hibberd and Onions, p. 259.

27 Eksteins, pp. 233–34.

28 Fussell, pp. 115–16; Hastings, pp. 296–97, 440; Hayward, pp. 46–69.

29 Hastings, p. 433.

30 Hayward, pp. 70–95; Hastings, p. 192; Piper, pp. 181–83; Kramer, p. 292, referring to terminology used by von Beseler in the context of the German atrocities in Belgium.

31 Hochschild, pp. 148–51.

32 Hochschild, pp. 118–19, 226.

33 Original German text: "*Der Krieg ist für die Reichen, die Armen stellen die Leichen.*"

34 Hayward, pp. 31–45.

35 Piper, pp. 186–87; "Belgium's imperialist rape of Africa." About the Belgian atrocities in the Congo, see Plumelle-Uribe, pp. 96–117.

36 Hastings, pp. 439–40; Fussell, pp. 86, 89.

37 Barthas, p. 423; Robert, p. 58.

38 Simpson, p. 33.

39 Hastings, p. 559; Rousseau (1999), pp. 235–43.

40 Fussell, p. 168.

41 Quoted in Fussell, p. 240.

42 Hibberd and Onions, p. 28.

43 Gurney quotation from Clapham, p. 78; Brittain quotation from Hibberd and Onions, p. 18.

44 Hastings, pp. 423, 425, 433; Fussell, pp. 175, 316.

45 Saint-Gille, *passim.*

46 Schorske, pp. 300–03.

CHAPTER 15

1 *Paths of Glory*, scene with young German woman: http://www.youtube.com/watch?v=pJH8hO7VlWE.

2 Rousseau (1999), p. 79; Losurdo (2006b), pp. 262–63; Ulrich, p. 117.

3 Cazals, p. 43; Rousseau (1999), pp. 37, 79; Losurdo (2006b), pp. 262–63; Connor,

p. 6; Ulrich, p. 117; Kolko (1994), pp. 127–28, 131, 136; Knightley, p. 108; Hastings, pp. 261, 425; Powell, pp. 121–22 ; Dorgelès, p. 112.

4   Quoted in Fussell, pp. 83–84.

5   http://www.forcespoetry.com/poemdetails.asp?ID=221.

6   Englund, p. 53–54; Hastings, p. 365.

7   Kolko (1994), pp. 127–28.

8   Robert, p. 58; Rousseau (1999), pp. 74–75, 78; Calzas, pp. 81–82; Miquel, pp. 81, 83–84.

9   Hastings, pp. 239, 302.

10   Rousseau (1999), pp. 33–40, 46–47.

11   Ulrich, p. 133.

12   Eksteins, pp. 174–75, 181.

13   Ulrich and Ziemann, p. 136.

14   Hastings, p. 529.

15   Miquel, p. 166; Horvat, p. 55.

16   Hastings, pp. 30, 539; Jackson, pp. 383–85; Johnson, p. 24.

17   Barthas, p. 292; Englund, p. 42; Hastings, p 402.

18   Miquel, p. 164; Rousseau (1999), pp. 281–83.

19   Hochschild, pp. 116, 126; Englund, p. 457.

20   "Enemy Aliens, Prisoners of War."

21   Fussell, p. 82; Mayer (2010), p. 307; Kolko (1994), pp. 45–46; Hochschild, pp. 126–27, 167, 233–34, 322; Hastings, pp. 350, 524; Sumpf (2014), p. 175; pictures in Friedrich, pp. 124–27, 238–41.

22   Kläber, p. 89–91. Full text on http://www.textlog.de/tucholsky-minuten-gehoer.html.

23   Hastings, pp. 230–33, 480; Kolko (1994), p. 128; Ulrich and Ziemann, pp. 44, 124; Markidès, p. 92.

24   Barthas, p. 69.

25   Hochschild, p. 137.

26   Barthas, p. 77; Kolko (1994), pp. 124–25; Rousseau (1999), pp. 83–85, 92–93; Markidès, p. 92; Hobohm, p. 140; Saint-Fuscien, p. 79.

27   Allard, pp. 107–08.

28   Robert, pp. 88–89; Rousseau (1999), pp. 109–14, 121–25; Kolko (1994), pp. 134–35; *14–18: Mourir pour la patrie*, p. 120; Guéno and Laplume, p. 39; Taylor-Whiffen; Englund, p. 51; Markidès, *passim*, and especially pp. 23, 27–32, 63–71.

29   Das (2011a), p. 81; Kolko (1994), pp. 136, 214; Taylor-Whiffen; Hochschild, pp. 233, 242; Rousseau (2006), p. 66; see the detailed study by Oram.

30   Fussell, pp. 118–19; Robertson, pp. 80–81.

31   Kläber, pp. 32–33; Pittalis, p. 205.

32   Knightley, p. 108.

33   Richard Anderson as a young French staff officer: http://www.youtube.com/

watch?v=KJDkLgwJopQ.

34 Horvat, p. 45; de Schaepdrijver, p. 213; Saint-Fuscien, p. 86.

35 Quoted in Dare Hall, p. 15.

36 Guéno and Laplume, p. 112; see also Rousseau (1999), pp. 254–55; Miquel, p. 180; Markidès, p. 92.

37 Hastings, pp. 539–40.

38 Hibberd and Onions, p. 141.

39 Winn, pp. 15–16; Hibberd and Onions, p. 212.

40 Firchow, p. 113.

41 Nicot, p. 146; Hastings, pp. 428, 440.

42 Ashworth, *passim*; Barthas, p. 304; Englund, pp. 182, 210, footnote 223; Hochschild, p. 131, 173; Kolko (1994), pp. 134–35; Hastings, pp. 526–27; Guéno and Laplume, pp. 78–79; Peacock, p. 14; Rousseau (1999), p. 100; Markidès, p. 22.

43 Fussell, pp. 123–24; Hayward, pp. 99–101; Cook, pp. 37–38; Hochschild, p. 173.

44 Hochschild, p. 131.

45 See e.g. Rousseau (2006), p. 138.

46 Barthas, p. 81; *14–18: Mourir pour la patrie*, pp. 170–77; Guéno and Laplume, p. 80

47 Drouin, p. 51; Miquel, pp. 152–53.

48 Hastings, pp. 556–57.

49 Christmas in the Trenches, 1914, see: https://www.youtube.com/watch?v=-gx2cAUo7i4.

CHAPTER 16

1 Fischer (1967), p. 37; Powell, p. 116.

2 Peeters, p. 119; Piper, p. 79; Münkler, pp. 110–17; Miquel, pp. 123–24; de Schaepdrijver, pp. 91–92.

3 Le Naour, pp. 30–33; *14–18: Mourir pour la patrie*, p. 132; Hastings, pp. 341–42.

4 Münkler, p. 201.

5 Münkler, pp. 194–200.

6 Duroselle, pp. 86–89; Peacock, pp. 61; Peeters, pp. 143–51, 169; de Schaepdrijver, pp. 173–79.

7 Piper, pp. 88–94; Münkler, pp. 207–10; Breverton, p. 79.

8 "Max Hoffmann."

9 Keay, p. 471.

10 Canali, p. 29; "The 1914 actions in Mesopotamia."

11 Englund, pp. 184, 267–69; Münkler, pp. 319–26; Breverton, pp. 151–52; "The tragedy of Kut."

12 Omer-Cooper, p. 159.

13 Segesser, pp. 110–20; Omer-Cooper, pp. 165–67; Münkler , pp. 328–33; Canales and

De Rey, pp. 93–120; Moyd.

14 Segesser, pp. 120–27; Schirokauer, pp. 311–12.

CHAPTER 17

1 Hastings, p. 515; Peacock, pp. 64–65, 78–79. More about the barbed wire in Englund, p. 63.

2 Barthas, introduction by Chrisje Brants, pp. 8–9; A. Becker, p. 114; Fussell, p. 37.

3 Hochschild, p. 136; Englund, pp. 67, 98.

4 Hibberd and Onions, p. 201.

5 Hibberd and Onions, p. 256–57.

6 Barthas, pp. 15, 204, 211; Miquel, pp. 155–60; Fussell, pp. 43–45; *14–18: Mourir pour la patrie*, pp. 141–43; Rouaud, pp. 52–53.

7 Fussell, pp. 43–44.

8 Fussell, pp. 41–44, 48, 120–21.

9 Hibberd and Onions, p. 67.

10 The situation was described like this in Fussell, p. 51.

11 "Lark"; "Nachtigall."

12 The full text of the poem can be found on http://www.warmuseum.ca/cwm/exhibitions/remember/flandersfields_e.shtml.

13 Baldin, p. 4; Fussell, p. 49.

14 Rousseau (1999), p. 77; Barthas, p. 251; see also Münkler, pp. 377–80.

15 Hochschild, p. 137; Guéno and Laplume, p. 55.

16 Englund, p. 311; Rousseau (1999), p. 251; Duroselle, p. 422.

17 See http://www.westernfrontassociation.com/great-war-people/48-brothers-arms/372-songs-war.html.

18 Fussell, pp. 46–48, 51–52, 242; Hastings, p. 519; de Schaepdrijver , pp. 183–85, 194.

19 The full text is to be found on http://www.firstworldwar.com/poetsandprose/binyon.htm.

20 Fussell, p. 49; Hibberd and Onions, pp. 152–53.

21 Miquel, pp. 67, 166–68; Rousseau (1999), pp. 193–95; Nicot, pp. 48–49; Barthas, p. 16 (introduction by Chrisje Brants), p. 92; Guéno and Laplume, p. 121; Saint-Fuscien, pp. 105–06; Daughton, pp. 50–55.

22 Kläber, p. 39; Hastings, pp. 408, 498, 509.

23 Breverton, pp. 119–20, 125, 128–30; Barthas, pp. 109, 182; Miquel, pp. 160–63; Fussell, pp. 48–49, 164; Robertson, pp. 37, 67; Dorgelès, p. 57.

24 Lyrics of "Any Soldier to His Son": http://www.forcespoetry.com/poemdetails.asp?ID=221.

25 Connor, p. 8.

26 Barthas, p. 448; Rousseau (1999), pp. 117–19.

27 Fussell, pp. 87–88, 171; Dare Hall; Allard, pp. 52–53; Miquel (2000), pp. 168–69.

28   Rousseau (1999), p. 76.

29   Barthas, pp. 8, 172.

30   Hastings, pp. 505, 509; Englund, p. 216.

31   Lyrics of "Tell Me Now": http://www.musicanet.org/robokopp/usa/tellmeno.htm.

32   Robertson, p. 57.

33   Roynette, pp. 23–24.

34   Quoted in Fussell, p. 88.

35   Lafon, pp. 40, 43; Loez and Mariot, pp. 21, 27; Kläber, pp. 39–40.

36   Barthas, p. 153.

37   Barthas, pp. 427–28; Loez and Mariot, p. 20; Hastings, p. 517; Englund, p. 64.

38   Kläber, pp. 39–40; Ulrich and Ziemann, p. 124:

39   Ulrich and Ziemann, p. 135. This was a variation of a verse of the poem "Die Ordensverteilung," "The distribution of honours," written in Menin, Belgium, in 1916, by Gottfried Rinker, a lieutenant in the Württemberg Army Corps, see http://www.lyrikheute.com/2012/05/blogbaustelle-hier-entsteht-ein-post.html and http://www.kriegstagebuch.gottfriedrinker.bplaced.net/gottfried.html.

40   Ulrich, p. 131.

41   Rousseau (1999), pp. 109, 116; Ulrich and Ziemann, pp. 43–45, 50, 122–23; Barthas, pp. 327, 381.

42   The generals' castle in *Paths of Glory*: http://www.youtube.com/watch?v=89y7pcYTQy4.

43   Knightley, p. 108; Hochschild, pp. 105, 127; Kläber, p. 94.

44   Barthas, p. 227.

45   Fussell, pp. 82–85; Hayward, p. 129; Barthas, p. 165.

46   Eksteins, pp. 104–05.

47   Quoted in Marwick, p. 55.

48   Roynette, p. 173; Barthas, p. 278.

49   Barthas, p. 448; Englund, p. 283; Saint-Fuscien, pp. 150–53.

50   Roynette, pp. 178–79.

51   Lyrics of Alfred Lichtenstein's poem, "Heimatschuß": http://gutenberg.spiegel.de/buch/5161/35.

52   Guéno and Laplume, pp. 48–49; Rousseau (2006), pp. 12, 75–77; Feltman, pp. 88, 91; Meyer, p. 122; Black and Boileau, p. 155; Sumpf (2014), pp. 137.

53   Roynette, p. 158.

54   Rousseau (1999), pp. 206–07.

55   "Analysis: Suicide in the Trenches by Siegfried Sassoon."

56   Kolko (1994), pp. 102–04; Eksteins, p. 155; Persico, p. 380, relying on a study by John Ellis and Michael Cox; Fussell, p. 41; Marwick, p. 55; Hochschild, p. 231; Wolff, p. 34; Saint-Fuscien, p. 187; Duroselle, p. 421.

57   http://www.bachlund.org/The_Bells_of_Hell.htm. See also Ferguson, pp. 364–65; Dorgelès, p. 110.

58   Hibberd and Onions, p. 145.

59   From the poem "And if a Bullet," quoted in Clapham, p. 56.

60   Lyrics of the German song "Bald, allzubalde": https://www.youtube.com/watch?v=pBiSRXFpIoo.

61   Barthas, introduction by Chrisje Brants, p. 10.

62   Ulrich and Ziemann, pp. 81–82, 92–95; Englund, p. 245, footnote.

63   Ulrich and Ziemann, p. 79; Rousseau (1999), p. 186.

64   Hibberd and Onions, p. 67.

65   Hibberd and Onions, pp. 284–85.

66   Barthas, p. 464.

CHAPTER 18

1   Hibberd and Onions, pp. 43, 46; Hochschild, p. 138.

2   Breverton, pp. 102–03.

3   Barthas, introduction by Chrisje Brants, p. 15.

4   Barthas, pp. 90, 105.

5   Barthas, p. 105.

6   Hibberd and Onions, p. 43.

7   Lyrics of «Bois-le-Prêtre»: http://www.histoiredefrance-chansons.com/index.php?param1=mil366.php.

8   Hochschild, pp. 162–68.

9   Lyrics of "Hanging On The Old Barbed Wire": http://www.antiwarsongs.org/canzone.php?lang=en&id=7606Wire'; Hibberd and Onions, p. 43.

10   Hochschild, pp. 162–68.

11   Miquel, pp. 229–32.

12   Barthas, pp. 157–58.

13   Duroselle (1994), p. 122; Miquel, p. 53.

14   Miquel, p. 232; Eslava Galán, p. 100; Barthas, pp. 94–95; Fussell, p. 50; Englund, pp. 162–63 ; A. Becker, p. 124.

15   Hochschild, p. 173.

16   Ulrich and Ziemann, pp. 89, 102–03, 106–07; Rousseau (1999), pp. 210–23; Kolko (1994), pp. 130–31; Breverton, pp. 181–84, 192–93.

17   Mueller and Mueller; Stone and Kuznick, pp. 20, 26; Hochschild, p. 142; Breverton, p. 77; Gowans (2013a) and (2015).

18   Hochschild, pp. 153, 155; Breverton, pp. 81–82.

CHAPTER 19

1   Münkler, pp. 333–42.

2   Lyrics of "Waltzing Matilda" on the internet site of Eric Bogle, http://ericbogle.net/

lyrics/lyricspdf/andbandplayedwaltzingm.pdf. The song can be heard on http://www.youtube.com/watch?v=471-ucVd7o0.

3   Rousseau , pp. 128–31.

4   Englund, pp. 111–12, 139–40.

5   Englund, pp. 111–12, 139–40; Losurdo (2006b), p. 219.

6   Del Boca, pp. 129, 130; Pittalis, pp. 49–55, 61–63; Hastings, p. 414; Ferro, pp. 67–68; Canfora (2006), p. 140; Canfora (2008), p. 172; Rousseau (2006), p. 89 ; Parenti (2014).

7   Feldbauer (2008a), pp. 77–78; Canfora (2006), pp. 137–41; Piper, pp. 298–308. See Rachschmir, pp. 77–83, for a thorough critique of the "legend of Mussolini's 'socialism'."

8   Englund, p. 146.

9   Del Boca, pp. 133–34, 139, 141–42; Kolko (1994), p. 135; Englund, p. 378; Rousseau (1999), p. 123; Cazals, p. 45.

10   Englund, pp. 172–73.

11   Del Boca, pp. 130–35, 138; Pittalis, pp. 71–72.

12   Quoted in Pittalis, p. 22.

13   "O Gorizia, tu sei maledetta," http://www.antiwarsongs.org/canzone.php?lang=it&id=47.

14   Sumpf (2014), pp. 12–13, 55–56, 86–87, 196–97, 218, 283, 299 ff.; Hochschild, pp. 156–57; Piper, pp. 176–78.

15   Duroselle, pp. 109, 269–70.

16   Iltchev, pp. 275–80; Duroselle, pp. 341–44; Englund, pp. 180, 279, 411, 433–34; Gillet, pp. 90–92; Miquel, pp. 56, 58, 161.

CHAPTER 20

1   Couliou, pp. 63–66.

2   Fussell, p. 182.

3   14–18: Mourir pour la patrie, p. 143; Barthas, p. 144; Loez and Mariot, pp. 29–30.

4   Miquel, pp. 251–52.

5   Lyrics of I Want to Go Home: http://www.musicanet.org/robokopp/english/iwantogo.htm.

6   Robert, pp. 58–59.

7   Lyrics of "Madelon": http://www.www.dutempsdescerisesauxfeuillesmortes.net/paroles/quand_madelon.htm. On "pays" as "little fatherland," see Cazals, p. 86.

8   Lyrics of "Der Treuer Husar": http://www.lieder-archiv.de/der_treue_husar-text_400194.html. This scene may be viewed on http://www.youtube.com/watch?v=GObO-KRkiZA.

9   Eksteins, p. 208.

10   Ulrich, p. 130.

11   Barthas, pp. 333, 339.

12   Englund, p. 308.

13   De Schaepdrijver, p. 188.

14   Hibberd and Onions, pp. 256–57.

15   Fussell, p. 87; Nicot, pp. 22–25; Rousseau (1999), p. 288. The Kern poem is quoted in Clapham, p. 11.

16   Fussell, pp. 86, 89, 289.

17   Barthas, pp. 353–54; Fussell, pp. 179–80; Nicot, pp. 149, 156.

18   Barthas, p. 88.

19   Barthas, pp. 136, 175, 187–88, 300–02, 370, 426; Fussell, p. 245.

20   Hochschild, pp. 130–31; Brown and Seaton, pp. 210–13; Sumpf (2014), pp. 106–09.

21   Barthas, p. 382.

22   British war veteran singing "We're Here Because We're Here": https://www.youtube.com/watch?v=UA730QtjOBE.

23   Nicot, pp. 144–45.

24   Rousseau (1999), pp. 14–16, 201; Ulrich and Ziemann, p. 87; Ulrich, pp. 129–30.

25   Barthas, p. 147.

26   Englund, p. 414.

27   Rousseau (1999), pp. 129–35; Rousseau (2006), p. 60.

28   Rousseau (1999), p. 129; Rousseau (2006), pp. 57–58

29   Couliou, p. 68.

30   Robert, pp. 40–41, 58–59; Horne, pp. 91–92.

31   Robert, pp. 61–63, 85–86; Horne, pp. 61–62.

32   Robert, p. 78–81.

33   Kolko (1994), p. 113; Schorske, pp. 302–06.

34   Sumpf (2014), p. 165; Englund, pp. 178–79.

35   Hastings, p. 414.

36   "The Group Scheme"; Black and Boileau, pp. 56–62.

37   "I Did Not Raise My Boy To Be A Soldier."

38   Text of "In Flanders' Fields": http://www.warmuseum.ca/cwm/exhibitions/remember/flandersfields_e.shtml.

39   Fussell, pp. 246–50; text of Rosenberg's poem: http://www.poetryfoundation.org/poetrymagazine/poem/2738.

40   I thank my brother, landscape architect Erik Pauwels, for this botanic information.

41   Fussell, pp. 246–50; Steven Connor, "Isaac Rosenberg: Birkbeck's War Poet," October 30, 2000, http://www.stevenconnor.com/rosenberg, pp. 9–10.

CHAPTER 21

1   Rouaud, p. 42.

2   Libardi, Orlandi, and Scudiero, p. 37; Miquel, p. 59.

3   Miquel, p. 261 ff.; *14–18: Mourir pour la patrie*, pp. 152–53; Ferguson, p. 285; Englund, pp. 253, 372; Duroselle, pp. 110–17; Piper, pp. 396–99; Breverton, pp. 122–23.

4   Keegan, p. 207 ff; Wolff, pp. 61–63. Haig-quotation in Wolff, pp. 62–63.

5   Hibberd and Onions, pp. 152–53.

6   Hochschild, p. 143.

7   Ferguson, p. 293; Fussell, pp. 13, 27, 29; Hochschild, pp. 196, 198, 206–07; Hibberd and Onions, pp. 152–53; Black and Boileau, pp. 136–39.

8   Hochschild, p. xviii.

9   Hochschild, pp. 180, 207.

10   Hochschild, pp. 209–10, 224.

11   Knightley, p. 100; Fussell, pp. 12, 175, 316; Ulrich and Ziemann, pp. 73, 95.

12   Hochschild, p. 214; Kolko (1994), p. 133.

13   Fussell, p. 243–245. Lyrics of the song: http://www.firstworldwar.com/audio/rosesofpicardy.htm.

14   Hibberd and Onions, p. 146.

15   Hibberd and Onions, pp. 143–44. *Sed miles* was an allusion to a famous poem by Henry Newbolt, "Clifton Chapel," dealing with someone who died young, *sed miles, sed pro patria*, that is, "but as a soldier, but for the fatherland."

16   Hochschild, pp. 211–12.

17   Fussell, pp. 71–74; Wolff, p. 28.

18   Fussell, pp. 41, 121, 131–33.

19   Hochschild, p. 194; Münkler, pp. 497–508; Canales and De Rey, pp. 145–51.

20   Ferro, pp. 78–79; Duroselle, pp. 339–41; Münkler, pp. 435–38; Englund, p. 271, footnote; Rousseau (2006), p. 72.

CHAPTER 22

1   Englund, p. 292.

2   Feltman, p. 92; Hochschild, p. 214; Ulrich and Ziemann, p. 67.

3   Text of the poem "Der Krieg ist für die Reichen": http://www.volksliederarchiv.de/text7129.html; Grünefeld, p. 343.

4   Englund, pp. 229, 361–62; Piper, p. 64.

5   Saint-Gille, *passim*; Hochschild, p. 218; Schramm, pp. 89–90; Schorske, pp. 308–09.

6   McKie.

7   Rousseau (2006), p. 98.

8   Hochschild, p. 215; Grünefeld, p. 380; Schmidt-Klingenberg.

9   Lyrics of the song "Mein Michel was willst du noch mehr?": http://www.volksliederarchiv.de/text1754.html and https://www.youtube.com/watch?v=4a55AtSWo60.

10   Ferguson, p. 271; Schorske, pp. 311–12.

11   Englund, pp. 241–42; de Schaepdrijver, pp. 215–19.

12   Dupeux, pp. 207–08; Horne, pp. 91–92; Rousseau (2006), pp. 93–95.

13   Englund, pp. 283, 301–02, 367; Dorgelès, pp. 243–44.

14   Bouloc (2008), pp. 193 ff., 282–83, 291 ff.; Duroselle, pp. 155–56; Pötzl, pp. 176–77.

15   Bouloc (2008), pp. 193 ff., 282–83, 291 ff.; Duroselle (1994), pp. 155–56; Pötzl, pp. 176–77.

16   Bouloc (2008), pp. 134–35, 208.

17   Boscus, pp. 231–36, 239; Bouloc (2008), p. 137; Robert, pp. 12–13, 154.

18   Cazals, p. 43.

19   Rogger (1983), pp. 259–60, 265; Sumpf (2014), pp. 135–36, 145; Rousseau (2006), pp. 100–01.

20   Horne, p. 53.

21   Marwick, pp. 90, 92, 96; Horne, pp. 78–80; Hastings, p. 414; Ferguson, pp. 173–75, 273, 445; Kolko (1994), pp. 108–09; Hochschild, pp. 249–50; Careless, p. 358.

22   Hochschild, pp. 186–90.

23   Jackson, pp. 394–402; Losurdo (2006b), pp. 153 (with quotation from A.J.P. Taylor), 215; Firchow, pp. 172–76.

24   Hochschild, pp. 183–85.

25   Firchow, p. 122.

26   Marwick, p. 111–12; Simpson, 33; Wolff, p. 35; Robertson, p. 66; Breverton, p. 285.

27   Lyrics of the parody of "Onward Christian Soldiers": http://www.fortunecity.com/tinpan/parton/2/christia.html.

28   Ulrich and Ziemann, pp. 109–11; de Schaepdrijver, pp. 191–93.

29   Hibberd and Onions, pp. 189–90.

30   Wolff, p. 33.

31   This brief treatment of the theme of sex and women relied on the following sources: Simpson, *passim*; Rousseau (1999), pp. 284–316, 319–34; Englund, p. 283; de Schaepdrijver, pp. 185, 191; Costello, p. 289; Pittalis, pp. 196–205; Eslava Galán, pp. 103–08; Dorgelès, pp. 155–57; Makepeace.

32   Robertson, p. 77.

33   Pittalis, p. 203.

34   Ulrich and Ziemann, pp. 137–38; Bonneure.

35   Van Bergen, p. 150.

36   Sumpf (2014), p. 47.

37   Rousseau (1999), pp. 284–316, 319–34; Englund, pp. 283, 292; Duroselle, pp. 429–30; Kogelfranz; de Schaepdrijver, pp. 185, 191; Münkler, pp. 380–86; lyrics of "I Wonder Who's Kissing Her Now": http://www.ww1photos.com/IWonderWhoseKissingHerNow.html.

38   "World War I and Dada"; "Dada: The Anti-War Art Movement"; "Dada and Surrealism."

CHAPTER 23

1   Duroselle, pp. 192-98; Miquel, p. 318 ff.

2   For a popular history of the Battle of Vimy, see the book by Pierre Berton.

3   Laserra, Leclercq, and Quaghebeur, pp. 209-10; "La chanson de craonne-1917."

4   Ulrich and Ziemann, pp. 99-101; Eslava-Galán, pp. 199-202. The Third Battle of
     Ypres is described in detail in the book by Leon Wolff, *In Flanders Fields*.

5   Quoted in Hochschild, p. 292.

6   Badsey, pp. 281-83.

7   Englund, p. 344-45, 460.

8   Kolko (1994), p. 135; Pittalis, pp. 212-22; Duroselle, pp. 332-33; Münkler, p. 604 ff.

9   Englund, pp. 267-69.

10   Pappé, pp. 66-68, 72; Engdahl, pp. 48-55; Nowell, pp. 116, 127; Piper, pp. 330-37;
     Pauwels (2008), pp. 227-29.

CHAPTER 24

1   Coopmans, pp. 121-23.

2   De Schaepdrijver, pp. 198, 205-06.

3   Horvat, pp. 46, 50; de Schaepdrijver, pp. 207, 213.

4   Quoted in Losurdo (2006b), pp. 113-14.

5   Horne, pp. 74-75; Robert, pp. 12-13, 171; Duroselle, p. 201.

6   Robert, pp. 119, 123-33; Englund, p. 374.

7   Robert, pp. 105, 112, 179.

8   Robert, pp. 116-17, 128-43, 157, 165-66, 246-47.

9   Barthas, p. 397.

10   Barthas, pp. 19, 378, 397-99; Loez, passim; Miquel, p. 338 ff.; Duroselle, pp. 202-06;
     Panel, pp. 6, 8 (footnote 46).

11   Barthas, pp. 406-07.

12   Kolko (1994), pp. 137-38.

13   *14-18: Mourir pour la patrie*, p. 167.

14   Nicot, pp. 117, 119, 125, 127, 130-31, 136-42, 150.

15   Hochschild, pp. 263-65, 274, 301-02; Wolff, pp. 42-45.

16   Hochschild, pp. 251, 314-15; Marwick, pp. 97, 103-04; Knightley, p. 103; Horne, pp.
     54-55.

17   Hochschild, pp. 279-80, 316.

18   Hibberd and Onions, p. 167.

19   Hibberd and Onions, p. 194.

20   Hibberd and Onions, p. 198.

21   Rousseau (2006), p. 68-69.

22 Rowe; Beckett, pp. 81–82.

23 Lyrics of "Tell Me Now": http://www.musicanet.org/robokopp/usa/tellmeno.htm.

24 Rousseau (1999), p. 67; Hochschild, p. 292; Kolko (1994), p. 136; Englund, p. 419, footnote.

25 Ferguson, p. 347.

26 Lyrics of "Back to Dear Old Blighty": http://www.firstworldwar.com/audio/takemebacktodearoldblighty.htm.

27 Ulrich and Ziemann, pp. 128–29.

28 Englund, p. 361.

29 Miquel, pp. 341–42.

30 Grünefeld, p. 346.

31 Losurdo (2006b), p. 114.

32 Barthas, pp. 296, 353–54; Panel, pp. 6–7; Saint-Fuscien, pp. 121–23.

33 Kolko (1994), pp. 139–40.

34 Mayer (2010), p. 3.

35 Grünefeld, p. 362.

36 Lyrics of "O Deutschland hoch in Ehren": http://www.altearmee.de/haltetaus.htm and https://www.youtube.com/watch?v=jyEW_hvzn1w.

37 Hastings, pp. 359, 547.

38 Kolko (1994), pp. 88–94, 101 (quotation on p. 94); Rousseau (2006), p. 91.

39 Ferguson, pp. 263–65.

40 Losurdo (2013), pp. 6–7.

41 Schorske, p. 313; Piper, pp. 415–16; Kolko (1994), pp. 113–14.

42 Kolko (1994), pp. 88–94, 101; Brady, p. 243; Rousseau (2006), pp. 111–12; Piper, pp. 309–10.

43 Kolko (1994), pp. 88–94, 101 (quotation on p. 94).

44 Kolko (1994), pp. 106, 112.

45 Marwick, p. 92.

46 Englund, p. 454; Robert, pp. 143–51, 160–61, 183; Duroselle (1994), p. 315 ff.

47 Piper, pp. 422–24; Münkler, pp. 589–90.

48 Quotation from Losurdo (2001), pp. 20–22.

49 Le Naour, pp. 117, 123–24, 129, 150–52, 168, 175–76, 189.

50 Eslava Galán, pp. 243–48.

51 Losurdo (2001), p. 23; Eksteins, pp. 180, 229 ff.; Lafon, p. 33; Hochschild, pp. 211–12; Englund, pp. 376–77.

52 Hibberd and Onions, p. 161.

CHAPTER 25

1 The influence of the Vatican on Catholic Americans in this context is described in Lacroix-Riz, pp. 15–17.

2 See Hoenicke Moore, p. 17 ff.

3 Losurdo (2006a), p. 292, and (2006b), pp. 154–55.

4 Stone and Kuznick, p. 5

5 Hochschild, pp. 247–48, 266–67; Swanson, pp. 71–72; *14–18: Mourir pour la patrie*, p. 95; Eslava-Galán, pp. 159–63.

6 Stone and Kuznick, p. 74; "American entry into World War I"; Duroselle, p. 286.

7 Duroselle, pp. 337–39.

8 Eslava Galán, pp. 245–46.

9 Ferguson, p. 436.

10 Zinn, pp. 353–54; Du Boff, p. 72; Oppelland, pp. 16–17; Elter, p. 26; Duroselle, pp. 164–65; Stone and Kuznick, pp. 67, 70; "American entry into World War I."

11 Hochschild, p. 314; Ferguson, pp. 328–29; Stone and Kuznick, p. 74; Swanson, pp. 175–76; Engdahl, p. 61.

12 Chad Williams; Kolko (1994), p. 126; Zinn, pp. 355, 361.

13 Losurdo (2006b), p. 209.

14 Fischer (1998), p. 183.

15 Zinn, pp. 346–49.

16 Zinn, pp. 356–59; Stone and Kuznick, p. 13; Ferguson, pp. 222–23; Losurdo (2006b), p. 214.

17 Zinn, pp. 363–64; Losurdo (2006b), p. 207; Elter, pp. 39, 55; Stone and Kuznick, pp. 7–8, 11–12, 14–15; Knightley, pp. 122–23; Tracy.

18 Losurdo (2006b), p. 98; Baker, pp. 3, 389.

19 Ferguson, p. 227.

CHAPTER 26

1 Englund, pp. 335–36.

2 Kolko (1994), pp. 88–94, 101 (quotation on p. 94).

3 Lewin (2005), pp. 293–94; Mayer (2010), p. 4.

4 Rogger (1983), pp. 266–69; Kolko (1994), p. 128; Lewin, p. 294.

5 Englund, pp. 340–41; Sumpf (2014), pp. 326–27.

6 Mayer (2000), pp. 242–44; Hochschild, pp. 263–64, 273.

7 Sumpf (2014), pp. 100–02; Lewin, pp. 293–94; Englund, p. 384.

8 Losurdo (2006b), p. 116; Kolko (1994), pp. 140–42, 169–77; Sumpf (2015).

9 Losurdo (2006b), pp. 99–101, 115, with references to Arthur Rosenberg and François Furet; Lewin, p. 293.

10 Shannon.

11   Stone and Kuznick, p. 28.

12   Losurdo (2006b), pp. 98, 219; Canfora (2008), p. 229; Knightley, pp. 148–51; Hochschild, p. 293; MacMillan (2001), p. 67; Breverton, pp. 132–33, 135–37; Crim.

13   Tilly, p. 294 ff.; Losurdo (2006b), p. 212.

14   Barthas, p. 445; Hochschild, pp. 216, 310; Cazals, p. 31; Catherine, pp. 91–92; Daughton, p. 49; Hill, passim; Whalan, p. 286; Miquel, pp. 331, 411–12.

15   Rousseau (2006), pp. 39–41; Cazals, p. 54; Duroselle, pp. 327–31.

16   Das (2011a), p. 78.

17   Das (2011a), p. 71 ff.; Losurdo (2010), passim.

18   Keay, p. 470.

19   Losurdo (2010 and 2013a), passim. On Churchill's view of Gandhi, see Hari, p. 2, referring to Richard Toye's book, *Churchill's Empire: The World That Made Him and the World He Made*.

20   Viên, pp. 164–65, 175–77; Hill, pp. 62–65.

21   Schirokauer, pp. 314–16; MacMillan (2001), p. 322 ff.

22   See the study by Xu Guoqi, *Strangers on the Western Front: Chinese Workers in the Great War*.

CHAPTER 27

1   Soete, pp. 20–27. See also the detailed study by Wheeler-Bennett.

2   De Schaepdrijver, pp. 209, 211, 242; Barthas, introduction by Chrisje Brants, p. 17.

3   Lyrics of the song "When this bloody war is over": http://www.traditionalmusic.co.uk/folk-song-lyrics/When_This_Bloody_War_is_Over(2).htm; see also http://www.youtube.com/watch?v=tjRIfIc6QPI.

4   Fussell, p. 116; Knightley, p. 105; Englund, pp. 220–21, footnote; Cazals, pp. 30–31; Baldin, p. 4. On the British use of horse carcasses, see Breverton, p. 281. For a commentary on the film *War Horse*, see Pauwels (2012).

5   Ferguson, p. 285.

6   For an excellent treatment of this offensive, see Miquel, p. 380 ff., and Münkler, p. 687 ff.

7   Fussell, pp. 17, 177–78; Münkler, p. 686.

8   Duroselle, p. 364 ff.; Münkler, p. 694.

9   Fussell, pp. 17–18. See also Ferguson, pp. 350–51, who writes that the Germans "wasted precious time in plundering."

10   Ferguson (1998), pp. 311–13, 368–73, 386–87; Faulkner, p. 26; Piper, pp. 430–31; Miquel, pp. 414–15.

11   Text of the poem "Ballade vom toten Soldaten": http://woerterwasserfall.forumsfree.de/t411-bertolt-brecht-legende-vom-toten-soldieren. See also http://www.youtube.com/watch?v=tQPiuxe-a_I.

12   Here we follow the account provided by Deist (1992).

13   Englund, p. 474.

14   Münkler, p. 682; Breverton, p. 113.

15   Rousseau (2006), p. 85; Baldin, p. 3; Faulkner, p. 6.

16   Miquel, pp. 411–12.

17   Pauwels (2011).

18   Engdahl, pp. 46–48; Nowell, pp. 95–96, 108–10; *14–18: Mourir pour la patrie*, pp. 98–99; Rousseau (1999), pp. 187–88; Miquel (2000), p. 27; Münkler, p. 715.

19   Newman, p. 144.

20   Iltchev, p. 283; Mazower, p. 108; Rousseau (2006), p. 114

21   Münkler, p. 704, referring specifically to the military historian Wilhelm Deist.

22   Münkler, pp. 704–07; Knightley, pp. 110–11; Ferguson, p. 352; Hochschild, pp. 330–31, 338; Rousseau (2006), pp. 74–75; Piper, p. 432.

23   Hibberd and Onions, p. 255.

24   Hochschild, pp. 337, 341; de Schaepdrijver, pp. 251–52; Persico, pp. 348–50; Black and Boileau, pp. 371–76; Breverton, p. 250.

25   Persico, p. 378; Black and Boileau, pp. 374–76; Fussell, p. 196.

CHAPTER 28

1   Englund, pp. 428–29.

2   Robert, pp. 12–13, 171–79, 183, 186–90, 214–18, 289.

3   Robert, pp. 208–12, 226–29; Hochschild, pp. 334–35.

4   Robert, pp. 269–74, 279–82; Rousseau (2006), pp. 108–09.

5   Robert, pp. 253–56.

6   Robert, pp. 12–13, 304–07, 309–13, 319–25, 328–29, 339–56, 399, 402; Dupeux, pp. 206–08.

7   Marwick, p. 109–10, 120–21; Ferguson, p. 396.

8   Hastings, p. 414; Hochschild, p. 352; Marwick, pp. 144–53; Childs, pp. 1–2; Kolko (1994), p. 178.

9   Marwick, pp. 169–72.

10   Losurdo (2010) and (2013a), passim.

11   Englund, p.471; Mueller and Mueller.

12   Kolko (1994), p. 146–148.

13   Schmidt-Klingenberg, p. 146.

14   Sohn-Rethel, pp. 152–53; Stone and Kuznick, p. 33.

15   Kolko (1994), pp. 148–56.

16   Ferguson, pp. 421–25.

17   Newman, pp. 143–47.

18   Kolko (1994), pp. 161–65; Piper, pp. 311–12; Feldbauer (2008a), pp. 80–83; Rousseau (2006), p. 112. For an excellent short history of the *biennio rosso*, Italy's "two red years" (1919-1920), see the book by Paleni.

19   De Schaepdrijver, pp. 237–38, 289–90, 299–300; Hobsbawm (1994), pp. 331–32.

20   Zimmermann.

21   Parenti (1995), pp. 68–69.

22   Parenti (1995), pp. 68–69; Pauwels (2015), pp. 42–44; Stone and Kuznick, pp. 16, 34–35.

23   Careless, p. 358.

24   Bethell, pp. 357–60; Williamson, p. 317.

25   Knightley, pp. 138, 153–55; Canfora (2008), pp. 223–24; Stone and Kuznick, pp. 28–29.

26   Münkler, p. 556.

27   Quoted in Abousnnouga and Machin, p. 79.

28   Losurdo (2013), pp. 161–62; Sumpf (2014), pp. 380.

29   Mayer (2000), p. 268; MacMIllan (2001), p. 73.

30   Kolko (1994), p. 136; Knightley, pp. 138, 157–61, 163–68; Stone and Kuznick, pp. 28–29; Robert, pp. 293–302; Marwick, pp. 144–53; Feldbauer (2008a), p. 82; MacMillan (2001), pp. 71–73; Shannon; Hill, p. 63.

31   MacMillan (2001), p. 73.

CHAPTER 29

1   Englund, p. 505.

2   For more details, see the detailed study by Margaret MacMillan, *Paris 1919.*

3   Hibberd and Onions, pp. 248–49.

4   Hibberd and Onions, pp. 82–83.

5   Mayer (2010), p. 3. See also Hans-Ulrich Wehler's essay "Der zweite Dreißigjährige Krieg."

6   Robert, p. 370.

CHAPTER 31

1   Canfora (2008), p. 355, points out that the religious revolution which the Reformation happened to be similarly became a national revolution in countries such as England and in major parts of Germany and Switzerland; see also Canfora (2013), pp. 18–19.

2   Kolko (1994), pp. 177–79.

3   Engelmann, p. 7.

4   Hochschild, p. xv.

5   Mazower, pp. 35, 126.

6   Arnstein, p. 225.

7   Le Naour, pp. 200–01.

8   Kolko (1994), p. 72.

9   Martens, pp. 16–17, 25.

10   Englund, p. 221; Kolko (1994), p. 66 ff.; Mayer (2010), p. 302.

11   Kolko (1994), pp. 69–72; Dupeux, pp. 203–25; Marwick, pp. 94–95.

12   Marwick, pp. 94–95, 168–69.

13   Lukács, pp. 72–73.

14   Kolko (1994), p. 154. More on the early elite support for Hitler in Pauwels (2013), part one, chapter 2.

15   Feldbauer (2008a), pp. 83–85, 93–107; Feldbauer (2008b), parts 5 and 6; Kolko (1994), pp. 165–67; Canfora (2008), p. 161; Lacroix-Riz (1996), pp. 86–88.

16   Canfora (2008), pp. 232–33; Hochschild, p. 368.

17   Feldbauer (2008b), part 6.

18   For details about Hitler's advent to power, see Pauwels (2013), part one, chapter 4.

19   Pauwels (2009), p. 79 ff.

20   Kolko (1994), p. 122.

21   See e.g. Pauwels (2009), pp. 29–30, 37–40.

22   Pauwels (2009), pp. 69–77.

23   Pauwels (2015), pp. 44–46.

24   Mayer (2010), p. 4.

25   See the studies of Annie Lacroix-Riz (2006 and 2008).

CHAPTER 31

1   Luciano Canfora, the Italian historian of the democratic idea, emphasizes in this historic context "the powerful elements of social democracy," and credits them to the influence of the Soviet constitution of 1936, which included guaranteed employment and free education and condemned racism, see Canfora (2008), pp. 256–68.

2   Dumolyn.

3   See e.g. Pauwels (2015), pp. 89–90, for the reasons of this wage increase.

4   Whitaker, p. 60.

5   Losurdo (2010, pp. 126–30.

6   Losurdo (2013), pp. 5–6; Gowans (2013b).

7   Laslett, p. 220.

8   Koller, p. 137; Whalan, p. 290.

9   Whalan, p. 289.

10   See e.g. the statistics (produced by economist Elise Gould) cited in Foster and Yates, pp. 8–9.

11   Hobsbawm (1994), p. 331; Canfora (2008), p. 258 ff.; Gowans (2013b).

12   Losurdo (2013), p. 5.

13   See e.g. Lacroix-Riz (1996), pp. 429 ff., 450–57, Feldbauer (2008b), part 10, and the studies by Giovanni Maria Pace and Gerald Steinacher.

14   Petras, referring to the book by Frances Stonor Saunders, *Who Paid the Piper: The CIA and the Cultural Cold War.*

15   Ganser; also Feldbauer (2008b), part 10.

16   Traverso, p. 55.

17   Canfora (2013), p. 26.

18   B. Becker.

19   Reference is made to the book by Roger Keeran and Thomas Kenny, *Socialism betrayed: Behind the Collapse of the Soviet Union.*

20   Parenti (2011); see also the remarks about the Schwarzenbergs in Bussmann and Tröger, pp. 414–15.

21   Feldbauer (2008b), part 17; more about Stepinac in Deschner, pp. 640–45.

22   See e.g. the undated article by Andrzej Dominiczak, "Church and State in Post-Communist Poland."

23   See Gowans (2013c) and the articles by Richard Pipes concerning Romania and by Sabine Kergel on women in former East Germany.

24   MacKinnon and Lehmann.

25   For intelligent and stimulating reflections on the development of China and a comparison with Russia, see Losurdo (2007a), p. 157 ff.

26   A great philanthropist and democrat, at least according to his own website, http://www.georgesoros.com.

27   As Luciano Canfora has explained, electoral victories are typically "fabricated," i.e. produced much as industry manufactures commodities, via massive "investments" and by means of expensive electoral "machinery," which means that the individuals and organizations disposing of most capital are very likely to win; see Canfora (2008), p. 212.

28   Dumolyn; see also Pauwels (2015), pp. 217–18.

29   Pauwels (2015), pp. 218–220.

30   Quoted in Joll, p. 317.

BIBLIOGRAPHY

Gil Abousnnouga and David Machin, *The Language of War Monuments*, Bloomsbury Academic, London and New York, 2013.

Giorgio Agamben, *État d'exception*, Éditions du Seuil, Paris, 2003.

"Alfred Charles William Harmsworth, Viscount Northcliffe," http://www.britannica.com/EBchecked/topic/419541/Alfred-Charles-William-Harmsworth-Viscount-Northcliffe.

Jules Allard, *Journal d'un gendarme 1914–1916*, Bayard, Montrouge, 2010.

"American entry into World War I," http://en.wikipedia.org/wiki/American_entry_into_World_War_I.

"Analysis: Suicide in the Trenches by Siegfried Sassoon," https://www.iggy.net/content/blog/analysis-suicide-in-the-trenches-by-siegfried-sassoon.

Walter L. Arnstein, *Britain Yesterday and Today: 1830 to the Present*, 2nd edition, D.C. Heath, Lexington, 1971. (Original edition: 1966)

Tony Ashworth, *Trench warfare, 1914–1918: the live and let live system*, Holmes & Meier, New York, 1980.

Stephen Badsey, *Doctrine and Reform in the British Cavalry 1880–1918*, Ashgate, Aldershot and Burlington, 2008.

Nicholson Baker, *Human Smoke: The Beginnings of World War II, the End of Civilization*, Simon & Schuster, New York, 2008.

Damien Baldin, "De la contiguïté anthropologique entre le combattant et le cheval," *Revue historique des armées*, 2007, http://rha.revues.org/473.

Louis Barthas, *De oorlogsdagboeken van Louis Barthas 1914–1918*, EPO, Berchem, 1998.

Annette Becker, *La Grande Guerre d'Apollinaire: Un poète combattant*, Texto, Paris, 2014.

Brian Becker, "It was the CIA that helped Jail Nelson Mandela. Crocodile tears to mask US imperialism's role as the enemy of African liberation," *Global Research*, July 20, 2013, http://www.globalresearch.ca/it-was-the-cia-that-helped-jail-nelson-mandela/5343409.

Ian F.W. Beckett (ed.), *1917: Beyond the Western Front*, Brill, Leiden and Boston, 2009.

"Belgium's imperialist rape of Africa," *World Socialist Web Site*, September 6, 1999, http://www.wsws.org/en/articles/1999/09/king-s06.html.

Richard L. Berke, "Trent Lott and His Fierce Freshmen," *The New York Times*, February 2, 1997, http://www.nytimes.com/1997/02/02/magazine/trent-lott-and-his-fierce-freshmen.html.

Carl Bernstein, "Cover Story: The Holy Alliance," February 24, 1992, http://content.time.com/time/magazine/article/0,9171,159069,00.html.

Pierre Berton, *Vimy*, McClelland & Stewart Limited, Toronto, 1986.

Leslie Bethell (ed.), *The Cambridge History of Latin America.Volume IV: C. 1870 to 1930*, Cambridge University Press, Cambridge, 1986.

Carey L. Biron, "Uzbekistan Still Using Child Slaves To Pick Cotton," October 20, 2014, http://www.mintpressnews.com/uzbekistan-still-using-child-slaves-to-pick-cotton/197884.

Dan Black and John Boileau, *Old Enough to Fight: Canada's Boy Soldiers in the First World War*, James Lorimer, Toronto, 2013.

Jerome Blum, *The End of the Old Order in Rural Europe*, Princeton University Press, Princeton, 1978.

Maurice Bologne, *L'insurrection proletarienne de 1830 en Belgique*, Aden, Brussels, 2005. (Original edition: 1929)

Jochen Bölsche,"Ein Hammerschlag auf Herz und Hirn," in Stephan Burgdorff and Klaus Wiegrefe (eds.), *Der Erste Weltkrieg: Die Ur-Katastrophe des 20. Jahrhunderts*, 3rd edition, Deutsche Verlags-Anstalt, Munich, 2014, pp. 54–58. (Original edition: 2004)

Bonneure, Kristien, "Het frontparadijs — Heinrich Wandt," http://www.cobra.be/cm/cobra/projecten/wereldoorlog-I/1.1787141.

Alain Boscus, "La perturbation des identités syndicales et militants," in François Bouloc, Rémy Cazals, and André Loez (eds.), *Identités Troublées 1914–1918: Les appartenances sociales et nationales à l'épreuve de la guerre*, Privat, Toulouse, 2011, pp. 227–41.

François Bouloc, *Les profiteurs de guerre 1914–1918*, Complexe, Paris, 2008.

François Bouloc, "La part des aspirations démocratiques dans la parole et l'expérience combattantes," in François Bouloc, Rémy Cazals, and André Loez (eds.), *Identités Troublées 1914–1918: Les appartenances sociales et nationales à l'épreuve de la guerre*, Privat, Toulouse, 2011, pp. 85–98.

Sean Brady, "Les démonstrations populaires et l'expérience Italienne de la Grande Guerre: la province sicilienne de Catane (mai-juin 1917)," in François Bouloc, Rémy Cazals, and André Loez (eds.), *Identités Troublées 1914–1918: Les appartenances sociales et nationales à l'épreuve de la guerre*, Privat, Toulouse, 2011, pp. 243–54.

Fernand Braudel, *Grammaire des civilisations*, Arthaud, Paris, 1987.

Leo Braudy, *From Chivalry to Terrorism: War and the Changing Nature of Masculinity*, Vintage, New York, 2003.

Terry Breverton, *Breverton's First World War Curiosities*, Amberley, Stroud, 2014.

Jean Bricmont, *Impérialisme humanitaire*. Aden, Brussels, 2005.

Malcolm Brown and Shirley Seaton, *Christmas truce: the Western Front, December 1914*, Pan, London, 1994.

Robert Craig Brown, "'Whither are we being shoved?': Political Leadership in Canada during World War I," in J.L. Granatstein and R.D. Cuff (eds.), *War and Society in North America*, Thomas Nelson, Toronto, 1971, pp. 104–19.

Stephan Burgdorff and Klaus Wiegrefe (eds.), *Der Erste Weltkrieg: Die Ur-Katastrophe des 20. Jahrhunderts*, 3rd edition, Deutsche Verlags-Anstalt, Munich, 2014. (Original edition: 2004)

"Business as usual," http://www.thisdayinquotes.com/2009/11/for-churchill-business-as-usual-was.html.

Michael Bussmann and Gabriele Tröger, *Tschechien*, 3rd edition, Michael Müller Verlag, Erlangen, 2011. (Original edition: 2005)

Kathryn Byrnes, "A Summary of Hermann Hesse's Demian," 1998, http://www.gss.ucsb.edu/projects/hesse/works/demian.pdf.

Carlos Canales and Miguel Del Rey, *La Gran Guerra: Grandeza y dolor en las trincheras*, Edaf, Madrid, 2014.

Mauro Canali, *Mussolini e il petrolio iracheno: L'Italia, gli interessi petroliferi e le grandi potenze*, Einaudi, Turin, 2007.

Luciano Canfora, *1914*, Sellerio, Palermo, 2006.

Luciano Canfora, *La democrazia: Storia di un'ideologia*, Laterza, Bari, 2008. (Original edition: 2004)

Luciano Canfora, *Intervista sul Potere*, Laterza, Bari, 2013.

J.M.S. Careless, *Canada: A Story of Challenge*, Stoddart, Toronto, 1970.

Julián Casanova, *Europa contra Europa 1914–1945*, Critica, Barcelona, 2011.

Lucas Catherine, *Loopgraven in Afrika (1914–1918): De vergeten oorlog van de Congolezen tegen de Duitsers*, EPO, Berchem, 2013.

Rémy Cazals, *Les mots de 14–18*, Presses Universitaires du Mirail, Toulouse, 2003.

David Childs, *The Two Red Flags: European Social Democracy and Soviet Communism since 1945*, Routledge, London and New York, 2000.

Stéphanie Claisse, "Au Poilu et au Jass inconnus . . . Mémoires de 14–18 dans l'entre-deux-guerres," *Cahiers électroniques de l'imaginaire*, n° 2, 2003–2004, pp.167–91, http://www.uclouvain.be/cps/ucl/doc/ucl/documents/cahiers2.pdf.

Marcus Clapham (ed.), *Poetry of the First World War*, Macmillan, London, 2013.

Christopher Clark, *The Sleepwalkers: How Europe Went to War in 1914*, Harper, London, 2012.

Humphrey Cobb, *Paths of Glory*, Penguin, London and New York, 2010.

M.J. Cohen and John Major, *History in Quotations*, Cassell, London, 2004.

Steven Connor, "Isaac Rosenberg: Birkbeck's War Poet," October 30, 2000, http://www. stevenconnor.com/rosenberg.

Tim Cook, "Black-hearted Traitors, Crucified Martyrs, and the Leaning Virgin: The Role of Rumor and the Great Canadian Soldier," in Jennifer D. Keene and Michael S. Neiberg (eds.), *Finding Common Ground: New Directions in First World War Studies*, Brill, Leiden and Boston, 2011, pp. 21–42.

Jean Batist Coopmans, *Verhaal uit den Groote Oorlog van 4 augustus 1914 tot 11 november 1918 [in] België, Nederland Frankrijk, Duitschland*, manuscript in the archive of the author.

John Costello, *Love, Sex and War: Changing Values, 1939–45*, Pan, London, 1985.

Benoist Couliou, "Ulysse et Damoclès. L'identité sociale des combattants français et leur perception de la durée (août 1914-décembre 1915)," in François Bouloc, Rémy Cazals, and André Loez (eds.), *Identités Troublées 1914–1918: Les appartenances sociales et nationales à l'épreuve de la guerre*, Privat, Toulouse, 2011, pp. 61–72.

Brian Crim, "Total War as Total Health: Race, Space and Genocide on the Eastern Front, 1941–1945," s.d., https://www.libraryofsocialscience.com/reviews/Mineau.html.

James Cross, "Romanians say communism was better than capitalism," October 17, 2010, http://www.canadaka.net/forums/international-politics-f2/romanians-say-communism-was-better-than-capitalism-t92392.html.

Raf Custers, *Grondstoffenjagers*, EPO, Berchem, 2013.

"Dada and Surrealism," http://www.oxfordartonline.com/public/page/themes/ dadaandsurrealism.

"Dada: The Anti-War Art Movement," http://www.arthistoryarchive.com/arthistory/dada/ arthistory_dada.html.

Zoe Dare Hall, "JB Priestley: the officer class killed most of my friends," *The Telegraph*, January 5, 2014, Inside the First World War-supplement, p.15.

Santanu Das, "Imperialism, Nationalism and the First World War in India," in Jennifer D. Keene and Michael S. Neiberg (eds.), *Finding Common Ground: New Directions in First World War Studies*, Brill, Leiden and Boston, 2011, pp. 67–85. (2011a)

Santanu Das, *Race, Empire and First World War Writing*, Cambridge University Press, Cambridge, 2011. (2011b)

James P. Daughton, "Sketches of the Poilu's World: Trench Cartoons from the Great War," in Douglas Mackaman and Michael Mays (eds.), *World War I and the Cultures of Modernity*, University Press of Mississippi, Jackson, 2000, pp. 35–67.

Richard B. Day and Daniel Gaido (eds.), *Discovering Imperialism: Social Democracy to World War I*, Brill, Leiden and Boston, 2012.

Wilhelm Deist, *Militär und Innenpolitik im Weltkrieg 1914–1918*, 2 volumes, Droste, Düsseldorf, 1970.

Wilhelm Deist, "Verdeckter Militärstreik im Kriegsjahr 1918?" in Wolfram Wette (ed.), *Der Krieg des Kleinen Mannes: Eine Militärgeschichte von unten*, Piper, Munich, 1992, pp.146–67.

Angelo Del Boca, *Italiani, brava gente?: Un mito duro a morire*, 4th edition, Neri Pozza, Vicenza, 2010. (Original edition: 2005)

Gita Deneckere, *1900: België op het breukvlak van twee eeuwen*, Lannoo, Tielt, 2006.

Sophie de Schaepdrijver, *De Groote Oorlog: Het Koninkrijk België tijdens de Eerste Wereldoorlog*, Atlas, Amsterdam, 1997.

Karlheinz Deschner, *Abermals krähte der Hahn: Eine kritische Kirchengeschichte*, 6th edition, Goldmann, Munich, 1996. (Original edition: 1962)

Andrzej Dominiczak, "Church and State in Post-Communist Poland," http://www.zoominfo. com/CachedPage/?archive_id=0&page_id=980148832&page_url=//www.iheu.org/ modules/wfsection/article.php?articleid=525&page_last_updated=2005-05-05T07:06:2 9&firstName=Kazimierz&lastName=Kapera.

Roland Dorgelès, *Les Croix de bois*, Albin Michel, Paris, 1919. "Drôle de date pour un nom de rue: le 22 novembre!," *Action Antifa Alsace*, March 22, 2010, https://antifalsace. wordpress.com/2010/03/22/drole-de-date-pour-un-nom-de-rue-le-22-novembre.

Dominique Drouin, *Villemandeur dans la Grande Guerre: un village du Loiret dans nos mémoires (1914–1918)*, n.p., 2006.

Richard B. Du Boff, *Accumulation and Power: An Economic History of the United States*, M.E. Sharpe, Armonk, NY and London, 1989.

Jan Dumolyn, "1302 was een revolutie, maar dan wel een linkse," http://egbertjs.wordpress.com/?s=dumolyn.

Georges Dupeux, *La société française 1789–1970*, Armand Colin, Paris, 1974.

Jean-Baptiste Duroselle, *La Grande Guerre des Français 1914–1918: L'incompréhensible*, Perrin, Paris, 1994.

Dietrich Eichholtz, "Ökonomie, Politik und Kriegführung: Wirtschaftliche Kriegsplanungen und Rüstungsorganisation bis zum Ende der 'Blitzkriegsphase'," in Dietrich Eichholtz (ed.), *Krieg und Wirtschaft: Studien zur deutschen Wirtschaftsgeschichte 1939–1945*, Metropol, Berlin, 1999, pp. 9–41. (1999a)

Dietrich Eichholtz, "Unfreie Arbeit — Zwangsarbeit," in Dietrich Eichholtz (ed.), *Krieg und Wirtschaft: Studien zur deutschen Wirtschaftsgeschichte 1939–1945*, Metropol, Berlin, 1999, pp.129–55. (1999b)

Dietrich Eichholtz (ed.), *Krieg und Wirtschaft: Studien zur deutschen Wirtschaftsgeschichte 1939–1945*, Metropol, Berlin, 1999. (1999c)

Modris Eksteins, *Rites of Spring: The Great War and the Birth of the Modern Age*, Lester & Orpen Dennys, Toronto, 1989.

Geoff Eley, *From Unification to Nazism: Reinterpreting the German Past*, Allen and Unwin, Boston, 1986.

Andreas Elter, *Die Kriegsverkäufer: Geschichte der US-Propaganda 1917–2005*, Suhrkamp, Frankfurt, 2005.

"Enemy Aliens, Prisoners of War: Canada's First World War Internment Operations, 1914–1920," http://www.pc.gc.ca/eng/pn-np/ab/banff/natcul/histoire-history/internement-internment.aspx.

William F. Engdahl, *A Century of War: Anglo-American Oil Politics and the New World Order*, Edition Engdahl, Wiesbaden, 2011.

Bernt Engelmann, *Einig gegen Recht und Freiheit: Ein deutsches Anti-Geschichtsbuch 2. Teil*, C. Bertelsmann, Munich, 1975.

Peter Englund, *The Beauty and the Sorrow: An Intimate History of the First World War*, Vintage, London, 2012.

Juan Eslava Galán, *La Primera Guerra Mundial contada para escépticos*, Planeta, Barcelona, 2014.

"Expressionismus (Literatur)," https://de.wikipedia.org/wiki/Expressionismus_(Literatur).

Neil Faulkner, *No Glory: The Real History of the First World War*, Stop The War Coalition, London, 2013.

Gerhard Feldbauer, *Geschichte Italiens: Vom Risorgimento bis heute*, PapyRossa, Cologne, 2008. (2008a)

Gerhard Feldbauer, "Benedikt XVI. und das Bündnis der Kurie mit Reaktion und Faschismus," http://www.offen-siv.net/2008/08–01_Feldbauer-Papst.pdf. (2008b)

Brian K. Feltman, "Letters from Captivity: The First World War Correspondence of the German Prisoners of War in the United Kingdom," in Jennifer D. Keene and Michael S. Neiberg (eds.), *Finding Common Ground: New Directions in First World War Studies*, Brill, Leiden and Boston, 2011, pp. 87–110.

Niall Ferguson, *The Pity of War*, Basic Books, New York, 1999.

Marc Ferro, *La Grande Guerre*, Gallimard, Paris, 1969.

Alvin Finkel, "Origins of the welfare state in Canada," in Leo Panitch (ed.), *The Canadian State: Political Economy and Political Power*, University of Toronto Press, Toronto, 1977, pp. 344–370.

Peter Edgerly Firchow, *The Death of the German Cousin: Variations on a Literary Stereotype, 1890–1920*, Bucknell University Press, Lewisburg, 1986.

Fritz Fischer, *Germany's Aims in the First World War*, W.W. Norton & Co., New York, 1967.

Fritz Fischer, "World Policy: World Power and German War Aims," in H.W. Koch (ed.), *The Origins of the First World War: Great Power Rivalry and German War Aims*, Macmillan, London and Basingstoke, 1972, pp. 79–144.

Fritz Fischer, *Hitler war kein Betriebsunfall: Aufsätze*, 4th edition, Beck, Munich, 1998. (Original edition: 1992)

John Bellamy Foster and Michael D. Yates, "Piketty and the Crisis of Neoclassical Economics," *Monthly Review*, 2014, Volume 66, Issue 6, November 2014, http://monthlyreview.org/2014/11/01/piketty-and-the-crisis-of-neoclassical-economics.

Ernst Friedrich, *Krieg dem Kriege! Guerre à la Guerre! War against War! Oorlog aan den Oorlog!*, 24th edition, 2001, Frankfurt, 1992. (Original edition: 1924)

Paul Fussell, *The Great War and Modern Memory*, Oxford University Press, London, 1977.

Filippo Gaja, *Il secolo corto: La filosofia del bombardamento. La storia da riscrivere*, Maquis, Milan, 1994.

"Gala Contemplating the Mediterranean Sea which at Twenty Meters Becomes the Portrait of Abraham Lincoln (Homage to Rothko)," http://thedali.org/exhibit/gala-contemplating-mediterranean-sea.

Daniele Ganser, *NATO's Secret Armies: Operation Gladio and Terrorism in Western Europe*, Routledge, New York, 2005.

Imanuel Geiss, "Origins of the First World War," in H.W. Koch (ed.), *The Origins of the First World War: Great Power Rivalry and German War Aims*, Macmillan, London and Basingstoke, 1972, pp. 36–78.

Olivier Gillet, *Les Balkans: Religions et nationalisme*, Ousia, Brussels, 2001.

Hermann Glaser, *Literatur des 20. Jahrhunderts in Motiven. Band I: 1870 bis 1918*, Beck, Munich, 1978.

Bertrand Goujon, "Insertion et distinction nobiliaire parmi les combattants français de la grande guerre," in François Bouloc, Rémy Cazals, and André Loez (eds.), *Identités Troublées 1914–1918: Les appartenances sociales et nationales à l'épreuve de la guerre*, Privat, Toulouse, 2011, pp. 47–60.

Stephen Gowans, "Should the US bomb Syria?" *What's left*, May 11, 2013, https://gowans.wordpress.com/2013/05/11/should-the-us-bomb-syria. (2013a)

Stephen Gowans, "The Revolution Will Not Be Televised . . . Nor Will It Be Brought To You By Russell Brand, Oliver Stone Or Noam Chomsky," *What's left*, November 9, 2013, https://gowans.wordpress.com/2013/11/09/the-revolution-will-not-be-televised-nor-will-it-be-brought-to-you-by-russell-brand-oliver-stone-or-noam-chomsky. (2013b)

Stephen Gowans, "Seven Myths about the USSR," December 23, 2013, https://gowans.wordpress.com/2013/12/23/seven-myths-about-the-ussr. (2013c)

Stephen Gowans, "The Concept of WMD, and its Use against Syria, in the Propaganda Systems of Western States," *What's left*, May 20, 2015, https://gowans.wordpress.com/2015/05/20/the-concept-of-wmd-and-its-use-against-syria-in-the-propaganda-systems-of-western-states.

J.L. Granatstein and R.D. Cuff (eds.), *War and Society in North America*, Thomas Nelson and Sons, Toronto, 1971.

H.C. Grünefeld (ed.), *Die Revolution marschiert. Band 2: Kampflieder der Unterdrückten und der Verfolgten 1806–1930*, Reinhard Welz, Mannheim, 2006.

Jean-Pierre Guéno and Yves Laplume (eds.), *Paroles de Poilus: Lettres et carnets du front 1914–1918*, Librio, Paris, 1998.

Johann Hari, "Not his finest hour: The dark side of Winston Churchill," *The Independent*, October 28, 2010, http://www.independent.co.uk/news/uk/politics/not-his-finest-hour-the-dark-side-of-winston-churchill-2118317.html.

Donald J. Harvey, *France Since the Revolution*, Collier-Macmillan, New York and London, 1968.

Max Hastings, *Catastrophe: Europe goes to War 1914*, Knopf, London, 2013.

P.H.S. Hatton, "Britain and Germany in 1914: The July Crisis and War Aims," in H.W. Koch (ed.), *The Origins of the First World War: Great Power Rivalry and German War Aims*,

Macmillan, London and Basingstoke, 1972, pp. 30–35.

Mike Hawkins, *Social Darwinism in European and American Thought, 1860–1945: Nature as Model and Nature as Threat*, Cambridge University Press, Cambridge, 1997.

James Hayward, *Myths & Legends of the First World War*, Sutton, Stroud, 2002.

Richard Heijster, *Krieg: Ieper, het martyrium van 14/18 door Duitse ogen*, Lannoo, Tielt, 2006.

Dominic Hibberd and John Onions, *The Winter of the World: Poems of the Great War*, Constable, London, 2008.

Kimloan Hill, "Sacrifices, sex, race: Vietnamese experiences in the First World War," in Santanu Das (ed.), *Race, Empire and First World War Writing*, Cambridge University Press, Cambridge, 2011, pp. 53–69.

Adolf Hitler, *Mein Kampf*, Reynal and Hitchcock, New York, 1939.

Martin Hobohm, "Soziale Heeresmißstände im Ersten Weltkrieg," in Wolfram Wette (ed.), *Der Krieg des Kleinen Mannes: Eine Militärgeschichte von unten*, Piper, Munich 1992, pp. 136–45.

Eric Hobsbawm, *The Age of Capital 1848–1875*, New American Library, New York, 1979. (Original edition: 1975)

Eric Hobsbawm, *The Age of Empire 1875–1914*, Abacus, London, 1994. (Original edition: 1987)

Adam Hochschild, *To End all Wars: A Story of Loyalty and Rebellion, 1914–1918*, Houghton Mifflin Harcourt, Boston and New York, 2011.

Michaela Hoenicke Moore, *Know Your Enemy: The American Debate on Nazism, 1933–1945*, Cambridge University Press, Cambridge, 2010.

John N. Horne, *Labour at War: France and Britain 1914–1918*, Oxford University Press, Oxford, 1991.

Stanislas Horvat, *De vervolging van militairrechtelijke delicten tijdens Wereldoorlog I: De werking van het Belgisch krijgsgerecht*, VUB, Brussels, 2009.

"I Did Not Raise My Boy To Be A Soldier," http://www.antiwarsongs.org/canzone.php?id=2670.

Ivan Iltchev, *La rose des Balkans: Histoire de la Bulgarie des origines à nos jours*, Colibri, Sofia, 2002.

Mario Isnenghi and Giorgio Rochat, *La Grande Guerra 1914–1918*, Sansoni, Milan, 2004.

"Italian Futurism," http://www.italianfuturism.org/manifestos/foundingmanifesto.

David Jablonsky, "Churchill, The Victorian Man of Action," *Parameters*, vol. 23, winter 1993–1994, pp. 74–90, http://www.dtic.mil/cgi-bin/GetTRDoc?AD=ADA515731.

T.A. Jackson, *Ireland Her Own: An Outline History of the Irish Struggle for National Freedom and Independence*, Lawrence & Wishart, London, 1971. (Original edition: 1947)

Nuala C. Johnson, *Ireland, the Great War and the Geography of Remembrance*, Cambridge University Press, Cambridge, 2003.

James Joll, "1914: The Unspoken Assumptions," in H.W. Koch (ed.), *The Origins of the First World War: Great Power Rivalry and German War Aims*, Macmillan, London and Basingstoke, 1972, pp. 307–28.

John Keay, *India: a History*, Folio Society, London, 2003.

John Keegan, *The Face of Battle: A Study of Agincourt, Waterloo and the Somme*, Vintage Books, Harmondsworth, 1976.

Jennifer D. Keene and Michael S. Neiberg (eds.), *Finding Common Ground: New Directions in First World War Studies*, Brill, Leiden and Boston, 2011.

Roger Keeran and Thomas Kenny, *Socialism betrayed: Behind the Collapse of the Soviet Union 1917–1991*, iUniverse, New York and Bloomington, 2010.

Tim Kendall (ed.), *Poetry of the First World War: An Anthology*, Oxford University Press, Oxford, 2013.

Sabine Kergel, "Ce qu'ont perdu les femmes de l'Est," *Le Monde diplomatique*, May 2015.

Kurt Kläber (ed.), *Der Krieg: Das Erste Volksbuch vom Großen Krieg*, Berlin Internationaler Arbeiter-Verlag, Berlin, 1929.

Paul Knevel and Marg van der Burgh (eds.), *Muziek, Oorlog en Vrede: Muzikaal commentaar op vijf eeuwen oorlog*, Thoth, Bussum, 2001.

Phillip Knightley, *The First Casualty: From the Crimea to Vietnam: The War Correspondent as Hero, Propagandist, and Myth Maker*, Harcourt, New York and London, 1975.

H.W. Koch, "Social Darwinism as a Factor in the 'New Imperialism'," in H.W. Koch (ed.), *The Origins of the First World War: Great Power Rivalry and German War Aims*, Macmillan, London and Basingstoke, 1972, pp. 329–54.

Siegfried Kogelfranz, "Schlange vorm Bordell," in Stephan Burgdorff and Klaus Wiegrefe (eds.), *Der Erste Weltkrieg: Die Ur-Katastrophe des 20. Jahrhunderts*, 3rd edition, Deutsche Verlags-Anstalt, Munich, 2014, pp. 150–53. (Original edition: 2004)

Gabriel Kolko, *The Triumph of Conservatism: A Reinterpretation of American History, 1900–1916*, Collier-MacMillan, Chicago, 1963.

Gabriel Kolko, *Century of War: Politics, Conflicts, and Society Since 1914*, The New Press, New York, 1994.

Christian Koller, "Representing Otherness: African, Indian and European soldiers' letters and memoirs," in Santanu Das (ed.), *Race, Empire and First World War Writing*, Cambridge University Press, Cambridge, 2011, pp. 127–42.

Alan Kramer, "'Greueltaten': Zum Problem der deutschen Kriegsverbrechen in Belgien und Frankreich 1914," http://www.europa.clio-online.de/_Rainbow/documents/keiner%20f%C3%BChlt%20sich%202/kramer.pdf.

Reinhard Kühnl, *Krieg und Frieden: Von den Kolonialkriegen und den Weltkriegen bis zur 'neuen Weltordnung' der USA*, Distel, Heilbronn, 2003.

Annie Lacroix-Riz, *Le Vatican, l'Europe et le Reich: de la Première guerre mondiale à la guerre froide*, Armand Colin, Paris, 1996.

Annie Lacroix-Riz, *Le choix de la défaite. Les élites françaises dans les années 1930*, Armand Colin, Paris, 2006.

Annie Lacroix-Riz, *De Munich à Vichy. L'assassinat de la Troisième République (1938–1940)*, Armand Colin, Paris, 2008.

Annie Lacroix-Riz, *Aux origines du carcan européen (1900–1960): La France sous influence allemande et américaine*, Delga, Paris, 2014.

Paul Lafargue, *Les luttes de classe en Flandre de 1336–1348 et de 1379–1385*, Aden, Brussels, 2003.

Alexandre Lafon, "Être camarade. Identité(s) et liens de sociabilité dans l'armée française (1914–1918)," in François Bouloc, Rémy Cazals, and André Loez (eds.), *Identités Troublées 1914–1918: Les appartenances sociales et nationales à l'épreuve de la guerre*, Privat, Toulouse, 2011, pp. 33–46.

"Lark," http://en.wikipedia.org/wiki/Lark.

Annamaria Laserra, Nicole Leclercq, and Marc Quaghebeur (eds.), *Mémoires et antimémoires littéraires au XXe siècle: la Première Guerre mondiale*, vol. 1, Peter Lang, Brussels, 2008.

Peter Laslett, *The World We Have Lost*, Methuen, London, 1971.

Gustave Le Bon, *The Crowd: a Study of the Popular Mind*, Viking Press, New York, 1960.

Jacques Le Gall, *La question coloniale dans le mouvement ouvrier en France (1830–1962). De la conquête de l'Algérie (1830) aux indépendances africaines (1962)*, Éclairage, Pantin, 2013.

Jean-Yves Le Naour, *Claire Ferchaud: La Jeanne d'Arc de la grande guerre*, Hachette Littératures, Paris, 2007.

Lenin [Vladimir Ulyanov], *Imperialism, the Highest Stage of Capitalism*, new edition, Progress Publishers, Moscow, 1963, http://www.marxists.org/archive/lenin/works/1916/imp-hsc (Original edition: 1916).

Adam Levine-Weinberg, "Germany Before the World Wars: Preventive War or *Innenpolitik*?" http://papers.ssrn.com/sol3/papers.cfm?abstract_id=1642043##.

Moshe Lewin, *The Soviet Century*, Verso, London and New York, 2005.

Massimo Libardi, Fernando Orlandi, and Maurizio Scudiero, *'Qualcosa di immane': L'arte e la grande guerra*, Silvy, Scurelle, 2012.

André Loez, *14–18. Les refus de la guerre. Une histoire des mutins*, Folio, Paris, 2010.

André Loez and Nicolas Mariot, "Brassage des corps et distances sociales: la découverte du peuple par la bourgeoisie intellectuelle dans les tranchées de 1914–1918," in François Bouloc, Rémy Cazals, and André Loez (eds.), *Identités Troublées 1914–1918: Les appartenances sociales et nationales à l'épreuve de la guerre*, Privat, Toulouse, 2011, pp. 17–32.

Domenico Losurdo, *Democrazia o bonapartismo. Trionfo e decadenza del suffragio universale*, Bollati Boringhieri, Turin, 1993.

Domenico Losurdo, *Heidegger and the Ideology of War: Community, Death, and the West*, Humanity Books, New York, 2001.

Domenico Losurdo, *Contrastoria del liberalismo*, second edition, Laterza, Rome and Bari, 2006. (Original edition: 2005)

Domenico Losurdo, *Le révisionnisme en histoire: Problèmes et mythes*, Albin Michel, Paris, 2006. (2006b)

Domenico Losurdo, *Fuir l'histoire?: La révolution russe et la révolution chinoise aujourd'hui*, Delga, Paris, 2007. (2007a)

Domenico Losurdo, *Il linguaggio dell'Impero: Lessico dell'ideologia americana*, Laterza, Rome and Bari, 2007.

Domenico Losurdo, *La non-violenza: Una storia fuori al mito*, Laterza, Bari, 2010.

Domenico Losurdo, *La lotta di classe: Una storia politica e filosofica*, Laterza, Bari, 2013.

Georg Lukács, *Die Zerstörung der Vernunft: Band I: Irrationalismus zwischen den Revolutionen*, Hermann Luchterhand, Darmstadt and Neuwied, 1973.

Douglas Mackaman and Michael Mays (eds.), *World War I and the Cultures of Modernity*, University Press of Mississippi, Jackson, 2000.

Mark MacKinnon and John Lehmann, "How Putin helped resurrect the Russian Orthodox Church," *The Globe and Mail*, January 16, 2014.

Margaret MacMillan, *Paris 1919: Six Months that Changed the World*, Random House, New York, 2003.

Margaret MacMillan, *The War that Ended Peace: The Road to 1914*, Allen Lane, Toronto, 2013.

Clare Makepeace, "Sex and the Somme: The officially sanctioned brothels on the front line laid bare for the first time," October 29, 2011, http://www.dailymail.co.uk/news/article-2054914/Sex-Somme-Officially-sanctioned-WWI-brothels-line.html.

Paul Markidès, *14–18: Les sacrifiés massacrés par l'armée française*, Le Temps des Cerises, Pantin, 2009.

Ludo Martens, "De Eerste Wereldoorlog, de Oktoberrevolutie en de Belgische Socialisten," *Marxistische Studies*, Brussels, April 1996, pp. 7–32.

Cédric Marty, "Le corps à corps au prisme des identités sociales," in François Bouloc, Rémy Cazals, and André Loez (eds.), *Identités Troublées 1914–1918: Les appartenances sociales et nationales à l'épreuve de la guerre*, Privat, Toulouse, 2011, pp. 73–84.

Marwick, Arthur, *Britain in the Century of Total War: War, Peace and Social Change 1900–1967*, Penguin Books, Harmondsworth, 1970 (Original edition: 1968).

"Max Hoffmann," http://www.firstworldwar.com/bio/hoffmann.htm.

Arno J. Mayer, *De hakenkruistocht. Tegen rood en jood*, EPO, Berchem, 1999.

Arno J. Mayer, *The Furies: Violence and Terror in the French and Russian Revolutions*, Princeton University Press, Princeton and Oxford, 2000.

Arno J. Mayer, *The Persistence of the Old Regime: Europe to the Great War*, Verso, London and Brooklyn, 2010. (Original edition: 1981)

Mark Mazower, *The Balkans: A Short History*, Modern Library, New York, 2002.

Robin McKie, "From fertiliser to Zyklon B: 100 years of the scientific discovery that brought life and death," November 3, 2013, http://www.theguardian.com/science/2013/nov/03/fritz-haber-fertiliser-ammonia-centenary.

Fritjof Meyer, "Lenin arbeitet nach Wunsch," in Stephan Burgdorff and Klaus Wiegrefe (eds.), *Der Erste Weltkrieg: Die Ur-Katastrophe des 20. Jahrhunderts*, 3rd edition, Deutsche Verlags-Anstalt, Munich, 2014, pp. 121–26. (Original edition: 2004)

Seumas Milne, "First World War: an imperial bloodbath that's a warning, not a noble cause," *The Guardian*, January 8, 2014, http://www.theguardian.com/commentisfree/2014/

jan/08/first-world-war-imperial-bloodbath-warning-noble-cause.

Pierre Miquel, *Les Poilus: La France sacrifiée*, Plon, Paris, 2000.

Annika Mombauer, "The Fischer Controversy 50 years on: Conference Report," October 2011, http://www.open.ac.uk/Arts/fischer-controversy.

Michelle Moyd, "'We don't want to die for nothing': *Askari* at war in German East Africa, 1914–1918," in Santanu Das (ed.), *Race, Empire and First World War Writing*, Cambridge University Press, Cambridge, 2011, pp. 90–107.

John Mueller and Karl Mueller, "Sanctions of Mass Destruction," *Foreign Affairs*, vol. 78, n° 3, May-June 1999, pp. 43–53.

Rolf-Dieter Müller, *Der Feind steht im Osten: Hitlers geheime Pläne für einen Krieg gegen die Sowjetunion im Jahr 1939*, Ch. Links Verlag, Berlin, 2011. (2011a)

Rolf-Dieter Müller, "Das 'Unternehmen Barbarossa' als wirtschaftlicher Raubkrieg," in Gerd R. Ueberschär and Wolfram Wette (eds.), *Der deutsche Überfall auf die Sowjetunion:'Unternehmen Barbarossa', 1941*, Fischer Taschenbuch, Frankfurt, 2011, pp. 125–57. (2011b)

Herfried Münkler, *Der Große Krieg: Die Welt 1914 bis 1918*, 4th edition, Rowohlt, Berlin, 2014 (Original edition: 2013).

"Nachtigall," http://de.wikipedia.org/wiki/Nachtigall.

John Paul Newman, "Les héritages de la Première Guerre mondiale en Croatie," in François Bouloc, Rémy Cazals, and André Loez (eds.), *Identités Troublées 1914–1918: Les appartenances sociales et nationales à l'épreuve de la guerre*, Privat, Toulouse, 2011, pp. 141–52.

Jean Nicot, *Les Poilus ont la parole. Dans les tranchées: lettres du front 1917–1918*, Complexe, Brussels, 1998.

Gregory P. Nowell, *Mercantile States and the World Oil Cartel, 1900–1939*, Cornell University Press, Ithaca, 1994.

J.D. Omer-Cooper, *History of Southern Africa*, James Currey, London, 1994.

Torsten Oppelland, "Der lange Weg in den Krieg (1900–1918)," in Klaus Larres and Torsten Oppelland (eds.), *Deutschland und die USA im 20. Jahrhundert: Geschichte der politischen Beziehungen*, Wissenschaftliche Buchgesellschaft, Darmstadt, 1997, pp. 1–30.

Gerard Christopher Oram, *Military Executions During World War I*, Palgrave, New York, 2004.

Giovanni Maria Pace, *La via dei demoni. La fuga in Sudamerica dei criminali nazisti: segreti, complicità, silenzi*, Sperling & Kupfer, Milan, 2000.

Bruno Paleni, *Italie 1919–1920: Les deux années rouges. Fascisme ou révolution?* Les bons caractères, Pantin, 2011.

Louis Panel, "La gendarmerie dans la bataille de Verdun (février-octobre 1916)," *Revue historique des armées*, n° 242, 2006, http://rha.revues.org/4182.

Marthe, Joseph, Lucien, and Marcel Papillon, *'Si je reviens comme je l'espère': Lettres du front et de l'arrière 1914–1918*, Grasset, Paris, 2003.

Ilan Pappé, *A History of Modern Palestine: One Land, Two Peoples*, Cambridge University Press, Cambridge, 2006.

Michael Parenti, *Blackshirts & Reds: Rational Fascism and the Overthrow of Communism*, City Lights Books, San Francisco, 1997.

Michael Parenti, *Democracy for the Few*, 6th edition, Bedford/St. Martin's, Boston, 1995. (Original edition: 1974)

Michael Parenti, "Must we adore Vaclav Havel?", December 18, 2011, http:// michaelparentiblog.blogspot.ca/2011/12/must-we-adore-vaclav-havel-by-michael.html.

Michael Parenti, "1918," November 2014, http://www.michaelparenti.org/1918.html.

Jacques R. Pauwels, *De Canadezen en de bevrijding van België 1944–1945*, EPO, Berchem, 2004.

Jacques R. Pauwels, *Een geschiedenis van de namen van landen en volkeren*, EPO, Berchem, 2006.

Jacques R. Pauwels, *Het Parijs van de sansculotten. Een reis door de Franse Revolutie*, EPO, Berchem, 2007.

Jacques R. Pauwels, *Europese namen voor de wereld*, EPO, Berchem, 2008.

Jacques R. Pauwels, "Hitler's Failed Blitzkrieg against the Soviet Union. The "Battle of Moscow" and Stalingrad: Turning Point of World War II," December 6, 2011, http://www.globalresearch.ca/70-years-ago-december-1941-turning-point-of-world-war-ii/28059.

Jacques R. Pauwels, "Hollywood: War Horses and the Great War of 1914–1918: A Comment on Steven Spielberg's most recent movie," *Global Research*, January 3, 2012, http://www.globalresearch.ca/hollywood-war-horses-and-the-great-war-of-1914–1918/28481.

Jacques R. Pauwels, *Big business avec Hitler*, Aden, Brussels, 2013.

Jacques R. Pauwels, *The Myth of the Good War: America in the Second World War*, revised edition, James Lorimer, Toronto, 2015. (Original edition: 2002)

A.J. Peacock, "An Alternative Guide to the Western Front (From Nieuport to Pfetterhouse)," *Gun Fire*, n° 21, 1990.

Joop Peeters, *De Duitse inval in België 1914*, Aspekt, Soesterberg, 2009.

Joseph E. Persico, *Eleventh Month, Eleventh Day, Eleventh Hour: Armistice Day, 1918. World War I and Its Violent Climax*, Random House, New York, 2005.

James Petras "The CIA and the Cultural Cold War Revisited," *Monthly Review*, Volume 51, Issue 6, November 1999, http://monthlyreview.org/1999/11/01/the-cia-and-the-cultural-cold-war-revisited.

"Piece Work," http://www.marxists.org/glossary/terms/p/i.htm.

Ernst Piper, *Nacht über Europa: Kulturgeschichte des Ersten Weltkriegs*, Propyläen, Berlin, 2013.

Richard Pipes, "Flight From Freedom: What Russians Think and Want," *Foreign Affairs*, May-June 2004, https://www.foreignaffairs.com/articles/russia-fsu/2004-05–01/flight-freedom-what-russians-think-and-want.

Edoardo Pittalis, *La Guerra di Giovanni. L'Italia al Fronte: 1915–1918*, Biblioteca dell'Immagine, Pordenone, 2006.

Rosa Amelia Plumelle-Uribe, *La férocité blanche. Des non-Blancs aux non-Aryens: génocides occultés de 1492 à nos jours*, Albin Michel, Paris, 2001.

Norbert F. Pötzl, "Verkäufer des Todes," in Stephan Burgdorff and Klaus Wiegrefe (eds.), *Der Erste Weltkrieg: Die Ur-Katastrophe des 20. Jahrhunderts*, third edition, Deutsche Verlags-Anstalt, Munich, 2014, pp. 172–77. (Original edition: 2004)

Nicos Poulantzas, *Fascisme et dictature*, Le Seuil, Paris, 1974.

Alexander E. Powell, *Fighting in Flanders*, McClelland, Goodchild & Stewart, Toronto, 1915.

14–18: Mourir pour la patrie, Le Seuil, Paris, 1992.

P.J. Rachschmir, *Der Ursprung des Faschismus*, Progress/Globus, Moscow and Vienna, 1981.

Erich Maria Remarque, *All Quiet On The Western Front*, Random House, New York, 1996.

Jean-Louis Robert, *Les Ouvriers, la Patrie et la Révolution: Paris 1914–1919*, Presses Universitaires de Franche-Comté, Paris, 1995.

Heather Robertson, *A Terrible Beauty: The Art of Canada at War*, James Lorimer, Toronto, 1977.

Bruce Robinson, "The Pals Battalions in World War One," March 10, 2011, http://www.bbc.co.uk/history/british/britain_wwone/pals_01.shtml.

Hans Rogger, "Russia in 1914," *Journal of Contemporary History*, vol.1, n° 4, October 1966, pp. 95–119.

Hans Rogger, *Russia in the Age of Modernisation and Revolution 1881–1917*, Routledge, London and New York, 1983.

Thomas Rohkrämer, "Der Gesinnungsmilitarismus der 'kleinen Leute' im Deutschen Kaiserreich," in Wolfram Wette (ed.), *Der Krieg des Kleinen Mannes: Eine Militärgeschichte von unten*, Piper, Munich, 1992, pp. 95–109.

Laura Root, "'Temporary Gentlemen' on the Western Front: Class Consciousness and the British Army Officer, 1914–1918," January 1, 2006, http://digitalcommons.unf.edu/cgi/viewcontent.cgi?article=1071&context=ojii_volumes.

Arthur Rosenberg, *Democracia y lucha de clases en la antigüedad*, El Viejo Topo, Barcelona, 2006.

Kristin Ross, "L'internationalisme au temps de la Commune," *Le Monde diplomatique*, May 2015.

Jean Rouaud, *Éclats de 14*, Dialogues, Paris, 2014.

Frédéric Rousseau, *La guerre censurée. Une histoire des combattants européens de 14–18*, Le Seuil, Paris, 1999.

Frédéric Rousseau, *La Grande Guerre en tant qu'expériences sociales*, Ellipses Marketing, Paris, 2006.

Laura Rowe, "'Their Lordships Regret That . . .': Admiralty Perceptions of and Responses to Allegations of Lower Deck Disquiet," in Jennifer D. Keene and Michael S. Neiberg (eds.), *Finding Common Ground: New Directions in First World War Studies*, Brill, Leiden and Boston, 2011, pp. 43–65.

Odile Roynette, *Les mots des tranchées: L'invention d'une langue de guerre 1914–1919*, Armand Colin, Paris, 2010.

John Ruskin, *The Complete Works of John Ruskin LL.D in twenty-six volumes. Volume Fifteen: The Crown of Wild Olive*, Reuwee, Watley and Walsh, Philadelphia, 1891.

Emmanuel Saint-Fuscien, *A vos ordres? La relation d'autorité dans l'armée française de la Grande Guerre*, EHESS, Paris, 2011.

Anne-Marie Saint-Gille, "Mutations des identités pacifistes allemandes entre 1914 et 1918–1919," in François Bouloc, Rémy Cazals, and André Loez (eds.), *Identités Troublées 1914–1918: Les appartenances sociales et nationales à l'épreuve de la guerre*, Privat, Toulouse, 2011, pp. 255–67.

Frances Stonor Saunders, *Who paid the Piper?: The CIA and the Cultural Cold War*, Granta, London, 1999.

Conrad Schirokauer, *A Brief History of Chinese Civilization*, Harcourt Brace Gap College, New York, 1991.

Michael Schmidt-Klingenberg, "Der Kampf in den Küchen," in Stephan Burgdorff and Klaus Wiegrefe (eds.), *Der Erste Weltkrieg: Die Ur-Katastrophe des 20. Jahrhunderts*, third edition, Piper, Munich, 2014, pp. 134–46. (Original edition: 2004)

Carl E. Schorske, *German Social Democracy 1905–1917: The Development of the Great Schism*, New York, Harper & Row, 1972. (Original edition: 1955)

Gottfried Schramm, "1914: Sozialdemokraten am Scheideweg," in Carola Stern and Heinrich August Winkler (eds.), *Wendepunkte deutscher Geschichte 1848–1990*, C.H. Beck, Frankfurt, 1997, pp. 71–97.

Daniel Marc Segesser, *Der Erste Weltkrieg in globaler Perspektive*, Marix Verlag, Wiesbaden, 2010.

Phil Shannon, "ANZACs vs Bolsheviks," May 8, 2010, https://www.greenleft.org.au/node/44033.

David Simpson, "Morale and Sexual Morality Among British Troops in the First World War," in Douglas Mackaman and Michael Mays (eds.), *World War I and the Cultures of Modernity*, University Press of Mississippi, Jackson MI, 2000, pp. 20–34.

Lieven Soete, *Het Sovjet-Duitse niet-aanvalspact van 23 augustus 1939: Politieke zeden in het interbellum*, EPO, Berchem, 1989.

Alfred Sohn-Rethel, *The Economy and Class Structure of German Fascism*, Free Association, London, 1987.

Mark Solomon, *The Cry Was Unity: Communists and African Americans, 1917–1936*, University Press of Mississippi, Jackson, MI, 1998.

Christian Staas and Volker Ullrich, "Deutsche Geschichte vom zweiten zum 'Dritten Reich'," February 8, 2011, http://www.zeit.de/zeit-geschichte/2010/04/Interview.

Gerald Steinacher, *Nazis auf der Flucht. Wie Kriegsverbrecher über Italien nach Übersee entkamen*, Fischer Taschenbuch, Frankfurt, 2010.

Carola Stern and Heinrich August Winkler (eds.), *Wendepunkte deutscher Geschichte 1848–1990*, C.H. Beck, Frankfurt, 1997.

Dave Stockton, "The Great Unrest: Organising the Rank and File 1910–1914" and "The Great Unrest: How militant miners created a movement of the rank and file," http://www.workerspower.co.uk/2012/05/rank-and-file-history and http://www.workerspower.co.uk/2012/06/rank-and-file-histor.

Oliver Stone and Peter Kuznick, *The Untold History of the United States*, Gallery Books, New York, 2012.

Richard Stumpf, "Die Matrosenrevolte in Wilshelmshaven 1918," in Wolfram Wette (ed.), *Der Krieg des Kleinen Mannes: Eine Militärgeschichte von unten*, Piper, Munich, 1992, pp. 168–80.

Alexandre Sumpf, *La Grande Guerre oubliée: Russie, 1914–1918*, Perrin, Paris, 2014.

Alexandre Sumpf, "Le complot bolchevique et l'a(r)gent allemand," *Le Monde Diplomatique*, June 2015.

David Swanson, *War Is A Lie*, David Swanson, Charlottesville, 2010.

A.J.P. Taylor, *English History 1914–1945*, Oxford University Press, New York and Oxford, 1965.

Peter Taylor-Whiffen, "Shot at Dawn: Cowards, Traitors or Victims," http://www.bbc.co.uk/history/british/britain_wwone/shot_at_dawn_01.shtml.

"The Group Scheme," http://www.1914-1918.net/derbyscheme.html.

"The 1914 actions in Mesopotamia," http://www.1914-1918.net/mespot1914.html.

"The tragedy of Kut," http://www.theguardian.com/world/2002/nov/20/iraq.features11.

David Thomson, *Democracy in France since 1870*, Oxford University Press, London and New York, 1969.

Charles Tilly, *Le rivoluzioni europee 1492–1992*, Laterza, Bari, 1993.

James F. Tracy, "'Progressive' Journalism's Legacy of Deceit," *Global Research*, July 20, 2012, http://www.globalresearch.ca/index.php?context=va&aid=31996.

Enzo Traverso, *L'histoire comme champ de bataille: interpréter les violences du XXe siècle*, La Découverte, Paris, 2011.

Barbara W. Tuchmann, *The Proud Tower: A Portrait of the World before the War 1890–1914*, Ballantine, New York, 1994.

Bernd Ulrich, "Die Desillusionierung der Kriegsfreiwilligen von 1914," in Wolfram Wette (ed.), *Der Krieg des Kleinen Mannes: Eine Militärgeschichte von unten*, Piper, Munich, 1992, pp. 110–26.

Bernd Ulrich, Jakob Vogel, and Benjamin Ziemann (eds.), *Untertan in Uniform: Militär und Militarismus im Kaiserreich 1871–1914. Quellen und Dokumente*, S. Fischer Verlag, Frankfurt, 2001.

Bernd Ulrich and Benjamin Ziemann (eds.), *Frontalltag im Ersten Weltkrieg. Wahn und Wirklichkeit: Quellen und Dokumente*, Fischer Taschenbuch, Frankfurt, 1995.

"United States home front during World War I," http://en.wikipedia.org/wiki/United_States_home_front_during_World_War_I.

Leo Van Bergen, *Before My Helpless Sight: Suffering, Dying and Military Medicine on the Western Front, 1914–1918*, Ashgate, Farnham/Surrey and Burlington/VT, 2009.

Jef Verschueren, "Het grote taboe. Braaf nationalisme, vroeger en nu," *De Standaard*, February 23, 2013.

Nguy n Kh c Vi n, Vi t Nam: A Long History, Foreign Languages Publishing House, Hanoi, 2009.

Eugen Weber, *France, Fin de Siècle*, Belknap/Harvard University Press, Cambridge and London, 1986.

Hans-Ulrich Wehler, "Der zweite Dreißigjährige Krieg," in Stephan Burgdorff and Klaus Wiegrefe (eds.), *Der Erste Weltkrieg: Die Ur-Katastrophe des 20. Jahrhunderts*, third edition, Deutsche Verlags-Anstalt, Munich, 2014, pp. 23–35. (Original edition: 2004)

James Weinstein, *The Decline of Socialism in America 1912–1925*, Vintage, New York, 1969.

Stanley Weintraub, *Silent Night: The Story of the World War I Christmas Truce*, Free Press, New York, 2001.

Manfred Weißbecker, *Das Firmenschild: Nationaler Sozialismus. Der deutsche Faschismus und seine Partei 1919 bis 1945*, PapyRossa, Cologne, 2011.

Wolfram Wette, "Die unheroischen Kriegserinnerungen des Elsässer Bauern Dominik Richert aus den Jahren 1914–1918," in Wolfram Wette (ed.), *Der Krieg des Kleinen Mannes: Eine Militärgeschichte von unten*, Piper, Munich, 1992, pp. 127–35.

Wolfram Wette (ed.), *Der Krieg des Kleinen Mannes: Eine Militärgeschichte von unten*, Piper, Munich, 1992.

Mark Whalan, "Not only war: the First World War and African American Literature," in Santanu Das (ed.), *Race, Empire and First World War Writing*, Cambridge University Press, Cambridge, 2011, pp. 283–300.

John W. Wheeler-Bennett, *Brest-Litovsk: The Forgotten Peace March 1918*, W.W. Norton, New York, 1971. (Original edition: 1938)

Reg Whitaker, "Images of the state in Canada," in Leo Panitch (ed.), *The Canadian state: political economy and political power*, University of Toronto Press, Toronto, 1977, pp. 28–68.

"Wilfred Nevill," http://en.wikipedia.org/wiki/Wilfred_Nevill.

Chad Williams, "African Americans and World War I," s. d., http://exhibitions.nypl.org/africanaage/essay-World-war-i.html.

Eric Williams, *Capitalism & Slavery*, University of North Carolina Press, Chapel Hill and London, 1994. (Original edition: 1944)

Edwin Williamson, *The Penguin History of Latin America*, Penguin, London, 1992.

Heinrich August Winkler, "1866 und 1878: Der Liberalismus in der Krise," in Carola Stern and Heinrich August Winkler (eds.), *Wendepunkte deutscher Geschichte 1848–1990*, Fischer Taschenbuch, Frankfurt, 1997, pp. 43–70.

Kieron Winn, "The Poetry of Herbert Read," in David Goodway (ed.), *Herbert Read Reassessed*, Liverpool University Press, Liverpool, 1998, pp.13–29.

Michel Winock, *La belle époque: La France de 1900 à 1914*, Perrin, Paris, 2002.

Leon Wolff, *In Flanders Fields: The 1917 Campaign*, Penguin, Harmondsworth, 1979.

"World War I and Dada," http://www.moma.org/learn/moma_learning/themes/dada.

Guoqi Xu, *Strangers on the Western Front: Chinese Workers in the Great War*, Harvard University Press, Cambridge MA, 2011.

Adrian Zimmermann, "Class Struggle and Class Compromise in the Netherlands and Switzerland (1914–1950)," Glasgow, April 11–14, 2012, https://www.academia.edu/1268707/Class_Struggle_and_Class_Compromise_in_the_Netherlands_and_Switzerland_1914-1950_.

Howard Zinn, *Geschiedenis van het Amerikaanse volk*, EPO, Berchem, 2007.

INDEX

Adenauer, Konrad, 543
Adrian, Louis Auguste, 331
Agadir Crisis, 147
Agathon, 150–151
Agnelli, Giovanni, 341, 543
Agrarian Party, 350
Agricultural Revolution, 34
Alacoque, Marguerite-Marie, 534
Alain (Chartier, Émile), 261
Alexander II, 170
Alexander-Sinclair, Edwyn, 511
Allard, Jules, 268
Alldeutsche Verband (Pan-German League), 113
Allenby, Edmund, 416, 417
Allende, Salvador, 560–561
American Civil War, 444
American Communist Party, 133
American Expeditionary Force (AEF), 229
American Federation of Labor (AFL), 457
American Holocaust, 34
American Patriotic League, 458
American War of Independence, 28, 117
Amritsar Massacre, 498, 554
Anastasia censorship, 211
ancien régime
    aristocrats and, 15, 29–32, 37
    authoritarian regimes and, 545
    Belgium, 214
    beneficiaries, 564
    bourgeoisie, 54, 59, 161
    China, 474
    Church and, 59, 125, 152, 558, 562, 564–565
    Europe, 38, 526, 562
    France, 25–26, 530
    Germany, 214, 288
    Hungary, 503, 540
    Italy, 542–543
    peasants in, 262
    pursuit of war, 159
    Russian, 152, 463, 512, 538
    world wide, 539
Anderson, Richard, 271
Anglicans, 30, 127, 159, 160, 186, 252, 400–401
anti-Semitism, 58, 69–70, 83,

88–89, 563–564
ANZAC (Australian and New Zealand Army Corps), 337–338
Apollinaire, Guillaume, 190, 206, 296, 331
Aragon, Louis, 408
Arendt, Hannah, 558
Armenian Genocide, 76
"Armenian Militia" (*Fedayi*), 339
Aron, Raymond, 558
Aryans
    Americans and, 445
    development of, 86–89, 539
    Germans as, 70–71, 116
    Social Darwinists, 89–90
    Superior races, 103
Ascaris, 292–293
Asquith, Cyril, 258
Asquith, Herbert Henry, 154, 157, 159
Asquith, Raymond, 9
Asquith Cabinet, 154, 157
Astor, Waldorf, 249
"Ataturk" (Kemal, Mustafa), 337
Atlantic Ocean, 34, 42, 48, 107, 451, 458, 506
Australian and New Zealand Army Corps, 337–338
Avanti, 344

Baden-Powell, Robert, 51
Balfour Declaration, 417
Balkan Wars, 109, 149, 177
Barbarossa, Frederik I, 112
Barbusse, Henri, 195
Barlach, Ernst, 205
barrage, 332, 379
Barthas, Louis
    battles, 327
    bugs, 307–308
    Christmas truce, 279
    the Church, 187
    diseases, 318
    food and drink, 306
    fraternization, 358–361
    friendly fire, 240
    industrialists, 362
    insubordination, 317, 423–424
    mistreatment of soldiers, 261, 267, 298–299

monuments and sacrifice, 324
    officer privileges, 310–313, 316
    officers removal, 277, 315
    orders from officers, 330, 353, 355
    peace, desire for, 356
    prisoner treatment, 274
    servility, 182–183
    smells, 302
Basel Congress, 192
BASF, 106, 391
Battle of Caporetto, 364, 415, 486
Battle of Coronel, 243
Battle of Dien Bien Phu, 552
Battle of Dobro Polje, 487
Battle of Gumbinnen, 242
Battle of Heligoland, 242
Battle of Jutland, 384–385, 447
Battle of Kosovo, 169
Battle of Le Cateau, 238, 267
Battle of Loos, 328–329, 330
Battle of Mons, 246–247, 249, 269, 285
"Battle of Peterloo," 59
Battle of Sarikamis, 289, 338–339
Battle of Tannenberg, 238–239, 242, 284, 288
Battle of the Frontiers, 268
Battle of the Marne
    accommodations after, 315
    desertions, 513
    events before, 244
    Germany and, 242, 297–298, 325
    Joffre and, 395
    second, 481, 486
    troop movements, 285, 288
Battle of the Masurian Lakes, 238, 284, 288
Battle of the Mines at Messines, 412–413
Battle of the Piave, 416, 486
Battle of the Reims, 481, 486
Battle of the Silver Helmets, 236
Battle of the Somme, 375, 380–383, 385, 414, 480
Battle of Verdun
    colonial soldiers in, 471
    comforts in trenches, 298

death numbers, 320, 410
equipment used during, 331, 373–374, 377, 483
evolution of, 373–377, 380–384
friendly fire, 240
Haig and, 376
peace, 388, 513
remembrance of, 338
"sacred road," 384
soldiers following, 380
Battle of Waterloo, 30
Battle of Ypres, 286
Battle of Ypres, Third, 409
Baudrillart, Alfred-Henri-Marie, 206
Bayer, 106, 334
Bay of Kiao-Chao, 111, 173
Bebel, August, 138, 153
Becker, Annette, 244
Becker, Jean-Jacques, 424
Beckmann, Max, 180, 242
Begbie, Harold, 253
Bell, Daniel, 558
Belle Époque
chauvinism, 150
class structure, 225
fear and tensions, 134–144
fondness for war, 94, 96, 151, 161
patriarchal powers, 212
Belloc, Hilaire, 97
Benoist, Charles, 138–139
Bergson, Henri, 283
Berlin, Isaiah, 558
Bernstein, Eduard, 130, 132, 193–194, 255
Beveridge, William Henry, 556
Beveridge Report, 556
Bishop of Ghent, 74
Black and Tans, 498
Black Hand, 142
Blohm & Voss, 435
Boches (Germans)
fraternizations with, 358
French perception of, 71
nicknames, 229
peace, 355
in racial war, 225
singing with, 279–280
translation of, 11, 496
Boer War, 291–292
Bogle, Eric, 338
Bolsheviks
defeatist attitude, 366
Kornilov and, 463
Lenin, 200–201
October Revolution, 434

peace and, 460, 464
political convictions, 464
propaganda by, 348
totalitarianism and, 215
Bonaparte, Napoleon, 28, 30
Borden, Mary, 297
Bottomley, Horatio, 71, 248
Bouloc, François, 208, 218, 394
Bourbon Monarchy, 223
bourgeoisie, haute. *See* haute bourgeoisie
bourgeoisie, petite. *See* petty bourgeoisie
Boxer Rebellion, 90, 474
Boyer, Lucien, 328
Boy Scouts, 51
Braudel, Fernand, 15, 139–140, 203–204
Brecht, Bertolt, 482
Brel, Jacques, 9, 176
Breton, André, 408
Briand, Aristide, 448
Brissot, Jacques Pierre, 94
British Expeditionary Force (BEF), 106, 239, 246, 284, 315, 330
British Labour Party, 131, 135, 498
British Workers' League, 249
Brittain, Vera, 253
Brodie, John Leopold, 331
Brooke, Rupert, 174
Brusilov, General, 385
Brusilov Offensive, 319, 386
Bund (General Union of Jewish Workers of Lithuania, Poland, and Russia), 74
Bund neues Vaterland (League for a New Fatherland), 255
Burckhardt, Jakob, 94–95
Burke, Edmund, 33, 89
Burns, Robert, 363
Bush, George W., 123, 416, 569

Cadorna, Luigi, 213, 346–347, 416
Café Liégeois, 237
Cameron, David, 266
Canfora, Luciano, 215, 560
Cannan, May Wedderburn, 489
"Capitaine Danrit" (Driant, Émile), 144
Carnot, Sadi, 170
Catherine, Lucas, 470
Catholic Church, 15, 534, 542, 549, 557, 562–564
Catholic Zentrum, 83
cavalry
aristocrats and, 231–232, 237, 272, 415

bourgeoisie protection, 59
Haelen, 236
nobility and, 162
role of, 177, 183, 376, 414–415, 418, 537
strategy and, 325, 330
strength of, 81
as weapons, 334
Cecil, Robert, Lord, 398
Central Powers
American feelings towards, 446
armistice, 476–477
blockade of, 451
conditions in, 220
countries in, 336–337
described, 103–104
economics of war and, 484
India and, 290
Italy and, 349–350
morale of, 246
supporters of, 454–455
war with, 289, 342, 385
CGT (*Confédération generale du travail*), 139, 195–196, 200, 269
Chalmers Mitchell, Peter, 157
Chamberlain, Neville, 547
Charles I (Emperor), 502
Chartier, Émile (Alain), 261
Chaucer, Geoffrey, 300
Cher Ami, 375
Chesterton, G. K., 248
Chomsky, Noam, 454
Chrysanthemum Revolution, 502
Churchill, Winston
attack plans, 336–337, 447
Black and Tans, 498
Bolsheviks, 466, 509
democrats vs. dictators, 466
fascinations, 94, 100, 172
Germany, 173
industry, 217
nonviolence, 473
October Revolution, 465
plebeians, 543
racism and, 467–468
CIA, 558–559, 561–562, 570
Citroën, 221
Claes, Ernest, 178
Class, Heinrich, 100
Clemenceau, Georges, 209, 215, 439, 493–494, 520
Cobb, Humphrey, 11, 269
Cogge, Karel, 286
Cold War, 466, 550–551, 553,

556–559, 561, 566–568
colonialism, 80, 125, 132, 291, 448
Comintern (Communist International), 528
Comité des Forges, 217, 396, 535
Committee on Public Information (CPI), 454
Communist International (Comintern), 528
Conan Doyle, Arthur, 155, 248
Confédération generale du travail (CGT), 139, 195–196, 200, 269
Congregation of the Immaculate Heart of Mary (Scheut Missionaries), 125
Connolly, James, 73, 399
Conrad, Joseph, 93
Constantine, H. F., 245–246
Constantine I, 350–351
Cook, Tim, 278
coolies (labourers), 219, 469–471, 474, 484
Cossacks, 250, 258
Count of Württemberg, 510
Cowan, Walter, 511
Cowper, William, 252
CPI (Committee on Public Information), 454
Creel, George, 454, 457
Currie, Arthur, 489
Curzon, Lord, 485
Czech Legion, 509

Dadaism, 408
Daensism, 73
Dahrendorff, Ralf, 435
Dali, Salvador, 14, 17, 19–20, 573
D'Annunzio, Gabriele, 158
Danube Monarchy. See Habsburg Empire
Dartford, R. C. G., 321
Darwin, Charles, 83–101, 104, 112, 115–116, 119, 124, 157, 467
Dax, Colonel, 13–14, 227, 271, 310
de Bonald, Louis-Gabriel, 89
Debs, Eugene, 138, 200, 457
de Candole, Alec, 321
de Castelnau, General, 227, 232
de Chateaubriand, François René, 33
Defence of India Act, 472–473
Defence of the Realm Act (DORA), 209–212
De Gaulle, Charles, 63, 277
Degeyter, Pierre, 67

de Gobineau, Joseph, 89
de Kostrowitzky, Guglielmo Apollinare (Apollinaire, Guillaume), 190, 206, 296, 331
de Lafayette, Marquis, 445
de Langle de Cary, General, 232
Del Boca, Angelo, 213
De Maistre, Joseph, 89
de Maud'huy, General, 232
Democratic Party, 436, 456–457
Democratic Party (Sozialdemokratische Partei Deutschland, SPD), 61, 436
Deng Xiaopeng, 475
Derby, Lord (Edward Stanley), 368
Derby Scheme, 368
de Schaepdrijver, Sophie, 94, 237, 284, 304, 401, 420, 478, 505
desertion
    discipline and, 430, 486–488
    morale, 348
    peace and, 461, 513
    penalties, 268–269, 363–364
    statistics, 182, 268–269, 345, 420, 424, 432, 478
d'Espèrey, Franchet, 232
Deterding, Henri, 538–539
de Tocqueville, Alexis, 85, 94
de Trentinian, General, 232
Deutsche Vaterlandspartei, DVLP (German Fatherland Party), 439–440
de Villar, Étienne, 268
de Villaret, General, 232
Diaz, Armando, 416
Dickens, Charles, 34
Diem clan, 560
Diggers, 229
Diner-Denes, Josef, 241
Directoire regime, 28, 30, 94
disease
    bombs and, 144
    causes of, 309
    civilians with, 498
    desertion by, 238, 318, 405–406
    doctors treating, 309
    poverty and, 35
    soldiers with, 35, 286, 290, 471
    supplies and, 44–45
Dix, Otto, 408
Dixon, F. J., 211

DORA (Defence of the Realm Act), 209–212
Dorgelès, Roland, 403
doughboys, 229
Douglas, Kirk, 13, 310
Downton Abbey, 36, 532
Dreyfus Affair, 65, 212, 227
Driant, Émile ("Capitaine Danrit"), 144
Dual Monarchy. See Habsburg Empire
Ducal, Charles, 202
Duchamp, Marcel, 408
Duisberg, Carl, 334
Duke of Urach, 510
Duma, 196–197, 205, 209
Dumolyn, Jan, 551, 567
Dunlop, 105, 484
DuPont, 451
Duroselle, Jean-Baptiste, 394
DVLP, Deutsche Vaterlandspartei (German Fatherland Party), 439–440
Dylan, Bob, 127

Easter Rising, 387, 399–400
Ebert, Friedrich, 500–501
Ebert-Groener agreement, 500–501
Edward VIII, 544
Eisenhower, Dwight, 63
Eksteins, Modris, 12, 91, 187, 193, 263
Elisabeth, Empress ("Sissi"), 170
Ellison, George, 489
Éluard, Paul, 408
Engels, Friedrich, 34, 42, 57, 153, 163, 193, 196
Englund, Peter, 224, 535
Enlightenment, 30–32, 52, 57, 86, 91
Entente Cordiale, 103, 106, 163, 219
Ernst, Max, 408
Espionage Act, 456–457, 569
Ewer, W. N., 517

Fasci d'Azione Rivoluzionario (Fasci of Revolutionary Action), 344
Fasci of Revolutionary Action (Fasci d'Azione Rivoluzionario), 344
Faulkner, Neil, 46, 48
Fedayi ("Armenian Militia"), 339
Ferchaud, Claire, 441
Ferguson, Niall
    Britain's aid to France, 172

capitalist interests, 122, 435
casualty statistics, 374
dissention, 209–210
Ludendorff, 213
religious observance, 205
state capitalism, 217
US involvement, 452–453
Ferro, Marc, 343
feudalism, 51, 538
Field Punishment Number
One, 270
First Battle of Ypres, 286
First Socialist International, 67
Fischer, Fritz, 12, 222, 546
Fisher, John (First Sea Lord),
106–107, 336
flame-thrower, 328, 334, 534,
537
Foch, Ferdinand, 227, 476, 481,
488, 510
Ford, Henry, 89, 468, 544
Ford, S. Gertrude, 427
Fourteen Points, 464, 502
France, Anatole, 362
Franco, Francisco, 544–545
Franco-Prussian War, 29, 39,
517
Frankau, Gilbert, 71, 402
Franz-Joseph, 238, 245, 536
fraternizations, 278, 358, 361
Friedrich-Wilhelm of Prussia,
148
free corps, 500, 541–542,
541–543
French, John, 232, 315, 330
French Revolution, 15, 17, 19,
25–35, 52–53
    church and state separa-
    tion, 563
    equality, 530
    Hitler and, 161
    influence of, 161, 418,
    492–493, 550
    Jewish influence in, 89
    liberty but not democ-
    racy, 85
    nationalism, 68
    social equality, 57
    war with exterior enemies
    vs., 94
Freud, Sigmund, 244, 441
Front National, 126, 571
Furet, François, 27
Fussell, Paul
    dirt and disease, 312
    "In Flanders' Field" and,
    370
    language and reality, 177
    plundering and loss of
    momentum, 481–482

"Roses of Picardy," 381
smells around the trench-
es, 301
staff officers vs. soldiers,
316
symbolism in art, 370,
381
trenches length, 296
understanding from
others, 357–358
war as conservative activity, 95
Futurism, 98

Gallieni, General, 285
Gandhi, Mahatma, 472–473,
552
Ganser, Daniele, 559
Garde indigène, 473
Garibaldi, Giuseppe, 73–74,
341
Garrod, H. W., 326
gas (for vehicles), 485
gas (poison), 9, 278, 326, 328,
332–334, 391, 402, 534
gas mask, 326
Geeraert, Hendrik, 286
Geiss, Imanuel, 112, 147
General Union of Jewish
Workers of Lithuania,
Poland, and Russia (Bund),
74
Gentile, Giovanni, 98
George V, 154
German Fatherland Party, DVLP
(Deutsche Vaterlandspartei),
439–440
Gibbs, Philip, 358
Girondins, 94
Glaser, Hermann, 100
Goebbels, Josef, 71
Gompers, Samuel, 457
Gorki, Maxim, 367
Gowans, Stephen, 556
Graves, Robert, 316–317, 329,
383, 442
Great Depression, 507, 548,
568
Great Labour, Socialist, and
Democratic Convention, 426
Grey, Viscount Edward, 157
Groener, Wilhelm, 468,
500–501
Grosz, George, 408
Guesde, Jules, 198
Guggisberg, Frederick Gordon,
97
Gunther, Henry, 490
Gurney, Ivor, 253

Haase, Hugo, 181, 193
Habermas, Jürgen, 435
Habsburg Empire, 441
    alliances, 102, 385, 445
    cavalry vs. soldiers, 231
    counterrevolution, 30
    death and war, 441
    democracy after war,
    501–503
    desertions in, 238
    end of, 487
    feudal political system, 42
    German language, 264
    governing class, 37, 42
    minority repression, 149
    nationalism movements,
    53, 73
    peace treaties, 517
    social movements and,
    148
    Triple Alliance, 103–104
    war of movement, 288
Habsburgs
    Americans and, 445
    Catholic Church, 454–
    455
    Central Powers, 103–104
    defeat of, 231
    desertions, 238
    minorities, 75, 149
    punishments of troops,
    271
Haider, Jörg, 563
Haig, Douglas
    arsenal, 377
    authority of army, 212
    casualties, 239, 346, 373,
    376
    casualty numbers, 239
    cavalry as powerful
    weapon, 232, 376
    colonial conquests, 81
    economy and war, 122
    headquarters of, 10
    promotions, vying for,
    328–329
    trenches, 330
    whisky, 122
Halifax, Lord, 544
Hardie, James Keir, 181, 200,
248, 399
Hardy, Thomas, 248
Harmsworth, Alfred (Viscount
Northcliffe), 157
Hastings, Max
    alliances, 342
    antiwar voices, 254
    Belgian neutrality, 172
    democracy and war,
    147–148

fraternization, 274–275
morale of soldiers, 226,
243
reconsideration, 208
social layers of soldiers,
208
workers' frustrations, 367
Haumont, Georges, 271–272
haute bourgeoisie
ambitions of factions
in, 222
army authority, 65
army officers and, 231
asceticism virtues and, 96
counterrevolution and, 17
democracy and, 61,
85–86
equality with proletar-
ians, 530
factions and wealth, 36
needs following revolu-
tion, 26–28
Paris Commune, 39–44
plutocrats, 41
power of, 207–208
revolution, 95, 161
theatre and, 54
Havel, Vaclav, 562
Hay, John, 119
Haywood, "Big Bill," 457
Heartfield, John, 408
Henderson, Arthur, 181
Heraclitus, 95
Hereros, 143
Hervé, Gustave, 135
Herzfeld, Helmut, 408
Herzl, Theodor, 74, 81
Hesse, Hermann, 203, 205
Heym, Georg, 97
Hitler, Adolf
advent to power, 543, 545
alliances with, 547
ambitions, 47
appeasement policy, 515
authoritarian system, 501,
544
democracy and war, 175,
206
dictatorship in France,
233
fascism, 442
France defeat, 549
fraternization of soldiers,
277
life details, 47, 115, 161,
215, 543
living space, 114
Mein Kampf, 175
military loans, 546
minister of propaganda, 71

national-socialism, 541–
542, 545
Nazism, 468
poison gas survival, 333
racial superiority, 88–89
Soviet Union obliteration,
547–548
supplies and winning
wars, 484–485,
538–539
territorial expansion, 80,
547
Vichy regime, 441
"wanted" war, 546–547
Ho, Chi Minh, 74, 474–475,
513, 539, 560
Hobbes, Thomas, 38
Hobohm, Martin, 226
Hobsbawm, Eric
capitalists interest in war,
122–123
democracy, 86, 146
imperialism and racism,
77
militarism, 50
Russian Revolution, 506
socialism, 132, 140, 199
socialists and revolutionaries, 135
"wanted" war, 149, 174
women's rights, 142
working class, 57–58
Hochschild, Adam
casualties and Germany's
losses, 238–239
cynicism of soldiers, 382
Easter Rising, 399
on Haig, 378–379
heroism of military,
378–379
internationalism, 277
nobility losses after wars,
532
pacifists, 200
socialism, 427
US involvement in war,
452
working class and armed
services, 184
Hoechst, 106
Hoffmann, Max, 288
Hohenzollerns, 103, 231, 445
Holliday, William, 398
Home Rule, 75, 154, 264, 399,
472
Hook, Sidney, 558
Hopi, 252
Horne, Cyril Morton, 300
Horne, John H., 216
horses

deaths, 235, 301, 302,
307, 376, 479
exhaustion, 284, 302
generals and, 395
labourers and, 469
peasants and, 179
problems with, 415
processing plants, 479
shipping to Palestine, 414
shortage of, 483, 486
as weapons, 531
Horthy, Miklós, 503, 514, 540,
544–545
Hotchkiss, 393
House, Edward M., 369
House of Lords, 37, 63, 154
Howard, Geoffrey, 160
Hugo, Victor, 35
L'Humanité, 195
Hussein, Saddam, 454
Husserl, Edmund, 440

IG Farben, 106
imperialism
Africa and, 125
benefits, 48, 67, 77, 122,
128, 132
Bolsheviks and, 539
Bonapartist, 28
capitalism and, 121–123
the Church and, 125
civil war avoided by, 79
in colonies, 78, 124, 559
costs vs. benefits of, 122
futurism and, 98
Great War and, 21
labourers, 121, 194, 195
material interests, 104,
484
nationalism and, 52,
67–83
psychological role, 77
racism and, 86
redistribution of colonies,
110
socialism and, 67–83
social reform and, 78
state power and, 83
United States and, 133
war and, 118–120, 484
western, 570
Independent Labour Party,
181, 200
Independent Social-
Democratic Party of
Germany (Unabhängige
Sozialdemokratische Partei
Deutschlands, USPD), 436
Indians
coolie system, 46

independence of, 472, 498
labourers for Europe, 469
language barriers, 264
prisoners of wars, 290
relationships with prole-
tarians, 470
wars against, 81, 82
wars for England, 90, 471
Indians (North American), 34,
118, 445–446, 473
Industrial revolution, 37, 40,
44, 334, 555
Industrial Workers of the World
(Wobblies), 135, 458
"In Flanders' Fields," 301,
369–371
Inquisition, 545
International Monetary Fund,
570
International Red Cross, 265,
345
International Workers'
Association, 67
"Internationale," the, 359
ITT, 561

Jackson, T. A., 264
Jacobins, 94, 512
Jaurès, Jean
assassination of, 176, 183,
192, 195, 572
capitalism and war, 122
Guesde and, 198
Péguy and, 151
socialism achievement,
130–131
war and liberalism, 151
Jews
as an "other," 69
army authority and, 65,
231
Aryan community infiltra-
tion, 88–89, 90
Bolsheviks, 467, 468
cause of social problems,
88–89
inciting revolutions, 91,
467–468
international people, 541
nationalist movement
of, 74
Nazi Germany, 454, 468
rejection by nobility, 54
repression of, 457
Russian refugees, 349, 445
socialism and, 70,
137–138
Zionism, 81
Joan of Arc, 126, 152, 191, 206,
285, 534, 549, 580

Joffre, Joseph
Battle of Marne, 285
Belgium defence against,
286
colonies and promo-
tions, 81
headquarters, 315
Plan XVII, 283
poilus and, 327
powers, 212, 395
publication bans on
losses, 243
John Bull, 70, 191, 248
John Paul II, 562–563
Johnson, Lyndon B., 553
Johnson, Nuala C., 74, 154
Jones, Paul, 458
J. P. Morgan & Co., 535
Jünger, Ernst, 441, 480
Junius Pamphlet, 196
Junkers, 43, 60, 536

Kaddafi, Muammar, 454
Kaiser. See William II (Wilhelm
II)
Károlyi, Mihály, 502
Kautsky, Karl, 129
Kemal, Mustafa ("Ataturk"),
337
Kennedy, John F., 553
Kerensky, Alexander, 196, 460,
462, 463, 465
Kern, Jerome, 254, 357
Kiel Canal, 106–107
Kipling, Rudyard, 70, 142, 191,
248, 328
Kirchner, Ernst Ludwig, 242
Kitchener, Horatio Herbert
(Lord)
army named after, 183–
184, 375–376
duration of war, 176
letter from John French,
232
poisonous gas, 334
propaganda, 191
sexual abstention policy,
405
war outbreak, 173
Knights of Liberty, 458
Koch, Hansjoachim Wolfgang,
40, 71
Koestler, Arthur, 558
Kolchak, General, 509
Kolko, Gabriel
Americans and Socialist
Party rise, 138
Bourgeoisie as winner in
war, 534
British Labour Party, 131

class character in army,
226
degrading incidents of
underlings, 259
democratic reforms and
end of war, 529
Lenin and defeatism, 201
morale of soldiers, 433,
437–438
officers roles, 267
poilus counter-culture, 424
popular masses less
respectful of elite, 254
post-traumatic stress disorder, 332
repressive movements in
war, 544–545
revolution in Russia, 497
shell-shock syndrome,
332
soldiers roles, 267,
437–438
SPD and Germany's rul-
ers, 131
war illusion, 177
Kornilov, Lavr, 462–466
Kriegsausschuß der deutschen
Industrie (War Committee of
German Industry), 217
Kropotkin, Peter, 197
Krupp
German industry, 106
Michelin vs., 484
power of industrialists,
536
profits from state orders,
49, 221, 435
state orders for weapons,
43, 46
weapons, 236, 537
Kubrick, Stanley, 11, 13, 55,
258
Ku Klux Klan, 458
Ku, Béla, 503, 540

labour
Africa as a source of, 469
aristocracy, 128
child, 564
colonies providing,
45–47, 52, 105, 469,
470–471
imperialism and, 104,
121, 128
liberalism, 153
movement in Europe,
57–58, 95, 366, 391,
495
obedience, 342
strikes by, 221, 421 (See

also strikes)
unions and, 422
United States, 448
wages and productivity
of, 555
women recruited, 219
labourers (coolies), 219
Lacroix-Riz, Annie, 110
Lady of the Limp, 384
laissez faire, 26, 31, 458, 535
landowners
Anglo-Irish gentry, 154
authoritarian state, 542,
544
Bolsheviks and, 465
China's, 475
Eastern European, 514
labour needed by, 46
loss of power, 533, 536,
551
political parties, 439–440
privileges of, 26, 562
profits, 220
redistribution of land,
502, 532
South Africa, 291–292
tenants, 300
territorial acquisitions,
124, 223, 342
United States, 42
Langbehn, Julius, 85
Lansdowne, Lord, 106
Lateran Agreements, 542
Law, Bonar, 154
Lawrence, Thomas Edward
("Lawrence of Arabia"), 109,
416–417
"Lawrence of Arabia"
(Lawrence, Thomas Edward),
109, 416–417
League for a New Fatherland
(*Bund neues Vaterland*), 255
Lebensraum, 47, 80, 114
Le Bon, Gustave, 85, 95, 577, 612
Le Chapelier, 26
Le Creusot, 393
Lee, Joseph, 273
Lefkowitz, Joseph, 519
Leftwich, Joseph, 519
Le Naour, Jean-Yves, 187
Lenin
assassination attempts
on, 466
Bolsheviks, 200–201, 548
colonies and revolution,
132
death, 528
defeatism, 201, 366
democracy in Western
world, 556

France, 494
Germans and, 473
Imperialism, 45
Latin-America, 508
October Revolution, 460,
464–465
oppressed people, 467
peace, 464–465
portrayal of, 465–466
Russian trip, 77
Shell Oil hatred of, 538
socialism, 131, 344
Leopold II, 74, 250
Leo XIII, Pope, 84
Le Queux, William, 157
Levine-Weinberg, Adam, 165
Lewis, Wyndham, 98, 287
Liberalism, 31, 35, 153
Liberal Party, 37
Liberation theology, 563
Liberty bonds, 453
Lichtenstein, Alfred, 180, 318
Liebknecht, Karl, 50, 193, 367,
390, 442, 500
Lincoln, Abraham, 14, 507
Lippmann, Walter, 454
Lissauer, Ernst, 172
Little, Frank, 458
Lloyd George, David
army and feelings for, 212
army rank differences, 316
Belgium as reason to enter
war, 254
democracy and dictator-
ship, 247
dictatorship of, 215
industrialists input into government, 396–397, 535
Irish insurrection, 399
Mussolini and, 543
opposition in govern-
ment, 209
reforms, 154, 427
revolutions in Europe,
512
Russia as enemy, 510
social unrest, 496–497
strikes by workers, 397,
497
totalitarian war cabinet,
438
war and civil war, 155
Loez, André, 353
London, Jack, 144
Losurdo, Domenico
class conflict, 20, 435, 556
class fusion, 41
colony independence, 552
democracy at embryonic
stage, 473

Judaism, 468
totalitarian systems, 215
Louis-Philippe, 39
Louis XIV, 29
Louis XVI, 25
Ludendorff, Erich
battles with Russians, 288
DVLP support of, 440
general but not aristo-
crat, 65
military dictatorship, 213,
438
offensive against Allies,
476
offensive in summer of
1918, 499
peace, pressure for, 436
resignation from army,
499
Second Battle of Marne,
486
spring offensive, 480
tanks used by Germans,
485–486
totalitarian systems, 215
vehicles effect on victory,
483–484
Ludlow Massacre, 455
Ludwig II of Bavaria, 33
Lukács, Georg, 536
Lumumba, Patrice, 560
Lusitania, 443, 447
Luther, 16, 89, 188
Lutheranism, 30, 533
Luxemburg, Rosa
corporate taxes during
war, 394
Marxists, 131
murder of, 500, 541
pacifist opposition, 200,
390
rebellious slaves, 91
revolutionary role, 131
Spartacist League, 255
SPD Reichstag member,
193

MacDonald, Ramsay, 181, 248
MacMillan, Margaret, 111, 156,
178, 514
Macpherson, Cluny, 326
Macready, George, 269
Malaparte, Curzio (Suckert, Kurt
Erich), 420
Malthus, Thomas, 35, 79, 100,
239, 346
Mandela, Nelson, 561
Mangin, Charles, 10, 240
Mann, Heinrich, 188
Mann, Thomas, 101, 174, 440

Mannerheim, Carl Gustaf Emil, 514, 544
Manning, Chelsea (Bradley), 456
Mao, Zedong, 475, 539, 565
Marc, Franz, 205
March on Rome, 542
Marinetti, Filippo Tommaso, 98
Mariot, Nicolas, 353
"Marseillaise," the, 11, 420, 425, 534
Martin, Marie Françoise-Thérèse (Saint Theresa of Lisieux), 152
Martyrs of Vingré, 268
Marwick, Arthur
    businessman and power, 536
    Lloyd George and totalitarianism, 438
    Representation of the People Act, 495
    socialism, 154, 156
    union leaders and the army, 196
    war, 182, 426
    working conditions for lower orders, 498
Marx, Karl
    background, 70
    Belgium and capitalism, 37
    Chinese and ideas of revolution, 475
    Communist Manifesto, 52
    hierarchies in army and industries, 52
    International Workers' Association, 67
    pauperization and revolution, 128, 437
    proletariat, 26
    social conflict, 20
    socialist revolution, 57
    socialists and information, 262
    wage systems, 218
Marxism, 95, 474, 508
Masefield, John, 179
Massis, Henri, 150–151
Maude, Frederick Stanley, 416
Maugham, William Somerset, 466
Mayer, Arno
    aristocracy and support of church, 159
    armistice in 1919, 520
    army and losses, 239
    Bolsheviks support by others, 512

bourgeois industrialists, 42–43, 54
    deserters killing each other, 463
    elite foreign policy, 147
    fondness for war, 94, 161, 548
    Futurists, 98
    nationalism and conservatives, 72
    Nietzsche, 90
    noble governing class, 42, 93
    "overfearful" elite of socialism, 140, 146
    popular masses and socialism, 128
    revolution derailment, 27
    revolutions and war, 134, 148, 434, 461
    royalty internationalism, 55
Mazower, Mark, 512
McCrae, John, 301, 369, 371
McCutcheon, John, 281
McKinley, William, 170
Mehring, Franz, 193, 390
Mensheviks, 196, 464
Merton, Robert K., 252, 577
MI-6 (Military Intelligence, Section 6), 214
Michelin, 105, 484
Michels, Robert, 130
militarism
    antidote to radicalism, 95
    British soldiers and, 471
    churches as centres for indoctrination, 186
    class hegemony, 50
    democracy neutralized by, 127
    desertion and, 182
    feudal ideology and, 43
    futurists and, 98
    Gallipoli, 338
    German, 196
    national economies and, 52
    nationalism and, 53
    poppies and, 371
    proletarians, 56, 83
    propaganda and, 186, 195
    schools as centers for indoctrination, 186
Military Intelligence, Section 6 (MI-6), 214
Mill, John Stuart, 62
Millerand, Alexandre, 130
Milner, Alfred, 249
Mindaugas II, 510

Mitchell, Peter Chalmers, 157
Mobutu, Sese Seko, 559–560
Monatte, Pierre, 200
Montague, Charles Edward, 253
Morel, Edmund Dene, 398, 470
Morillon, Gervais, 276, 278
Moroccan Crisis, 147
mouchards, 215
multinationals, 564, 566
Münkler, Herfried, 285, 287
Murray, Gilbert, 400
Mussolini, Benito
    authoritarian systems led by, 544
    elite support of, 545
    fascism, 344
    life details, 542–549
    loans to pay for military, 546
    plebeians and war, 346–347
    revolutionary movement and, 542
    socialism discovered at front lines, 442
    steps back, 542–543
    mustard gas, 333

Naidu, Sarojini, 471
Napoleon III, 39, 63
National Association against Social Democracy (Reichsverband gegen die Sozialdemokratie), 147
nationalism
    allies against Russia, 510
    bourgeoisie and, 65, 73, 75
    business and, 52
    church and, 186
    classes within, 69
    described, 68
    Eastern Europe, 140, 563–564
    economic advantages, 53–54
    ethnic minorities within, 73
    futurists and, 98
    imperialism and, 55, 67–83
    internationalism vs., 68
    Irish, 154, 400
    jingoism as variety of, 52–53
    poppies, 371–372
    revolution externalized, 28, 53, 68
    rivals and support of, 75

romanticism, 32
socialism and, 74, 79,
  129–130, 204
South-Slav, 149
war and, 156, 170, 225,
  276–277, 503
NATO, 558–559, 567–568, 571
naval blockade, 220, 391–392,
  431
NCF (No-Conscription
  Fellowship), 398
neurasthenia, 332, 555
Nevill, Wilfred, 97
Newfoundland Regiment, 378
New Statesman, 254
Nicholas II, 163, 339, 349,
  536, 565
Nietzsche, Friedrich
  Darwinism, 83–101
  democratization and
    war, 99
  elite rule through force,
    91–93
  Futurism, 98
  Jews inciting revolutions, 91
  meeting with elite
    European and
    Americans, 90–91
  Paris Commune con-
    demned by, 40
  philosophy embraced by
    United States, 118–119
  Social Darwinism, 83–101
  soldiers' character
    improvements, 99
  war to prevent revolu-
    tion, 18
Nivelle, Robert, 410
nobility, 38–55
  ancien régime wanted by,
    152, 158–159
  army authority, 65, 99,
    228, 231–232, 387,
    501, 531
  in Belgium, 36–37, 214
  bourgeoisie and, 26–27,
    40–41, 44, 534–535,
    565
  bureaucratization, 64
  Catholic Church and, 152,
    159–160, 534, 542
  cavalry favoured by, 376,
    415
  counterrevolution by, 30,
    40, 530–532, 540
  democracy effect on,
    84–85, 91
  described, 17
  France and bourgeois
    regime, 39

French Revolution and,
  15, 25
in Germany, 42–43
as governing class, 42,
  216
imperialism favoured
  by, 123
international links of, 55
Jews in Germany and, 54
liberalism, 31
nationalism, 32, 53
poisonous gas use by, 334
political preferences,
  40–41
poverty seen as natural
  by, 35
power of, 37, 222, 231,
  534
proletarian dangers,
  56–57, 59, 67
social revolution, 39, 139,
  141
territorial acquisitions, 18,
  77, 124, 152, 223, 464
war and goals of, 159–
  163, 438
wealth reduction, 36
weapon production and
  profits, 48–49
No-Conscription Fellowship
  (NCF), 398
Nolte, Emil, 215
Nolte, Ernst, 344
Norman, Montagu, 544
Northern Ireland, 498
Noske, Gustav, 129
Notre-Dame-de-Lorette, 299,
  325–327
Nye Committee, 449, 452

Occitan, 263
October Crisis, 211
October Revolution, 434, 460–
  461, 464–465, 473
oil
  Dutch Royal families and,
    123
  efficiency of, 107–108
  imperialism, 106, 112,
    122, 484
  in Middle East, 108–109,
    417, 570–571
  in war, 102, 485–486
  wars over, 123, 164,
    288–290, 538, 570
Olten soviet, 506
Orthodox Church, 30, 127,
  152, 159–160, 564–565
Orwell, George, 558
Ottoman Empire

Armenians in, 141,
  338–339
British assistance, 76
British plan of attack on,
  336–337
capitulation, 418, 517
casualties of war, 241
Central Powers, 288–289
the Entente and, 341
Gallipoli and, 337
German railway project,
  108–109, 113
Germany and, 108
Greece and, 351
Indians under British rule
  and, 472
Middle East and, 108
Muslims within, 289
oil within, 289
peace conference of Great
  War, 448, 466
religions, 68, 533
Sykes-Picot Agreement,
  417
territory, 109, 111
Versailles Treaty, 517
Owen, Wilfred, 189, 270, 428,
  430

Pacha, Enver, 289, 339
pacifism
  Britain and, 200, 248, 371
  elite and, 145, 156, 176
  Germany and, 255
  reforms and, 255
  United States, 446, 456
  women and, 98, 142, 407
  workers support of, 161
Pais, Sidónio, 441
Pan-German League (*Alldeutsche
  Verband*), 113
Panhard-Levassor, 421
Pankhurst, Sylvia, 182, 200, 398
Papini, Giovanni, 346
Parenti, Michael, 342, 446, 507
Pareto, Vilfredo, 91, 95
Paris Commune
  bourgeoisie and, 39–40,
    57
  democracy and, 91
  Franco-Prussian conflict,
    16
  repression and, 60
  revolutionary tradition,
    220
  Third Republic, 39
Paris Peace Conference, 448,
  450, 537, 538
Parr, John, 232, 489
Passchendaele, 413–414

Paths of Glory, 11
    class conflict, 13–14
    compassion, 271, 332
    elite view of soldiers, 227
    entertainment, 403
    executions and, 251, 269
    French and German con-
      flict, 11, 13–14
    good guys and bad, 257
    internationalism, 55
    officers class, 271, 403
    officers vs. soldiers, 227,
      271, 310, 315
    religion and, 251
    returning home, 335
    trenches in water and
      mud, 299
Patriot Act, 509
Patriotic Order of Sons of
    America, 458
Péguy, Charles, 151
Penrose, Charles, 305–306, 377
Pentagon system, 568
Pershing, John J., 81
Pétain, Philippe, 233, 268, 373,
    424, 441, 549
petite bourgeoisie. *See* petty
    bourgeoisie
petty bourgeoisie
    Bolsheviks and, 511
    described, 13, 58
    France and, 207
    Gallic republic and, 150
    Germany, 440
    nationalism, 71
    political power and, 39
    revolution and, 27, 36
    social climbing opportun-
      ities, 441
    values of elite, 127–128
Picot, Georges, 417, 466
Pilsudksi, Józef, 544
Pinochet, General, 559–560,
    563
piottes, 264, 401, 419
Piper, Ernst, 242, 440
Pirelli, Alberto, 341, 543
Plan XVII, 283
Plekhanov, George, 197
poilus
    casualty statistics, 325, 330
    "Chanson de Craonne"
      ("Song of Craonne"),
      411
    comforts in trenches,
      298, 306
    described, 11
    desire to return home,
      318, 354, 423
    diseases to leave front, 318

    dissention, 330
    feelings for elite, 356
    fraternization with other
      side, 279–280, 360
    industrialists, 362
    "*Internationale*," the, 423
    language difficulties, 263
    martyrs of Vingré, 268
    morale, 365
    mutinies, 410, 424–425
    Notre-Dame-de-Lorette,
      327
    in *Paths of Glory*, 13,
      257–258
    patriotism lacking, 353
    poppies, 372
    privileges of officers, 265
    "Song of Craonne"
      ("*Chanson de*
      Craonne"), 411
    suicides of, 319
    war weariness, 421, 425
Poincaré, Raymond, 151, 164,
    171, 356
police force, colonial, 473
Polish-Lithuanian Union, 545
Pope, Jessie, 188
Pope John Paul II, 562–563
populists, 545
post-traumatic stress disorder,
    332
Potiorek, Oskar, 311
Pottier, Eugène, 67
Poulantzas, Nicos, 43
POW camps, 265
Price, George, 489
Priestley, J. B., 272
Princip, Gavrilo, 169
prohibition, 60, 210–211, 218,
    314, 411
propaganda, 246–250
    anti-German, 155
    Bolsheviks, 201, 348
    churches, 159, 454
    in Cold War, 559
    distribution in Europe,
      49, 202
    distribution methods, 70
    elements of, 246–248
    elite involvement in, 249
    in enemy camp, 76
    in Europe, 246
    "In Flanders' Fields,"
      369–371
    in Germany, 147
    in Great Britain, 156, 248
    in Italy, 265
    messages of, 246–248
    for military service, 190
    Mussolini's, 344

    nationalist, 70
    scepticism of, 250
    target of, 249
    in totalitarian systems,
      215
    in United States, 119,
      454, 569
prostitution, 316, 318, 393,
    403–404, 404–405, 406
Protestant Reformation, 16
Protestants
    coercion into services, 251
    French, 86
    in Germany, 206
    Irish rebels and, 400
    propaganda against
      Germany, 454
    socialist parties and, 138
    superiority of, 88
    sympathy of Germans,
      445
    volunteer service,
      154–155
Putin, Vladimir, 565

racism, 69–72, 127, 133, 141,
    225, 564, 604
Rathenau, Walther, 217, 535
raw materials
    Africa and, 47
    agreements about, 45
    as assets, 47
    blockades to Germany,
      384–385
    colonies, 18, 45, 469, 484
    control over, 104
    Eastern Europe and, 480
    Germany at disadvantage
      in, 112–113, 485
    imperialism and, 67, 77,
      121, 194, 340, 484
    Japan taking, 111
    multinationals in Russia,
      566
    neocolonialism, 448, 570
    state as hunters for, 46
    United States, 118
    war for, 19, 21
Razaf, Andy (Razafkeriefo,
    Andrea), 554
Razafkeriefo, Andrea (Razaf,
    Andy), 554
Read, Herbert, 274
Reagan, Ronald, 63, 562–563,
    567, 569
Red Army, 551, 558
Red Cross, 265, 345
Reed, John, 5, 507
Reichsrat, 148
Reichstag

accountability to Kaiser
vs., 213–214
authority over army, 63
constitution, 500
described, 60–61
peace negotiations resolution, 300, 436
social democrats in, 138
social economic order of
the, 199
socialists, 147–148
universal suffrage, 66
war budget, 192–193, 255
Wilhelm II and, 148
*Reichsverband gegen die
Sozialdemokratie* (National
Association against Social
Democracy), 147
Remarque, Erich Maria, 186,
332
Remington, 451
Renan, Ernest, 80
Renault, 483, 485, 494
Renoir, Jean, 176
Representation of the People Act,
495
Republic of the Two Nations
(Polish-Lithuanian Union),
545
Rerum Novarum, 84
resistance
Africa, 48
of colonial people, 132
to democratization pro-
cess, 91
French, 374, 549
German, 291–293, 488
German colonies, 224
Ghandi and, 552
Independent Labour
Party, 200
Ottoman troops, 290
propaganda to reduce,
245
Serbian, 287
Réveilhac, Géraud, 240, 269
revolutionary syndicalism, 135
Rhodes, Cecil, 67, 79, 118,
132, 224
Richert, Dominik (Dominique),
251, 314, 355, 487
Ridley, Lady, 265
Rilke, Rainer Maria, 205
Risorgimento, 73
Roberts, Lord Frederick, 155, 157
Robespierre, Maximilien,
27–28, 32, 39, 94
Rockefellers, 435, 485
Rogger, Hans, 174, 396
Roma, 69

Roman Empire, 112, 176, 341
Romanovs, 231, 238
Romanticism
described, 31–34
fixation on Middle Ages,
191, 351, 387
Joan of Arc and, 126
Nationalism and, 68
Zeitgeist, 191
Romero, Bishop, 563
Roosevelt, Theodore, 94, 119,
445, 446, 553
Rosenberg, Isaac, 190, 258,
308–309, 370
Rothschild, Lord, 55, 417
Rothschilds, 281
Rouaud, Jean, 179
Rousseau, Frédéric, 30, 251,
259, 262, 484
Royal Navy
in Baltic Sea, 511
blockade of Germany,
516
comforts in, 260
discontent in, 429
fear of, 243
Great War naval battle,
384
powerless to u-boats,
334–335
victories, 242
Ruskin, John, 92
Russell, Bertrand, 200, 398, 610
Russian Civil War, 510, 539,
547, 557
Russian-Japanese war, 147
Russian Revolution, 16, 468
American Communist
Party affected by, 132
aristocrats support of, 512
Bolsheviks responsible
for, 466–467
Bolshevism in United
States, 507
British democratic reforms
as a result of, 496
democratization in
Europe and, 506
described, 433–434
financial losses to com-
panies, 538
French Revolution and,
493–494
Germans affected by, 488,
496
Great War experience
and, 463
Hitler's feelings about,
161
Marxism and, 474

planned by Jews, 89, 468
precursor to Great War, 29
socialism success and, 426
War Measures Act after,
211
working class affected by,
473–474, 501

Sacred Heart of Jesus, 126, 285
"sacred union"
democratization sus-
pended, 206–209
parliamentary activities
suspended, 216
rejection of, 344, 365,
394–395, 422
social agitation stopped
by, 234
source of, 197
workers affected by, 217,
221, 225
worker's unions and, 492
Saint Theresa of Lisieux (Martin,
Marie Françoise-Thérèse), 152
Salandra, Antonio, 343
Salazar, Antonio di Oliveira,
441, 544
Salvarsan, 406
Salvation Army, 51
sans-culottes, 15, 26, 28, 34
Sarajevo assassination, 76, 136,
150, 164, 169–171, 340, 516
Sassoon, Siegfried, 187, 274,
317, 319, 428, 592, 606
Scheidemann, Philipp, 199, 500
Schemua, Blasius, 148
Scheut Missionaries
(Congregation of the
Immaculate Heart of Mary),
125
Schlieffen Plan, 164, 236,
283–284, 287, 526
Schneider, Adolphe and Eugène,
393, 396
Schorske, Carl E., 199, 208
Schrecklichkeit, 237, *250*
Schumacher, Hermann, 223
Schumpeter, Joseph, 40
Schwarzenbergs, 562, *605*
Schwarzenegger, Arnold, 63
Scotland Yard, 155, 214
Scott, Walter, 33
Second Balkan War, 349
Second Battle of Messines,
412–413
Second Battle of the Marne,
481, 486
Second Empire, 39
Secret Intelligence Service (SIS),
466

Secret Service Bureau, 214
Sedition Act, 456
Selective Service Act (*Selective
 Draft Act*), 453
Sembat, Marcel, 198–199
September program, 223
serfdom, 30
Seven-Years War, 28
Shakespeare, 263, 300
Shanks, Edward, 323
Shaw, George Bernard, 383, 399
Shell, 123, 538
Shelley, Mary, 33
shell-shock, 332, 555
Sinn Fein movement, 400
"Sissi" (Empress Elisabeth), 170
slavery, 27–28, 39, 47, 93, 219,
 258, 469, 526
Smith, Adam, 31, 35, 46
Smithsonian Institution, 375
Smuts, Jan Christiaan, 292
snitches, 215
Social Darwinism, 18, 83–101,
 87, 89, 119
Social Democratic Party, SPD
 (*Sozialdemokratische Partei
 Deutschland*), 61, 436
socialism, 56–66
 bourgeoisie and, 43
 colonialism and, 80–81
 nationalism used against,
  72–77
 Nietzschean concept of
  war and, 94–95
 organisations created
  under, 18
 perceptions of, 68–69
 racism vs., 71
Socialist Labour Party, 426
Solzhenitsyn, Alexander, 238
Sombart, Werner, 116
Sonnino, Sidney, 343
Soros, George, 566
*Sozialdemokratische Partei
 Deutschland*, SPD (Social
 Democratic Party), 61, 436
Spaak, Paul-Henri, 558
Spanish-American War, 110
Spanish flu, 498
Spartacists, 499, 500
SPD, Social Democratic Party
 (*Sozialdemokratische Partei
 Deutschland*), 61, 436
Spengler, Oswald, 89
squadristi, 542
Stalin, Joseph, 528–529, 548,
 551, 556, 561, 565, 615
Standard Oil, 485
Stanley, Edward (Lord), 368
Stanley, Edward (Lord Derby), 368

Steffens, Lincoln, 507
Stepinac, Aloïs, 563
Stinnes, 435
Stoddard, Lothrop, 88
Stolypin, Piotr, 152, 159
Storm troops, 413, 442, 500,
 537
Strauss, Johann, 55
strikes, 101, 136–141, 211, 218,
 492–496, 504–508, 520, 556
Suckert, Kurt Erich (Malaparte,
 Curzio), 420
Sudeten, 547
Suharto, General, 560
suicide ditch, 305
Sumpf, Alexandre, 179, 218,
 319, 349
Sun, Yat-Sen, 144
Sykes, Mark, 417, 466
Sykes-Picot Agreement, 417,
 466

Taliban, 178
Tarde, Alfred, 150–151
Taylor, A. J. P., 210, 399
terrorism, 559, 568, 571
Thatcher, Margaret, 567, 569
The *Daily Mail*, 97, 191, 248
The Good Soldier Svejk, 238
The Guardian, 110–111
The Nation, 209
The Socialist, 426
The Times, 71, 156, 191, 248,
 266, 466
Third Battle of Ypres, 409,
 412–414, 598
Third International
 (Communist International,
 Comintern), 528
Third Republic, 39, 48, 60, 63,
 150–151, 395, 441
Thomas, Albert, 198–199, 395,
 492, 585
Thomson, Basil, 155, 214
Thyssen, 106, 536
Thyssen, August, 223
Tisza, Duke István, 171
Toller, Ernst, 242
Tomlinson, A. E., 382
Tommies, 229, 271, 275,
 299–310, 315, 323, 328–
 331, 377–378, 382–384,
 429–430, 480
Ton, Duc Thang, 513
Tories, 143, 154, 554
Townshend, Charles, 290
Traverso, Enzo, 559
Treaty of Brest-Litovsk, 477,
 502, 509–510
Treaty of Moscow, 521

Treaty of Riga, 521
Treaty of Tartu, 521
Treaty of the XXIV Articles, 173
Treaty of Versailles, 474–475,
 516–519
trench foot, 296, 298
trench warfare
 bordellos, 404
 death as escape from,
  319, 323
 duration, 287, 526
 equipment and supplies,
  325, 330–331
 living conditions, 299
 officers, 313–314
Triple Alliance, 103
Triple Entente, 103–104, 164
Trotsky, Leon, 366, 477, 507
Trudeau, Pierre Elliott, 211
Tuchman, Barbara, 131
Tucholsky, Kurt, 259, 266
Twain, Mark, 128

U-boat, 334, 447
Ulstermen, 155, 399
Ulyanov, Vladimir Ilitch. *See*
 Lenin
*Unabhängige Sozialdemokratische
 Partei Deutschlands*, USPD
 (Independent Social-
 Democratic Party of
 Germany), 436
Union of Democratic Control
 (UDC), 398
unions
 advantages to belonging,
  422
 advantages to elites, 200
 anti-Hamitic, 72
 Catholic Church and,
  84, 128
 collaboration with gov-
  ernments, 195–197,
  199, 457–458
 conferences, 366
 infiltrators hired by
  employers, 215
 labour movement, 57,
  137–138
 Marxism and, 18
 membership increasing,
  394, 422–423, 504
 Mussolini against,
  542–543
 peace demonstrations, 181
 political input, 216
 recognition, 494, 540
 rights violations, 217–
  218, 343
 socialist parties, 139

strikes and, 58, 221, 392,
394, 397–398, 492
wages, 392
war effort support, 181,
194, 366
union sacrée. *See* "sacred
union"
Untermensch (under-man), 88
USPD, Independent Social-
Democratic Party of
Germany (*Unabhängige
Sozialdemokratische Partei
Deutschlands*), 436

Van Beek, Theo, 381
Vandervelde, Emile, 131–132,
196
Venizelos, Eleftherios, 350–351
Verbindungsperson (liaison
agent), 215
Vertrauensperson (trusted person), 215
Vichy, France, 441, 549, 612
Victor Emmanuel III, 343
Victoria, Queen, 55, 73
Vienna Congress, 30
vigilantes, 458
Vimy Ridge, 327, 330
Viviani, René, 197
V-Leute. See Verbindungsperson
and *Vertrauensperson*
Volksgeist, 32
Voltaire, 30
von Bernhardi, Friedrich, 92
von Bethmann-Hollweg,
Theobald, 173, 222
von Bismarck, Otto, 43
von Bissing, Moritz, 213–214,
417
von der Goltz, Colmar, 117
von Falkenhayn, Erich, 373–
374, 377
von Herder, Johann Gottfried,
32
von Hindenburg, Paul, 65, 213,
288, 436
von Hötzendorf, Franz Conrad,
115
von Lettow-Vorbeck, Paul, 292
von Moltke, Helmuth Johannes
Ludwig (Moltke the
Younger), 96, 115, 164,
284–285, 373
von Moltke, Helmuth Karl
Bernhard (Moltke the Elder),
96, 115
von Sanders, Otto Liman, 337
von Schlieffen, Alfred, 103
von Spee, Maximilian, 243
von Tirpitz, Alfred, 95

von Treitschke, Heinrich, 43, 92
von Wilamowitz-Moellendorff,
Ulrich, 188
vorticism, 98
Vorwärts, 170, 200

Wagner, Richard, 128
Wahl, Maurice, 577
Walesa, Lech, 79
War Committee of German
Industry (*Kriegsausschuß der
deutschen Industrie*), 217
War Measures Act, 201–211
war profiteers, 221, 362, 387,
393, 396, 425, 492, 538
Warsaw Pact, 558, 567
Washington, George, 64, 444,
447, 558, 560
Weatherley, Frederick E., 381
Weber, Max, 64
Weimar Republic, 500–501,
543
welfare state, 550, 552, 554–
555, 567–569, 571, 609
Wells, H. G., 144, 192, 248
Whiskey Rebellion, 118
White Fathers (*Pères Blancs*),
125
white feather, 188
Whitlock, Brand, 214
Wild West, 47, 87, 113, 118,
547
Wilhelm (II) Karl Florestan
Gero Crescentius, 510
William II (Wilhelm II), 157,
164, 205, 213–214, 432,
436, 499
Willis, George, 259, 297, 308,
356
Wilson, Trevor, 333
Wilson, Woodrow, 369, 446–
447, 457, 464, 507, 538
Winnipeg General Strike, 507
Winock, Michel, 77, 130, 136,
207
Wobblies (Industrial Workers of
the World), 135, 458
Wojtyla, Karol, 562–563
Women's Social and Political
Union (WSPU), 142
Worm, Anne-Marie, 126
Wyatt, H. F., 92

Xinhai Revolution, 144

Yankees, 229, 478, 482
yellow press, 250, 356–356
Yeltsin, Boris, 562, 565
YMCA, 406
yperite, 333

Ypres, First Battle of, 286
Ypres, Third Battle of, 409

Zetkin, Clara, 255
Zhou Enlai, 475
Zimmerwald Conference, 366
Zweig, Stefan, 204

ABOUT THE AUTHOR

JACQUES R. PAUWELS has taught European history at the University of Toronto, York University and the University of Waterloo. He is the author of several books on twentieth-century history, including *The Myth of the Good War*, in which he provides a revisionist look at the role of the United States and other Allied countries in the Second World War. An independent scholar, Pauwels holds PhDs in history and political science. He lives in Brantford, Ontario.